REFERENCE

WITHDRAWN
USJ Library

The Pius XII Library

SAINT JOSEPH
COLLEGE

West Hartford, Connecticut 06117

REFERENCE

AMERICANS WITH DISABILITIES ACT HANDBOOK
THIRD EDITION
VOLUME 2

SUBSCRIPTION NOTICE

This Aspen Law & Business product is updated on a periodic basis with supplements to reflect important changes in the subject matter. If you purchased this product directly from Aspen Law & Business, we have already recorded your subscription for the update service.

If, however, you purchased this product from a bookstore and wish to receive future updates and revised or related volumes billed separately with a 30-day examination review, please contact our Customer Service Department at 1-800-234-1660, or send your name, company name (if applicable), address, and the title of the product to:

ASPEN LAW & BUSINESS
A Division of Aspen Publishers, Inc.
7201 McKinney Circle
Frederick, MD 21701

AMERICANS WITH DISABILITIES ACT HANDBOOK

THIRD EDITION

VOLUME 2

HENRY H. PERRITT, JR.

Professor of Law
Villanova University
School of Law

A PANEL PUBLICATION

This text is printed on acid-free paper.

Copyright © 1990, 1991, 1993, 1995, 1997 by John Wiley & Sons, Inc.

All rights reserved. Published simultaneously in Canada.

IBM is a registered trademark of International Business Machines Corporation. WordPerfect is a registered trademark of Corel Corporation Limited. Microsoft and Windows are registered trademarks of Microsoft Corporation.

Reproduction or translation of any part of this work beyond that permitted by Section 107 or 108 of the 1976 United States Copyright Act without the permission of the copyright owner is unlawful. Requests for permission or further information should be addressed to the Permissions Department, John Wiley & Sons, Inc., 605 Third Avenue, New York, NY 10158-0012.

This publication is designed to provide accurate and authoritative information in regard to the subject matter covered. It is sold with the understanding that the publisher is not engaged in rendering legal, accounting, or other professional services. If legal advice or other expert assistance is required, the services of a competent professional person should be sought.

Library of Congress Cataloging-in-Publication Data

Perritt, Henry H.
    Americans with Disabilities Act handbook / Henry H. Perritt, Jr.—
3rd ed.
      p.   cm. — (Employment law library)
    Includes index.
    ISBN 0-471-16754-1 (cloth : set : alk. paper)
    1. Handicapped—Employment—Law and legislation—United States.
2. Architecture and the physically handicapped—Law and legislation—
United States.   3. Discrimination against the handicapped—Law and
legislation—United States. I. Title. II. Series.
KF3469.P47   1997
342.73 ' 087—dc21   97-6383
                                                        CIP
                                                       Rev.

 Published by Panel Publishers
Formerly published by John Wiley & Sons, Inc.

ISBN 0-471-16754-1 (set)
ISBN 0-471-16755-X (vol. 1)
ISBN 0-471-16756-8 (vol. 2)
ISBN 0-471-18494-2 (vol. 3)
ISBN 0-471-18507-8 (disk)

Printed in the United States of America

10 9 8 7 6 5 4 3

SUMMARY CONTENTS

SUMMARY CONTENTS

Volume 3

DETAILED CONTENTS

Volume 2

Volume 3

Short Reference List

Appendixes

Tables

Cases

United States Code Citations

Index

SHORT REFERENCE LIST

Short Reference	Full Reference
ADA	Americans with Disabilities Act, Pub. L. No. 101–336, 104 Stat. 327 (1990) (codified at 42 U.S.C. §§ 12101–12213; 47 U.S.C. §§ 225, 711 (1994))
Title I	ADA §§ 101–108, 42 U.S.C. §§ 12111–12117 (1994)
Title II	ADA §§ 201–246, 42 U.S.C. §§ 12131–12165 (1994)
Title III	ADA §§ 301–310, 42 U.S.C. §§ 12181–12189 (1994)
Title IV	ADA §§ 401–402, 47 U.S.C. §§ 225, 711 (1994)
Title V	ADA §§ 501–514, 42 U.S.C. §§ 12201–12213 (1994)
ADAAG	Americans with Disabilities Act Accessibility Guidelines
ADEA	Age Discrimination in Employment Act, 29 U.S.C. §§ 621–634 (1994)
ATBCB	Architectural and Transportation Barriers Compliance Board
Civil Rights Act of 1964	42 U.S.C. chapter 21 (1994)
Civil Rights Act of 1991	42 U.S.C. §§ 1981a, 2000e to 2000e-17 (1994)
Congressional Accountability Act of 1995	2 U.S.C. chapter 24 (Supp. 1996)
DOJ	Department of Justice
DOT	Department of Transportation
EEOC	Equal Employment Opportunity Commission
Fair Housing Act	42 U.S.C. §§ 3601–3631 (1994)

FCC   Federal Communications Commission

House Commerce
  Report   H.R. Rep. No. 485, 101st Cong., 2d Sess., pt. 4 (1990)

House Conference
  Report   H.R. Conf. Rep. No. 596, 101st Cong., 2d Sess., *reprinted in* 136 Cong. Rec. H4582 (daily ed. July 12, 1990)

House Judiciary
  Report   H.R. Rep. No. 485, 101st Cong., 2d Sess., pt. 3 (1990)

House Labor
  Report   H.R. Rep. No. 485, 101st Cong., 2d Sess., pt. 2 (1990)

House Public
  Works Report   H.R. Rep. No. 485, 101st Cong., 2d Sess., pt. 1 (1990)

IDEA   Individuals with Disabilities Education Act, 20 U.S.C. §§ 1400–1491 (1994)

McDonnell
Douglas   McDonnell Douglas v. Green, 411 U.S. 792 (1973)

MGRAD   Minimum Guidelines and Requirements for Accessible Design

Q&A   U.S. Department of Justice, *Questions and Answers* (rev. Sept. 1992)

Rehabilitation Act
of 1973   29 U.S.C. §§ 701–709, 720–724, 730–732, 740, 741, 750, 760–764, 770–776, 780–787, 790–794 (1994)

Senate Report   S. Rep. No. 116, 101st Cong., 1st Sess. (1989)

TDD   Telecommunications device for the deaf

Title II of the
  Civil Rights
  Act of 1964   42 U.S.C. §§ 2000a to 2000a-6 (1994)

Title VII   Civil Rights Act of 1964, 42 U.S.C. §§ 2000e to 2000e-16 (1994)

UFAS   Uniform Federal Accessibility StandardsFair Housing Act 42 U.S.C. §§ 33601–3631 (1994)

CHAPTER 10

FORMS AND PROCEDURES FOR TITLE I COMPLAINTS

§ 10.1   Introduction and Overview

Lawsuits under Title I of the Americans with Disabilities Act (ADA)[1] begin not with complaints in federal or state court but with charges filed with the Equal Employment Opportunity Commission (EEOC) (see **Form 10–1**). Accordingly, this chapter begins with forms for EEOC charges, illustrating several different kinds of violations of the ADA. See **Forms 10–2** through

---

[1] Pub. L. No. 101–336, 104 Stat. 327 (1990) (codified at 42 U.S.C. §§ 12101–12213 (1994); 47 U.S.C. §§ 225, 711 (1994) [hereinafter ADA]; *see also* ADA §§ 101–107, 42 U.S.C. §§ 12111–12117 (1994) [hereinafter Title I].

10–5. The chapter then presents analytical material regarding the drafting of complaints and offers form language on specific requirements in federal complaints, such as jurisdiction allegations. See **Forms 10–6** through **10–10.** The chapter also moves into more comprehensive complaints presenting several different styles and actual contexts. For example, an intervenor's complaint is included, which is of particular interest in ADA cases because of the possibility that the EEOC would file suit first and that the victim would like to participate in that lawsuit and therefore exercise the right granted by Title VII of the Civil Rights Act of 1964,[2] incorporated by reference into the ADA. See **Form 10–10.**

Because fear of publicity may deter disabled plaintiffs from pursuing their rights, the chapter evaluates the criteria for allowing plaintiffs to proceed anonymously and provides not only a sample of an affidavit in support of a motion to proceed anonymously but also an accompanying motion and draft order granting leave to proceed anonymously.

This chapter, as well as other chapters in **Volume 2,** contains forms and proceedings from a mock liability trial. The materials associated with the mock trial of liability are identified as such in the section headings. These materials support other mock trial materials in other chapters.

§ 10.2   EEOC Charge Form

FORM 10–1
SAMPLE EEOC CHARGE FORM

Please immediately complete the entire form and return it to the U.S. Equal Employment Opportunity Commission (EEOC). REMEMBER, a charge of employment discrimination must be filed within the time limits imposed by law, generally within 180-300 days of the alleged discrimination.

ALLEGATIONS OF EMPLOYMENT DISCRIMINATION

Full Name _____

Address _____

City/State/Zip Code _____

Area Code/Telephone Number (Home) _____

Date of Birth _____

---

[2] 42 U.S.C. §§ 2000e–2000e-16 (1994) [hereinafter Title VII]; *see also* Civil Rights Act of 1964, 42 U.S.C. Ch. 21 (1994) [hereinafter Civil Rights Act of 1964].

Social Security Number _____

Company Name   _____

Address (location where you actually worked or sought employment)

_____

_____

City/State/Zip Code   _____

Main Telephone Number (area code if known)   _____

Type of Business _____

_____

_____

Approximate Number of Employees _____

BASIS - reasons you believe the action was taken against you, giving specifics. When you check a basis specify your class (e.g., sex - female, etc).

Race _____

Age   _____

Color   _____

Disability _____

Sex   _____

Retaliation   _____

Religion   _____

Other (explain briefly)   _____

National Origin _____

DATE OF HARM: _____

TYPE OF HARM: (e.g., discharge, denied hire, harassment, etc.)

EMPLOYMENT HISTORY (date of hire, position hired into, date sought employment and position applied for, each position held, dates in each position, etc.)

BRIEF EXPLANATION OF WHAT OCCURRED (be sure to give names and titles of persons involved, incidents and dates of each incident, etc.)

WITNESSES to any of the above actions: (give name, home telephone number, address if known, and a brief explanation of what each person should be able to tell EEOC)

Please provide the name of an individual, at a different address, who is in the local area and who would know how to reach you.

Name _____

Relationship _____

Address _____

City/State/Zip Code _____

Telephone Number/Area Code _____

Miscellaneous Information: _____

QUESTIONNAIRE

( ) I want to file a charge.

( ) I DO NOT WANT to file a charge at this time.

( ) I want to speak with an EEOC Representative before this is filed as a charge.

( ) I can be contacted at (area code/telephone number)

The best days and times to contact me are _____.

( ) I have not filed a charge concerning the alleged harm (information provided) with any other agency.

( ) I have filed a charge on the alleged harm (information provided) with the following agency/agencies:

Name of Agency _____

Date Filed _____

Agency Docket Number   _____

I am scheduled for an interview with the following named Agency: _____

Date of Interview   _____

Interviewer Name   _____

Location of Interview _____

I have received a QUESTIONNAIRE to be completed from the following named Agency:

_____

_____

Signature   _____

Date   _____

Commentary.   ADA claims that have not been presented to the EEOC may not be included in a civil action. This means that the scope of federal or state court litigation is circumscribed by the scope of the EEOC charge.[3]

§ 10.3   —Failure to Make Reasonable Accommodations for Person with MS (Mock Trial)

FORM 10–2
SAMPLE CHARGE: FAILURE TO MAKE REASONABLE ACCOMMODATIONS FOR PERSON WITH MS

On [August 5, 1992], I was terminated from [Eastern Pharmaceuticals, Incorporated (Eastern)]. I was hired by [Eastern] as an accounting clerk on [July 7, 1972]. Since then, I have received several promotions and on [July 11, 1989], I became a staff accountant. As a staff accountant, my essential job functions included: (1) producing financial reports through spreadsheet applications, (2) operating an adding machine to perform various mathematical functions, maintaining the general ledger, and (3) communicating with outside vendors and Eastern's purchasing agents regarding fixed asset acquisitions. At all times, my work performance was average or above average. [Eastern] has employed more than 25 employees for the preceding year.

---

[3] §§ **9.15–9.17.**

On [June 26, 1991], I was diagnosed with multiple sclerosis (MS) and suffered from blurry vision and slurred speech. At that time, [Eastern] provided a magnification screen that enabled me to read the computer screen. It also re-routed my incoming calls so that another employee could answer my calls. At all relevant times, [Ms. Lisa Brown], [Eastern]'s accounting manager, knew of my disability. On [July 28, 1992], I suffered another MS attack. My eyesight and speech deteriorated further and I had difficulty with walking and coordination of muscle movement.

I was informed by [Ms. Brown] that I was terminated for my inability to perform the essential functions of a staff accountant and that the necessary accommodations would cause [Eastern] undue hardship. Furthermore, she pointed out that the employment was terminable at will by either party.

I believe that [Eastern] failed to make reasonable accommodations for my disability because

1.   With reasonable accommodations, I would have been able to perform the essential job functions of a staff accountant.

2.   On [July 30, 1992], I requested the following accommodations:

a.   Having a reader communicate written messages and computer information to me

b.   Having a speaker communicate oral messages from me, and

c.   Having the office area of [Eastern]'s facility made "handicapped friendly."

On [August 5, 1992], [Ms. Brown] informed me that the accommodations were unreasonable and would create undue financial hardship for [Eastern]. She stated that I could no longer perform my essential job functions. Furthermore, she suggested that there were many "healthy" individuals who could perform the job without the changes.

3.   The staff accountant position requires experience in the type of accounting system used by [Eastern] which takes years to master. The tasks of reading and speaking can be done by our existing secretaries with minimal intrusion into their current jobs. Making the office "handicapped friendly" entails larger information signs (*e.g.,* EXIT), better lighting, and handrails in the hallways.

§ 10.4   —Intentional Discrimination for History of Cancer

FORM 10–3
SAMPLE CHARGE: INTENTIONAL DISCRIMINATION OF HISTORY OF CANCER

On [date] I was denied an opportunity for employment as a chemical process engineer with [company name]. I have 15 years of experience as a process engineer in a Fortune 100 company and I have received numerous awards for outstanding work performance. Other then my history of cancer, I have no other disabilities that would effect my work performance. [Company name] has 200 employees.

I was informed on [date], by [company name]'s personnel manager, [name], that I was qualified for the position but they were unable to offer me the job because of my past history of cancer.

I believe I was discriminated against on the basis of my disability (past history of breast cancer) because

1.   The person who was hired was less qualified than I.

2.   On [date], I interviewed with three vice-presidents, [names]. They were impressed with my credentials and told me that I would be hired if I passed the medical examination. However, after the routine prehiring medical examination which included questioning on my past history of cancer, [company name] first raised doubts concerning my employment.

3.   [Company name] consistently stated they were concerned with its growing medical costs and that my employment would increase its medical costs.

4.   [Company name] used my past history of cancer in its hiring decision.

§ 10.5 —Refusal to Accommodate a Disabled (Blind) Person

FORM 10–4
SAMPLE CHARGE: REFUSAL TO ACCOMMODATE DISABLED (BLIND) PERSON

On [date], I was denied an opportunity for employment as a telemarketer with the [company name]. Currently, I am a customer service representative. My current duties include answering customer questions regarding our products. I have worked for [company name] for 5 years with good to average work evaluations for each year. [Company name] has 200 employees with revenues of $1.5 million.

On [date], my supervisor, [name], informed me that the current telemarketing system required a person with eyesight; therefore, she stated that I did not have the essential skills necessary for the job. She also informed me that the necessary modifications to enable a blind person to work as a telemarketer would cause undue financial hardships for the company.

I believe I was discriminated against on the basis of my disability (blindness) because

1.   On [date], a job posting listed a telemarketing position. The next day, I went to [supervisor's name] to apply for the position. [Name] encouraged me to apply. On [date], [name], manager of telemarketing, telephoned me to set up an appointment. On [date], I interviewed with [manager's name]. When we first met, he was shocked to learn that I was blind. He was impressed with my communications skills, but he told me that there were other candidates he still had to interview.

2.   In my work performance evaluations, I have consistently received high marks in communication skills.

3.   With current technological advances, modifications to the telemarketing system is feasible without causing undue hardship to the company. These include Braille keyboards and software which allows computers to speak words displayed on the screen. These modifications would cost less than $5000.

4.   [Company name] failed to make reasonable modifications to its existing facilities to accommodate a blind employee. I was not given equal opportunities to advance, and I was relegated to a lesser job than my qualifications warranted.

§ 10.6   —Retaliation

FORM 10–5
SAMPLE CHARGE: RETALIATION

On [date], I was fired by [company name]. I have been with the company for 30 years and I have received satisfactory work performance reviews each year, including the current year. [Company name] employs 200 people.

My supervisor,[name], informed me that my employment was terminated because of unsatisfactory work performance. I did not have an employment contract with [company name] and therefore [name] stated that it was a terminable at will employment contract.

I believe I was retaliated against on the basis of my reporting the company's noncompliance with the Americans with Disabilities Act because

1.   On [date], I noticed that the access to the front of the building was not wheelchair accessible, although 5 employees use wheelchairs. The building is only wheelchair accessible through the delivery entrance in the rear of the building. I notified my manager, [name], of this discrepancy and asked that the front door be made wheelchair accessible. [Name] said he would look into it. When no action was taken by [date], I asked [name] about our previous conversation. [Name] stated that the disabled had access through the delivery door and that was adequate. At that time, I informed [name] that unless the front doors were made wheelchair accessible, I would report it to the EEOC. [Name] told me not to cause any trouble or I would regret it. After waiting three weeks, I filed a complaint with the EEOC stating [name]'s noncompliance with the ADA on [date]. Within two weeks, I was fired from the company.

2.   People with worse work performance reviews than mine are still with the company.

§ 10.7   Complaint Drafting Styles

Counsel have much room for discretion, advocacy, and their own artistic instinct in drafting the complaints. Although notice pleading is the theory both in federal court[4] and in an increasing number of state court systems, ADA complaints in the real world serve more purposes then giving bare bones notice to the defendant about the factual controversy alleged and about the legal claims asserted.

---

[4] Leatherman v. Tarrant County Narcotics Intelligence & Coordination Unit, 507 U.S. 163 (1993) (reversing application of "heightened" pleading requirement in municipal Civil Rights Act of 1964 liability case).

Virtually all of the complaints reproduced in this chapter and in **Chapter 11** reflect multiple purposes. They tell a story as well as giving notice. This helps to create not only a sympathetic perspective but also a context within which the legal claims and specific factual allegations material to the claims can be understood.

Dividing the complaint into jurisdiction, parties, and common fact sections facilitates the structuring of the subsequent specific legal counts in an understandable way without undue repetition.

In drafting a complaint, counsel should remember that its paragraphs will be used throughout the litigation as a way of framing issues and legal contentions. Organizing the complaint so that efficient references can be made to parts of it later on is desirable.

It is helpful drafting discipline to review a preliminary draft complaint by imagining the perspective of the opponent's position and the opponent's answers to the draft. Drafting an answer to a draft complaint can reveal areas for refinement, such as when allegations are not sufficiently particularized to permit them to be admitted or denied. This exercise may also reveal unintended admissions in the preliminary draft complaint.

§ 10.8 —Allegation of Jurisdiction

It is important to allege jurisdiction correctly in a complaint. The following examples from official Form 2 of the Federal Rules of Civil Procedure illustrate two different allegations of jurisdiction.

Jurisdiction founded on diversity of citizenship and amount.

Plaintiff is a [citizen of the State of [name]] [corporation incorporated under the laws of the State of [name] having its principal place of business in the State of [name]] and defendant is a corporation incorporated under the laws of the State of [name] having its principal place of business in a State other than the State of [name]. The matter in controversy exceeds, exclusive of interest and costs, the sum of fifty thousand dollars.[5]

Jurisdiction founded on the existence of a federal question.

The action arises under [the Constitution of the United States, Articles ___, Section ___]; [the ___ Amendment to the Constitution of the United States, Section ___]; [the Act of ___, ___ Stat. ___; U.S.C., Title ___, § ___]; [the Treaty of the United States (here describe the treaty)] as hereinafter more fully appears.[6]

---

[5] Official Form 2, Fed. R. Civ. P.

[6] *Id.*

§ 10.9   — Complaint (Mock Trial)

FORM 10–6
SAMPLE COMPLAINT FOR MOCK TRIAL

UNITED STATES DISTRICT COURT FOR THE [EASTERN]
DISTRICT OF [PENNSYLVANIA]

[Steven Lyons],

Plaintiff

v.   Civil Action No. [92-0130]

[Eastern Pharmaceuticals, Incorporated],

Defendant.

COMPLAINT FOR JURY TRIAL

I.   JURISDICTION

1.   This action arises under the Americans with Disabilities Act of 1990 (ADA), 42 U.S.C. § 12201.

2.   Plaintiff brings this action pursuant to ADA § 107(a), 42 U.S.C. § 12117(a).

3.   ADA § 107(a), 42 U.S.C. § 12117(a), incorporates by reference Title VII of the Civil Rights Act of 1964 (Title VII), 42 U.S.C. § 2000e-5, which grants jurisdiction to this Court.

4.   All preconditions to jurisdiction under § 706 of Title VII, 42 U.S.C. § 2000e-5(f)(3), have been satisfied.

a.   Plaintiff filed a charge of employment discrimination on the basis of disability with the Equal Employment Opportunity Commission (EEOC) within 180 days of the alleged employment discrimination on the basis of disability against him.

b.   The EEOC issued a "right to sue" letter to plaintiff on [February 15, 1993].

c.   Plaintiff filed this complaint within 90 days of receiving the "right to sue" letter from the EEOC.

II.   PARTIES

5.   Plaintiff is a citizen of the United States and a resident of [Norristown], [Pennsylvania].

6.   Plaintiff has multiple sclerosis (MS). MS substantially limits plaintiff in the major life activities of reading, speaking and walking.

7.   Plaintiff is an individual with a "disability" within the meaning of ADA § 3(2), 42 U.S.C. § 12102(2).

8.   Plaintiff, with the reasonable accommodations of:

a.   Having a reader communicate written messages and computer information to him,

b.   Having a speaker communicate oral messages from him, and

c.   Having the office area of [Eastern Pharmaceuticals, Incorporated (Eastern)]'s facility made "handicapped friendly,"

can perform the essential functions of his job as a staff accountant in [Eastern]'s finance department.

9. Plaintiff is a "qualified individual with a disability" within the meaning of ADA § 101(8), 42 U.S.C. § 12111(8).

10. Plaintiff has been a "qualified individual with a disability" since [June 26, 1991].

11. Defendant, [Eastern], is a [Delaware] corporation with its manufacturing plant and principal place of business in [Fort Washington], [Pennsylvania.]

12. [Eastern] is a "person" within the meaning of ADA § 101(7), 42 U.S.C. § 12111(7), and Title VII, § 701(a), 42 U.S.C. § 2000e(a).

13.   [Eastern] is engaged in an "industry affecting commerce" within the meaning of ADA § 101(7), 42 U.S.C. § 12111(7), and Title VII §§ 701(g)–(h), 42 U.S.C. §§ 2000e(g)–(h).

14.   [Eastern] employed more than 25 employees for each working day in more than 20 weeks during the preceding year.

15.   [Eastern] is an "employer" within the meaning of ADA § 101(5)(A), 42 U.S.C. § 12111(5)(A).

16.   [Eastern] is a "covered entity" within the meaning of ADA § 101(2), 42 U.S.C. § 12111(2).

III.   FACTS

17.   [Eastern] hired Plaintiff on [July 7, 1972] for the position of accounting clerk. After several promotions, plaintiff was employed as a staff accountant in [Eastern]'s finance department. [Eastern] promoted plaintiff to the position of staff accountant on [July 11, 1989]. Plaintiff worked continuously at [Eastern] from [July 7, 1972] to [August 5, 1992].

18.   [Lisa Brown]. [Eastern]'s accounting manager, was plaintiff's direct supervisor at all relevant times.

19.   Plaintiff's essential job functions as a staff accountant were: producing financial reports through spreadsheet applications; operating an adding machine to perform various mathematical functions; maintaining the general ledger; and communicating with outside vendors and [Eastern]'s purchasing agents regarding fixed asset acquisitions.

20.   On [June 26, 1991], Plaintiff was diagnosed with MS. At that time, plaintiff suffered from blurry vision and slurred speech.

21.   At all relevant times, [Ms. Brown] knew that plaintiff had MS.

22.   [Eastern] provided plaintiff with a device that magnifies the computer screen and also re-routed Plaintiff's incoming calls so that another employee answered the phone for him.

23.   Plaintiff was able to perform the essential functions of his job as staff accountant after [Eastern] provided the reasonable accommodations listed in paragraph 22.

24.   On [July 28, 1992], Plaintiff suffered another MS attack. After this attack, Plaintiff's eyesight and speech deteriorated further and he began to have difficulty walking and coordinating muscle movement.

25.   Plaintiff requested the additional reasonable accommodations listed in allegation 8 to enable him to continue performing his essential job functions.

26.   [Ms. Brown] refused to make reasonable accommodations for plaintiff's disability and terminated him on [August 5, 1992].

27.   The decisions made and the actions taken by [Ms. Brown] enumerated in allegation 26 were within the course and scope of her employment at [Eastern].

28.   [Eastern]'s refusal to make reasonable accommodations for plaintiff's known disability constitutes discrimination against Plaintiff due to his disability in violation of ADA § 102(b)(5)(A), 42 U.S.C. § 12112(b)(5)(A).

29.   [Eastern] acted with malice or with reckless indifference toward plaintiff's federally protected rights as a qualified individual with a disability when it refused to make reasonable accommodations for plaintiff's known disability.

30.   As a result of [Eastern]'s discrimination on the basis of disability, plaintiff suffered and continues to suffer economic losses, mental anguish, pain and suffering and other nonpecuniary losses.

IV.   PRAYER FOR RELIEF

Plaintiff demands judgment against [Eastern] for:

31.   Salary and benefits, and accrued interest thereon, from [August 5, 1992] until entry of judgment against [Eastern].

32.   Compensatory damages for plaintiff's mental anguish, pain and suffering and other nonpecuniary losses.

33.   Reinstatement to the position of staff accountant in [Eastern]'s finance department at the salary rate in effect on [August 5, 1992].

34.   Reasonable accommodations, as listed in allegation 8, so that Plaintiff can perform his essential job functions.

35.   Punitive damages in an amount to be determined at trial.

36.   Plaintiff's attorneys' fees and costs of this action.

37.   Such other relief as may be just and equitable.

> [Louis Watt], Attorney for Plaintiff
> [1234 Main Street]
> [Villanova], [Pennsylvania] 19085

§ 10.10   —Title I HIV Discrimination

FORM 10–7
SAMPLE TITLE I HIV DISCRIMINATION COMPLAINT

IN THE UNITED STATES DISTRICT COURT

FOR THE [judicial district] OF [state]

[JOHN DOE], M.D. (orthopedic surgeon)

Plaintiff

v.

[name] HEALTH CORPORATION

Defendant

and

[name] MEDICAL CENTER

Defendant

and

[name] HEALTH PLAN

Defendant

and

[Dr. A],

Defendant

and

[Dr. B],

Defendant.

Civil Action No. [number]

Jury Trial Demanded

COMPLAINT

INTRODUCTION

1.   [John Doe], M.D., is a doctor infected with Human Immunodeficiency Virus (HIV). For many years he practiced at [name] Medical Center—until the Center's management learned of his HIV status. The Center's Medical Board, echoing the views of most public health officials and medical experts, found that [Dr. Doe]'s infection did not pose a significant risk of harm to his patients, and recommended that he be allowed to continue his practice without restriction. Instead, the Defendants, heeding fear instead of facts, have prevented [Dr. Doe] from resuming his medical practice. Their discriminatory actions violate the Rehabilitation Act of 1973, and the Americans with Disabilities Act. [Dr.

Doe] brings this action to vindicate his right, and the rights of other qualified people with disabilities, to fair treatment and equal opportunity.

JURISDICTION AND VENUE

2.   This Court has jurisdiction over the subject matter of this Complaint pursuant to 28 U.S.C. § 1331, 28 U.S.C. § 2000d-7, and principles of pendent and ancillary jurisdiction.

3.   Venue is proper in this Court pursuant to the provisions of 28 U.S.C. § 1391.

PLAINTIFF

4.   Plaintiff, [John Doe], M.D., is a resident of [state] and an orthopedic surgeon who, since [year], has been associated with Defendants Health Corporation, Medical Center, and Health Plan. [Dr. Doe]'s identity is known to the Defendants and has been supplied to the Court in his verification annexed to Plaintiff's motion for leave to proceed in pseudonym and to seal records.

DEFENDANTS

5.   Defendant Health Corporation is a corporation doing business in [state] and is a subsidiary of [name] Health Corporation, operating two acute care hospitals providing medical services to patients throughout the [region]. The two hospitals comprising [name] Medical Center are [name] in [city, state] and [name] in [city, state].

6.   Defendant Medical Center is a corporation doing business in [state] and is a subsidiary of [name] Health Corporation, operating two acute care hospitals providing medical services to patients throughout the [region]. The two hospitals comprising [name] Medical Center are [name] in [city, state] and [name] Hospital in [city, state].

7.   Defendant Health Plan is a corporation doing business in this state with principal office at [address] and it contracts with various health care providers to provide health care services to [name] Health Plan subscribers, all of whom are Medicaid program recipients. Subscribers of [name] Health Plan who require hospitalization receive inpatient care at [name] Medical Center and other hospitals. Outpatient services to [name] Health Plan subscribers are provided in the private offices of participating health care practitioners.

8.   [Name] Health Plan, [name] Health Corporation, and [name] Medical Center, including its surgical operations, are programs or activities receiving federal funds, including funds under the Medicare and Medicaid programs.

9.   [Name] Health Plan, [name] Health Corporation, and [name] Medical Center employ in excess of twenty-five people and have gross receipts in excess of one million dollars.

10.   Defendant [Dr. A] is Executive Vice President of [name] Health Corporation, and at all times relevant to this Complaint was acting in that capacity.

11.   Defendant [Dr. B] is Senior Vice President for Professional Affairs and Medical Director, [name] Health Corporation of Southeastern [state], and at all times relevant to this Complaint was acting in that capacity.

12.   HIV is the retrovirus believed to cause AIDS. HIV impairs the human immune system, ultimately destroying key cells that help protect the body against disease. People infected with the virus may enjoy apparent health, relatively minor illnesses, or the fatal constellation of infections and cancers known as AIDS.

13.   Although current data indicate that a high percentage of people infected with HIV will eventually develop AIDS, it is usually many years before debilitating symptoms appear. Unless prevented by the ignorance and prejudice of others, people who have the virus are very often able to continue their working lives on the same basis as before the diagnosis of their infection.

14.   HIV is transmitted by intimate sexual contact involving the exchange of infected semen or blood; by exposure to infected blood through transfusion or needle-stick; and by perinatal exposure and breastfeeding from mother to child. Because of the sexual and perinatal modes of transmission, people with HIV are impaired in their reproductive activities.

15.   Despite careful investigation throughout the world, particularly in the past two years, health officials have found not one single case of HIV transmissions from a medical doctor or surgeon to a patient in the course of providing care.

16.   Possible HIV transmission in the course of providing health care has been limited to one cluster of cases involving a [state] dentist with HIV. DNA analysis indicated that five patients had been infected by their dentist, although the actual mode of transmission has never been determined. The dentist disregarded standard infection control guidelines, and may even have infected the patients intentionally.

17.   According to state and federal health officials, the risk of HIV transmission from infected health care provider to patient is extremely low and can be further minimized by rigorous adherence to barrier precautions.

THE FACTS OF [DR. DOE]'S LOSS OF PRIVILEGES

18.   In [date], [Dr. Doe] learned that he was infected with HIV. He was also diagnosed with Kaposi's sarcoma, a cancer associated with AIDS.

19.   [Dr. Doe] has an outstanding professional record.

20.   [Dr. Doe] has always rigorously adhered to barrier precautions.

21.   [Dr. Doe] has always employed surgical techniques that minimize the chances of his being cut and exposing a patient to his blood.

22.   [Dr. Doe] has cut himself during surgery only a few times in six years of practice, and has never to his knowledge exposed a patient to his blood.

23.   On or about [date], Plaintiff, having secured a promise of confidentiality, discussed his HIV infection with [Dr. C], Director of Surgery at [name] Hospital.

24. Immediately thereafter, [Dr. C], without Plaintiff's permission, disclosed Plaintiff's HIV infection to Defendants [Dr. A] and [Dr. B].

25.   Under public health recommendations in effect at that time, [Dr. Doe] should have been evaluated by an expert review panel, guided by appropriate state and local health officials, to determine on an individualized basis whether he posed a significant risk to his patients. The guidelines further recommended that notification of past patients be considered only on a case-by-case basis after consultation with state and local health officials.

26.   After learning of [Dr. Doe]'s HIV infection, Defendants did not consult with appropriate local, state, or federal health officials, nor did they convene an expert review panel.

27.   Indeed, Defendants did not seek the advice of any expert in the transmission of HIV, nor did any of the Defendants possess such expertise.

28.   Instead, and in the absence of any evidence whatsoever that [Dr. Doe] posed a significant risk to his patients, Defendants' immediate response was to seek [Dr. Doe]'s prompt resignation. On or about [date], Plaintiff was contacted by Defendant [Dr. B], who demanded a letter from Plaintiff promising that Plaintiff would never again under any circumstances perform surgery at Defendant hospitals. Defendant [Dr. B] stated that this demand was made on behalf of the Defendant [name] Medical Center.

29.   Further, on or about [date], Defendants informed [Dr. Doe] through counsel that they wished to notify every single patient whom [Dr. Doe] had ever operated on that an orthopedic surgeon who had operated on them had tested HIV-positive. The Defendants did not seek the advice or assistance of the state health department or any other public health authority in deciding to make this release.

30.   On [date], despite [Dr. Doe]'s willingness to cooperate with a review of his qualifications and safety record as recommended by applicable public health guidelines, Defendants filed a petition under the [state] Confidentiality of HIV-Related Information Act, seeking court permission to notify all of [Dr. Doe]'s surgical patients, the press and the public of the fact that he had tested HIV-positive. The order was granted on [date].

31.   The only public health official who participated in the notification controversy was a representative of the [state] Department of Health, who appeared as a witness for Plaintiff in opposition to the disclosure Petition filed by Defendants.

32.   On [date], Defendants sent registered letters to 1,050 patients stating that a doctor who had participated in their surgical procedure had tested positive for HIV. The letter stated that the risk of infection in surgery was "extremely remote."

33.   The next day the Defendants held a press conference, informing the news media that an orthopedic surgeon who had been on staff at [name] Medical Center since [date] and who was affiliated with [name] Hospital, had tested positive for HIV and that letters had been sent to all of his patients notifying them of same.

34.   The notification, while not directly disclosing [Dr. Doe]'s name, did make [Dr. Doe]'s identity easily discernible and easily ascertainable. Members of the press, coworkers, patients, and friends were able to deduce his identity within hours.

35.   On or about [date], in connection with the public announcement of [Dr. Doe]'s infection, Defendant [Dr. A] advised Plaintiff by letter that "your clinical privileges pertaining to the performance of any and all inpatient and/or outpatient diagnostic or therapeutic invasive procedures at [name] Medical Center are hereby immediately suspended outlined below because of concerns for patient safety."

36.   Defendant [Dr. A] suspended Plaintiff pursuant to [Medical Staff By-law 9.6 (a)], which relates to "an immediate danger to the health of any individual" and "in the best interest of patient care."

37.   Defendant's suspension of [Dr. Doe] ignored compelling evidence that HIV-infected health care workers as a class do not pose a significant risk to patients. The Defendants likewise failed to consider [Dr. Doe]'s own impeccable record of patient care and his scrupulous adherence to infection control guidelines.

38.   The Defendants' blanket notification of his past patients had produced no cases of HIV believed by health authorities to have been caused by exposure to [Dr. Doe.]

39.   Despite its assertion that [Dr. Doe] posed a threat to patient health, [Dr. A]'s letter purported to state certain conditions under which he would be allowed to continue his operative practice, including prior clearance by an internal review panel of each operation and the notification of each prospective patient of [Dr. Doe]'s HIV infection.

40.   On the next occasion that [Dr. Doe] sought to schedule surgery at [name] Medical Center, he was informed by a hospital official that he did not have surgical privileges at the hospital and that therefore the surgery could not take place.

41.   Following these events, patient referrals to Plaintiff from the medical staff at [name] Medical Center, which heretofore had been a common occurrence, precipitously dropped to zero and Plaintiff's name was not given out on Defendants' telephone referral line.

42.   On [date], the Medical Board of [name] Medical Center convened to hear [Dr. Doe]'s appeal of the suspension imposed by Defendant [Dr. A]. At said hearing, both sides presented testimony on the issue of whether [Dr. Doe] posed any risk to patients in surgery.

43.   On [date], the Center's Medical Board recommended by unanimous vote that [Dr. Doe] be reinstated to full privileges without any restriction whatsoever.

44.   On [date], the Board of Directors of defendant [name] Medical Center rejected the Medical Board's recommendation.

45.   On [date], the Board of Directors reached a final decision that purported to reinstate [Dr. Doe]'s surgical privileges on the condition that he inform each patient of his HIV infection prior to performing any invasive procedure.

46.   Defendants' action in requiring such notification is based on Defendants' questionable ethical and tort liability concerns, rather than a well-founded belief that the risk of HIV transmission posed by [Dr. Doe] is significant.

47.   The theoretical possibility of HIV transmission is much lower than many other health care risks commonly accepted by patients and which do not trigger any such mandatory disclosure requirements.

48.   Defendants are fully aware that a requirement of patient notification effectively prevents [Dr. Doe] from continuing to maintain an economically viable practice.

49. [Dr. Doe] is a fully qualified orthopedic surgeon, able to perform safely all the duties of his profession, and to meet the obligations associated with admitting privileges at the Defendant hospital.

COUNT I

REHABILITATION ACT OF 1973

50. [Dr. Doe] incorporates by reference paragraphs 1 through 48 as though fully set forth herein.

51. This Count I is brought against all Defendants.

52. [Dr. Doe] is an individual with handicaps within the meaning of § 504 of the Rehabilitation Act of 1973, 29 U.S.C. § 794.

53. [Dr. Doe] was, at all times relevant to this Complaint, otherwise qualified to pursue the duties attendant to his surgical privileges at the hospital. [Dr. Doe] does not pose a significant risk of harm to his patients.

54. Defendants failed to carry out an individualized assessment of [Dr. Doe] and any risk he might pose to patients, nor, having concluded that HIV-infected surgeons as a class pose only a remote risk to patients, did they offer a reasonable accommodation to the disability they perceived.

55. Solely by reason of his handicap, [Dr. Doe] was excluded from participation in, denied the benefits of, and subjected to discrimination under programs and activities receiving federal funds.

WHEREFORE, [Dr. Doe] asks this Court to enter judgment:

a. Declaring that the Rehabilitation Act Defendants have discriminated against [Dr. Doe] in violation of the Rehabilitation Act of 1973, 29 U.S.C. § 794;

b. Ordering that the Rehabilitation Act Defendants shall pay actual and compensatory damages resulting from Defendants' discriminatory acts, in an amount to be proved at trial;

c. Ordering the full restoration of [Dr. Doe]'s medical privileges without discriminatory restrictions;

d. Awarding [Dr. Doe] the costs and expenses of this action, including attorneys' fees and interest; and

e.   Awarding [Dr. Doe] such other and further relief as the Court shall deem just and proper.

COUNT II

TITLE III OF THE AMERICANS WITH DISABILITIES ACT

56.   [Dr. Doe] incorporates by reference paragraphs 1 through 54 as though fully set forth herein.

57.   This Count II is brought against all Defendants.

58.   [Dr. Doe] is a qualified individual with a disability within the meaning of § 101 of the Americans with Disabilities Act, 42 U.S.C. § 12111.

59.   [Dr. Doe] was, at all times relevant to this Complaint, otherwise qualified to pursue his duties attendant to his surgical privileges at the hospital. [Dr. Doe] does not pose a significant risk of harm to his patients.

60.   Solely because of his handicap, [Dr. Doe] was denied participation in and enjoyment of the privileges of a place of public accommodation in violation of Title III of the Americans with Disabilities Act, 42 U.S.C. § 12182.

WHEREFORE, [Dr. Doe] asks this Court to enter judgment:

a.   Declaring that the Americans with Disabilities Act Defendants have discriminated against [Dr. Doe] in violation of the Americans with Disabilities Act, 42. U.S.C. §§ 12111 *et seq.*;

b.   Ordering the full restoration of [Dr. Doe]'s medical privileges;

c.   Awarding [Dr. Doe] the costs and expenses of this action, including attorneys' fees and interest; and

d.   Awarding [Dr. Doe] such other and further relief as the Court shall deem just and proper.

Respectfully submitted,

[attorney name]

[address]

[telephone number]

Attorney I.D. [number]

§ 10.11   —Mentally Retarded
Employment Applicant

FORM 10–8
SAMPLE COMPLAINT FOR MENTALLY RETARDED
EMPLOYMENT APPLICANT

UNITED STATES DISTRICT COURT FOR THE

DISTRICT OF [NEW JERSEY]

[name],

Plaintiff

v.   Civil Action, File [number]

[name],

Defendant.

COMPLAINT FOR JURY TRIAL

I. JURISDICTION

1.   This action arises under the Americans with Disabilities Act of 1990 (ADA), 42 U.S.C. § 12201.

2.   Plaintiff brings this action pursuant to ADA § 107(a), 42 U.S.C. § 12117(a).

3.   ADA § 107(a), 42 U.S.C. § 12117(a), incorporates by reference Title VII of the Civil Rights Act of 1964 (Title VII), 42 U.S.C. § 2000e-5, which grants jurisdiction to this Court.

4.   All preconditions to jurisdiction under § 706 of Title VII, 42 U.S.C. § 2000e-5(f)(3), have been satisfied.

a.   Plaintiff filed a charge of employment discrimination on the basis of disability with the Equal Employment Opportunity Commission (EEOC) within 180 days of the alleged employment discrimination on the basis of disability against her.

b.   The EEOC issued a "right to sue" letter to plaintiff on [date].

c.   Plaintiff filed this complaint within 90 days of receiving the "right to sue" letter from the EEOC.

II.   PARTIES

5.   Plaintiff is a citizen of the United States and a resident of [city, state].

6.   Plaintiff is mentally retarded. Mental retardation substantially limits plaintiff in the major life activity of learning.

7.   Plaintiff is an individual with a "disability" within the meaning of ADA § 3(2), 42 U.S.C. § 12102(2).

8.   Plaintiff can perform the essential functions of cashier at [defendant] without any reasonable accommodations.

9.   Plaintiff is a "qualified individual with a disability" within the meaning of ADA § 101(8), 42 U.S.C. § 12111(8).

10.   Defendant, [company name], is a [state] corporation with its restaurants and principal place of business in [city, state].

11.   [Defendant] is a "person" within the meaning of ADA § 101(7), 42 U.S.C. § 12111(7), and Title VII § 701(a), 42 U.S.C. § 2000e(a).

12.   [Defendant] purchases all of its rolls from [supplier], a [state] corporation with its Bakery and principal place of business in [city, state].

13.   [Defendant] is engaged in an "industry affecting commerce" within the meaning of ADA § 101(7), 42 U.S.C. § 12111(7), and Title VII § 701(g)-(h), 42 U.S.C. §§ 2000e(g)–(h).

14.   [Defendant] employed more than 25 employees for each working day in more than 20 weeks during the preceding year.

15.   [Defendant] is an "employer" within the meaning of ADA § 101(5)(A), 42 U.S.C. § 12111(5)(A).

16.   [Defendant] is a "covered entity" within the meaning of ADA § 101(2), 42 U.S.C. § 12111(2).

III.   FACTS

17.   Plaintiff responded to a "Help Wanted" sign in [defendant]'s window on [date]. Plaintiff applied for the position of cashier at [name].

18.   The essential job functions of cashier at [defendant] are: (1) greeting customers, (2) repeating customer orders into a microphone which broadcasts into the kitchen, (3) picking up customer orders from the cooks, (4) delivering the food to the customers, and (5) operating the cash register.

19.   [Name], [defendant]'s president and sole stockholder, made all of [defendant]'s hiring decisions at all relevant times.

20.   [Defendant's president] told plaintiff that plaintiff was the most qualified applicant for the position.

21.   [Defendant's president] told plaintiff that he could not hire her because he thought that the customers would feel awkward placing their orders with someone who was mentally retarded.

22.   [Defendant]'s limitation and classification of plaintiff in a way that adversely affected plaintiff's status as an applicant for employment constitutes discrimination against plaintiff due to her disability in violation of ADA § 102(b)(1), 42 U.S.C. § 12112(b)(1).

23.   [Defendant] acted with malice or with reckless indifference toward plaintiff's federally protected rights as a qualified individual with a disability when it limited and classified plaintiff in a way that adversely affected her status as an applicant for employment.

24.   As a result of [defendant]'s discrimination on the basis of disability, plaintiff suffered and continues to suffer economic losses, mental anguish, pain and suffering and other nonpecuniary losses.

IV.   PRAYER FOR RELIEF

Plaintiff demands judgment against [defendant] for:

25.   Salary and benefits, and accrued interest thereon, from [date] until entry of judgment against [defendant].

26.   Compensatory damages for plaintiff's mental anguish, pain and suffering and other nonpecuniary losses.

27.   Injunctive relief, requiring [defendant] to hire plaintiff for the position of cashier at the salary rate in effect on [date].

28.   Punitive damages in an amount to be determined at trial for this matter.

29.   Plaintiff's attorneys fees and costs of this action.

30.   Any other and further relief as may be just and equitable.

[name], Attorney for Plaintiff

[address]

§ 10.12   —EEOC v. A.I.C. Complaint

FORM 10–9
EEOC v. A.I.C. COMPLAINT

IN THE UNITED STATES DISTRICT COURT

FOR THE [NORTHERN DISTRICT] OF [ILLINOIS]

[EASTERN DIVISION]

U.S. EQUAL EMPLOYMENT OPPORTUNITY COMMISSION,

Plaintiff,

v.   Civil Action No. [number]

[A.I.C. SECURITY INVESTIGATIONS, LTD.];

[A.I.C. INTERNATIONAL, LTD.];

and [unnamed defendant C],

Defendants.

COMPLAINT AND JURY DEMAND

NATURE OF THE ACTION

This is an action under Title I of the Americans with Disabilities Act of 1990 and Title I of the Civil Rights Act of 1991, to correct unlawful employment practices on the basis of disability and to make whole [Charles L. Wessel ("Wessel")]. Defendants discharged [Wessel], a qualified individual with a disability, cancer, from his position as Executive Director, because of his disability.

JURISDICTION AND VENUE

1.   Jurisdiction of this Court is invoked pursuant to 28 U.S.C. §§ 451, 1331, 1337, 1343, and 1345. This action is authorized and instituted pursuant to § 107(a) of the Americans with Disabilities Act of 1990 (ADA), 42 U.S.C.

§ 12117(a), which incorporates by reference §§ 706(f)(1) and (3) of Title VII of the Civil Rights Act of 1964 ("Title VII"), 42 U.S.C. §§ 2000e-5(f)(1) and (3), and pursuant to § 102 of the Civil Rights Act of 1991, 42 U.S.C. § 1981(A).

2.   The employment practices hereafter alleged to be unlawful were and are now being committed in the [Northern District] of [Illinois], [Eastern] Division.

PARTIES

3.   Plaintiff, Equal Employment Opportunity Commission (the "Commission"), is an agency of the United States of America charged with the administration, interpretation and enforcement of Title I of the ADA and is expressly authorized to bring this action by § 107(a) of the ADA, 42 U.S.C. § 12117(a), which incorporates by reference § 706(f)(1) of Title VII, 42 U.S.C. § 2000e-5(f)(1).

4.   At all relevant times, Defendant [A.I.C. Securities, Inc. ("A.I.C.")] has been and is now an [Illinois] corporation doing business in the State of [Illinois] and the City of [Chicago], and has continuously had and does now have at least twenty-five (25) employees.

5.   At all relevant times, Defendant [A.I.C. International, Ltd. ("A.I.C. International")] has been and now is an [Illinois] corporation which wholly owns Defendant [A.I.C.].

6.   At all relevant times, Defendant [C] has been the owner of [A.I.C. International] and [A.I.C.], and is an agent of an Employer within the meaning of § 101(5)(A) of the ADA, 42 U.S.C. § 12111(5)(A).

7.   At all relevant times Defendant [A.I.C.] has continuously been engaged in an industry affecting commerce within the meaning of Section 101(5) of the ADA , 42 U.S.C. § 12111(5), and § 107(7) of the ADA, 42 U.S.C. § 12117(7), which incorporates by reference §§ 701(g) and (h) of Title VII, 42 U.S.C. §§ 2000e(g) and (h).

8.   At all relevant times, Defendant [A.I.C.] has been a covered entity under § 101(2) of the ADA, 42 U.S.C. § 12111(2).

STATEMENT OF CLAIMS

9.   More than thirty (30) days prior to the institution of this lawsuit, [Wessel] filed a Charge with the Commission alleging violations of Title I of the ADA by Defendants [A.I.C.], [A.I.C. International] and [C]. All conditions precedent to the institution of this lawsuit have been fulfilled.

10.   Since at least [July 26, 1992], Defendants have engaged in unlawful employment practices in violation of the ADA §§ 102(a), 102(b)(1) and 102 (b)(5)(B), 42 U.S.C. §§ 12112(a), 12112(b)(1) and 12112(b)(5)(B), at their [Chicago], [Illinois] facility. These practices include but are not limited to Defendants'

discharge of [Wessel], a qualified individual with a disability, who was able to perform the essential functions of his position with or without reasonable accommodation, because of his disability, cancer; and Defendants' discharge of [Wessel]
based on the need to make reasonable accommodations to his possible future
physical impairments.

11.   The effect of the practices complained of above has been to deprive
[Wessel] of equal employment opportunities and otherwise adversely affect his
status as an employee because of his disability.

12.   The unlawful employment practices complained of above were and are
intentional.

PRAYER FOR RELIEF

WHEREFORE, the Commission respectfully prays that this Court:

A.   Grant a permanent injunction enjoining Defendant [A.I.C.], its owners,
officers, management personnel, employees, agents, successors, assigns; enjoining [Defendant C], and all persons in active concert or participation with them,
from engaging in any employment practice which discriminates on the basis of
disability;

B.   Order Defendants [A.I.C.], [A.I.C. International] and [Defendant C] to
institute and carry out policies, practices, and programs which provide equal
employment opportunities to qualified individuals with disabilities, and which
eradicate the effects of past and present unlawful employment practices;

C.   Order Defendants [A.I.C.], [A.I.C. International] and [C] to make whole
[Wessel] by providing him with appropriate lost earnings and insurance premiums, with pre-judgment interest, in amounts to be proved at trial, and other
affirmative relief necessary to eradicate the effects of its unlawful employment
practices, including, but not limited to reinstatement of [Wessel] to the position
of Executive Director;

D.   Order Defendants [A.I.C.], [A.I.C. International] and [C] to make whole
[Wessel] by providing compensation for pecuniary losses, including but not
limited to costs to be incurred for health and life insurance premiums and costs
of seeking new employment, in amounts to be determined at trial;

E.   Order Defendants [A.I.C.], [A.I.C. International] and [C] to make whole
[Wessel] by providing compensation for non-pecuniary losses, including emotional pain, suffering, inconvenience and mental anguish in amounts to be
proven at trial;

F.   Grant such further relief as the Court deems necessary and proper; and,

G.   Grant the Commission its costs in this action.

JURY TRIAL DEMANDED

The Commission requests a jury trial on all questions of face raised by the Complaint.

§ 10.13   —Intervenor's Complaint

FORM 10–10
SAMPLE INTERVENOR'S COMPLAINT

IN THE UNITED STATES DISTRICT COURT

FOR THE DISTRICT OF [district]

[Lance Butzer]

v.   Civil Action No. [number]

[Intercounty Trucking, Inc.]

Complaint in Intervention and Jury Trial Demand

JURISDICTION AND VENUE

1.   Jurisdiction in this claim under Title I of the Americans with Disabilities Act ("ADA"), 42 U.S.C. § 12101-12117 (Supp. 1990), is granted by 42 U.S.C. § 2000e-5(f), incorporated by reference by § 107 of the ADA, 42 U.S.C. § 12117. This case involves a federal question and thus jurisdiction also exists under 28 U.S.C. § 1331.

2.   Plaintiff/intervenor filed a charge with the EEOC within 180 days of the discriminatory acts alleged herein.

3.   All of the acts alleged in this complaint took place in the [district] and [state].

PARTIES

4.   The plaintiff, [Lance Butzer], is a [25]-year-old male who lives at [address].

5.   Plaintiff lost his left leg above the knee in a farm accident when he was fourteen years old, and thus is a person with a disability under the ADA.

6.   Defendant [Intercounty Trucking] is a corporation that operates a trucking line in several states, with offices at [address].

7.   Defendant [Intercounty Trucking] is engaged in an industry affecting commerce and employs more than 25 employees for more than 20 weeks in the current year and this is an "employer" and a "covered entity" under Title I of the ADA.

COUNT I—AMERICANS WITH DISABILITIES ACT

8.   On [September 1, 1992], plaintiff applied for employment as a [truck driver] with defendant.

9.   Plaintiff was qualified to perform the essential functions of that position.

10.   Defendant's personnel director told plaintiff that he would not be hired because of his disability.

11.   Plaintiff asked to discuss possible accommodations for his disability.

12.   Defendant's personnel director refused to discuss accommodation.

13.   Defendant violated its duty under the ADA, 42 U.S.C. § 12112, not to discriminate against a qualified individual with a disability because of the disability of such individual.

14.   Defendant, through its personnel director, expressed wilful disregard of defendant's duties under the ADA.

RELIEF

15. WHEREFORE, plaintiff requests

A.   An order compelling defendant to hire him as a [truck driver].

B.   An order for backpay and other appropriate equitable relief.

C.   A judgment for compensatory and punitive damages.

D.   Attorneys' fees.

JURY TRIAL DEMAND

The plaintiff/intervenor requests a jury trial on all questions of fact.

In some courts, the jury trial demand must be made in a separate document.

It is convenient if the paragraph numbers in the intervenor's complaint correspond to the paragraph numbers in the EEOC complaint. If they do, it is easy for the motion for intervention to show common transactions and issues of fact and law.

§ 10.14 Proceeding Anonymously

In ADA cases, plaintiffs may wish to proceed anonymously (that is, use a fictitious name) to protect against blacklisting by employers or public disclosure of their disability. Generally, the use of fictitious names is frowned upon as against public policy. However, courts have found that legitimate reasons exist for allowing plaintiffs to use fictitious names. These include retaliation, disclosure of utmost personal information, and threat of harm. Nevertheless, the plaintiff's interests must be balanced against those of the public and the defendant in disclosing of the plaintiff's real name.

Section 9.11 analyses the case law involving fictitious names.

The courts differ on the procedure for the use of fictitious names. In *Roe v. New York*,[7] the district court held that under Federal Rule of Civil Procedure 10(a) a valid complaint must contain the plaintiff's real name. Without the plaintiff's real name, no action was commenced.[8] The court suggested the following three alternatives for overcoming this procedural hurdle:

1. Filing a complaint under the plaintiff's true name, then requesting a protective order or leave to amend the complaint to shield the plaintiff's identity

2. Using pseudonyms in the complaint but setting forth the plaintiff's true name in an attached letter

---

[7] 49 F.R.D. 279 (S.D.N.Y. 1970). Plaintiffs R. Roe, M. Moe, S. Soe, and J. Joe filed a complaint seeking an injunction and money damages after alleging they received inadequate care in state training schools. The plaintiffs used pseudonyms because they were juvenile delinquents who were concerned with embarrassment, harassment, and ridicule. Furthermore, they argued that disclosure would hamper their attempts to assimilate into the community.

[8] The *Roe* complaint did not contain the real names of any of the plaintiffs. The defendants moved to dismiss because the complaint did not contain anyone's real name, which violated Fed. R. Civ. P. 10(a). The plaintiffs offered to provide their real names under protective provisions, and the plaintiffs also submitted affidavits containing their true names. However, the court dismissed the claim stating "if a complaint does not identify any plaintiff in the title or otherwise, then its filing is ineffective to commence an action." *Id.* at 281. The court looked at Fed. R. Civ. P. 3, which provides: "A civil action is commenced by filing a complaint with the court." The court found that the complaint filed was invalid because it did not meet the requirements of Fed. R. Civ. P. 10(a).

3.   Using a fictitious name in the complaint but verifying the complaint by signing the plaintiff's true name.[9]

Other courts allow plaintiffs to file a claim using fictitious names, then examine the plaintiffs' need for anonymity.[10] Given the possibility of dismissal if the complaint does not contain a plaintiff's real name, the better solution seems to be to file a claim using the real name and then to seek a protective order.

§ 10.15   —Affidavit in Support of Motion to Proceed Anonymously

FORM 10–11
SAMPLE AFFIDAVIT IN SUPPORT OF MOTION TO
PROCEED ANONYMOUSLY

UNITED STATES DISTRICT COURT

[WESTERN DISTRICT] OF [NEW YORK]

[MARIE C. DOE]

Plaintiff,

vs.

[state] STATE BOARD OF LAW EXAMINERS,

Defendant.

---

[9] Roe v. New York, 49 F.R.D. 279, 281 (S.D.N.Y. 1970).

[10] In Doe v. Hallock, 119 F.R.D. 640 (S.D. Miss. 1987), Jane Doe filed a complaint using a pseudonym. The defendants filed a motion to dismiss, relying on Roe v. New York, 49 F.R.D. 279 (S.D.N.Y. 1970). They argued that no suit was commenced under Fed. R. Civ. P. 3 because the complaint did not contain the name of the real party, which violated Fed. R. Civ. P. 10(a). Consequently, the defendants alleged that the court lacked subject matter jurisdiction as well as personal jurisdiction over the parties. Defendants further asserted that because the complaint was not properly filed, the court had no authority to issue summons, thereby rendering process insufficient. However, the court held that increasing numbers of parties have sought for a variety of reasons to sue anonymously to keep their identities confidential and, in fact, "a practice has developed permitting individuals to sue under fictitious names" under certain circumstances. *See* Doe v. Deschamps, 64 F.R.D. 652, 653 (D. Mont. 1974) (noting host of cases have been prosecuted under fictitious names since Roe).

CIV. NO. ___

AFFIDAVIT IN SUPPORT OF MOTION TO PROCEED ANONYMOUSLY

STATE OF [state]

COUNTY OF [name]

[Plaintiff], being duly sworn, deposes and says:

1.   I am the Plaintiff in this action and I make this Affidavit in support of my motion to file and prosecute this action anonymously. I am a candidate for admission to the [state] State Bar, and I am scheduled to take the [state] State Bar Examination on[date], in [city, state]. I suffer a severe visual handicap, and I desire to file this action to compel the [state] State Board of Law Examiners to provide reasonable accommodations to me. I am supplying with this affidavit copies of the complaint and other materials which I proposed to file herein.

2.   I seek to file this action anonymously, under the name [Marie C. Doe], to protect my privacy. I am a permanent resident of [city, state], and I intend to make my home in this community. I hope to be able to practice law in [city].

3.   Throughout my education and working experience, I have sought to minimize my visual handicap. Although I have from time to time received accommodations from schools and testing authorities, I have attempted insofar as has been possible to live and work without reference to my disability. In my working experience, I have been able to function competently by compensating for my lack of vision. Although everyone who knows me is aware that I always wear thick glasses, very few people have knowledge of the severity of my visual handicap.

4.   In this action, my medical condition and my background will necessarily be disclosed. Given the newness of the Americans with Disabilities Act, I believe my case may indeed come to the attention of the public both in [city] and beyond. I am fearful that I will come to be known as a "blind lawyer," and that potential employers and clients will be hesitant to hire or be represented by me. I have great concern the public disclosure of my condition might ruin the career I hope to pursue.

5.   I believe no prejudice would impose upon the defendant [state] State Board of Law Examiners if this action proceeds anonymously. The defendant will, of course, be aware of my identity, and I do not believe that any legitimate interest of the defendant will be compromised if my identity is not disclosed to the public.

6.   I therefore respectfully request that an order be entered allowing me to proceed to file and prosecute this action anonymously.

DATED: [date]

§ 10.16 —Order Granting Leave to
Proceed Anonymously

FORM 10–12
SAMPLE ORDER GRANTING LEAVE TO
PROCEED ANONYMOUSLY

UNITED STATES DISTRICT COURT

[judicial district] OF [state]

[MARIE C. DOE]

Plaintiff,

vs.

[state] STATE BOARD OF LAW EXAMINERS,

Defendant.

CIV. NO. [number]

ORDER GRANTING LEAVE TO PROCEED ANONYMOUSLY

The named plaintiff having moved this Court for an order authorizing her to file and prosecute this action anonymously, and the Court having given the matter due deliberation, it is

ORDERED, that the Plaintiff may file and prosecute this action anonymously by substituting the name [Marie C. Doe] for her true name; and it is further

ORDERED, that the Affidavit in support of the plaintiff's motion to proceed anonymously shall be served on defendant for purposes of informing defendant of the named plaintiff's identity, that defendant and its employees, agents and representatives shall not disclose the name of the plaintiff in connection with the proceedings in this action, that all parties to this action shall substitute the name [Marie C. Doe] for the true name in all papers and proceedings to be filed and had in this action, and that the affidavit in support of the motion to proceed anonymously shall be sealed by this Court and shall not be made a matter of public record.

Dated: [city, state]

[date]

CHAPTER 11

COMPLAINTS UNDER TITLES II AND III

§ 11.1   Introduction and Overview

This chapter parallels **Chapter 10** except that it contains Americans with Disabilities Act (ADA)[1] complaints made under Titles II[2] and III.[3] See **Forms 11–1** through **11–15.** The material in **Chapters 9** and **10** pertaining to styles of complaints and proceeding anonymously is equally applicable to complaints

---

[1] Pub. L. No. 101–336, 104 Stat. 327 (1990) (codified at 42 U.S.C. §§ 12101–12213 (1994); 47 U.S.C. §§ 225, 711 (1994) [hereinafter ADA].

[2] ADA 201–246, 42 U.S.C. §§ 12131–12165 (1994) [hereinafter Title II].

[3] ADA 301–310, 42 U.S.C. §§ 12181–12189 (1994) [hereinafter Title III].

drafted in this chapter. On the other hand, it is not necessary to file charges with the EEOC for Title III claims; it is possible to go directly to federal court after giving notice to a state or local agency with jurisdiction.[4]

§ 11.2   Movie Theater Access

FORM 11–1
SAMPLE COMPLAINT: MOVIE THEATER ACCESS

IN THE UNITED STATES DISTRICT COURT

FOR [judicial district]

[name],

[address]

Plaintiff,

v.   Civil Action No. [number]

[name],

[address]

SERVE:

[name],

[address]

Defendant.

AMENDED COMPLAINT

(Discrimination on the Basis of Disability)

JURISDICTION

1.   Jurisdiction of this Court is founded on 28 U.S.C. §§ 1331, 1441.

---

[4] 42 U.S.C. §§ 2000a-3(c), 2000a-3(d) (1994).

PARTIES

2.   [Plaintiff] is an adult resident of [state]. He is a wheelchair user due to a spinal cord injury.

3.   Defendant [name], is a corporation incorporated under the laws of the state of [state name], with its principal place of business located in the state of [state]. Defendant is licensed to do business and is doing businessatthe motion picture house known as [name], located at [address].

FACTS

4.   Defendant operates a motion picture house known as [name], located at [address]. One of the nine theatres, known as the [name], has a seating capacity in excess of 300 persons. Each of the other eight theatres has a seating capacity of fewer than 300 persons.

5.   On [date], Plaintiff went to the [name] Theatre for the purpose of viewing a movie. Plaintiff purchased a ticket for a movie entitled *Bugsy* and proceeded into the theatre known as [name]. Plaintiff wished to sit near the middle of the theatre. The only wheelchair seating area in [name], however, is behind the back row of seats. Defendant prohibits persons in a wheelchair, such as the Plaintiff, from sitting in the aisles or in any place other than the designated wheelchair seating area, and therefore Defendant segregates such persons, including Plaintiff, in the back of the theater regardless of their seating location preference.

6.   On or about [date], Plaintiff learned that in the eight theaters in the [name] Theatres other than [name], the only wheelchair seating area is located in the back row of seats, or behind the back row or seats. In each of the theaters, Defendant prohibits persons in a wheelchair, such as the Plaintiff, from sitting in the aisles or in any place other than the designated wheelchair seating area, and therefore Defendant segregates such persons, including Plaintiff, in the back of the theater regardless of their seating location preference.

7.   In the [name] theater, Defendant has not provided more than merely two wheelchair seating spaces, has not located wheelchair seating spaces so that they are dispersed throughout the entire seating area of the [name] theater, and evidently does not intend to do so.

8.   As a direct and proximate result of the Defendant's denial to Plaintiff of a reasonable choice of wheelchair seating areas in its theaters, Plaintiff has suffered and will suffer inconvenience, embarrassment, humiliation, emotional distress, and the indignity and stigma of discrimination.

CAUSE OF ACTION

COUNT I

(Violation of Americans with Disability Act)

9.   At all times relevant to this action, the Americans with Disabilities Act of 1990 (ADA), 42 U.S.C. § 12101 *et seq.,* was in full force and effect in the United States.

10.   The ADA expressly prohibits, inter alia, discrimination on the basis of disability in the full and equal enjoyment of the goods, services, facilities, privileges, advantages, or accommodations of any place of public accommodation by any person who owns, leases (or lease to), or operates a place of public accommodation. Under the terms of the ADA, discrimination includes a failure to remove architectural barriers, where such removal is readily achievable. The ADA requires that goods, services, facilities, privileges, advantages, and accommodations be afforded to an individual with a disability in the most integrated setting appropriate to the needs of the individual.

11.   The ADA expressly provides that a person with a disability is not required to engage in a futile gesture if such person has notice that a place of public accommodation does not intend to comply with the ADA.

12.   Plaintiff is an individual with a disability within the meaning of the ADA because Plaintiff has a physical impairment that substantially limits one or more of Plaintiff's major life activities.

13.   The [name]Theatres is a place of public accommodation with in the meaning of the ADA because it is a motion picture house, the operations of which affect commerce.

14.   Defendant is a person who owns, leases, or operates a place of public accommodation within the meaning of the ADA because Defendant owns, leases, or operates the [name] Theatres.

15.   Defendant is in violation of the ADA because it discriminates against Plaintiff on the basis of disability in the full and equal enjoyment of the services, facilities, privileges, advantages, or accommodations of the [name] theater at the [name] Theatres; because it does not afford to Plaintiff the services, facilities, privileges, advantages, and accommodations of the [name] theater in the most integrated setting appropriate to Plaintiff's needs; and because it has failed to undertake readily achievable removal of architectural barriers in the [name] theater.

16.   Plaintiff has actual notice that Defendant does not intend to comply with the ADA in respect to the number and location of wheelchair seating

spaces in the [name] theater because Defendant has expressly refused to comply so when Plaintiff specifically requested it to do so.

COUNT II

(Violation of [state] Human Rights Act)

17.   At all times relevant to this action, the [state] Human Rights Act, [cite statute] (Human Rights Act), was in full force and effect in [state].

18.   The Human Rights Act expressly prohibits, inter alia, the direct or indirect denial to any person, on account of physical handicap, of the full and equal enjoyment of the goods, services, facilities, privileges, advantages, and accommodation of any place of public accommodation.

19.   Plaintiff is a person with a physical handicap within the meaning of the Human Rights Act because Plaintiff has a bodily disablement which is the result of injury and for which reasonable accommodation can be made.

20.   Defendant is a place of public accommodation within the meaning of the Human Rights Act.

21.   On [date], Defendant violated the Human Rights Act because it denied Plaintiff, based on Plaintiff's physical handicap, the full and equal enjoyment of the services, facilities, privileges, advantages, and accommodations of the [name] Theatres.

22.   Defendant is in further violation of the Human Rights Act because it denies Plaintiff, based on Plaintiff's physical handicap, the full and equal enjoyment of the services, facilities, privileges, advantages, and accommodations or all the other theaters at the [name] Theatres.

23.   As a direct and proximate result of Defendant's violation of the Human Rights Act, Plaintiff has suffered inconvenience, embarrassment, humiliation, emotional distress, and the indignity and stigma of discrimination.

COUNT III

(Tortious Failure to Furnish Facilities to a Member of the Public)

24.   At all times relevant to this action, Defendant was under a noncontractual duty to furnish to the public without discrimination the facilities of the [name] Theatres.

25.   At all times relevant to this action, Plaintiff was entitled to use and enjoy the facilities of the [name] Theatres.

26.   On [date], Defendant violated its duty to furnish to the public without discrimination the facilities of the [name] Theatres because Defendant failed to provide Plaintiff the services, facilities, privileges, advantages, or accommodations of the [name] Theatres in an appropriate, nonsegregated and dignified setting.

27.   Defendant has further breached its duty to furnish to the public without discrimination the facilities of all the other theaters at the [name] Theatres because defendant has failed to provide Plaintiff the services, facilities, privileges, advantages, or accommodations of the other theaters at the [name] Theatres in an appropriate, nonsegregated and dignified setting.

28.   As a direct and proximate result of Defendant's breach of its duty to furnish to the public without discrimination the facilities of its [name] Theatres, Plaintiff has suffered and will suffer inconvenience, embarrassment, humiliation, emotional distress, and the indignity and stigma of discrimination.

WHEREFORE, Plaintiff [name] respectfully requests that the Court grant him the following relief:

(a)   An order directing Defendant to alter the [name] theater at the [name] Theatres to make such facility readily accessible to and usable by the individuals with disabilities, in accordance with the ADA Accessibility Guidelines for Buildings and Facilities, by providing six accessible wheelchair seating spaces, by providing at least one companion-fixed seat next to each wheelchair seating area, and by locating the wheelchair seating spaces so that they are dispersed throughout the entire seating area of the [name] theater;

(b)   An order directing Defendant to alter all the other theaters at the [name] Theatres to make such facilities readily accessible to and usable by individuals with disabilities, in accordance with the Human Rights Act, by locating a reasonable number of wheelchair seating spaces so that they are dispersed throughout the entire seating area of each theater, and by providing at least on companion-fixed seat next to each wheelchair seating area;

(c)   Entry of a money judgment against Defendant, awarding Plaintiff compensatory damages in the full and just amount of [Twenty-Five Thousand Dollars ($25,000.00)];

(d)   An award to Plaintiff of attorneys' fees, including litigation expenses, and costs;

(e)   An award to Plaintiff of such other and further legal and equitable relief as the Court deems just and proper.

JURY TRIAL DEMAND

Plaintiff requests a trial by jury on all aspects of this case.

Respectfully submitted,

[name]

[address]

[telephone number]

Counsel for Plaintiff

§ 11.3 Department Store Access

FORM 11–2
SAMPLE COMPLAINT: DEPARTMENT STORE ACCESS

SUPERIOR COURT OF [judicial district]

Civil Division

[name],

[address]

Plaintiff,

v.   Civil Action No. [number]

[name],

[address]

SERVE: [name]

[address]

Defendant.

COMPLAINT

(Discrimination on the Basis of Disability)

JURISDICTION

1.   Jurisdiction of this Court is founded on [statute].

PARTIES

2.   [Plaintiff] is an adult resident of [state] and is a wheelchair user due to a spinal cord injury.

3.   Defendant [name] is a corporation incorporated under the laws of [state], with its principal place of business located in [state]. Defendant is licensed to do business and is doing business at the retail store known as [store name], located at [address].

FACTS

4.   On [date], Plaintiff went to Defendant's store known as [store name], located at [address], for the purpose of shopping for clothes. In attempting to enter the store and use its facilities, Plaintiff encountered several architectural barriers.

5.   The floor buttons on the elevator car control panels were too high for Plaintiff to reach readily.

6.   The spout of the drinking fountain on the second floor adjacent to the public elevators, was too high for Plaintiff to use readily.

7.   No public accessible route was provided for Plaintiff into the public toilet facilities located on the seventh floor of [store name].

8.   The only route provided for Plaintiff to the public toilet facilities located on the seventh floor of [store name] passed through nonpublic service areas of the store, and involved use of the nonpublic freight elevator.

9.   No accessible route was provided for Plaintiff into the public toilet facilities located at the Down Under level of [store name].

10.   As a direct and proximate result of Defendant's denial to Plaintiff of appropriate and dignified access into and use of [store name], Plaintiff suffered inconvenience, embarrassment, humiliation, emotional distress, and the indignity and stigma of discrimination.

CAUSES OF ACTION

COUNT I

(Violation of Americans with Disabilities Act)

11.   At all times relevant to this action, the Americans with Disabilities Act of l990 (ADA), 42 U.S.C. § 12101 *et seq.,* was in full force and effect in the United States.

12.   The ADA expressly prohibits, inter alia, discrimination on the basis of disability in the full and equal enjoyment of the goods, services, facilities, privileges, advantages, or accommodations of any place of public accommodation by any person who owns, leases (or leases to), or operates a place of public accommodation. Under the terms of the ADA, discrimination includes a failure to remove architectural barriers, where such removal is readily achievable. The ADA requires that goods, services, facilities, privileges, advantages, and accommodations be afforded to an individual with a disability in the most integrated setting appropriate to the needs of the individual.

13.   Plaintiff is an individual with a disability within the meaning of the ADA because he has a physical impairment that substantially limits one or more of his major life activities.

14.   [Store name] is a place of public accommodation within the meaning of the ADA because it is a sales establishment the operations of which affect commerce.

15.   Defendant is a person who owns, leases, or operates a place of public accommodation within the meaning of the ADA because Defendant owns, leases, or operates [store name].

16.   On [date], Defendant violated the ADA because it discriminated against Plaintiff on the basis of disability in the full and equal enjoyment of the goods, services, facilities, privileges, advantages, or accommodations of [store name]; because it did not afford to Plaintiff the goods, services, facilities, privileges, advantages, and accommodations of [store name] in the most integrated setting appropriate to Plaintiff's needs; and because it failed to undertake readily achievable removal of architectural barriers.

COUNT II

(Violation of [state] Human Rights Act)

17.   At all times relevant to this action, [state] Human Rights Act, [cite statute] (Human Rights Act), was in full force and effect in [state].

18.   The Human Rights Act expressly prohibits, inter alia, the direct and indirect denial to any person, on account of physical handicap, of the full and equal enjoyment of the goods, services, facilities, privileges, advantages, and accommodations of any place of public accommodation.

19.   Plaintiff is a person with a physical handicap within the meaning of the Human Rights Act because Plaintiff has a bodily disablement which is the result of injury and for which reasonable accommodation can be made.

20.   Defendant is a place of public accommodation within the meaning of the Human Rights Act.

21.   On [date], Defendant violated the Human Rights Act because it denied Plaintiff, based on Plaintiff's physical handicap, the full and equal enjoyment of the goods, services, facilities, privileges, advantages, and accommodations of [store name].

COUNT III

(Tortious Failure to Furnish Facilities to a Member of the Public)

22.   At all times relevant to this action, Defendant was under a noncontractual duty to furnish to the public without discrimination the facilities of [store name].

23.   At all times relevant to this action, Plaintiff was entitled to the facilities of [store name].

24.   On [date], Defendant violated its duty to furnish to the public without discrimination the facilities of [store name] because Defendant failed to provide Plaintiff a means of appropriate, nonsegregated, independent, and dignified access to and usage of the facilities of [store name].

25.   As a direct and proximate result of Defendant's breach of its duty to furnish to the public without discrimination the facilities of [store name], Plaintiff suffered inconvenience, embarrassment, humiliation, emotional distress, and the indignity and stigma of discrimination.

WHEREFORE, Plaintiff [name] respectfully requests that the Court grant him the following relief:

(a)   An order directing Defendant to remove the architectural barriers at the elevators, water fountains, and toilet facilities of [store name] to make such facilities readily accessible to and usable by individuals with disabilities, consistent with the ADA Accessibility Guidelines for Buildings and Facilities;

(b)   Entry of a money judgment against Defendant, awarding Plaintiff compensatory damages in the full and just amount of [Twenty-Five Thousand Dollars ($25,000.00)];

(c)   An award to Plaintiff of his attorneys' fees, including litigation expenses, and costs; and

(d)   An award to Plaintiff of such other and further legal and equitable relief as the Court deems just and proper.

JURY TRIAL DEMAND

Plaintiff requests a trial by jury on all aspects of this case.

Respectfully submitted,

[name]

[address]

[telephone number]

Counsel for Plaintiff

§ 11.4   Hotel Access

FORM 11–3
SAMPLE COMPLAINT: HOTEL ACCESS

SUPERIOR COURT OF [judicial district]

Civil Division

[name],

[address]

Plaintiff,

v.   Civil Action No. [number]

[name]

[address]

SERVE: [name]

[address]

Defendant.

COMPLAINT

(Discrimination on the Basis of Disability)

JURISDICTION

1.   Jurisdiction of this Court is founded on [statute].

PARTIES

2.   [Plaintiff] is an adult resident of [state] and is a wheelchair user due to a spinal cord injury.

3.   Defendant [name] is a corporation incorporated under the laws of [state], with its principal place of business located in [state]. Defendant is licensed to do business and is doing business at the hotel known as the [hotel name], located at [address].

FACTS

4.   On [date], Plaintiff went to Defendant's hotel known as [hotel name], located at [address], for the purpose of eating brunch at the restaurant known as [name], located on the first floor of the hotel. Plaintiff sought to use the toilet facilities located on the first floor of the hotel. The toilet facilities, however, were not readily accessible to or usable by Plaintiff.

5.   Plaintiff found one toilet stall evidently intended for use by persons who use a wheelchair. The round door knob on the toilet stall door, however, was extremely difficult for the Plaintiff to operate.

6.   Grab bars were not provided around the water closet.

7.   The lavatory provided in the toilet stall was not in operation.

8.   Adequate knee clearance was not provided under the public lavatories for Plaintiff in the wheelchair.

9.   The public lavatory faucets were difficult for Plaintiff to operate because they were not operable with one hand and because they required grasping, which is difficult for Plaintiff to do.

10.   Upon seeking to exit the toilet facilities, Plaintiff discovered that there was inadequate clearance on the latch side of the door to permit him to swing the door open. Consequently, Plaintiff had to call for assistance to exit the toilet facilities.

11.   As a direct and proximate result of Defendant's denial to Plaintiff of toilet facilities that were readily accessible to and usable by persons such as Plaintiff who use a wheelchair, Plaintiff suffered inconvenience, embarrassment, humiliation, emotional distress, and the indignity and stigma of discrimination.

CAUSE OF ACTION

COUNT I

(Violation of Americans with Disabilities Act)

12.   At all times relevant to this action, the Americans with Disabilities Act of 1990 (ADA), 42 U.S.C. § 12101 *et seq.,* was in full force and effect in the United States.

13.   The ADA expressly prohibits, inter alia, discrimination on the basis of disability in the full and equal enjoyment of the goods, services, facilities, privileges, advantages, or accommodations of any place of public accommodation by any person who owns, leases (or leases to), or operates a place of public accommodation. Under the terms of the ADA, discrimination includes a failure to remove architectural barriers, where such removal is readily achievable.

14.   Plaintiff is an individual with a disability within the meaning of the ADA because Plaintiff has a physical impairment that substantially limits one or more major life activities.

15.   The [hotel name] is a place of public accommodation within the meaning of the ADA because it is a hotel the operations of which affect commerce.

16.   Defendant is a person who owns, leases, or operates a place of public accommodation within the meaning of the ADA because Defendant owns, leases, or operates the [hotel name].

17.   On [date], Defendant violated the ADA because it discriminated against Plaintiff on the basis of disability in the full and equal enjoyment of goods, services, facilities, privileges, advantages, or accommodations of the [hotel name], and because it failed to undertake readily achievable removal of architectural barriers.

COUNT II

(Violation of [state] Human Rights Act)

18.   At all times relevant to this action, [state] Human Rights Act, [cite statute] (Human Rights Act), was in full force and effect in [state].

19.   The Human Rights Act expressly prohibits, inter alia, the direct or indirect denial to any person, on account of physical handicap, of the full and equal

enjoyment of the goods, services, facilities, privileges, advantages, and accommodations of any place of public accommodation.

20.   Plaintiff is a person with a physical handicap within the meaning of the Human Rights Act because of a bodily disablement which is the result of injury and for which reasonable accommodation can be made.

21.   Defendant is a place of public accommodation within the meaning of the Human Rights Act.

22.   On [date], Defendant violated the Human Rights Act because it denied Plaintiff, based on Plaintiff's physical handicap, the full and equal enjoyment of goods, services, facilities, privileges, advantages, and accommodations of the [hotel name].

COUNT III

(Tortious Failure to Furnish Facilities to a Member of the Public)

23.   At all times relevant to this action, Defendant was under a noncontractual duty to furnish to the public without discrimination the facilities of [hotel name].

24.   At all times relevant to this action, Plaintiff was entitled to the facilities of [hotel name].

25.   On [date], Defendant violated its duty to furnish to the public without discrimination the facilities of [hotel name] because Defendant failed to provide Plaintiff a means of appropriate, nonsegregated, independent, and dignified access to [hotel name].

26.   As a direct and proximate result of Defendant's breach of its duty to furnish to the public without discrimination the facilities of [hotel name], Plaintiff suffered inconvenience, embarrassment, humiliation, emotional distress, and the indignity and stigma of discrimination.

WHEREFORE, Plaintiff [name] respectfully requests that the Court grant him the following relief:

(a)   An order directing Defendant to remove the architectural barriers in the toilet facilities of [hotel name] and to alter its facilities at [hotel name] to make such facilities readily accessible to, and usable by, individuals with disabilities, in accordance with the ADA Accessibility Guidelines for Buildings and Facilities;

(b)   Entry of a money judgment against Defendant awarding Plaintiff compensatory damages in the full and just amount of [Twenty-Five Thousand Dollars ($25,000.00)];

(c)   An award to Plaintiff of his attorneys' fees, including litigation expenses, and costs; and

(d)   An award to Plaintiff of such other and further legal and equitable relief as the Court deems just and proper.

JURY TRIAL DEMAND

Plaintiff requests a trial by jury on all aspects of this case.

Respectfully submitted,

[name]

[address]

[telephone number]

Counsel for Plaintiff

§ 11.5   Clothing Store Access

FORM 11–4
SAMPLE COMPLAINT: CLOTHING STORE ACCESS

SUPERIOR COURT OF [judicial district]

Civil Division

[name]

[address]

Plaintiff,

v.   Civil Action No. [number]

[name],

[address]

SERVE: [name]

[address]

Defendant.

<u>COMPLAINT</u>

(Discrimination on the Basis of Disability)

<u>JURISDICTION</u>

1.   Jurisdiction of this Court is founded on [statute].

<u>PARTIES</u>

2.   [Plaintiff] is an adult resident of [state] and is a wheelchair user due to a spinal cord injury.

3.   Defendant [name] is a corporation incorporated under the laws of [state], with its principal place of business located in [state]. Defendant is licensed to do business and is doing business at the retail store known as [store name] located at [address].

<u>FACTS</u>

4.   On [date], Plaintiff went to Defendant's store located at [address] for the purpose of shopping for clothes. Plaintiff entered the store through the doors at the only public entrance, located at [address]. Plaintiff, in a wheelchair, was unable to proceed into the store, however, because there was a change in level of approximately 15 inches between the doors and the floor of the store. The only means provided for traversing the change in level was three stairs; no ramp, elevator, wheelchair lift device, or other means of wheelchair access at the entrance was provided.

5.   In order for Plaintiff to gain entry into [store name], a manager escorted Plaintiff out of the store, up the street, into the lobby of the adjoining office building, up an elevator, and then through an emergency exit door which was locked from the outside and is not a public entrance to [store name].

6.   As a direct and proximate result of Defendant's denial to Plaintiff of appropriate and dignified access into [store name], Plaintiff suffered inconvenience, embarrassment, humiliation, emotional distress, and the indignity and stigma of discrimination.

<u>CAUSE OF ACTION</u>

<u>COUNT I</u>

(Violation of Americans with Disabilities Act)

7.   At all times relevant to this action, the Americans with Disabilities Act of 1990 (ADA), 42 U.S.C. § 12101 *et seq.*, was in full force and effect in the United States.

8.   The ADA expressly prohibits, inter alia, discrimination on the basis of disability in the full and equal enjoyment of the goods, services, facilities, privileges, advantages, or accommodations of any place of public accommodation by any person who owns, leases (or leases to), or operates a place of public accommodation. Under the terms of the ADA, discrimination includes a failure to remove architectural barriers, where such removal is readily achievable. The ADA requires that goods, services, facilities, privileges, advantages, and accommodations be afforded to an individual with a disability in the most integrated setting appropriate to needs of the individual.

9.   Plaintiff is an individual with a disability within the meaning of the ADA because of a physical impairment that substantially limits one or more major life activities.

10.   [Store name] is a place of public accommodation within the meaning of the ADA because it is a clothing store the operations of which affect commerce.

11.   Defendant is a person who owns, leases, or operates a place of public accommodation within the meaning of the ADA because Defendant owns, leases, or operates [store name].

12.   On [date], Defendant violated the ADA because it discriminated against Plaintiff on the basis of disability in the full and equal enjoyment of the goods, services, facilities, privileges, advantages, or accommodations of [store name]; because it did not afford to Plaintiff the goods, services, facilities, privileges, advantages, and accommodations in the most integrated setting appropriate to Plaintiff's needs; and because it failed to undertake readily achievable removal of architectural barriers.

<u>COUNT II</u>

(Violation of [state] Human Rights Act)

13.   At all times relevant to this action, the [state] Human Rights Act, [cite statute] (Human Rights Act), was in full force and effect in [state].

14.   The Human Rights Act expressly prohibits, inter alia, the direct or indirect denial to any person, on account of physical handicap, of the full and equal enjoyment of the goods, services, facilities, privileges, advantages, and accommodations of any place of public accommodation.

15.   Plaintiff is a person with a physical handicap within the meaning of the Human Rights Act because of a bodily disablement which is the result of injury and for which reasonable accommodation can be made.

16.   Defendant is a place of public accommodation within the meaning of the Human Rights Act.

17.   On [date], Defendant violated the Human Rights Act because it denied Plaintiff, based on his physical handicap, the full and equal enjoyment of goods, services, facilities, privileges, advantages, and accommodations of [store name].

<u>COUNT III</u>

(Tortious Failure to Furnish Facilities to a Member of the Public)

18.   At all times relevant to this action, Defendant was under an on contractual duty to furnish to the public without discrimination the facilities of [store name].

19.   At all times relevant to this action, Plaintiff was entitled to the facilities of [store name].

20.   On [date], Defendant violated its duty to furnish to the public without discrimination the facilities of [store name] because Defendant failed to provide Plaintiff a means of appropriate, nonsegregated, independent, and dignified access to [store name].

21.   As a direct and proximate result of Defendant's breach of its duty to furnish to the public without discrimination the facilities of [store name], Plaintiff suffered inconvenience, embarrassment, humiliation, emotional distress, and the indignity and stigma of discrimination.

WHEREFORE, Plaintiff [name] respectfully requests that the Court grant him the following relief:

(a)   An order directing Defendant to remove the architectural barriers at the entrance to its [store name] to make such facilities readily accessible to and usable by individuals with disabilities, in accordance with the ADA Accessibility Guidelines for Buildings and Facilities.

(b)   Entry of a money judgment against Defendant, awarding Plaintiff compensatory damages in the full and just amount of [Twenty-Five Thousand Dollars ($25,000.00)];

(c)   An award to Plaintiff of his attorneys' fees, including litigation expenses, and costs; and

(d)   An award to Plaintiff of such other and further legal and equitable relief as the Court deems just and proper.

<u>JURY TRIAL DEMAND</u>

Plaintiff requests a trial by jury on all aspects of this case.

Respectfully submitted,

[name]

[address]

[telephone number]

Counsel for Plaintiff

§ 11.6   Accommodation in Bar Exam

FORM 11–5
SAMPLE COMPLAINT: ACCOMMODATION IN BAR EXAM

UNITED STATES DISTRICT COURT

[judicial district] OF [state]

[name]

Plaintiff,   CIV. NO. [number]

v.

[state] BOARD OF LAW EXAMINERS

Defendant.

DEMAND FOR JURY TRIAL

Plaintiff [name], by and through her attorneys, [names], brings this Complaint against Defendant [state] Board of Law Examiners and states as follows:

INTRODUCTION

1.   This action seeks preliminary and permanent injunctive relief against Defendant [state] Board of Examiners (Law Examiners) based on the Law Examiners' discriminatory conduct against Plaintiff, a disabled person. Plaintiff is registered to take the [date] [state] Bar Examination and has requested certain accommodations in the manner in which the Bar Examination is administered. These accommodations are necessary to insure that the Bar Examination is accessible to Plaintiff, who suffers from severe visual disabilities.

2.   The Law Examiners have refused to grant Plaintiff sufficient accommodations, which refusal violates the ADA, 42 U.S.C. § 12101 *et seq.* The ADA requires that all persons who offer examinations related to licensing for professional and trade purposes do so in a place and manner accessible to persons

with disabilities. 42 U.S.C. § 12189. In addition, the ADA prohibits public entities such as the Law Examiners from discriminating against disabled persons. 42
U.S.C. § 12132. The ADA further provides that defendants who violate the
ADA are liable for the costs of litigation, including attorneys' fees, pursuant to
specific provisions of the ADA and the Civil Rights Act of 1964.

PARTIES

3.   Plaintiff is an individual residing in [city, state].

4.   Defendant [state] Board of Law Examiners is an instrumentality of
[state], with its principal place of business in [city, state]. Among other functions, the Law Examiners prepare and administer the biannual [state] Bar
Examination, the professional licensing examination required for admission to
practice law in [state].

JURISDICTION AND VENUE

5.   This Court has jurisdiction over this action under:

a.   28 U.S.C. § 1331 for civil actions arising under the laws of the United
States;

b.   42 U.S.C. § 12188(a)(1), which incorporates the provisions of 42 U.S.C.
§ 2000a-(3)(a), providing for civil actions by any person being subjected to discrimination on the basis of disability in violation of Title III of the ADA; and

c.   42 U.S.C. § 12133, which incorporates the provisions of 29 U.S.C.
§ 794a, for violations of Title II of the ADA.

6.   Venue in this District is proper under 28 U.S.C. § 1391(b)(2) and 42
U.S.C. § 2000e-5(f) in that the acts of discrimination complained of occurred in
this District.

FACTS

7.   Plaintiff is a [year] graduate of the [name] School of Law. Prior to enrollment in law school, Plaintiff attended [name] College and later [name] University.
Plaintiff graduated from [name] University with a Bachelor of Science Degree in
1987 and a Master of Science Degree in 1990.

8.   Plaintiff suffers from a severe visual disability. As set forth in the affidavit of
[name], M.D., attached hereto as Exhibit A, Plaintiff has marked myopia (nearsight-
ness) and bilateral partial amblyopia, which means that, although her eyes are normal in form and physiological function, Plaintiff is unable to achieve anything
approaching 20\20 vision. Neither corrective lenses nor surgery will bring
Plaintiff's vision close to normal levels. Because of the visual disability, plaintiff

has an extremely difficult time reading and finds it nearly impossible to read normal-sized print.

9.   In addition to myopia and bilateral partial amblyopia, Plaintiff also suffers from severe ocular fatigue. Plaintiff's visual difficulties worsen when reading over extended periods of time, and Plaintiff develops blurring, tearing, and burning, and requires frequent breaks to rest her eyes. The disabling impact these visual difficulties have on Plaintiff's reading skills directly affects Plaintiff's ability to take the Bar Examination under normal conditions.

10.   Plaintiff's visual impairment has been recognized and documented for the past 21 years. Plaintiff has been under the continual care of [name], M.D., a licensed ophthalmologist, since 1972. Plaintiff was referred to Dr. [name] at age [14] due to her severe visual problems. As Dr. [name] wrote in his [date] letter to the Law Examiners, "Her vision is not able to be corrected to full normal levels by either her glasses or by contact lenses . . . . She cannot develop 20\20 vision or anywhere near it." A copy of this letter is attached hereto as Exhibit B.

11.   Plaintiff's visual disability has been recognized by the [state] Department of Vocational Rehabilitation, through which Plaintiff received large print books and other assistance while in high school.

12.   On [date], Plaintiff was tested at the [name] Medical Center in [city, state]. At [name], Plaintiff was examined by the University's Director of Cornea Service, [name], M.D. Dr. [name] diagnosed Plaintiff's condition as extreme myopia and strabismic myopia. In a letter dated [date], a copy which is attached as Exhibit C, Dr. [name] wrote that the examination revealed:

> [Plaintiff's] corrected acuity with her present glasses was 25\50 in the right eye and 20\70 in the left eye. Neither eye improved with pinpoint . . . . Manifest refraction over her current glasses did not improve acuity in either eye. Manifest refraction together with retinoscopy without her glasses again did not improve acuity in either eye. A stereopsis exam revealed failure to see even the wings of the fly on the Titmus test.

In addition, Dr. [name] noted that Plaintiff's poor vision "keeps her from performing routine daily tasks such as driving and reading comfortably." In discussing Plaintiff's options for the future, Dr. [name] noted that Plaintiff's decreased visual acuity is due to her amblyopia, which is a "permanent, lifelong problem which with current technology cannot be corrected."

13.   Because of Plaintiff's visual disability, Plaintiff received special accommodations for the Law School Admissions Test, including a large print exam, extra time to take the exam, and a special testing room.

14.   Plaintiff also received special accommodations for examinations at [name] Law School. The Committee on Law Students with Special Needs determined that Plaintiff's disability necessitated large-print exam materials and extra

time to take examinations. Plaintiff was also permitted to reschedule exams to allow for rest days between tests.

15.   In [date], Plaintiff received special testing conditions for the Multi-State Professional Responsibility Exam (MPRE), held in [city, state]. Plaintiff received a large print exam, a separate testing room, and extra time to take the exam. Plaintiff was also permitted to use a straight-edge ruler and her own lamp for enhanced lighting. Plaintiff received a passing score on the MPRE.

16.   Following Plaintiff's graduation from law school in [date], Plaintiff began preparing to take the [date] [state] Bar Examination.

17.   In [date], Plaintiff submitted an application to sit for the [month] Bar Examination. As part of the application, Plaintiff submitted a request for special testing conditions pursuant to the Rules of the [state] Board of Law Examiners. [Statute]. Plaintiff provided documentation of her disability in the form of a letter from Dr. [name], dated [date]. A copy of Dr. [name]'s letter is attached hereto as Exhibit D.

REQUEST TO THE LAW EXAMINERS FOR SPECIAL TESTING CONDITIONS

18.   Because of Plaintiff's severe visual disability, Dr. [name] advised the Law Examiners that Plaintiff required special accommodations on the Bar Examination. In a [date] letter to the Law Examiners, Dr. [name] stated:

> There is no question that [plaintiff] can do the work and I believe there is no question that [plaintiff] can pass the exam, but because of special visual problems she does need certain aids:
> 2. Because of her visual difficulty, Plaintiff develops blurring, tearing, and burning, and that is why she needs rest every 30-60 minutes during an exam.
> 3. [Plaintiff's] visual problems make it impossible for her to 'skim' material, so needs more time to take an exam.
> 6. With ocular fatigue during a long exam, sometimes people like [plaintiff] have difficulty in following a line, and it is helpful to allow them to use a ruler.
> 7. If it is possible, larger print would be helpful-perhaps over ten point print.

Dr. [name] specifically requested that Plaintiff be given extra time for the [date] Bar Examination. He also recommended the following accommodations: (1) a separate examination room with extra lighting; (2) use of a pen rather than pencil; (3) yellow-lined paper rather than white; and (4) handwritten answers to multiple choice questions. As a disabled person, these accommodations were necessary to ensure Plaintiff a fair and equal opportunity to perform on the [month] Bar Examination. Without these accommodations, especially the requirement of extra time, Plaintiff would not be afforded an equal opportunity to demonstrate her knowledge and ability.

19.   In a letter dated [date], the Law Examiners notified Plaintiff that they were willing to grant some, but not all, of her requests for special testing conditions. A

copy of the Law Examiners' letter is attached as Exhibit E. Plaintiff received the following accommodations:

1.   The exam time was increased to time and one-half. On [date], the test schedule was from 7:30 A.M. to 5:45 P.M. with 45 minutes for lunch, and on [date] from 7:30 A.M. to 5:30 P.M., with one hour for lunch.

2.   The exam materials were enlarged.

3.   Plaintiff could bring her own lamp.

4.   The answers to multiple choice questions could be written out, rather than placed on a computer scoring test.

5.   Plaintiff was permitted to use a straight-edge ruler.

[date] EXAMINATION

20.   Plaintiff sat for the Bar Examination on [date]. The time and one-half schedule increased the normal time of the exam on [date] from 6-1/2 to 9-1/2 hours and on [date] from 6 hours to 9 hours.

21.   Plaintiff's disability makes it extremely difficult to read; it takes much longer to read exam questions than nondisabled persons. Further, Plaintiff suffers from blurring and ocular fatigue during long periods of reading. As a result, the schedule forced Plaintiff to use all of the additional examination time just to complete and finish the exam, without affording an opportunity to rest her eyes.

22.   The testing conditions for the [date] Bar Examination did not provide Plaintiff with an equal opportunity to perform.

23.   In [date], Plaintiff received notification that she had failed the [date] Bar Examination. Plaintiff began to prepare to retake the examination scheduled for [date].

REAPPLICATION FOR THE BAR EXAMINATION

24.   On or about [date], Plaintiff again requested special accommodations for the Bar Examination. She again provided documentation of the disability and requested additional testing time, with the specific provision that the exam be administered over four days. In a letter dated [date], a copy of which is attached hereto as Exhibit B, Dr. [name] described the special request:

The most important special testing arrangement is extra time. [Plaintiff] advises me that she was allotted additional time to take the exam in [month]. Her exam schedule was from 7:30 A.M. to 5:45 P.M. on [date] and 7:30 A.M. to 5:30 P.M. on [date]. In all probability, this schedule exacerbated [Plaintiff's] disability. Because it takes her longer to read through the testing materials, [Plaintiff] ended up reading and writing during the extra time for the exam, rather than resting her eyes. [Plaintiff]'s eye fatigue was aggravated by the schedule. A more reasonable accommodation would be to permit her to take the two-day exam over a period of four days.

Unless she receives this special accommodation, Plaintiff will be severely disadvantaged as compared to nondisabled individuals taking the Bar Examination.

25.   On or about [date], Plaintiff was notified that while some of the accommodations she requested will be granted, Plaintiff will not be provided with a four-day schedule to take the [month] Bar Examination. While the Law Examiners will permit Plaintiff to create her own schedule over two days, this "accommodation" is deceiving. As described by Dr. [name], a longer daily exam schedule will only exacerbate Plaintiff's visual difficulties. The denial of her request to take the exam over four days denies Plaintiff the opportunity to take the Bar Examination in a manner equivalent to nondisabled persons.

26.   On or about [date], Plaintiff filed an appeal to the Law Examiners of their decision of [date]. In a verified petition, Plaintiff requested that the Law Examiners reconsider their denial of her request to take the exam over four days. Plaintiff proposed a test schedule with five hours of testing on each of the four days, plus 15-minute breaks on the hour if needed and a lunch break. In an affidavit dated [date], Dr. [name] described the proposal:

> It is my recommendation that if the examination time periods are limited to five hours per day for four days, plus 15-minute breaks every hour if needed and a break for lunch, this schedule would result in a more accurate reflection of [plaintiff's] abilities. With the 15-minute breaks, she would have an opportunity to rest her eyes. With a limitation on the number of hours of testing in a given day, she would have an opportunity to rest her eyes during the evening hours.

The appeal was filed pursuant to the Rules of the Board of Law Examiners. [Statute]. A copy of the verified petition, along with Dr. [name]'s affidavit, is attached hereto as Exhibit F.

27.   As of the date of this complaint, the Law Examiners have not advised Plaintiff of their decision on the appeal. Based on discussions with a representative of the Law Examiners, Plaintiff does not expect that the Law Examiners will revise their decision, and the appeal will be denied.

COUNT I (Violation of 42 U.S.C. § 12189)

28.   Plaintiff incorporates by reference the allegations contained in paragraphs 1 through 27 herein as if set forth in their entirety.

29.   Plaintiff is a qualified individual with a disability because she has a physical impairment that substantially limits one or more major life functions. Plaintiff suffers from visual disabilities which severely limit the manner in which she is able to perform important life activities. In addition, Plaintiff is disabled because she has a record of having a physical impairment that substantially limits one or more major life functions and because she has been regarded as having such impairment.

30.   The ADA, 42 U.S.C. § 12189, requires that the Law Examiners, as a person offering examinations related to licensing for professional and trade purposes, must offer such examinations in a place and manner accessible to persons with disabilities, such as Plaintiff. In order for the Bar Examination to be accessible to Plaintiff, the Law Examiners must provide the accommodations set forth in Dr. [name]'s letter of [date] and affidavit of [date], including the request that the exam be administered over four days.

31.   Despite the request for the accommodations required by the ADA, the Law Examiners have refused to grant Plaintiff the accommodations necessary for the Bar Examination to be administered in a manner accessible to a person with specific and documented visual disabilities. Because of its refusal to grant the reasonable accommodations, the Law Examiners are in violation of 42 U.S.C. § 12189.

32.   The Law Examiners' violation of the ADA has caused immediate and irreparable injury to Plaintiff, including jeopardizing Plaintiff's ability to take the Bar Examination in a fair and reasonable manner and to ensure the same opportunity to pass the Bar Examination as is provided to individuals who are not disabled. Plaintiff's aptitude and achievement levels will not be accurately reflected under the testing conditions proposed by the Law Examiners.

33.   The Law Examiners' violation of the ADA has also damaged Plaintiff's access to an equal opportunity to be admitted to practice law in [state]. In addition, the Law Examiner's refusal to provide necessary accommodations to a disabled person has caused Plaintiff to suffer mental distress, humiliation, and public embarrassment.

COUNT II (Violation of 42 U.S.C. § 12132)

34.   The Plaintiff incorporates by reference the allegations contained in paragraphs 1 through 33, herein as set forth in their entirety.

35.   Plaintiff is a qualified individual with a disability because of a physical impairment that substantially limits one or more major life functions. Plaintiff suffers from visual disabilities which severely limit the manner in which she is able to perform important life activities. In addition, Plaintiff is disabled because of a record of having a physical impairment that substantially limits one or more major life functions and because Plaintiff has been regarded as having such impairment.

36.   Plaintiff has met the essential eligibility requirements to take the Bar Examination in [state]. However, because of visual disabilities, Plaintiff requires the reasonable accommodations set forth in Dr. [name]'s letter of [date], and affidavit of [date], in order to have an equal chance of passing the Bar Examination.

37.   The ADA, 42 U.S.C. § 12132, prohibits public entities, such as the Law Examiners, from discriminating against a qualified individual with a disability in the provision of services, programs, or activities. In addition, § 12132 prevents a public entity from excluding a person with a disability from participation in or receipt of the benefit of its services, programs, or activities.

38.   Despite Plaintiff's request for accommodations based on disability, the Law Examiners have refused to grant the accommodations necessary to ensure that the Bar Examination is administered in a manner accessible to a person with visual disabilities. Accordingly, the Law Examiners have discriminated against Plaintiff, by excluding her from participation and denying the benefits of the Bar Examination. This discrimination and denial of benefits is solely attributable to Plaintiff's disability. By refusing to provide the requested accommodations, the Law Examiners have violated 42 U.S.C. § 12132.

39.   The Law Examiners' violation of the ADA has caused immediate and irreparable injury to Plaintiff, including jeopardizing her ability to take the Bar Examination in a fair and reasonable manner and to provide her with the same opportunity to pass the Bar Examination as is provided to individuals who are not disabled.

40.   The Law Examiners' violation has also damaged Plaintiff's access to an equal opportunity for admission to practice law in [state]. In addition, the refusal of the Law Examiners to provide reasonable accommodations to Plaintiff as a disabled person has caused her to suffer mental distress, humiliation, and public embarrassment. The Board's discrimination against Plaintiff has or may also result in the following damages: (1) additional costs which have been paid to enroll in preparation courses for the exam; (2) additional examination fees which have been paid to the Law Examiners; and (3) other special damages.

RELIEF REQUESTED

WHEREFORE, Plaintiff prays that this Court enter judgment on her belief as follows:

(1)   A preliminary and permanent mandatory injunction requiring that the [state] Board of Law Examiners extend to Plaintiff the following accommodations in the manner of taking the [date] [state] Bar Examination and any future Bar Examinations, if necessary:

(a)   To take the examination in a separate room, isolated from other Bar candidates;

(b)   To be allowed to hand mark answer letters as opposed to filling in the computer-scored answer sheet with respect to multiple choice questions;

(c)   To be provided with a large print exam and be allowed to use a straight-edge ruler; and

(d)   To be allotted additional time to take the examination over a four-day period, with approximately five hours of testing each day, plus 15-minute breaks on the hour, if needed, and a lunch break.

(2)   Monetary relief against the Board under Count 11 in an amount not less than [$1,200], recoverable pursuant to 42 U.S.C. § 12133, which incorporates the provisions of 29 U.S.C. § 794a:

(3)   Attorneys' fees, including litigation expenses and costs, incurred by Plaintiff in this action, recoverable pursuant to the provisions of 42 U.S.C. § 12205, 29 U.S.C. § 794a and 42 U.S.C. § 1988; and such other and further relief as this Court may deem proper and necessary.

Dated: [date]

Signed: [attorney for plaintiff]

§ 11.7   —Affidavit of Expert #1

FORM 11–6
SAMPLE EXPERT AFFIDAVIT

UNITED STATES DISTRICT COURT

[judicial district] OF [state]

[name],

Plaintiff,

v.

[state] BOARD OF LAW EXAMINERS,

Defendant.

AFFIDAVIT

[state]

[county]

[name], being duly sworn, deposes and says:

1.   I am an ophthalmologist in private practice in [city, state]. I am a clinical professor of ophthalmology at the [name] School of Medicine and the Department of Ophthalmology at the [name] University. A copy of my curriculum vitae is attached hereto [not included].

2.   [Plaintiff] has been a patient of mine since [date], at which time she was referred to me because of a severe visual impairment. I make this affidavit at [Plaintiff]'s request in connection with her action against the [state] Board of Law Examiners (Law Examiners).

3.   [Plaintiff] has been very myopic (nearsighted) with myopic astigmatism since infancy. Her vision is not correctable to full normal levels by either glasses or by contact lenses. With visual aids, [plaintiff]'s vision is 20/50 in the right eye and 20/70 in the left eye.

4.   In addition to marked nearsightedness, [plaintiff] has bilateral partial amblyopia, which means that although her eyes are normal in form and physiologic function, [plaintiff] cannot develop 20/20 vision or anywhere near it. As a result of the condition, [plaintiff] suffers from a "lazy eye" condition, which might also be called a dimness of vision.

5.   In [year], I referred [plaintiff] to Dr. [name], Professor of Ophthalmology at [name] Medical Center. [Plaintiff] had informed me that she was frustrated with her condition and was interested in exploring the possibility of a surgical procedure to improve her eyesight. Unfortunately, Dr. [name] concluded that she was unable to improve [plaintiff]'s eyesight at this time and that the decreased visual acuity cannot be corrected. A copy of Dr. [name]'s most recent letter to me is attached hereto.

6.   Despite [plaintiff]'s visual disability, she has been able to graduate successfully from [name] University and [name] Law School. [Plaintiff] has informed me that she has been provided with extra time on examinations and has been afforded large print examination materials.

7.   These testing accommodations are necessary in order to afford [plaintiff] an equal opportunity to perform. Long periods of sustained reading are impossible for [plaintiff]. After reading continuously for a period of approximately 45 minutes, she develops blurring, tearing, and burning in the eyes and suffers from an acute form of ocular fatigue. This condition clearly affects her ability to read at a normal rate. In order to demonstrate her abilities on an equal basis, [plaintiff] must be afforded rest time throughout a period of continuous reading.

8.   In [date], [plaintiff] requested a letter from me as her ophthalmologist to the Law Examiners, outlining her disability and my recommendations on special testing conditions. Prior to sending the letter, [plaintiff] advised me that she had several conversations with representatives from the Law Examiners, and they had indicated to her that they were willing to provide no more than "time and one-half" for the exam. It was on this basis that I included the request for this accommodation.

9.   Later in [year], I was informed by [plaintiff] that the Law Examiners had provided her with an exam schedule which in my opinion exacerbated the visual impairment. The exam schedule was from 7:30 A.M. to 5:45 P.M. on [date]. As I have described above, it takes [plaintiff] longer to read through the testing materials. The additional time allotted by the Law Examiners was probably used by [plaintiff] for reading and writing, rather than testing. [Plaintiff]'s acute ocular fatigue could only have been aggravated by this schedule.

10.   [Plaintiff] requested that I provide an additional letter to the Law Examiners for her reapplication for the [date] exam. In my letter dated [date], I was critical of the exam schedule which had been provided to [plaintiff] for the [month] exam. I suggested that the exam be administered to [plaintiff] over a four-day period.

11.   It is my recommendation that the examination time periods should be limited to five hours per day for four days, plus 15-minute breaks every four hours, if needed, and a break for lunch. This schedule would result in a more accurate reflection of [plaintiff]'s abilities. With the 15-minute breaks, she would have an opportunity to rest her eyes. With a limitation on the number of hours of testing in a given day, [plaintiff] would have an opportunity to rest her eyes during the evening hours.

12.   [Plaintiff] advises me that the Law Examiners have agreed to permit her to set her own hours over the two days of the [month] exam. Unfortunately, the longer the exam is on a given day, the less likely [plaintiff] will adequately perform. She, like any nondisabled individual, will become tired with a prolonged schedule. With acute ocular fatigue, the proposed schedule does not provide [plaintiff] with a fair and equal opportunity to perform.

13.   Therefore, I am recommending that [plaintiff] be provided with the special testing conditions which I have outlined in my [date] letter to the Law Examiners and a test schedule in which the exam will be spread out over a four-day period of time with approximately five hours of testing each day, plus 15-minute breaks on the hour, if needed, and a lunch break.

[Attach curriculum vitae.]

ATTACHMENT

Dear Dr. [name]:

This is a follow-up letter on your patient, [plaintiff], who, as you recall, is a pleasant, thirty-four-year-old with a history of strabismic amblyopia and high myopia.

[Plaintiff] returned to the [name] Eye Center on [date] for re-evaluation and advice concerning possible ways to correct her myopia. She has a history of contact lens intolerance (hard lens) and claims to have poor vision from her glasses. [Plaintiff] is distraught over the fact that poor visual acuity keeps her from performing routine daily tasks such as driving and reading comfortably.

On examination, [plaintiff]'s corrected acuity with her present glasses was 20/50 in the right eye and 20/70 in the left eye. Neither eye improved with pinhole. She is currently wearing a −1 1.75 + 1.50 × 11 0 in the right and −1 2.25 +1.00 × 070 in the left. She has bilateral 2.25 adds. Manifest refraction over current glasses did not improve acuity in either eye. Manifest refraction together with retinoscopy without glasses again did not improve acuity in either eye. Both pupils were reactive without afferent pupillary defect. [Plaintiff]'s extraocular motility exam revealed a small esotropia in primary gaze at three meters. A stereopsis exam revealed failure to see even the wings of the fly on the Titmus test. Dilated fundus exam revealed a grossly normal posterior pole with myopic cups.

We referred [plaintiff] to our Contact Lens Clinic for a trial fitting of soft contact lenses (because of intolerance to hard lenses in the past) and she was able to be fit comfortably but had no improvement in vision. The lenses used had a base curve of 8.8 and a diameter of 14.5.

We informed [plaintiff] that the goal of any refractive surgery would be to free her from dependence on glasses and not to gain an improvement in visual acuity. We explained that the decreased visual acuity is due to amblyopia, which is a permanent, life-long problem which with current technology cannot be corrected. Options for the future include excirner laser surgery and epikeratophakia. Since the excimer laser has been used in high myopes only recently and the test results are still pending, she agreed to wait at least six months to a year in order that the results of longer-term follow-up are available for these patients. We also discussed the fact that epikeratophakia, although it can eliminate a large part of her myopia, will result in a probable reduction in contrast sensitivity and possible overall correctable vision; however, epikeratophakia is reversible.

Meanwhile, the options available to [plaintiff] are the following: She may continue with glasses, making sure she has a spare pair at all times in case of breakage. Alternatively, she can try to wear the soft contact lenses in an attempt to reduce dependence on thick glasses; however, she was noted to have a low tear film during the recent exam and in exams in the past. [Plaintiff] does wish to wait until the results of the high myopia excimer trial are further established, at which time she may return to discuss either that procedure or epikeratophakia in the future if so desired. Another important thing to consider is that of low vision aids, especially telescopes and reading-type magnifying devices, which may make life a little bit easier. We informed her that [name] Institute has an excellent Low Vision Clinic, unless you have a particular favorite of your own.

As always, please feel free to call with any questions or concerns, regarding this interesting patient.

[name], M.D., F.A.C.S.

Professor of Ophthalmology

Director, Cornea Service

§ 11.8   —Affidavit of Expert #2

FORM 11–7
SAMPLE EXPERT AFFIDAVIT

UNITED STATES DISTRICT COURT

[judicial district] OF [state]

[name],

Plaintiff,

v.   CIV. NO. [number]

[state] BOARD OF LAW EXAMINERS,

Defendant.

AFFIDAVIT

[state]

[county]

[name], being duly sworn, deposes and says:

1.   I am an attorney-at-law duly admitted to practice in [state]. I am a clinical instructor at [name] School of Law.

2.   1 am personally familiar with the examination accommodations which were provided to [plaintiff], due to her disability while she was a student at [name] Law School. During [plaintiff's] three years at the Law School, from [date], through [date], I was a member of the Committee on Law Students with Special Needs (the Committee).

3.   The Committee acts upon requests for reasonable accommodations from qualified law students who have disabilities. These requests are denied or granted depending upon documentation of the nature of disability and the accommodations which are requested due to an individual's disability.

4.   Upon [plaintiff]'s arrival at [name] School, she advised the Committee of her need for reasonable accommodations due to her disability. [Plaintiff] is visually impaired and is very nearsighted and suffers from significant eye fatigue.

5.   On or about [date], the Committee received a letter from Dr. [name] of [city] concerning [plaintiff]'s visual impairment and her needs and requirements for the taking of examinations. This letter was considered by the Committee in granting special testing conditions to accommodate [plaintiff]'s disability. A copy of Dr. [name]'s letter is attached hereto as Exhibit A.

6.   For each examination period during [plaintiff]'s three years at [name] Law School, she was provided with the following special testing conditions:

a.   Additional time.

b.   Large print examination materials.

c.   Separate testing room.

7.   Normally, [plaintiff] was provided either "time and one-half" or "doubletime" for her examinations. If an examination was scheduled for three hours, from 9:00 A.M. to 12:00 noon, [plaintiff] would be provided with additional time to take the examination until 2:00 P.M. If an examination was scheduled for seven hours, from 9:00 A.M. to 5:00 P.M., she would be asked to return the examination the following morning. As a result of the accommodation of additional time for the examinations, [plaintiff] was never forced to take two examinations on the same day.

8.   [Plaintiff] was also permitted to reschedule her examinations during the two week examination periods. She would reschedule her examinations to provide a day or two of rest time between each examination.

9.   Before each semester's examination period, someone from the Committee, usually myself, interviewed [plaintiff] to determine her needs for the examinations and to assess where her condition had improved. The Committee determined that [plaintiff]'s condition remained the same. She was entitled to the same special testing conditions which had previously been granted to her to reasonably accommodate her disability.

10.   I can personally attest to the severity of [plaintiff]'s visual impairment. I assisted her in the completion of her application for the [state] Bar Examination in [date]. She simply could not read the instructions because the print was too small.

11.   It was the Committee's judgment that [plaintiff]'s requests for accommodations were reasonable and conservative given her disability. The accommodations which were provided were appropriate given her disability and afforded her an opportunity to participate equally in the Law School curriculum with nondisabled peers. These special accommodations did not give her an advantage over other nondisabled students. These special accommodations were necessary to provide [plaintiff] with an equal opportunity to perform on law school examinations. [Plaintiff] received a law degree in good standing from [name].

[name]

§ 11.9   Discriminatory Testing

FORM 11–8
SAMPLE COMPLAINT: DISCRIMINATORY TESTING

IN THE UNITED STATES DISTRICT COURT

FOR [judicial district]

THE UNITED STATES OF AMERICA,

c/o U.S. Department of Justice,

[Civil Rights Division],

[Public Access Section],

[P.O. Box 66738],

[Washington, D.C.] [20035-6738],

Plaintiff,   CV-[number]

v.

[name]

[address],

Defendant.

COMPLAINT

(for violations of the Americans with Disabilities Act)

The United States of America alleges:

1.   This action is brought by the United States to enforce the Americans with Disabilities Act of 1990 (ADA), 42 U.S.C. § 12101 *et seq.,* against [defendant].

2.   This Court has jurisdiction of this action under 42 U.S.C. §§ 12188(b)(1)(B) and 12189, and 28 U.S.C. §§ 1331 and 1345.

3.   Venue is proper in [state] pursuant to 28 U.S.C. § 1391, as the claim arose in that Defendant does business in [state].

4.   Defendant [name] is an unincorporated association that offers a course designed to prepare its students for the national Certified Public Accountant (CPA) examination. [Defendant]'s course is offered at approximately one hundred twenty (120) cities throughout the nation. [Defendant]'s course has been offered in [1992] and will be offered in [month] [1993] at [location], [address]. It has been offered in [1992] and will be offered in [1993] at other locations in cities that surround [state] and that may serve [state] residents, including the cities of [name] and [name] in [state], and [city] and [city] in [state]. [Defendant] has solicited in [state] for students for all of the named locations.

5.   Defendant [name] has more than 25 employees and gross annual receipts of more than [$1,000,000].

6.   Defendant [name], through its partners and officers, is a person offering a course related to applications, licensing, certification, or credentialing for secondary or postsecondary educational, professional, or trade purposes within the meaning of 42 U.S.C. § 12189 and the Department of Justice's implementing regulation, 28 C.F.R. pt. 36 at § 36.309.

7.   Defendant [name] is a private entity that operates a place of education and/or a place of public gathering and is therefore a public accommodation within the meaning of Title III of the ADA, 42 U.S.C. § 12101 *et seq.,* and its implementing, regulation at 28 C.F.R. § 36.104.

8.   Persons with hearing impairments that substantially limit their hearing or other major life activities or who are deaf are individuals with disabilities

within the meaning of 42 U.S.C. § 12101 *et seq.,* and its implementing regulation, at 28 C.F.R. § 36.104.

9.   In its operation of its CPA review course, Defendant [name] has refused to furnish sign language interpreters and/or other appropriate auxiliary aids or services for a person who is deaf, [injured party], for whom such aids or services would provide effective communication.

10.   [Injured party] is a person who is deaf and for whom communication in a group educational setting such as that offered by [defendant] is ineffective without the provision of qualified sign language interpreters and/or other appropriate auxiliary aids or services.

11.   [Injured party] attended the first six lectures of the [date] [defendant]'s course: three in [state] and three in [city, state]. Prior to the commencement of the course, [injured party] requested [defendant] to provide interpreter services. Defendant refused to furnish appropriate aids or services, including qualified interpreter services, and [injured party] was unable to complete the course because of this refusal.

12.   [Injured party) has informed Defendant [name] that he intends to take [defendant]'s course beginning [date], in [state]. He has requested that [defendant] provide interpreter services. Defendant has not agreed to furnish such services for the course beginning in [date].

13.   [Defendant]'s general policy is not to furnish qualified sign language interpreters that would provide effective communication for students who are deaf or who have hearing impairments and who request them. The general policy is to provide only instructors' notes, transcripts of pre-recorded audio lectures, and transparencies.

COUNT I

14.   The conduct of Defendant [name] described in paragraphs 1 through 13 constitutes discrimination on the basis of a disability in violation of § 302 of the ADA, 42 U.S.C. § 12182, and its implementing regulation at 28 C.F.R. part 36 because the conduct of Defendant [name] constitutes:

a.   Discrimination against individuals on the basis of disability in the full and equal enjoyment of the goods, services, facilities, privileges, advantages, or accommodations of a place of public accommodation, in violation of ADA § 302(a) and 28 C.F.R. § 36.201 (a);

b.   Subjecting an individual, or class of individuals, on the basis of disability or disabilities to a denial of the opportunity to participate in or benefit from the goods, services, facilities, privileges, advantages, or accommodations of a place of public accommodation, or affording an opportunity that is not equal to that afforded others, in violation of 42 U.S.C. §§ 12182(b)(1)(A)(i) and (ii) and 28 C.F.R. § 36.202;

c.   A failure to make reasonable modifications in policies, practices, or proce-dures, in violation of 42 U.S.C. § 12182(b)(2)(A)(ii) and 28 C.F.R. § 36.302(a); and

d.   A failure provide auxiliary aids and services, in violation of 42 U.S.C. § 12182(b)(2)(A)(iii) and 28 C.F.R. § 36.303.

15.   [Defendant]'s policy and practice as described herein or refusing to fur-nish qualified sign language interpreters and/or other appropriate auxiliary aids or services that would provide effective communication for persons with hear-ing impairments or persons who are deaf constitutes (a) a pattern or practice of discrimination within the meaning of 42 U.S.C. § 12188(b)(1)(B)(i) and 28 C.F.R. § 36.503(a); and (b) discrimination against [injured party] and others similarly situated and raises an issue of general public importance within the meaning of 42 U.S.C. § 12188(b)(1)(B)(ii) and 28 C.F.R. § 36.503(b).

COUNT II

16.   The conduct of Defendant [name] described in paragraphs 1 through 13 constitutes discrimination on the basis of a disability in violation of § 302 of the ADA, 42 U.S.C. § 12189, and its implementing regulation at 28 C.F.R. § 36.309.

17.   [Defendant]'s policy and practice as described herein of refusing to furnish qualified sign language interpreters and/or other appropriate auxiliary aids and ser-vices that would provide effective communication for persons with hearing impair-ments or who are deaf other than instructors' notes, transcripts of a pre-recorded lecture, and transparencies constitutes a pattern or practice of discrimination within the meaning of 42 U.S.C. § 12188(b)(1)(B)(i) and 28 C.F.R. § 36.503(b).

PRAYER FOR RELIEF

WHEREFORE, the United States prays that the Court:

A.   Declare that the discriminatory practices of Defendant [name], as set forth above, violates the ADA, 42 U.S.C. §§ 12101 *et seq.,* and the U.S. Department of Justice's implementing regulation at 28 C.F.R. part 36;

B.   Enjoin Defendant [name], its partners, officers, agents, and employees, and all other persons in active concert or participation with any of them, from discriminating on the basis of a disability against any individuals seeking to take their course;

C.   Enjoin Defendant [name], its partners, officers, agents, and employees, and all other persons in active concert or participation with any of them, from failing to furnish to students with disabilities appropriate auxiliary aids and ser-vices that would provide effective communication;

D.   Enjoin Defendant [name], its partners, officers, agents, and employees, and all other persons in active concert or participation with any of them, from failing to furnish [injured party] with qualified sign language interpreters and/or other appropriate auxiliary aids or services that would provide effective communication for the duration of his participation in [defendant]'s course, whether the [date] course or any others to follow;

E.   Award monetary damages to [injured party] and other similarly situated person who have been discriminated against by Defendant [name] to compensate them for injuries resulting from such discrimination;

F.   Assess a civil penalty in an amount authorized by 42 U.S.C. § 12188(b)(2)(C), to vindicate the public interest; and

G.   Order such other appropriate relief as the interests of justice may require.

JURY DEMAND

A.   The United States of America requests a jury trial on all questions of fact or combine questions of law and fact raised by this complaint.

Respectfully Submitted,

[name]

Attorney General

[name]

United States Attorney

§ 11.10   **AIDS Discrimination in Medical Treatment**

FORM 11–9
SAMPLE COMPLAINT: AIDS DISCRIMINATION IN
MEDICAL TREATMENT

UNITED STATES DISTRICT COURT

[judicial district] FOR [state]

[name],

Plaintiff,

v.   CASE NO. [number]

[Defendant A],

[Defendant B],

[Defendant C],

[Defendant D],

[DOES] 1 through 20,

Defendants.

COMPLAINT FOR VIOLATIONS OF:

1)   AMERICANS WITH DISABILITIES ACT

2)   § 504 OF THE REHABILITATION ACT OF 1973 [29 U.S.C. § 794]

3)   [State] CIVIL CODE SECTION 51

4)   [State] CIVIL CODE SECTION 54.1

5)   [State] BUSINESS AND PROFESSIONS CODE SECTION 17200

6)   INTENTIONAL INFLICTION OF EMOTIONAL DISTRESS

7)   NEGLIGENT INFLICTION OF EMOTIONAL DISTRESS

DEMAND FOR JURY TRIAL

JURISDICTION

1.   This Court has subject matter jurisdiction pursuant to 28 U.S.C. § 1331 for claims arising under the Americans with Disabilities Act (ADA). There is an actual controversy between Plaintiff and Defendants. This Court also has subject matter jurisdiction pursuant to 28 U.S.C. §§ 1343(3) and (4) for claims arising under § 504 of the Rehabilitation Act, as amended, 29 U.S.C. § 794.

INTRODUCTION

2.   By this action, Plaintiff [name] challenges the legality of the policy and practice of Defendants [names], and others employed by or otherwise associated with them, of arbitrarily and unlawfully discriminating against persons with Acquired Immunodeficiency Syndrome (AIDS) or persons infected with the Human Immunodeficiency Syndrome (HIV) by denying these individuals full and equal access to and enjoyment of medical services and facilities provided by Defendants, solely because these individuals have AIDS or are infected with HIV.

3.   As a direct result of Defendants' arbitrary and injustifiably discriminatory acts, Plaintiff has been severely harmed and disadvantaged. Plaintiff has been enforced to suffer extreme pain, degradation, and humiliation by Defendants' arbitrary and unjustifiable refusal to provide necessary medical treatment and services.

4.   Accordingly Plaintiff respectfully requested that this Court enjoin Defendants, and each of them, from continuing to engage in their unjustifiable practice of denying individuals access to and the use and benefit of medical services and facilities, based wholly or partly on the fact that the individuals have AIDS or are HIV-infected. Plaintiff also requests that this Court award damages to compensate for the harm that Plaintiff has suffered as a result of Defendants' unlawful discriminatory practices. Plaintiff further requests a grant of exemplary damages in an amount sufficient to punish Defendants for their invidious and discriminatory conduct and to set an example of Defendants.

VENUE

5.   Pursuant to 28 U.S.C. §§ 1391(b)(2) and 1391(c), venue is proper in the [judicial district] of [state] in that the events and omissions giving rise to the claims herein arose in [name] County and Defendants' residences are in [name] County.

PARTIES

6.   Plaintiff [name] is an adult resident of the City and County of [name] who sought the medical services of Defendants in the County of [name], [state]. [Plaintiff] is infected with HIV and has been diagnosed with AIDS. [Plaintiff] disclosed his diagnosis to Defendants who refused, on that basis, to provide [plaintiff] with necessary medical services.

7.   Defendant [A] is a physician licensed to do, and doing, business in [state], City and County of [name], where [A] engages in the offering and providing of medical services and related goods to the general public.

8.   Defendant [B] is a [state] partnership whose partners are Defendants [C] and [D], Defendants [B, C, and D] offer and provide medical services and related goods to the general public in [state], City and County of [name].

9.   Defendants [Does] 1 through 20 are individuals who are employed by, associated with, or otherwise acting as authorized representatives or agents of Defendants [A, B, C, and/or D].

10.   Plaintiff is ignorant of the true names and capacities of Defendants sued herein as Does 1 through 20, inclusive, and therefore sues herein as Does 1 through 20, inclusive, and therefore sues these Defendants by their fictitious names. Plaintiff will amend this Complaint to allege their true names and capacities when this information is ascertained. Plaintiff is informed and believes and, on

that basis, alleges that each fictitiously named Defendant is intentionally or negligently responsible in some manner for the occurrences herein alleged, and Plaintiff's injuries as herein alleged were proximately caused by these Defendants' intentional or negligent misconduct.

11.   At all times herein mentioned, Defendants, and each of them, were the agents, representatives, principals, and/or employees of each other and, in doing the things herein alleged, were acting within the course and scope of said agency or employment.

FACTUAL ALLEGATIONS

12.   Since AIDS was first identified in 1981, over 200,000 people in the United States have been diagnosed with the disease. AIDS is an immune disorder caused by the HIV. An estimated 1.5 million Americans are HIV-infected. HIV infection manifests itself in the body by a continuum of conditions associated with immune dysfunction. HIV attacks certain of the body's white blood cells (T-lymphocytes), and undermines that part of the body's immune system, which normally combats infections and malignancies. An individual infected with HIV may have little damage to his or her immune system, or may suffer from significant, life-threatening illnesses, without having been diagnosed as having AIDS. AIDS, as defined for reporting purposes by the Centers for Disease Control (CDC), is currently marked by the presence of HIV infection plus the presence of one or more opportunistic infections or malignancies, dementia, or wasting syndromes. Persons who are infected with HIV, and who exhibit symptoms of some illnesses relating to the suppression of the immune system, but who have not been diagnosed with AIDS, are sometimes referred to as having an AIDS-related condition (ARC).

13.   According to the CDC, the United States Occupational Safety and Health Administration (OSHA), and the [state] Patient Protection Act of 1991 (the Patient Protection Act), health care providers must consider the blood and certain of the bodily fluids of <u>all</u> patients to be potentially infectious of HIV as well as other disease agents (for example, Hepatitis B). The CDC recommends, and OSHA and the Patient Protection Act require, that protective measures to prevent exposure to blood be used for all patients. Such measures, known as 'universal precautions," include barrier precautions (such as the use of facemasks or shields, and sterile gloves), safe handling of waste disposal procedures, and the careful sterilization of all equipment.

14.   The vast majority of HIV-infected individuals do not know they are infected. Health care professionals therefore cannot rely upon a patient's disclosure in order to be informed of a patient's infectious status. The use of universal precautions has been demonstrated to be an effective—indeed, the most effective—method of reducing the risk of potential infection to a health care provider or other patients by HIV or other infectious agents. Seeking to identify which patients may be HIV-infected and refusing such persons treatment or services is

likely to promote a false sense of security in a health care professional and runs the risk that universal precautions will not be carefully observed.

15.   The standard of care recommended by medical professional societies, including the American Medical Association (AMA) and the [state] Medical Association, is in accord with the CDC—universal precautions should be used for all patients and no patient should be refused service solely because of his or her AIDS or HIV status. The AMA's ethical policy specifically provides that "[a] physician may not ethically refuse to treat a patient whose condition is within the physician's current realm of competence solely because the patient is seropositive [for HIV]." Plaintiff in this action was denied Defendants' medical services based solely on being HIV-infected.

16.   On [date], at approximately [1:00 P.M.], Plaintiff [name] badly cut his left palm when a drinking glass shattered while he was washing the dishes at home. He bled quite profusely. After controlling the bleeding, Plaintiff called information for the phone number of the nearest urgent care center. Plaintiff was given the number of and called the Defendants' facilities, doing business under the name of [B], for precise directions. While preparing to leave for the facility, Plaintiff realized there could be a potential problem with his care because he has AIDS. Plaintiff again called Defendants' facilities to ensure he would receive the emergency treatment needed and so he would not be wasting the time of the trip, which could hinder recovery from the injury. The person to whom Plaintiff spoke assured Plaintiff that his AIDS status was not a problem and that he would be treated for the wound.

17.   Plaintiff was driven to Defendants' facility by a friend and dropped off. The friend agreed to return for Plaintiff when Plaintiff called and asked to be picked up. Plaintiff had earlier wrapped his injured left hand in a towel. Plaintiff checked in and proceeded to fill out the requisite forms for the clinic. Prior to completing the form, which lacked any inquiry about AIDS and HIV status, an employee of the Defendants informed Plaintiff that the doctor at the care unit claimed not to treat patients who are HIV-positive.

18.   Plaintiff requested to hear this denial of medical services from the doctor. The doctor, Defendant [A], repeated that [A] would not treat people infected with the HIV virus. Plaintiff asked to get this in writing, to which Defendant [A] assented. On a prescription form which [A] signed and dated, [A] wrote, "This is to inform you that I do not treat patient (sic) with HIV positive in our clinic. Advised to go to County ER for treatment." A true and correct copy of this prescription is attached hereto as Appendix A. Plaintiff told Defendant [A] he had no transportation to another care facility. Defendants made no offer to assist Plaintiff in obtaining transportation to another facility.

19.   Defendant [A] never questioned Plaintiff about the severity of the wound, nor did [A] ask him to unwrap the towel so as to allow visual inspection of plaintiff's hand. Defendants provided no care or assistance to Plaintiff whatsoever,

although Plaintiff was in need of emergency medical care. When Plaintiff ultimately was able to obtain medical care elsewhere, the wound was so serious as to require multiple sutures.

FIRST CAUSE OF ACTION

(Violation of the ADA)

20.   Plaintiff realleges and incorporates herein by reference each and every allegation contained in paragraphs 1 through 19 above.

21.   The Americans with Disabilities Act (ADA) prohibits discrimination on the basis of disability in the full and equal enjoyment of goods, services, facilities, privileges, advantages, and accommodations of any place of public accommodation by any person who owns, leases (or leases to), or operates a place of public accommodation. 42 U.S.C. § 12182(a).

22.   At all times mentioned herein, Defendants' medical offices have been a "place of public accommodation" within the meaning of the ADA. The ADA specifically states that a professional office of a health care provider and/or a hospital is a public accommodation. 42 U.S.C. § 12181(7)(F).

23.   At all times mentioned herein, Defendants [B, C, and D] owned and operated a place of public accommodation. At all times mentioned herein, Defendant [A] operated a place of public accommodation.

24.   AIDS and HIV infection are disabilities within the meaning of the ADA.

25.   Through the conduct described above, Defendants have discriminated against Plaintiff solely on the basis of his disability by denying him the full and equal enjoyment of the services, facilities, and accommodations otherwise available to members of the general public.

26.   Defendants should be ordered to take all steps necessary to ensure full enjoyment of all rights guaranteed by the ADA. Plaintiff is entitled to such injunctive relief under the ADA.

SECOND CAUSE OF ACTION

(Violation of § 504 of the Federal Rehabilitation Act of 1973 [29 U.S.C. § 701 *et seq.*])

27.   Plaintiff realleges and incorporates herein by reference each and every allegation contained in paragraphs 1 through 19 above.

28.   Section 504 of the Federal Rehabilitation Act of 1973 [29 U.S.C. § 794] (hereafter § 504) provides, in pertinent part, that no otherwise qualified handicapped person "shall, solely by reason of his or her handicap, be excluded from the participation under any program or activity receiving Federal financial assistance." Plaintiff is and was regarded by Defendants to be a handicapped person for purposes of § 504. Plaintiff is and was qualified to receive the medical services and/or treatments offered by Defendants.

29.   By virtue of the fact that Defendants receive Medicare funding, Defendants receive federal financial assistance within the meaning of § 504. Defendants are thus prohibited from excluding, denying benefits to, or discriminating against handicapped persons, including, but not limited to, persons who are infected with HIV or who have AIDS, solely on the basis of such person's handicap in connection with Defendants' provision of medical services.

30.   Defendants, and each of them, have violated Plaintiffs' rights under § 504 by failing and refusing to provide necessary medical treatment and/or access to Defendants' facilities, services, and accommodations, based solely on Plaintiff's handicapped status.

31.   In order to prevent Defendants from continuing to violate § 504, Defendants should be enjoined and prohibited from the unlawful and invidiously discriminatory practice of failing or refusing to provide necessary medical treatment, services, and/or access to Defendants' facilities to persons who have, or are perceived to have, AIDS or who are or are perceived to be HIV-infected, based solely on those facts or perceptions. Defendants should be further ordered to take all steps necessary to ensure the full enjoyment of rights guaranteed by § 504. Plaintiff is entitled to such relief pursuant to 29 U.S.C. § 794a.

32.   As a further and proximate result of Defendants' unlawfully discriminatory failure or refusal to provide Plaintiff necessary medical treatment and/or access to the facilitates, services, and/or accommodations of Defendants' offices, based solely on Plaintiff's handicap, Plaintiff has suffered harm in the form of denied medical treatment, physical pain, shame, humiliation, degradation, and emotional distress entitling Plaintiff to actual damages in an amount to be determined at trial.

33.   Pursuant to 29 U.S.C. § 794a(b), Plaintiff is also entitled to reasonable costs and attorneys' fees.

THIRD CAUSE OF ACTION

(Violation of [statute])

34.   Plaintiff realleges and incorporates herein by reference each and every allegation contained in paragraphs 1 through 19 above.

35.   [Statute] provides that"[all] persons within the jurisdiction of this state are free and equal, and no matter what their . . . physical disabilities are entitled to the full and equal accommodations, advantages, facilities . . . or services in all business establishments of every kind whatsoever."

36.   At all times mentioned herein, Defendants' medical offices have been a "business establishment" within the meaning of [statute], which expressly includes all business establishments "of every kind whatsoever."

37.   Through the conduct described above, Defendants, and each of them, have denied Plaintiff the full and equal enjoyment of Defendants' "accommodations, advantages, facilities or services" by refusing Plaintiff medical treatment and/or services to which he is entitled, solely because of his disability.

38.   Defendants' practices are discriminatory per se because they treat Plaintiff and other similar-situated persons as an outcast group, based solely on their disability.

39.   Plaintiff is informed and believes, and on that basis alleges, that Defendants, and each of them, are and at all times herein relevant have been engaged in conduct resistant to Plaintiff's full enjoyment of rights guaranteed him by [statute].

40.   In order to prevent Defendants from continuing to violate [statute], Defendants should be enjoined and prohibited from the unlawful and invidiously discriminatory practice of failing or refusing to provide necessary medical treatment, services, and/or access to Defendants' facilities to persons who have or are perceived to have AIDS or who are or are perceived to be HIV-infected, based solely on those facts or perceptions. Defendants should be further ordered to take all steps necessary to ensure the full enjoyment of all rights guaranteed under [statute]. Plaintiff is entitled to such injunctive relief under [statute].

41.   As a direct and proximate result of Defendants' discriminatory practices, Plaintiff has suffered actual damages in the form of denied medical treatment, physical pain, shame, humiliation, degradation, and emotional distress in an amount to be determined at trial. Pursuant to [statute], Plaintiff is entitled to actual damages in an amount to be determined at trial.

42.   Pursuant to [statute], Plaintiff is also entitled to such additional amount as may be determined at trial, up to a maximum of three times the amount of actual damage but in no case less than [two hundred and fifty ($250)] per violation, as well as reasonable attorneys' fees.

43.   In committing the acts described above, Defendant[A] acted maliciously and oppressively with a conscious, reckless, willful, and callous disregard of Plaintiff's rights, and with the intent of depriving Plaintiff of rights guaranteed by

[statute]. Plaintiff is therefore entitled to exemplary and punitive damages in an amount sufficient to punish and set an example of Defendant [A].

FOURTH CAUSE OF ACTION

(Violation of [statute])

44.   Plaintiff realleges and incorporates herein by reference each and every allegation contained in paragraphs 1 through 19 above.

45.   [Statute] provides that "physically disabled persons shall be entitled to full and equal access, as other members of the general public, to accommodations . . . . [and] facilities . . . of all . . . places of public accommodation . . . to which the general public is invited, subject only to the conditions and limitations established by law, or state or federal regulations, and applicable alike to all persons."

46.   At all times mentioned herein, Defendants' medical offices have been a "place of public accommodation" within the meaning of [statute].

47.   Through the conduct described above, Defendants, and each of them, have denied Plaintiff, solely on the basis of his disability, access to public accommodations otherwise available to members of the general public who are not physically disabled.

48.   In order to prevent Defendants from continuing to violate [statute], Defendants should be enjoined and prohibited from the unlawful and invidiously discriminatory practice of failing or refusing to provide necessary medical treatment, services, and/or access to Defendants' facilities to persons who have or are perceived to have AIDS or who are or are perceived to be HIV-infected, based solely on those facts or perceptions. Defendants should be further ordered to take all steps necessary to ensure the full enjoyment of all rights guaranteed by [statute]. Plaintiff is entitled to such injunctive relief under [statute].

49.   As a direct and proximate result of Defendants' discriminatory practices, Plaintiff has suffered actual damages in the form of denied medical treatment, physical pain, shame, humiliation, degradation, and emotional distress. Pursuant to [statute], Plaintiff is entitled to actual damages in an amount to be determined at trial.

50.   Pursuant to [statute], Plaintiff is also entitled to such additional amount as may be determined at trial, up to a maximum of three times the amount of actual damage but in no case less than two hundred and fifty dollars ($250) per violation, as well as reasonable attorneys' fees.

51.   In committing the acts described above, Defendant [A] acted maliciously and oppressively, with a conscious, reckless, willful, and callous disregard of Plaintiff's right to full and equal access to Defendants' place of public accommodation equivalent to that of members of the general public who are not disabled. Plaintiff is therefore entitled to exemplary and punitive damages in an amount sufficient to punish and set an example of Defendant [A].

FIFTH CAUSE OF ACTION

(Violation of [statute])

52.   Plaintiff realleges and incorporates herein by reference each and every allegation contained in paragraphs 1 through 19 above.

53.   By engaging in the conduct described above, Defendants, and each of them, have engaged in unlawful business practices prohibited by [statute].

54.   In order to prevent Defendants from continuing to commit unlawful business practices, Defendants should be enjoined and prohibited from the unlawful and invidiously discriminatory practice of failing or refusing to provide necessary medical treatment, services, and/or access to Defenclants' facilities to persons who have or are perceived to have AIDS or who are or are perceived to be HIV-infected, based solely on those facts or perceptions. Defendants should be further ordered to take all steps necessary to ensure that persons with AIDS or who are HIV-infected are not unlawfully denied necessary medical treatment, service, and/or access to Defendants' facilities, based solely on the fact that such persons have AIDS or are HIV-infected. Plaintiff is entitled to such relief pursuant to [statute].

SIXTH CAUSE OF ACTION

(Intentional Infliction of Emotional Distress)

55.   Plaintiff realleges and incorporates herein by reference each and every allegation contained in paragraphs 1 through 19 above.

56.   Defendants' extreme and outrageous conduct, as described above, was done with intent to cause, or with reckless disregard of the probability of causing, Plaintiff to suffer severe emotional distress in the form of mental anguish and suffering, humiliation, shame, shock, degradation, and extreme and enduring physical pain.

57.   Defendants' conduct was made more extreme and outrageous because Plaintiff was seeking emergency medical services and Defendants knew, or should have known, of their ethical duty to treat such a patient. As a result of this special relationship and Plaintiff's need for medical services, Defendants knew, or should have known, of Plaintiff's particular susceptibility to emotional

distress, and that such injury was substantially certain to occur as a result of Defendants' conduct.

58.   As a proximate result of Defendants' extreme and outrageous conduct, Plaintiff has suffered humiliation, mental anguish, emotional and physical distress, and has been injured in mind and body in degrees and amounts to be determined at trial.

59.   The aforementioned acts of Defendant [A] were willful, reckless, malicious, oppressive, and done with a callous disregard of the consequences substantially certain to occur and justify an award of exemplary and punitive damages against Defendant [A].

SEVENTH CAUSE OF ACTION

(Negligent Infliction of Emotional Distress)

60.   Plaintiff realleges and incorporates herein by reference each and every allegation contained in paragraphs 1 through 19 above.

61.   At all times herein relevant, Defendants were bound by their common law and statutory duties to provide medical services, treatment, and full and equal access to their place of business to all persons on an equivalent basis regardless of their physical disability. As a result of Defendants' failure to fulfill these duties, Plaintiff has suffered substantial and enduring emotional injury.

62.   Defendants knew, or should have known, that their failure to provide necessary medical treatment, services, or full and equal access to their facilities to Plaintiff because of his HIV status would foreseeably cause Plaintiff serious emotional and physical distress.

63.   Defendants breached their duty to exercise due care by refusing to provide services to or treat Plaintiff solely on the basis of Plaintiff's HIV status.

64.   As a proximate result of Defendants' acts or omissions as described above, Plaintiff has suffered serious emotional distress in the form of shame, humiliation, degradation, and physical injuries in an amount to be determined at trial.

PRAYER FOR RELIEF

WHEREFORE, Plaintiff prays for judgment as follows:

1.   For injunctive relief ordering Defendants, and each of them to:

a.   refrain from discriminating in any manner, by failing or refusing to extend to any individual who has, or is regarded as having, AIDS or who is or is regarded as being infected with HIV, the full and equal enjoyment of and access to Defendants' treatment, services, and/or facilities of any kind whatsoever, on the basis (either in whole or in part) of the fact or perception that such individual has AIDS or an AIDS-related condition, or is infected with HIV;

b.   train and educate each and every individual physician, staff member and all other personnel employed or associated with Defendants' facilities, regarding the actual risks in treating patients with AIDS or who are HIV-infected, and the precautionary measures which must or should be taken to prevent transmission of the disease, including, but not limited to, the use of universal precautions;

c.   train and educate each and every individual physician, staff member, and all other personnel to maintain the confidentiality of Defendants' patients and potential patients' medical and health information, and to disclose such information only as, and to the extent, necessary for that patient's medical treatment or care, and only to such persons as are necessary to ensure that patient full and competent medical care and treatment.

2.   For an award of compensatory damages to Plaintiff equal to the injury suffered due to Defendants' discriminatory practices, in an amount to be determined at trial.

3.   For an award of such additional amount as may be determined at trial, up to a maximum of three times the amount of actual damage but in no case less than [two hundred and fifty dollars ($250)] for each violation of [statutes], as provided by [statute].

4.   For an award of exemplary and punitive damages against Defendant [A] in an amount sufficient to punish and set an example of [A].

5.   For an order awarding Plaintiff costs of suit, including litigation expenses out-of-pocket expenses, and reasonable attorneys' fees, in accordance with all applicable provisions of law, including, but not limited to, the provisions of 29 U.S.C. § 12205; 29 U.S.C. § 794a(b); and [state statutes].

6.   For such other and further relief as the Court may deem just and proper.

§ 11.11   Theater Discrimination Complaint

This section reproduces an actual complaint filed in an ADA Title III case. (All proper names have been substituted with fictitious names.) This complaint is notable because of the effective use of an introductory statement (paragraphs 1 to 7) to give a "big picture" of the claim, the class action allegations in paragraphs 14 to 20, and the careful pleading of facts that link the transaction to specific statutory prohibitions in paragraphs 22 to 25.

FORM 11–10
SAMPLE COMPLAINT: THEATER DISCRIMINATION

IN THE UNITED STATES DISTRICT COURT

FOR THE DISTRICT OF [state]

[JANE DOE], a minor by her parent and natural guardian, [ALICE DOE],

and

[RICHARD ROE], on behalf of themselves and all other similarly situated individuals,

Plaintiffs,

CIVIL ACTION No. [number]

vs.

[ABC, INC.], Owner of The Arena,

Defendant.

CLASS ACTION
COMPLAINT

I.   INTRODUCTION

1.   The Arena discriminates against adults and children who are disabled by refusing to sell them seats on the floor level, during those events when nondisabled persons are permitted to sit on the floor level.

2.   On July 12, 1990, Congress enacted the Americans with Disabilities Act, 42 U.S.C. §§ 12101 *et seq.*, establishing the most important civil rights for persons with disability in our country's history.

3.   The congressional statutory findings include:

a.   "some 43,000,000 Americans have one or more physical or mental disabilities";

b.   "historically, society has tended to isolate and segregate individuals with disabilities and, despite some improvements, such forms of discrimination against individuals with disabilities continue to be a serious and pervasive social problem";

c.   "discrimination against individuals with disabilities persists in such critical areas as . . . public accommodations";

d.   "individuals with disabilities continually encounter various forms of discrimination, including . . . the discriminatory effects of architectural . . . barriers"; and

e.   "the continuing existence of unfair and unnecessary discrimination and prejudice denies people with disabilities the opportunity . . . to pursue those opportunities for which our free society is justifiably famous. 42 U.S.C. § 12101(a).

4.   Congress went on to state explicitly the purpose of the Americans with Disabilities Act, to be:

a.   "to provide a clear and comprehensive national mandate for the elimination of discrimination against individuals with disabilities";

b.   "to provide clear, strong, consistent, enforceable standards addressing discrimination against individuals with disabilities"; and

c.   "to invoke the sweep of Congressional authority . . . to regulate commerce, in order to address the major areas of discrimination faced day to-day by people with disabilities." 42 U.S.C. § 12101 (b).

5.   Congress gave public accommodations one and a half years to implement the Act. The effective date was January 26, 1992.

6.   Nevertheless, the Arena at [Main Street], [Anytown], [State] has not eliminated barriers that prevent persons who use wheelchairs from sitting, like nondisabled persons, on the ground floor of this stadium.

7.   Plaintiffs have repeatedly requested defendant to make its stadium accessible. After months of futile negotiations that have resulted neither in the removal of architectural barriers nor in a commitment to remove those barriers, plaintiffs seek to redress their rights under the Americans with Disabilities Act and request this Court to issue declaratory and injunctive relief against defendant to end the ongoing discrimination.

II.   JURISDICTION

8.   This court has jurisdiction under 28 U.S.C. §§ 1331 and 1343.

9.   Plaintiffs' claims are authorized by 28 U.S.C. §§ 2201 and 2202, and 42 U.S.C. § 1983.

III.   PARTIES

10.   [Alice Doe] is the mother and guardian of [Jane Doe], a [four]-year-old child who uses a wheelchair for mobility. They are residents of [Big County], [State].

11.   [James Noe] is a resident of [Townsville], [State], and he uses a wheelchair for mobility.

12.   [Richard Roe] is a resident of [Big city], [State], and he uses a wheelchair for mobility.

13.   [ABC] is a [state] corporation which owns and operates [The Arena], a public stadium and arena, located at [Main Street], [Anytown], [State].

IV.   CLASS ACTION ALLEGATIONS

14.   Plaintiffs [Doe], [Noe], and [Roe] bring this action on behalf of all other persons similarly situated, pursuant to Rule 23(a) and (b)(2) of the Federal Rules of Civil Procedure. The class members consist of all persons who use wheelchairs for ambulation, who wish to attend basketball games and other entertainment at [The Arena], who wish to sit on the floor level, and for whom [The Arena] presents architectural barriers to accessibility to the floor-level seating.

15.   The exact size of the class is unknown to the plaintiffs but they believe the size of the class is so numerous that joinder of all members is impracticable.

16.   There are questions of law or fact common to the class; to wit, the plaintiffs' rights under the Americans with Disabilities Act have been wrongfully denied.

17.   The claims of the named plaintiffs are typical of the claims of the class; to wit, the defendant has abridged named and class plaintiffs' rights under the Americans with Disabilities Act and has violated their rights protected by federal regulations.

18.   The defendant has acted or refused to act on grounds generally applicable to the class, thereby making appropriate injunctive and declaratory relief with respect to the class as a whole.

19.   The named plaintiffs will fairly and adequately protect the interests of the class.

20.   Plaintiffs' counsel is experienced in litigating class actions.

V.   FACTS

21.   One of the most important parts of the Americans with Disabilities Act was Title III, known as the "Public Accommodations and Services Operated by Private Entities." 42 U.S.C. § 12181 *et seq.*

22.   Congress included a "motion picture house, theater, concert hall, stadium, or other place of exhibition or entertainment" as a public accommodation covered by the Act. 42 U.S.C. § 12181(7)(C).

23.   Defendant's business at [Main Street] is a stadium and/or arena at which sporting and other entertainment events take place.

24.   As relevant to the present action, discrimination includes "a failure to remove architectural barriers . . . that are structural in nature, in existing facilities . . . where such removal is readily achievable." 42 U.S.C. § 121 82(b)(2)(A)(iv).

25.   In the event that the removal of the barrier was not readily achievable, the United States Department of Justice has by regulation required that the public accommodation [be made] available through alternative methods, if these methods are "readily achievable." 28 C.F.R. § 36.305(a).

26.   [Jane Doe] is a [four]-year-old child who has severe cerebral palsy and requires a special stroller and/or wheelchair for mobility.

27.   [Jane Doe] attends school in [Town], [State].

28.   Her mother, [Alice Doe], wanted to take [Jane] to [The Arena] to see "Sesame Street Live."

29.   [Mrs. Doe] ordered tickets from [The Arena]'s box office via telephone and advised defendant that her daughter required handicapped seating.

30.   Defendant's agents assured [Mrs. Doe], when she purchased the tickets, that there was accessible seating on the floor level.

31.   [Jane] and her mother were assured they would be seated on the floor level next to the stage and that such seating was accessible.

32.   They paid for the most expensive seats for the show.

33.   Parking in the "handicapped parking area" was not close to the entrance of [The Arena], nor on a direct path to accessible seating.

34.   When they entered [The Arena], they found no accessible symbols for persons in a wheelchair to the floor level. Rather, they saw only steps.

35.   Plaintiffs asked the usher about their alleged accessible tickets, and the usher told them that handicapped seating was handled through the information booth, which was located halfway around the building.

36.   At the information booth, plaintiffs were told that all handicapped seating is in Section C—the furthest point from the stage.

37.   Accessible seating in Section C is not on the floor or near the stage, where [Mrs. Doe] had paid for her seats.

38.   [James Noe] is the Executive Director of the [Happy Valley Project] with industry, a nonprofit organization that is affiliated with the [Major Rehabilitation Hospital] and which assists businesses and industries to hire people with disabilities, including advising them on the accommodations that may be necessary. He has also worked as the Adjunct Instructor in Neuropsychology at [Large] University, and a Coordinator in the [Regional Spinal Cord and Injury Center] of [Happy Valley].

39.   [Mr. Noe] uses a wheelchair for mobility.

40.   [James Noe] was Chairperson of the Mayor's Commission for People with Disabilities, as well as the President of Transition to Independent Living, a Vice President of United Cerebral Palsy of [State] and [Vicinity], and a President of [Happy Valley Wheelchair Athletic Association].

41.   [James Noe] is a major league and college basketball fan, and he also plays wheelchair basketball.

42.   In [March 19__], when the NCAA Basketball Playoffs were held at [The Arena], [Mr. Noe] was forced to sit on the last row of Section C because the defendant refuses to sell tickets on the floor level to persons who use wheelchairs.

43.   Similarly, when [James Noe] goes to basketball games, he must sit in Section C far from the game.

44.   [Mr. Noe] and his companion, who must sit behind him in Section C and whose view is partially blocked, want to purchase tickets for seats on the floor level, but they have been prevented by defendant's policy.

45.   [Richard Roe] is [28] years old and received a spinal cord injury playing football in college.

46.   For the past nine years, he has used a wheelchair and plays wheelchair basketball.

47.   [Mr. Roe] is the Sports Director for [WWWW-FM], a local radio station.

48.   In order for him to adequately perform his employment, he, like other reporters, must visit the locker rooms after a game and interview the players.

49.   For some time, after the basketball games, [Mr. Roe] took the freight elevator from [The Arena]'s mezzanine seating level to the floor level, where he was able to roll to the locker room.

50.   Without explanation, defendant told him that he could no longer use the freight elevator. As a consequence of this decision, plaintiff [Roe] cannot adequately be a sports reporter.

51.   A few years ago, [The Arena] built new steps to the entrance for advance ticket purchases and for the press. From this entrance, reporters walk no stairs, but use a ramp to gain access both to the floor level of [The Arena] and to the athletes' locker room.

52.   By building a ramp as part of these new steps, defendant can make [The Arena]'s floor level accessible to persons who use wheelchairs.

53.   [The Arena] also has a tunnel to the floor level which is used to transport equipment, food, and buses for the athletes.

54.   A ramp for persons who use wheelchairs could be built adjacent to the existing ramp, and persons who use wheelchairs would have access to the floor level.

55.   In [The Arena] there is also an elevator that is used primarily for freight.

56.   Defendant could easily make alterations to this existing elevator for persons who use wheelchairs.

57.   Thus, there are three ways to make [The Arena] accessible for persons with disabilities who wish to purchase seats on the floor level: (1) build a ramp adjacent to the recently constructed stairs; (2) build a ramp adjacent to the existing tunnel; or (3) convert the freight elevator to the passenger elevator.

VI.   CLAIMS

First

58.   Pursuant to the Americans with Disabilities Act, 42 U.S.C. § 12182(b)(2)(A)(iv), and the federal regulations promulgated pursuant to this Act, defendant was to make [The Arena] stadium at [Main Street], [Anytown], [State], accessible by January 26, 1992. To date, it has not.

59.   By failing to remove architectural barriers where such removal is readily achievable, defendant discriminated against the plaintiff in violation of the Americans with Disabilities Act.

Second

60.   Pursuant to the Americans with Disabilities Act, 42 U.S.C. § 12182(a), and the federal regulations promulgated by the U.S. Department of Justice, 28 C.F.R. § 36.305, if removal of a barrier is not readily achievable, accommodation must be made available through alternative methods.

61.   By failing to permit plaintiffs and their wheelchairs down the existing ramp and by failing to modify the existing elevator, defendant discriminated against plaintiffs in violation of the Americans with Disabilities Act.

Third

62.   Pursuant to the Americans with Disabilities Act, 42 U.S.C. § 12182(a), and the federal regulations promulgated pursuant to this Act, defendant cannot discriminate against persons with disabilities solely based on their disability.

63. Defendant's policy of prohibiting persons who use wheelchairs from purchasing tickets on the floor level and limiting the number of available seats for persons with disabilities discriminates against plaintiffs in violation of the Americans with Disabilities Act.

PRAYER FOR RELIEF

WHEREFORE, plaintiffs respectfully pray;

1.   That this Court assume jurisdiction;

2.   That this Court issue an injunction enjoining defendant from continuing its discrimination;

3.   That this Court award plaintiffs appropriate compensatory damages, attorney fees, and such additional or alternative relief as may be just, proper, and equitable.

Dated: [date]

Respectfully submitted, [names]

Attorneys for Plaintiffs

§ 11.12 HIV Discrimination

This complaint is notable because it involves HIV, because it involves denials of service rather than barriers to physical access, and because it includes multiple state claims, including common-law claims that are allegedly within the supplemental jurisdiction of the federal court.

FORM 11–11
SAMPLE COMPLAINT: HIV DISCRIMINATION

UNITED STATES DISTRICT COURT

DISTRICT FOR [state]

[RICHARD ROE],

Plaintiff,

vs.   CASE NO. [number]

[BETTY BETA, MD];

[CITY CARE CENTER],

DOES 1 through 20.

Defendants.

COMPLAINT FOR VIOLATIONS OF:

1) AMERICANS WITH DISABILITIES ACT

2) SECTION 504 OF THE REHABILITATION ACT OF 1973 (29 U.S.C. SECTION 794)

3) [CIVIL CODE SECTION 51]

4) [CIVIL CODE SECTION 54.1]

5) [BUSINESS AND PROFESSIONS CODE SECTION 17200]

6) [INTENTIONAL INFLICTION OF EMOTIONAL DISTRESS]

7) [NEGLIGENT INFLICTION OF EMOTIONAL DISTRESS]

DEMAND FOR JURY TRIAL

JURISDICTION

1.   This Court has subject matter jurisdiction pursuant to 28 U.S.C. § 1331 for claims arising under the Americans with Disabilities Act. There is an actual controversy between Plaintiff and Defendants. This Court also has subject matter jurisdiction pursuant to 28 U.S.C. §§ 1343(3) and (4) for claims arising under § 504 of the Rehabilitation Act, as amended, 29 U.S.C. § 794.

INTRODUCTION

2.   By this action, Plaintiff [Richard Roe] challenges the legality of the policy and practice of Defendants [Allen Alpha], and [Dr. Betty Beta, M.D.], [City Care Center], [Ken Kappa], and others employed by or otherwise associated with them, of arbitrarily and unlawfully discriminating against persons with Acquired Immunodeficiency Syndrome ("AIDS") or who are infected with the Human Immunodeficiency Syndrome ("HIV") by denying these individuals full and equal access to and enjoyment of medical services and facilities provided by Defendants, solely because these individuals have AIDS or are infected with HIV.

3.   As a direct result of Defendants' arbitrary and injustifiably discriminatory acts, Plaintiff has been severely harmed and disadvantaged. Plaintiff has been enforced to suffer extreme pain, degradation, and humiliation by Defendants' arbitrary and unjustifiable refusal to provide necessary medical treatment and services.

4.   Accordingly, Plaintiff respectfully requested that this Court enjoin Defendants, and each of them, from continuing to engage in their unjustifiable practice of denying individuals access to and the use and benefit of medical services and facilities, based wholly or partly on the fact that the individuals have AIDS or are HIV-infected. Plaintiff also requests that this Court award him damages to compensate him for the harm that he has suffered as a result of Defendants' unlawful discriminatory practices. Plaintiff further requests a grant of exemplary damages in an amount sufficient to punish Defendants for their invidious and discriminatory conduct and to set an example of Defendants.

VENUE

5.   Pursuant to 28 U.S.C. §§ 1391 (b)(2) and 1391 (c), venue is proper in the District of [state] in that the events and omissions giving rise to the claims herein arose in [name] County and Defendants' residences are in [name] County.

PARTIES

6.   Plaintiff [Richard Roe ("Roe")] is an adult resident of the City and County of who sought the medical services of Defendants in the [name] County

of [state] Roe is infected with the Human immunodeficiency Virus (HIV) and has been diagnosed with Acquired Immune Deficiency Syndrome ("AIDS"). [Roe] disclosed his diagnosis to Defendants who refused, on that basis, to provide [Roe] with necessary medical services.

7.   Defendant [Betty Beta, M.D. ("Beta")] is a physician licensed to do and doing business in the State of [name], City and County of [name] where she engages in the offering and providing of medical services and related goods to the general public.

8.   Defendants [City Care Center] is a partnership whose partners are Defendants [Ken Kappa ("Kappa")] and [Allen Alpha ("Alpha")]. Defendants [City Care Center], [Kappa], and [Alpha] offer and provide medical services and related goods to the general public in the State of [name], City and County of [name].

9.   Defendants [Does 1 through 20] are individuals who are employed by, associated with, or otherwise acting as authorized representatives or agents of Defendants [Beta] and/or [City Care Center] and/or [Alpha] and/or [Kappa].

10.   Plaintiff is ignorant of the true names and capacities of Defendants sued herein as [Does 1 through 20], inclusive, and therefore sues these Defendants by their fictitious names. Plaintiff will amend this Complaint to allege their true names and capacities when this information is ascertained. Plaintiff is informed and believes and on that basis alleges that each fictitiously named Defendant is intentionally or negligently responsible in some manner for the occurrences herein alleged, and Plaintiff's injuries as herein alleged were proximately caused by these Defendants' intentional or negligent misconduct.

11.   At all times herein mentioned, Defendants, and each of them, were the agents, representatives, principals and/or employees of each other and, in doing the things herein alleged, were acting within the course and scope of said agency or employment.

12.   Since Acquired Immune Deficiency Syndrome ("AIDS"), was first identified in 1981, over 200,000 people in the United States have been diagnosed with the disease. AIDS is an immune disorder caused by the Human Immunodeficiency Virus ("HIV"). An estimated 1.5 million Americans are HIV-infected. HIV infection manifests itself in the body by a continuum of conditions associated with immune dysfunction. HIV attacks certain of the body's white blood cells (T-lymphocytes), and undermines that part of the body's immune system, which normally combats infections and malignancies. An individual infected with HIV may have little damage to his or her immune system, or may suffer from significant, life-threatening illnesses, without having been diagnosed as having AIDS. AIDS, as defined for reporting purposes by the Centers for Disease Control ("CDC"), is currently marked by the presence of HIV infection plus the presence of one or more opportunistic infections or malignancies, dementia, or wasting syndrome. Persons who are

infected with HIV, and who exhibit symptoms of some illnesses relating to the suppression of the immune system, but who have not been diagnosed with AIDS, are sometimes referred to as having an AIDS-related condition ("ARC").

13.   According to the CDC, the United States Occupational Safety and Health Administration ("OSHA"), and the [state] Patient Protection Act of 1991 (the 'Patient Protection Act'), health care providers must consider the blood and certain of the bodily fluids of all patients to be potentially infectious of HIV as well as other disease agents, (e.g., hepatitis B). The CDC recommends and OSHA and the Patient Protection Act require that protective measures to prevent exposure to blood be used for all patients. Such measures, known as 'universal precautions," include barrier precautions (such as the use of face masks or shields, and sterile gloves), safe handling of waste disposal procedures, and the careful sterilization of all equipment.

14.   The vast majority of HIV-infected individuals do not know they are infected. Health care professionals therefore cannot rely upon a patient's disclosure to be informed of a patient's infectious status. The use of universal precautions has been demonstrated to be an effective-indeed, the most effective-method of reducing the risk of potential infection to a health care provider or other patients by HIV or other infectious agents. Seeking to identify which patients may be HIV infected and refusing such persons treatment or services is likely to promote a false sense of security in a health care professional and runs the risk that universal precautions will not be carefully observed.

15. The standard of care recommended by medical professional societies, including the American Medical Association (the "AMA") and the [state] Medical Association, is in accord with the CDC's-universal precautions should be used for all patients and no patient should be refused service solely because of his or her AIDS or HIV status. The AMA's ethical policy specifically provides that "[a] physician may not ethically refuse to treat a patient whose condition is within the physician's current realm of competence solely because the patient is seropositive (for HIV)." Plaintiff in this action was denied Defendants' medical services based solely on the fact that he was HIV-infected.

16.   On [date], at approximately [time], Plaintiff [Roe] badly cut his left palm when a drinking glass shattered while he was washing the dishes at home. He bled quite profusely. After he controlled the bleeding, Plaintiff called information for the phone number of the nearest urgent care center. Plaintiff was given the number of and called the Defendants' facilities, doing business under the name of [City Care Center], for precise directions. While preparing to leave for the facility, Plaintiff realized there could be a potential problem with his care because he has AIDS. Plaintiff again called Defendants' facilities to ensure he would receive the emergency treatment he needed and so he would not be wasting the time of the trip, which could hinder recovery from his injury. The person to whom Plaintiff spoke assured Plaintiff that his AIDS status was not a problem and that he would be treated for his wound.

17. Plaintiff was driven to Defendants' facility by a friend and dropped off. The friend agreed to return for Plaintiff when Plaintiff called and asked to be picked up. Plaintiff had earlier wrapped his injured left hand in a towel. Plaintiff checked in and proceeded to fill out the requisite forms for the clinic. Prior to completing the form, which lacked any inquiry about AIDS and HIV status, an employee of the Defendants informed Plaintiff that the doctor at the care unit said she does not treat patients who are HIV positive.

18. Plaintiff requested to hear this denial of medical services from the doctor herself. The doctor, Defendant [Betty Beta, M.D.], repeated that she would not treat people infected with the HIV virus. Plaintiff asked to get this in writing, to which Defendant [Beta] assented. On a prescription form which [Beta] signed and dated she wrote, "This is to inform you that I do not treat patient (sic) with HIV positive in our clinic. Advised to go to County ER for treatment." A true and correct copy of this prescription is attached hereto as Appendix A. Plaintiff told Defendant [Beta] he had no transportation to another care facility. Defendants made no offer to assist Plaintiff in obtaining transportation to another facility.

19. Defendant [Beta] never questioned Plaintiff about the severity of his wound, nor did she ask him to unwrap the towel so as to allow her visually to inspect his hand. Defendants provided no care or assistance to Plaintiff whatsoever, although he was in need of emergency medical care. When Plaintiff ultimately was able to obtain medical care elsewhere, his wound was so serious as to require multiple sutures.

FIRST CAUSE OF ACTION

(Violation of the Americans with Disabilities Act)

20. Plaintiff realleges and incorporates herein by reference each and every allegation contained in paragraphs 1 through 19 above.

21. The Americans with Disabilities Act (the "ADA") prohibits discrimination on the basis of disability in the full and equal enjoyment of goods, services, facilities, privileges, advantages, and accommodations of any place of public accommodation by any person who owns, leases (or leases to), or operates a place of public accommodation (42 U.S.C. § 12182(a)).

22. At all times mentioned herein, Defendants' medical offices have been a "place of public accommodation" within the meaning of the ADA. The ADA specifically states that a professional office of a health care provider and/or a hospital is a public accommodation (42 U.S.C. § 12181(7)(F)).

23. At all times mentioned herein, Defendants [City Care Center], [Kappa], and [Alpha] owned and operated a place of public accommodation. At all times mentioned herein, Defendant [Beta] operated a place of public accommodation.

24.   AIDS and HIV infection are disabilities within the meaning of the ADA.

25.   Through the conduct described above, Defendants have discriminated against Plaintiff, solely on the basis of his disability, by denying him the full and equal enjoyment of the services, facilities, and accommodations otherwise available to members of the general public.

26.   Defendants should be ordered to take all steps necessary to ensure full enjoyment of all rights guaranteed by the ADA. Plaintiff is entitled to such injunctive relief under the ADA.

SECOND CAUSE OF ACTION

(Violation of § 504 of the Federal Rehabilitation Act of 1973, 29 U.S.C. §§ 701 *et seq.*)

27.   Plaintiff realleges and incorporates herein by reference each and every allegation contained in paragraphs 1 through 1 9 above.

28.   Section 504 of the Federal Rehabilitation Act of 1973, 29 U.S.C. § 794 (hereafter, "Section 504"), provides, in pertinent part, that no otherwise quali- fied handicapped person "shall, solely by reason of his or her handicap, be excluded from the participation under any program or activity receiving Federal financial assistance . . . ." Plaintiff is and was regarded by Defendants to be a handicapped person for purposes of Section 504. Plaintiff is and was qualified to receive the medical services and/or treatments offered by Defendants.

29.   By virtue of the fact that Defendants receive Medicare funding, Defendants receive federal financial assistance within the meaning of Section 504. Defendants are thus prohibited from excluding, denying benefits to, or discriminating against handicapped persons, including but not limited to persons who are infected with HIV or who have AIDS, solely on the basis of such persons' handicap, in connec- tion with Defendants' provision of medical services.

30.   Defendants, and each of them, have violated Plaintiff's rights under Section 504 by failing and refusing to provide necessary medical treatment and/or access to Defendants' facilities, services, and accommodations, based solely on Plaintiff's handicapped status.

31.   To prevent Defendants from continuing to violate Section 504, Defendants should be enjoined and prohibited from the unlawful and invidiously discrimina- tory practice of failing or refusing to provide necessary medical treatment services, and/or access to Defendants' facilities to persons who have or are perceived to have AIDS or who are or are perceived to be HIV-infected, based solely on those facts or perceptions. Defendants should be further ordered to take all steps neces- sary to ensure the full enjoyment of rights guaranteed by Section 504. Plaintiff is entitled to such relief pursuant to 29 U.S.C. § 794a.

32.   As a further and proximate result of Defendants' unlawfully discriminatory failure or refusal to provide Plaintiff necessary medical treatment and/or access to the facilities, services, and/or accommodations of Defendants' offices, based solely on Plaintiff's handicap, Plaintiff has suffered harm in the form of denied medical treatment, physical pain, shame, humiliation, degradation, and emotional distress entitling him to his actual damages in an amount to be determined at trial.

33.   Pursuant to 29 U.S.C. § 794a(b), Plaintiff is also entitled to his reasonable costs and attorneys' fees.

THIRD CAUSE OF ACTION

(Violation of the [state] Civil Rights Act [Civil Code § 511])

34.   Plaintiff realleges and incorporates herein by reference each and every allegation contained in paragraphs 1 through 19 above.

35.   [Civil Code § 51 (the "Act")] provides that "[all] persons within the jurisdiction of this state are free and equal, and no matter what their . . . physical disabilities are entitled to the full and equal accommodations, advantages, facilities . . . or services in all business establishments of every kind whatsoever."

36.   At all times mentioned herein, Defendants' medical offices have been a "business establishment" within the meaning of the Act, which expressly includes all business establishments "of every kind whatsoever."

37.   Through the conduct described above, Defendants, and each of them, have denied Plaintiff the full and equal enjoyment of Defendants' "accommodations, advantages, facilities or services" by refusing Plaintiff medical treatment and/or services to which he is entitled, solely because of his disability.

38.   Defendants' practices are discriminatory per se because they treat Plaintiff and other similarly situated persons as an outcast group, based solely on their disability.

39.   Plaintiff is informed and believes, and on that basis alleges, that Defendants, and each of them, are and at all times herein relevant have been engaged in conduct resistant to Plaintiff's full enjoyment of rights guaranteed him by the Act.

40.   To prevent Defendants from continuing to violate the Act, Defendants should be enjoined and prohibited from the unlawful and invidiously discriminatory practice of failing or refusing to provide necessary medical treatment, services, and/or access to Defendants' facilities to persons who have or are perceived to have AIDS or who are or are perceived to be HIV-infected, based solely on those

facts or perceptions. Defendants should be further ordered to take all steps necessary to ensure the full enjoyment of all rights guaranteed under the Act. Plaintiff is
entitled to such injunctive relief under [Civil Code § 52(c)(3)].

41.   As a direct and proximate result of Defendants' discriminatory practices, Plaintiff has suffered actual damages in the form of denied medical treatment, physical pain, shame, humiliation, degradation, and emotional distress in
an amount to be determined at trial. Pursuant to [Civil Code § 52(a)], Plaintiff is
entitled to actual damages in an amount to be determined at trial.

42.   Pursuant to [Civil Code § 52(a)], Plaintiff is also entitled to such additional amount as may be determined at trial, up to a maximum of three times
the amount of actual damage but in no case less than [two hundred and fifty
dollars ($250)] per violation, as well as reasonable attorneys' fees.

43.   In committing the acts described above, Defendant [Beta] acted maliciously and oppressively with a conscious, reckless, willful, and callous disregard of Plaintiff's rights, and with the intent of depriving him of rights
guaranteed by the Act. Plaintiff is therefore entitled to exemplary and punitive
damages in an amount sufficient to punish and set an example of Defendant
[Beta].

FOURTH CAUSE OF ACTION

(Violation of [Civil Code § 54.1])

44.   Plaintiff realleges and incorporates herein by reference each and every
allegation contained in paragraphs 1 through 19 above.

45.   [Civil Code § 54.1(a)] provides that "physically disabled persons shall
be entitled to full and equal access, as other members of the general public, to
accommodations, . . . [and] facilities . . . of all . . . places of public accommodation . . . to which the general public is invited, subject only to the conditions
and limitations established by law, or state or federal regulations, and applicable alike to all persons."

46.   At all times mentioned herein, Defendants' medical offices have been a
place of public accommodation" within the meaning of [Civil Code § 54.1].

47.   Through the conduct described above, Defendants, and each of them,
have denied Plaintiff, solely on the basis of his disability, access to public
accommodations otherwise available to members of the general public who are
not physically disabled.

48.   To prevent Defendants from continuing to violate [Civil Code § 54.1],
Defendants should be enjoined and prohibited from the unlawful and invidiously discriminatory practice of failing or refusing to provide necessary medical

treatment, services, and/or access to Defendants' facilities to persons who have or are perceived to have AIDS or who are or are perceived to be HIV-infected, based solely on those facts or perceptions. Defendants should be further ordered to take all steps necessary to ensure the full enjoyment of all rights guaranteed by [Civil Code § 54.1]. Plaintiff is entitled to such injunctive relief under [Civil Code § 55].

49.   As a direct and proximate result of Defendants' discriminatory practices, Plaintiff has suffered actual damages in the form of denied medical treatment, physical pain, shame, humiliation, degradation, and emotional distress. Pursuant to [Civil Code § 54.3], Plaintiff is entitled to actual damages in an amount to be determined at trial.

50.   Pursuant to [Civil Code § 54.3], Plaintiff is also entitled to such additional amount as may be determined at trial, up to a maximum of three times the amount of actual damage but in no case less than [two hundred and fifty dollars ($250)] per violation, as well as reasonable attorneys' fees.

51.   In committing the acts described above, Defendant [Beta] acted maliciously and oppressively, with a conscious, reckless, willful, and callous disregard of Plaintiff's right to full and equal access to Defendants' place of public accommodation equivalent to that of members of the general public who are not disabled. Plaintiff is therefore entitled to exemplary and punitive damages in an amount sufficient to punish and set an example of Defendant [Beta].

FIFTH CAUSE OF ACTION

(Violation of [Business and Professions Code §§ 17200 *et seq.*])

52.   Plaintiff realleges and incorporates herein by reference each and every allegation contained in paragraphs 1 through 19 above.

53.   By engaging in the conduct described above, Defendants, and each of them, have engaged in unlawful business practices prohibited by [Business and Professions Code ("B&P Code") § 17200].

54.   To prevent Defendants from continuing to commit unlawful business practices, Defendants should be enjoined and prohibited from the unlawful and invidiously discriminatory practice of failing or refusing to provide necessary medical treatment, services, and/or access to Defendants' facilities to persons who have or are perceived to have AIDS or who are or are perceived to be HIV infected, based solely on those facts or perceptions. Defendants should be further ordered to take all steps necessary to ensure that persons with AIDS or who are HIV-infected are not unlawfully denied necessary medical treatment, service, and/or access to Defendants' facilities, based solely on the fact that such persons have AIDS or are HIV-infected. Plaintiff is entitled to such relief pursuant to [B&P Code §§ 17202 through 17204].

SIXTH CAUSE OF ACTION

(Intentional Infliction of Emotional Distress)

55.   Plaintiff realleges and incorporates herein by reference each and every allegation contained in paragraphs 1 through 19 above.

56.   Defendants' extreme and outrageous conduct, as described above, was done with intent to cause, or with reckless disregard of the probability of causing, Plaintiff to suffer severe emotional distress in the form of mental anguish and suffering, humiliation, shame, shock, degradation, and extreme and enduring physical pain.

57.   Defendants' conduct was made more extreme and outrageous because Plaintiff was seeking emergency medical services and Defendants knew or should have known of their ethical duty to treat such a patient. As a result of this special relationship and Plaintiff's need for medical services, Defendants knew or should have known of Plaintiff's particular susceptibility to emotional distress, and that such injury was substantially certain to occur as a result of Defendants' conduct.

58.   As a proximate result of Defendants' extreme and outrageous conduct, Plaintiff has suffered humiliation, mental anguish, and emotional and physical distress, and has been injured in mind and body in degrees and amounts to be determined at trial.

59.   The aforementioned acts of Defendant [Beta] were willful, reckless, malicious, oppressive, and done with a callous disregard of the consequences substantially certain to occur and justify an award of exemplary and punitive damages against Defendant [Beta].

SEVENTH CAUSE OF ACTION

(Negligent Infliction of Emotional Distress)

60.   Plaintiff realleges and incorporates herein by reference each and every allegation contained in paragraphs 1 through 19 above.

61.   At all times herein relevant, Defendants were bound by their common law and statutory duties to provide medical services, treatment, and full and equal access to their place of business to all persons on an equivalent basis regardless of their physical disability. As a result of Defendants' failure to fulfill these duties, Plaintiff has suffered substantial and enduring emotional injury.

62.   Defendants knew, or should have known, that their failure to provide necessary medical treatment, services, or full and equal access to their facilities

to Plaintiff because of his HIV status would foreseeably cause Plaintiff serious emotional and physical distress.

63. Defendants breached their duty to exercise due care by refusing to provide services to or treat Plaintiff, solely on the basis of Plaintiff's HIV status.

64. As a proximate result of Defendants' acts or omissions as described above, Plaintiff has suffered serious emotional distress in the form of shame, humiliation, degradation, and physical injuries in an amount to be determined at trial.

PRAYER FOR RELIEF

WHEREFORE, Plaintiff prays for judgment as follows:

1. For injunctive relief ordering Defendants, and each of them to:

a. refrain from discriminating in any manner, by failing or refusing to extend to any individual who has or is regarded as having AIDS or who is or is regarded as being infected with HIV, the full and equal enjoyment of and access to Defendants' treatment, services and/or facilities of any kind whatsoever, on the basis (either in whole or in part) of the fact or perception that such individual has AIDS or an AIDS-related condition, or is infected with HIV;

b. train and educate each and every individual physician, staff member, and all other personnel employed or associated with Defendants' facilities, regarding the actual risks in treating patients with AIDS or who are HIV-infected, and the precautionary measures which must or should be taken to prevent transmission of the disease, including but not limited to the use of universal precautions;

c. train and educate each and every individual physician, staff member, and all other personnel to maintain the confidentiality of Defendants' patients and potential patients' medical and health information, and to disclose such information only as and to the extent necessary for that patient's medical treatment or care, and only to such persons as are necessary to ensure that patient full and competent medical care and treatment.

2. For an award of compensatory damages to Plaintiff equal to the injury he has suffered due to Defendants' discriminatory practices, in an amount to be determined at trial.

3. For an award of such additional amount as may be determined at trial, up to a maximum of three times the amount of actual damages but in no case less than [two hundred and fifty dollars ($250)] for each violation of [Civil Code § 51] and for each violation of [Civil Code § 54.1], as provided by [Civil Code §§ 52 and 54.3].

4.   For an award of exemplary and punitive damages against Defendant [Beta] in an amount sufficient to punish and set an example of her.

5.   For an order awarding Plaintiff his costs of suit, including litigation expenses, out-of-pocket expenses, and reasonable attorneys' fees, in accordance with all applicable provisions of law, including but not limited to the provisions of 29 U.S.C. § 12205; 29 U.S.C. § 794a(b); [Civil Code §§ 52], [54.3], and [55]; and [Code of Civil Procedure § 1021.5].

6.   For such other and further relief as the Court may deem just and proper.

§ 11.13   Wrongful Institutionalization

FORM 11–12
SAMPLE COMPLAINT: WRONGFUL INSTITUTIONALIZATION

IN THE UNITED STATES DISTRICT COURT

FOR [judicial district] OF [state]

[Plaintiff A],

[Plaintiff B],

[Plaintiff C],

[Plaintiff D],

[Plaintiff E],

Plaintiffs,

v.   CIVIL ACTION [number]

[Defendant A], individually and in official capacity as Superintendent, [name] Hospital,

and

[Defendant B], in official capacity as Secretary, [state] Department of Public Welfare,

Defendants.

AMENDED COMPLAINT

I.	Introduction

1.	[Plaintiff A] was born on [date]. Since [year], when she was [26]-years-old—and for the last forty years—she has been unnecessarily and illegally institutionalized.

2.	[Plaintiff A] is institutionalized at [name] Hospital, an institution for persons with mental illness, even though she is not mentally ill. Rather, she had traumatic brain injury, a physiological condition. She could live in the community with appropriate services.

3.	[Plaintiffs B, C, and D] are institutionalized in a nursing home. They have, respectively, sarcoidosis, multiple sclerosis, and stroke effects. They all use wheelchairs and with community-based attendant services could reside in the community.

4.	Plaintiffs are exactly the type of persons Congress had in mind in 1990, when Congress enacted the Americans with Disabilities Act (ADA), 42 U.S.C. § 12101.

5.	The Congressional statutory findings include:

a.	"historically, society has tended to isolate and segregate individuals with disabilities, and despite some improvements, such forms of discrimination against individuals with disabilities continue to be a serious and pervasive problem";

b.	"discrimination against individuals with disabilities persists in such critical areas as . . . institutionalization";

c.	"individuals who have experienced discrimination on the basis of disability have often had no legal recourse to redress such discrimination";

d.	"individuals with disabilities continually encounter various forms of discrimination, including . . . segregation";

e.	"the Nation's proper goals regarding individuals with disabilities are to assure . . . independent living." 42 U.S.C. § 12101(a).

6.	Plaintiffs have been and are currently discriminated against in the exact manner Congress found existed throughout the country. Each of the above Congressional findings of fact apply to the plaintiffs:

(a)	they have been isolated and <u>segregated</u>; they have been <u>institutionalized</u>;

(b)   they have had <u>no legal redress</u>; and

(c)   their goal, like Congress', is <u>independent</u> living.

7.   In addition to violating plaintiff's rights under the ADA, defendants also violate [Plaintiff A]'s rights under the Fourteenth Amendment to the United States Constitution.

II.   <u>Jurisdiction</u>

8.   This Court has jurisdiction under 28 U.S.C. §§ 1331 and 1334.

9.   Plaintiff's claims are authorized by 28 U.S.C. §§ 2201 and 2202 and 42 U.S.C. § 1983.

III.   Parties

10.   Plaintiff [A] is a [66]-year-old person who is a resident of [name] County.

11.   Plaintiff [B] is a [44]-year-old person who is a resident of [name] County.

12.   Plaintiff [C] is a [56]-year-old person who is a resident of [name] County.

13.   Plaintiff [D] is a [44]-year-old person who is a resident of [name] County.

14.   Plaintiff [E] is a nonprofit corporation whose members are persons with disabilities. [E] represents persons with disabilities who live in institutions and nursing homes and who could live in the community with appropriate attendant care and other medical treatment and services. [E]'s purpose, among others, is to assist persons with disabilities who are in institutions and nursing homes but who could live in the community in noninstitutional housing. [E]'s organizational purpose is adversely affected by defendants' refusal to comply with the ADA and to refuse to provide necessary community-based attendant care services. [E] suffers direct and concrete injury as a result of defendants' actions. [E]'s members and potential members are injured when defendants refuse to comply with the ADA but, instead, continue to discriminate against persons with disabilities.

15.   Defendant [A] is the Superintendent of the [name] Hospital and is responsible for the day-to-day operations at [name] Hospital, including the proper discharge planning, as well as implementation of the discharge plans.

16.   Defendant [B] is the Secretary of the [state] Department of Public Welfare (DPW) and is statutorily responsible for the policies and operations of DPW, including the Office of Mental Health, the [name] Hospital, and the Office of Medical Assistance (which includes payments for nursing home and community-based attendant care).

V.   Factual Background

A.   [Plaintiff A]

17.   When she was [three] years old, [A] experienced cerebral trauma as a result of being hit by a trolley car in [city]. For the next few years, she did not speak.

18.   She attended a Catholic school where she took "special education" classes. At the age of [18] and in [8th] grade, she "graduated." [A] can read and write.

19.   In [1953], when she was [27] and living with her parents, [A] attempted suicide and was admitted to [name] Hospital.

20.   She was then transferred to [name] Hospital where she was treated for "depression" and received electroshock "therapy treatment."

21.   [A] remained in [name] Hospital until [1971] when she was placed in a boarding home, where she was raped and beaten, became hysterical, and had to be restrained.

22.   [A] was taken to [name] Hospital on [date]. Staff at [name] Hospital noted its diagnostic impression: Organic Brain Syndrome due to head injury and mild mental retardation without psychosis.

23.   At the time of [A]'s admission to [name] Hospital in [1971], its clinical staff recommended that discharge planning be commenced immediately. To date, [21] years later, [A] has not been discharged.

24.   [Name] Hospital is a facility for persons with mental illnesses. [A] has an organic brain injury—not a mental illness.

25.   [Name] Hospital does not have appropriate and adequate programs to treat and habilitate persons with Organic Brain Syndrome.

26.   [A] has expressed a strong desire to leave [name] Hospital for a long time. Her sisters reside in [city], where they are very active in their parish, and [A] has had numerous "day visits" to her sisters' home. She has familiarity with that area of the city and ·has expressed a strong preference to live near her sisters and their

church. Understandably, due to her [1971] experience in a boarding home, [A] is anxious about where she will live and the type of a community program she will receive.

27.   Plaintiff [A] could benefit from living in a "family-style" supported home where she can live with women similar to her age and social functioning. Due to her disabilities and length of her institutionalization, she will require support staff on a 24-hour basis, like that provided in community-living arrangements for persons who have other developmental disabilities.

28.   Although defendants have recommended since [1971] that [A] be discharged from [name] Hospital, no one has developed an appropriate discharge plan or required that it be funded and implemented. The plaintiff has never been placed in a supervised setting appropriate to her needs.

29.   Besides her organic brain injury, [A] has a hypertensive cardiovascular disease and adult-onset of insulin-dependent diabetes mellitus, which require support and monitoring.

30.   Even though she is not mentally ill, [A] receives Mallaril 25 mg per day, a psychotropic medicine which, in fact, may induce diabetic retinopathy.

31.   [A] works one and one-half days a week at a sheltered workshop, which she enjoys very much because she can socialize there.

32.   Although she has the potential to reacquire adaptive, functional, life skills focused on the maintenance of a home, meal preparation, and personal care skills, she cannot learn these skills at [name] Hospital but only in a community-based program.

33.   Due to the length of time she has been institutionalized, she will require appropriate clinical, programmatic, and habilitative services.

34.   Defendants have failed to implement the [name] Hospital professionals' recommendations to discharge the plaintiff.

35.   Defendants have failed to develop or to assure the provision of adequate aftercare for persons with Organic Brain Syndrome.

36.   As a result of defendants' policies and practices, [A] has remained confined in [name] Hospital unnecessarily and contrary to professional recommendations.

37.   As a result of defendants' policies and practices, [A] has been confined to [name] Hospital which does not provide her with treatment that is as effective, or as habilitative, as she could receive in the community.

38.   As a result of defendants' policies and practices, [A] continues to be institutionalized at [name] Hospital and unnecessarily segregated from the community.

B.   [Plaintiffs B, C, and D]

39.   [B] is a mother of two daughters, ages 18 and 15. When [B] was thirty years old, she was diagnosed as having sarcoiclosis in her lungs, a systematic disease that may affect any organ of the body.

40.   In [1981], the disease affected her ability to ambulate. Today she uses a wheelchair for mobility.

41.   Prior to her disease, [B] lived with her father. Because his house was not wheelchair accessible and because [B] required attendant care which she could not afford, she was institutionalized in a nursing home in [1988].

42.   [B] receives only [$30] a month from Supplemental Security Income (SSI). Using her wheelchair for ambulation, [B] attends community college three days a week and sometimes goes out to dinner.

43.   Even though she is able to get in and out of bed alone, [B] requires attendant care for some personal care.

44.   She wishes to live with her daughters in the community and wants Defendant [B] and Medical Assistance to pay for attendant care instead of paying for her nursing home care.

45.   [C] was diagnosed with Multiple Sclerosis (MS) in [1973], a year after she was in an automobile accident.

46.   From [1973] to [1978], she continued to work at two jobs—a seamstress and key punch operator.

47.   In [1978], [C] started to use a wheelchair for mobility. She needs assistance in washing and grooming, which she received from a private nurse whom [C] used when she was living at home.

48.   After her funds were depleted, [C] could no longer afford attendant care and she was institutionalized in a nursing home in [1991].

49.   [C] wishes to live in a community and wants Defendant [B] and Medical Assistance to pay for her attendant care instead of paying for her nursing home care.

50.   [D] had a cerebro-vascular accident (commonly known as a stroke) in [1989], which affects her left side.

51.   She uses a wheelchair for ambulation.

52.   In [1991], because she could not afford an attendant in the community, [D] was institutionalized in a nursing home.

53.   [D] requires assistance in grooming and personal hygiene, but with assistance has visited her daughter in the community.

54.   She wishes to live in the community and wants defendant [B] and Medical Assistance to pay for attendant care instead of paying for her nursing home care.

55.   The professional nursing home staff believe that [plaintiffs B, C, and D] could live in the community if they had appropriate attendant care.

56.   As a result of Defendant [B]'s policies and practices, [plaintiffs B, C, and D] remain confined to a nursing home unnecessarily and contrary to professional recommendations, remain institutionalized and unnecessarily segregated from the community, and do not receive as effective treatment as they could receive in the community.

Causes of Action

Count I

57.   Contrary to the recommendation of defendants' and the nursing home's own professionals that [plaintiffs A, B, C, and D] be placed and served in an appropriate community program, Defendant [B] violates 42 U.S.C. §§ 12132 and 12182(b)(1)(B) and 28 C.F.R. § 35.130(d), which require defendants to provide services to them "in the most integrated setting appropriate to the needs of qualified individuals with disabilities."

58.   Defendant [B]'s provision of services to plaintiffs only either in [name] Hospital or nursing home institutional settings, which are less effective than treatment in the community and which are unnecessary for their treatment, violates 42 U.S.C. §§ 12132 and 12182(b)(1)(A)(iii) and 28 C.F.R. § 35.130(b)(1)(iv) in that the services at [name] Hospital and nursing homes are unnecessarily "separate" and not as "effective" as services [plaintiffs A, B, C, and D] could receive in the community.

59.   Defendant [B]'s policies and procedures violate 42 U.S.C. §§ 12132 and 12182(b)(1)(A)(ii) and (b)(2)(A)(ii) and (iii) and 28 C.F.R. §§ 35.130(b)(7) and (8) in that they have failed with regard to named plaintiffs to make reasonable modifications to afford them appropriate community-based services and to terminate the discrimination and the institutional segregation.

Count II

60.   Defendants [A and B] violate [plaintiff A]'s due process rights under the Fourteenth Amendment by failing to comply with the judgment of the professionals treating [plaintiff A] that she receive services in an appropriate community setting other than in a state mental hospital.

PRAYER FOR RELIEF

WHEREFORE, plaintiffs pray that this Court:

1.   Assume jurisdiction over their cases.

2.   Enjoin defendants from violating plaintiffs' rights under the ADA and the Fourteenth Amendment.

3.   Order defendants to issue a Request for Proposals to establish an appropriate community-based program in [city] for [plaintiff A].

4.   Order defendants to provide attendant care in the community for [plaintiffs B, C, and D].

5.   Award plaintiffs compensatory damages for the years of unnecessary institutionalization and award such other relief as may be just, proper, and equitable, including reasonable attorneys' fees and costs.

Respectfully submitted,

[name]

[address]

[telephone number]

[name]

[address]

[telephone number]

Attorneys for Plaintiffs

Dated: [date]

§ 11.14   Inaccessible Recreational Facility

FORM 11–13
SAMPLE COMPLAINT: INACCESSIBLE RECREATIONAL FACILITY

IN THE UNITED STATES DISTRICT COURT

FOR THE [judicial district] OF [state]

[Plaintiff A], a minor, by her parent and natural guardian, [name],

and

[Plaintiffs B and C], on behalf of themselves and all other similarly situated individuals,

Plaintiffs,

v.   Civ. Action No.

[name], Owner of [arena name],

Defendant.

CLASS ACTION

COMPLAINT

I.   INTRODUCTION

1.   [Defendant], a public stadium and arena, discriminates against adults and children who are disabled by refusing to sell them seats on the floor level, during those events when nondisabled persons are permitted to sit on the floor level.

2.   On July 12, 1990, Congress enacted the Americans with Disabilities Act (ADA), 42 U.S.C. § 12101 *et seq.,* establishing the most important civil rights for persons with disability in our country's history.

3.   The Congressional statutory findings include:

a.   "some 43,000,000 Americans have one or more physical or mental disabilities . . .";

b.   "historically, society has tended to isolate and segregate individuals with disabilities and, despite some improvements, such forms of discrimination against individuals with disabilities continue to be a serious and pervasive social problem";

c.   "discrimination against individuals with disabilities persists in such critical areas as . . . public accommodations";

d.   "individuals with disabilities continually encounter various forms of discrimination, including . . . the discriminatory effects of architectural . . . barriers"; [and]

e.   "the continuing existence of unfair and unnecessary discrimination and prejudice denies people with disabilities the opportunity . . . to pursue those opportunities for which our free society is justifiably famous." 42 U.S.C. § 12101(a).

4.   Congress went on to state explicitly the purpose of the ADA to be:

(1)   "to provide a clear and comprehensive national mandate for the elimination of discrimination against individuals with disabilities";

(2)   "to provide clear, strong, consistent, enforceable standards addressing discrimination against individuals with disabilities"; [and]

(3)   "to invoke the sweep of Congressional authority . . . to regulate commerce, in order to address the major areas of discrimination faced day-to-day by people with disabilities." 42 U.S.C. § 12101(b).

5.   Congress gave public accommodations one and a half years to implement the Act. The effective date was January 26, 1992.

6.   Nevertheless, [defendant], at [address], [city, state], has not eliminated barriers that prevent persons who use wheelchairs from sitting, like nondisabled persons, on the ground floor of this stadium.

7.   Plaintiffs have repeatedly requested defendant to make its stadium accessible. After months of futile negotiations that have resulted neither in the removal of architectural barriers nor in a commitment to remove those barriers, plaintiffs seek to redress their rights under the ADA and request this Court issue declaratory and injunctive relief against defendant to end the ongoing discrimination.

II.   JURISDICTION

8.   This Court has jurisdiction under 28 U.S.C. §§ 1331 and 1343.

9.   Plaintiffs' claims are authorized by 28 U.S.C. §§ 2201 and 2202, and 42 U.S.C. § 1983.

III.   PARTIES

10.   [Name] is the parent and guardian of [plaintiff A], a [four]-year-old child who uses a wheelchair for mobility. They are residents of [name] County, [state].

11.   [Plaintiff B] is a resident of [city, state] and uses a wheelchair for mobility.

12.   [Plaintiff C] is a resident of [city, state] and uses a wheelchair for mobility.

13.   [Defendant] is a [state] corporation which owns and operates [name], a public stadium and arena, located at [address].

IV.   CLASS ACTION ALLEGATIONS

14.   Plaintiffs [A, B, and C] bring this action on behalf of all other persons similarly situated, pursuant to Rules 23(a) and (b)(2) of the Federal Rules of Civil Procedure. The class members consist of all persons who use wheelchairs for ambulation, who wish to attend basketball games and other entertainment at [arena], who wish to sit on the floor level, and for whom [arena] presents architectural barriers to accessibility to the floor level seating.

15.   The exact size of the class is unknown to the plaintiffs, but they believe the size of the class is so numerous that joinder of all members is impracticable.

16.   There are questions of law or fact common to the class; to wit, the plaintiffs' rights under the ADA have been wrongfully denied.

17.   The claims of the named plaintiffs are typical of the claims of the class; to wit, the defendant has abridged, named, and classed plaintiffs' rights under the ADA and has violated their rights protected by federal regulations.

18.   The defendant has acted or refused to act on grounds generally applicable to the class, thereby making appropriate injunctive and declaratory relief with respect to the class as a whole.

19.   The named plaintiffs will fairly and adequately protect the interests of the class.

20.   Plaintiffs' counsel is experienced in litigating class actions.

V.   FACTS

21.   One of the most important parts of the ADA was Title III, known as the "Public Accommodations and Services Operated by Private Entities." 42 U.S.C. § 12181 *et seq.*

22.   Congress included a "motion picture house, theater, concert hall, stadium, or other place of exhibition or entertainment" as a public accommodation covered by the Act. 42 U.S.C. § 12181(7)(C).

23.   Defendant's business at [address] is a stadium and/or arena at which sporting and other entertainment events take place.

24.   As relevant to the present action, discrimination includes "a failure to remove architectural barriers . . . that are structural in nature, in existing facilities . . . where such removal is readily achievable." 42 U.S.C. § 12182(b)(2)(A)(iv).

25.   In the event that the removal of the barrier was not readily achievable, the United States Department of Justice has by regulation required that the public accommodation [be made] available through alternative methods, if these methods are readily achievable." 28 C.F.R. § 36.305(a).

26.   [Plaintiff A] is a [four]-year-old child who has severe cerebral palsy and requires a special stroller and/or wheelchair for mobility.

27.   [Plaintiff A] attends school at [name] in [city, state].

28.   [Plaintiff A]'s mother, [name], wanted to take [plaintiff A] to [arena] to see "Sesame Street Live."

29.   [Plaintiff A's mother] ordered tickets from [arena]'s box office via telephone and advised defendant that [plaintiff A] required handicapped seating.

30.   Defendant's agents assured [plaintiff A's mother] when she purchased the tickets that there was accessible seating on the floor level.

31.   [Plaintiff A] and her mother were assured they would be seated on the floor level next to the stage and such seating was accessible.

32.   They paid for the most expensive seats for the show.

33.   Parking in the "handicapped parking area" was not close to the entrance of [arena], nor on a direct path to accessible seating.

34.   When they entered [arena], they found no accessibility symbols for persons in a wheelchair to the floor level. Rather, they saw only steps.

35.   Plaintiffs asked the usher about their alleged accessible tickets, and the usher told them that handicapped seating was handled through the information booth, which was located halfway around the building.

36.   At the information booth, plaintiffs were told that all handicapped seating is in Section C—the furthest point from the stage.

37.   Accessible seating in Section C is not on the floor or near the stage, where [plaintiff's mother] had paid for her seats.

38.   [Plaintiff B] is the Executive Director of [name], a nonprofit organization that is affiliated with the [name] Hospital and which assists businesses and industries to hire people with disabilities, including advising them on the accommodations that may be necessary. He has also worked as the Adjunct Instructor in Neuropsychology at [name] University, and a Coordinator in the Regional Spinal Cord and Injury Center of [name].

39.   [Plaintiff B] uses a wheelchair for mobility.

40.   [Plaintiff B] was Chairperson of the Mayor's Commission for People with Disabilities, as well as the President of Transition to Independent Living, a Vice President of United Cerebral Palsy of [city] and [vicinity], and a President of [name] Wheelchair Athletic Association.

41.   [Plaintiff B] is a college basketball fan, and he also plays wheelchair basketball.

42.   In [date], when the NCAA Basketball playoffs were held at [arena], [plaintiff B] was forced to sit on the last row of Section C because the defendant refuses to sell tickets on the floor level to persons who use wheelchairs.

43.   Similarly, when [plaintiff B] goes to games, he must sit in Section C far from the game.

44.   [Plaintiff B] and his companion, who must sit behind him in Section C and whose view is partially blocked, want to purchase tickets for seats on the floor level but they have been prevented by defendant's policy.

45.   [Plaintiff C] is [28] years old and received a spinal cord injury playing football in college.

46.   For the past nine years, he has used a wheelchair and plays wheelchair basketball.

47.   [Plaintiff C] is the Sports Director for [WWWW-FM], a local radio station.

48.   In order for him adequately to perform his employment, he, like other reporters, must visit the locker rooms after a game and interview the players.

49.   For some time, after the games, [plaintiff C] took the freight elevator from [arena]'s mezzanine seating level to the floor level where he was able to roll to the locker room.

50.   Without explanation, defendant told him that he could no longer use the freight elevator. As a consequence of this decision, [plaintiff C] cannot adequately be a sports reporter.

51.   A few years ago, [arena] built new steps to the entrance for advance ticket purchases and for the press. From this entrance, reporters walk no stairs but use a ramp to gain access both to the floor level of [arena] and to the athletes' locker room.

52.   By building a ramp as part of these new steps, defendant can make [arena]'s floor level accessible to persons who use wheelchairs.

53.   [Arena] also has a tunnel to the floor level, which is used to transport equipment, food, and buses for the athletes.

54.   A ramp for persons who use wheelchairs could be built adjacent to the existing ramp, and persons who use wheelchairs would have access to the floor level.

55.   In [arena] there is also an elevator that is used primarily for freight.

56.   Defendant could easily make alternations to this existing elevator for persons who use wheelchairs.

57. Thus, there are three ways to make [arena] accessible for persons with disabilities who wish to purchase seats on the floor level: (1) build a ramp adjacent to the recently-constructed stairs; (2) build a ramp adjacent to the existing tunnel; or (3) convert the freight elevator to the passenger elevator.

VI.   CLAIMS

First

58.   Pursuant to the ADA 42 U.S.C. § 12182(b)(2)(A)(iv), and the federal regulations promulgated pursuant to this Act, defendant was to make [arena] at [address] accessible by January 26, 1992. To date, it has not.

59.   By failing to remove architectural barriers where such removal is readily achievable, defendant discriminated against the plaintiff in violation of the ADA.

Second

60. Pursuant to the ADA, 42 U.S.C. § 12182(a), and the federal regulations promulgated by the U.S. Department of Justice, 28 C.F.R. § 36.305, if removal of a barrier is not readily achievable, accommodation must be made available through alternative methods.

61. By failing to permit plaintiffs and their wheelchairs down the existing ramp and by failing to modify the existing elevator, defendant discriminated against plaintiffs in violation of the ADA.

Third

62. Pursuant to the ADA, 42 U.S.C. § 12182(a), and the federal regulations promulgated pursuant to this Act, defendant cannot discriminate against persons with disabilities solely based on their disability.

63. Defendant's policy of prohibiting persons who use wheelchairs to purchase tickets on the floor level and limiting the number of available seats for persons with disabilities discriminates against plaintiffs in violation of the ADA.

PRAYER FOR RELIEF

WHEREFORE, plaintiffs respectfully pray;

1. That this Court assume jurisdiction;

2. That this Court issue an injunction enjoining defendant from continuing its discrimination;

3. That this Court award plaintiffs appropriate compensatory damages, attorneys' fees, and such additional or alternative relief as may be just, proper, and equitable.

Respectfully submitted,

[name]

[address]

[telephone number]

Dated [date]

§ 11.15   Attendant Care Services

FORM 11–14
SAMPLE COMPLAINT: ATTENDANT CARE SERVICES

IN THE UNITED STATES DISTRICT COURT

FOR THE [district] DISTRICT OF [state]

[plaintiff], by her next friend [plaintiff's mother]

Plaintiff,

v.   CIVIL ACTION NO. [number]

[defendant A], Secretary of the

Department of Public Welfare,

[defendant B], Deputy Secretary for

Social Programs, and

[HOMEMAKER SERVICES OF THE METROPOLITAN AREA],

Defendants.

COMPLAINT

I.   INTRODUCTION

1.   [Plaintiff], a young woman with serious physical disabilities, brings this action by her mother and next friend, [name], to enjoin defendants' refusal to provide attendant care services to individuals with cognitive limitations.

2.   Pursuant to [state statute], [state] has established a program to provide personal care attendants to persons with serious physical disabilities to assist them in daily living activities (the "Attendant Care Program").

3.   Defendants refuse to provide attendant care services to persons who have cognitive limitations and physical disabilities. Although [plaintiff's] physical disabilities qualify her for attendant care services, her cognitive impairments led defendants to terminate her attendant care services.

4.   Defendants' refusal to provide attendant care services to plaintiff due to her cognitive impairments violates Title II of the Americans with Disabilities Act, 42 U.S.C. §§ 12131–12134.

II.   JURISDICTION AND VENUE

5.   This Court has subject matter jurisdiction pursuant to 28 U.S.C. § 1331. Plaintiff's claims are authorized by 28 U.S.C. §§ 2201 and 2202 and by 42 U.S.C. §§ 12101 *et seq.*

III.   PARTIES

6.   Plaintiff is a [28]-year-old resident of [city, state]. She brings this action through her mother and next friend, [name], who also is a resident of [city, state].

7.   Defendant [A] is the Secretary of the [state] Department of Public Welfare ("DPW"). She is responsible for the operation of DPW, including its Office of Social Programs ("OSP") which implements the [Attendant Care Program]. She is sued in her official capacity.

8.   Defendant [B] is the Deputy Secretary of OSP which is responsible for the implementation of the [Attendant Care Program]. She is sued in her individual and official capacities.

9.   Defendant [Homemaker Services of the Metropolitan Area ("HSMA")] is a [state] nonprofit corporation. Under contract with DPW, [HSMA] provides attendant care services to individuals in [city, state].

IV.   FACTS

10.   [Plaintiff] was born on [date].

11.   In [August 1982], [plaintiff] was involved in an automobile accident which resulted in a severe head injury. Her condition is described as spastic quadriplegia level of C7 post-traumatic. As a result of the accident, plaintiff has lost the use of her legs and her arms, with the exception of her left hand. She is unable to speak, but she can communicate through head and eye signaling. She does have cognitive limitations.

12.   [Plaintiff] lives with her family members who are her primary caretakers. She requires substantial assistance in all daily living and self-care activities, including eating, toileting, bathing, and getting out of bed.

13.   Around [1984], [state] first began to address the needs of [state] residents with severe physical handicaps for assistance in daily living.

14.   DPW contracted with several nonprofit corporations, including defendant [HSMA], to supply attendants to such individuals to assist them in the basic functions of daily living in their own homes.

15.   In [1986], the [state] legislature enacted the [state statute], codifying the developing [Attendant Care Program]. The Act became effective on [July 1, 1987].

16.   The purpose of the [state statute] is to provide hands-on, physical assistance to persons who are not able to perform daily living functions due to their disabilities. Such services enable individuals with physical disabilities to live in their own homes and communities. To the maximum extent feasible, attendants operate under the supervision of the consumers of the services.

17.   Under the [state statute], only "eligible individuals" are entitled to participate in the [Attendant Care Program]. "Eligible individual" is defined as-

Any physically disabled person 18 through 59 years of age who meets all of the following requirements:

(1)   Experiences any medically determinable physical impairment which can be expected to last for a continuous period of not less than 12 months.

(2)   Is capable of selecting, supervising and, if needed, firing an attendant.

(3)   Is capable of managing his own financial and legal affairs.

(4)   Because of physical impairment, requires assistance to complete functions of daily living, self-care and mobility, including, but not limited to, those functions included in the definition of attendant care services. [state statute] (emphasis added).

18.   In [1987], after the enactment of the [state statute], plaintiff applied for personal care services from [Resources for Living Independently ("RLI")]. DPW had contracted with [RLI] to provide attendant care services in the geographic area in which plaintiff was then residing.

19.   [RLI] evaluated plaintiff and determined that she was eligible for 33 hours of personal care services each week due to her physical impairments. [RLI] assigned attendants to assist [plaintiff] in washing, toileting, brushing her teeth, eating, and transferring to her wheelchair.

20.   Due to [plaintiff]'s cognitive limitations, a family member assisted with the attendant's activities. For example, when [plaintiff]'s mother was at work, another family member was presented to direct that attendant.

21.   In [February 1992], [plaintiff]'s family moved to [city, state].

22.   Defendant [HSMA], under contract with DPW, provides attendant care services to persons living in [city, state].

23.   In [December 1992], [plaintiff] was terminated from the [Attendant Care Program] as a result of [HSMA]'s determination that she was ineligible for attendant care services solely because she was unable to direct her attendant.

24.   Since [plaintiff] has been terminated from the [Attendant Care Program], she spends more time confined to her bed and receives less stimulation. [Plaintiff]'s family has great difficulty in providing her with the care that she needs.

V.   CLAIM

25.   This count is asserted pursuant to the Americans with Disabilities Act ("ADA"), 42 U.S.C. § 12101 *et seq.,* against all defendants.

26.   Plaintiff is a qualified individual with a disability as that term is defined by Title I of the ADA, 42 U.S.C. § 12131(2).

27.   DPW, OSP, and [HSMA] (as a contractor providing DPW services) are public entities—as that term is defined by Title II of the ADA, 42 U.S.C. § 12131(1).

28.   Under the [state statute], defendants exclude persons with cognitive limitations, such as plaintiff, from participation in the [Attendant Care Program] and deny them access to attendant care services even though they have severe physical disabilities and so require attendant care.

29.   Defendants fail to provide reasonable accommodations for persons who need attendant care and who also have cognitive limitations to enable them to participate in the [Attendant Care Program]. For example, defendants do not permit family members to direct the services of an attendant for a person with cognitive limitations.

30.   Defendants have violated Title II of the ADA, 42 U.S.C. § 12132, by excluding plaintiff from participation in the [Attendant Care Program] and denying her attendant care services due to her disability, i.e., her cognitive impairment, and by failing to permit a reasonable accommodation to enable her to take part in the [Program] and receive the services.

VI.   PRAYER FOR RELIEF

WHEREFORE, plaintiff prays that this Court:

1.   Assume jurisdiction over this case.

2.   Declare that defendants' exclusion of persons with cognitive disabilities from the [Attendant Care Program] and their denial of attendant care services of those individuals violates the Americans with Disabilities Act.

3.   Order injunctive relief requiring defendants to provide attendant care to plaintiff.

4.   Award such other relief as may be just, proper and equitable, including reasonable attorneys' fees and costs.

Respectfully submitted,

[Attorneys for Plaintiff]

[Attorney A]

Attorney I.D. No. [number]

[address]

[city, state] [zip code]

[telephone number]

and

[Attorney B]

Attorney I.D. No. [number]

[address]

[city, state] [zip code]

[telephone number]

Dated: [date]

§ 11.16   Air Carrier Services

FORM 11–15
SAMPLE COMPLAINT: AIR CARRIER SERVICES

IN THE UNITED STATES DISTRICT COURT

FOR THE [district] DISTRICT OF [state]

[name],

Plaintiff,

vs.   CIVIL ACTION NO. [number]

[name],

Defendant.

JURY TRIAL DEMANDED

COMPLAINTS UNDER TITLES II AND III

COMPLAINT

I.   Introduction

1.   Plaintiff [name and occupation], uses an electrically powered wheelchair for ambulation. Despite the congressional enactment of the Air Carrier Access Act, 49 U.S.C. app. § 1374(c), Defendant [name ("Airline")] discriminated against plaintiff.

2.   [Airline] refused to provide Plaintiff with the use of a ground wheelchair to make a flight connection, failed to stow his electric wheelchair to ensure its arrival on the same flight, and failed to train its employees to know that his non-spill gel battery need not be separated from his wheelchair. [Airline]'s actions violate the Air Carrier Access Act, 49 U.S.C. app. § 1374(c), and the federal regulations duly promulgated thereunder, 14 C.F.R. §§ 382.39(a)(1) and (3), 382.41(f)(3) and (g)(2), and 382.43(a).

3.   Plaintiff seeks compensatory and punitive damages, as well as declaratory and injunctive relief to require compliance with the federally promulgated regulations.

II.   Jurisdiction and Venue

4.   This Court has jurisdiction over the claims set forth in this Complaint under 28 U.S.C. §§ 1331 and 1343. Plaintiff's claims are authorized by the Air Carriers Access Act, 49 U.S.C. app. § 1374(c), 28 U.S.C. §§ 2201 and 2202, and 42 U.S.C. § 1983.

5.   Venue is appropriate pursuant to 28 U.S.C. § 1391 because [Airline] transacts business in this District and a substantial part of the events giving rise to Plaintiff's claim occurred in this District.

III.   Parties

6.   Plaintiff is a resident of [city, state].

7.   Defendant, a [Delaware] Corporation, is an air carrier engaged in interstate commerce. [Airline] operates flights into and out of the [city] International Airport.

IV.   Factual Background

8.   Plaintiff received a doctorate in philosophy degree in clinical psychology in [1978].

9.   On [December 20, 1979], Plaintiff was in an automobile accident which caused "C-5 quadriplegia" (complete lesion of the spinal cord). He is paralyzed in the bottom half of both his arms and below his mid-chest to his feet.

10.   Plaintiff was hospitalized for nine months after the automobile accident, including seven months in a rehabilitation hospital, after which he resumed his professional career.

11.   Plaintiff has a private practice in individual and family psychology. He writes a bimonthly column for [newspaper] entitled "Healing"; he hosts a weekly talk show on [National Public Radio]; he supervises advanced clinical studies at [city, state]; he lectures frequently; and he has written a book [title].

12.   Plaintiff uses an electrically powered wheelchair for ambulation. His wheelchair is his legs. He uses his wheelchair 17 hours a day.

13.   With his wheelchair, Plaintiff is able to be independent. He works and has an active social life in the community.

14.   Periodically, Plaintiff's work requires that he travel by airplane.

15.   On [April 9, 1994], Plaintiff purchased a round-trip ticket on [Airline] to fly from [city, state] to [city, state] to attend and speak at the [convention].

16.   Plaintiff cannot take his electric wheelchair into the cabin of the plane. Instead, he checks his wheelchair along with his other baggage, and airlines provide him with an "aisle chair" to transport him to and from the cabins of their planes.

17.   Aisle chairs are narrowly designed to permit passage through the aisles of airplanes. They are shaped like handcarts used to transport merchandise, except they have two small rear wheels. Aisle chairs are tipped backward to push the individual and the aisle chair through the plane's cabin.

18.   Aisle chairs are not designed or intended to be used for transporting persons with disabilities beyond the plane's cabin.

19.   Plaintiff checked his electric wheelchair in [city, state] for his flight to [city, state].

20.   [Airline]'s flight to [city, state] required that Plaintiff change planes in [city, state]. The flight to [city] from [city] was scheduled to depart thirty minutes after the arrival in [city] of the flight from [city]. When Plaintiff arrived in [city], [Airline] personnel took him off the plane in an aisle chair.

21.   Once outside the plane's cabin, [Airline] was supposed to supply him with a manual wheelchair—not the aisle chair—to enable him to transport himself (with the assistance of his attendant) to his connecting flight. However, after he disembarked from the airplane, [Airline] personnel informed him that no manual wheelchair was available to transport him to the gate where he would make his flight connection. An [Airline] flight attendant told Plaintiff that an elderly, nondisabled woman, who had departed from the same flight, had taken the only ground wheelchair, and that the wheelchairs were available on a "first come, first served" basis.

22.   Without a manual wheelchair, Plaintiff could not take himself to the gate of his connecting flight.

23.   To transport Plaintiff to his connecting flight, [Airline] used the narrow aisle chair. [Airline] personnel pushed him in that narrow device to the street, and informed him that [Airline] would send a van to transport him to the connecting flight. [Airline] personnel then left Plaintiff (on the aisle chair) and his attendant alone to wait for the van.

24.   Plaintiff waited in the aisle chair on the street for thirty minutes (past the time his flight to [city] was scheduled to depart) until the van arrived. During that time, Plaintiff did not know if he would make his connecting plane or if his electrically powered wheelchair would make the connection to [city]. He was afraid he would not have his wheelchair, thereby immobilizing and terrifying him.

25.   The van [Airline] dispatched to transport Plaintiff was not equipped for an aisle chair. Plaintiff had to bend over to enter the van on that chair. The aisle chair could not be strapped or locked down so that when the driver, who drove quickly, made turns, the aisle chair tipped to the side. Plaintiff was extremely frightened of being injured during the ride. The ride on the van, while sitting in the aisle chair, was one of the most harrowing experiences of his life.

26.   As a result of being forced to sit for more than thirty minutes on the aisle chair, Plaintiff exacerbated his decubitus ulcer (a "pressure sore"), since he could not shift his body to relieve the pressure.

27.   While being strapped into the aisle chair, Plaintiff felt like "a helpless cripple."

28.   Plaintiff ultimately did make his connecting flight to [city]. When he arrived at [city], Plaintiff went to the baggage area to retrieve his electric wheelchair, since [Airline] did not bring it to meet him at the plane. When his electric wheelchair arrived, the frame was damaged and an employee of [Airline] gave him the name of a repair shop in [city].

29. For his return flight from [city] to [city], Plaintiff arrived at the airport one hour before his departure time, his normal procedure.

30. Plaintiff's electric wheelchair (which cannot be folded) uses a "gel" battery. The acid in gel batteries cannot be spilled, and so these batteries can be transported safely without removal from the wheelchairs.

31. When Plaintiff checked in, he verbally informed both the [Airline] ticket agent and the [Airline] baggage supervisor that his battery was a gel battery. Plaintiff also provided that information in writing on the wheelchair. The battery itself also plainly states that it is "gel." Plaintiff informed [Airline] verbally and in writing that because the wheelchair has a gel battery, the battery did not have to be removed from the wheelchair. Both the ticket agent and the baggage supervisor in [city] assured him it would be "no problem; the battery will not be taken apart."

32. In [city] as usual, Plaintiff was the last person to be taken off the plane and he was forced to wait a long time.

33. While waiting to disembark, an [Airline] supervisor told Plaintiff that his wheelchair did not make the flight "because it took so long to take the wires off the battery in [city]." Plaintiff was devastated, since his wheelchair for him is like a pair of legs are for a nondisabled person. The loss of his wheelchair was "like someone saying I borrowed your legs and misplaced them."

34. [Airline] offered him a voucher for supper and a manual wheelchair in which to wait.

35. [Airline] left him unattended and therefore immobilized for much of the time.

36. When his electric wheelchair arrived a few hours later, [Airline] had wired it incorrectly so that when he pushed the directional stick to the right, the chair went to the left.

37. Plaintiff's experiences with [Airline] left him feeling "castrated" by people who just did not care about him.

38. As a direct and proximate result of [Airline]'s willful, wanton and malicious disregard of Plaintiff's civil rights, Plaintiff experienced great physical duress, mental anguish, emotional pain and suffering, embarrassment, feeling of extreme humiliation, and other injuries.

39. Unless [Airline] is enjoined from continuing its discriminatory practices, Plaintiff will be unable to use the airline for future air travel.

V.   Claim

Air Carrier Access Act

40.   Congress enacted the Air Carrier Access Act, 49 U.S.C. app. § 1374(c), in March 1986. The Air Carrier Access Act was enacted to ensure that air carriers do not discriminate against people with disabilities in the provision of transportation, both in the air and on the ground in the airports. Among other things, Congress hoped to prevent "humiliating and degrading" practices of airlines.

41.   [Airline] is an air carrier within the meaning of the Air Carrier Access Act, 49 U.S.C. app. § 1374(c), and is required to comply with the federal regulations promulgated pursuant to the Air Carrier Access Act, including

a.   14 C.F.R. § 382.39(a)(1) ("delivering carrier . . . [is] responsible for assistance in making flight connections and transportation between gates. This assistance shall include . . . the use of ground wheelchairs . . .");

b.   14 C.F.R. § 382.39(a)(3) ("carriers shall not leave the handicapped passenger unattended in a ground wheelchair, boarding wheelchair, or other device, in which the passenger is not independently mobile, for more than 30 minutes.");

c.   14 C.F.R. § 382.41(f)(3) ("carriers shall provide for the timely return of passengers' wheelchairs as close as possible to the door of the aircraft . . . . Wheelchairs shall be stowed in the baggage compartment with priority over other cargo and baggage");

d.   14 C.F.R. § 382.41(g)(2) ("carriers shall transport electric-powered wheelchairs secured in an upright position, so that batteries need not be separated from the wheelchair in order to comply with DOT hazardous materials rules."); and

e.   14 C.F.R. § 382.43(a) ("when wheelchairs . . . are disassembled by the carrier for storage, the carrier shall reassemble them . . . [and] shall be returned to the passenger in the condition received by the carrier.").

42.   [Airline] violated the Air Carrier Access Act, *inter alia*, by refusing to provide Plaintiff with a ground wheelchair in [city] for assistance in traveling to his connecting flight, by refusing to return his wheelchair to the door of the aircraft in [city] by disassembling his battery and separating it from his wheelchair, by failing to store his wheelchair on the flight to [city] before other cargo and baggage and by returning his wheelchair to him in [city] and [city] in a damaged condition.

VI.   Prayer for Relief

WHEREFORE, Plaintiff respectfully prays:

1.   That this Court assume jurisdiction.

2.   That this Court issue a declaratory judgment and an injunction enjoining Defendant from violating the Air Carrier Access Act and the regulations promulgated pursuant to the Act.

3.   That the Court award Plaintiff appropriate compensatory damages, including damages for emotional distress.

4.   That the Court award appropriate punitive damages for the willful, wanton and malicious disregard of Plaintiff's federally protected civil rights by [Airline]. [Airline] stranded Plaintiff at the [city] Airport on an unstable, narrow aisle chair in which he was unable to move and then drove him in a van rapidly through the airport, causing the aisle chair (which was not strapped down) to tip and tilt. [Airline] also willfully, wantonly, and maliciously disregarded Plaintiff's civil rights by unnecessarily disassembling his wheelchair, resulting in Plaintiff's arrival in [city] before his wheelchair. The amounts shall be large enough to deter [Airline]'s future misconduct of travellers with disabilities and not less than [$500,000].

5.   That the Court award such additional or alternative relief as may be just, proper and equitable under the circumstances, including an award of reasonable attorneys' fees and expenses.

VII.   Jury Demand

Plaintiff demands a trial by jury for all of the issues that a jury properly may decide, and for all of the requested relief that a jury may award.

Respectfully submitted,

[attorneys for plaintiff]

[attorney A]

Attorney I.D. No. [number]

[address]

[city, state] [zip code]

[telephone number]

and

[attorney B]

Attorney I.D. No. [number]

[address]

[city, state] [zip code]

[telephone number]

Although this complaint asserts claims under the Air Carrier Access Act[5] rather than directly under the ADA, its factual allegations are appropriate models for similar problems that might arise under the ADA. For example, a place of public accommodation might mistreat a disabled person as the airline allegedly did in this case.

---

[5] 49 U.S.C. app. §§ 1305(a), 1374(c) (1994).

CHAPTER 12

POST-COMPLAINT MOTIONS, SUPPORTING MEMORANDA, AND ANSWERS

§ 12.1   Introduction and Overview

This chapter provides forms, associated commentary, and analysis for post-complaint and prediscovery activities for Americans with Disabilities Act

(ADA)[1] litigation. It includes motions to dismiss, answers, motions to intervene, notices of removal to federal court, and motions to remand to state court.

§ 12.2 Motions

The Federal Rules of Civil Procedure and most state rules permit considerable flexibility in drafting motions. See **Forms 12–1** through **12–7.** Typically, the motion must provide notice to the judge and to the opposing parties of the relief sought and the specific grounds supporting the request for relief.[2] In addition, Federal Rule of Civil Procedure 6 and similar state rules require notice of the filing of a motion. This notice typically includes dates upon which a response is due and any hearing date for the motion. Many local rules and good practice also militate in favor of including a draft order with the motion, which the judge approving the motion simply may sign. There is no reason that multiple requests for relief may not be included in the same motion.

Although there is no apparent rule against including legal and factual argument in the motion itself, it is more usual to confine the motion to a specification of the relief sought, the factual allegations, and a brief summary of the grounds asserted with the argument and the full development of authority in a separate memorandum attached to the motion.

§ 12.3 —Notice of Motion and Proof of Service

FORM 12–1
SAMPLE NOTICE OF MOTION AND PROOF OF SERVICE

IN THE UNITED STATES DISTRICT COURT

FOR THE [NORTHERN] DISTRICT OF [ILLINOIS]

[EASTERN] DIVISION

U.S. EQUAL EMPLOYMENT OPPORTUNITY COMMISSION,

Plaintiff   Civil Action No. [92 C 7330]

v.

---

[1] Pub. L. No. 101–336, 104 Stat. 327 (1990) (codified at 42 U.S.C. §§ 12101–12213 (1994); 47 U.S.C. §§ 225, 711 (1994) [hereinafter ADA].

[2] Fed. R. Civ. P. 7(b)(1) (requiring that motions be in writing and state with particularities supporting grounds). Local rules typically require that advance notice of motions be given.

[A.I.C. SECURITY INVESTIGATIONS, LTD.];

[A.I.C. INTERNATIONAL, LTD.]; and [unnamed defendant C],

Defendants.

Honorable [Marvin E. Aspen]

Magistrate Judge [Ronald A. Guzman]

NOTICE OF MOTION

To: [attorney A]
Equal Employment Opportunity Commission
[536 South Clark Street]
[Chicago, IL 60605]

[attorney C]

[attorney D]

PLEASE TAKE NOTICE, that on [Thursday], the [4th] day of [March, 1993], at [2:00], or as soon thereafter as this motion may be heard, the undersigned shall appear before Magistrate Judge [Ronald A. Guzman], or any judge sitting in his stead, in the U.S. District Court for the [Northern] District of [Illinois], [Eastern] Division, [219 South Dearborn Street], [Chicago], [Illinois] [60604] and there and then present the accompanying Defendants' Emergency Motion in Limine to Exclude from Evidence Plaintiff's Exhibit No. 26-"Disability Evaluation Under Social Security."

By: [attorney A]
[WESSELS & PAUTSCH, P.C.]
[330 East Kilbourn Ave., Suite 1475]
[Milwaukee, WI 53202]
[(414) 291-0600]

PROOF OF SERVICE

The undersigned hereby certifies that true and correct copies of this NOTICE OF MOTION and DEFENDANTS' EMERGENCY MOTION IN LIMINE TO EXCLUDE FROM EVIDENCE PLAINTIFFS' EXHIBIT NO. 26-"DISABILITY EVALUATION UNDER SOCIAL SECURITY" were served upon the above-noticed individuals via hand delivery on this [4th] day of [March, 1993].

[attorney B]

Subscribed and sworn by me this [4th] day of [March 1993]

Notary Public

§ 12.4 —Omnibus Certificate of Service

FORM 12–2
SAMPLE OMNIBUS CERTIFICATE OF SERVICE

IN THE UNITED STATES DISTRICT COURT

FOR THE [NORTHERN] DISTRICT OF [ILLINOIS]

[EASTERN] DIVISION

U.S. EQUAL EMPLOYMENT OPPORTUNITY COMMISSION,

Plaintiff,   Civil Action No. [92 C 7330]

v.

[A.I.C. SECURITY INVESTIGATIONS, LTD.];

[A.I.C. INTERNATIONAL, LTD.]; and [unnamed defendant C],

Defendants.

Judge Marvin E. Aspen

Magistrate Judge Guzman

CERTIFICATE OF SERVICE

The undersigned hereby certifies that true and correct copies of this DEFEN-
DANTS' RESPONSE TO PLAINTIFFS' OBJECTION TO DEFENDANTS' CALLING
[JODIE C]. AS A WITNESS AT TRIAL, OBJECTION TO PLAINTIFFS' DEPOSITION
DESIGNATING OF [CHARLES H. WESSEL], RESPONSE TO PLAINTIFFS' MOTION
IN LIMINE, STATEMENT OF CAUSE OF ACTION and LIST OF EXHIBITS THEY
WILL USE AT TRIAL were served, via facsimile and by depositing same in the
United States mail, first-class postage prepaid, to the above-noticed individuals on
this [5th] day of [February], [1993], addressed to the following:

To: [attorney A]
[attorney B]
Equal Employment Opportunity Commission
[536 S. Clark Street]
[Chicago, IL 60605]

[A.I.C. attorney C]

[A.I.C .attorney D]

§ 12.5 —Motion to Intervene and
Supporting Memorandum

FORM 12–3
SAMPLE MOTION TO INTERVENE

IN THE UNITED STATES DISTRICT COURT

FOR THE DISTRICT OF [state]

EEOC and [Lance Butzer]

v.   Civil Action No. [93-4444]

[Intercounty Trucking, Inc.]

MOTION TO INTERVENE AS PLAINTIFF

1.   Intervenor is the victim of disability discrimination on whose behalf the Equal Employment Opportunity Commission ("EEOC") filed a complaint in this civil action on [December 15, 1992].

2.   Intervenor is granted a right to intervene in an action brought by the EEOC under 42 U.S.C. § 2000e-5(f) because he is the "person aggrieved" in the action brought by the EEOC.

3.   Intervenor also is granted a right to intervene by Fed. R. Civ. P. 24(a), because a statute of the United States confers an unconditional right to intervene, as set forth in paragraph (2) of this motion.

4.   Intervenor also is granted a right to intervene by Fed. R. Civ. P. 24(a) because:

A.   Intervenor claims violation of a right not to be subjected to discrimination in violation of the ADA based on the same transition giving rise to the EEOC's civil action;

B.   Intervenor's ability to protect his ADA rights may as a practical matter be impaired or impeded by the disposition of this action; and

C.   The intervenor's interest is not adequately represented by the EEOC.

5.   If the court finds that intervenor is not entitled to intervene as of right, intervenor nevertheless should be allowed to intervene under Fed. R. Civ. P. 24(b), because:

A.   Intervenor's claim, as shown in his Complaint in intervention, presents one or more questions of fact or law common to the EEOC's complaint in this action.

B.   Intervention will not unduly delay or prejudice the rights of the original parties to this action.

WHEREFORE, intervenor requests an order granting this motion and making him a party plaintiff to this action.

FORM 12–4
SAMPLE MEMORANDUM IN SUPPORT OF MOTION
TO INTERVENE

IN THE UNITED STATES DISTRICT COURT

FOR THE DISTRICT OF [state]

EEOC and [Lance Butzer]

v.   Civil Action No. [93-4444]

[Intercounty Trucking, Inc.]

MEMORANDUM IN SUPPORT OF MOTION TO INTERVENE AS PLAINTIFF

Plaintiff/intervenor is entitled to intervene under Fed. R. Civ. P. 24, which allows intervention as of right,

• "upon timely application . . ."

• "(1) when a statute of the United States confers an unconditional right to intervene," or

• "(2) when the applicant claims an interest relating to the property or transaction which is the subject of the action and the applicant is so situated that the disposition of the action may as a practical matter impair or impede the applicant's ability to protect that interest, "unless the applicant's interest is adequately represented by existing parties."

[Fed. R. Civ. P. 24] is intended to enlarge the opportunity for intervention, see [Moore & Levi, *Federal Intervention,* 45 Yale L.J. 565 (1936)], and was amended in [1966] to break the circularity of cases allowing intervention as of right only by parties who could show that they would be precluded by the result of the case in which they sought to intervene. See [*Atlantis Development Corp. v. United States*, 379 F.2d 818 (5th Cir. 1967) (reversing denial of intervention to absentee who would not be bound by preclusion but who was within scope of 1966 amendments; explaining intended congruence among [Rules 20, 19, 23 and 24] and comparing nearly identical language)]; [Advisory Committee Notes to 1966 Amendments Federal Rules of Civil Procedure, Rule 24, 39 F.R.D. 69, 110 (1966)] (amendments intended to overturn result in [*Sam Fox Publishing Co. v. United States*, 366 U.S. 683 (1961)] and to eliminate requirement that proposed intervenor show that he would be bound by res judicata as precondition for intervention as of right).

This case presents a compelling case for intervention as of right, most directly because [§ 706(f) of the Civil Rights Act of l964], [42 U.S.C. § 2000e-5(f)(1988)], gives an individual victim the right to intervene in suit brought by EEOC on his behalf. [*General Telephone Co. v. EEOC*, 446 U.S. 318, 326 (1980) (explaining relationship between EEOC and victim standing under Title VII)]. This unconditional right to intervene is granted to the "aggrieved party" in a suit brought by the EEOC. The movant is the "aggrieved party" in this suit because he is the one who filed the charge on which this lawsuit is based. [*Spirt v. TIAA*, 93 F.R.D. 627, 640 (S.D.N.Y. 1982) ("person aggrieved" under § 2000e-5(f) means person who filed original charge, or whose grievance is close enough to charge to permit that person to file suit under Title VII)]. Title VII's procedural provisions govern ADA actions like this one. [ADA § 107, 42 U.S.C. § 2117]:

> The powers, remedies, and procedures set forth in [sections 705, 706, 707, 709, and 710 of the Civil Rights Act of 1964 (42 U.S.C. 2000e-4, 2000e-5, 2000e-6, 2000e-8, and 2000e-9)] shall be the powers, remedies, and procedures this title provides to the Commission, to the Attorney General, or to any person alleging discrimination on the basis of disability in violation of any provision of this Act, or regulations promulgated under section 106, concerning employment.

Even if [§ 506(f)] were not enough, movant also meets the prerequisites for intervention as of right under [Rule 24(a)(2)]. His claim is exactly the same claim that is at the nucleus of the EEOC's action. *Compare* [¶¶ ___ to ___] of Complaint in Intervention], attached hereto, *with* [¶¶ ___ to ___ of EEOC Complaint]. It is thus based on the same transactions as the EEOC's claim. His ability to protect his ADA rights may as a practical matter be impaired or impeded by the disposition of this action and his interest is not adequately represented by the EEOC, in part because the EEOC has less interest than he in obtaining compensatory and punitive damages.

This is not a case like [*Worlds v. Department of Health and Rehabilitative Services*, 929 F.2d 591, 594–95 (11th Cir. 1991) (dismissing appeal by Title VII intervenor properly denied intervention for failure to meet second requirement of Fed. R. Civ. P. 24(a)(2))], where the motion to intervene came after the case had advanced to the point where the scope of evidence to be presented had already been narrowed, thus actually advantaging the intervenor if he remained outside. The intervenor in [*Worlds*] had similar [Title VII] claim, similar enough to meet the "interest" requirements of [Rule 24(a)], but not identical, as in the instant case. The

[*Worlds*] intervenor thus would have been prejudiced to the extent of stare decisis, but not preclusion. The prejudice resulting from denial of intervention in this case thus is much stronger than in [*Worlds*].

Even if there is some doubt about movant's entitlement to intervene as of right, he should be allowed permissive intervention under [Rule 24(b)]. The common nucleus of factual transactions produces many common issues of fact. There will be no prejudice from allowing him to be a party. See generally [*Spirt v. TIAA*, 93 F.R.D. 627 (S.D.N.Y. 1982) (denying limited permissive intervention to EEOC for purpose of opposing one motion, and denying intervention to individual intervenors, under careful review of requirements of Fed. R. Civ. P. 24(a) and (b))].

Finally, this motion is timely. Timeliness of a motion to intervene should be governed by when the notice of the opportunity to intervene actually was received and the prejudice to existing parties and to judicial efficiency from permitting intervention at the time requested. If a party received notice or should have had actual notice from an effort to give notice under the circumstances, and the party delayed requesting intervention without excuse, intervention should be denied as untimely. The second consideration, prejudice to existing parties and to efficiency, depends on whether there were evidentiary proceedings before the request to intervene is received. Under these criteria, this plaintiff/intervenor's motion is timely.

§ 12.6 —Memorandum in Opposition to Motion to Dismiss Certain Defendants

FORM 12–5
SAMPLE MEMORANDUM IN OPPOSITION OF MOTION TO DISMISS CERTAIN DEFENDANTS

IN THE UNITED STATES DISTRICT COURT

FOR THE [NORTHERN] DISTRICT OF [ILLINOIS]

[EASTERN] DIVISION

U.S. EQUAL EMPLOYMENT OPPORTUNITY COMMISSION,

Plaintiffs,

v.   Civil Action No. [92 C 7330]

[A.I.C. SECURITY INVESTIGATIONS, LTD.];

[A.I.C. INTERNATIONAL, LTD.]; AND [unnamed defendant C],

Defendants.

Magistrate Judge [Guzman]

PLAINTIFFS' MEMORANDUM IN OPPOSITION TO MOTION TO DISMISS

DEFENDANTS [A.I.C. INTERNATIONAL, LTD.] AND [unnamed defendant C]

Plaintiff, Equal Employment Opportunity Commission (the "Commission" or "EEOC") and Intervening Plaintiff, [Charles Wessel], hereby submit this Memorandum in Opposition to Motion to Dismiss Defendants [A.I.C. International, Ltd.], and [C].

42 U.S.C. § 1981a provides for the recovery of compensatory and punitive damages in Title VII and ADA cases. Specifically, § 1981a provides that a complaining party may recover compensatory and punitive damages as allowed in subsection V of this section, in addition to any relief authorized by § 706(g) of the Civil Rights Act of 1964 [42 U.S.C. § 2000e-5(g)], from the respondent." 42 U.S.C. § 1981a(2). Defendants apparently contend that Congress' use of the term "respondent" somehow limits the scope of § 1981a, narrowing the types of employers from whom damages are recoverable. A review of § 1981a, the ADA, and Title VII finds no support for Defendants' argument.

The ADA defines the term *employer* for the first two years following the effective date of the statute as "a person engaged in an industry affecting commerce who has 25 or more employees for each working day in each of 20 or more calendar weeks in the current or preceding year, and any agent of such person." 42 U.S.C. § 12111(5). The ADA does not define the term "respondent." Title VII provides the identical definition of the term employer, with the exception that the number of employees required is fifteen. [*See* 42 U.S.C. § 2000e(b)]. In addition, Title VII defines the term *respondent* as "an employer. . . ." 42 U.S.C. § 2000e(n). Thus, for the purposes of Title VII, the terms "employer" and "respondent" are used interchangeably. There does not appear to be any principled basis for providing a different meaning to the term respondent under the ADA and, in fact, the Regulations and the Interpretive Guidance provide that the term "employer" is to be given the same meaning under the ADA as it is given in Title VII. [29 C.F.R. § 1630.2] and the [EEOC Interpretive Guidance] thereto. Therefore, if [A.I.C. International, Ltd.] and [defendant C] are employers within the meaning of the ADA and Title VII, then they are also respondents within the meaning of § 1981a and are subject to its compensatory and punitive damage provisions.

[A.I.C. International, Ltd.] is an employer under the ADA, because it can be consolidated with [A.I.C. Security Investigations, Ltd.] under the integrated enterprise doctrine, making both entities the employer of [Charles Wessel]. There are four factors to consider in determining whether consolidation of separate entities under the integrated enterprise doctrine is appropriate. They are: (1) interrelation of operation, (2) common management, (3) centralized control of labor relations, and (4) common ownership or financial control. [*Armbruster v. Quinn*, 711 F.2d 1332, 1337 (6th Cir. 1983)]; [*Baker v. Stuart Broadcasting Co.*, 560 F.2d 389, 392

(8th Cir. 1977)]; [*Smith v. Jones Warehouse, Inc.,* 590 F. Supp. 1206, 1208 (N.D. Ill. 1984)]. In [*Armbruster,* 711 F.2d at 1337–38], the court stated:

> While each factor is indicative of interrelation and while control over the elements of labor relations is a central concern... the presence of any single factor in the Title VII context is not conclusive. All four criteria need not be present in all cases, and even when no evidence of common control of labor relations policy is presented, the circumstances may be such that the single-employer doctrine is applicable. (Citations omitted.)

The element of common ownership is clearly satisfied in this case. [A.I.C. Security Investigations, Ltd.] is a wholly-owned subsidiary of [A.I.C. International, Ltd.]. [Defendant C] is the sole shareholder of [A.I.C. International Ltd.]. Thus there is no dispute that the entities share common ownership.

The record also reflects that [A.I.C. International] and [A.I.C. Security Investigations] share common management. Specifically, the evidence establishes that [defendant C] is sole shareholder of both [A.I.C. International] and [A.I.C. Security Investigations] and that the offices of [A.I.C. International] hold the same position in the management structure of [A.I.C. Security Investigations]. Therefore, the element of common management is also certified in this case.

The record also reflects that there is interrelation of operations in that [A.I.C. International] and [A.I.C. Security Investigations] share the same facility. In addition [A.I.C. International] is a holding company for [A.I.C. Security Investigations] which has no employees and conducts no business of its own. Thus, the business conducted by [A.I.C. Security Investigations] is the business of [A.I.C. International]. It is well-settled that the term "employer" is liberally construed to give effect to the remedial purpose of Title VII. [*Armbruster,* 711 F.2d at 1336]. There is sufficient evidence in the record to demonstrate that [A.I.C. International] and [A.I.C. Security Investigations] are an integrated enterprise; therefore, [A.I.C. International] is an employer for purposes of the ADA.

[Defendant C] is also an employer for purposes of the ADA in that she is an agent of [A.I.C. Security Investigations]. In [*Jones v. Continental Corp.,* 789 F.2d 1225 (6th Cir. 1986)], the [Sixth Circuit] noted that "the law is clear that individuals may be held liable for violations of [§ 1981], and as agents of an employer under Title VII." [*Id.* at 1231 (citations omitted)]. A person is an agent under § 2000e(b) if he participated in the decision-making process that forms the basis of the discrimination. [*Levendos v. Stem Entertainment, Inc.,* 909 F.2d 747 (3d Cir. 1990) (citations omitted)]. In [*Paroline v. Unisys Corp.,* 879 F.2d 100 (4th Cir. 1989)], the [Fourth Circuit] noted that "a[n] individual qualifies as an 'employer' under Title VII if he or she serves in a supervisory position and exercises significant control over the plaintiff's hiring, firing, or conditions of employment." [*Id.* at 104 (*vacated in part on rehg,* 900 F.2d 27 (4th Cir. 1990))]. *See also* [*Hamilton v. Rodgers,* 791 F.2d 439, 443 (5th Cir. 1986) ("A person is an agent under § 2000e(b) if he participated in the decision-making process that forms the basis of the discrimination. To hold otherwise would encourage supervisory personnel to believe that they may violate Title VII with impunity.")]; [*Owens v. Rush,* 636 F.2d 283, 287 (10th Cir. 1980) (it is clear for purposes of Title VII an elected county sheriff is an agent of the county for all matters properly committed to his discretion including the hiring and firing of employees.")]; [*Ditch v. Board of County Commissioners,* 650 F Supp. 1245, 1251 (D. Kan. 1986) ("[I]t is not a great revelation to hold that agents . . . can be held personally liable as employers under [Title VII]. In fact, such a holding makes perfect sense and is mandated by the language of the statute.")]; [*Hendrix v. Fleming Companies,* 650 F. Supp. 301, 303 (W.D. Okla. 1986) (personal liability is imposed under Title VII as result of active discriminatory conduct by the individual)]; [*Tafoya v. Adams,* 612 F. Supp. 1097, 1104 (D. Colo. 1985) ("Officials and supervisors having responsibility and power to employ personnel and to control their conditions of employment have been held subject to Title VII")].

In this instance, the evidence reveals that [defendant C] participated in the decisionmaking process forming the basis of the discrimination in that she instructed [Beverly K.] to discharge [Charles Wessel]. Thus, [defendant C] exercised significant control over the firing, and under the reasoning of [*Paroline*], she is an agent and, consequently, an employer for purposes of the ADA. [879 F.2d 100, 104].

Because both [A.I.C. International] and [defendant C] are employers within the meaning of Title VII, they are liable for damages under § 1981a. Therefore, Defendants' Motion to Dismiss should be denied.

Respectfully Submitted,

[name]

Trial Attorney
Equal Employment Opportunity Commission
[536 South Clark, Room 982]
[Chicago, Illinois 60605]
[(312) 886-9120]

[A.I.C. attorney C]

§ 12.7   —Motion to Dismiss for Failure to Exhaust

FORM 12–6
SAMPLE MOTION TO DISMISS COMPLAINT

MOTION TO DISMISS COMPLAINT UNDER [FED. R. CIV. P. 12(b)(6)]

1.   The complaint filed in this case asserts claims based only on Title I of the Americans with Disabilities Act (ADA), 42 U.S.C. § 12111 to 12117.

2.   Title I of the ADA utilizes the remedies and procedures of Title VII of the Civil Rights Act of 1964. 42 U.S.C. § 12117(a) (incorporating by reference 42 U.S.C. §§ 2000e-4 to 2000e-9).

3.   Title VII of the Civil Rights Act of 1964 requires that claims of discrimination be filed with the Equal Employment Opportunity Commission (EEOC) or, in certain circumstances with state or local antidiscrimination agencies before a claim cognizable by the United States District Courts arises. 42 U.S.C. §§ 2000e-5(b), (c).

4.   The plaintiff has not alleged in her complaint any such filing with the EEOC or a state or local agency.

5.   On information and belief, neither the plaintiff nor anyone on her behalf has filed a charge with the EEOC or a state or local antidiscrimination agency alleging the acts of discrimination alleged in the complaint.

6.   In addition, 42 U.S.C. § 2000e-5(e) requires that the plaintiff receive a "Right to Sue Letter" from the EEOC as a prerequisite to filing a claim in federal court.

7.   The plaintiff has not alleged receipt of such a right to sue letter.

8.   On information and belief plaintiff has not received a Right to Sue Letter.

9.   Wherefore the defendant prays that this court dismiss the complaint.

Commentary.   The motion to dismiss is broad enough to cover two situations: (1) a situation in which no charge of any kind covering the plaintiff and the defendant has been filed; and (2) a situation in which a charge has been filed but does not cover the parties or the discriminatory acts alleged in the complaint. In the second type of situation, a motion to dismiss might be objectionable because it does not give sufficiently particular notice of the defect in the complaint.

The motion is asserted under Rule 12(b)(6) of the Federal Rules of Civil Procedure rather than for lack of jurisdiction under Rule 12(b)(1) because the overwhelming case law says that filing with the EEOC is not a jurisdictional prerequisite but merely an exhaustion requirement. For the same reason, the motion does not request dismissal with prejudice because this would be inappropriate. Instead, the district court should dismiss the complaint without prejudice, permitting refiling after EEOC procedures have been exhausted.

§ 12.8   —Motion to Strike Claim for Compensatory and Punitive Damages

FORM 12–7
SAMPLE MOTION TO STRIKE CLAIM FOR COMPENSATORY AND PUNITIVE DAMAGES

MOTION TO STRIKE CLAIM FOR COMPENSATORY AND
PUNITIVE DAMAGES

1.   Paragraphs [number] and [number] of the complaint in this case request compensatory and punitive damages.

2.   The only claim asserted is one under Title III of the Americans with Disabilities Act (ADA), 42 U.S.C. §§ 12181–12189.

3.   Title III of the ADA does not authorize either compensatory or punitive damages. Rather, 42 U.S.C. § 12188 authorizes only equitable relief.

4.   Wherefore the defendant prays that this court strike paragraphs [number] and [number] from the complaint.

§ 12.9   Drafting Answers

Rule 8 of the Federal Rules of Civil Procedure requires that a defendant do one of three things in response to each allegation in a complaint: (1) admit it, (2) deny it, or (3) deny it for reason of insufficient information to admit or deny. See **Forms 12–8** through **12–11**.

Rule 11 of the Federal Rules of Civil Procedure increasingly imposes costs on counsel who deny allegations with an inappropriate basis for the denial. Furthermore, Federal Rule of Civil Procedure 8(d) contains a trap because it provides that any specific allegation that is not denied is deemed admitted. Thus, if the plaintiff includes multiple allegations in a single paragraph, it is important for the answer to dissect the paragraph into those specific allegations that are admitted and those that are denied. Federal Rule of Civil Procedure 9 requires that certain allegations be challenged specifically, further reinforcing the desirability of particularity in answers.

Of particular importance in ADA litigation is the requirement in Rule 8(c) of the Federal Rules of Civil Procedure to plead affirmative defenses. For example, it is quite clear in ADA Title I[3] litigation that "undue hardship" is an affirmative defense and it must be pleaded as such.[4] Similarly, in ADA Title III[5] litigation, the following defenses are affirmative defenses and must be pleaded as such:

1. The criteria tending to exclude the disabled are necessary for provision of goods or services[6]
2. The modification of practices or steps to provide auxiliary aids and services would fundamentally alter the nature of the goods or services offered[7]
3. The removal of architectural barriers is not readily achievable[8]
4. The provision of alternative methods for removal of architectural barriers is not readily achievable.[9]

Federal Rule of Civil Procedure 8(c), however, has a catchall, requiring that "any other matter constituting an avoidance or affirmative defense" must be pleaded affirmatively. The best practice is to interpret this provision as requiring that any new factual allegation the defendant wishes to make at trial must be pleaded affirmatively. Thus, if the defendant wishes to take the position in Title I litigation that the plaintiff failed to request accommodation and that this is a prerequisite to the employer's duty to accommodate, then this failure should be asserted affirmatively.

Of course, the subject matter of motions permitted under Rule 12 of the Federal Rules of Civil Procedure also may be asserted in the answer. Indeed, if the affirmative defenses are not asserted either by motion before the answer is filed or by an answer or other responsive pleading, they are waived.

---

[3] ADA §§ 101–108, 42 U.S.C. §§ 12111–12117 (1994) [hereinafter Title I].

[4] ADA § 102(b)(5)(A), 42 U.S.C. § 12112(b)(5)(A) (1994).

[5] ADA §§ 301–310, 42 U.S.C. §§ 12181–12189 (1994) [hereinafter title III].

[6] ADA § 302(b)(2)(A)(i), 42 U.S.C. § 12182(b)(2)(A)(i) (1994).

[7] ADA § 302(b)(2)(A)(ii), 42 U.S.C. § 12182(b)(2)(A)(ii) (1994); ADA § 302(b)(2)(A)(iii), 42 U.S.C. § 12182(b)(2)(A)(iii) (1994).

[8] ADA § 302(b)(2)(A)(iv), 42 U.S.C. § 12182(b)(2)(A)(iv) (1994).

[9] ADA § 302(b)(2)(A)(v), 42 U.S.C. § 12182(b)(2)(A)(v) (1994).

§ 12.10   Sample Answer: Title II Testing Case

FORM 12–8
SAMPLE ANSWER: TITLE II TESTING CASE

UNITED STATES DISTRICT COURT

[judicial district] OF [state]

[name],

Plaintiff,   [case number]

v.

[state] BOARD OF LAW EXAMINERS,

Defendant.

ANSWER

The defendant, [state] Board of Law Examiners, by its attorney, [name], Attorney General of the State of [state], [name], Assistant Attorney General, of counsel, as and for its Answer to the complaint herein, alleges as follows:

1.   Admits the allegations contained in paragraphs 3, 4, 15, 17, 19, 20, 29 and 35 of the complaint. [References are to complaint in **Form 11–5, § 11.6.**]

2.   Denies the allegations contained in paragraphs 22, 31, 32, 33, 38, 39 and 40 of the complaint.

3.   Denies knowledge or information sufficient to form a belief as to the truth or falsity of the allegations contained in paragraphs 9, 11, 12, 13, 14 and 16 of the complaint.

4.   As to the allegations contained in paragraph 1:

a. Sentence 1 consists of the plaintiff's characterization of the relief she seeks and, as such requires no response. The defendant denies so much of said sentence that alleges that it took any discriminatory action against the plaintiff.

b. Admits the allegations contained in sentence 2.

c. Admits so much of sentence 3 which alleges that the plaintiff suffers from severe visual disabilities, and denies the remainder of said sentence.

5.   As to the allegations contained in paragraph 2:

a. Denies the allegations contained in sentence I.

b. As to the remaining allegations of the said paragraph, respectfully refers the court to the statutes cited therein for the full and accurate contents thereof.

6.   The allegations contained in paragraphs 5 and 6 consist of the plaintiff's interpretations of the law, which require no response. To the extent that a response is necessary, the defendant respectfully refers the court to the statutes cited therein for the full and accurate contents thereof. The defendant specifically denies that this Court has jurisdiction over this action pursuant to Title III of the Americans with Disabilities Act (ADA).

7.   As to the allegations contained in paragraph 7:

a. Admits that the plaintiff is a 1992 graduate of the [name] School of Law.

b. Denies knowledge or information sufficient to form a belief as to the truth or falsity of the remainder of said paragraph.

8.   As to the allegations contained in paragraph 8:

a.   Admits that the plaintiff suffers from a severe visual disability, and that the plaintiff has annexed an affidavit from [Dr. A], M.D.

b.   Denies knowledge or information sufficient to form a belief as to the truth or falsity of the remainder of said paragraph.

9.   As to the allegations contained in paragraph 10:

a.   Admits that Dr. [A] wrote a letter to the Law Examiners on [date], as set forth more fully in Exhibit B to the complaint.

b.   Denies knowledge or information sufficient to form belief as to the truth or falsity of the remainder of said paragraph, including the truth or falsity of the matters set forth in Dr. [A]'s letter.

10.   As to the allegations contained in paragraph 18:

a.   Admits that Dr. [A] wrote a letter dated [date], to the Law Examiners in which he expressed his opinions with respect to the plaintiff's condition and the accommodations which he deemed appropriate for the plaintiff to take the Bar Exam. The defendant respectfully refers to that letter for the full and accurate contents thereof.

b.   Denies knowledge or information sufficient to form belief as to the truth or falsity of the remainder of said paragraph.

11.   As to the allegations contained in paragraph 21:

a. Admits sentences 1 and 2 thereof.

b. Denies knowledge or information sufficient to form a belief as to the truth or falsity of the allegations contained in sentence 3 thereof.

12.   As to the allegations contained in paragraph 23:

a.   Admits sentence 1 thereof.

b.   Denies knowledge or information sufficient to form a belief as to the truth or falsity of the allegations contained in sentence 2 thereof.

13.   As to the allegations contained in paragraph 24:

a.   Denies so much of said paragraph which alleges that unless the plaintiff is allowed four days to take the examination she will be severely disadvantaged as compared to non-disabled individuals taking the Bar Examination.

b.   Denies knowledge or information sufficient to form a belief as to the truth or information sufficient to form remaining allegations thereof.

14.   As to the allegations contained in paragraph 25:

a.   Admits sentence 1.

b.   Denies so much of sentence 2 which alleges that the accommodation is "deceiving," and admits the remainder of said sentence.

c.   Denies sentences 3 and 4 thereof.

15.   Admits the allegations contained in paragraph 26, with the exception that, while the defendant admits that Dr. [A] recommends certain accommodations, denies that such accommodations were necessary in order to satisfy the requirements of the ADA.

16. Admits so much of paragraph 27 which alleges that as of the date of the complaint the Law Examiners had not advised the plaintiff of their decision on plaintiff's appeal. The defendant affirmatively asserts that the plaintiff's appeal was denied, as set forth in the Board's letter of [date].

17.   As to the allegations contained in paragraphs 29 and 35, admits that the plaintiff has submitted documentation indicating that she has a physical impairment which substantially limits one or more of her major life functions and denies knowledge or information sufficient to form a belief as to the truth or falsity of the remainder of said paragraph.

18. As to the allegations contained in paragraph 30:

a. The allegations contained in sentence 1 thereof consist of the plaintiff's interpretations of the law, which require no response. To the extent that a response is necessary, the defendant respectfully refers the court to the statutes cited therein for the full and accurate contents thereof.

b. Denies the allegations contained in sentence 2 thereof.

19. As to the allegations contained in paragraph 36:

a. Admits sentence 1 thereof.

b. Denies sentence 2 thereof.

20. The allegations contained in paragraph 37 consist of the plaintiff's interpretations of the law, which require no response. To the extent that a response is necessary, the defendant respectfully refers the court to the statutes cited therein for the full and accurate contents thereof.

21. Denies each and every other allegation of the complaint to which a response has not heretofore been interposed.

AS A FIRST AFFIRMATIVE DEFENSE, THE DEFENDANT ALLEGES THAT:

22. The complaint fails to state a cause of action upon which relief may be granted.

AS A SECOND AFFIRMATIVE DEFENSE, THE DEFENDANT ALLEGES THAT:

23. That the alleged conduct was, in whole or in part, properly within the discretionary authority committed to the defendant to perform its official functions, and that the relief prayed for would constitute an improper intrusion by the federal judiciary into said discretionary authority.

AS A THIRD AFFIRMATIVE DEFENSE, THE DEFENDANT ALLEGES THAT:

24. The plaintiff was not deprived of any right, privilege or immunity secured to her under the United States Constitution, the [state] Constitution or the laws of the United States or the [state].

AS A FOURTH AFFIRMATIVE DEFENSE, THE DEFENDANT ALLEGES THAT:

25. The defendant, at all times relevant hereto, acted under the reasonable belief that its actions were in accordance with federal law. At no time relevant hereto, did any of the Board members/defendants act in contravention of clearly established federal statutory or constitutional rights of plaintiff of which a reasonable

person should have known. Therefore, the defendant is qualifiedly immune from liability in damages.

AS A FIFTH AFFIRMATIVE DEFENSE, THE DEFENDANT ALLEGES THAT:

26.   The extension of time sought by the plaintiff does not constitute a reasonable modification of the bar examination within the meaning of the ADA.

WHEREFORE, defendant demands judgment dismissing the complaint and granting such other and further relief as this Court may deem just and proper, including attorneys' fees, costs, and disbursements.

§ 12.11   —Title I Case with Affirmative Defenses (Mock Trial)

FORM 12–9
SAMPLE ANSWER AND DEFENSES: TITLE I CASE

UNITED STATES DISTRICT COURT FOR THE [EASTERN]

DISTRICT OF [PENNSYLVANIA]

[Steven Lyons], Plaintiff

v.   Civil Action, File Number [820130]

[Eastern Pharmaceuticals, Incorporated],

Defendant.

ANSWER

I.   JURISDICTION

1.   Defendant, [Eastern], denies the allegation of paragraph 1. [References are to **Form 10–6, § 10.9.**]

2.   [Eastern] admits that plaintiff seeks to bring this action pursuant to § 107(a) of the Americans with Disabilities Act of 1990 (ADA), 42 U.S.C. § 12117(a), but denies that ADA § 107(a), 42 U.S.C. § 12117(a) applies.

3.   [Eastern] admits the allegations in paragraph 3.

4.   [Eastern] is without knowledge or information sufficient to form a belief as to the truth of the allegations of paragraph 4 that plaintiff satisfied all preconditions to jurisdiction.

II.   PARTIES

5.   [Eastern] admits the allegations in paragraph 5.

6.   [Eastern] is without knowledge or information sufficient to form a belief as to the truth of the allegations of paragraph 6 that plaintiff has multiple sclerosis ("MS") and that MS limits plaintiff in the major life activities of reading, speaking and walking.

7.   [Eastern] is without knowledge or information sufficient to form a belief as to the truth of the allegation of paragraph 7 that plaintiff is an individual with a "disability" within the meaning of ADA § 101 (8), 42 U.S.C. § 12111(8).

8.   [Eastern] denies the allegations of paragraph 8 that plaintiff can perform the essential functions of the job of staff accountant in Eastern's finance department with the reasonable accommodations of: (a) having a reader communicate written messages and computer information to him, (b) having a speaker communicate oral messages from him, and (c) having the office area of [Eastern]'s facility made "handicapped friendly."

9.   [Eastern] denies the allegation of paragraph 9 that plaintiff is a "qualified individual with a disability" within the meaning of ADA § 101(8), 42 U.S.C. § 12111(8).

10.   [Eastern] denies the allegation of paragraph 10 that plaintiff has been a "qualified individual with a disability" since June 26, 1991.

11.   [Eastern] admits the allegations in paragraph 11.

12.   [Eastern] admits the allegation in paragraph 12.

13.   [Eastern] admits the allegation in paragraph 13.

14.   [Eastern] admits the allegations in paragraph 14.

15.   [Eastern] admits the allegation in paragraph 15.

16.   [Eastern] admits the allegation in paragraph 16.

III.   FACTS

17.   [Eastern] admits the allegations in paragraph 17.

18.   [Eastern] admits the allegation in paragraph 18.

19.   [Eastern] admits the allegations in paragraph 19.

20.   [Eastern] is without knowledge or information sufficient to form a belief as to the truth of the allegations of paragraph 20 that plaintiff was diagnosed with MS on June 26, 1991, and that plaintiff suffered from blurry vision and slurred speech.

21.   [Eastern] denies the allegation of paragraph 21 that [Lisa Brown] knew at all relevant times that plaintiff had MS.

22.   [Eastern] admits the allegations in paragraph 22.

23.   [Eastern] admits the allegations in paragraph 23.

24.   [Eastern] is without knowledge or information sufficient to form a belief as to the truth of the allegations of paragraph 24 that plaintiff suffered another MS attack on [July 28, 1992], and that after this attack, plaintiff's eyesight and speech deteriorated further and that he began to have difficulty walking and coordinating muscle movement.

25.   [Eastern] admits the allegation of paragraph 25 that plaintiff requested the additional accommodations listed in allegation 8, but denies that the accommodations will enable him to continue performing his essential job functions.

26.   [Eastern] admits the allegation of paragraph 26 that [Ms. Brown] terminated plaintiff on [August 5, 1993], but denies that [Ms. Brown] refused to make reasonable accommodations for plaintiff.

27.   [Eastern] denies the allegations of paragraph 27 that [Ms. Brown]'s decisions and actions were within the course and scope of her employment at [Eastern].

28.   [Eastern] denies the allegation of paragraph 28 that its actions constitute discrimination against plaintiff in violation of ADA § 102(b)(5)(A), 42 U.S.C. § 12112(b)(5)(A).

29.   [Eastern] denies the allegation of paragraph 29 that [Eastern] acted with malice or with reckless indifference toward plaintiff's federally protected rights.

30.   [Eastern] denies the allegation of paragraph 30 that [Eastern] discriminated against plaintiff, and is without knowledge or information sufficient to form a belief as to the truth of the allegation that plaintiff suffered and continues to suffer economic losses, mental anguish, pain and suffering, and other nonpecuniary losses.

IV.   PRAYER FOR RELIEF

1.   [Eastern] denies the allegations of paragraph 1.

2.   [Eastern] denies the allegations of paragraph 2.

3.   [Eastern] denies the allegations of paragraph 3.

4.   [Eastern] denies the allegations of paragraph 4.

5.   [Eastern] denies the allegations of paragraph 5.

6.   [Eastern] denies the allegations of paragraph 6.

7.   [Eastern] denies the allegations of paragraph 7.

FIRST DEFENSE

The complaint fails to state a claim against [Eastern] upon which relief can be granted.

SECOND DEFENSE

[Eastern] did not discriminate against plaintiff because providing the reasonable accommodations which plaintiff requested would have caused [Eastern] to suffer an "undue hardship" within the meaning of ADA § 101(10), 42 U.S.C. § 12111(10).

THIRD DEFENSE

Plaintiff failed to mitigate the damages alleged in the complaint.

FOURTH DEFENSE

[Eastern] had fewer than [501] employees in each of 20 weeks of the preceding year. Therefore, compensatory and punitive damages are limited to [$200,000] pursuant to 42 U.S.C. § 1981a(b)(3).

[John Black], Attorney for Defendant
[1111 Cherry Street]
[Philadelphia], [Pennsylvania] [19105]

§ 12.12   —Title I Case (EEOC)

FORM 12–10
SAMPLE ANSWER: TITLE I CASE

IN THE UNITED STATES DISTRICT COURT

FOR THE [NORTHERN] DISTRICT OF [ILLINOIS]

[EASTERN] DIVISION

U.S. EQUAL EMPLOYMENT OPPORTUNITY COMMISSION,

Plaintiff,   Civil Action No.: [92 C 7330]

v.

[A.I.C. SECURITY INVESTIGATIONS, LTD.];

[A.I.C. INTERNATIONAL, LTD.]; and [unnamed defendant C],

Defendants.   Honorable [Marvin E. Aspen]

DEFENDANTS' ANSWERS AND DEFENSES

NOW COME Defendants, [A.I.C. SECURITY INVESTIGATIONS, LTD.]; [A.I.C. INTERNATIONAL, LTD.]; and [C], by and through their attorneys, [WESSELS & PAUTSCH, P.C.], by [Charles W. Pautsch], [attorney A], and [attorney B], and as for their Answer and Defenses to the Complaint in the above-captioned cause, deny each and every averment of said Complaint, except and only to the extent as is hereinafter expressly admitted, qualified or modified:

NOTICE OF ACTION

This is an action under Title I of the Americans With Disabilities Act of 1990 and Title I of the Civil Rights Act of 1991, to correct unlawful employment practices on the basis of disability and to make whole [Charles H. Wessel ("Wessel")]. Defendants discharged [Wessel], a qualified individual with a disability, cancer, from his position as Executive Director because of his disability.

ANSWER: Defendants admit this action has been filed under Title I of the Americans With Disabilities Act of 1990 ("the Act") and Title I of the Civil Rights Act of 1991. Defendants deny that they have committed any unlawful employment practices or discharged [Charles H. Wessel ("Wessel")] because of any disability. Defendants further deny that [Wessel] was a qualified individual as that term is defined in the Act. Defendants lack information or knowledge sufficient regarding the truth or veracity of whether [Wessel] has a disability, as that term is defined in the Act, and therefore deny same.

JURISDICTION AND VENUE

1.   Jurisdiction of this Court is invoked pursuant to 28 U.S.C. §§ 451, 1331, 1337, 1343, and 1345. This action is authorized and instituted pursuant to § 107(a) of the Americans With Disabilities Act of 1990 ("ADA"), 42 U.S.C. § 12117(a), which incorporates by reference §§ 706(f)(1) and (3) of Title VII of the Civil Rights Act of 1964 (Title VII), 42 U.S.C. §§ 2000e-5 (f)(1) and (3), and pursuant to § 102 of the Civil Rights Act of 1991, 42 U.S.C. § 1981a.

ANSWER: Defendants admit.

2.   The employment practices here after alleged to be unlawful were and are now being committed in the [Northern] District of [Illinois], [Eastern] Division.

ANSWER: Defendants deny that they have committed or are now committing any unlawful employment practices. Defendants admit that [Wessel] was employed by [A.I.C. Security Investigations, Ltd.] in the [Northern] District of [Illinois], [Eastern] Division.

PARTIES

3.   Plaintiff, Equal Employment Opportunity Commission (the "Commission"), is an agency of the United States of America charged with the administration, interpretation and enforcement of Title I of the ADA and is expressly authorized to bring this action by § 107(a) of the ADA, 42 U.S.C. § 12117(a), which incorporates by reference § 706(f)(1) of Title VII, 42 U.S.C. § 2000e-5(f)(1).

ANSWER: Defendants admit.

4.   At all relevant times, Defendant [A.I.C. Securities, Inc. ("A.I.C.")] (sic) has been and is now an [Illinois] corporation doing business in the State of [Illinois] and the City of [Chicago], and has continuously had and does now have at least twenty-five (25) employees.

ANSWER: Defendants deny, upon information and belief, that any corporation named [A.I.C. Securities, Inc.] exists as an [Illinois] corporation. Defendants affirmatively state that at all relevant times, Defendant [A.I.C. Security Investigations, Ltd. ("A.I.C.")] has been and is now doing business in the State of [Illinois] and the City of [Chicago], and has continuously had and does now have at least twenty-five (25) employees.

5.   At all relevant times, Defendant [A.I.C. International, Ltd. ("A.I.C. International")] has been and now is an [Illinois] corporation which wholly owns Defendant [A.I.C.].

ANSWER: Defendants admit.

6.   At all relevant times, Defendant [C] has been the owner of [A.I.C. International] and [A.I.C.], and is an agent of the Employer within the meaning of § 101(5)(A) of the ADA, 42 U.S.C. § 12111(5)(A).

ANSWER: Defendants deny that at all relevant times Defendant [C] has been the owner of [A.I.C. International] and [A.I.C.] Defendants affirmatively state that as of approximately [date] Defendant [C] became the sole shareholder of [A.I.C. International] and [A.I.C.]. Defendants deny that at all relevant times Defendant [C] was an agent of the Employer. Defendants do affirmatively state that as of approximately [July 6, 1992] Defendant [C] became President of [A.I.C. International].

7.   At all relevant times Defendant [A.I.C.] has continuously been engaged in an industry affecting commerce within the meaning of § 101(5) of the ADA, 42 U.S.C. § 12111(5), and § 107(7) of the ADA, 42 U.S.C. § 12117(7), which incorporates by reference §§ 701 (g) and (h) of Title VII, 42 U.S.C. §§ 2000e(g) and (h).

ANSWER: Defendants admit.

8.   At all relevant times, Defendant [A.I.C.] has been a covered entity under § 101(2) of the ADA, 42 U.S.C. § 12111(2).

ANSWER: Defendants admit.

STATEMENT OF CLAIMS

9.   More than thirty (30) days prior to the institution of this lawsuit, [Wessel] filed a Charge with the Commission alleging violations of Title I of the ADA by Defendants [A.I.C.], [A.I.C. International] and [C]. All conditions precedent to the institution of this lawsuit have been fulfilled.

ANSWER: Defendants admit.

10.   Since at least July 26, 1992, Defendants have engaged in unlawful employment practices in violation of the ADA §§ 102(a), 102(b)(1) and 102(b)(5)(B), 42 U.S.C. §§ 12112(a), 12112(b)(1), and 12112(b)(5)(B), at their [Chicago], [Illinois] facility. These practices include, but are not limited to, Defendants' discharge of [Wessel], a qualified individual with a disability, who was able to perform the essential functions of his position with or without reasonable accommodation, because of his disability, cancer; and Defendants' discharge of [Wessel] based on the need to make reasonable accommodations to his possible future physical impairments.

ANSWER: Defendants deny.

11.   The effect of the practices complained of above has been to deprive [Wessel] of equal employment opportunities and otherwise adversely affect his status as an employee because of his disability.

ANSWER: Defendants deny.

12.   The unlawful employment practices complained of above were and are intentional.

ANSWER: Defendants deny.

DEFENSES

1.   As and for their first affirmative defense, Defendants assert that [Wessel] was terminated for legitimate business reasons.

2.   As and for their second affirmative defense, Defendants assert that [Wessel] has failed to mitigate his damages.

3.   As and for their third affirmative defense, Defendants assert that at the time of [Wessel]'s termination he was not a qualified individual.

4.   As and for their fourth affirmative defense, Defendants assert that at the time of [Wessel]'s termination he could not, with or without reasonable accommodation, perform the essential functions of his employment position.

5.   As and for their fifth affirmative defense, Defendants assert that they provided to [Wessel] reasonable accommodations and that any further accommodation would have imposed an undue hardship upon Defendants.

6.   As and for their sixth affirmative defense, Defendants assert that [Wessel] did not meet job-related qualification standards consistent with business necessity because he posed a direct threat to the health or safety of others in the work place.

7.   As and for their seventh affirmative defense, Defendants assert that at all relevant times they made a good faith effort, in consultation with Plaintiff, to reasonably accommodate him, to the extent he informed Defendants that such accommodations were needed, and to the extent such accommodations would not cause an undue hardship on the operation of the business (§ 1981 a(a)(3)), and acted in good faith in all particulars in connection with Plaintiff's employment with Defendants.

WHEREOF, Defendants, by their attorneys, respectfully request this Honorable Court to dismiss the Complaint filed herein and grant Defendants such just and equitable relief as the Court deems proper.

§ 12.13 —Title II Case with Affirmative Defenses

FORM 12–11
SAMPLE ANSWER AND DEFENSES: TITLE II CLAIM

IN THE UNITED STATES DISTRICT COURT

FOR THE [judicial district] OF [state]

[plaintiffs' names],

Individually and on behalf of all others similarly situated

v.   [case number]

[defendant A], individually, and in his official capacity as Secretary of the [state] Department of Transportation and [defendant B], individually, and in his official capacity as the Commissioner of the [city] Streets Department

CITY OF [name]'s RESPONSE TO PLAINTIFF'S COMPLAINT IN CIVIL ACTION ON BEHALF OF [defendant B], BOTH INDIVIDUALLY AND IN HIS OFFICIAL CAPACITY WITH AFFIRMATIVE DEFENSES

Defendant, City of [name], by and through its undersigned counsel, answers this Complaint of Plaintiff, as follows:

1.   Denied. The allegations in paragraph 1 are untrue, inaccurate and misleading as they are stated.

2.   Denied. The allegations in paragraph 2 are untrue, inaccurate and misleading as they are stated.

3.   Denied. The allegations in paragraph 3 are conclusions of law which require no responsive pleadings under the Federal Rules of Civil Procedure and are therefore, specifically denied. Strict proof is demanded at time of trial.

4.   Denied. The allegations in paragraph 4 are conclusions of law which require no responsive pleadings under the Federal Rules of Civil Procedure and are therefore, specifically denied. Strict proof is demanded at time of trial.

5.   Denied. The allegations in paragraph 5 are conclusions of law which require no responsive pleadings under the Federal Rules of Civil Procedure and are therefore, specifically denied. Strict proof is demanded at time of trial.

6.   Denied. The allegations in paragraph 6 are conclusions of law which require no responsive pleadings under the Federal Rules of Civil Procedure and are therefore, specifically denied. Strict proof is demanded at time of trial.

7.   Denied. The allegations in paragraph 7 are untrue, in accurate and misleading as they are stated. The allegations in paragraph 7 are conclusions of law which require no responsive pleadings under the Federal Rules of Civil Procedure and are therefore, specifically denied. Strict proof is demanded at time of trial. By way of further answer, [defendant B] did not enter into any reconstruction contracts post [date], which did not comply with the Americans with Disabilities Act of 1990 (ADA). The contract in question was bid on [date]. (See Exhibit A-1). This project was a single contract in which work commenced prior to [date]. The [name] Highway District's resurfacing project did not alter the curbs in the areas where curb reconstruction occurred, ramps where placed at the direction of the project engineer.

8–9.   Denied. All allegations pertaining to jurisdiction are denied and strict proof thereof demanded at the trial of this case. Moreover, the averments, in paragraphs 8–9 of Plaintiff's Complaint deal with conclusions of law which require no responsive pleadings under the Federal Rules of Civil Procedure, and are therefore denied, and strict proof thereof demanded at the trial of this case.

10–21. Denied. After reasonable investigation, the answering defendants are without knowledge or information sufficient to form a belief as to the truth of the averments in paragraphs.

22.   Denied. After reasonable investigation, the answering defendants are without knowledge or information sufficient to form a belief as to the truth of the averments in paragraph 22 of Plaintiff's Complaint, and therefore, deny the allegations therein and demand strict proof thereof at the trial of this case. The allegations in paragraph 22 are conclusions of law which require no responsive pleadings under the Federal Rules of Civil Procedure and are therefore, specifically denied. Strict proof is demanded at time of trial.

23.   Denied. The averments of paragraph 23 of Plaintiff's Complaint are not directed to the answering defendant and require no responsive pleadings under the Federal Rules of Civil Procedure, and are therefore denied, and strict proof thereof demanded at the trial of this case.

24.   Admitted in part. Denied in part. It is admitted that [defendant B] is the Commissioner of the [city] Streets Department. After reasonable investigation, the City of [name] is without knowledge or information sufficient to form a belief as to the truth of the remaining averments contained in paragraph 24, and therefore, the City of [name] denies the remaining averments.

25.   Denied. After reasonable investigation, the answering defendants are without knowledge or information sufficient to form a belief as to the truth of the averments in paragraph 25 of Plaintiff's Complaint, and therefore, deny the allegations therein and demand strict proof thereof at the trial of this case. The allegations in paragraph 25 are conclusions of law which require no responsive pleadings under the Federal Rules of Civil Procedure and are therefore, specifically denied. Strict proof is demanded at time of trial.

26–31. Denied. The allegations in paragraphs 26–31 are conclusions of law which require no responsive pleadings under the Federal Rules of Civil Procedure and are therefore, specifically denied. Strict proof is demanded at time of trial. After reasonable investigation, the answering defendants are without knowledge or information sufficient to form a belief as to the truth of the averments in paragraphs 26-31 of Plaintiff's Complaint, and therefore, deny the allegations therein and demand strict proof thereof at the trial of this case.

32–34. Denied. The allegations in paragraphs 32–34 are conclusions of law which require no responsive pleadings under the Federal Rules of Civil Procedure and are therefore, specifically denied. Strict proof is demanded at time of trial.

35.   Admitted.

36–37. Denied. The allegations in paragraphs 36–37 are conclusions of law which require no responsive pleadings under the Federal Rule of Civil Procedure and are therefore, specifically denied. Strict proof is demanded at time of trial.

38.   Admitted on behalf of Defendant [B].

39.   Denied. The allegations in paragraph 39 are untrue, inaccurate and misleading as they are stated.

40.   Denied. The averments of paragraph 40 of Plaintiff's Complaint are not directed to the answering defendant and require no responsive pleadings under the Federal Rules of Civil Procedure, and are therefore denied, and strict proof thereof demanded at the trial of this case.

41–42. Denied. After reasonable investigation, the answering defendants are without knowledge or information sufficient to form a belief as to the truth of the averments in paragraphs of Plaintiff's Complaint, and therefore, deny the allegations therein and demand strict proof thereof at the trial of this case.

43.   Denied. The allegations in paragraph 43 are untrue, inaccurate and misleading as they are stated.

44–53. Denied. After reasonable investigation, the answering defendants are without knowledge or information sufficient to form a belief as to the truth of the averments in paragraphs 44–52 of Plaintiff's Complaint, and therefore, deny the allegations therein and demand strict proof thereof at the trial of this case.

54–55. Denied. The allegations in paragraphs 54–55 are conclusions of law which require no responsive pleadings under the Federal Rules of Civil Procedure and are therefore, specifically denied. Strict proof is demanded at time of trial.

56.   Denied. The allegations in paragraph 56 are conclusions of law which require no responsive pleadings under the Federal Rules of Civil Procedure and are therefore, specifically denied. Strict proof is demanded at time of trial. Furthermore, the allegations in paragraph 56 are untrue, inaccurate and misleading as they are stated.

WHEREFORE, the defendant City of [name], denies that it is liable on the cause of action declared upon. By way of further answer, the City of [name] on behalf of [defendant B] prays that this Court deny plaintiff's prayer for relief on the issues of jurisdiction, class certification, injunctive relief, and any fees.

FIRST AFFIRMATIVE DEFENSE

The Plaintiff's Complaint fails to state a cause of action upon which relief can be granted.

SECOND AFFIRMATIVE DEFENSE

All allegations pertaining to jurisdiction are denied and strict proof thereof demanded at the trial of this case.

THIRD AFFIRMATIVE DEFENSE

It is averred that Plaintiff's Complaint is replete with allegations which are vague, argumentative, and conclusionary in nature and require no responsive pleadings under the Federal Rules of Civil Procedure. Therefore, all such allegations are denied and strict proof thereof demanded at the trial of this case.

FOURTH AFFIRMATIVE DEFENSE

It is averred that Plaintiff's Complaint is replete with allegations which deal with conclusions of law which require no responsive pleadings under the Federal Rules of Civil Procedure, and are therefore denied and strict proof thereof demanded at the trial of this case.

FIFTH AFFIRMATIVE DEFENSE

Plaintiff has failed to exhaust appropriate state remedies.

SIXTH AFFIRMATIVE DEFENSE

It is averred that each defendant asserts every defense available to [defendant B] and/or it under the existing Civil Rights Act.

SEVENTH AFFIRMATIVE DEFENSE

It is averred that at all times concerned with this litigation, the answering Defendant acted in a manner which was proper, reasonable, lawful, and in the exercise of good faith.

EIGHTH AFFIRMATIVE DEFENSE

It is averred that a defendant official of a municipal corporation, in the exercise of his executive and/or ministerial duties of his employment, is not liable for any alleged violation of plaintiff's civil rights, unless he was personally present and personally directed an invasion of plaintiff's civil rights.

Respectfully submitted,

[name]

§ 12.14   Removal of a Civil Action

A defendant can remove a state civil action to federal court if the district court has original jurisdiction over the claim.[10] Therefore, a claim can be removed if there is either diversity jurisdiction or federal question jurisdiction over the claim.[11] Removal based on diversity jurisdiction is fairly straightforward. If there is diversity of citizenship and if the amount in controversy exceeds $50,000, exclusive of interest and costs, the defendant can remove the action to federal court.[12] Removal based on federal question jurisdiction, though, can be complicated and is discussed here in relation to the ADA.

The best way to discuss removal based on federal question jurisdiction involving the ADA is to use hypothetical examples. This section contains Example 1, an easy example which is progressively altered in Examples 2 and 3 (see § 12.15) to reflect the nuances of removal and the ADA. Deeper analysis of removal is found in § 9.26.

Example 1: Removal Based on Federal Question Jurisdiction

James Miller was employed as an oil tanker captain by the shipping division of Pelican Oil, Inc. (Pelican) from January 1986 until December 1992. Miller is a recovered alcoholic. He has not had a drink since successfully completing a two-month intensive treatment program at the Betty Ford Clinic in December 1988. All of Miller's supervisors and coworkers knew of Miller's drinking problem and the treatment he received.

Nobody at Pelican ever brought up Miller's bout with alcohol until shortly after the infamous Exxon *Valdez* oil spill in 1989. After this environmental tragedy, Miller's coworkers began to tease Miller about his alcoholism. At first, Miller took the jokes in stride; however, the good-natured jokes did not cease. In fact, they escalated into statements that ridiculed and belittled Miller about his earlier disease.

Six months after the Alaskan oil spill, while he was still being tormented by his coworkers, Miller asked his supervisor, Richard Sherman, to intervene on his behalf. Miller told Sherman that everyone at Pelican was driving him crazy due to a disease from which he had recovered. Sherman said that he was aware of what was going on and that he would speak to Miller's coworkers to stop the harassment. Sherman failed to take any action on Miller's behalf.

---

[10] 28 U.S.C. § 1441(a) (1994).

[11] *Id.* § 1441(b).

[12] *Id.* §§ 1331, 1441(b).

The jokes and taunts against Miller continued with no letup for another six months. Miller approached Sherman again. This time, Miller asked to be transferred to another ship. Sherman said that he would try to accommodate Miller. Again, Sherman did nothing.

Finally, in December 1992, when Miller could no longer withstand the endless barrage of ridicule and scorn he was facing, he resigned from Pelican. Miller has been unable to find employment since leaving Pelican. Furthermore, his daily routine now consists solely of watching CNN in the hope of viewing an update on the status of the Alaskan cleanup effort.

In January 1993, Miller filed a charge with the EEOC alleging discrimination by Pelican in violation of the provisions of the ADA. In July 1993, Miller received a right to sue letter from the Commission. Two weeks later, Miller filed a complaint in state court under the ADA, alleging discrimination by Pelican due to his record of having a disability.

The provision for removal of a civil action to federal court is located in 28 U.S.C. § 1441(b), if the action arises under the Constitution, treaties, or laws of the United States. Because Miller's complaint invokes a federal statute, the ADA, Pelican can clearly remove the cause of action to federal court. Pelican's notice of removal would be drafted like **Form 12–12** in § **12.15.**

§ 12.15 —Notice of Removal

FORM 12–12
SAMPLE NOTICE OF REMOVAL

United States District Court for the

[Eastern] District of [Pennsylvania]

[James Miller],

Plaintiff

v.   Civil Action, File Number [12345]

[Pelican Oil, Incorporated],

Defendant.

NOTICE OF REMOVAL

To the judges of the United States District Court for the [Eastern] District of [Pennsylvania]:

The above-entitled action is civil in nature and within the original jurisdiction of this Court and may therefore be removed to this Court from the Court of Common Pleas of [Montgomery County], [Pennsylvania] pursuant to 28 U.S.C. § 1441, in that:

(a)   Plaintiff's complaint alleges:

(1)   Plaintiff has a record of having a disability of which Defendant's employer was aware.

(2)   Defendant employer failed to make reasonable accommodations for Plaintiff's record of having a disability.

(3)   Plaintiff is otherwise qualified to perform the essential functions of the position.

(4)   Defendant employer discriminated against Plaintiff because of Plaintiff's record of having a disability.

(b)   This action arises under the employment title of the Americans with Disabilities Act of 1990 (ADA), ADA §§ 101–108, 42 U.S.C. §§ 12111–12117, the provisions of which are applicable and brought into operation by Plaintiff's complaint.

(c)   Since the above-described action arises under the employment title of the ADA, ADA §§ 101–108, 42 U.S.C. §§ 12111–12117, this Court would have original jurisdiction of this action without regard to the amount in controversy, or diversity of citizenship, pursuant to 42 U.S.C. § 12117; the action may therefore be removed to this Court pursuant to 28 U.S.C. § 1441(a).

Respectfully Submitted,

[Ronald Dewey], Attorney for Defendant
[5678 Main Street]
[Villanova], [Pennsylvania] [19085]

Commentary.   The removal request is captioned Notice of Removal and not Petition for Removal, pursuant to the 1988 amendment to 28 U.S.C. § 1446.[13] The amendment also changed the requirements of a removal request. No longer is a verified petition for removal necessary; rather, only a notice of removal, signed pursuant to Rule 11 of the Federal Rules of Civil Procedure, is required. Furthermore, instead of pleading the facts supporting

---

[13] Judicial Improvements and Access to Justice Act, Pub. L. No. 100-702 § 1016, 102 Stat. 4669-70 (1988) (codified in miscellaneous sections 5 U.S.C., 18 U.S.C., and 28 U.S.C. (1994)).

removal, the removing party now need state only the grounds for removal and attach a copy of all process, pleadings, and orders served upon the removing party.[14] The grounds for removal can easily be extracted from the complaint. Congress changed the pleading requirements to make the removal process simpler.[15] The changes also reflect the modern distaste for verified pleadings.[16]

As demonstrated in Example I in § **12.14,** a federal question must appear on the face of the plaintiff's properly pleaded complaint for the cause of action to be removable. This is the "well-pleaded complaint rule" of *Louisville & Nashville Railroad v. Mottley.*[17] The *well-pleaded complaint rule* states that if the complaint is well pleaded and does not invoke a federal question on its own, the cause of action generally is not removable. Furthermore, the well-pleaded complaint rule precludes removal of a state cause of action on the grounds that the defendants contend that their defense will invoke a federal question. After all, as masters of the complaint, plaintiffs can rely on whatever law they wish.

Example 2: State Discrimination Statute Violation

This example also uses the same facts as Example I in § **12.14,** except that instead of filing an ADA claim, Miller files a complaint alleging violation of a state discrimination statute in state court. Because the complaint does not invoke a federal question, under the well-pleaded complaint rule, it cannot be removed.

Example 3: Intentional Infliction of Emotional Distress

This example also uses the same facts as Example I in § **12.14,** except that instead of filing an ADA claim, Miller alleges the intentional infliction of emotional distress in state court.

In this situation, the cause of action is not removable under the well-pleaded complaint rule. If Miller's claim for intentional infliction of emotional distress were removed to federal court, he would be able to move successfully for remand back to state court. Miller's motion for remand would be drafted like **Form 12–13** in § **12.16.**

---

[14] *Id.*

[15] H.R. Rep. No. 889, 100th Cong., 2d Sess. 134 (1988), *reprinted in,* 1988 U.S.C.C.A.N. 5982, 6032.

[16] *Id.*

[17] 211 U.S. 149 (1908).

§ 12.16   —Motion to Remand Removed Action

FORM 12–13
SAMPLE MOTION TO REMAND REMOVED ACTION

United States District Court for the

[Eastern] District of [Pennsylvania]

[James Miller],

Plaintiff

v.   Civil Action, File Number [12345]

[Pelican Oil, Incorporated],

Defendant.

MOTION TO REMAND REMOVED ACTION

Plaintiff moves this Court for an order remanding the above-entitled action to the Court of Common Pleas of [Montgomery County], [Pennsylvania] on the grounds that the action was improperly removed and is not within the jurisdiction of this Court. The action does not invoke a claim or right arising under the Constitution, treaties or laws of the United States, contrary to the allegations of Defendant, as set forth in its notice of removal of the action to this Court. There is also no other basis for this Court's jurisdiction of the above-entitled action, since Plaintiff's cause of action against Defendant arises solely under state law, as construed and applied by the courts of the State of [Pennsylvania].

Respectfully Submitted,

[Joel Casey], Attorney for Plaintiff
[4321 Market Street]
[Philadelphia], [Pennsylvania] [19128]

CHAPTER 13

DISCOVERY

§ 13.1   Introduction and Overview

This chapter presents forms and other materials related to discovery for Americans with Disabilities Act (ADA)[1] cases. It provides a significant amount of strategic and tactical analysis for discovery techniques utilizing time extensions (see **Forms 13–1** through **13–5**), as well as the full text of Rule 26 of the Federal Rules of Civil Procedure (see **§ 13.3**), which changes federal discovery by imposing uniform obligations of disclosure and limiting the use of depositions and interrogatories.

---

[1] Pub. L. No. 101–336, 104 Stat. 327 (1990) (codified at 42 U.S.C. §§ 12101–12213 (1994); 47 U.S.C. §§ 225, 711 (1994) [hereinafter ADA].

It is important to understand that modern discovery significantly shapes the subsequent handling of a lawsuit by forming the record on which summary judgment can be based and by identifying the specific evidence and issues for trial.

DISCOVERY APPROACHES

§ 13.2 Discovery Strategy

Counsel for any party in an ADA case should formulate a clear strategy for discovery. The strategy should distinguish the roles of interrogatories (see **Forms 13–15** to **13–24**) and depositions (see **Forms 13–6** to **13–14**) and assign an appropriate place to requests for production of documents and things (see **Forms 13–25** to **13–29**) and requests for physical and mental examinations (see **Forms 13–30** and **13–31**). Counsel also should recognize that modern discovery serves two different purposes: (1) the discovery of specific facts and evidence; and (2) the preservation and packaging of evidence for use in summary judgment proceedings and at trial.

The second purpose is particularly important in ADA litigation. The best way for a plaintiff to show the qualifications of the plaintiff may be to demonstrate in a videotape deposition the plaintiff actually performing the essential functions in controversy. This possibility makes videotape depositions particularly important and increases the likelihood that plaintiff's counsel may wish to arrange for the deposition of the plaintiff.

Videotape depositions can also be of particular value to defendants in ADA litigation. If the plaintiff has unusual difficulty performing certain functions, an effective way to prove this may be to ask the plaintiff to perform those functions during a videotape deposition. Or, if the plaintiff has a mental disability that causes outbursts or other behavioral problems, it is effective to capture these during a videotape deposition. The videotape deposition then could be used at trial either for direct evidence or for impeachment purposes.

Obviously, the possibility and importance of these trial-oriented discovery techniques make it essential to anticipate their use by opponents. Demonstrative depositions are persuasive only if the assumptions underlying the demonstration match the position of the opponent. For example, the ADA defers—at least to some extent—to the employer's definition of the essential functions of positions. The probative value and probable admissibility of a deposition demonstrating the plaintiff's performance of job functions is greater if the job functions demonstrated are the ones defined unilaterally by the employer. If the plaintiff and the defendant disagree about the essentiality of certain job functions, it is possible that a deposition structured around the plaintiff's definition of essential job functions would be admissible, but there would be additional challenges to its materiality and relevancy.

From the opposing perspective, the defendant obviously is in a better position to protect its interests at a demonstrative deposition if the defendant knows what functions will be demonstrated, based on the plaintiff's position. Accordingly, an important part of the discovery strategy, the discovery conference, and the joint discovery planning process must be to determine whether the opponent intends to use videotape depositions and demonstrations in depositions. In this way, the parties can use the appropriate discovery tools to determine the scope of any demonstrations.

§ 13.3   Rule 26: General Provisions Governing Discovery; Duty of Disclosure

This section provides the full text of subsection (a) and of paragraphs (b)(1) and (2) of Rule 26 of the Federal Rules of Civil Procedure, adopted by the Supreme Court in April 1993. This rule went into effect on December 1, 1993.

(a)   Required Disclosures; Methods to Discover Additional Matter.

(1)   Initial Disclosures. Except to the extent otherwise stipulated or directed by order or local rule, a party shall, without awaiting a discovery request, provide to other parties:

(A)   the name and, if known, the address and telephone number of each individual likely to have discoverable information relevant to disputed facts alleged with particularity in the pleadings, identifying the subjects of the information;

(B)   a copy of, or a description by category and location of, all documents, data compilations, and tangible things in the possession, custody, or control of the party that are relevant to disputed facts alleged with particularity in the pleadings;

(C)   a computation of any category of damages claimed by the disclosing party, making available for inspection and copying as under Rule 34 the documents or other evidentiary material, not privileged or protected from disclosure, on which such computation is based, including materials bearing on the nature and extent of injuries suffered; and

(D)   for inspection and copying as under Rule 34 any insurance agreement under which any person carrying on an insurance business may be liable to satisfy part or all of a judgment which may be entered in the action or to indemnify or reimburse for payments made to satisfy the judgment.

Unless otherwise stipulated or directed by the court, these disclosures shall be made at or within 10 days after the meeting of the parties under subdivision (f). A party shall make its initial disclosures based on the information then reasonably available to it and is not excused from making its disclosures because it has not fully completed its investigation of the case or because it challenges the sufficiency of another party's disclosures or because another party has not made its disclosures.

(2)   Disclosure of Expert Testimony.

(A)   In addition to the disclosures required by paragraph (1), a party shall disclose to other parties the identity of any person who may be used at trial to present evidence under Rules 702, 703, or 705 of the Federal Rules of Evidence.

(B)   Except as otherwise stipulated or directed by the court, this disclosure shall, with respect to a witness who is retained or specially employed to provide expert testimony in the case or whose duties as an employee of the party regularly involve giving expert testimony, be accompanied by a written report prepared and signed by the witness. The report shall contain a complete statement of all opinions to be expressed and the basis and reasons therefor; the data or other information considered by the witness in forming the opinions; any exhibits to be used as a summary of or support for the opinions; the qualifications of the witness, including a list of all publications authored by the witness within the preceding ten years; the compensation to be paid for the study and testimony; and a listing of any other cases in which the witnesses has testified as an expert at trial or by deposition within the preceding four years.

(C)   These disclosures shall be made at the times and in the sequence directed by the court. In the absence of other directions from the court or stipulation by the parties, the disclosures shall be made at least 90 days before the trial date or the date the case is to be ready for trial or, if the evidence is intended solely to contradict or rebut evidence on the same subject matter identified by another party under paragraph (2)(B), within 30 days after the disclosure made by the other party. The parties shall supplement these disclosures when required under subdivision (e)(1).

(3)   Pretrial Disclosures. In addition to the disclosures required in the preceding paragraphs, a party shall provide to other parties the following information regarding the evidence that it may present at trial other than solely for impeachment purposes:

(A)   the name and, if not previously provided, the address and telephone number of each witness, separately identifying those whom the party expects to present and those whom the party may call if the need arises;

(B)   the designation of those witnesses whose testimony is expected to be presented by means of a deposition and, if not taken stenographically, a transcript of the pertinent portions of the deposition testimony; and

(C)   an appropriate identification of each document or other exhibit, including summaries of other evidence, separately identifying those which party expects to offer and those which the party may offer if the need arises.

Unless otherwise directed by the court, these disclosures shall be made at least 30 days before trial. Within 14 days thereafter, unless a different time is specified by the court, a party may serve and file a list disclosing (1) any objections to the use under Rule 32(a) of a deposition designated by another party under subparagraphs (B) and (ii) any objection, together with the grounds therefor, that may be made to the admissibility of materials identified under subparagraph (C). Objections not so disclosed, other than objections under Rules 402 and 403 of the Federal Rules of Evidence, shall be deemed waived unless excused by the court for good cause shown.

(4) Form of Disclosures; Filing. Unless otherwise directed by order or local rule, all disclosures under paragraphs (1) through (3) shall be made in writing, signed, served, and promptly filed with the court.

(5) Methods to Discover Additional Matter. Parties may obtain discovery by one or more of the following methods: depositions upon oral examination or written questions; written interrogatories; production of documents or things, or permission to enter upon land or other property under Rule 34 or 45(a)(1)(C), for inspection and other purposes; physical and mental examinations; and requests for admission.

(b) Discovery Scope and Limits. Unless otherwise limited by order of the court in accordance with these rules, the scope of discovery is as follows:

(1) In General. Parties may obtain discovery regarding any matter, not privileged, which is relevant to the subject matter involved in the pending action, whether it relates to the claim or defense of the party seeking discovery or to the claim or defense of any other party, including the existence, description, nature, custody, condition, and location of any books, documents, or other tangible things and the identity and location of persons having knowledge of any discoverable matter. The information sought need not be admissible at the trial if the information sought appears reasonably calculated to lead to the discovery of admissible evidence.

(2) Limitations. By order or by local rule, the court may alter the limits in these rules on the number of depositions and interrogatories and may also limit the length of depositions under Rule 30 and the number of requests under Rule 36. The frequency or extent of use of the discovery methods otherwise permitted under these rules and by any local rule shall be limited by the court if it determines that: (i) the discovery sought is unreasonably cumulative or duplicative, or is obtainable from some other source that is more convenient, less burdensome, or less expensive; (ii) the party seeking discovery has had ample opportunity by discovery in the action to obtain the information sought; or (iii) the burden or expense of the proposed discovery outweighs its likely benefit, taking into account the needs of the case, the amount in controversy, the parties' resources, the importance of the issues at stake in the litigation, and the importance of the proposed discovery in resolving the issues. The court may act upon its own initiative after reasonable notice or pursuant to a motion under subdivision (c).

Commentary.   The remainder of the rule has been omitted.

§ 13.4 Discovery Checklist

_____   1.   Obligations under Federal Rules of Civil Procedure 26(b)(1), 26(g), and local rules

_____   Sanctions under Federal Rules of Civil Procedure 16, 26, 37

_____ 2. Filing and Service Requirements

_____   Nonfiling of discovery materials under Federal Rules of Civil Procedure 5(d)

_____   All discovery requests/responses

_____   Confidential materials

_____   Defer transcribing/filing depositions

_____   Filing when needed in connections with motions

_____   Reports regarding discovery

_____   Periodic reports

_____   Filing abbreviated notices of discovery requests/ responses

_____   Reducing service requirements under Federal Rule of Civil Procedure 5(c)

_____   Use of liaison counsel/coordinating secretaries

_____   Special service on need-to-know basis

_____   Use of electronic bulletin boards, databases accessible through the Internet, and/or joint databases to track requests and status

_____ 3. Preclusion (failure to disclose proposed facts/proof/evidence may result in preclusion from use at trial)

_____ 4. Identification of Issues for Discovery Purposes

_____   Issues for early discovery

_____   Sources of information (documents/witnesses/other litigation)

_____   Existence of compiled/computerized data

_____   Issues for early discovery

_____   Class action discovery

_____   Special issues for early resolution

_____   Limiting scope of discovery

_____   Time periods

_____   Priority to particular claims/defenses

_____   Damage issues—whether to defer

_____   Interrelationship between discovery and issues

_____   Revision of discovery plan in light of intervening discovery and refinement/modification of issues

_____   Attempt to structure discovery so that any additional discovery will be supplementary, not duplicative

____   5.   Control of Discovery
        ____   Limitations
        ____   Time limits
        ____   Completion of all discovery (or set trial date)
        ____   Schedule for completing particular phases/forms
        ____   Limits based on issues
        ____   Priority of specified issues
        ____   Deferring discovery on specified issues
        ____   Limits on quantity
        ____   Number/length of depositions
        ____   Number of interrogatories
        ____   Requiring joint interrogatories/document requests
        ____   Precluding discovery already obtained by coparties
        ____   Special situations
        ____   Class members/representatives
        ____   Limitations on scope of discovery from class representatives and counsel
        ____   Approval from court before discovery from class members
        ____   Limits on quantity/scope/form of discovery from class members
        ____   Discovery outside country
            ____   Advance approval from court required
            ____   Need shown
            ____   Specific information/documents sought
        ____   Sequencing of discovery
        ____   Identify sources of information
        ____   Location/form of documents
        ____   Identification/location of witnesses
        ____   Computerized data; summaries
        ____   Governmental studies/reports
        ____   Other litigation
        ____   Priority of discovery on specific issues, time periods, geographic areas. Common discovery before individual discovery
        ____   Sequencing common discovery, with concurrent individual discovery. Priority/preference according to party
        ____   From one side before other side
        ____   By one side before other side

____   Alternatively by weeks/months
____   According to form of discovery
____   Document production
____   Depositions
____   Interrogatories
____   Requests for Admission
____   Reducing cost/time of discovery
____   Cooperation among counsel
____   Stipulations
____   Informal discovery
____   Document inspection
____   Interviews of possible witnesses
____   Consultation before formal discovery requests prepared
____   Nontechnical reading of discovery requests
____   Disclosing/providing similar information already available
____   Combining forms of discovery (requests for admission, document requests, interrogatories, identification of potential deponents)
____   Conference-type depositions
____   Limiting number of counsel
____   Resolving discovery disputes
____   Good-faith effort by counsel to resolve voluntarily
____   Procedures for obtaining court ruling
____   Form of motion/request—written or oral
____   When briefs required/permitted
____   Telephonic conferences
____   Reference to magistrates
____   Appointment of special master
____   Use of other judges on special matters (for example, privileges)
____   Depositions in other districts
____   Monitoring progress of discovery
____   Periodic written reports
____   Reports at conferences
____   Sanctions for failure to meet schedules

____   6.   Privileges and Confidential Information
____   Identify potential problem areas

_____   Discovery from parties

_____   Discovery from third-parties

_____   Access sought by others

_____   Related litigation

_____   News media; public interest groups

_____   Governmental investigations

_____   Confidential orders

_____   To whom disclosure authorized without prior court approval

_____   Extent of disclosure to clients

_____   Disclosure to experts

_____   Disclosure for trial support services

_____   Execution of agreements precluding further disclosure

_____   Counsel in related litigation

_____   Procedures for additional disclosures

_____   Advance notification of proposed disclosure

_____   Disputes whether documents should be considered confidential; declassification

_____   Power of court to modify terms of order

_____   Special terms regarding depositions

_____   Availability of protection to third parties

_____   Subpoenas from other courts/agencies

_____   Copying

_____   Claims of privilege, including work product protection

_____   Possible avoidance of or delaying certain discovery

_____   Need to identify items for which privilege claimed

_____   Use of another judge/magistrate for in camera inspections

_____   Need for appointment of special master

_____   Consideration of nonwaiver agreements

_____   7.   Documents

       _____   Identification system

       _____   Same number throughout litigation

       _____   When copies separately identified

       _____   Log of documents produced; relationship to computer databases on electronic bulletin boards and access through Internet

       _____   Preservation orders

      ____ Modification of interim order against destruction

      ____ Exemption to avoid unnecessary hardship

      ____ Limiting scope as issues narrowed

      ____ Procedure for giving advance notice of proposed destruction

      ____ Expiration

____ Return of documents after litigation concluded

____ Retention for specified period of time

____ Special problems with computerized data

      ____ Format compatibility

      ____ Identification of existing data/printouts

      ____ Description of files/fields/records; other documentation

      ____ Direct communications between parties' experts

      ____ Identification of data prepared/compiled for trial

      ____ Time for disclosure

      ____ Format

      ____ Preservation of source documents

      ____ Verification

      ____ Production of source documents

      ____ Inquiry regarding input, storage, retrieval

      ____ Opportunity for testing

      ____ Feasibility of requiring admission regarding accuracy production

      ____ In machine-readable form

      ____ Formats

      ____ Protection of confidential information, including programming

      ____ Requests for special programming/formats

      ____ Cost

      ____ Feasibility of jointly developed trial support systems

      ____ Accessibility through Internet

____ Coordinating requests for documents

____ Joint request for production

____ Limiting request to documents not previously produced

____ Standard/deemed requests in multiple litigation

_____   Discovery from third parties
_____   Sufficient advance notice
_____   Applicability of confidentiality orders
_____   Cost-sharing
_____   Outside district
_____   Exercise of powers outside district
_____   Use of special master to supervise

_____ 8. Depositions
        _____   Limitations
        _____   Number/length of depositions
        _____   Requiring court approval
        _____   Depositions of class members
        _____   Depositions outside country
        _____   Cost-saving measures
        _____   Informal interviews
        _____   Tape-recorded interviews
        _____   Tape-recorded depositions
        _____   Encouragement by court
        _____   Stipulations as to submission/filing
        _____   Provision for transcriptions
        _____   Tape recording as supplement to regular reporting
        _____   Telephonic depositions
        _____   Video depositions
        _____   Stipulations as to oath
        _____   Restrictions on attendance/coaching
        _____   Providing documents to deponent
        _____   Written questions under Federal Rule of Civil Procedure 31
        _____   Conference-type depositions
        _____   Affidavit from proposed deponent claiming no knowledge
        _____   Limited attendance by counsel
        _____   Authorizing supplemental examination after review of transcript
        _____   Participation by telephone
        _____   Providing written questions under Federal Rule of Civil Procedure 30(c), 31
        _____   Deferring transcription/filing until need arises

_____ Adoption of previously given depositions/report/affidavit

_____ Videotaped depositions; teleconferencing

_____ Scheduling

_____ Time periods

_____ Exclusive periods for particular parties

_____ Preferential rights during specified periods

_____ According to subject matter

_____ Special time periods for deposing experts

_____ Arranging depositions in logical or geographic sequence

_____ Conducting depositions in central locations

_____ Multiple, concurrent depositions

_____ Ordinarily no postponement for attorney scheduling conflicts

_____ Other litigation

_____ Cross-noticing

_____ Adoption of previously given testimony

_____ Coordination of scheduling

_____ Order to show cause why not usable in other cases

_____ Disputes

_____ Telephonic presentations

_____ Acting as deposition judge outside district

_____ Use of master/magistrate/judge to supervise deposition

_____ Guidelines

_____ Improper objections; suggesting answers

_____ Instructions not to answer

_____ Privileges

_____ Bad faith/oppressive examination

_____ Who may be present

_____ Advance approval for telephonic and nonstenographic depositions

_____ Confidential information-examination/production

_____ Providing copies of documents to deponent/other counsel

_____ Procedures for supplemental examination

_____ Procedures for obtaining court ruling

_____ 9. Interrogatories

_____ Uses

    ____ Identify witnesses/documents
    ____ Identification/description of computerized data
    ____ Specific information known in part by different persons
    ____ Initial discovery of expert opinions
    ____ Explain denials of requests for admission
    ____ Contention interrogatories
    ____ Timing
    ____ Scope
    ____ Limitations
    ____ Number
    ____ Restricting over-inclusive definitions
    ____ Scope/purpose; timing
    ____ No repetition of interrogatories previously answered
    ____ Exchange in machine-readable form, including electronic mail (e-mail) or the World Wide Web
    ____ Improving utility
    ____ Consolidated interrogatories in multiple-party litigation
    ____ Standard/master interrogatories in multiple litigation
    ____ Use of answers from other litigation
    ____ Nontechnical reading
    ____ Respond with available information similar to that requested
    ____ Successive responses as information obtained
    ____ Resolving disputes promptly—voluntarily if possible
    ____ Continuing obligation to supplement

____ 10. Stipulations; Admissions; Uncontested/Contested Facts
    ____ Timing; adequate opportunity for discovery
    ____ Acknowledging facts that will not be disputed or contested
    ____ Federal Rule of Civil Procedure 36 procedures
    ____ Timing
    ____ Duty to make reasonable inquiry
    ____ Obligation to clarify denial, admit other parts
    ____ Interrogatories to clarify further
    ____ Negotiated stipulations
    ____ Timing
    ____ Use of special master to facilitate

_____ Development of uncontested/contested facts; statements of contentions and proof

_____ Sequential preparation

_____ Timetable

_____ Scope

    _____ All facts

    _____ Principal facts

    _____ Facts that may be admitted and, if admitted, will reduce scope of trial

    _____ Fact of particular issues (for example, summary judgment)

_____ Use of special hearings (for example, class certification, preliminary injunctions)

_____ Interlineation/deletion to clarify position

_____ Annotations by reference to witnesses/documents

_____ Permissive

_____ Mandatory, with preclusive effect

_____ Objections

    _____ Not basis for refusing to admit

    _____ Requiring certain objections (for example, authentication)

    _____ Requiring all objections

    _____ Effect

_____ Admitted for purpose of trial; when independent evidence permitted

_____ Precluding proof of unlisted facts

_____ Sanctions under Federal Rule of Civil Procedure 36 for unwarranted denial

_____ Withdrawal from admission under Federal Rule of Civil Procedure 36 standards

_____ 11. Special Problems

_____ Expert opinions

_____ At initial conference

_____ Identify subjects on which expert opinions may be offered

_____ Set timetables for

    _____ Identifying experts to be called

    _____ Disclosure of reports/information under Federal Rule of Civil Procedure 26

_____   Deposing experts
_____ Any revision to opinions/reasons
_____ Materials on which opinions based
_____ General requirement for preservation/production
_____ Consider whether aborted/discarded preliminary studies should be preserved/produced
_____ Potential problem when using information protected by attorney-client privilege or work product doctrine
_____ Disclosure of publications/treatises
_____ Critiques of opinions by other experts—time for disclosure
_____ Costs of depositions
_____ Paid by deposing party under Federal Rule of Civil Pro-cedure 26
_____ Each party by agreement pays costs to own expert
_____ Limiting length of deposition
_____ Pretrial consideration of objections to expert's qualifications or opinions
_____ Discovery from court-appointed expert(s)
_____ Governmental investigations/reports
_____ Early identification of relevant investigations/reports
      _____   Production
      _____   From parties
      _____   From public records
      _____   Subpoena
      _____   Requests under Freedom of Information Act[2]
      _____   Grand jury materials
_____ Admissibility
_____ Discovery regarding trustworthiness
_____ Pretrial consideration of objections
_____ Summaries; compilations
_____ Timetable for disclosure
_____ Production of underlying data
_____ Verification procedures
_____ Detect/correct errors if feasible
_____ Stipulation as to estimated range of errors
_____ Polls; surveys; other sampling techniques

---

[2] 5 U.S.C. § 552 (1994).

_____   Timetable for disclosure of potential use

_____   Consultation between experts prior to conducting survey

_____   Disclosure of results/underlying data

_____   Admissibility

_____   Discovery

_____   Pretrial consideration of objections

_____   Settlements

_____   Continuing duty to disclose settlements/special agreements

_____   Discovery regarding fairness/adequacy of proposed class settlements

_____   Discovery not postponed for settlement discussions

_____   Potential problems with settlements limiting discovery

_____   Attorneys' fees

_____   Scope of discovery

_____   Inquiry into hourly rates of opposing counsel[3]

TIME EXTENSIONS

§ 13.5   Motion to Extend Discovery Time

FORM 13–1
SAMPLE MOTION TO EXTEND DISCOVERY TIME

DEFENDANTS' MOTION FOR ENLARGEMENT OF TIME IN WHICH TO CONDUCT DISCOVERY

Defendants, [A.I.C. SECURITY INVESTIGATIONS, LTD.]; [A.I.C. INTERNATIONAL, LTD.]; and [unnamed defendant C], by and through their attorneys, [WESSELS AND PAUTSCH, P.C.], by [Charles A. Pautsch], [attorney A], and [attorney B], pursuant to Rule 6(b), Fed. R. Civ. P., hereby requests this Court to enlarge the time in which parties to this action may conduct discovery and state in support hereof as follows:

1.   This action was filed by Plaintiff on [November 5, 1992].

2.   On or about [November 12, 1992], this Court, upon motion of Plaintiff, set forth an order closing discovery in this matter as of [January 1, 1993].

---

[3] Adapted from Manual for Complex Litigation 2d § 40.2 (1985).

3.   Thus far Plaintiff has taken the depositions of six (6) individuals, five (5) of whom are current employees of Defendants, has scheduled depositions for two (2) more employees of the Defendant companies, and has sought to depose the individually named Defendant [C].

4.   Defendants have served upon Plaintiff answers to interrogatories, documents in response to a Rule 34, Fed. R. Civ. P., document requests, and objections to certain written discovery inquiries.

5.   Thus far Defendants have taken the depositions of two (2) treating physicians and two (2) individuals. Defendants intend to depose two (2) additional individuals prior to [December 31, 1992].

6.   Plaintiff has served upon Defendants answers to interrogatories.

7.   On [November 17, 1992], Defendants served upon Plaintiff Defendants' First Requests for Production of Documents. According to this Court's [November 12, 1992], Order, Plaintiff's responses to Defendants' First Request for Production of Documents were due on [November 27, 1992].

8.   As of the date below, Defendants have not received from Plaintiff responses to Defendants' First Requests for Production of Documents.

9.   On [December 1, 1992], Defendants sent to Plaintiff a Notice of Deposition for [Charles H. Wessel ("Wessel")].

10.   Plaintiff refused to produce [Wessel] for his deposition scheduled for [December 10, 1992].

11. Plaintiff has failed to set forth an adequate reason for the failure of [Wessel] to appear for his deposition, did not seek a protective order, and has produced no verification that [Wessel] is unfit to be deposed.

12. Defendants promptly filed a Motion to Compel the attendance of [Charles H. Wessel] for deposition.

13. On or about [December 15, 1992], this Court referred Defendants' Motion to Compel the Attendance of [Charles H. Wessel] for Deposition to Magistrate Judge [Guzman] for determination. Thus far there has been no ruling on Defendants' Motion nor has a hearing date for said motion been set.

14.   If Defendants are not allowed to depose [Wessel] prior to trial, they will be unfairly prejudiced.

15.   On [November 13, 1992], Defendants made a motion to this Court for an Order allowing the physical and mental examination of [Wessel].

16.   On or about [November 24, 1992], this Court referred Defendants' Motion to Magistrate Judge [Guzman] for determination. Thus far there has been no ruling on Defendants' Motion nor has a hearing date been set for said motion.

17.   Defendants have retained a physician who can make a physical and mental examination of [Wessel] within a reasonable time after this Court so orders.

18.   If Defendants are not allowed a physical and mental examination prior to trial, they will be unfairly prejudiced.

19.   Due to upcoming holidays, it will be near impossible to complete discovery before [January 1, 1993].

WHEREFORE, in light of the foregoing, Defendants, through counsel, respectfully request that:

1)   the discovery deadline in this action be moved to [Friday], [January 22, 1993]; and

2)   the pre-trial conference, presently scheduled for [January 15, 1993], be moved ahead accordingly.

Dated this [22nd] Day of [December], [1992].

§ 13.6   Motion to Extend Time for Written Discovery/Supporting Affidavit

FORM 13–2
SAMPLE MOTION TO EXTEND TIME FOR WRITTEN DISCOVERY

IN THE UNITED STATES DISTRICT COURT

FOR THE [NORTHERN] DISTRICT OF [ILLINOIS]

[EASTERN] DIVISION

U.S. EQUAL EMPLOYMENT OPPORTUNITY COMMISSION,

Civil Action No. [92 C 7330]

Plaintiff,

v.

[A.I.C. SECURITY INVESTIGATIONS, LTD.];

[A.I.C. INTERNATIONAL, LTD.]; and [unnamed defendant C]

Honorable [Marvin E. Aspen]

Defendants.

DEFENDANTS' MOTION FOR ENLARGEMENT OF TIME IN WHICH TO RESPOND TO PLAINTIFF'S WRITTEN DISCOVERY

Defendants, [A.I.C. SECURITY INVESTIGATIONS, LTD.], [A.I.C. INTERNA-TIONAL, LTD.], and [C], by and through their attorneys, [WESSELS & PAUTSCH, P.C.], by [Charles W. Pautsch], [attorney A], and [attorney B], pursuant to Rule 6(b), Fed. R. Civ. P., hereby requests that this Honorable Court grant Defendants an extension of time in which to respond to Plaintiff's written discovery and state in support hereof as follows:

1.   On or about [November 9, 1992], Plaintiff Equal Employment Oppor-tunity Commission (EEOC) served upon Defendants its First Set of Interrogatories, First Request for Production of Documents, and First Request for Admissions.

2.   Along with the discovery requests served upon Defendants, as refer-enced in paragraph one above, Plaintiff also filed a motion with this Court to expedite discovery asking that the Court order (1) that all written discovery be answered by any party within seven days of receipt, and (2) that all discovery be completed by [December 31, 1992].

3.   Upon information and belief, on or about [November 12, 1992], this Court, without the parties coming forward for argument, granted Plaintiff's motion. Defendants' attorneys were never served with the Court's order and have knowl-edge of it only through subsequent conversations with the Court's Minute Clerk.

4.   The undersigned counsel for Defendants subsequently discussed the Court's order over the telephone with Attorney [name] of the EEOC and each party agreed that the Court's Order meant Defendants' answers to Plaintiff's First Set of Written Discovery would be due on or before [November 24, 1992].

5.   That upon the date Defendants' attorneys were served with Plaintiff's First Request for Production of Documents, First Set of Interrogatories, and First Request for Admissions, the same were immediately forwarded to the Defendants' place of business in order to facilitate the gathering of the requested information.

6.   Plaintiff's First Set of Interrogatories to Defendants number in excess of 50, including sub-parts, and that Plaintiff's First Request for Production of Documents requests voluminous materials.

7.   Defendants in good faith have attempted to respond to Plaintiff's First Set of Interrogatories and First Request for Production of Documents by

[November 24, 1992], but, however, were unable to comply with such an expedited deadline.

8.   On or about [November 18, 1992], Defendants served upon the EEOC Defendants' Responses to Plaintiff's First Request for Admissions.

9.   Defendants' delay in serving their responses to Plaintiff's First Set of Interrogatories and First Request for Production of Documents was the result of excusable neglect.

10.   That Defendants will need until [December 15, 1992], to set forth adequately responses to the EEOC's First Set of Interrogatories and First Request for Production of Documents.

WHEREOF, Defendants request an order allowing them until [December 15, 1992], in which to set forth responses to Plaintiff's First Set of Interrogatories and First Request for Production of Documents.

FORM 13–3
SAMPLE AFFIDAVIT IN SUPPORT OF MOTION TO EXTEND TIME

IN THE UNITED STATES DISTRICT COURT

FOR THE [NORTHERN] DISTRICT OF [ILLINOIS]

[EASTERN] DIVISION

U.S. EQUAL EMPLOYMENT OPPORTUNITY COMMISSION,

Plaintiff,

Civil Action No. [92 C 7330]

v.

[A.I.C. SECURITY INVESTIGATIONS, LTD.];

[A.I.C. INTERNATIONAL, LTD.]; and [unnamed defendant C]

Honorable [Marvin E. Aspen]

Defendants.

AFFIDAVIT OF [attorney B]
STATE OF [WISCONSIN]
COUNTY OF [MILWAUKEE]

The affiant [attorney B], being first duly sworn upon oath, hereby deposes and states as follows:

1.   Affiant is an attorney duly admitted to practice before this Honorable Court and has filed and appearance on behalf of the Defendants in the above-captioned cause.

2.   Neither Affiant nor any other attorney of the law firm of [Wessels & Pautsch, P.C.] was served with the Court's Order dated [November 12, 1992], expediting discovery in the above-captioned cause, and affiant only has knowl-edge of the Court's [November 12, 1992], Order through conversation with the Court's Minute Clerk.

3.   After receiving knowledge of the Court's [November 12, 1992], Order expediting discovery, affiant talked with [Attorney A], attorney for Plaintiff, regarding an interpretation of the Order and agreed that the Order instructed Defendants to set forth responses to Plaintiff's First Set of Written Discovery on or before [November 24, 1992].

4.   On or about [November 9, 1992], Affiant, on behalf of Defendants, we served with Plaintiff's First Set of Interrogatories and First Request for Production of Documents. On that same day Affiant immediately forwarded via facsimile Plaintiff's First Request for Production of Documents and First Set of Interro-gatories to Defendants' place of business in order to facilitate the gathering of the requested information.

5.   That I have read these five (5) paragraphs and two (2) pages, and certify by my signature below that they are true and correct to my best information and belief.

§ 13.7   Response to Motion to Extend Time for Discovery (EEOC)

FORM 13–4
SAMPLE RESPONSE TO MOTION TO EXTEND TIME FOR DISCOVERY

EEOC'S RESPONSE TO DEFENDANTS' MOTION FOR ENLARGEMENT OF TIME IN WHICH TO CONDUCT DISCOVERY

Plaintiff, the Equal Employment Opportunity Commission (the "EEOC"), respectfully submits this Memorandum in response to Defendants' Motion for Enlargement of Time in Which to Conduct Discovery.

This is an action under the Americans With Disabilities Act (ADA), 42 U.S.C. § 12101 *et seq.*, in which the EEOC alleges that [Charles H. Wessel ("Wessel")]

was discharged from his employment because of his disability, terminal brain cancer. [Wessel] suffers from malignant brain tumors, and his condition has been diagnosed as terminal. See depositions of Drs. [A] and [B].

Because of [Wessel]'s condition, EEOC requested, and the Court ordered, a discovery cutoff date of [December 31, 1992], and a date for final pre-trial order of [January 15, 1993]. Defendants now seek a three-week extension of those dates. EEOC respectfully requests that the Motion be denied, because any delay in setting the case for trial may result in [Wessel] being unable to testify and because Defendants' Motion demonstrates on its face that no extension is necessary.

Defendants' Motion relies on two bases for an extension: that EEOC has not yet responded to an outstanding document request; that the Court has not yet ruled upon Defendants' Motion for a Mental and Physical Examination of [Charles H. Wessel]. None of these bases justifies an extension of discovery cutoff.

EEOC produced its investigative file to Defendants on [November 24, 1992]. The documents sought in Defendants' First Request for Production of Documents were documents belonging to [Wessel], and those obtained by the EEOC were produced on [December 28, 1992].

Defendants' Motions to Compel a Second Deposition by [Wessel] and to compel a Mental and Physical Examination have been fully briefed. In the event that the Court were to order that either take place, they would, of course, need to be scheduled outside of the discovery period. This would not, however, require any extension of discovery for any other purpose.[4]

As set forth in Defendants' Motion for Enlargement of Time, both parties have noticed and taken numerous depositions during the discovery period. In addition, Defendants have subpoenaed voluminous documents from health care providers and others. Defendants have not noticed any depositions, other than that of [Wessel], which they have been unable to schedule. Defendants do not claim a need for any discovery in addition to that which is the subject of the two pending motions; therefore no extension of time is necessary.

This is an unusual case in that Plaintiff's most important evidence, [Wessel]'s testimony, may be unavailable if the matter is not brought quickly to trial.[5] Defendants have identified no discovery which they need, which has not been

---

[4] There is also a pending Motion to Compel answers to interrogatories and answers to document requests filed by EEOC and fully briefed by the parties. Ruling on that motion will not require any delay in the discovery cutoff date. Similarly, ruling on a pending motion by Defendants to disqualify counsel for A.I.C. should not be permitted to delay discovery.

[5] Wessel's videotape deposition was taken on November 5, 1992, in response to a Petition to Perpetuate Testimony made by Wessel and by the defendants. That deposition will not be as probative of the issues in the case as live testimony by Wessel would be.

either obtained or is the subject of pending motions. No extension of discovery is necessary, and EEOC therefore requests that the dates for discovery cutoff and for final pre-trial order stand, and that the matter be set for trial at the earliest convenient date.

§ 13.8   Transcript of Hearing on Defendants' Request for Extension of Time for Discovery

FORM 13–5
SAMPLE HEARING TRANSCRIPT ON REQUEST FOR EXTENSION OF TIME

IN THE UNITED STATES DISTRICT COURT

FOR THE [NORTHERN] DISTRICT OF [ILLINOIS]

[EASTERN] DIVISION

U.S. EQUAL EMPLOYMENT OPPORTUNITY DIVISION

Plaintiff,

v.

[A.I.C. SECURITY INVESTIGATIONS, LTD.];

[A.I.C. INTERNATIONAL, LTD.]; and [unnamed defendant C],

Defendants.

Docket No. [92 C 7330]

[Chicago, Illinois]

[December 29, 1992]

TRANSCRIPTS OF PROCEEDINGS BEFORE THE HON. [MARVIN E. ASPEN]

APPEARANCES:

For the Plaintiff:

[plaintiff attorney A] and

[plaintiff attorney B]

(United States Equal Employment Opportunity Commission)

[536 South Clark St.]

[Chicago], [Illinois] [60605]

For Defendant [A.I.C.]:

[WESSELS & PAUTSCH], by

[defense attorney B]

[330 East Kilbourn Avenue]

[Milwaukee], [Wisconsin] [53202]

For Defendant [Wessel]:

[injured party's attorney]

[address]

Court reporter:

[court reporter]

[address]

[telephone number]

THE CLERK: [92 C 7330], EEOC versus [A.I.C. Security Investigations]

[DEFENSE ATTORNEY B]: Good morning, your Honor,

THE COURT: Good morning.

[DEFENSE ATTORNEY B]: [Defense attorney B name] appearing on behalf of the defendants.

[PLAINTIFF ATTORNEY A]: [Plaintiff attorney A] and [Plaintiff attorney B] representing the EEOC.

[INJURED PARTY'S ATTORNEY]: [Injured party's attorney name], your Honor, I am appearing on behalf of—for [attorney D], who represents Charles Wessel. She was unable to be here today and she requested that I appear here for her.

THE COURT: Okay, I don't have the motion here. I think I might have left it on my desk, Gladys, with—I know what it's about.

Do you have an objection to the extension of time for—

[PLAINTIFF ATTORNEY A]: Yes, your Honor, the EEOC, we do have an objection to the extension of time.

Your Honor, this is a case under the Americans with Disabilities Act. Charles Wessel has terminal cancer. His prognosis is not good. He is at the moment well, he will be able to testify.

The discovery cutoff at this point is December 31st, and both sides' have virtually completed all discovery. There are a couple of pending motions, and if those were granted some additional discovery would be necessary but I don't think that would require an extension on other matters.

Our primary concern is to get the case to trial, and what we would ask for is an early trial date. Then beyond that we would have no particular concern about discovery until then.

THE COURT. Yes.

[DEFENSE ATTORNEY]: If I may reply.

We feel that discovery is not almost over. This case has been on the expedited docket and our client is working with a small administrative staff that has been overburdened, especially in the past month, attempting to comply with numerous discovery requests, written discovery and the many depositions. We have had twelve depositions scheduled together in December. It's been a short month, only 19 working days. We haven't had time to conduct discovery—complete discovery.

We have asked for the deposition of Mr. Wessel, who is the subject of the case, and without moving for a protective, order—

THE COURT: What you have asked for, really, is an extension of about a month, right, to complete discovery?

[DEFENSE ATTORNEY]: 21 days, I believe. Until January 22nd, I believe.

THE COURT: It's not realistic if the case is going to be tried in that time period anyway. So I am going to allow the motion, but I am not going to give you any further extensions, so you're going to have to do what you have to do during that time period. If you don't complete discovery in that period it won't be done.

I will also set the date for filing the written pre-trial order in open court. Let's set that down for February the 9th at 10:00 o'clock.

How long is it going to take to try this case?

[PLAINTIFF ATTORNEY A]: Four or five days I would think, your Honor.

[DEFENSE ATTORNEY]: We believe longer than that, your Honor.

THE COURT: Okay. I am going to—who's the Magistrate Judge in this case? [defense attorney]: Guzman.

[PLAINTIFF ATTORNEY A]: Guzman.

THE COURT: All right. Do you have any objections to Magistrate Judge Guzman trying the case?

[PLAINTIFF ATTORNEY A]: No, your Honor. We want the earliest possible trial date.

THE COURT: Okay.

[DEFENSE ATTORNEY]: Your Honor, at this time I would like to be able to discuss with other counsel an objection to that. At this point we are going to maintain an objection to that.

THE COURT: I'm sorry?

[DEFENSE ATTORNEY B]: At this point we are going to maintain an objection going to the Magistrate.

THE COURT. It would be helpful, because otherwise I am going to have to interrupt another trial to try this case, and I will; it's going to be tried quickly.

Why don't you—

[DEFENSE ATTORNEY B]: Can we have time to consider that?

THE COURT. Sure. Come back Friday at—

THE CLERK: Friday is a holiday, Judge.

THE COURT: Okay. Why don't you come back on January the 12th at 9:30, if you want, and let me know at that time whether your clients will accept it, all right?

DEPOSITIONS

§ 13.9   Order for Deposition Guidelines

FORM 13–6
SAMPLE ORDER FOR DEPOSITION GUIDELINES

It is ORDERED that depositions be conducted in accordance with the following rules:

1.   Cooperation. Counsel are expected to cooperate with, and be courteous to, each other and deponents.

2.   Stipulations. Unless contrary to an order of the court, the parties (and, when appropriate, a nonparty witness) may stipulate in any suitable writing to alter, amend, or modify any practice relating to noticing, conducting, or filing a deposition. Stipulations for the extension of discovery cutoffs set by the court are not, however, valid until approved by the court.

3.   Scheduling. Absent extraordinary circumstances, counsel shall consult in advance with opposing counsel and proposed deponents in an effort to schedule depositions at mutually convenient times and places.

4.   Attendance.

(a)   Who may be present. Unless otherwise ordered under Fed. R. Civ. P. 26(c), depositions may be attended by counsel of record, members and employees of their firms, attorneys specially engaged by a party for purpose of the deposition, and potential witnesses. While the deponent is being examined about any stamped confidential document or the confidential information contained therein, persons to whom disclosure is not authorized under the Confidentiality Order shall be excluded.

(b)   Unnecessary attendance. Unnecessary attendance by counsel is discouraged and may not be compensated in any fee application to the court. Counsel who have only marginal interest in a proposed deposition or who expect their interests to be adequately represented by other counsel may elect not to attend and the conduct pursuant to paragraph 13(b) of this order supplemental interrogation of the deponent should a review of deposition reveal the need for such examination.

5.   Conduct.

(a)   Examination. Each side should ordinarily designate an attorney to conduct the principal examination of the deponent, and examination by other attorneys should be limited to matters not previously covered.

(b)   Objections. The only objections that should be raised at the deposition are those involving a privilege against disclosure or some matter that may be remedied if presented at the time, such as to the form of the question or the responsiveness of the answer. Objections on other grounds are unnecessary and should generally be avoided. All objections should be concise and must not suggest answers to (or otherwise coach) the deponent. Argumentative interruptions will not be permitted.

(c)   Directions not to answer. Directions to the deponent not to answer are improper except on the ground of privilege or to enable a party or deponent to present a motion to the court for termination of the deposition on the ground that it is being conducted in bad faith or in such a manner as unreasonably to annoy, embarrass, or oppress the party or the deponent. When a privilege is claimed, the witness should nevertheless answer questions relevant to the existence, extent, or waiver of the privilege, such as the date of a communication, who made the statement, to whom the contents of the statement have been disclosed, and the general subject matter of the statement.

(d)   Private consultation. Private conference between deponents and their attorney during the actual taking of the deposition are improper except for the purpose of determining whether a privilege should be asserted. Unless prohibited by the court for good cause shown, such conferences may, however, be held during normal recesses and adjournments.

6.   Documents.

(a)   Production of documents. Witnesses subpoenaed to produce numerous documents should ordinarily be served at least 30 days before the scheduled deposition. Depending upon the quantity of documents to be produced, some time may be needed for inspection of the documents before the interrogation commences.

(b)   Confidentiality order. A copy of the Confidentiality Order shall be provided to the deponent before the deposition commences if the deponent is to produce or may be asked about documents which may contain confidential information.

(c)   Copies. Extra copies of documents about which counsel expect to examine the deponent should ordinarily be provided to opposing counsel and the deponent. Deponents should be shown a document before being examined about it except when counsel seek to impeach or test the deponent's recollection.

7.   Depositions of witnesses who have no knowledge of the facts. An officer, director, or managing agent of a corporation or a governmental official served with a notice of a deposition or subpoena regarding a matter about which such person has no knowledge may submit to the noticing party a reasonable time before the date noticed an affidavit so stating and identifying a person within the corporation or government entity believed to have such knowledge. Notwithstanding such affidavit, the

noticing party may proceed with the deposition, subject to the right of the witness to seek a protective order.

8. Expert witnesses. Leave is granted to depose expert witnesses in addition to or in lieu of discovery through interrogatories. Objection to such depositions may be made by motion.

9. Tape-recorded depositions. By indicating in its notice of a deposition that it wishes to record the deposition by tape recording in lieu of stenographic recording (and identifying the person before whom the deposition will be taken), a party shall be deemed to have moved for such an order under Fed. R. Civ. P. 30(b)(4). Unless an objection is filed and served within [number of] days after such notice is received, the court shall be deemed to have granted the motion pursuant to the following terms and conditions.[6]

(a) Transcript; filing. Subject to the provision of paragraph 12, the party noticing the deposition shall be responsible for preparing a transcript of the tape recording and for filing within applicable time limits this transcript together with the original tape.

(b) Right of other parties. Other parties may at their own expense arrange for stenographic recording of the deposition, may obtain a copy of the tape and transcript upon payment of a pro-rata share of the noticing party's actual cost, and may prepare and file their own version of the transcript of the tape recording.

10. Videotaped depositions. By indicating in its notice of a deposition that it wishes to record the deposition by videotape (and identifying the proposed videotape operator), a party shall be deemed to have moved for such an order under Fed. R. Civ. P. 30(b)(4). Unless an objection is filed and served within [number of] days after such notice is received, the court shall be deemed to have granted the motion pursuant to the following terms and conditions.[7]

(a) Stenographic recording. The videotaped deposition shall be simultaneously recorded stenographically by a qualified court reporter. The court reporter shall on camera administer the oath or affirmation to the official record of the deposition for purposes of Fed. R. Civ. P. 30(e) (submission to witness) and 30(f) (filing exhibits).

(b) Cost. The noticing party shall bear the expense of both the videotaping and the stenographic recording. Any party may at its own expense obtain a copy of the videotape and the stenographic transcript.

Requests for taxation of these costs and expenses may be made at the conclusion of the litigation in accordance with applicable law.

---

[6] This provision is unnecessary under the 1993 amendments to Fed. R. Civ. P. 30(b).

[7] *Id.*

(c)   Video operator. The operator(s) of the videotape recording equipment shall be subject to the provisions of Fed. R. Civ. P. 28(c). At the commencement of the deposition the operator(s) shall swear or affirm to record the proceedings fairly and accurately.

(d)   Attendance. Each witness, attorney, and other person attending the deposition shall be identified on camera at the commencement of the deposition. Thereafter, only the deponent (and demonstrative materials used during the deposition) will be videotaped.

(e)   Standards. The deposition will be conducted in a manner to replicate to the extent feasible, the presentation of evidence at a trial. Unless physically incapacitated, the deponent shall be seated at a table or in a witness box except when reviewing or presenting demonstrative materials for which a change in position is needed. To the extent practicable, the deposition will be conducted in a neutral setting, against a solid background, with only such lighting as is required for accurate video recording. Lighting, camera angle, lens setting, and field of view will be changed only as necessary to record accurately the natural body movements of the deponent or to only as necessary to record satisfactorily the voices of counsel and the deponent. Eating and smoking by deponents or counsel during the deposition will not be permitted.

(f)   Interruptions. The videotape shall run continuously throughout the active conduct of the deposition. Videotape recording will be suspended during all "off the record" discussions.[8]

(g)   Examination; exhibits; rereading. The provisions of paragraph 5 and 6 of this order apply to videotaped depositions. Rereading of questions or answers, when needed, will be done on camera by the stenographic court reporter.

(h)   Index. The videotape operator shall use a counter on the recording equipment and after completion of the deposition shall prepare a log, cross-referenced to counter numbers, that identified the positions on the tape at which examination by different counsel begins and ends, at which objections are made and examination resumes, at which exhibits are identified, and at which any interruption of continuous tape recording occurs, whether for recesses, "off the record" discussions, mechanical failure, or otherwise.

(i)   Filing. The operator shall preserve custody of the original videotape in its original condition until further order of the court. Subject to the provisions of paragraph 12 of this order, the original of the tape recording, together with the operator's log index and a certificate of the operator attesting to the accuracy of the tape, shall be filed with the Clerk. No part of a videotaped deposition shall be released or made available to any member of the public unless authorized by the court.

---

[8] If, as in this sample order, a simultaneous stenographic transcript is being made, many courts prefer that the off-the-record discussions be eliminated from the videotape.

(j)   Objections. Requests for pre-trial rulings on the admissibility of evidence obtained during a videotaped deposition shall be accompanied by appropriate pages of written transcript. If the objection involves a matter peculiar to the videotaping, a copy of the videotape and equipment for viewing the tape shall also be provided to the court.

(k)   Use at trial, purged tapes. A party desiring to offer a videotape deposition at trial shall be responsible for having available appropriate playback equipment and a trained operator. After the designation by all parties of the portions of a videotape to be used at trial, an edited copy of the tape, purged of unnecessary portions (and any portions to which objections have been sustained), [may/shall] be prepared by the offering party to facilitate continuous playback, but a copy of the edited tape shall be made available to other parties at least [number of] days before it is used, and the unedited original of the tape shall also be available at the trial.

11.   Telephonic depositions. By indicating in its notice of a deposition that it wishes to conduct the deposition by telephone, a party shall be deemed to have moved for such an order under Fed. R. Civ. P. 30(b)(7). Unless an objection is filed and served within [number of] days after such notice is received, it is deemed that the court shall have granted the motion. Other parties may examine the deponent telephonically or in person. However, all persons present with the deponent be identified in the deposition and shall not by word, sign, or otherwise, coach or suggest answers to the deponent.

12.   Waiver of transcription and filing. The parties and deponents are authorized and encouraged to waive transcription and filing of depositions that prove to be of little or no usefulness in the litigation or to agree to defer transcription and filing until the need for using the depositions arises.

13.   Use; supplemental depositions.

(a)   Use. Depositions may, under the conditions prescribed in Fed. R. Civ. P. 32(a)(1)–(4), or as otherwise permitted by the Federal Rules of Evidence, be used against any party (including parties later added and parties in cases subsequently filed in, removed to, or transferred to this court as part of this litigation)

(1)   who was present or represented at the deposition,

(2)   who had reasonable notice thereof, or

(3)   who, within 30 days after the filing of the deposition (or, if later, within 60 days after becoming a party in this court in any action which is part of this litigation), fails to show just cause why such deposition should not be usable against such party.

(b)   Supplemental depositions. Each party not present or represented at a deposition (including parties later added and parties in cases subsequently filed in, removed to, or transferred to this court) may, within 30 days after the filing of the deposition (or, if later, within 60 days after becoming a party in this court in any action which is a part of this litigation), request permission to conduct a supplemental deposition of the deponent, including the right to take such deposition telephonically and by nonstenographic means. If permitted, the deposition shall be treated as the resumption of the deposition originally noticed; and each deponent shall, at the conclusion of the initial deposition be advised of the opportunity of nonattending parties to request a resumption of such deposition, subject to the right of the deponent to seek a protective order. Such examination shall not be repetitive of the prior interrogation.

14.   Rulings.

(a)   Immediate presentation. Disputes arising during depositions that cannot be resolved by agreement and that, if not immediately resolved, will significantly disrupt the discovery schedule or require a rescheduling of the deposition, may be presented by telephone to the court. (If the judge will not be available during the period while the deposition is being conducted, the dispute may be addressed to Magistrate [name]. The presentation of the issue and the court's ruling will be recorded as part of the deposition.

(b)   Extraterritorial jurisdiction. The undersigned will exercise by telephone the authority granted under 28 U.S.C. § 1407(b) to act as district judge in the district in which the deposition is taken.[9]

Date: [date]

United States District Judge[10]

§ 13.10   Telephone Depositions versus Depositions on Written Interrogatories

Rule 31 of the Federal Rules of Civil Procedure permits depositions to be taken where the presiding officer reads written questions submitted in advance by the party convening the deposition. This technique may be appropriate if the deponent is some distance away, making it expensive for the person taking the deposition to travel to the place at which it is taken. On the other hand, telephone depositions also are authorized by the Federal

---

[9] This specifies the power to exercise authority over nonparty deponents outside the district circuit or intercircuit assignment.

[10] These deposition guidelines have been adapted from *Sample Deposition Guidelines*, in Manual for Complex Litigation 2d § 41.38 (1985).

Rules of Civil Procedure 30, and they preserve much of the spontaneity and ability to follow up questions and answers that are lost in depositions on written interrogatories. Accordingly, when distance is a problem, telephonic depositions are preferable to depositions on written questions.

The discovery plan now required by Federal Rules of Civil Procedure 16 and 26 can ensure that telephonic depositions as well as videotapes and other modern technologies play their appropriate role in the overall discovery plan.

§ 13.11   Notice of Video Deposition

FORM 13-7
SAMPLE NOTICE OF VIDEO DEPOSITION

To: [each party and his or her attorney]

You are hereby notified that the deposition of [name of plaintiff] will be taken by oral examination pursuant to Rule [number] of the Federal Rules of Civil Procedure by videotape before [name of court reporter or other person authorized to administer oath] at [location] at [city, state] on [date] at [time].

The deponent is obligated by Rule 30 to appear, and may bring counsel. Others named in this notice may appear and examine the deponents.

Federal Rule 30 permits you to make your own arrangements for the preparation of a traditional transcript of this deposition. The videotape will remain in the custody of the person before whom it is taken and copies will be made available to you at your cost.

Commentary.   In *State ex rel. Anderson v. Miller*,[11] the Oregon Supreme Court granted mandamus against a trial court judge who prohibited a videotape deposition. The pertinent Oregon rule of civil procedure not only allowed depositions to be videotaped if so specified in the notice of deposition but also provided for protective orders to eliminate harassment or unduly burdensome discovery. In prohibiting the use of videotape, the trial judge simply expressed his view that videotaping was unnecessary and might impose a certain amount of inconvenience. The Oregon Supreme Court said that the trial judge was substituting his policy judgment for that of the rule drafters and concluded that mandamus was the appropriate remedy for this abuse of discretion. However, in *Cherry Creek School District No. 5 v. Voelker*,[12] the Colorado Supreme Court reversed the intermediate court. The court found plaintiff not entitled to videotape plaintiff's deposition after the end of discovery and on the eve of

---

[11] 882 P.2d 1109 (Or. 1994).

[12] 859 P.2d 805, 810 (Colo. 1993).

trial because she was unable to attend trial. The plaintiff's inability to attend had long been known and the videotape deposition, even though a superior means of presenting testimony compared with a reading discovery deposition, would have worked an inconvenience on the defendant.

§ 13.12   Notice of Unknown Corporate Deponent

FORM 13–8
SAMPLE NOTICE OF UNKNOWN CORPORATE DEPONENT

To: [each party and his or her attorney]

You are hereby notified that the deposition of [name of corporation] will be taken by oral examination pursuant to the Federal Rules of Civil Procedure before [name of court reporter or other person authorized to administer oath] by videotape at [location], at [city, state] on [date] at [time].

[Name of corporation] is directed, pursuant to Fed. R. Civ. P. 30(b)(6) to designate one or more of its officers, directors, managing agents, or other persons to appear on its behalf and testify on each of the subject matters set forth below:

1.   The employment history of the plaintiff in this action

2.   The knowledge possessed by any employee of the corporation as to physical or mental disabilities, real or perceived, of the plaintiff

3.   Any request for accommodation to disability made by the plaintiff

4.   Any discussions, analysis, reports, or correspondent from, by, or to employees of the corporation with respect to the disabilities of the plaintiff or possible accommodation to disabilities by the corporation.

The deposition will continue from day to day until completed. Parties and their attorneys other than the corporation and the designated deponent may appear and examine the witness. The corporation is obligated to appear through its designated officer, director, managing agent, or other person.

Any party may cause a traditional transcript to be made of the deposition at its own expense. The videotape will be retained in the custody of the officer taking the deposition and copies will be made available to any party at that party's request and expense.

§ 13.13 Notice of Deposition/Response Letter

FORM 13-9
SAMPLE NOTICE OF DEPOSITION

IN THE UNITED STATES DISTRICT COURT

FOR THE [NORTHERN] DISTRICT OF [ILLINOIS]

[EASTERN] DIVISION

U.S EQUAL EMPLOYMENT OPPORTUNITY COMMISSION,

Plaintiff,

and

Civil Action [No. 92 C 7330]

[A.I.C. SECURITY INVESTIGATIONS, LTD.];

[A.I.C. INTERNATIONAL, LTD.];

and [unnamed defendant C]

Honorable [Marvin E. Aspen]

Defendants.

NOTICE OF DEPOSITION

To: [plaintiff attorney A]

Equal Employment Opportunity Commission

[536 South Clark Street]-[Room 982]

[Chicago], [IL] [60605]

[defense attorney D]

PLEASE TAKE NOTICE that, pursuant to Rule 30 of the Federal Rules of Civil Procedure, the Defendants, [A.I.C. SECURITY INVESTIGATIONS, LTD.], [A.I.C. INTERNATIONAL, LTD.], and [unnamed defendant C], by and through their attorneys, [WESSELS & PAUTSCH, P.C.], by [Charles W. Pautsch], [attorney A] and [attorney B] will take the deposition upon oral examination of the following:

DEPONENT: [Charles H. Wessel]

DATE: [Thursday], [December 10, 1992]

TIME: [10:00 A.M.]

PLACE: [Wessels & Pautsch, P.C.],

[Dunham Center]

[2035 Foxfield Drive]

[St. Charles], [IL] [60174]

FORM 13–10
SAMPLE RESPONSE LETTER TO DEPOSITION NOTICE

[December 4, 1992]

[defense attorney B]
[Wessels & Pautsch, P.C.]
[330 East Kilbourn Avenue]
[Suite 1475]
[Milwaukee], [WI] [53202]
Re: EEOC v. A.I.C., *et al.*
[92 C. 7330] [(N.D. Ill.)]

Dear [attorney B]:

I am writing to you concerning the Notice of Deposition for [Charles H. Wessel] which we received today. As I advised [defense attorney A] this afternoon, we consider another deposition of [Mr. Wessel] to be unduly burdensome in light of the lengthy deposition he has already given.

If you believe that there are areas which need to be covered which were not inquired about during the previous deposition, please let met know. If not, we will move for a protective order.

I will give you a call on [Monday],[December 7], so that we can have a conference as required by Rule [12(k)] of the Local Rules of the [Northern District] of [Illinois].

I look forward to hearing from you.

[plaintiff attorney A]

§ 13.14 Motion to Compel Deposition of Victim

FORM 13–11
SAMPLE MOTION TO COMPEL DEPOSITION OF VICTIM

IN THE UNITED STATES DISTRICT COURT

FOR THE [NORTHERN] DISTRICT OF [ILLINOIS]

[EASTERN] DIVISION

U.S EQUAL EMPLOYMENT OPPORTUNITY COMMISSION,

Plaintiff,

and   Civil Action No. [92 C 7330]

[A.I.C. SECURITY INVESTIGATIONS, LTD.];

[A.I.C. INTERNATIONAL, LTD.];

and [unnamed defendant C]

                                                        Honorable [Marvin E. Aspen]

Defendants.

DEFENDANTS' MOTION TO COMPEL ATTENDANCE
OF CHARLES H. WESSEL FOR DEPOSITION

Defendants [A.I.C. SECURITY INVESTIGATIONS, LTD.], [A.I.C. INTERNA-TIONAL, LTD.], and [C], by and through their attorneys, [WESSELS & PAUTSCH, P.C.], by [Charles W. Pautsch], [attorney A], and [attorney B], pursuant to Rule 37, Fed. R. Civ. P., hereby move this Honorable Court for an Order compelling the attendance of [Charles H. Wessel] for Deposition and state in support hereof as follows:

1.   On [November 5, 1992], prior to the instigation of this present action, [Charles H. Wessel ("Wessel")] was deposed by his attorney, [attorney C], pursuant to a Court Order made by Judge [Kocoras] upon [Wessel]'s Petition to Perpetuate Testimony under Rule 27, Fed. R. Civ. P.

2.   On [November 5, 1992], counsel for Defendants had a limited opportunity to cross-examine [Wessel]. (See Memorandum in support hereof, served herewith and incorporated herein.)

3.   Prior to [November 5, 1992], counsel for Defendants had no opportunity whatsoever to conduct any background discovery, including the collection and review of documents and medical records.

4.   On [November 5, 1992], Plaintiff Equal Employment Opportunity Commission ("EEOC") filed this present action on behalf of [Wessel] and served the Complaint upon Defendants on or about [November 10, 1992].

5.   On [November 12, 1992], this Court ordered discovery to be conducted on an expedited basis with discovery closing [December 31, 1992].

6.   On [December 1, 1992], Defendants' counsel sent to Plaintiff EEOC via facsimile and U.S. Mail a Notice of Deposition instructing Plaintiff EEOC to have [Wessel] appear for his deposition on [Thursday], [December 10, 1992], at [10:00 A.M.] (See copy of Notice of Deposition and Proof of Service attached hereto as Exhibit No. 1 and incorporated herein.)

7.   On [Friday], [December 4, 1992], [attorney A], attorney for Plaintiff EEOC, sent a letter to Defendants' counsel expressing a desire to conduct a [12(k)] (Local Court General Rule [12(k)]) conference on [December 7, 1992]. (See letter attached hereto as Exhibit No. 2 and incorporated herein.)

8.   On [Monday, December 7, 1992], [attorney B], another attorney for Plaintiff EEOC, telephoned Defendants' counsel; however, Defendants' counsel was in meeting and unable to take Attorney [B]'s telephone call. (See copy of message note attached hereto as Exhibit No. 3 and incorporated herein.)

9.   Twice on [Monday], [December 7, 1992], at approximately [1:00 P.M.] and [3:00 P.M.], Defendants' counsel [B] returned the telephone call of EEOC Attorney [B]; however, EEOC Attorney [B] did not accept the calls and did not return the message left by Defense Attorney [B]. (See Affidavit of [defense attorney B] attached hereto and incorporated herein.)

10.   On [Tuesday], [December 8], [1992], one of Defendants' counsel, [attorney A], telephoned Plaintiff's EEOC Attorney [A], and was informed by her that Plaintiff refuses to produce [Wessel] for deposition.

11.   Prior to the date of filing of this present motion, Defendants' attorneys' attempts to engage in personal consultation have been unsuccessful due to no fault of Defendants' attorneys. [Local Court Gen. Rule 12(k)].

12.   Prior to the date of filing of this present motion, Plaintiff EEOC has not moved for a protective order pursuant to Rule 26(c), Fed. R. Civ. P., nor has Plaintiff put forward a legitimate reason for not producing [Wessel] for deposition.

WHEREOF, Defendants respectfully request the Court to set forth an Order:

(1)   commanding [Charles H. Wessel] to appear for deposition; and

(2)   awarding Defendants just and equitable relief pursuant to Rule 37(d), Fed. R. Civ. P., including, but not limited to, reasonable attorneys' fees and costs for having to file this present motion.

FORM 13–12
SAMPLE AFFIDAVIT FOR MOTION TO COMPEL

IN THE UNITED STATES DISTRICT COURT

FOR THE [NORTHERN] DISTRICT OF [ILLINOIS]

[EASTERN] DIVISION

U.S. EQUAL EMPLOYMENT OPPORTUNITY COMMISSION,

Plaintiff,

and   Civil Action No. [92 C 7330]

[A.I.C. SECURITY INVESTIGATIONS, LTD.];

[A.I.C. INTERNATIONAL, LTD.]; and [unnamed defendant C]

                                            Honorable [Marvin E. Aspen]

Defendants.

AFFIDAVIT OF [attorney B]

STATE OF [WISCONSIN]

COUNTY OF [MILWAUKEE]

I, [attorney B], being first duly sworn under oath, deposes and states:

1.   Affiant is an attorney duly admitted to practice before this Court and has filed an Appearance on behalf of the Defendants in the above-captioned action.

2.   On [Monday], [December 7, 1992], the affiant received a written telephone message from his secretary, [name], the Attorney [B] from the Equal Employment Opportunity Commission ("EEOC") had telephoned.

3.   At approximately [1:00 P.M.] on [December 7, 1992], affiant telephoned the EEOC in [Chicago] and asked for Attorney [B]. The person answering the

phones at the EEOC indicated that [attorney B] was unavailable to come to the phone. The affiant then asked the receptionist at the EEOC to take down his name and number and have [attorney B] return the call.

4. At approximately [3:00 P.M.] on [Monday], [December 7, 1992], the affiant made a second telephone call to the EEOC and asked for Attorney [B]. The person answering the phones for the EEOC indicated that [attorney B] was still not available to talk. The affiant requested that a telephone message be given to [attorney B] so she could promptly return affiant's phone call.

5. On [Monday], [December 7, 1992], the affiant was at his office until approximately [6:30 P.M.] and did not at any time receive a telephone call from either Attorney [B] or Attorney [A].

6. I have read these six (6) paragraphs and two (2) pages, and certify by my signature below that they are true and correct to my best information and belief.

§ 13.15 Defendant's Motion to Compel Deposition of Victim's Wife

FORM 13–13
SAMPLE MOTION TO COMPEL DEPOSITION OF VICTIM'S WIFE

DEFENDANTS' MOTION TO COMPEL DEPONENT [ALICE E. WESSEL]

Defendants, [A.I.C. SECURITY INVESTIGATIONS, LTD.]; [A.I.C. INTERNA-TIONAL, LTD.]; and [unnamed defendant C], by and through their attorneys [WESSEL AND PAUTSCH, P.C.], by [Charles A. Pautsch], [attorney A], and [attorney B], pursuant to Rule 37(a)(2), Fed. R. Civ. P., hereby move this Honorable Court to set forth an Order compelling Deponent [Alice H. Wessel] to answer certain questions posed to her at deposition and state in support hereof as follows:

1. On [January 27, 1993], [Alice H. Wessel] was deposed at the offices of the Equal Employment Opportunity Commission ("EEOC") pursuant to a subpoena issued to her under Rule 45, Fed. R. Civ. P. by Defendants' attorneys, [Wessel & Pautsch, P.C.]

2. Deponent [Alice H. Wessel] was represented at the deposition by Attorney [C].

3. During the course of the deposition of [Alice H. Wessel], Attorney [C] instructed his client not to answer a number of questions posed to her based upon an assertion of spousal privilege.

4.   During the course of this deposition, the parties presented an argument to this Court via a telephone conference call on the deponent's refusal to testify regarding assets of she and her husband, the Plaintiff in intervention, [Charles Wessel] (which issue was ruled upon during said conference with the Court), and also regarding the deponent's refusal to answer any questions concerning communications between the deponent and [Charles Wessel].

5.   The Court proposed that the parties stipulate to the deponent's answering the objectionable questions and that the transcript be sealed and forwarded to the Court for its ruling on the asserted application of spousal privilege; when the deponent's counsel refused to so stipulate, the Defendants were instructed to certify to the Court any objected to questions pursuant to the Federal Rules of Civil Procedure.

6.   Accordingly, the Defendants hereby move to compel the deponent [Alice Wessel]'s testimony on questions posed on the following pages, and lines (hereinafter referenced as TR [Page #], [Line #s]) of the attached transcript: [enumerated page citations omitted].

(See transcript of deposition of [Alice H. Wessel] filed herewith and incorporated herein.)

7.   Defendants are entitled to the questions set forth in paragraph six (6) above. (See Memorandum in support of his motion filed herewith and incorporated herein.)

WHEREFORE, Defendants respectfully request this Court to set forth an Order compelling Deponent [Alice H. Wessel] to answer the foregoing questions noted from the transcript of her [January 27, 1993] deposition. Defendants further request attorneys' fees and costs in having to prepare and file this present motion and attorneys' fees and costs in reconvening the deposition of [Alice H. Wessel].

Dated this [8th] day of [February], [1993].

§ 13.16   Order to Compel Attendance at Deposition

FORM 13–14
SAMPLE ORDER TO COMPEL ATTENDANCE AT DEPOSITION

IN THE UNITED STATES DISTRICT COURT

FOR THE [NORTHERN] DISTRICT OF [ILLINOIS]

[EASTERN] DIVISION

U.S. EQUAL EMPLOYMENT OPPORTUNITY COMMISSION,

Plaintiff,

and   Civil Action No. [92 C 7330]

[A.I.C. SECURITY INVESTIGATIONS, LTD.];

[A.I.C. INTERNATIONAL, LTD.]; and [unnamed defendant C]

Honorable [Marvin E. Aspen]

Defendants.

ORDER

Pending is Defendants' [A.I.C. SECURITY INVESTIGATIONS, LTD.]; [A.I.C. INTERNATIONAL, LTD.]; and [defendant C] ("Defendants") motion to compel attendance of plaintiff [Charles H. Wessel ("Wessel")] for deposition. For the reasons listed below [Mr. Wessel] is hereby ordered to appear.

BACKGROUND FACTS

This is an action under the Americans With Disabilities Act, 42 U.S.C. § 12101 *et seq.*, ("the Act") alleging that [Charles Wessel ("Wessel")] was terminated from his employment because of his disability, terminal cancer. On [November 5, 1992], prior to the commencement of this action, [Wessel] was deposed by defense Attorney [C] and [B], pursuant to a Court Order entered by the Honorable [Charles Kocoras] upon [Wessel]'s Petition to Perpetuate Testimony under Federal Rules of Civil Procedure 37. At this time counsel for Defendants had no opportunity to conduct any background discovery, including the collection and review of documents and medical records. At the time of the deposition, it appears that Defendants had been forwarded a list of all the medical practitioners who had provided treatment or examined [Mr. Wessel]'s medical condition or status. This list included the hospitals where [Mr. Wessel] had been treated. [Mr. Wessel] did not have any medical records in his possession with one exception, he had the last two MRIs which were performed on him at the [Center for Magnetic Imaging]. He did not, however, have the radiologist's report which interpreted those MRIs. At this time, [Mr. Wessel]'s attorney also produced payment records provided by [Mr. Wessel]'s insurance company.

On [November 6,1992], the Equal Employment Opportunity Commission ("EEOC") filed the instant complaint on behalf of [Wessel] and served the Complaint upon Defendants on or about [November 10, 1992]. On [December 1, 1992], Defendants' counsel sent to the EEOC a Notice of Deposition instructing the EEOC to have [Wessel] appear for his deposition on [Thursday], [December 10, 1992], at [10:00 A.M.]. On [Tuesday], [December 8, 1992], one of Defendants' counsel, [attorney A], telephoned [Wessel]'s attorney at the EEOC, [attorney A], and was informed by her that [Wessel] would not be produced for his deposition.

Prior to the filing of this motion, negotiations pursuant to [Local Court Gen. Rule 12(k)] proved unsuccessful.

The EEOC objects to producing [Wessel] because such a deposition would be unduly burdensome, and because of alleged misstatements made in Defendants' Motion to Compel Attendance. In particular, the EEOC points out that the initial Petition to Perpetuate Testimony of [Wessel] as well as to Produce Documents and for a Physical and Mental Examination were initiated by Defendants. Similarly, the EEOC argues that defendants counsel had ample opportunity to examine [Wessel] during the [November 5, 1992] deposition. The EEOC also points out that attorneys for Defendants requested and received information and documents from [Wessel]'s attorneys in accordance with an order issued by Judge [Kocoras] at a hearing on [October 15, 1992].

The EEOC further argues that it would be unduly burdensome to produce [Wessel] a second time especially in light of the fact that he was questioned extensively concerning his medical condition and its effect upon his ability to perform his job duties. The EEOC contends that Defendants have made no showing that there were material issues which were not covered during the deposition.

DISCUSSION

While I agree with the EEOC that Defendants have failed to make a showing of the material issues not covered during [Mr. Wessel]'s deposition of [November 5, 1992], it is also clear that Defendants were required to take [Mr. Wessel]'s deposition with little or no medical evidence as to [Mr. Wessel]'s terminal cancer condition. The list of health care providers forwarded to Defendants counsel on [October 21, 1992], would not have adequately prepared Defendant for this deposition nor would the two MRI's.

As provided in the Act, the Act currently provides for a three-pronged definition of disability which provides as follows:

A person with disability is

(a)   a person with a physical or mental impairment that substantially limits that person in some major life activity;

(b)   a person with a record of such a physical or mental impairment; or

(c)   a person who is regarded as having such an impairment.

ADA § 3; 42 U.S.C. § 12102(2)

The EEOC regulations to the ADA, which implement the employment title of the law (Title I), repeat this three-prong definition of disability. [*See* 29 C.F.R. § 1630.2(g)]. As indicated by the definition, this impairment must be one that substantially limits the person in a major life activity. [*Id.*] In determining whether a person is substantially limited in a life activity, the potential limitation must be analyzed without regard to the existence of mitigating devices or medicines. See [29 C.F.R. § 1630.2(h),(j) (EEOC GUIDANCE at 35741)]. While most serious medical conditions do have a substantial impact on basic life activities, this impact on [Mr. Wessel] must be established by [Mr. Wessel] to enjoy the protection of the Act.

Further, [Mr. Wessel] must show that he is a qualified individual with a disability. Under the ADA, a "qualified individual with a disability" is a person who, with or without reasonable accommodation can perform the "essentials functions" of the job that the person holds or desires. ADA § 101(8). [Mr. Wessel]'s qualifications or lack thereof could be used by Defendants as a defense.

In light of the fact that [Mr. Wessel]'s condition is a cerebral progressive condition and the effects of this condition vary from case to case, it is only appropriate that [Mr. Wessel] appear for a second deposition where the limitations of his medical condition as well as the essential functions of the job are explored. Defendants could not have adequately prepared for this line of questioning without having reviewed [Mr. Wessel]'s medical records.

I am limiting, however, the scope of this second deposition in accordance with Fed. R. Civ. P. 26(c) from questioning [Mr. Wessel] on issues not covered in the [November 5, 1992] deposition. Fed. R. Civ. P. 26(c) provides that a court may limit the discovery of a party "to protect a party . . . from annoyance, embarrassment, oppression, or undue burden or expense" on a showing of good cause.

Defendants are not to take this opportunity to harass [Mr. Wessel]. If such becomes the case, [Mr. Wessel] may petition the court for a protective order.

INTERROGATORIES

§ 13.17   Drafting Interrogatories

The author of interrogatories must never forget that interrogatories are answered in an adversarial context. If the form of an interrogatory affords room for an opponent to object or to give a vague or unhelpful answer, the opponent is motivated to do so. Accordingly, interrogatories should be narrowly framed, precise, and unambiguous. When preparing interrogatories, it is even more useful than in complaint drafting to change roles or have someone play devil's advocate to see what kinds of objections or useless responses can be made to a preliminary draft of interrogatories. Properly drafted interrogatories support motions for sanctions if an opponent is unresponsive.

One useful technique for minimizing unhelpful responses is to provide branching questions, for example, "State what accommodations you provided plaintiff; if you provided no accommodation, state why not." This reduces the probability of the respondent getting off the hook with a simple "no," or "none were provided."

When a court order or local rule limits the number of interrogatories that may be propounded without special permission,[13] attention must be given to efficiency in drafting interrogatories. For example, by asking, "Who was involved in the decision not to provide accommodation to plaintiff's disability?," only one interrogatory is used. By asking, "Was A involved in deciding not to accommodate plaintiff's disability? Was B involved in failing to accommodate plaintiff's disability? Was C involved in failing to accommodate plaintiff's disability?," three interrogatories are used.

It is more convenient for everyone if interrogatories are propounded and answered in computer-readable form.

§ 13.18   Objections to Interrogatories

Federal Rule of Civil Procedure 33(a) authorizes objections to interrogatories rather than answers, as long as the objections are asserted with particularity and are served more or less contemporaneously with the answers. Counsel objecting to interrogatories should consider at least the following objections, which are usually valid if supported by the form of the question in the underlying factual circumstances:

1. Outside the scope of discovery, for example, privileged or not likely to lead to admissible evidence
2. Vague or ambiguous
3. Overbroad (for example, all documents pertaining to the employer's personnel policies or actions taken pursuant thereto)
4. Unduly burdensome, in light of the cost to respond and the probable utility to the propounding party
5. Request for purely legal conclusions.

The following objections are not likely to be sustained:

1. Inadmissible information
2. Information available to requesting party through other sources

---

[13] Even if Congress postpones or rejects these amendments, a growing number of judges and local rules already limit the number of interrogatories.

3.   Requests an admission
4.   Opinions or contentions.

Objections can be asserted in the response to the interrogatories or, if they relate to an entire set of interrogatories, they may be asserted in a request for a protective order.

§ 13.19   Interrogatory Preparation

The following is a list of the types of information to be requested in interrogatories in an ADA case:

1.   Names of persons providing statements to the responding person or entity
2.   Persons who have been interviewed in connection with the litigation
3.   Other persons with knowledge of the transactions material to the litigation
4.   Existence, nature, description, location, and custodian of documents, including witness statements
5.   Summaries of technical data and statistics, reports, studies, personnel policies, and position evaluations and descriptions material to the litigation and reflecting an employer's overall approach to accommodation under the ADA
6.   Business and corporate information, including the state of incorporation, the relationship between the employing entity and its corporate affiliates, and the assets and income of both the employing entity and its corporate affiliates for relevant time periods
7.   Names of expert witnesses who will testify at trial, or who have been retained or consulted whether or not they will testify.[14]
8.   Opinions and basis for opinions of experts expected to testify at trial
9.   Existence and extent of insurance coverage
10. Information that may be pertinent to an ultimate writ of execution, with appropriate attention to possible garnishment
11. Facts pertinent to establishing personal jurisdiction
12. Basis for contentions expressed or implied by the pleadings or anticipated in amendments to the pleadings.[15]

---

[14] By limiting discovery of facts and opinions held by experts who are not expected to be called, Fed. R. Civ. P. 26(b)(4)(B) implies that the names of such experts are discoverable. Moreover, the phrase "who has been retained or specially employed" implies that the facts known to and opinions held by experts who are regular employees are discoverable like any other information.

[15] Fed. R. Civ. P. 33(b) expressly permits "contention interrogatories."

Interrogatories typically are divided into sections, which include:

1. Prefaces explaining the request and the authority for making the request, including time limits for answering
2. Instructions, including a reminder to conduct a reasonable investigation and an obligation to include information, even if it is hearsay
3. Definitions, including definitions of commonly used words like "describe," "document," and "identify."

§ 13.20 Interrogatories with Detailed Definitions

FORM 13–15
SAMPLE INTERROGATORIES WITH DETAILED DEFINITIONS

[JKL]'S FIRST SET OF INTERROGATORIES TO THE DEFENDANTS

The Plaintiff, [JKL Corporation], hereby requests that the defendants each answer the following interrogatories in accordance with Rule 33 of the Federal Rules of Civil Procedure.

Definitions and Instructions

1. As used herein, the designation ["JKL"] refers to the named plaintiff [JKL Corporation] and any and all predecessor or successor companies, corporations, partnerships, or other business entities; any company, corporation, partnership, or other business entity affiliated with [JKL] or owned by it in whole or in part; and the partners, directors, agents, employees, and attorneys of any of them, including all persons acting or purporting to act on behalf of, or who are subject to the direction or control of, any of the foregoing.

2. The term "document" or "documents" as used herein shall mean any recordation of any intelligence or information, and includes, wherever applicable and without limitation, letters, correspondence, memoranda, notes, reports, compilations, data, notebooks, work papers, graphs, charts, blueprints, books, ledgers, drawings, sketches, schematic diagrams, layouts, logic diagrams, flow charts, part lists, photographs, movies, slides, video recordings, diaries, sales literature, brochures, employee handbooks, employee benefit plans, summary plan descriptions, agreements, minutes of meetings, punch cards, magnetic disks, diskettes, tape or wire, optical disks, printout sheets, and any and all other writings, typings, printings, drafts, copies and/or mechanical, electronic or photographic reproduction or recordations thereof in the possession, custody, or control of the defendants or any of its representatives, or known to any of the foregoing, whether or not prepared by the defendants. "Document" or "documents" also includes all copies which are not identical with the original.

3.   "Water Recreation Equipment" means boats, skis, motorized ski equipment, as well as related and unrelated equipment used for recreational boating.

4.   "Individual Defendant(s)" mean [defendant A], [defendant B], [defendant C], or [defendant D] individually and in any permutation.

5.   Whenever an interrogatory or response refers to a document, the answer shall state the following information with respect to each such document:

(a)   the date appearing on such document, and if no date appears thereon, the answer shall so state and shall give the date or approximate date such document was prepared.

(b)   the identifying or descriptive code number (including production number if already produced), file number, title, or label of such document.

(c)   the general nature or description of such document (i.e., whether it is a letter, memorandum, drawing, etc.) and the number of pages of which it consists.

(d)   the name of the person who signed such document, and if it was not signed, the answer shall so state and shall give the name of the person or persons who prepared it.

(e)   the name of the person to whom such document was addressed and the name of each person other than such addressee to whom such document or copies thereof were given or sent

(f)   the name of the person(s) having possession, custody, or control of such document and any copy thereof.

(g)   whether or not any draft, copy, or reproduction of such document contains or has been subject to any postscript, notation, change, amendment, or addendum not appearing on said document itself, and if so, the answer shall identify as herein required each such draft, copy, or reproduction.

(h)   the source or origin of said document and, if the document was not generated by defendants, specify from whom the document was obtained and identify said person and their relationship to defendants.

(i)   if any such document was, but is no longer in the possession or subject to the control of defendant, state what disposition was made of it and when.

(j)   if any such document is claimed to be privileged, in addition to the foregoing information, state as to each such document:

(i)   the basis on which the claim of privilege is asserted, and

(ii)   a general description of the content thereof.

6.   The term "communication" refers to any exchange or transfer of information whether documentary, oral or otherwise.

7.   The term "things" refers to any physical object other than documents, including without limitation models, structures, components, circuit boards, prototypes, or other devices, and any parts, portions, or assemblies thereof.

8.   Whenever an interrogatory or response refers to a person, state to the extent known, his or her:

(a)   full name;

(b)   present or last known home address;

(c)   present or last known business address;

(d)   present or last known title or occupation;

(e)   present or last known employer; and

(f)   if associated with defendants, the period of times so associated, the nature of the association, and the area of responsibility during such times.

9.   Whenever an interrogatory or response refers to a company, corporation, partnership, joint venture, foundation, educational institution, or other entity, state to the extent known its:

(a)   full name;

(b)   address;

(c)   state of incorporation;

(d)   location or its headquarters;

(e)   location or the divisions), branch(es), or office(s) which is (are) connected with or handled the matter(s) referred to in the interrogatory; and

(f)   identify the person or persons acting or purporting to act on behalf of the entity in connection with the matter(s) referred to in the interrogatory.

10.   Whenever an interrogatory or response refers to "information" or "beliefs," to the extent known:

(a)   identify the person, document, communication, or other source of said of said information or belief;

(b)   identify the person or other recipient of said information or belief;

(c)   state the date said information or belief was communicated;

(d)   state what information or belief was communicated;

(e)   identify all acts, transactions, occurrences, or other activities under-taken to verify or otherwise investigate the veracity of said information or belief;

(f)   state what information was relied upon to form any belief; and,

(g)   identify all documents and communications referring or relating to said information or belief or the information referred to in subsections (a)–(f) hereof.

11.   Whenever an interrogatory or response refers to or seeks a description of an act, transaction, occurrence, dealing omission, or instance, state to the extent known:

(a)   the state, including year, month, and date, when it occurred;

(b)   the place where it occurred;

(c)   the identity of each person participating therein;

(d)   on whose behalf each said person participated or purported to participate.

(e)   the nature, subject matter, and circumstances surrounding it;

(f)   the nature and substance of all communications occurring during, or in connection with it; and

(g)   identify all documents referring or relating thereto or the information referred to in subsections (a)–(f) hereof.

12.   Whenever an interrogatory seeks the basis for an allegation, include all facts, beliefs, acts, transactions, occurrences, dealings, omissions, instances, and communications, and identify all documents and persons that refer or relate to said allegation.

13.   These interrogatories shall be deemed continuing so that with respect to any interrogatory herein, or part thereof, as to which defendants, after answer-ing, acquire additional knowledge or information, [JKL] requests that a supple-mental response be made within thirty (30) days after acquiring such additional knowledge or information.

INTERROGATORY NO. 1

Identify all related and predecessor corporations and business entities (includ-ing subsidiaries, divisions, affiliated, or parent corporations) of the defendant

[ABC] and identify each officer, director, employee, and shareholder for such corporation or business entity.

INTERROGATORY NO. 2

Identify the persons, with tenure dates, who have had for the past ten years responsibility for the following functions of defendant [ABC], its predecessors, and related corporations identified in the Answer to Interrogatory No. 1:

(a)   chief executive officer;

(b)   chief operating officer or general manager;

(c)   manufacturing;

(d)   sales;

(e)   engineering;

(f)   research and development;

(g)   patent activities;

(h)   contract and license;

(i)   the manufacture, marketing, sale, or distribution of water treatment equipment;

(j)   personnel or human resources;

(k)   labor relations;

(l)   employee benefits;

(m)   risk management;

(n)   training;

(o)   legal;

(p)   Board of Directors;

(q)   Treasurer; and

(r)   Secretary.

INTERROGATORY NO. 3

Describe any and all business relationships which presently exist or have in the past existed between or among each of the defendants (in any combination or permutation) and locate and identify all documents and things which refer to, relate to or comment upon any such relationship.

INTERROGATORY NO. 4

Identify all documents and things in the possession, custody, or control of [ABC] and/or the Individual Defendants which:

(a)   any Individual Defendant obtained during or by reason of his employment at [JKL] or during any period of consultancy for [JKL];

(b)   embody or in any way refer to information obtained during and by reason of any individual Defendant's employment at [JKL]; and/or

(c)   embody or in any way refer to information secured, directly or indirectly, from [JKL].

INTERROGATORY NO. 5

As to each individual Defendant for the whole of the time period subsequent to his employment at [JKL] and for [RDP] from [1988] to the present, identify all documents and things which were at one time in his or its possession, custody, or control, which are no longer in his or its possession, custody, or control and which:

(a)   constitute documents or things of [JKL]; and/or

(b)   embody, or in any way, refer to information secured, directly or indirectly, from[JKL].

INTERROGATORY NO. 6

State whether any representative of [ABC] (including the Individual Defendants for the time periods subsequent to the respective dates of termination of their employment at [JKL]) has ever seen any documents, or excerpts thereof, or orally received any information which refers to, relates to, or comments upon:

(a)   the plaintiff's mental or physical condition;

(b)   the plaintiff's ability to perform job functions;

(c)   any request for modification in job functions for plaintiff;

(d)   any evaluation of plaintiff's performance and conduct as an employee; and

(e)   plaintiff's prospects for future employment with any defendant.

INTERROGATORY NO. 7

If the response to any part of Interrogatory No. 6 is affirmative, state for each occurrence:

(a)   when and where each such document was seen or such oral information was received;

(b)   by whom and to whom each document was shown or such oral information disclosed;

(c)   how each such document or oral information was obtained;

(d)   whether [ABC] and/or any individual Defendant now has each such document,

and, if not, when and how it lost possession thereof and the present location of each such document; and

(e)   identify all such documents presently in the possession, custody or control of any defendant.

INTERROGATORY NO. 8

Identify all documents which refer or relate in any way to a need or desire on the part of defendant [ABC] to respond to or meet its obligations under any law covering mental or physical disabilities in:

(a)   employees;

(b)   suppliers; and

(c)   customers.

§ 13.21   Sample Employee Interrogatories for ADA Claim

FORM 13–16
SAMPLE EMPLOYEE INTERROGATORIES FOR ADA CLAIM

§ 1 Reasons for Employee Termination and Employer Justification

1)   Why was the plaintiff/employee terminated?

2)   Are there any documents reflecting this reason for termination? Please describe briefly each such document, and provide copies of them.

3)   What, if anything, was the plaintiff told was the reason for termination? By whom? When? Please give dates and names of persons participating, and describe what was said to the plaintiff and by the plaintiff on each occasion.

4)   At what time did you begin contemplating the discharge of the plaintiff? Please state the exact date.

5)   Did the plaintiff ever make any complaints about your policies or practices? If the answer is "yes," provide dates, times, summary of the complaints, and identify by name, address, and telephone number the person to whom the complaint was made.

6)   Please describe the incident or series of incidents that prompted you first to consider terminating the plaintiff. In your answer, please describe exactly what the plaintiff did or did not do.

7)   What was your response to this conduct of the plaintiff include the date, the name of any person designated to act in your behalf, and the action you took.

8)   If you told the plaintiff about plaintiff's conduct, please state as precisely as you can what you said, and state the time, date, and place of this communication. If you communicated to the plaintiff in writing, please describe the content of the communication, and state the date the communication was sent or given to the plaintiff.

9)   Why do you feel that the plaintiff's conduct could not be tolerated, consistent with the business needs of your firm?

§ 2 Contract Formation and Terms of the Employment Relation

10)   Was the employee/plaintiff ever told anything orally, or in writing, regarding how long employment would last, or the conditions under which the employment would end?

11)   Did you ever tell the plaintiff that it would take a certain discrete period of time to complete fully the task or tasks for which she was hired? If so, state the date and circumstances under which the statement was made, and the time period mentioned.

12)   Did you ever represent to the plaintiff that the job would last for a specific length of time? If so, how long?

13)   Did you ever represent to the plaintiff that plaintiff's job was dependent on the performance of tasks, or on the fulfillment of certain conditions? If so, please specify the date on which the representations were made, by whom, in what form, and the precise details of the tasks and conditions.

14)   Did you ever represent to the plaintiff that plaintiff would never have to worry about being discharged? If so, state the time, place, and form of the representation, and the name of the person(s) who made such a representation.

15)   Did you ever represent to the plaintiff that all employees of the company would be treated fairly? If so, state the time, date, place, and form of such representations, and the name of the person(s) who made the representations.

16)   Did you ever represent to the plaintiff that plaintiff would be dismissed if plaintiff engaged in certain conduct or failed to meet certain performance requirements? If so, please state the time, date, and place such representations were made, the name of the person(s) who made the representations, and the form of the representations.

17)   Do you believe that you treat your employees fairly? If so, please state your reasons why. How do you ensure that first-level supervisors treat your employees fairly?

18)   Do you have a written personnel policy handbook, or an employee manual? If so, please state when it was created, describe any revisions made since it was created, and describe its contents. Please provide a copy.

19)   What is the purpose of the employee handbook or manual?

20)   Do you give the employee manual or policy handbook to the employees? If so, please state when the manual or policy handbook is given to employees.

21)   Was the plaintiff given a copy of the employee handbook or manual? If so, please state the time, date, and place of the distribution.

22)   Did a person authorized to make representations on your behalf explain the meaning of the handbook or policy manual to the plaintiff? If so, please state the name of the person who made such representation, as well as his/her address and position/job title. In addition, please describe the explanation that this representative made at the time of distribution of the manual or handbook.

23)   Do other documents exist that were written in connection with the creation of the employee handbook or manual? If so, please describe their content.

24)   Who wrote the employee handbook or manual? Please state their names, addresses, and positions.

25)   Do you believe the employee handbook or manual to be apart of the plaintiff's employment contract with you? If not, please state your reasons for this belief.

26) Is there any reason why the plaintiff would believe that you do not follow the policies articulated or procedures outlined in the handbook or manual? If so, please give your reasons.

27) When you gave the plaintiff the handbook or manual, did you intend to be bound by it? If not, please explain why.

28) Do you expect employees to comply with provisions of the handbook or manual? Which provisions?

29) Do you have a standard application for employment form? If the answer is "yes" please provide a copy.

30) Did the plaintiff fill out an application for employment form? If the answer is "yes," please provide a copy.

31) Why do you think that the plaintiff came to work for you?

32) After you hired the plaintiff, were you aware of any offers made to plaintiff for new employment? If so, please state the date and substance of the offers, to the best of your knowledge.

33) Did the plaintiff discuss these offers with anyone in your enterprise? If the answer is "yes," summarize the nature of such discussions and state what was said to the plaintiff.

34) After you hired the plaintiff, did plaintiff arrive for work at the stated time? Please state the date upon which plaintiff's work began.

§ 3 Procedures Utilized in Connection with the Termination

35) When the plaintiff was terminated, what procedure was followed? Please list each step, the result, the date upon which the step was taken, and the person in charge of administering the particular steps.

36) Please describe any additional actions that you took, or actions taken by any person designated by you to act, in response to any conduct by the plaintiff.

37) If you told the plaintiff anything regarding plaintiff's conduct, please state as well as you can what you said, and the date, time, and place of such statements.

38) If you had any written communication with the plaintiff regarding plaintiff's conduct, please describe the content of the communication, and the date on which it was sent or given to the plaintiff.

39)   Did you at any time cause anyone to investigate any fact of the plaintiff's life, including conduct on or off the job? If so, please state the investigator's name, address, and time period during which the investigations were conducted.

40)   If an investigation was made of the plaintiff, were reports made to you? If the answer is "yes," please state the date on which the reports were made, the nature of the reports, and their content.

41)   What means were used to investigate the plaintiff? Please describe the means in detail.

42)   If an investigation of the plaintiff was made, were any reports made? If so, please state the dates of the reports, and their nature and content.

43)   Did you ever tell the plaintiff that plaintiff would be terminated on a date other than the date the plaintiff was actually terminated? If so, please state the date and place such statements were made, and the name, address, and position of the person who made the statements.

44)   If you did not tell the plaintiff prior to the date that plaintiff was terminated that plaintiff would be terminated, please explain why you did not?

45)   Was the decision to terminate the plaintiff subject to review by someone else before the termination was effected? If so, by whom?

46)   Before you terminated the plaintiff's employment, did you consider how the plaintiff would feel when plaintiff was terminated? If you did, please describe your thoughts at the time.

47)   Do you believe that the plaintiff expected to be terminated? If so, please state your reasons for this belief.

48)   Was the plaintiff afforded any kind of internal hearing or review before plaintiff was terminated? If so, please describe, giving the dates and the names of the persons participating in each step. Are there any written records or documents summarizing, or otherwise memorializing, what transpired while these procedures were being followed? Please describe each of these documents.

49)   If you personally terminated the plaintiff, please describe the plaintiff's reaction to the termination. If another employee terminated the plaintiff, please state the person's name, address, and position.

50)   When you were contemplating terminating the employment of the plaintiff, did you talk with anyone about this pending decision? If so, please state the person's name, address, and position (if employed by you), and describe the nature and content of the communication.

51)   During the termination, was any other person present? If so, please state the person's name, address, and position, if employed by you.

52)   Did the plaintiff undertake to arbitrate or mediate the termination? If so, please describe the steps taken, the results, the dates upon which the steps were taken, and the names and addresses of all persons involved.

53)   After the plaintiff's termination, did you communicate with any other person about the decision, excluding attorneys? If so, state the other person's name, address, and position (if your employee), and describe the nature and content of the discussion.

§ 4 Employer's Assessment of the Plaintiff's Job Performance

54)   Are there any written evaluations of the plaintiff's performance during plaintiff's tenure with the company? Do you have any other documents reflecting the plaintiff's performance during the time that plaintiff was employed by you? If so, please describe, and please provide copies of such documents.

55)   Do you have documents describing your initial evaluation of the plaintiff prior to the time plaintiff started working for you? If do, please describe them, and provide copies.

56)   Do you have any documents describing any disciplinary action taken against the plaintiff? If so, please describe, and provide copies.

57)   Was the plaintiff ever counseled in any way regarding plaintiff's conduct or performance? If so, please give the dates, and names of persons participating in such counseling. What was said on each occasion to the plaintiff and by the plaintiff?

58)   How would you characterize the plaintiff's overall work performance?

59)   Did the plaintiff receive any awards or commendations? If so, please gives that dates and describe.

60)   Why did the plaintiff's employment continue for as long as it did?

§ 5 Discovering Similarly Situated Personnel

61)   Have any other employees ever been terminated for the same reason as the plaintiff? Please give the names of these employees and the dates of termination.

62)   What other employees performed at the same level as the plaintiff and engaged in conduct similar to the plaintiff's? Please give the names and a brief summary of their performance, conduct, and any personnel actions taken.

63) Who, if anyone, is now filling the plaintiff's job?

64) Is anyone now performing the plaintiff's job duties? Who?

§ 6 Background Information About the Employer

65) Describe the nature of your business. Include the number of employees, the type of work they do, and the institutions or persons they serve, if applicable.

66) How many distinct plants or facilities are part of the employing enterprise? Please provide a list of all such plants and facilities.

67) What is the legal form of the employing enterprise (partnership, corporation, proprietorship)?

68) In what state is the employing enterprise registered or incorporated?

69) If the employing enterprise is a corporation, is the stock publicly traded? If so, what is its symbol, and on which exchange is it traded?

70) If the employing enterprise is a corporation, please provide a list of the ten most significant owners of stock in the company.

71) Are you required to be licensed by state, local, or federal governments to perform your business functions? If so, please describe the licenses held, and provide the name and address of the issuing agency.

72) Are you subject to any state or federal civil service laws or regulations? If so, please briefly describe their nature, or state in what publication they may be found.

73) When did the plaintiff first begin working for you? Please state the exact date.

74) Who was the plaintiff's supervisor?

75) Who made the decision to terminate the plaintiff's employment?

76) Has this person ever terminated any other employees? If so, please give the employee's names and the dates of termination.

§ 7 Witness Identification

77) What are the names, phone numbers, and addresses of employees who can testify to (i) employer policies or statements, or (ii) conduct showing employer policy, practice, and performance, or (iii) conduct of the plaintiff?

§ 8 Other Formal Proceedings Related to the Termination

78)   Was any hearing held on an unemployment claim by the plaintiff? Were any other documents or records made memorializing the hearing?

79)   Did the company contest any claim for unemployment benefits made by the plaintiff? If not, why not? Do you have any internal procedures for grievance processing? If so, please state (i) when such procedures came into effect, (ii) the name, address, and position of the person or persons responsible for administering them, and (iii) the nature of the procedures.

80)   Did you have in effect any arbitration or mediation procedure, either formal or informal, at the time of plaintiff's termination? If so, please describe the steps taken under this procedure, and describe the procedure as a whole.

81)   Do you know of any company or official investigation or inquiry into the circumstances surrounding the plaintiff's termination?

§ 9 Reasonable Accommodation by Employer/Undue Hardship

82)   Did your company perform a preemployment medical examination on the plaintiff? If so, were any major medical problems discovered? Please attach a copy of the doctor's written report pertaining to the plaintiff's examination. Does your company as a practice subject all employees to a medical examination prior to the commencement of their employment?

83)   When the plaintiff began working for you, did you believe her to be a "qualified individual with a disability," as defined by the Americans with Disabilities Act ("ADA"), 42 U.S.C. § 12101 *et seq.*?

84)   If the answer to the preceding question is "yes," what mental or physical impairment did you or do you believe the plaintiff to have? Please explain.

85)   Do you contend that you attempted to make a "reasonable accommodation," as defined by the ADA, to cope with the plaintiff's disability? What steps, if any, did you take to accommodate the plaintiff's disability?

86) Do you contend that to make an accommodation for the plaintiff's disability would constitute an "undue hardship," as defined by the ADA? If the answer is "yes," please state in some detail why such an accommodation would constitute an undue hardship.

87)   Why is the plaintiff, in your opinion, no longer qualified to perform plaintiff's job? What essential job functions is the plaintiff unable to perform?

88)   Are there any other jobs with your company similar to the plaintiff's former job that plaintiff would be capable of performing? Did you attempt to have

the plaintiff try another job after you concluded that plaintiff was no longer capable of performing plaintiff's previous job?

89)   Do you contend that even if you make reasonable accommodations, the plaintiff still will be unable to perform essential job functions? If so, please specifically describe what functions plaintiff cannot perform.

90)   Do you contend that the demand for accommodation for the plaintiff requires elimination of an essential function of the job? If you do, identify the function or functions.

91)   What do you believe would be the economic cost to you in order to accommodate the disability of the plaintiff?

92)   Would it be possible for you to reassign the plaintiff to a lower-graded position because you cannot make the accommodations to allow the plaintiff to remain in plaintiff's former position?

93)   Could you conceivably restructure the plaintiff's job requirements in order to allow plaintiff to continue working in the position occupied prior to the termination of employment?

94)   Do you have any employees who suffer from the same disability as the plaintiff? If so, please state their names, positions, and addresses.

95)   Do you contend that the plaintiff's disability poses a health or safety threat to other employees of your company? Do you contend that the plaintiff's disability poses a direct threat to plaintiff? Specifically identify the threat or threats.

96)   Do you contend that the plaintiff has a substance abuse problem? If so, what leads you to this conclusion? Please provide copies of any drug test results or relevant other materials. Do you believe that the plaintiff has ever completed a supervised drug rehabilitation program?

97)   Do you have notices posted in accessible format to applicants, employees, and members describing the applicable portions of the ADA? If so, where are such notices posted? Please provide a specific geographical description.

98)   What major life activities of the plaintiff do you believe are substantially limited by plaintiff's disability?

99)   Are there certain preemployment tests associated with the plaintiff's former job that you believe plaintiff is presently unable to pass? If so, please describe the tests as best you can, and provide a copy of them, if possible. Are all entering employees subject to this examination regardless of disability?

100) Do you contend that business necessity forces you to deny continuing employment to the plaintiff, given plaintiff's disability? Please describe in detail what business necessity, if any, makes you unable to make a reasonable accommodation for the plaintiff's disability.[16]

§ 13.22   First Interrogatories (EEOC)

FORM 13–17
SAMPLE FIRST INTERROGATORIES (EEOC)

IN THE UNITED STATES DISTRICT COURT

FOR THE [NORTHERN] DISTRICT OF [ILLINOIS]

[EASTERN] DIVISION

U.S. EQUAL EMPLOYMENT OPPORTUNITY COMMISSION,

Plaintiffs,

Civil Action No. [92 C 7330]

v.

[A.I.C. SECURITY INVESTIGATIONS, LTD.];

[A.I.C. INTERNATIONAL, LTD.]; and [unnamed defendant C],

Defendants.   Judge [Marvin E. Aspen]

EQUAL EMPLOYMENT OPPORTUNITY COMMISSION'S
FIRST SET OF INTERROGATORIES TO DEFENDANTS

Pursuant to Rule 33 of the Federal Rules of Civil Procedure, Plaintiff Equal Employment Opportunity Commission (the "EEOC") hereby propounds the following Interrogatories to Defendants [A.I.C. Security Investigations, Ltd. ("A.I.C.")]; [A.I.C. International, Ltd. ("A.I.C. International")], and [defendant C], to be answered fully in writing and under oath within forty-five (45) days from the date of receipt of this request, or such shorter period as may be ordered by the Court.

---

[16] These interrogatories were compiled by Mark R. Lisker, assistant to Henry H. Perritt, Jr., in June 1993.

DEFINITIONS AND INSTRUCTIONS

For each of these Interrogatories, and unless a different meaning is clearly required by the context, the following definitions shall apply:

1. "Defendants" as used herein includes Defendants and their attorneys and agents, including, but not limited to, any agent or consultant employed by said attorneys in connection with this litigation received to Plaintiff's First Set of Interrogatories or First Request for Production of Documents.

2. "Person" as used herein refers to a natural person, or, if applicable, any form of legal entity such as a partnership, association, or corporation.

3. "Document" as used herein refers to and includes, but is not limited to, all writings of any kind, including the original and all nonidentical copies (whether different from the original by reason of notations made on such copies, or otherwise) of all letters, telegrams, memoranda, reports, forms, invoices, advertisements, statements, studies, contracts, calendar or diary entries, pamphlets, notes, charts, diagrams, plans, outlines, tabulations, proposals, minutes and records of meetings, conferences, and telephone or other communications, and every form of mechanical, electronic or electrical recording or date compilation, including all forms of machine or computer storage or retrieval.

4. "Identify," when used herein with respect to a document, means to state the title of the document; the date of the document, the author(s) of the document, the addressees of the document, a detailed description of the contents of the document, and the present location and possessor(s) of the original and each copy of the document.

5. "Identify" when used in reference to a person, means to state the name, social security number, last known business address, last known home address, and last known position held by the person being identified.

6. If asked to state the facts upon which Defendants base an allegation or contention, state all of the facts known or available to Defendants, whether in possession of Defendants' attorneys, or other agents, and state the identity of the person who has knowledge of said facts, together with the identity of any documents relating to each of said facts.

7. If Defendants identify any documents which have been lost, discarded, or destroyed, such documents shall be identified in a written response as completely as possible, including the following information: author, addressee, date, subject matter, date of disposal, person authorizing the disposal, and person disposing of the document.

INTERROGATORIES

1.   With respect to Defendant [A.I.C.], state:

a.   Its correct legal name;

b.   Any other names by which [A.I.C.] has been known, and dates when such name was used;

c.   The state and date of incorporation;

d.   The identification of all officers from [January 1, 1986], to the present;

e.   The identification of its owners from [January 1, 1986], to the present;

f.   Its relationship to [A.I.C. International] and to [defendant C].

g.   The number of its employees on [July 29, 1992], and the identity of all documents reflecting the number of employees on that date;

h.   The number of its employees on [November 5, 1992], and the identity of all documents reflecting the number of employees on that date.

2.   With respect to [A.I.C. International], state:

a.   Its correct legal name;

b.   Any other names by which [A.I.C. International] has been known, and dates when such name was used;

c.   The State and date of its incorporation;

d.   The identification of all officers from [January 1, 1986], to the present;

e.   The identification of its owners from [January 1, 1986], to the present;

f.   The nature of its business;

g.   The number of its employees on [July 29, 1992], and the identification of all documents reflecting the number of employees on that date;

h.   The number of its employees on [November 5, 1992], and the identification of all documents reflecting the number of employees on that date; and

i.   The names and the nature of all businesses held by [A.I.C. International], and the number of employees of each such business on [July 29, 1992], and on [November 5, 1992].

3.   State every reason for the termination of [Charles H. Wessel ("Wessel")], and identify all documents which relate to or support such reasons, and all persons having knowledge of any such reason.

4.   With respect to the decision to terminate [Wessel]:

a.   Identify all persons who participated in the decision and the nature of their participation;

b.   State the date, location, and identity of all participants with respect to all conversations between any of the persons identified in subpart a with each other and/or with [Wessel] concerning the termination and the reasons for the termination;

c.   State the substance of each conversation identified in subpart b.

d.   Identify all documents reflecting any such conversations.

5.   Identify all customers of [A.I.C.] whose contracts were overseen by an [A.I.C.] employee other than [Wessel] from [January 1, 1992], through [July 31, 1992].

6.   Identify all customers of [A.I.C.] whose contracts were overseen by an [A.I.C.] employee other than [Wessel] from [January 1, 1992], through [July 31, 1992]. For each such customer state:

a.   The name of the [A.I.C.] employee who had responsibility for the account;

b.   The date on which the [A.I.C.] employee assumed responsibility for the account;

c.   The identity of the individual who represented the customer with respect to the account.

7.   Identify all conversations between [defendant C], or any employee of Defendants, whether in person or by telephone, with any physician or employee of a physician, concerning [Wessel]'s health and/or his ability to work. For each such conversation state:

a.   The date of the conversation;

b.   The identity of the participants;

c.   The substance of the conversation;

d.   The identity of any documents which reflect the conversation.

8.   With respect to [Wessel], state:

a.   His date of hire;

b.   His salary at hire;

c.   The dates and amounts of all salary increases throughout his employment, and the identity of the person(s) determining each such salary increase;

d.   The dates and amounts of all bonuses paid to [Wessel] throughout his employment, and the identity of the person(s) determining each such bonus;

9.   Describe every accommodation offered to [Wessel] because of his disability, and with respect to each such accommodation state:

a.   Whether [Wessel] requested the accommodation, and, if so, on what date;

b.   The identity of the person(s) who decided to make the accommodation;

c.   Whether the accommodation was necessary in order to allow [Wessel] to perform the essential functions of the job;

d.   The date on which the accommodation was made, and if the accommodation was a continuing one;

e.   The identity of all documents reflecting or pertaining to such accommodation.

10.   Describe any accommodation [Wessel] requested which was not made by Defendants. For each such requested accommodation, state:

a.   The date the accommodation was requested;

b.   The identity of the person(s) denying the accommodation;

c.   Every reason that the accommodation was denied;

d.   If defendants claim that the accommodation would have created an undue hardship, describe the nature of the undue hardship;

e.   The identity of all documents which reflect or pertain to the requested accommodation and its denial.

11.   Identify and describe each essential function and each marginal function of the position of Executive Director of [A.I.C.].

12.   Describe each essential function of the position of Executive Director which was reassigned to another employee between [January 1, 1987], and [August 1, 1992]. For each such reassignment state:

a.   The date of the reassignment;

b.   The identity of the person making the reassignment;

c.   The identity of the person(s) to whom the essential function was reassigned;

d.   The duration of the reassignment;

e.   The identity of the person(s) who have performed the function since [August 1, 1992];

f.   The identity of all documents which reflect or pertain to the transfer of the essential function.

13.   State the annual earnings of [A.I.C.] for each year from 1987–1992.

14.   State every reason for the termination of [another individual] and identify all documents which relate to or refer to the reasons for his termination, and identify all persons with knowledge of any reason for the termination of [another individual].

15.   For each refusal to Admit a Request to Admit propounded by EEOC, describe all facts which support the refusal to admit and identify all persons with knowledge of said facts, and all documents which reflect or pertain to such facts.

§ 13.23   Objections to Interrogatories and First Request for Production (EEOC)

FORM 13–18
SAMPLE OBJECTIONS TO INTERROGATORIES AND FIRST REQUEST FOR PRODUCTION (EEOC)

IN THE UNITED STATES DISTRICT COURT

FOR THE [NORTHERN] DISTRICT OF [ILLINOIS]

[EASTERN] DIVISION

U.S. EQUAL EMPLOYMENT OPPORTUNITY COMMISSION,

Plaintiffs,

Civil Action No. [92 C 7330]

v.

[A.I.C. SECURITY INVESTIGATIONS, LTD.];

[A.I.C. INTERNATIONAL, LTD.]; and [unnamed defendant C],

Defendants.   Judge [Marvin E. Aspen]

DEFENDANTS' OBJECTIONS TO PLAINTIFF'S FIRST SET OF INTERROGATORIES AND FIRST REQUEST FOR PRODUCTION OF DOCUMENTS

Defendants, [A.I.C. SECURITY INVESTIGATIONS, LTD.], [A.I.C. INTERNATIONAL, LTD.], and [defendant C], by and through their attorneys, [WESSELS & PAUTSCH, P.C.], by [Charles W. Pautsch], [attorney A], and [attorney B], hereby sets forth the following objections to Plaintiff Equal Employment Oppor-tunity Commission's First Set of Interrogatories and First Request for Production of Documents:

Interrogatory No. 13: State the annual earnings of [A.I.C.] for each year from [1987]–[1992].

OBJECTION: Defendants object. The information sought by Interrogatory No. 13 is not reasonably calculated to lead to the discovery of admissible evidence and would be unduly burdensome to produce. In addition, Defendants object because the term "annual earnings" is vague.

Interrogatory No. 14: State every reason for the termination of [David P.] and identify all documents which relate to or refer to the reasons for his termination, and identify all persons with knowledge of any reason for the termination of [David P.].

OBJECTION: Defendants object. The information sought by Interrogatory No. 14 is not reasonably calculated to lead to the discovery of admissible evidence.

Interrogatory No. 15: For each refusal to admit a Request to Admit propounded by EEOC, describe all facts which support the refusal to admit and identify all persons with knowledge of said facts, and all documents which reflect or pertain to such facts.

OBJECTION: Defendants object. The information sought in part by Interrogatory No. 15 was either properly objected to in Defendants' responses to Plaintiff's Request to Admit or seeks legal conclusions which do not constitute proper inquiries under Rule 33, Fed. R. Civ. P. In addition, Defendants object because the information sought in part by Interrogatory No. 15 seeks extended narrative which Plaintiff will have a proper opportunity to gather through depositions. Furthermore, Defendants object to Interrogatory No. 15 because it is vague.

Request No. 2: Personnel files of [Charles H. Wessel ("Wessel")], [Victor V.], [David P.], [Lawrence R.], [Edward B.], [Jan D.], and [Beverly K.].

OBJECTION: Defendants object. The documents which Request No. 2 seek are not reasonably calculated to the discovery of admissible evidence and would impose an unreasonable burden and expense upon Defendants in having, to produce such documents. Without waiving said objection, Defendants state that they will produce the personnel files of [Charles H. Wessel].

Request No. 3: All contracts between [A.I.C.] and its customers which were overseen by [Wessel] from [February 1, 1986], through [July 31, 1992].

OBJECTION: Defendants object. The documents which Request No. 3 seek are not reasonably calculated to lead to the discovery of admissible evidence and would impose an unreasonable burden and expense upon Defendants in having to produce such document. In addition, Defendants object because the contracts which Request No. 3 seek are confidential containing proprietary information, and therefore are not properly discoverable.

Request No. 3: All documents which show profits and liabilities for [A.I.C.] for the years [1987]–[1992], including but limited to, year-end balance sheets or financial statements.

OBJECTION: Defendants object. The documents which request No. 3 seek are not reasonably calculated to lead to the discovery of admissible evidence and would impose and unreasonable burden and expense upon Defendants in having to produce such documents. In addition, such documents are confidential containing proprietary information, and therefore are not properly discoverable.

Dated this [27th] day of [November], [1992].

§ 13.24   Plaintiff's Motion to Compel

FORM 13–19
SAMPLE PLAINTIFF'S MOTION TO COMPEL

IN THE UNITED STATES DISTRICT COURT

FOR THE [NORTHERN] DISTRICT OF [ILLINOIS]

[EASTERN] DIVISION

U.S. EQUAL EMPLOYMENT OPPORTUNITY COMMISSION,

Plaintiffs,

v.

Civil Action No. [92 C 7330]

[A.I.C. SECURITY INVESTIGATIONS, LTD.];

[A.I.C. INTERNATIONAL, LTD.]; and [unnamed defendant C],

Defendants.   Judge [Marvin E. Aspen]

PLAINTIFF'S MOTION TO COMPEL

Plaintiff, the Equal Employment Opportunity Commission (the "EEOC"), respectfully moves the Court, pursuant to Rule 37 of the Federal Rules of Civil Procedure, for an Order compelling Defendants [A.I.C. Security Investigations, Ltd.], [A.I.C. International, Ltd.], and [defendant C] [(collectively "A.I.C.")] to respond to EEOC's First Set of Interrogatories and EEOC's First Request for Production of Documents. In support of its Motion, EEOC states as follows:

1.   This is an action brought pursuant to the Americans with Disabilities Act of 1990 (ADA), 42 U.S.C. § 12101 *et seq.,* alleging that [A.I.C.] discharged [Charles H. Wessel], a qualified individual with a disability, because of his disability, terminal cancer. The action was filed on [November 5, 1992], and, because of the nature of the disability, EEOC moved for expedited discovery.

2.   On [November 6, 1992], EEOC served [A.I.C.], by facsimile mail to their attorney, with EEOC's First Set of Interrogatories, (attached as Exhibit 1) and First Request for Production of Documents (attached as Exhibit 2).

3.   On [November 12, 1992], the Court granted EEOC's Motion for Expedited Discovery and ordered that all written discovery is to be answered by any party within seven days of receipt. The Order also provided a discovery cutoff date of [December 31, 1992]. Pursuant to the Order, responses to EEOC's written discovery were due no later than [November 17, 1992].

4. On [November 30, 1992], EEOC received Defendants' Objections to Plaintiff's First Set of Interrogatories and First Request for Production of Documents (attached as Exhibit 3). No responses were received to the Interrogatories and Document Requests to which there were no objections.

5.   On [December 1, 1992], a telephone conference was conducted pursuant to [Rule 12(k)] of the Local Rules of the [Northern District] of [Illinois]. Participants were [A], attorney for the EEOC, [B], attorney for the EEOC, and [defense attorney B], attorney for [A.I.C.]. During the conference it was agreed that [A.I.C.] would withdraw its objections to certain Interrogatories and Document Requests if EEOC would agree to a protective order concerning proprietary information. [A.I.C.] maintains its objections to Interrogatory 14 and Document Request 3.

6.   During the [12(k)] conference [defense attorney B] stated that he would attempt to provide Interrogatory answers by [December 4, 1992]. He did not know when the requested documents would be available.

7.   As of the date of this Motion, no responses have been received.

For the foregoing reasons, EEOC respectfully requests that the Court issue an Order compelling [A.I.C.] to provide forthwith full responses to EEOC's First Set of Interrogatories and First Request for Production of Documents, including those objected to by[A.I.C.]. In further support of its Motion, EEOC submits a Memorandum, and requests that the case be set for a Pre-Trial conference pursuant to Rule 16(a) of the Federal Rules of Civil Procedure.

§ 13.25   —Memorandum Supporting Motion to Compel Answers to Interrogatories

FORM 13–20
SAMPLE MEMORANDUM SUPPORTING MOTION TO COMPEL ANSWERS TO INTERROGATORIES

IN THE UNITED STATES DISTRICT COURT

FOR THE [NORTHERN] DISTRICT OF [ILLINOIS]

[EASTERN] DIVISION

U.S. EQUAL EMPLOYMENT OPPORTUNITY COMMISSION,

Plaintiff,

v.

Civil Action No. [92 C 7330]

[A.I.C. SECURITY INVESTIGATIONS, LTD.];

[A.I.C. INTERNATIONAL, LTD.]; and [unnamed defendant C]

Defendants.   Judge [Marvin E. Aspen]

EEOC REPLY MEMORANDUM IN SUPPORT OF MOTION TO COMPEL

Plaintiff, Equal Employment Opportunity Commission (the "EEOC") respectfully submits this Reply Memorandum in support of its Motion to Compel Answers to its First Interrogatories and First Request for Production of Docu-ments.

Since the filing of EEOC's Motion, the Court on [December 8, 1992] granted Defendants' [("A.I.C.'s")] Motion for an extension of time to answer written discovery to [December 15, 1992]. On [December 7, 1992], EEOC received responses to

EEOC's First Interrogatories, in which [A.I.C]. maintained its objections discussed in the previous Memoranda. [A.I.C.] further objected to two additional Interrogatories, which EEOC counsel had believed to be resolved. See Letter from [EEOC attorney A] to [A.I.C. attorney B], dated [December 2, 1992], attached as Exhibit 1; Letter from [A.I.C. attorney B] to [EEOC attorney A] dated [December 3, 1992], attached as Exhibit 2. The Answers to Interro-gatories were not made under oath as required by Rule 33 of the Federal Rules of Civil Procedure. This Memorandum will address Defendants' continued objections: 1) to production of information concerning the termination of [David P.]; 2) to information concerning [A.I.C.]'s annual earnings; 3) to identification of documents and persons with knowledge concerning [A.I.C.]'s failure to admit certain requests for admissions; and 4) to information concerning contracts overseen by [Charles Wessel].

1.   In their Memorandum in Response to the Motion to Compel, [A.I.C.] asserts that it should not be compelled to provide information concerning the reasons for the termination of [David P.], former President of [A.I.C.], and [Wessel]'s immediate supervisor, because "the reasons for his [David P.'s] termination from [A.I.C. International, Ltd.] do not relate in any way to the issues to be tried." Defendants' Memorandum, p. 2. The argument is refuted by Defendants' subpoena of [David P.] for deposition on [December 16, 1992], requiring him to produce any and all documents which relate in any way to "(1) [David P.]'s termination of employment with [A.I.C. International, Ltd.]" (Attached as Exhibit 3.)

2.   Interrogatory 13 requests information concerning the annual earnings of [A.I.C.]. Defendants objected on grounds of relevance, burdensomeness, and vagueness. EEOC counsel believed that these objections had been withdrawn, based on EEOC's willingness to agree to a protective order covering any propri-etary information. See Exhibits I and 2. However, the earnings of the Division of which [Wessel] was Executive Director are obviously relevant to his capabilities as the Manager of the Division. There is minimal burden in producing audited financial statements, as testified to by [Philip W.], Comptroller of [A.I.C.], at his deposition on [December 8, 1992].

3.   Interrogatory 15 requests facts concerning [A.I.C.]'s refusals to admit, and identification of documents which support such refusals and persons with knowledge of the alleged facts. During the [12(k)] conference, EEOC agreed to limit the request to identification of documents and witnesses. See Exhibit 1. The disputed requests to admit concern [Wessel]'s ability to perform the essen-tial functions of his job (Requests 9 and 10), [Wessel]'s qualifications (Request 13), and his disability (Requests 11 and 12). EEOC is clearly entitled to all docu-ments pertaining to, and witnesses with knowledge of, these issues.

4.   Finally, Defendants' objection to producing customer contracts overseen by [Wessel] during his tenure as Executive Director is without merit. In its Answers to Interrogatories, [A.I.C.] admits that one of the essential functions of the Executive Director position is to "direct and represent the company regarding customer relations." Answer to Interrogatory 11. Defendants' "most important"

objection to production of the documents, that they contain valuable proprietary information, fails to acknowledge that EEOC has offered to agree to a protective order which would require confidentiality of any proprietary information.

For the foregoing reasons, and for the reasons set forth in EEOC's previous memorandum, EEOC respectfully requests that Defendants be ordered to submit Answers to Interrogatories under oath, that they be compelled to Answer Interrogatory 14 concerning the reasons for the termination of [David P.], and that they be ordered to produce contracts overseen by [Wessel] during his tenure as Executive Director.

§ 13.26   Defendants' Motion to Compel Answers to Interrogatories and Responses to Requests for Admission

FORM 13–21
SAMPLE MOTION TO COMPEL ANSWERS TO INTERROGATORIES AND RESPONSES TO REQUESTS FOR ADMISSION

IN THE UNITED STATES DISTRICT COURT

FOR THE [NORTHERN] DISTRICT OF [ILLINOIS]

[EASTERN] DIVISION

U.S. EQUAL EMPLOYMENT OPPORTUNITY COMMISSION,

Plaintiff,

v.

Civil Action No. [92 C 7330]

[A.I.C. SECURITY INVESTIGATIONS, LTD.];

[A.I.C. INTERNATIONAL, LTD.]; and [unnamed defendant C],

Defendants.

Honorable [Marvin E. Aspen]

Magistrate Judge [Ronald A. Guzman]

DEFENDANTS' EMERGENCY MOTION TO COMPEL ANSWERS
TO DEFENDANTS' SECOND SET OF INTERROGATORIES AND
REQUESTS FOR ADMISSIONS TO PLAINTIFF [WESSEL]

Defendants, [A.I.C. SECURITY INVESTIGATIONS, LTD.], [A.I.C. INTERNA-
TIONAL, LTD.], and [unnamed defendant C], by and through their attorneys,
[WESSELS & PAUTSCH, P.C.], by [Charles W. Pautsch], [attorney A] and [attor-
ney B], pursuant to Rule 37, Fed. R. Civ. P., and [Local Court General Rule 12],
hereby set forth their Emergency Motion to Compel Answers to Defendants'
First Requests for Admissions to Plaintiff Equal Employment Opportunity
Commission as follows:

1.   On [January 19, 1993], Defendants served upon Plaintiff [Wessel]
Defendants' Second Set of Interrogatories to be answered pursuant to Court Order,
within seven (7) days of receipt.

2.   Defendants' Second Set of Interrogatories to Plaintiff [Wessel] seek
information reasonably calculated to lead to the discovery of admissible evidence. Specifically, Defendants' Second Set of Interrogatories inquires into the
financial status of Plaintiff [Wessel]. Such information is relevant to this action
since Plaintiff's claim of compensatory and punitive damages is premised, in
part, upon allegations that the Defendants' actions caused [Wessel] extreme
financial hardship after his termination.

3.   Defendants' Second Set of Interrogatories to Plaintiff [Wessel] violate no
rules of procedure and were served in a timely fashion.

4.   On [January 22, 1993], Defendants served upon Plaintiff [Wessel]
Defendants' First Set of Requests for Admissions.

5.   Thereafter attorneys for Plaintiff [Wessel] have taken the position that
Defendants' First Set of Requests for Admissions are untimely and have refused
to answer same.

6.   Defendants' First Set of Requests for Admissions to Plaintiff [Wessel]
violate no rules of procedure and were served in a timely fashion.

7.   Attempts to resolve the foregoing discovery conflicts would be futile in
light of Plaintiff's position that Defendants' discovery is untimely, irrespective of
the Court's Order that discovery could proceed until [January 22, 1993].

WHEREFORE, Defendants respectfully request this Court to set forth an Order
compelling Plaintiff [Wessel] to set forth responses to Defendants' Second Set of
Interrogatories and Defendants' First Request for Production of Documents and to
grant Defendants' costs and attorneys' fees incurred in bringing this present motion.

Dated this [25th] day of [January], [1993].

[A.I.C. SECURITY INVESTIGATIONS, LTD.];

[A.I.C. INTERNATIONAL, LTD.]; and [unnamed defendant C]

By: [defense attorney A]

§ 13.27 Responses to Interrogatories

FORM 13–22
SAMPLE RESPONSE TO INTERROGATORIES

DEFENDANTS' [___], [___], and [___] ANSWERS TO
PLAINTIFF'S INTERROGATORIES

1. [R ___] Company]: [January 1, 1978]–[June 30, 1980], sole proprietorship.

[R.B.C., Inc., d/b/a RBC Company]: [July 1, 1980] to present.

Officers: [___ Sr.], President;

Board of Directors: [___ Sr.], [___], [___, Jr.], [___], [___].

Shareholders: [___, Jr.], [___] and [___] .

2. a.   [Robert W. M___, Jr.], [1978]–present.

b .   [Robert W. M___, Sr.], [1978]–present.

c.   [Paul G. M[___], [September 1978]–present.

d.   [Richard W. M___], [1978]–present.

e.   [Paul G. M___] and [Richard W. M___], [September 1978]–present.

f.   [Robert W. M___, Sr.], [T.H. Wentz], [Dorothy S. M___], [Robert W. M___, Jr.], [Richard W. M___] and [Paul G. M___].

g.   [Dorothy S. M___], [1978]–present.

3.   All of the Defendants, with the exception of Defendants [K] and [G,] are employees of [RBC]. [K] has been employed as a consultant on an independent contractor basis. [G] is not currently employed, but in the past has been employed

on an independent contractor basis. All documents relating to the business relationships between the Defendants are contained in their individual personnel files, which, insofar as they are relevant, are available for inspection and copying in the office of [RBC].

4. a.   All documents are being copied and will be supplied to Plaintiff. In addition to the documents which are in the process of being copied, Defendant [W] upon leaving, retained three manuals identified as follows: [Personnel Policy Manual for Supervisors]; [Handling Employee Problems]; [Writing Employee Evaluations]. Copies of these documents will be made available if requested.

Except for [K], all documents which were in the possession of the individual defendants when they left [JKL]'s employ have been produced. No documents have been destroyed or otherwise discarded or removed from the control of any of the answering Defendants. With respect to [K], shortly after his consulting relationship with [JKL] terminated, [JKL] sent a representative to [K]'s offices who removed a large number of documents. [K] does not recall the identity of each of these documents.

5.   Defendants object to interrogatory number 5 insofar as it assumes that Defendants are aware of the identity of each customer or supplier of [JKL]. Insofar as this interrogatory requests information relating to contracts between [RBC Company] and [JKL], correspondence relating to such contacts is attached. Furthermore, each of the individual defendants had contact with [Robert W. M_, Sr.], and other representatives of [RBC] before they were offered and accepted employment. Such information is available in the individual defendants' personnel files. [Robert W. M_, Sr.], met with [H.D.] in [March 1985] in [RBC]'s [Delaware] office about employment. [M_] contacted [J.S.] in the [Spring] of [1985]. He has also had contact with [J.W.], [A.I.] and [G.E.]. [Robert M_] had contact with several others who remain in [JKL]'s employ. Defendants object to interrogatory number 5 insofar as it requests information relating to contacts between [RBC Company] and others who may currently be employed by [JKL] on the grounds that such contacts were confidential and are privileged. Defendants are unwilling to supply this information to Plaintiff until the terms of a confidentiality agreement and protective order have been negotiated by the parties.

6.a.   No.

b.   No.

c.   Defendants were aware that [JKL]'s Material Handling Division was having financial trouble. Defendants also were told that [JKL] had instituted an employee performance monitoring program.

d.   Yes, [RBC] was told about [ABC]'s disability by [J.B.] in [June], [1993].

e.   Defendants do not understand what information Plaintiff seeks in response to this interrogatory, and if it is clarified, Defendants will respond accordingly.

7.   See reply to number 6. No documents exist.

8.   None, except insofar as other documents produced or made available reflect such a desire.

9.   Yes

a.   [Robert W. M___], President, overall involvement in design, development, manufacturer marketing, etc. of water recreation equipment.

[J.G.], designer, provided design services to [RBC] on contract basis.

[___], draftsman/designer.

[___], draftsman.

[___], draftsman.

[___, Jr.], draftsman.

[___], engineering consultant.

b.   The time sheets of the individual defendants, as well as lists of [RBC]'s product codes are available at Defendant's offices and will be made available to Plaintiff upon execution of an acceptable confidentiality agreement and protective order.

c.   Previously supplied.

d.   [___]: Contract employee [4/29/85]–[4/30/85]. Full-time employee 5/1/85 to present.

[___]: Contract employee [4/11/85]–[4/29/85]. Full-time employee [5/1/85] to present.

[___]: Full-time employee [4/15/85] to present.

[___: Jr.]: Contract employee [8/12/85]–[8/31/85]. Full-time employee [9/1/85] to present.

[K]: Engineering consultant [1982] to present.

[G]: [June 5, 1985], contract employee.

e.   Objected to as being a request for privileged material. Moreover the request is overbroad and unrelated to any specific product that is at issue in this proceeding. This interrogatory seeks, essentially, every document in Defendant's offices, and the request is burdensome. Without waiver of this objection, Defendants are willing to advise that no written contracts exists between [RBC] and any of the individual defendants.

10.   No.

11.a. [Robert W. M___ Sr.], [Richard W. M___], [Robert W. ___, Jr.] and [Paul G. M___].

b.   [Robert W. M___, Sr.], [Richard W. M___], [Robert W. M___, Jr.] and [Paul G. M___].

c.   [Robert W. M___, Sr.], [Richard W. M___], [Robert W. M___, Jr.] and [Paul G, M___].

d.   [Robert W. M[___, Sr.], [Richard W. M___], [Robert W. M___, Jr.] and [Paul G. M___].

e.   Personnel files will be available as previously noted. These files contain resumes of the Defendants.

12.   See answer to 11e.

13.   The specific duties and assignments are listed on the individual defendants' time sheets, which will be made available once the conditions noted previously are satisfied. Defendants object to providing listings of every trip undertaken by any of them on the grounds that the information will lead to the disclosure of the identities of [RBC]'s suppliers. This information is considered confidential by Defendants and is privileged.

14. a. Yes. [RBC] was contacted by [H] regarding employment when the company was located in [Newark], [Alabama]. During the meeting with [Mr. H], he was instructed by [RBC]'s representatives to disclose any impediments to his ability to perform job functions. During their interviews with [RBC], [A] and [M] were instructed to make the same disclosures.

b.   No documents exist.

c.   No documents exist.

15.   Insofar as this interrogatory seeks information relating to [RBC]'s development and manufacture of water recreation equipment, it is objected to as being overbroad and burdensome. This interrogatory seeks virtually every document relating to [RBC]'s business. The interrogatory makes no effort to limit its request or to have it relate to matters which are in dispute in this litigation. With respect to [JKL]'s products, Defendants have no documents other than those previously supplied.

16.   All [JKL] documents which Defendants retained are being supplied.

17.   See answer to 16.

18.   See answer to 16.

19.   Yes.

20.   With respect to all of the individual defendants, such information will be made available to Plaintiff upon execution of an appropriate confidentiality agreement and protective order. Upon execution on an appropriate confidentiality agreement and protective order, such information will be made available. Former [JKL] employees contacted, in addition to the individual defendants, are: [H.C.], [G.G.], [J.W.] and [A.S.].

VERIFICATION

I, [Robert W. M___], verify that I am the President of [RBC Company]; as such I am authorized to make this verification on its behalf; and that the foregoing Answers to Interrogatories are true and correct to the best of my knowledge, information and belief. I understand that false statements herein are made subject to the penalties of [18 Pa. Cons. Stat. Ann. § 4904] relating to unsworn falsification to authorities.

§ 13.28 —Supplemental Responses to Interrogatories (EEOC)

FORM 13–23
SAMPLE SUPPLEMENTAL RESPONSES TO
INTERROGATORIES (EEOC)

IN THE UNITED STATES DISTRICT COURT

FOR THE [NORTHERN DISTRICT] OF [ILLINOIS]

[EASTERN] DIVISION

U.S. EQUAL OPPORTUNITY COMMISSION

Plaintiff,

v.

Civil Action No.: [No. 92-C-7330]

[A.I.C. SECURITY INVESTIGATIONS, LTD.];

[A.I.C. INTERNATIONAL, LTD.]; AND [unnamed defendant C],

Defendants.

Judge [Marvin E. Aspen]

Magistrate Judge [Guzman]

EQUAL EMPLOYMENT OPPORTUNITY COMMISSION'S
SUPPLEMENTAL RESPONSES TO DEFENDANTS' FIRST SET OF
INTERROGATORIES TO PLAINTIFF

Interrogatory No. 36: List all experts retained by Plaintiff or [Wessel] in anticipation of litigation and state:

(a)   the name of the expert;

(b)   the specialty of the expert;

(c)   the address and telephone number of the expert.

Supplemental Response:

[A], M.D., Radiation Oncology, [address], [telephone number].

[C], M.D., Neurology, [address], [telephone number].

Respectfully submitted,

[attorney A]

Supervisory Trial Attorney

Equal Employment Opportunity Commission

[536 South Clark], [Room 982]

[Chicago], [Illinois] [60605]

[(312) 353-7546]

§ 13.29 —Order to Compel Answers

FORM 13–24
SAMPLE ORDER TO COMPEL ANSWERS

IN THE UNITED STATES DISTRICT COURT

FOR THE [NORTHERN] DISTRICT OF [ILLINOIS]

[EASTERN] DIVISION

U.S. EQUAL OPPORTUNITY COMMISSION

Plaintiff,

v.   No. [92-C-7330]

[A.I.C. SECURITY INVESTIGATIONS, LTD.];

[A.I.C. INTERNATIONAL, LTD.]; AND [unnamed defendant C],

Defendants,

ORDER

Pending is plaintiff's motion to compel pursuant to Rule 37 of the Federal Rules of Civil Procedure, for an order compelling Defendants, [A.I.C. Security Investigations, Ltd.], [A.I.C. International, Ltd.], and [unnamed defendant C] [(collectively "A.I.C.")] to respond to the EEOC's First Set of Interrogatories and the EEOC's First Request for Production of Documents. For the reasons listed below, plaintiff's motion is hereby granted in part and denied in part.

BACKGROUND FACTS

This is an action brought pursuant to the Americans With Disabilities Act of 1990 (ADA), 42 U.S.C. § 12101 *et seq.*, alleging that [A.I.C.] discharged [Charles Wessel] because of his disability, terminal cancer. On [November 6, 1992], the EEOC served [A.I.C.], with the EEOC's First Set of Interrogatories, and First Request for Production of Documents.

DISCUSSION

Defendants have objected to Plaintiff's Interrogatory No. 14, which inquires into the reasons for the termination of [David P.], the former president of [A.I.C. International, Ltd.]. This interrogatory also seeks documents pertaining to his termination and a list of all persons with knowledge of [David P.]'s termination. Defendants claim that the information sought is not reasonably calculated to lead to the discovery of admissible evidence. Plaintiff responds that the reason for seeking information regarding [David P.]'s termination is that Defendants may use this evidence at trial.

I agree with Defendants that plaintiff has failed to establish that Interrogatory No. 14 seeks information that is reasonably calculated to lead to discovery of admissible evidence. Further, I assume that [Mr. P.]'s entire personnel file is being produced pursuant to Document Request No. 2, which Defendants have failed to raise any objections to. In light of this, Plaintiffs' Motion to Compel Answers to Interrogatory No. 14 is hereby denied.

Plaintiffs also seek, through its request for Document No. 3, all contracts between [A.I.C. Security Investigations, Ltd.] (a subsidiary of [A.I.C. International, Ltd.]) and its customers which were overseen by [Mr. Wessel] from [February 1, 1986] through [July 31, 1992]. Defendants object to this request for three reasons. First, Defendant objected because such documents are not easily calculated to lead to the discovery of admissible evidence. Defendants contend that these contracts have no bearing on the issue of whether [Wessel] was able to perform the essential functions of his job position. Second, the production of these contracts over more than a [six]-year period is unduly burdensome. Third, Defendants object because the contracts in question are confidential and contain valuable proprietary information.

I agree with Defendants that the production of this information would divulge information that could create irreparable harm. The terms of a contract between a business and its customers are often confidential and Plaintiff has failed to establish that the specific terms of the contracts are relevant. I have concluded, however, that the number of contracts [Mr. Wessel] negotiated and monitored during his employment with defendant is entirely relevant for purposes of determining what the job requires and whether [Wessel] is a qualified person. In light of such, Defendants are hereby ordered to compile a list summarizing the contracts [Mr. Wessel] was responsible for securing and/or monitoring. This list is to indicate the name of the client, the date the contract was negotiated, and any other information the Defendants deem appropriate to include.

Defendants are further ordered to produce information concerning [A.I.C.]'s annual earnings pursuant to interrogatory 13. I agree with Plaintiff that the annual earnings of [A.I.C.] are obviously relevant to [Wessel]'s capabilities as Manager of the Division. As Plaintiff points out, there is minimal burden in producing audited financial statements.

Likewise, Defendants are hereby ordered to answer Interrogatory 15. The disputed Requests to Admit concern [Wessel]'s ability to perform essential functions of his job, [Wessel]'s qualifications, and his disabilities. The EEOC is clearly entitled to all documents pertaining to witnesses with knowledge of these issues.

CONCLUSION

Plaintiff's motion to compel is hereby GRANTED IN PART and DENIED IN PART.

The parties are to contact my clerk to schedule a Pre-Trial Conference.

SO ORDERED

Enter: [January 29, 1993]

[Ronald A. Guzman]

United States Magistrate Judge

REQUEST FOR PRODUCTION OF DOCUMENTS

§ 13.30   Request for Production of Documents

FORM 13–25
SAMPLE REQUEST FOR PRODUCTION OF DOCUMENTS

PLAINTIFF'S FIRST REQUEST FOR PRODUCTION OF
DOCUMENTS AND THINGS

Plaintiff, [ABC Corporation ("ABC")], hereby requests, pursuant to Rule 34, Fed. R. Civ. P. that defendants permit plaintiff to inspect and copy the following documents and things on or before the date specified in Rule 34.

For purposes of this request the term "employment policies" means letters, memoranda, and notes of meetings as well as formal personnel procedure manuals or employee handbooks. The abbreviations ["ABC"] and ["JKL"] include any parent, subsidiary, affiliates or related corporations or business entities. The term "Individual Defendants" means [defendant A], [defendant B], [defendant C], [defendant D], and [defendant E], both individually and in all permutations.

1.   All documents and things requested to be identified in [X]'s First Set of Interrogatories to Defendants.

2.   All agreements (including employment agreements) of any kind, type or description between any of the Individual Defendants and: (a) [X]; (b) [JKL].

3.   All documents and things obtained directly or indirectly by any of the individual Defendants from [JKL].

4.   Identify any and all employment advertisements of [JKL] including particularly all advertisements referring in any way to equal opportunity.

5.   All employment agreements between [X] and [JKL].

6.   All personnel policies.

7.   All documents referring to [X]'s disability or [ABC]'s ability to perform job functions, essential or otherwise.

§ 13.31   Response to Request for Production

FORM 13–26
SAMPLE RESPONSE TO REQUEST FOR PRODUCTION

REPLY OF DEFENDANTS TO PLAINTIFF'S REQUEST FOR
PRODUCTION OF DOCUMENTS

1.   Supplied, except to those to which we have previously objected. Defendants incorporate their objections contained in their Answers to Interrogatories as appropriate.

2. a. None in possession of Defendants.

b.   None exist.

3.   Supplied.

4.   Attached.

5.   See reply to 2a above.

§ 13.32   First Request for Production (EEOC)

FORM 13–27
SAMPLE FIRST REQUEST FOR PRODUCTION

IN THE UNITED STATES DISTRICT COURT

FOR THE [NORTHERN] DISTRICT OF [ILLINOIS]

[EASTERN] DIVISION

U.S. EQUAL EMPLOYMENT OPPORTUNITY COMMISSION,

Plaintiff,

v.

Civil Action No. [92-C-7330]

[A.I.C. SECURITY INVESTIGATIONS, LTD.];

[A.I.C. INTERNATIONAL, LTD.]; and [unnamed defendant C],

Defendants.   Judge [Marvin E. Aspen]

EQUAL EMPLOYMENT OPPORTUNITY COMMISSION'S FIRST REQUEST FOR PRODUCTION OF DOCUMENTS TO DEFENDANTS

Plaintiff Equal Employment Opportunity Commission (the "EEOC"), pursuant to Rule 34 of the Federal Rules of Civil Procedure, hereby requests that Defendants [A.I.C. Security Investigations, Ltd. ("A.I.C.")]; [A.I.C. International, Ltd. ("A.I.C. International")]; and [unnamed defendant C] produce the documents listed in this Request which are within their possession, custody, or control, for inspection and copying at the office of the EEOC, [536 South Clark Street], [Room 982], [Chicago], [Illinois], within 45 days from the date of receipt of this Request, or within such shorter period as may be ordered by the Court.

DEFINITIONS AND INSTRUCTION

1.   This request incorporates by reference the definitions and instructions contained in EEOC's First Set of Interrogatories to Defendants.

2.   With respect to any document that Defendants deem privileged and withhold from production, Defendants shall provide a written response on the date of the production pursuant to this Request, setting forth as to each document:

a.   The date appearing on the document or if not date appears, the date on which the document was prepared;

b.   The identity of the person(s) to whom the document was addressed;

c.   The identity of the person(s) to whom the document or a copy there of was sent or with whom the document was discussed;

d.   The identity of the person(s) who prepared it;

e.   The general nature or description of the subject matter and contents of the document and the number of pages of which it consists;

f.   The identity of the person(s) who has custody of the document; and

g.   The specific ground(s) on which the claim of privilege rests.

DOCUMENTS TO BE PRODUCED

1.   All documents identified in Defendants' Answers to EEOC's First Set of Interrogatories.

2.   Personnel files of [Charles H. Wessel ("Wessel")], [Victor V.], [David P.], [Lawrence R.], [Edward B.], [Jan D.], and [Beverly K.].

3.   All contracts between [A.I.C.] and its customers which were overseen by [Wessel] from [February 1, 1986] through [July 31, 1992].

4.   All EEO-1 reports filed with the joint Reporting Committee for the years [1986]–[1992] for [A.I.C.], [A.I.C. International], and for each other entity held by [A.I.C. International].

5.   All documents which describe or relate to the essential functions of the position of Executive Director of [A.I.C.] for each year from [1986] through [1992], including, but not limited to written job description, written performance evaluations, and written performance goals.

6.   All documents which describe or relate to the essential functions of the positions held by [David P.], [Lawrence R.], [Edward B.], [Jan D.], and [Beverly K.] for each year from [1986] through [1992].

7.   All documents which relate or refer to [Wessel]'s medical condition, including but not limited to, notes of conversations with his doctors and letters from doctors concerning his condition, internal memoranda between Defendants' employees; documents prepared by [Wessel] concerning his medical condition, and letters or notes of conversations between Defendants and outside experts.

8.   All documents pertaining to policies of [A.I.C.] concerning sick leave and/or attendance.

9.   All documents which reflect or relate to attendance and/or time off from work by [Wessel] from [1987]–[1992].

10.   All documents which support the contention that [Wessel] was unable to perform any essential function of his job from [1987]–[1992].

11.   All documents which support the contention that [Wessel] was unable to perform any marginal function of his job from [1987]–[1992].

12.   All documents which support the contention that any essential function of the position of Executive Director was transferred from [Wessel] to another employee or agent of [A.I.C.] from [January 1, 1992] to [July 31, 1992].

13.   All documents which show profits and liabilities for [A.I.C.] for the years [1987]–[1992], including but not limited to, year-end balance sheets or financial statements.

14.   All documents which describe or relate to Defendants' policies with respect to termination or management employees, including but not limited to policies with respect to discharge, layoff, retirement, permanent disability retirement.

15.   All documents which reflect or relate to any accommodations provided to [Wessel], or considered for [Wessel].

§ 13.33   Request for Production under Rule 34 (Refusal to Hire)

FORM 13–28
SAMPLE REQUEST FOR PRODUCTION OF DOCUMENTS
(REFUSAL TO HIRE)

Plaintiff [A.B.] requests defendant [C.D.] to respond within [number] days to the following request:

That defendant produce and permit plaintiff to inspect and copy each of the following documents:

(1)   Any written statement of the job description and/or essential job functions of the position that the plaintiff applied for;

(2)   All documents reflecting the reason why the plaintiff was not hired;

(3)   Any written personnel policy or handbook or employee manual;

(4)   Any documents written in connection with the creation of the employee handbook or manual;

(5)   The standard application for employment form, as well as the completed application form filled out by the plaintiff;

(6)   Any written communication between your company and the plaintiff regarding potential employment;

(7)   Any investigative reports made by you or for you of the plaintiff;

(8)   Any documents describing your initial evaluation of the plaintiff prior to your decision not to hire plaintiff;

(9)   Any publication that describes the nature of your business, including the number of employees, the type of work they do, and the institutions or persons they serve;

(10)   Any documents stating the number of offices or distinct plants or manufacturing facilities that are part of the employing enterprise, as well as listing the location of all such facilities;

(11)   A copy of the registration or incorporation certificate of the employing enterprise;

(12)   A list of the ten most significant owners of stock in the company, if the employing enterprise is a corporation;

(13)   A copy of the doctor's written report if a preemployment physical examination was conducted;

(14)   Any documents reflecting accommodations that you offered to make to deal with the plaintiff's disability;

(15)   A copy of all notices posted in accessible format to applicants, employees, and members describing the applicable portions of the ADA.

Signed: [attorney for plaintiff]

[address]

§ 13.34   Request for Production of Documents (Employee Termination)

FORM 13–29
SAMPLE REQUEST FOR PRODUCTION OF DOCUMENTS (EMPLOYEE TERMINATION)

Plaintiff [A.B.] requests defendant [C.D.] to respond within [number] days to the following request:

That defendant produce and permit plaintiff to inspect and copy each of the following documents:

(1)   Any written statement of the plaintiff's job description and/or listing of the essential job functions associated with plaintiff's position;

(2)   All documents reflecting the reason why the plaintiff was terminated;

(3)   Any written personnel policy, handbook or employee manual;

(4)   Any documents written in connection with the creation of the employee handbook or manual;

(5)   The standard application for employment form, as well as the completed application form filled out by the plaintiff;

(6)   Any written communication between your company and the plaintiff regarding plaintiff's conduct;

(7)   Any investigative reports made by you or for you of the plaintiff;

(8)   Any written records of any internal hearing or review afforded to the plaintiff prior to plaintiff's termination;

(9)   All written evaluations of the plaintiff's performance during plaintiff's tenure with the company, as well as any other documents reflecting the plaintiff's performance during the time that plaintiff was employed by you;

(10)   Any documents describing any initial evaluation of the plaintiff prior to the time plaintiff started working for you;

(11)   Any documents describing any disciplinary action taken against the plaintiff;

(12)   Any documents that describe the nature of your business, including the number of employees, the type of work they do, and the institutions or persons they serve;

(13)   Any documents stating the number of offices or distinct plants or manufacturing facilities that are part of the employing enterprise, as well as listing the location of all such facilities;

(14)   A copy of the registration or incorporation certificate of the employing enterprise;

(15)   A list of the ten most significant owners of stock in the company, if the employing enterprise is a corporation;

(16)   Any documents or records regarding any unemployment claim made by the plaintiff;

(17)   A copy of the doctor's written report if a preemployment physical examination was conducted;

(18)   Any documents reflecting accommodations made by you to deal with the plaintiff's disability;

(19)   A copy of all notices posted in accessible format to applicants, employees, and members describing the applicable portions of the ADA;

(20)   A copy of any preemployment tests that the plaintiff took, as well as an evaluation of the results.

Signed: [attorney for plaintiff]

[address][17]

§ 13.35   Request for Production of Computer-Readable Materials

Most enterprises, even relatively small ones, maintain some or all of their records in computer-readable form. Discovery requests should encompass such format. For example, in *Zapata v. IBP, Inc.*,[18] national origin discrimination plaintiffs included the following requests in their First Request for Production of Documents:

7.   A complete copy of all computer data, including but not limited to computer tapes, disks and hard copies of the computer data, including personnel and/or employment files for all employees of the [Garden City], [Kansas] and [Emporia], [Kansas] plants employed during any period of time between [January 1, 1988] to the present.

8.   A list of all computer codes and decoders related to the computer data requested in request 7.

9.   A complete copy of all dispensary records or documents, including computer records, for all employees of the [Garden City], [Kansas] and [Emporia], [Kansas] plants employed during any period of time between [January 1, 1988] to the present.

The defendants objected to these requests on the grounds that the personnel files and records of nonparty employees were irrelevant and immaterial, that the breadth and scope of the request would impose an undue burden and expense, and that some of the documents were privileged attorney-client communications or work product. The district court overruled these objections. It concluded that information on salaried employees was relevant because that would permit statistical analysis of promotion paths available. It overruled the objection on burdensomeness because the defendant failed to produce

---

[17] This document was compiled by Mark R. Lisker, assistant to Henry H. Perritt, Jr., in June 1993.

[18] Civ. A. No. 93-2366-EED, 1994 WL 649322 (D. Kan. Nov. 10, 1994).

specific facts showing how responding to the request for production would be burdensome.

This request can easily be tailored to an ADA action in which statistical evidence about other employees is likely to be or to lead to admissible evidence. The language of paragraph 8 can be improved upon, however. It would be better to refer to "copies of all computer programs or routines in such form as will permit the data to be read and analyzed." It also might be appropriate to delete the request for hard copies and to add a request for magnetic cassettes and optical media of any kind and magnetic cassettes.

When hearing-impaired persons are involved in ADA litigation, discovery may be sought of transcripts of telecommunication device for the deaf (TDD) communication. In *People v. Mid-Hudson Medical Group, PC,*[19] the district court applied conventional attorney work-product analysis to TDD transcripts to justify denying a motion for an order to compel disclosure. The court held "Hearing impaired lawyers deserve the same expectation of confidentiality as hearing lawyers. To hold otherwise would sanction opposing counsel's eavesdropping on TTY conversations between lawyers and their witnesses in anticipation [of] litigation."

PHYSICAL AND MENTAL EXAMINATION

§ 13.36   Motion for Physical and Mental Examination

FORM 13–30
SAMPLE MOTION FOR PHYSICAL AND MENTAL EXAMINATION

IN THE UNITED STATES DISTRICT COURT

FOR THE [NORTHERN] DISTRICT OF [ILLINOIS]

[EASTERN] DIVISION

U.S. EQUAL EMPLOYMENT OPPORTUNITY COMMISSION,

Plaintiff,

and

Civil Action No. [92 C 7330]

---

[19] 877 F. Supp. 143 (S.D.N.Y. 1995).

[A.I.C. SECURITY INVESTIGATIONS, LTD.];

[A.I.C. INTERNATIONAL, LTD.]; and [unnamed defendant C]

Defendants.

Honorable Judge [Marvin E. Aspen]

DEFENDANTS' MOTION FOR A PHYSICAL AND MENTAL EXAMINATION OF [CHARLES H. WESSEL]

Defendants, by and through their attorneys, [WESSELS & PAUTSCH, P.C.], by [Charles W. Pautsch], [attorney A] and [attorney B], and pursuant to Rule 35, Fed. R. Civ. P., hereby move this Court for an Order compelling [Charles H. Wessel] to submit to a physical and mental examination and states in support hereof as follows:

1.   On or about [November 5, 1992] the Equal Employment Opportunity Commission ('EEOC") filed this present action on behalf of [Charles H. Wessel ("Wessel")] alleging certain violations of the Americans with Disabilities Act ("ADA"), 42 U.S.C. § 12101 *et seq.,* on the part of Defendants.

2.   Within the EEOC's Complaint filed herein at paragraph ten (10), it states that [Wessel] was a qualified individual with a disability who was able to perform the essential functions of his job with or without reasonable accommodation.

3.   Defendants contend, *inter alia,* that [Wessel], due to his condition, could not perform the essential functions of his job with or without reasonable accommodation.

4.   Medical evidence and expert medical testimony will play a key role in determining issues at trial.

5.   The mental and physical condition of [Wessel] is in controversy.

6.   Defendants will be unduly prejudiced if unable to have [Wessel] examined by a physician.

7.   If allowed by this Court, [Wessel]'s examination will be performed by Dr. [Susan S.] (neurologist), located at [clinic name], [address], and [telephone number], on [Tuesday], [December 29, 1992] at [2:00 P.M.].

8.   If ordered by this Court, [Dr. S.] shall examine [Wessel]'s mental and physical capacity to function in his previous position with [A.I.C.] and produce a report enabling other experts in the fields of oncology and radiology to testify regarding [Wessel]'s ability to perform the essential functions of his prior position.

WHEREFORE, Defendants, by and through counsel, hereby respectfully request this Court to order a physical and mental examination of [Charles H. Wessel].

§ 13.37   Order to Compel Physical and
Mental Examination

FORM 13–31
SAMPLE ORDER TO COMPEL PHYSICAL AND
MENTAL EXAMINATION

IN THE UNITED STATES DISTRICT COURT

FOR THE [NORTHERN] DISTRICT OF [ILLINOIS]

[EASTERN] DIVISION

U.S. EQUAL OPPORTUNITY COMMISSION

Plaintiff,

v.   No. [92-C-7330]

[A.I.C. SECURITY INVESTIGATIONS, LTD.];

[A.I.C. INTERNATIONAL, LTD.]; and [unnamed defendant C],

Defendants.

ORDER

Pending is defendants' [A.I.C. Security Investigation, Ltd.]; [A.I.C. International, Ltd.]; and [defendant C]'s [(collectively "A.I.C.")] motion to compel [Charles H. Wessel] to submit to a physical and mental examination. For the reasons listed below, [A.I.C.]'s motion is hereby granted.

BACKGROUND FACTS

On or about [November 5, 1992], the Equal Opportunity Commission ("EEOC") filed this present action on behalf of [Charles H. Wessel ("Wessel")] alleging certain violations of the Americans with Disabilities Act (ADA), 42 U.S.C. §§ 12101 *et seq.* The EEOC in its complaint alleges that [Wessel] is an individual who was able to perform the essential functions of his job with or without reasonable accommodation. Defendants contend, however, that [Wessel] is not able to perform the essential functions of his job with or without reasonable accommodation. In light of this defense, [A.I.C.] argues that the mental and physical condition of [Wessel] is in controversy and that [A.I.C.] will be unduly prejudiced if they are unable to have [Wessel] examined by a physician.

DISCUSSION

The Act currently provides for a three-pronged definition of disability which states as follows:

A person with a disability is

(a)   a person with a physical or mental impairment that substantially limits that person in some major life activity;

(b)   a person with a record of such a physical or mental impairment; or

(c)   a person who is regarded as having such an impairment.

ADA, § 3; 42 U.S.C. § 12102(2)

The EEOC regulations to the ADA, which implement the employment title of the law (Title 1), repeat this three-pronged definition of disability. See [29 C.F.R. § 1620.2(g)]. As indicated by the definition, this impairment must be one that substantially limits the person in a major life activity, the potential limitation must be analyzed without regard to the existence of mitigating devices or medicines. See [29 C.F.R. §§ 1630.2(h), (j) (EEOC GUIDANCE at 35741)]. Although most serious medical conditions do have a substantial impact on basic life activities, this impact on [Mr. Wessel] must be established by [Mr. Wessel] to enjoy the protection of the Act.

Further, [Mr. Wessel] must show that he is a qualified individual with a disability. Under the ADA, a "qualified individual with a disability" is a person who, with or without reasonable accommodation can perform the "essential functions" of the job that the person holds or desires. ADA § 101(8). [Mr. Wessel]'s qualifications or lack thereof could be used by Defendants as a defense.

In light of the fact that [Mr. Wessel]'s condition is a cerebral progressive condition and the effects of this condition vary from case to case, it is only appropriate that [A.I.C.] be given the opportunity to have its medical experts examine [Mr. Wessel] from both a mental and physical perspective.

CONCLUSION

[Mr. Wessel] is hereby ordered to appear before [Doctor L.] for a mental and physical examination.

ORDERED

Enter: [February 2, 1993]

[Ronald A. Guzman]

United States Magistrate Judge

REQUESTS FOR ADMISSION

§ 13.38   Requests for Admission

The reason for requests for admissions (see **Form 13–32** to **13–34**) overlaps with the purpose of interrogatories and the preparation of pretrial orders and stipulated facts for partial summary judgment purposes. Now that the number of interrogatories is limited (under amendments to the Federal Rules of Civil Procedure transmitted to Congress in April 1993), it may be appropriate to shift some requests for admission from interrogatories to requests for admission explicitly denominated as such. On the other hand, the need for separately denominated requests for admission is diminished by the increasing formality and standardization of pretrial orders that declare uncontested facts. The form of requests should be such that each can be answered with a simple "admitted" or "denied." Obviously, they should be framed with such particularity that a "denied" response exposes the responder to sanctions if the request subsequently is proven. Form 25 appended to the Federal Rules of Civil Procedure illustrates the form:

Plaintiff [A.B.] requests defendant [C.D.] within [number] days after service of this request to make the following admissions for the purpose of this action only and subject to all pertinent objections to admissibility which may be interposed at the trial:

(1)   That each of the following documents, exhibited with this request, is genuine. [List the documents and describe each document.]

(2)   That each of the following statements is true. [List the statements.]

As with interrogatories, a preface and definition may be appropriate.

A request for admission should be more like questions asked on cross-examination than questions asked on direct examination. In other words, requests for admission, unlike interrogatories, should be closed-ended, and suitable for yes or no answers. It is important to ask, "Do you admit that plaintiff has been diagnosed with dyslexia?" instead of "From what mental disabilities does the plaintiff suffer?"

It is important to remember that limiting phrases or words, such as adjectives, gives the responding party wiggle room. Asking for an admission to the statement, "the plaintiff suffers from severe depression," permits a "denied" response based on the word "severe" when the responding party would admit that "the plaintiff suffers from depression."

With requests for admission, it is also wise to avoid compound assertions, because the responding party may deny all of the assertions based on a denial of one part.

§ 13.39 Motion to Compel Response to Requests for Admission

FORM 13–32
SAMPLE MOTION TO COMPEL REQUESTS FOR ADMISSION

IN THE UNITED STATES DISTRICT COURT

FOR THE [NORTHERN] DISTRICT OF [ILLINOIS]

[EASTERN] DIVISION

U.S. EQUAL EMPLOYMENT OPPORTUNITY COMMISSION,

Plaintiff,

v.

Civil Action No. [92 C 7330]

[A.I.C. SECURITY INVESTIGATIONS, LTD.];

[A.I.C. INTERNATIONAL, LTD.]; and [unnamed defendant C],

Defendants.

Honorable [Marvin E. Aspen]

Magistrate Judge [Ronald A. Guzman]

DEFENDANTS' EMERGENCY MOTION TO COMPEL ANSWERS
TO DEFENDANTS' FIRST REQUESTS FOR ADMISSION TO
PLAINTIFF EQUAL EMPLOYMENT OPPORTUNITY COMMISSION

Defendants, [A.I.C. SECURITY INVESTIGATIONS, LTD.]; [A.I.C. INTERNA-TIONAL, LTD.]; and [C], by and through their attorneys, [WESSELS & PAUTSCH, P.C.], by [Charles W. Pautsch], [attorney A] and [attorney B], pursuant to Rule 37, Fed. R. Civ. P., and [Local Court General Rule 12], hereby set forth their Emergency Motion to Compel Answers to Defendants' First Request for Admissions to Plaintiff Equal Employment Opportunity Commission (EEOC) as follows:

1.   On [January 22, 1993], Defendants served upon Plaintiff Equal Empl-oyment Opportunity Commission Defendants' First Set of Requests for Admissions.

2.   The Plaintiff, Equal Employment Opportunity Commission, has taken the position that Defendants' previously served Second Set of Interrogatories are untimely, and therefore, any attempts to resolve the foregoing discovery conflicts would be futile in light of Plaintiff's position that Defendants' discovery is untimely, irrespective of the Court's order that discovery could proceed until [January 22, 1993].

WHEREFORE, Defendants respectfully request this Court to set forth an Order compelling Plaintiff Equal Employment Opportunity Commission to set forth responses to Defendants' First Requests for Admissions within seven (7) days of ser-vice to grant Defendants costs and attorneys' fees incurred in bringing this motion.

Dated this [25th] day of [January], [1993].

[A.I.C. SECURITY INVESTIGATIONS, LTD.];

[A.I.C. INTERNATIONAL, LTD.]; and [defendant C]

By: [attorney A]

§ 13.40   Memorandum Supporting Plaintiff's Motion to Compel

FORM 13–33
SAMPLE MEMORANDUM SUPPORTING PLAINTIFF'S MOTION TO COMPEL

IN THE UNITED STATES DISTRICT COURT

FOR THE [NORTHERN] DISTRICT OF [ILLINOIS]

[EASTERN] DIVISION

U.S. EQUAL EMPLOYMENT OPPORTUNITY COMMISSION,

Plaintiff,

v.   Civil Action No. [92 C 7330]

[A.I.C. SECURITY INVESTIGATIONS, LTD.];

[A.I.C. INTERNATIONAL, LTD.]; and [unnamed defendant C]

Defendants.   Judge [Marvin E. Aspen]

MEMORANDUM IN SUPPORT OF PLAINTIFF'S MOTION TO COMPEL

Plaintiff, the Equal Employment Opportunity Commission (the "EEOC"), respectfully submits this Memorandum in support of its Motion to Compel.

This is an action brought pursuant to the Americans With Disabilities Act of 1990 (ADA), 42 U.S.C. § 12101 *et seq.,* alleging that [Charles H. Wessel ("Wessel")] was discharged from his employment by Defendants, [A.I.C. Security Investigations, Ltd.]; [A.I.C. International, Ltd.]; and [defendant C] [(collectively "A.I.C.")].

The facts pertaining to the Motion are not disputed. [Wessel] suffers from cancer, and his condition has been diagnosed as terminal. [Wessel] was hired by [A.I.C.] as Executive Director of [A.I.C.]'s security guard division in [February, 1986]. He held that position until his discharge on [July 29, 1992]. In that position he reported directly to the President of [A.I.C. International, Ltd.], [David P.], until [David P.]'s termination on [July 2, 1992], less than a month prior to [Wessel]'s discharge. [Wessel]'s duties include the oversight of contracts to provide security guards to managers of commercial property who were customers of [A.I.C.].

EEOC alleges that [Wessel] was, at the time of his discharge and continuing to the present, able to perform the essential functions of his position as Executive Director, with or without reasonable accommodations, an allegation denied by [A.I.C.]. EEOC's most important witness at trial will be [Wessel], if he remains able to testify. Because of his condition, his deposition was taken by videotape transcription on [November 5, 1992]. Also because of his condition, EEOC requested expedited discovery, and the Court ordered expedited discovery on [November 12, 1992]. EEOC also expects to call [David P.] to demonstrate, inter alia, that [Wessel] continued to perform his duties of oversight of contracts. [A.I.C.] intends to argue that [David P.] is a biased witness because of his own termination.

The Court's Order of [November 12, 1992], requires that all written discovery be answered within seven days of receipt, that discovery be concluded by [December 31, 1992], and that a Final Pre-Trial Order be filed with the court on [January 15, 1993].

The disputed discovery consists of Answers to Interrogatories and Requests for Production of Documents which were due on [November 17, 1992].[20] To date no answers have been received, although Defendants' Objections were mailed on [November 27, 1992].[21]

---

[20] The Counsel for the EEOC agreed on November 13, 1992, to an informal extension of time to provide answers by November 24, 1992.

[21] A.I.C.'s Answers to EEOC's First Request for Admissions, also due on November 17, 1992, were mailed to the EEOC on November 18, 1992. A.I.C.'s Answers to EEOC's Second Set of Interrogatories (dealing with proposed expert witnesses), which were due on November 30, 1992, were received on December 3, 1992. These responses are not the subject of the Motion.

EEOC respectfully submits that the Court should order that the answers be provided immediately. Rule 37(a) of the Federal Rules of Civil Procedure provides that a party may move the Court to compel answers to interrogatories and document requests if the opposing party fails to answer, as is the case here. EEOC has scheduled nine depositions between [December 4, 1992] and [December 28, 1992]. The written discovery responses will assist EEOC in preparing for those depositions.

EEOC also requests that the Court order [A.I.C.] to respond to Interrogatory 14 and Document Request 3, the discovery requests to which [A.I.C.] maintained its objections following the conference held pursuant to [Rule 12(k)] of the Local Rules for the [Northern] District of [Illinois]. Interrogatory 14 requests [A.I.C.] to [s]tate every reason for the termination of [David P.] and identify all documents which relate to or refer to the reasons for [David P.]'s termination, and identify all persons with knowledge of the reasons for the termination of [David P.]." Document Request 3 requests [A.I.C.] to produce "[a]ll contracts between [A.I.C.] and its customers which were overseen by [Wessel] from [February 1, 1986] through [July 31, 1992]."[22]

The general rule is that failure to make timely objection to a discovery request results in waiver of the objection, even if the objection is based on privilege. See [Davis v. Fendler, 650 F.2d 1154, 1160 (9th Cir. 1981)]; [United States v. 58.16 Acres of Land, 66 F.R.D. 570 (E.D. Ill. 1975)]. In this case the only objections are that "the . . . information sought is not reasonably calculated to lead to the discovery of admissible evidence," and, with respect to production of the contracts, undue burden. Here, where expedited discovery is so crucial, [A.I.C.] should be deemed to have waived any objection to the discovery sought.

In any event, the objections are without merit. Interrogatory 13 seeks information concerning [David P.], the former President of [A.I.C.]. He is expected to testify for EEOC, and his credibility may well be a major issue to be determined by the jury.[23] Reasons for his discharge are obviously relevant to a determination of that credibility.

Similarly, contracts overseen by [Wessel] requested by Document Request 3 are clearly relevant to the issue of whether [Wessel] was performing that particular essential function of his position. [A.I.C.] has made no attempt to demonstrate any undue burden which would be created by copying the contracts.

EEOC will be ready for trial on [January 15, 1993], when the Final Pre-Trial Order is filed. Because of the nature of the case, EEOC will ask for the earliest possible trial date. [A.I.C.]'s refusal to comply with the expedited discovery schedule should not be permitted to delay trial, and thus increase the possibility that [Wessel] may be unable to testify, or to obtain the relief of reinstatement which he seeks.

---

[22] EEOC had agreed to a protective order which would have protected any proprietary information contained in those contracts.

[23] A.I.C. had subpoenaed David P. for deposition on December 16, 1992.

For the foregoing reasons, EEOC respectfully requests that its Motion to Compel be granted. EEOC also requests that the case be set for a Pre-Trial Conference pursuant to Rule 16 of the Federal Rules of Civil Procedure, to resolve all discovery disputes and to set a trial date.

§ 13.41   Response to Motion to Compel (EEOC)

FORM 13–34
SAMPLE RESPONSE TO MOTION TO COMPEL

IN THE UNITED STATES DISTRICT COURT

FOR THE [NORTHERN] DISTRICT OF [ILLINOIS]

[EASTERN] DIVISION

U.S. EQUAL EMPLOYMENT OPPORTUNITY DIVISION

Plaintiff,

v.

Civil Action No. [92 C 7330]

[A.I.C. SECURITY INVESTIGATIONS, LTD.];

[A.I.C. INTERNATIONAL, LTD.]; and [unnamed defendant C],

Defendants.

Honorable [Marvin E. Aspen]

Magistrate Judge [Guzman]

PLAINTIFF EQUAL EMPLOYMENT OPPORTUNITY
COMMISSION'S RESPONSE TO DEFENDANT'S EMERGENCY
MOTION TO COMPEL ANSWERS TO FIRST REQUESTS
FOR ADMISSIONS

The Defendants have filed an Emergency Motion to Compel the Equal Employment Opportunity Commission ("EEOC") to respond to Defendant's First Set of Request for Admissions and Second Set of Interrogatories. Defendant's Motion misstates both the facts and the rules applicable to this matter. First, the Defendants' contention that the EEOC has refused to answer a Second Set of Interrogatories is simply wrong. The fact is that the Defendants never served the

EEOC with a Second Set of Interrogatories. Therefore, the EEOC cannot be compelled to answer discovery with which it was never served.

Next, Defendants' contention that their First Set of Requests for Admissions were timely served under the rules and must be answered by EEOC is likewise unfounded. On [December 29, 1992], Defendants requested and were granted by Judge [Aspen] an extension of the discovery cutoff date from [December 31, 1992] to [January 22, 1993]. Judge [Aspen] also stated to both parties at that time that there would be no more extensions of discovery beyond the [January 22, 1993] date. Specifically, Judge [Aspen] stated " . . . I am going to allow the motion, but I am not going to give you any further extensions, so you're going to have to do what you have to do during that time period. If you don't complete discovery in that period it won't be done." Transcript of the [December 29, 1992], hearing before the Honorable [Marvin Aspen] at pages 3, 4. Attached hereto as Exhibit 1.

On [January 19, 1993], the EEOC received a copy of Defendants' First Requests for Admissions. On [January 22, 1993], the EEOC informed Defendants' counsel by letter (Exhibit 2) that the thirty-four requests for Admissions were not timely under the Local Rules and that, as a result, the EEOC would not be submitting responses to the Requests. The EEOC also noted in its [January 22nd] letter that since twenty-four of the requests dealt with the authenticity of documents, the EEOC would be happy to discuss stipulations as to authenticity as a part of the pre-trial order process. On that same date, Defendants' counsel requested assistance in locating the Local Rule which supports the EEOC's position that Defendants' Requests for Admissions were not timely served. The EEOC informed Defendants' counsel by telephone which Local Rule applied, specifically, paragraph three of the Standing Order Establishing Pre-trial Procedure (Exhibit 3) which states:

> Except to the extent specified by the Court on motion of either party, discovery must be completed before the discovery closing date. Discovery requested before the discovery closing date, but not scheduled for completion before the discovery closing date, does not comply with this order.

On [January 25, 1993], counsel for Defendants informed the EEOC by letter that the Local Rule the EEOC had been relying on had been repealed in [1982] (Exhibit 4). On [January 26, 1993], the EEOC sent counsel for Defendants a copy of the rule in question showing that the rule is still in effect, and asked for Defendants' counsel to produce evidence to the contrary if any existed (Exhibit 5). Defendants have produced no such evidence.

The facts here are simple. Judge [Aspen] set a discovery cutoff date in this case of [January 22, 1993], and stated that all discovery in the case was to be completed by that date and that there would be no further extensions. In an effort to circumvent Judge [Aspen]'s order, Defendants chose not to serve further written discovery until three days prior to the close of discovery in direct contravention of the Local Rules for this District and in complete defiance of Judge [Aspen]'s order.

In sum, the Defendants are trying to do indirectly what Judge [Aspen] stated they would not be allowed to do directly—extend the discovery cutoff date in this case. The Defendants should not be allowed to circumvent either the discovery cutoff date or the requirements of the Local Rules by delaying service of written discovery until three days before the discovery cutoff and then seeking an order compelling the EEOC to answer them outside of the discovery period. To allow the Defendants' motion would reward Defendants for their decision to ignore the Local Rules of this District and would in effect nullify Judge [Aspen]'s clear order regarding the discovery cutoff in this case.

For the reasons stated herein, Defendants' motion should be denied in its entirety.

Respectfully submitted,

[EEOC attorney B]

Trial Attorney

ORDERS

§ 13.42   Points for Memorandum on Protective Order

Federal Rule of Civil Procedure 26(c) authorizes protective orders (see **Form 13–35**) to prevent "annoyance, embarrassment, oppression, or undue burden or expense." One of the clearest reasons for the entry of a protective order is to protect well-recognized privileges. The doctor-patient privilege is one such recognized privilege, and it clearly extends to any form of psychological counseling as long as the counselor is a professional.[24]

A person seeking a protective order must do so in advance, rather than by simply refusing to answer questions and then raising that privilege or other matter justifying a protective order after the fact.[25]

The language of the interrogatories attached as Exhibit A to the motion for a protective order demonstrate on their face a request for disclosure of information within the psychiatrist-patient privilege.[26]

---

[24] Cunningham v. Southlake Ctr. for Mental Health, 125 F.R.D. 474, 477 (N.D. Ind. 1989) (denying privilege to supervisor).

[25] *See* Hudson Tire Mart, Inc. v. Aetna Casualty & Sur. Co., 518 F.2d 671 (2d Cir.1975).

[26] Calloway v. Marvel Entertainment Group, 110 F.R.D. 45, 50 (S.D.N.Y. 1986) (question not implicating psychiatrist-patient privilege because dealing with communications outside scope of treatment).

§ 13.43   Motion for Protective Order

FORM 13–35
SAMPLE MOTION FOR PROTECTIVE ORDER

Plaintiff moves this court for an order pursuant to Fed. R. Civ. P. 26(c) prohibiting defendant from asking plaintiff questions in discovery that invade the psychiatrist patient privilege.

The basis for this motion is certain interrogatories propounded by the defendant, shown in Exhibit A to this motion, presenting the likelihood that plaintiff will be subject to sanctions for refusing to answer these questions unless a protective order is issued, and also making it probable that defendant will ask similar questions in depositions already scheduled or to be scheduled in the future.

This motion is based on the attachments, including the plaintiff's affidavit (Exhibit B) and the attached Memorandum of Law.

§ 13.44   Sample Order Referring Privilege Claims to Master

The likelihood of privilege claims in ADA litigation suggests that the convenience of court and counsel might be served by appointing a master to decide such claims. See **Form 13–36.**

FORM 13–36
SAMPLE ORDER REFERRING PRIVILEGE CLAIMS TO MASTER

Referral of Privilege Claims to Master

It appearing that submission of claims of privilege to a special master appointed under Fed. R. Civ. P. 53 is warranted by the expected volume of such claims and by the likelihood that in camera inspection may be needed to rule on these claims and should be accomplished, to the extent possible, by someone other than the judge to whom this litigation has been assigned, the court hereby, with the consent of the parties, ORDERS:

1.   Appointment. [Name] is appointed under Rule 53 as special master for the purpose of considering all claims of privilege (including assertion of protection against disclosure based on the "work product" doctrine) that may be asserted during the course of discovery in this litigation and for such other matters as may be referred to such master by the court, such as resolution of disputes under the Confidentiality Order.

2.   Procedures. The master shall have the rights, powers, and duties as provided in Rule 53 and may adopt such procedures as are not inconsistent with that rule or with this or other orders of the court. Until directed otherwise by the master or the court, any person asserting a privilege shall specifically identify the document or other communication sought to be protected from disclosure, including the date, the person making the statement, the persons to whom or in whose presence the statement was made, other persons to whom the contents were or have been revealed, the general subject matter of the communication (unless itself claimed to be privileged), the particular privileges) or doctrines) upon which protection against disclosure is based, and any other circumstances affecting the existence, extent, or waiver of the privilege. When appropriate, the master may require that this documentation of claims of privilege be verified.

3.   Reports. The master shall make findings of fact and conclusions of law with respect to the matters presented by the parties and report expeditiously to the court pursuant to Rule 53(e) as applicable in nonjury actions. Unless directed by the court or believed advisable by the master, the report shall not be accompanied by a transcript of the proceedings, the evidence, or the exhibits. Such parts of the report, if any, as may be confidential shall be filed under seal pending further order of the court.

4.   Fees and Expenses. Compensation at rates mutually agreeable to the master and the parties shall be paid to the master on a periodic basis by the parties. The master may employ other persons to provide clerical and secretarial assistance; such persons shall be under the supervision and control of the master, who shall take appropriate action to insure that such persons preserve the confidentiality of matter submitted to the master for review. Final allocation of these amounts shall be subject to taxation as costs at the conclusion of the case at the discretion of the court.

5.   Distribution. A copy of this order shall be mailed by the Clerk to the Special Master and to Liaison Counsel for the parties.

Dated: [date]

United States District Judge

CHAPTER 14

EARLY PRE-TRIAL PLANNING, MOTIONS FOR SUMMARY JUDGMENT, AND SUPPORTING MEMORANDA

§ 14.1 Introduction

This chapter presents materials for Amercians with Disabilities Act (ADA)[1] cases for initial pre-trial conferences (see **Form 14–1** in **§ 14.2**), scheduling (see **Form 14–2** in **§ 14.4**), for summary judgment (see **Forms 14–3** and **14–4** in **§§ 14.5** and **14.6** and **Form 14–5** in **§ 14.7**); and a reply memorandum on summary judgment (**Form 14–6**). A significant trend in modern civil procedure is to increase judicial management of cases by mandating more explicit scheduling and planning for the handling of discovery and the framing of issues for trial. Implicitly, this involves removing certain issues from the trial agenda by deciding them as a matter of law through summary judgment.

---

[1] Pub. L. No. 101-336, 104 Stat. 327 (1990) (codified at 42 U.S.C. 12101–12213 (1994); 47 U.S.C. §§ 225, 711 (1994) [hereinafter ADA].

§ 14.2   Rule 16: Pre-Trial Conferences, Scheduling, and Management

One of the 1993 amendments to the Federal Rules of Civil Procedure expands Rule 16 to make it more specific about judicial control of litigation. The full text of the amended rule follows.

FORM 14–1
PRE-TRIAL CONFERENCE

(b)   Scheduling and Planning. Except in categories of actions exempted by district court rule as inappropriate, the district judge, or a magistrate judge when authorized by district court rule, shall, after receiving the report from the parties under Rule 26(f) or after consulting with the attorneys for the parties and any unrepresented parties by a scheduling conference, telephone, mail, or other suitable means, enter a scheduling order that limits the time

(1)   to join other parties and to amend the pleadings;

(2)   to file motions; and

(3)   to complete discovery.

The scheduling order may also include

(4)   modifications of the times for disclosures under Rules 26(a) and 26(e)(1) and of the extent of discovery to be permitted;

(5)   the date or dates for conferences before trial, a final pre-trial conference, and trial; and

(6) any other matters appropriate in the circumstances of the case.

The order shall issue as soon as practicable but in any event within 90 days after the appearance of a defendant and within 120 days after the complaint has been served on a defendant. A schedule shall not be modified except upon a showing of good cause and by leave of the district judge or, when authorized by local rule, by a magistrate judge.

(c)   Subjects for Consideration at Pre-trial Conferences. At any conference under this rule consideration may be given, and the court may take appropriate action, with respect to

(1)   the formulation and simplification of the issues, including the elimination of frivolous claims or defenses;

(2)   the necessity or desirability of amendments to the pleadings;

(3)   the possibility of obtaining admissions of fact and of documents which will avoid unnecessary proof, stipulations regarding the authenticity of documents, and advance ruling from the court on the admissibility of evidence;

(4)   the avoidance of unnecessary proof and of cumulative evidence, and limitations or restrictions on the use of testimony under Rule 702 of the Federal Rules of Evidence;

(5)   the appropriateness and timing of summary adjudication under Rule 56;

(6)   the control and scheduling of discovery, including orders affecting disclosures and discovery pursuant to Rule 26 and Rules 29 through 37;

(7)   the identification of witnesses and documents, the need and schedule for filing and exchanging pretrial briefs, and the date or dates for further conferences and for trial;

(8)   the advisability of referring matters to a magistrate judge or master;

(9)   settlement and the use of special procedures to assist in resolving the dispute when authorized by statute or local rule;

(10)   the form and substance of the pre-trial order:

(11)   the disposition of pending motions;

(12)   the need for adopting special procedures for managing potentially difficult or protracted actions that may involve complex issues, multiple parties, difficult legal questions, or unusual proof problems;

(13) an order for a separate trial pursuant to Rule 42(b) with respect to a claim, counterclaim, cross-claim, or third-party claim, or with respect to any particular issue in the case;

(14)   an order directing a party or parties to present evidence early in the trial with respect to a manageable issue that could, on the evidence, be the basis for a judgment as a matter of law under Rule 50(a) or a judgment on partial findings under Rule 52(c);

(15) an order establishing a reasonable limit on the time allowed for presenting evidence; and

(16)   such other matters as may facilitate the just, speedy and in expensive disposition of the action.

At least one of the attorneys for each party participating in any conference before trial shall have authority to enter into stipulations and to make admissions regarding all matters that the participants may reasonably anticipate may be discussed. If appropriate, the court may require that a party or its representative be present or reasonably available by telephone in order to consider possible settlement of the dispute.

§ 14.3   Checklist for Initial Conference

The following checklist[2] is more comprehensive and detailed than the report of parties' planning meeting in § 14.4.

____   1.   Format for Conference
   ____   Establish/confirm agenda
   ____   Special instructions: for example, counsel must identify themselves for court and reporter when speaking
____   2.   Counsel
   ____   Appearances at conference
   ____   By counsel and parties
   ____   Other observers
   ____   Admission pro hac vice
   ____   Present/potential problems of disqualifications
   ____   Maintenance and filing of time and expense records
   ____   General policies
   ____   Avoidance of excessive attendance, unnecessary time
   ____   Obligations under Federal Rules of Civil Procedure 7, 11, 16, 26
   ____   Cooperation and courtesy; resolving disputes without resort to court
____   3.   Court
   ____   Present/potential problems of disqualification of judge
   ____   Assumption of active supervision over litigation
   ____   Policies and preferences of judge regarding such matter as communications with court, decorum
   ____   Suspension of local rules
   ____   Use of sanctions
   ____   Use of other judges and magistrates

---

[2] Adapted from checklist, Manual for Complex Litigation 2d § 40.1 (1985).

_____   4.   Preliminary Identification of Issues

_____   Brief outline by parties of positions and expected principal issues, supplementing any earlier written reports

_____   Jurisdictional/venue problems—whether to consider early or defer

_____   Issues for early determination

_____   Class action allegations

_____   Whether initial discovery should be limited to certain time periods, parties, claims, or defenses

_____   Identification of issues for early summary judgment determination

_____   Discovery needed; time to accomplish

_____   Schedule for motions, briefing, and submission

_____   Preliminary determination of issues on which discovery should be focused

_____   5.   Pleadings and Motions

_____   Suspension of time for filing certain pleadings and motions

_____   Filing of amended complaint(s) after discovery

_____   Deadlines

_____   Adding/changing claims or defenses

_____   Joining additional parties

_____   Counterclaims, cross-claims, third-party complaints

_____   Relief from deadlines if justified by discovery

_____   Standard and "deemed" pleadings, motions, and orders

_____   Refinement of issues

_____   Abandonment of frivolous issues

_____   Listing essential elements of cause of action/defense

_____   Statements of contentions/proof on specific claims/defenses

_____   Total or partial summary judgment; also Federal Rule of Civil Procedure 56(d)

_____   Discovery period

_____   Time for motions, briefs, and submission

_____   Early trial of special issues under Federal Rule of Civil Procedure 42(b)

_____   Early appellate review under Federal Rule of Civil Procedure 54(b), 28 U.S.C. § 1292(b) (1994), and so on.

_____   Exchange of pleadings, motions, and memoranda in electronic form

____ 6. Class Allegations

- ____ Probing behind allegations; potential for certification even if not alleged
- ____ Possible conflicts
- ____ Within class
- ____ Discovery for class certification purposes
- ____ Schedule; completion date
- ____ Discovery from class representatives
- ____ Extent to which discovery is permitted from class members
- ____ Time/procedure for presenting certification question
- ____ Whether formal motion required and when
- ____ Defining class in objective terms and identifying particular claims of class
- ____ Briefing; Statement of uncontested facts
- ____ Schedule
- ____ Identifying factual disputes on which evidentiary hearing needed
- ____ Proposed method and form of notice
- ____ Hearing
- ____ Date
- ____ Extent to which evidence is presented by affidavit, by witnesses

____ 7. Preliminary Plan for Discovery

- ____ Obligations under Federal Rule of Civil Procedure 26(a), (b), and (g)
- ____ Adoption of plan under Federal Rule of Civil Procedure 26(f)
- ____ Preliminary delineation of issues
- ____ Monitor and review as litigation progresses
- ____ Revise when justified
- ____ Limitations
- ____ Time limits and schedules
- ____ Using transcripts, interrogatories, and answers in electronic form
- ____ Completion of all discovery (or set trial date)
- ____ Schedule for particular segments of discovery
- ____ Sequencing of discovery
- ____ Identify sources of information (documents/witnesses)
- ____ Limits on quantity
- ____ General limitations

_____ Class members/representatives

_____ Discovery in other countries

_____ Procedures for resolving disputes

_____ Efforts by counsel to resolve voluntarily

_____ Procedures for obtaining court ruling

_____ Form of motion—written/oral

_____ When brief required/permitted

_____ Telephone conferences

_____ Use of magistrates

_____ Need for special master

_____ Special topics

_____ Confidential information; protective orders

_____ Documents

_____ Adoption of identification system

_____ Preservation

_____ Depositories

_____ Depositions

_____ Cross-noticing

_____ Use of videotape depositions

_____ Guidelines

_____ Deferred/supplemental depositions

_____ Interrogatories

_____ For what purposes

_____ Timing; scope

_____ Special limits on number

_____ Requests for admissions; stipulations

_____ Expert testimony

_____ Governmental investigations, reports

_____ Computerized data; other summaries

_____ Polls; surveys; sampling techniques

_____ Continuing duty to disclose settlement/special agreements

_____ Discovery databases: formats; remote access

_____ 8.   Special Appointments and Referrals

_____ Court-appointed expert (Federal Rule of Evidence 706) or magistrate/master (Federal Rule of Civil Procedure 53)

_____ Need; identification of subject matter

_____ Timing

_____ Procedure for selection

_____ Nominations by parties

_____ Suggestions by other groups; peremptory challenges

_____ Use of magistrate as special master

_____ Compensation

_____ Communications

_____ Extent to which expert/master may communicate ex parte with parties, parties' experts, or court

_____ Report from expert/magistrate/master

_____ Discovery from court-appointed expert

_____ Agreements as to effect of findings by court's expert/master

_____ Arbitration

_____ 9. Settlement

_____ Status of discussions

_____ Desirability of settlement conference

_____ Judge's role in facilitating negotiations

_____ Use of other resources/techniques

_____ Other judges/magistrates

_____ Special master(s)

_____ Special counsel

_____ Summary jury trial; minitrial

_____ Nonbinding arbitration

_____ Special problems

_____ Class actions

_____ Premature settlement discussions

_____ Settlement classes

_____ Secret agreements

_____ Most-favored-nation clauses

_____ Agreements limiting discovery

_____ Problems with late partial settlements

_____ Ethical considerations

_____ Discovery schedules not extended for settlement discussions

_____ 10. Trial

_____ Trial date—tentative or firm

_____ Statement of agreed/disputed facts; statement of contentions and proof listing of witnesses/exhibits

_____ Preliminary schedule

_____ Use of videotapes or computer-stored or -displayed materials

____   Identification of issues for severance and early trial

____   Interrelationship between jury and nonjury issues

____   Potential res judicata/collateral estoppel from other litigation

____ 11.   Further Conference(s)

____   Date of next conference—tentative or firm

____   Interim status reports

____   Additional conferences

____   Prescheduled

____   On request, as need arises

____   As particular phases of proceedings completed

____   To handle emergency matters

____ 12.   Preparation of Order

____   Drafts by counsel

____   Use of exhibits as attachments to order

____   Transcription by reporter of proceedings

§ 14.4   Report of Parties' Planning Meeting (Form 35)

Form 35 (see **Form 14–2**), provided in the Federal Rules of Civil Procedure, covers essentially the same issues as the checklist in § **14.3.** That checklist could be used as the starting point for a more detailed report of a planning meeting, in lieu of the simpler form that follows.

FORM 14–2
SAMPLE REPORT OF PARTIES' PLANNING MEETING

1. Pursuant to Fed. R. Civ. P. 26(f), a meeting was held on [date] at [place] and was attended by:

name for plaintiff(s) [name]

name for defendant(s) [name]

name for defendant(s) [name]

2. Pre-Discovery Disclosures. The parties [have exchanged/will exchange] by [date] the information required by [Fed. R. Civ. P. 26(a)(1)/Local Rules _____].

3. Discovery Plan. The parties jointly propose to the court the following discovery plan: (Use separate paragraphs or subparagraphs as necessary if parties disagree.)

Discovery will be needed on the following subjects: (brief description of subjects on which discovery will be needed).

All discovery commenced in time to be completed by [date]. (Discovery on [issue for early discovery] to be completed by [date])

Maximum of [___] interrogatories by each party to any other party. (Responses due [___] days after service.)

Maximum of [___] requests for admission by each party to any other party. (Responses due [___] days after service.)

Maximum of [___] depositions by plaintiff(s) and [___] by defendants).

Each deposition (other than of [___]) limited to maximum of [___] hours unless extended by agreement of parties.

Reports from retained experts under Rule 26(a)(2) due:

from plaintiff(s) by [date]

from defendant(s) by [date]

Supplementations under Rule 26(e) due [time/interval].

4. Other Items. (Use separate paragraphs or subparagraphs as necessary if parties disagree.)

The parties [request/do not request] a conference with the court before entry of the scheduling order.

The parties request a pre-trial conference in [month, year].

Plaintiff(s) should be allowed until [date] to join additional parties and until [date] to amend the pleadings.

Defendant(s) should be allowed until [date] to join additional parties and until [date] to amend the pleadings.

All potentially dispositive motions should be filed by [date].

Settlement [is likely/is unlikely/cannot be evaluated prior to [date]] (may be enhanced by use of the following alternative dispute resolution procedure:

Final lists of witnesses and exhibits under Rule 26(a)(3) should be due

from plaintiff(s) by [date]

from defendant(s) by [date]

Parties should have [___] days after service of final lists of witnesses and exhibits to list objections under Rule 26(a)(3).

The case should be ready for trial by [date] (and at this time is expected to take approximately [length of time]).

[Other matters.]

Date: [date]

§ 14.5   Sample Schedule Order

FORM 14–3
SAMPLE SCHEDULE ORDER

Schedule Order

It is ORDERED:

1. Discovery shall be conducted according to the following schedule:

Discovery Time

Interrogatories by all parties to ascertain identity and location of witnesses and documents, including computerized records

Document production by all parties

Lay witness depositions

___noticed by plaintiffs

___noticed by defendants

Expert(s):

Plaintiff

___identification; reports

___depositions

Defendant

___identification; reports

___depositions

Production of proposed computerized summaries and samples:

___by plaintiffs

___by defendants

Requests for admission and interrogatories by all parties

2.   Except for good cause shown,

(a) relief from the above schedule shall not be granted and all discovery shall be completed by [date];

(b) discovery shall be limited to matters occurring after [date], and before [date];

(c) no more than [___] interrogatories (including subparts) may be propounded to any party (exclusive of interrogatories seeking the identity and location of witnesses and documents);

(d) no more than [___] depositions may be taken by either plaintiffs or defendants, may take more than [___] days;

(e) no amendment of pleadings may be made after [date], and no additional parties may be joined as plaintiff, defendant, or third-party defendant after [date].

3. The parties are expected to be prepared for trial on all issues (except [___]) by [date].

Dated:

United States District Judge

SUMMARY JUDGMENT ISSUES

§ 14.6   Statement of Material Facts

FORM 14–4
SAMPLE STATEMENT OF MATERIAL FACTS

IN THE UNITED STATES DISTRICT COURT

FOR THE [NORTHERN] DISTRICT OF [ILLINOIS]

[EASTERN] DIVISION

U.S. EQUAL EMPLOYMENT OPPORTUNITY COMMISSION,

Plaintiff,   Civil Action No.: [92 C 7330]

v.

[A.I.C. SECURITY INVESTIGATIONS, LTD.];

[A.I.C. INTERNATIONAL, LTD.];

and [unnamed defendant C],   Honorable [Marvin E. Aspen]

Defendants.   Magistrate Judge [Guzman]

DEFENDANTS' STATEMENT OF MATERIAL FACTS

Defendants, [A.I.C. SECURITY INVESTIGATIONS, LTD. ("A.I.C.")], [A.I.C. INTERNATIONAL, LTD. ("A.I.C. INTERNATIONAL")], and [C], by and through their attorneys [WESSEL & PAUTSCH, P.C.], by [Charles W. Pautsch], [attorney A], and [attorney B], pursuant to Rule 56 of the Federal Rules of Civil Procedure, and [Rule 12(l)] of the General Rules of the United States District Court for the [Northern] District of [Illinois], hereby proffer the following materials facts to which there exists no material issue to be tried:

A.   ESSENTIAL FUNCTIONS OF [CHARLES WESSEL]'S POSITION

1.   [Charles Wessel (hereinafter, "Wessel")] was hired in [February], [1986], as the Executive Director of [A.I.C. Security Investigations, Ltd. (hereinafter, "A.I.C.")], a wholly owned subsidiary of A.I.C. International, Ltd. (hereinafter, "A.I.C. International"); [A.I.C.] was and is the largest division of [A.I.C. International] [citation to record].

2.   The Executive Director position which [Wessel] held was at all times during his employment the highest management position in [A.I.C.], and, accordingly, [Wessel] was responsible for the overall management and profitability of [A.I.C.] [citations to record].

3.   The business of [A.I.C.] at all pertinent times has been to provide security guards and related services for commercial and residential properties in and around [Chicago], [Illinois] [citations to record].

4.   The security guard business, as compared to other service industries, is highly competitive; it is a dynamic, unpredictable business that requires continual and prompt adaptations to the clients' needs as they arise [citation to record].

5.   The position of Executive Director for [A.I.C.] required, as an essential function, regular and predictable attendance of as many hours as necessary to meet the needs of the clients; it was not a "9 to 5" job [citation to record].

6.   The position of Executive Director for [A.I.C.] required, as an essential function, overall management and direction of the 300-plus employees of the company, from all management level personnel to watch commanders, and ultimately the hundreds of security guards employed by [A.I.C.] [citation to record].

7.   The position of Executive Director for [A.I.C.] required, as an essential function, dealing with labor unions . . . . supervising investigations . . . , and tracking litigation [A.I.C.] was involved in [citations to record].

8.   The position of Executive Director for [A.I.C.] required, as an essential function, the development of policy, site walk-throughs, handling labor matters, establishing price rates, and monitoring and disciplining subordinates [citation to record].

B.   [CHARLES WESSEL]'S CLAIMED DISABILITY

9.   When [Wessel] started with [A.I.C.], he had emphysema caused by smoking 2–4 packs of cigarettes/day for approximately 25 years and 8–10 cigars a day for 15 years, and he had a back injury rendering him 20-percent disabled under his V.A. disability.

10.   [Wessel] had cancer for 5 of the approximately 6 years he worked for [A.I.C.], with the first diagnosis of lung cancer in his left lung in [1987]; a recurrence of cancer in his right lung in [1991]; and, a diagnosis of inoperable brain tumors in early [April of 1992].

11.   The cancerous brain tumors are believed by [Wessel]'s doctors to have "metastasized" (i.e., moved to the brain from their primary site of development,

Wessel's lungs) approximately three to six months before they were diagnosed, sometime in late [1991] [citation to record].

12.   [Wessel]'s condition is believed by his doctors to be terminal and he was told sometime in [April 1992] that he had six to twelve months to live; his treatments since [April] of [1992] have been "palitative," that is, not for the purpose of a cure, but to prolong and assure some quality of [Wessel]'s life.

13.   [Wessel] was initially diagnosed in [April 1992] with 2 tumors, and subsequently in [June 1992], 2 additional tumors were diagnosed, for a total of 4.

C.   [CHARLES WESSEL]'S INABILITY TO CONTINUE TO PERFORM THE ESSENTIAL FUNCTIONS OF THE POSITION HE HELD AS EXECUTIVE DIRECTOR FOR [A.I.C.]

14.   As of [July 29, 1992], [Charles Wessel] was absent from work approximately 25 percent of the previous year:

(a)   he missed 16 days between [July 29th] and [August 13th, 1991], when he experienced a pneumothorax (collapsed lung) during what was supposed to have been a routine one-day biopsy [citation to record];

(b)   he missed 2 half days and one full day following the above, in [August] of [1991];

(c)   he missed approximately 33 days between [October 3rd] and [November 4th], [1991] for surgery to remove a portion of his right lung due to recurring cancer [citation to record];

(d)   he missed approximately 3 hours per day as a result of each day he received radiation treatments, which would have included:

(i)   several days in [December], [1991], following his lung operation;

(ii)   15 workdays in [April] and [May], [1992] (Ex. 2, 63.)

(iii)   several work days in [June], [1992]

(iv)   2 days in [July], [1992]

D.   [CHARLES WESSEL]'S RISK OF INJURY TO HIMSELF AND OTHERS

15.   An additional brain tumor in the occipital area of [Charles Wessel]'s brain was identified on or about [June 22, 1991] [citation to record].

16.   Dr. [A], [Wessel]'s primary treating physician, restricted [Wessel]'s driving because of lesions in the occipital lobe of the brain [citation to record].

17.   In [June] of [1992], [Wessel] developed new brain tumors in the parietal area of the brain [citation to record].

18.   [Wessel] experienced seizures in [December] of [1992] [citation to record].

19.   Dr. [B], a radiation oncologist treating [Wessel], informed [defendant C] in a telephone conversation that [Wessel] had been advised not to drive [citation to record].

20.   [Larry R.], the Executive Vice President of [A.I.C. International]'s Systems Division, offered [Wessel] a driver as an accommodation, which [Wessel] refused [citation to record].

Dated this [24th] day of [February], [1993].

[counsel for defendants]

§ 14.7   Response to Statement of Material Facts

FORM 14–5
SAMPLE RESPONSE TO STATEMENT OF MATERIAL FACTS

IN THE UNITED STATES DISTRICT COURT

FOR THE [NORTHERN] DISTRICT OF [ILLINOIS]

[EASTERN] DIVISION

U.S. EQUAL EMPLOYMENT OPPORTUNITY COMMISSION

AND [CHARLES H. WESSEL]

Plaintiffs,   Civil Action No. [92 C 7330]

v.

[A.I.C. SECURITY INVESTIGATIONS, LTD.];

[A.I.C. INTERNATIONAL, LTD.]; AND [unnamed defendant C],

Defendants.   Magistrate Judge [Guzman]

PLAINTIFFS' RESPONSE TO DEFENDANTS' STATEMENT OF MATERIAL FACTS

Pursuant to Rule 56 of the Federal Rules of Civil Procedure and [Rule 12(n)] of the General Rules of the United States District Court for the [Northern] District of [Illinois], Plaintiffs hereby file their response to Defendants' Statement of Material Facts.

Paragraph 1: The Plaintiffs admit this statement.

Paragraph 2: The Plaintiffs admit this statement.

Paragraph 3: The Plaintiffs admit this statement.

Paragraph 4: The security industry is a changing business requiring adaptation to resolve issues as they arise [citation to record].

Paragraph 5: The security industry is not always a nine-to-five business [citation to record].

Paragraphs 6, 7, and 8: The essential functions of the position of Executive Director at [A.I.C. Security Investigations, Ltd.] were the supervision over and responsibility for the guard division to ensure both profitability and legal compliance [citation to record].

Paragraphs 9 and 10: Defendants have not cited any support in the record for the information contained in these paragraphs. As the moving parties, Defendants have the burden of proving that there is no genuine issue of fact as to these assertions. Because Defendants failed to provide any support for these assertions, the statements should not be considered for purposes of the pending Motion for Summary judgment.

Paragraph 11: [Charles Wessel] was diagnosed with brain lesion in [April 1992]. There is no way of determining within a reasonable degree of medical certainty how long the brain tumors were present before they were diagnosed [citation to record].

Paragraphs 12 and 13: Defendants have not cited any support in the record of the information contained in these paragraphs. As the moving parties, Defendants have the burden of proving that there is no genuine issue of fact as to these assertions. Because Defendants failed to provide any support for these assertions, the statements should not be considered for the pending Motion for Summary judgment.

Paragraph 14:[3] Initially, Plaintiffs note that Defendants have not cited any support in the record for the assertions in subparagraphs (b), (d)(i), (d)(iii), and 400. As the moving parties, Defendants have the burden of proving that there is no genuine issue of fact as to these assertions. Because Defendants failed to provide any support for these assertions, the statements should not be considered for purposes of the pending Motion for Summary Judgment.

Plaintiffs admit subparagraphs 14(a) and (c); however, the statement that the 49 days that [Wessel] missed work represents twenty-five percent of the workdays between [July 1991] and [July 1992] is simply incorrect.

Paragraphs 15 and 17: In [June 1992], [Charles Wessel] was found to have a new small lesion, less than one centimeter, in the parietal area of the brain [citation to record].

Paragraph 16: The Defendants cite to pages 189–91 of Dr. [A]'s deposition in support of the statement; however, no such pages exist in the deposition transcript. Dr. [A], [Wessel]'s primary treating physician, never instructed [Charles Wessel] not to drive. As of [September 3, 1992], Dr. [A] would place some driving restrictions on Mr. [Wessel] [citations to record].

Paragraph 18: In [December 1992], [Wessel] experienced a seizure [citation to record].

Paragraph 19: Plaintiffs admit this paragraph.

Paragraph 20: [Charles Wessel] did not require a driver to and from his employment in 1991 and does not recall being offered a driver by [Larry R.] at that time. Deposition of [Charles Wessel] [(February 10, 1993)], p. 44, lines 20–24; and p. 45, lines 1–4.

Respectfully Submitted,

[attorney B]
Trial Attorney

Equal Employment Opportunity Commission
[536 South Clark], [Room 982]
[Chicago], [Illinois] [60605]
[(312) 886-9120]

[attorney D]
Attorney for [Charles Wessel]

---

[3] Defendants have two paragraphs numbered 13 (see § **14.6**), but they do not have a paragraph 14 in their statement. Therefore, the plaintiffs are labeling the second paragraph 13 as Paragraph 14 for purposes of this response.

§ 14.8   Reply Memorandum on Summary Judgment

FORM 14–6
SAMPLE REPLY MEMORANDUM ON SUMMARY JUDGMENT

DEFENDANTS' REPLY MEMORANDUM ON SUMMARY JUDGMENT

I. THE PLAINTIFFS HAVE NOT REBUTTED THE CONCLUSIVE EXPERT MEDICAL EVIDENCE THAT [CHARLES WESSEL] WAS UNABLE TO PERFORM THE ESSENTIAL FUNCTIONS OF HIS JOB

Defendants' motion for summary judgment was supported by uncontroverted medical opinions from both of [Wessel]'s treating physicians. (Defendants' initial memorandum, pages 16–17.) Defendants also supplied for the record medical opinions of the two physicians Defendants intend to call at trial, if necessary [citation to record]. As the record makes clear, all four physicians who would give expert medical testimony at trial have declared [Charles Wessel] unable to perform his former position of Executive Director for [A.I.C.]. This conclusive medical testimony is not disputed anywhere in the Plaintiffs' response.

Specifically, [Wessel]'s primary treating physician, Doctor [A], completed a medical report for the Bureau of Disability Determination Service, stating that [Wessel] was "frequently fatigued," was "unable to perform routine tasks" and was "unable to perform any work-related activities at this time" [citation to record].[4]

Defendants have also made pertinent portions of the deposition transcript of Doctor [B] a part of the record. Doctor [B] similarly indicated that [Wessel] was unable to perform his position.[5] Doctor [C] also testified that [Mr. Wessel] was not able to perform the essential function of his job as Executive Director at [A.I.C.] [citation to record].

Finally, Doctor [D], the only neurologist among the parties' expert witnesses for trial, testified:

---

[4] This opinion was rendered on or about August 24, 1992, one week after Doctor [A] examined Wessel. The most recent examination of Wessel prior to this August examination was performed on July 13, 1992. Because Wessel's last day of work for defendants was July 29, 1992, the August examination is the most relevant to Wessel's condition on his last day at work. This conclusion is particularly compelling in light of Doctor [B]'s testimony that, if anything, Wessel's condition had improved in August [citations to record].

[5] Defendants' citation in its original memorandum, page 17, incorrectly cited to page 67 rather than page 127. This was a typographical error. Page 163 may have been omitted from Defendants' Exhibit 4 of Doctor [B]'s deposition transcript, and it is attached hereto as Exhibit A, as a Supplement to Exhibit 4.

Q.   Okay. Dr. [D], do you have any opinions, within a reasonable degree of medical certainty, as to whether or not, in [July 1992], [Charles Wessel] was able to perform the essential functions of his job?

A.   I do.

Q.   And what is that opinion?

A.   Well, because of the neurological condition that [Mr. Wessel] had, it was my opinion that he was very likely to have cognitive impairments; neurological problems in terms of various functions involving reasoning, judgment, other personality-related functions that go along with having had metastic brain tumors, as well as a course of radiation therapy, as well as medications that he was receiving.

[citation to record].

II. THE PLAINTIFFS HAVE NO SUPPORTIVE MEDICAL EVIDENCE FOR A TRIAL

It comes as no surprise that Plaintiffs have completely ignored the medical opinions of even their own expert witnesses in their response. Their medical expert, Doctor [A], has admitted to supplying false medical reports to the bureau of Disability Determination Services on the very issue about which he is to testify at trial (i.e., [Wessel]'s ability to work).

On or about [August 24, 1992], Doctor [A] completed a medical report for the Bureau of Disability Determination Services in connection with [Wessel]'s application for social security disability benefits. . . . This medical report stated that [Wessel] was "frequently fatigued," was "unable to perform routine tasks" and was "unable to perform any work-related activities at this time" [citations to record].

By contrast, a little over one week after filling out this disability medical report, Doctor [A] signed an affidavit prepared for him by the EEOC . . . . This document provided: "I have assessed that [Mr. Wessel] can work full time in the position he held as Executive Director with A.I.C. Security" [citations to record].

On [December 18, 1992], Dr. [A] was confronted with these two contradictory medical reports at his deposition. Having testified in support of his EEOC affidavit that [Wessel] could work, Dr. [A] was asked to explain his conflicting medical report that Wessel could not work:

Q.   What does it state under No. 11 [of the report]?

A.   It states, "Patient is unable to perform any work-related activities at this time."

Q.   Do you want to distinguish between that and your previous testimony?

A.   The reason for this now is that he had been fired from his job, and we felt that he should be able to get some compensation because no one is going to hire him anymore. He is not going to be able to get any income at all, and so this is for the social security to say that, yes, he is not able to work.

Q.   And you know that by writing what you were writing under No. 11 that would help him qualify for benefits?

A.   That's correct.

Q.   Is it your testimony today that despite what you put in response to Question No. 11, that's not what you believe?

A.   Absolutely not.

Q.   You emphatically disagree with what you wrote on that?

A.   Yes.

Clearly, Doctor [A] was without any legitimate explanation for his two completely contradictory medical opinions. Instead, the doctor testified that one of the opinions—the one given to the Bureau of Disability Determination Services—was entirely fabricated because "we felt he [Wessel] should be able to get some compensation . . . ."

At the same time, Doctor [A] testified that he knew almost nothing about [Wessel]'s job at [A.I.C.] (including its title) even though he had signed the EEOC's affidavit that stated: "I am aware of the essential functions that comprise the job of Executive Director" [citation to record].[6]

Doctor [A] admittedly committed a felony by lying on the very issue which Plaintiffs are attempting to prove through his expert medical opinion. The Social Security Act contains severe criminal penalties for the filing of false medical reports, and upon conviction of such a felony, the law provides for a fine of not more than $5,000.00 or imprisonment for not more than five years, or both. 42 U.S.C. § 408(c); *cf.* [*United States v. Toler*, 440 F.2d 1242 (5th Cir. 1971)].

This Court is justified in excluding Doctor [A]'s opinions from its consideration of the merits of this case. The [Seventh] Circuit Court of Appeals has held that a Rule 702 (Fed. R. Evid.) Expert Witness' "declaration, full of assertion but empty of

---

[6] In fact, Doctor [A] testified that he was not under oath when he signed the EEOC affidavit. Furthermore, he admitted, "I sign a lot of things without reading them," so he was not sure if he had ever read the EEOC's affidavit [citations of record]. Defendants submit that, given the fact that Doctor [A] had just prepared a medical report on August 24 which stated that Wessel was unable to work, a proper investigation into the facts of this matter required more than just obtaining a busy doctor's signature on a form affidavit that he may not even have read.

the facts and reasons, won't get a case past summary judgment, for the judge must look behind [the expert's] ultimate conclusion . . ." (citations omitted; emphasis added). [*Mid-State Fertilizer Co. v. Exchange Nat'l Bank*, 877 F.2d 1333, 1339 (7th Cir. 1989)].

In this case, Doctor [A]'s testimony that he flat out lied about [Wessel]'s medical condition should be so offensive to the Court that anything he may say now is without one scintilla of value to the findings of fact in this action. As Judge [James M.] of this Court noted in [*Soderlund v. Ben Franklin Stores, Inc.*, 41 Fair Empl. Prac. Cas. (BNA) 1709, 1711 (N.D. Ill. 1986)], some testimony is so unworthy of consideration in court that it may be termed "incredible as a matter of law" (citing [*Draeger v. Jockey International, Inc.*, 583 F. Supp. 570 (S.D.N.Y.), *aff'd mem.*, 751 F.2d 368 (2d Cir. 1984)]).

Under circumstances such as these, the United States Court of Appeals for the [Seventh] Circuit has declared that District courts have a "duty to ignore sham issues in determining the appropriateness of summary judgment." [*Babrocky v. Jewel Food Co.*, 773 F.2d 857, 861 (7th Cir. 1985)].

In [*Babrocky*], the court of appeals stated that parties (or, Defendants submit, their expert witnesses) should not be allowed to create credibility issues contradicting their own earlier testimony: "Otherwise, the very purpose of the summary judgement motion—to weed out unfounded claims, specious denials, and sham defenses would be severely undercut." [*Id.* at 861]. Here, Doctor [A] must not be allowed to pick between his medical opinions, especially to state that his opinion of [August 24th] was a felonious lie, but that his opinion of [September 2nd] is now credible for this Court.

Significantly, Doctor [B] has never rendered any medical opinion about [Wessel]'s ability to work other than her assessment to the Bureau of Disability Determination Services that [Wessel] could not do so [citation to record]. Doctor [B] apparently will not contradict her earlier opinion that [Wessel] could not work, and in any event, Plaintiffs have not any favorable opinion from [Dr. B] for purposes of the instant motion.

Doctor [B] testified generally about the effects of tumors in various portions of the brain . . . but when asked specifics about memory processes, she replied: "That's really beyond area [sic] of, you know, my personal expertise since I'm not a neurologist or neurosurgeon" [citation to record].

At her deposition, Doctor [B] would only testify that the physiological aspects of the human brain fall outside her expertise and within the expertise of neurosurgeons and neurologists:

Q.   Is it safe to say generally that those portions of the brain we're talking about where [Mr. Wessel]'s tumors were in [April] are more related to motor functions?

A.   No, they are not so much related to motor functions. Really, the area which is referred to motor function is parietal [sic] area of the brain.

Again, I think you are trying to simplify the question, you know. The brain cannot be just separated, you know, nine or ten pieces. It is all connected together.

Q.   Again, the experts that talk about this type of subject would be a neurosurgeon or neurologist?

A.   That's correct.

[citation to record].

Given the uncontroverted fact that [Wessel] suffers from a dynamic neurological condition, and given the uncontroverted fact that [Wessel]'s position involved reasoning, judgment and, generally, running an entire company in the demanding security guard industry, no fair-minded jury could find that [Wessel] was qualified without the benefit of expert medical testimony.

All of the expert medical opinions in this record state that [Wessel] could not do the job anymore.

III.   GIVEN THE NATURE OF [WESSEL]'S ILLNESS AND HIS JOB, PLAINTIFFS CANNOT MEET THEIR PRIMA FACIE BURDEN TO SHOW THAT [WESSEL] WAS QUALIFIED WITHOUT COMPETENT EXPERT MEDICAL EVIDENCE

The instant action involved [Charles Wessel]'s condition of "metastatic cancer," that is, cancer initially of the lungs which subsequently moved to his brain in the form of multiple, growing tumors [citation to record].

[Wessel]'s position of Executive Director of [A.I.C.], as the top management position, meant that he ran the company [citation to record]. The essential functions of the position are, admittedly, largely intellectual.[7]

Given these facts, competent medical evidence is required in order to address the issue of [Wessel]'s ability to continue to perform, with or without reasonable accommodation, the essential functions of his job while suffering from a degenerative brain disease.

In [*School Board of Nassau County v. Arline,* 480 U.S. 273, 287 (1987)], the Supreme Court observed that "in most cases, the district court will need to conduct an individualized inquiry and make appropriate findings of fact" in order to determine if an individual is "qualified" for a particular job.

---

[7] However, the defendants do dispute the plaintiff's characterization of his job as purely mental.

The [*Arline*] court held that its inquiry "should include '[findings of]' facts based upon reasonable medical judgments given the state of medical knowledge" about [Arline]'s communicable disease. [(*Id.* at 288.)]

The instant action requires that the Court's inquiry include findings of fact based upon the reasonable medical judgments in the record concerning [Wessel]'s degenerative brain cancer. The [District of Columbia] Court of Appeals addressed a similar situation involving the complexities of diseases of the brain:

> Unlike some other handicaps, the causes and effects of manic-depressive syndrome and the extent to which the symptoms of the illness can be controlled by medication and therapy [i.e. "accommodated"] are beyond the ken of the average lay person. Where proof of an issue is related to a science or profession beyond the ken of an average lay person, expert testimony is required. (Citations omitted.)

[*American University v. DCCHR*, 57 Fair Empl. Prac. Cas. (BNA) 245, 250, 598 A.2d 416 (D.C. App. 1991)].

Indeed, expert medical testimony is a commonplace necessity in handicap/disability litigation. *See, e.g.,* [*Chiari v. City of League City*, 920 F.2d 311, 316 (5th Cir. 1991) (on review of district court's decision of summary judgment, court of appeals rejected Plaintiff's argument that "despite the testimony of three physicians, a jury still could find that he is capable of performing his job . . .")]; [*Sanders v. United Parcel Service*, 491 N.E.2d 1314, 1318, 142 Ill. App. 3d 362, 96 Ill. Dec. 854 (1986) (dismissal of complaint upheld where Plaintiff failed to provide medical documentation and therefore failed to meet initial burden on handicap claim)]; [*Connecticut General Life Insurance Co. v. DILHR*, 86 Wis. 2d 393, 407–8, 273 N.W.2d 206 (1979) (court's determination regarding alcoholism as a handicap "is a matter of expert medical opinion proved by a physician and not a layman")].

The circumstances of the present case call for expert medical opinions just as the Supreme Court required in [*Arline*], and just as numerous forums have required in similar case law. The neurological consequences of brain tumors in various portions of the brain simply are not within the knowledge of the lay person juror.

IV. THE PLAINTIFFS' RESPONSE TO DEFENDANTS' MOTION FOR SUMMARY JUDGMENT FAILS TO CREATE THE GENUINE ISSUES OF MATERIAL FACT NECESSARY TO TAKE THIS CASE TO TRIAL AND SUMMARY JUDGMENT IN DEFENDANTS' FAVOR IS THEREFORE APPROPRIATE

Plaintiffs concede that it is their burden to prove that [Wessel] was qualified for the position of Executive Director at the time of his discharge [citation to record]. Having admitted this burden, however, Plaintiffs have failed to designate specific facts showing a genuine issue for trial on the matter of whether [Wessel] was qualified to remain in his position beyond [July 29,1992].

Instead of putting forth specific facts that would create a genuine issue regarding the material fact of [Wessel]'s ability to continue working, Plaintiffs' memorandum treats the issue as though this were Defendants' burden, which they need only dis-prove.[8]

The only evidence Plaintiffs put forth in support of their prima facie burden to show that [Wessel] was qualified is that [Wessel] had "experience and expertise in the security industry." . . .[9] This misses the mark. [Wessel] would not have been hired as A.I.C.'s Executive Director in [1986] had he not had experience in the security industry. The relevant issue is whether [Wessel] was able to perform the essential functions of the job beyond [July, 1992] given his degenerative condition. In these regards, it must be noted that Plaintiffs' heavy reliance on [David P.] is meaningless considering Plaintiffs' admission that [David P.] was fired on [July 6, 1992] [citations to record].

The severe lack of probative evidence offered by Plaintiffs is simply insufficient to overcome Defendants' Motion for Summary Judgment, and Rule 56(c) of the Federal Rules of Civil Procedure provides that Summary Judgment "shall be ren-dered forthwith" where the moving party is entitled to judgment as a matter of law based upon the record before the court.

In [*EEOC v. Clay Printing Co.*, 955 F.2d 936, 942–43 (4th Cir. 1992)], the Court noted that "[i]n overcoming a motion for summary judgment," the EEOC has to "produce direct evidence" supporting its prima facie case. Holding that the EEOC failed to "marshall enough evidence," the Court upheld summary judgment, stating as follows:

> A fair-minded jury simply could not return a verdict for the EEOC on the evidence presented. [*Anderson v. Liberty Lobby, Inc.*, 477 U.S. 242, 252 (1986)]. "The mere existence of a scintilla of evidence in support of the plaintiff's position will be insuffi-cient; there must be evidence on which the jury could reasonably find for the plain-tiff." [*Id.*]

Here, Plaintiffs do not even attempt to rebut [Wessel]'s own admissions that he turned over his essential functions to his assistants. (See Defendants' initial memo-randum, pp. 15–16 and citations to evidence.) Furthermore, such transfers of

---

[8] For instance, the plaintiffs concede Wessel's short-term memory loss but argue that this fact does not evidence any impact upon Wessel's performance [citation to record].

[9] The plaintiffs' memorandum argues several points that are not supported in the record. First, the entire "factual Summary" is without one single citation to record evidence; second, the plaintiffs' assertion regarding the financial performance of A.I.C. is likewise unsupported by Fed. R. Civ. P. 56 evidence (defendants could show that A.I.C.'s prof-itability was actually drastically down in 1992 from 1991, had plaintiffs properly put the matter at issue in this motion); and finally, the plaintiffs' so-called "powerful" evidence that a subordinate on-site employee (that is, an employee who did not work at A.I.C.'s premises with Wessel) held Wessel in high esteem is less than the scintilla of evidence rejected on summary judgment in *Brownell* [citations to record]. *See* Brownell v. Figel, 950 F.2d 1285, 1289 (7th Cir. 1991).

essential functions do not even fall into the analysis of whether reasonable accommodations can be made.

In another handicap case involving the security guard industry (albeit, a managerial position was not involved), the Court of Appeals for the [Tenth] Circuit held that the company did not have to provide an assistant to a legally blind security guard. [Coleman v. Darden, 595 F.2d 533 (10th Cir. 1979)]. The court in [Coleman] reasoned that the "assistant" would be performing the job for the individual rather than assisting the individual to perform his job. [Id. at 536.]

Similarly, when [Wessel], as Executive Director, required that his "assistants" perform what had always been the essential functions of his job, in essence he ceased doing the job and was no longer "qualified." Again, these compelling facts are uncontroverted.

V. PLAINTIFFS HAVE FAILED TO RAISE ANY ISSUE OF MATERIAL FACT THAT DEFENDANTS ARE NOT ENTITLED TO SUMMARY JUDGMENT BECAUSE [WESSEL] POSED A DIRECT THREAT AS DEFINED IN THE ADA

Plaintiffs' memorandum [citation to record] does not raise any issues of fact on the matter of [Wessel]'s medically verified risk of injury to himself and others. Therefore, the following facts are now undisputed:

(1) [Wessel] was at risk of unpredictable seizures and was advised as early as [April], [1992] to avoid the use of an automobile [citation to record];

(2) Based upon the discovery of new tumors in the parietal area of his brain in [June], [1992], [Wessel] was considered by his physicians to be at an acute and heightened risk of seizures [citation to record];

(3) [Wessel] drove to, from, and during work and included his subordinate employees as passengers in his automobile [citation to record];

(4) Defendants offered [Wessel] a personal driver to pick him up at his house and take him to and from his work [citation to record];

(5) [Wessel] refused Defendants' offer of a driver [citation to record]; and

(6) [Wessel] continued driving despite his doctors advising him not drive [citation to record].

Instead of challenging these facts, Plaintiffs argue that the direct threat defense of ADA does not apply as a matter of law. Obviously, this is a matter to be decided by the Court and not a jury.

Plaintiffs' argument is based upon two erroneous legal arguments. First, they argue that Defendants' direct threat defense must fail because Defendants cannot establish that driving was an essential function of the position of Executive Director. Second, Plaintiffs apparently argue that Defendants may not assert the direct threat defense without proving that their motive was particular concern over the health or safety of [Wessel] and/or his subordinates. Both of these legal arguments must fail.

A. Under the ADA, a direct threat defense need only be "job-related" and in any event, getting to and from work was an essential function inherent in [Wessel]'s position.

It is expressly stated in the pertinent provisions of the ADA that the direct threat defense need only be "job-related." 42 U.S.C. §§ 12113(a), (b).

To apply the direct threat standard only to essential functions of the job would mean that employers would have to tolerate serious safety risks in all instances where a "direct threat" employee is performing only marginal functions or is simply on the employer's premises. Although the ADA mandates reasonable accommodations to avoid the risks involved with a direct threat employee, there clearly can be risks associated with nonessential functions that simply cannot be reasonably accommodated.[10]

For example, an engineer with Parkinson's disease poses no direct threat to safety while performing the essential functions of his engineering job. However, if in performing those essential functions, he needs to get to, from and about in the buildings he is inspecting, he may pose a serious risk to health and safety. These were the actual facts in the case of [*Chiari v. City of League City*, 920 F.2d 311 (5th Cir. 1991)].

The Court in [*Chiari*] held that the Plaintiff was not "otherwise qualified" under the Rehabilitation Act when three neurologists/neurosurgeons testified that his Parkinson's disease posed a significant risk to health and safety. [*Id.* at 316.]

In the instant action, Plaintiffs did not challenge their own expert witness, Dr. [B]'s, determination that [Wessel] posed a significant risk while driving due to the high probability of seizures. When [Wessel] in fact experienced seizures, Dr. [B] was not in the least surprised [citation to record].

As with [*Chiari*], driving did not comprise the majority of [Wessel]'s job, yet he clearly needed to get to and from work. Furthermore, [Wessel] himself testified that approximately 5 percent of his job involved making on-site visits, although he became more selective in [1992] [citation to record].

---

[10] Even the EEOC interpretative rules (29 C.F.R. § 1630.2(r)) do not go so far as to say that a threat must be directly connected to an essential function of the employer's job. To an extent, the rules could be read in the fashion argued in the plaintiffs' response. The defendants submit that the rules are inconsistent with the congressional directive that the threat be "job-related." 42 U.S.C. §§ 12113(a), (b).

Thus, driving was inherently an essential function of [Wessel]'s job, even though this is not required under the law.

Plaintiffs' hypothetical argument that [Wessel] could easily have used other modes of transportation is unavailing under the uncontroverted circumstances of this case. [Wessel] insisted on driving. [Wessel] drove despite his doctors' orders. [Wessel] refused Defendants' offer to provide a personal driver for him. These facts are not contested.

Under these circumstances, Defendants attempted to provide [Wessel] more than "reasonable accommodations," all to no avail.

Similar to [Wessel], the Plaintiff in [*Chiari*] argued to the Court that he should be able to make his own choices regarding his personal safety. [*Id.* at 316.] However, the [*Chiari*] Court upheld summary judgment against the Plaintiff based upon objective and credible medical evidence that [*Chiari*] posed a risk to health and safety, with no consideration given to the subjective arguments of [*Chiari*]. [*Id.* at 317.]

B. Plaintiffs' argument that defendants must show a genuine concern for [Wessel]'s health and safety sets a standard for the direct threat defense that does not exist in the law.

Plaintiffs' argument that Defendants may not assert the direct threat defense because their motives were in the wrong place is simply unavailing. Plaintiffs would have Defendants bear a burden of demonstrating genuine concern over the health and welfare of [Charles Wessel] in order to assert the defense. This is not the law.

The ADA requires only that "an individual shall not pose a direct threat to health or safety . . . ." 42 U.S.C. § 12113(b). This language does not support the Plaintiffs' conclusion that an employer's motive be humane versus financial versus any other motive. All that the law requires is that, as here, medical experts have determined that [Wessel] posed a significant risk to health and safety to either himself or other employees in the workplace, and that these circumstances caused his exclusion from work with Defendants.

VI. CONCLUSION

In a very recent civil rights action before this Court, District Judge [Charles N.] summarized [Seventh] Circuit and Supreme Court precedent on the circumstances that favor the granting of a motion for summary judgment:

> Rule 56(c) of the Federal Rules of Civil Procedure provides that for a party to prevail on a summary judgment motion "the pleadings, depositions, answers to inter-rogatories, and admissions on file, together with the affidavits, if any, [must] show that there is no genuine issue as to any material fact and the moving party us entitled to a judgment as a matter of law." Fed R. Civ. P. 56(c). Even though all reasonable

inferences are drawn in favor of the party opposing the motion, [*Beraha v. Baxter Health Care Corp.*, 956 F.2d 1436, 1440 (7th Cir. 1992)], a scintilla of evidence in support of the non-movant's position will not suffice to oppose a motion for summary judgment. [*Brownell v. Figel*, 950 F.2d 1285, 1289 (7th Cir. 1991)]. Instead, the non-moving party must elucidate specific facts demonstrating that there is a genuine issue for trial. [*Matsushita Elec. Indus. Co. v. Zenith Radio Corp.*, 475 U.S. 574, 586 (1986)]. Moreover, to preclude summary judgment the disputed facts must be those that might affect the outcome of the suit, [*First Indiana Bank v. Baker*, 957 F.2d 506, 508 (7th Cir. 1992)], and a dispute about a material fact is 'genuine' only if the evidence is such that a reasonable jury could return a verdict for the non-moving party. [*Anderson v. Liberty Lobby, Inc.*, 477 U.S. 242, 248 (1986)]. 'One of the principal purposes of the summary judgment rule is to isolate and dispose of factually unsupported claims and defenses . . . .' [*Celotex Corp. v. Catrett*, 477 U.S. 317, 323–24 (1986)]. Accordingly, the non-moving party is required to go beyond the pleadings, affidavits, depositions, answers to interrogatories and admissions on file to designate specific facts showing a genuine issue for trial. [*Bank Leurni Le-Isreal, B.M. v. Lee*, 928 F.2d 232, 236 (7th Cir. 1991)].

[*Seward v. General Motors Corp.*, 805 F. Supp. 623, 627 (N.D. Ill. 1992)].

Plaintiffs' response to Defendants' Motion for Summary Judgment leaves untouched the unanimous medical opinions that [Wessel] could not perform. There are no genuine issues of material fact on the expert medical opinions in this action.

As the nonmoving party, Plaintiffs were required to come forward with specific facts creating genuine issues for trial. This is particularly necessary as to issues which Plaintiffs concede are their burden to prove in order to maintain any action under the ADA, and they have failed to provide evidence under Rule 56(c) that would permit a rational jury to determine that [Wessel] was qualified to remain the Executive Director for [A.I.C.].

On the matter of [Wessel] having also been excluded as posing a direct threat to health and safety, Plaintiffs have likewise wholly ignored the uncontroverted medical consensus that [Wessel] indeed posed such a probable risk. The legal arguments Plaintiffs raise are for the Court's determination (not a jury) and the arguments are insufficient to avoid summary judgment,

Because no rational jury could return a verdict for Plaintiffs based upon the record now before the Court, Defendants are entitled to have their motion for summary judgment granted. *See* [*Anderson v. University of Wisconsin*, 841 F.2d 737 (7th Cir. 1988)].

Respectfully submitted this [1st] day of [March], [1993].

[name and address of counsel]

§ 14.9   Record for Summary Judgment

This section contains an actual court record (**Form 14–7**) from *Smith v. Kitterman*[11] and the portions of the deposition exchanges (**Form 14–8**) upon which the court based its record. In this case, the referenced deposition exchanges saved the plaintiff from summary judgment on the employer's argument that her carpal tunnel syndrome did not constitute a disability because it disqualified her from only one job. (In the court record, the cross-references to the deposition exchanges are indicated with asterisks.)

FORM 14–7
SAMPLE RECORD FOR SUMMARY JUDGMENT

The Court simply is not persuaded for purposes of summary judgment that Plaintiff's medical restrictions do not create "a significant barrier to employment in positions that are comparable in stature to her former position at [Kitterman]"—especially given her limited educational, training, and employment background. As to the different jobs Plaintiff has held since Defendant told her she could not return to [Kitterman], there is evidence before the Court that either (1) those jobs required her to perform restricted tasks prohibited by Plaintiff's doctor in her medical release report and/or tasks that caused her pain in connection with her carpal tunnel syndrome; [See **Form 14–8** at *.] (2) the jobs involuntarily [. . .] ended due to layoff; [See **Form 14–8** at **.] or (3) the jobs were not permanent or not available full-time. [See **Form 14–8** at ***.] Not only does this evidence to which Defendant cites fail to support Defendant's proposition that Plaintiff's "physical impairment has not created a significant barrier to employment positions that are comparable in stature to her former positions at [Kitterman]," but it actually flies in the face of such a conclusion given Plaintiff's sworn testimony regarding the duties of the full-time and permanent jobs she actually secured. Notably, beyond Defendant's conclusory allegations to the contrary, there is no evidence before the Court to dispute Plaintiff's claim that she is significantly restricted in the ability to perform a class of jobs or a broad range of jobs in various classes, when compared with the ability of a person with comparable training, qualifications, skills and abilities to perform those same jobs. See EEOC Interpretive Guide, § 1630.2(j) [footnotes omitted].

FORM 14–8
SAMPLE DEPOSITION EXCHANGE

*Q. In your position at [Bio Mat], is there anything that you do that causes you problems with your hands?

A. There is some things, yes.

[11] 897 F. Supp. 423, 427–28 (W.D. Mo. 1995).

Q. What would those things be?

A. For instance, like turning things, like the ratchet type thing. It causes pain, but I still do it, if I have to turn it really super hard. [Karen Smith] Dep. at 8-9.

Q. While you were working at [Henry Wurst], did you experience any problems with either your right hand or your left hand?

A. Yes, I did at different times, yes.

Q. What type of problems did you have?

A. Well, just normal problems like I always have, pain. [Karen Smith] Dep. at 12-13.

Q. What did you do for [Haldex]?

A. Put brakes together.

Q. Can you describe for me or tell me how you did that job, what was involved?

A. Yes. You had to—I guess I can tell you exactly how it was done. You had to put a lot of greasy parts together, and you had to screw them down, and you had to use an air driver to put them in.

    You had a lot of twisting and turning to do.

                        *   *   *

Q. Did you have any troubles with either your right hand or your left hand using the air driver?

A. Yes, I did.

Q. What about the twisting and the turning?

A. I had trouble with that.

Q. Which hand bothered you?

A. The right hand. [Karen Smith] Dep. at 21–22.

Q. [I]n October of '93, [Dr. Vilmer] gave you certain restrictions as far as the type of work you could perform. I was wondering if you're under any of the same restrictions today or different restrictions?

A. Well, I haven't been back to him. I do just what I have to do. I do it and if it hurts, I still do it anyway. [Karen Smith] Dep. at 14.

Q. What type of work did you do for [Westport Research]?

A. Electronics.

Q. What type of work was that?

A. We had to put boards together, electronic boards.

Q. Okay. To do this job, did you need to use small hand tools?

A. I had to use like little pliers. [Karen Smith] Dep. at 32–33.

* * *

**Q. How long did you work for [Stuart Hall]?

A. I think I worked for them three months.

Q. What caused you to leave [Stuart Hall]?

A. Layoff.

Q. [T]he work you did at [Stuart Hall], was [sic] there any tasks that you performed that would cause you problems with either your right or your left hand?

A. I really didn't have anything that I had to twist or pull or-

Q. So would that mean no?

A. That would mean no. [Karen Smith] Dep. at 27.

***Q. Before [Stuart Hall], where did you work?

A. Oh. Yeah, I was in [Interstate Inn], and I did that basically part-time.

Q. Did any of your job duties at [Interstate Inn] require twisting and turning with your hands?

A. No.

Q. Did you have to use small hand tools?

A. No.

Q. Why did you leave [Interstate Inn]?

A. Because I needed to make more money. [Karen Smith] Dep. at 27–29.

Q.   Do you have any recollection as to how long you were with [Westport Research]?

A.   I think I was with them for like a couple of months. However long the job lasted.

Q.   And it was a temporary position?

A.   Yes. [Karen Smith] Dep. at 33.

CHAPTER 15

PRE-TRIAL PROCESS

§ 15.1   Introduction and Overview

This chapter provides materials for Americans with Disabilities Act (ADA)[1] cases related to the pre-trial process (see **Forms 15–1** to **15–5**). The materials

---

[1] Pub. L. No. 101-336, 104 Stat. 327 (1990) (codified at 42 U.S.C. §§ 12101–12213 (1994); 47 U.S.C. §§ 225, 711 (1994)) [hereinafter ADA].

in this chapter and in **Chapter 16** are closely related because the pre-trial order (see **Forms 15–15** to **15–17**) resulting from a final pre-trial conference governs the course of the trial. In addition, as the *A.I.C.* pre-trial order (see **Form 15–18**) shows, a comprehensive pre-trial order actually contains material, such as rulings on facts (see **Forms 15–13** to **15–14**), evidentiary issues, and jury instructions that will take effect as the trial proceeds.

§ 15.2   Order of Reference

FORM 15–1
SAMPLE ORDER OF REFERENCE

UNITED STATES DISTRICT COURT

DISTRICT OF [name]

Plaintiff, [name]

v.   Docket No. [case number]

Defendant, [name].

ORDER OF REFERENCE

IT IS HEREBY ORDERED that the above-captioned matter be referred to United States Magistrate Judge [name] for all further proceedings and entry of judgment in accordance with Title 28 U.S.C. § 636(c) and the consent of the parties.

U.S. District Judge

§ 15.3   Motion to Extend Time for Pre-Trial Order

FORM 15–2
SAMPLE MOTION TO EXTEND TIME FOR PRE-TRIAL ORDER

DEFENDANTS' EMERGENCY MOTION FOR AN ENLARGEMENT
OF TIME FOR FILING THEIR FINAL PRE-TRIAL ORDER

The Defendants, [A.I.C. SECURITY INVESTIGATIONS, LTD.]; [A.I.C. INTERNATIONAL, LTD.]; and [unnamed defendant C], by and through their attorneys, [WESSELS & PAUTSCH, P.C.], by [Charles W. Pautsch], [attorney A], [attorney B], and [William H., Esq.], pursuant to Rule 6(b) of the Federal Rules of Civil Procedure, hereby move for an enlargement of time in which to file the parties' Final Pre-Trial Order in the above-captioned action based upon the following.

1.   By Order dated [December 29, 1992], the Court established [February 9, 1993], as the due date for the parties' Final Pre-Trial Order in the above-captioned action;

2.   On [December 8, 1992], Defendants filed their motion to compel the deposition of the Plaintiff in intervention, [Charles Wessel], after he had refused to appear for his deposition, noticed pursuant to the Federal Rules of Civil Procedure for [December 10, 1992].

3.   To date, there has been no ruling on Defendants' Motion to Compel and it is the Defendants' position that their ability to defend against this action is being severely prejudiced without this essential discovery.

4.   On or about [November 13, 1992], Defendants filed their Motion to Compel the Physical and Mental Examination of [Charles Wessel].

5.   To date, there has been no ruling on Defendants' Motion to Compel the foregoing examination of [Charles Wessel] and it is the Defendants' position that their ability to defend against this action is being severely prejudiced without this essential discovery.

6.   On [December 24, 1992], Defendants filed their motion to disqualify [attorney D] and the law firm of [firm name] from appearing on behalf of and representing [Charles Wessel] in this litigation due to an obvious conflict of interest in that [attorney D] is a witness in this action and she and her firm have rendered legal services to Defendant [A.I.C. Security Investigations, Ltd.] on matters of employment law related to this action.

7.   To date, there has been no ruling on Defendants' motion to disqualify counsel for Plaintiff [Charles Wessel], and it is Defendants' position that their ability to defend against this action is being severely prejudiced by the involvement of challenged counsel.

8.   This action was filed on or about [November 5, 1992], and, as a result of an expedited discovery schedule procured by motion of the Equal Employment Opportunity Commission, the cutoff for discovery was [December 31, 1992], a mere [35] working days ([56] actual days) from the initiation of this action by the Plaintiff and approximately one month after the Defendants' answer was due.

9.   By Order dated [December 29, 1992], the Court extended discovery until [January 22, 1993], with no further extensions permitted, and established [February 9, 1993] as the due date for final pre-trial orders; no other extensions have been granted.

10.   Pursuant to the above-referenced discovery timetable, Defendants scheduled three depositions for [Thursday], [January 21, 1993]; however, one of the depositions—that of [Alice Wessel]—was unexpectedly canceled without

notice based upon her attorney's ([attorney C] of the law firm [firm name]) representation that his flight to [Chicago] from [city] was canceled on that date due to the weather. By stipulation, the parties have agreed to reschedule [Alice Wessel]'s deposition on [Wednesday], [January 27, 1993], on account of the foregoing unavoidable "act of God."

11.   That Defendants are unable to obtain transcripts of depositions already taken until approximately early [February], and the deposition transcript of [Alice Wessel] may not be available until perhaps a week later—the current week of the due date for final pre-trial orders.

12.   Many responses to discovery are either still pending, incomplete, or challenged, and Defendants are currently attempting to resolve same or, if necessary, will move to compel responses.

13.   Because of all the foregoing, the Defendants are being unduly prejudiced in their defense of the charges brought in this litigation, and there will be no adequate opportunity for motions in limine, statements of stipulated/uncontested facts, schedules of exhibits, and all other materials necessary for full compliance with the Court's final pre-trial order.

WHEREFORE, the Defendants respectfully request that the final pre-trial order in this action, currently due on or before [February 9, 1993], be enlarged by a reasonable time period to allow for rulings on all pertinent outstanding motions and to allow for all discovery issues to be resolved; Defendants propose that a status conference be set in this matter in early [February] to determine the status of the foregoing matters and to set a subsequent date for the pre-trial order that will permit the parties an adequate opportunity to provide all required materials and documents.

Dated this [22nd] of [January], [1993].

§ 15.4   Statement of Cause of Action

FORM 15–3
SAMPLE STATEMENT OF CAUSE OF ACTION

IN THE UNITED STATES DISTRICT COURT

FOR THE [NORTHERN] DISTRICT OF [ILLINOIS]

[EASTERN] DIVISION

U.S. EQUAL EMPLOYMENT OPPORTUNITY COMMISSION,

Plaintiff,

v.   Civil Action No. [92 C 7330]

[A.I.C. SECURITY INVESTIGATIONS, LTD.];

[A.I.C. INTERNATIONAL, LTD.]; and [unnamed defendant C]

                                                Judge [Marvin E. Aspen]

Defendants.   Magistrate Judge [Guzman]

DEFENDANTS' STATEMENT OF CAUSE OF ACTION

Defendants, [A.I.C. SECURITY INVESTIGATIONS, LTD.]; [A.I.C. INTERNA-
TIONAL, LTD.]; and [defendant C], by and through their attorneys, [WESSELS &
PAUTSCH, P.C.], by [Charles W. Pautsch], [attorney A], and [attorney B], hereby
submit to this Honorable Court Defendants' Statement of Cause of Action:

1.   At the Pre-Trial Conference held [Thursday], [March 4, 1993], in the
above referenced case, the Court requested that Defendants submit a "Statement of
Cause of Action" to be read to the jury.

2.   Defendants submit as the "Statement of Cause of Action" as follows:

This is an action filed under the Americans With Disabilities Act of 1990 (the
"ADA"), in which Plaintiffs allege that Defendants discriminated against
[Charles H. Wessel] by discharging him from his employment because of a disability, cancer, in violation of the ADA. Defendants deny any violation of the
ADA occurred and instead contend, among other things, that [Charles Wessel]
was justifiably excluded from the position of Executive Director because he
could no longer perform the essential functions of that position.

Dated this [5th] day of [February], [1993].

§ 15.5   Checklist for Final Preparation for Trial

____   1.   Review of Proceedings
              ____   Schedule
              ____   Reports on completion of discovery
              ____   Items remaining to be completed
              ____   Requests for relief from deadlines/preclusion orders
              ____   Review statements of uncontested/contested facts, state-
                      ments of contention and proof, witness/documents lists
              ____   Outstanding motions
              ____   Rule on all outstanding motions

_____ Challenges to jurisdiction or venue

_____ Transfer under 28 U.S.C. §§ 1404 or 1406

_____ Summary judgment, including motions under Federal Rule of Civil Procedure 56(d)

_____ Motions seeking to limit period/scope of proof

_____ Issues regarding right to jury trial

_____ Possible rulings on objections to evidence

_____ Immediate rulings

_____ Schedule hearing under Federal Rule of Evidence 104

_____ Consider whether to recommend remand under 28 U.S.C. § 1407

_____ 2. Trial

_____ Set/modify/confirm date and place of trial

_____ Continuance only in extreme circumstances

_____ Deadline for partial settlements in class actions

_____ Trial schedule:

    _____ Normal hours

    _____ Days when no trial or trial day reduced

    _____ Holidays; recesses

_____ Consolidation under Federal Rule of Civil Procedure 42(a):

    _____ Class actions and individual actions

    _____ Jury and nonjury cases

    _____ Transfer as appropriate under 28 U.S.C. §§ 1404 or 1406

_____ Severance under Federal Rule of Civil Procedure 42(b):

    _____ Define/confirm issues for trial and those severed for later trial

_____ If both jury and nonjury issues to be tried:

    _____ Receive additional nonjury evidence at completion of trial

    _____ Receive additional nonjury evidence at close of each day

_____ Schedule for subsequent trials of severed issues:

    _____ Immediately after initial trial

    _____ Later, perhaps after additional discovery

_____ Order of proof/issue/evidence:

    _____ Standard order of presentation

    _____ Issues presented in specified sequence

_____ Plaintiffs' evidence presented in specified sequence, followed by defendants' evidence in same sequence

_____ Parties present all evidence on first issue before proceeding with evidence on next issue(s)

_____ Arguments presented as evidence on issue completed

_____ Verdict/findings on first issue before proceeding with evidence on next issue

_____ Jury selection:

_____ Principal jurors

_____ Number of peremptory challenges

_____ Selection of alternate jurors

_____ Number

_____ When disclosure made as to identity of alternates

_____ Stipulations:

_____ Agreement to receive verdict from remaining jurors, avoiding need to select alternatives

_____ Agreement to accept less than unanimous verdict

_____ Agreement on excusing juror after deliberations begin

_____ Agreement to accept nonjury decision if jury not unanimous

_____ Number of jurors to be called/impaneled

_____ Submission of suggested voir dire questions:

_____ Written questionnaires

_____ Before jury reports

_____ After jurors given initial instructions

_____ Special procedures to handle problems of publicity

_____ Review of practices used in court for exercising challenges

_____   3.   Witness and Exhibit Lists

_____ Deadline for submitting:

_____ Sequentially

_____ Concurrently by all parties

_____ Contents

_____ All potential witnesses and exhibits

_____ Exception for impeachment evidence

_____ Indicate whether probable or improbable

_____ Key witnesses and exhibits

____ Expected length of direct examination of witnesses

____ Nature of expected testimony

____ Depositions:

> ____ Indicate which witnesses to be presented by deposition

> ____ Designation of portions to be offered

> ____ Preparation of agreed summaries of depositions

____ Identify evidence to be offered against fewer than all parties

____ Provide copies of exhibits not previously produced

____ Responses

____ Cross-examination

____ Expected length

____ Additional substantive topics

____ Designation of additional portions of depositions

____ Objections to evidence:

> ____ Certain objections waived if not raised (for example, authenticity, best evidence, requirement for foundation)

> ____ All objections waived if not raised

> ____ Effect

____ Precluding evidence not listed:

> ____ Except solely for impeachment purposes

____ Authenticating/laying foundation for exhibits

____ Precluding all or certain objections not raised

____ 4. Limits on Evidence; Facilitating Presentation of Evidence

____ Precluding proof of facts not disclosed on statement of contentions or statement of contested facts

____ Precluding witnesses/exhibits not listed

____ Precluding expert testimony unless report filed

____ Limits on quantity of evidence

____ Preliminary steps:

> ____ Review lists of witnesses/exhibits in light of disputed facts

> ____ Consider views of counsel

> ____ Limit number of expert witnesses

> ____ Limit number of lay witnesses/exhibits on particular subjects

> ____ Limit time for presentation by parties

____ Limits on time for direct examination of own witnesses and on cross-examination of other witnesses

____ Limits on gross time for each party's case-in-chief

____ Depositions

____ Summaries

____ Selected extracts, purged of unnecessary materials

____ Adoption of prepared reports as direct testimony, subject to cross-examination

____ Permitting all/specified witnesses to remain in courtroom by not invoking Federal Rule of Evidence 615

____ Limiting cross-examination on additional subjects under Federal Rule of Evidence 611(b)

____ Pre-trial ruling on objections

____ Use of summaries or samples in lieu of voluminous source documents

____ 5. Briefs

    ____ Timetable:

        ____ Sequential

        ____ Concurrent

    ____ Supplemental briefs as trial progresses

    ____ Contents:

        ____ Specific issues or all probable issues

        ____ Jury voir dire

        ____ Suggested questions for oral examinations

        ____ Suggested written questionnaire

        ____ Suggested instructions

        ____ Initial instructions

        ____ Limiting instructions on particular evidence

        ____ Final instructions

        ____ Glossary/index of key terms, events, persons

        ____ Suggested special verdict/interrogatories

        ____ Proposed findings/conclusions in nonjury cases

____ 6. Administrative Details

    ____ Arrangements for facilities/equipment

    ____ Representatives from parties

    ____ Courtroom arrangement, tables, name plates

    ____ Witness/exhibit/conference rooms

    ____ Copying/computer equipment

_____ Exhibits:

    _____ Premarked and listed on clerk's exhibit sheets

    _____ Absent objection, deemed as offered and received when identified

    _____ Notify counsel before using (to avoid interruptions while they review/ locate copies)

    _____ Glossaries, indexes, demonstrative aids

    _____ Provide copies for court/jurors

    _____ Exhibit books

    _____ Enlargement/slides

    _____ Representatives assist clerk in maintaining/ indexing list of exhibits received

_____ Schedule of evidence:

    _____ Advance notification of expected order of presenting witnesses and documents

    _____ Notify of changes in schedule as soon as known

    _____ Notify of changes in deposition designations

    _____ Notify if portion of document to be offered

_____ Guidelines/discussion of courtroom protocol/decorum:

    _____ Examination of witnesses

    _____ Manner of making objections

    _____ Submission of exhibits to witnesses

    _____ Publication of exhibits to jurors

    _____ Side-bar/chambers conferences

    _____ How/when offer of proof made

    _____ Witness demonstrations

    _____ Approaching witnesses

    _____ Use of podium

_____ Transcript of proceedings:

    _____ Expedited/daily/hourly transcript

    _____ Representatives review daily

    _____ Suggested corrections submitted promptly to court

    _____ Whether to permit independent tape recording of proceedings

_____ Interpreters, translation of documents

_____ Special arrangements if jury to be sequestered:

    _____ Hotel/meals

    _____ Transportation

_____ Family visitation

_____ Recreation

_____ Security

_____ Schedule for interim conferences during trial:

_____ Jurors

_____ Note-taking

_____ Exhibit books

_____ Questions by jurors[2]

§ 15.6   Motion to Amend Witness List

FORM 15–4
SAMPLE MOTION TO AMEND WITNESS LIST

DEFENDANTS' MOTION TO AMEND WITNESS LIST

Defendants, [A.I.C. SECURITY INVESTIGATIONS, LTD.]; [A.I.C. INTERNA-TIONAL, LTD.]; and [unnamed defendant C], by and through their attorneys, [WESSELS & PAUTSCH, P.C.], by [Charles W. Pautsch], [attorney A], and [attorney B], hereby set forth their Motion to Amend Witness List as follows:

1.   On [Monday], [February 22, 1993], Defendants and Plaintiffs in the above referenced case filed a joint Pre-Trial Order.

2.   Within the Pre-Trial Order referenced to above was included Defendants' List of Witnesses.

3.   Due to an oversight by Defendants' counsel, [A], M.D. was left off of the Defendants' Witness List.

4.   Defendants now wish to add [Dr. A] to Defendants' Witness List.

5.   Plaintiffs will not be prejudiced in any manner by the adding of [Dr. A] to Defendants' Witness List since [Dr. A] was a treating physician of Plaintiff [Wessel] and was previously deposed in this matter.

WHEREFORE, Defendants respectfully request this Court to grant Defendants' Motion to Amend Witness List to add the name of [A], M.D.

Dated this [26th] day of [February], [1993].

---

[2] This checklist was adapted from Manual for Complex Litigation 2d § 40.3 (1985).

§ 15.7   Support for Calling Witness Named in
Pre-Trial Order

FORM 15–5
SAMPLE SUPPORT FOR CALLING WITNESS NAMED IN
PRE-TRIAL ORDER

IN THE UNITED STATES DISTRICT COURT

FOR THE [NORTHERN] DISTRICT OF [ILLINOIS]

[EASTERN] DIVISION

U.S. EQUAL EMPLOYMENT OPPORTUNITY COMMISSION,

Plaintiff

v.   Civil Action No. [92 C 7330]

[A.I.C. SECURITY INVESTIGATIONS, LTD.];

[A.I.C. INTERNATIONAL, LTD.]; and [unnamed defendant C],

                                         Honorable [Marvin E. Aspen]

Defendants.   Magistrate Judge [Ronald A. Guzman]

DEFENDANTS' RESPONSE TO PLAINTIFFS' OBJECTION TO
DEFENDANTS' CALLING [JODIE C.] AS A WITNESS AT TRIAL

Defendants, [A.I.C. SECURITY INVESTIGATIONS, LTD.]; [A.I.C. INTERNA-
TIONAL, LTD.]; and [unnamed defendant C], by and through their attorneys,
[WESSELS & PAUTSCH, P.C.], by [Charles W. Pautsch], [attorney A], and [attorney
B], hereby submit to this Honorable Court Defendants' Response to Plaintiffs'
Objection to Defendants' calling [Jodie C.] as a Witness at Trial and states in sup-
port hereof as follows:

1.   On [February 22, 1993], the parties submitted to the Court a Final Pre-
Trial Order signed by all parties.

2.   Schedule D-2, to the Final Pre-Trial Order is Defendants' List of Witnesses
with Plaintiffs' objections noted.

3.   Within Schedule D-2, Defendants list as a witness [Jodie C.] and Plaintiffs
object because she was not identified in answer to Plaintiff EEOC's First Set of
Interrogatories No. 3.

4.   Plaintiff EEOC's First Set of Interrogatories No. 3 states:

State every reason for the termination of [Charles H. Wessel ("Wessel")], and identify all documents which relate to or support reasons, and all persons having knowledge of any such reason.

5.   Defendants answered Plaintiff EEOC's Interrogatory No. 3 as follows:

ANSWER: [Charles H. Wessel] was terminated because he could not perform, with or without reasonable accommodation, the essential functions of his job position. See also defenses enumerated in Defendants' Answers and Defenses previously filed with the Court. Persons having knowledge of the reasons for [Wessel]'s termination are [defendant C], [Beverly K.], [Lawrence R.], [Ken D.], [Ed B.], and [Jan D.]. Defendants have not identified any documents which relate to or support such reasons. Investigation continues.

6.   Defendants in good faith answered Interrogatory No. 3, listing each and every individual who may have had involvement in the decision-making process and who may have had possible knowledge for the reasons for the decision which was made.

7.   The language of Plaintiff EEOC's Interrogatory No. 3 seeks, in part, those individuals with knowledge of the actual reasons for [Wessel]'s "termination." This interrogatory does not ask for individuals with knowledge of any fact which supports a claim or defense to this action.

8.   [Jodie C.] is an individual who worked in a separate division from [Wessel]. Her work station happened to be near the back entrance to the building. Thus, [witness] was able to observe Wessel entering and leaving the building on a daily basis. Also [witness] would see Wessel in the building at various times during the business day. [Witness] will testify to these facts.

9.   [Jodie C.] in no way was part of any decision-making process regarding [Wessel] nor was she privy to any information whatsoever regarding the decision-making process and the reasons for [Wessel]'s separation from employment, Thus, [witness] had no knowledge whatsoever of the information sought by Plaintiff EEOC Interrogatory No. 3. Her ignorance on the issues as to the reasons for [Wessel]'s "termination" was verified by the undersigned counsel for Defendants by a direct interview with her wherein she stated in essence that she did not have knowledge of the reasons why [Wessel] was not working at [A.I.C.] any longer. Defendants' counsel would be willing to set forth an affidavit to this effect if so requested by the Court.

10.   Plaintiffs cannot claim that they are surprised or suffer unfair prejudice due to Defendants' calling [Jodie C.] at trial. At [Charles Wessel]'s first deposition on [November 5, 1992], the same day this action was filed, [Wessel] testified in substance that he would pass [Jodie C.] when entering and leaving the building at [A.I.C.]. (See Transcript of [Wessel] Deposition of [11/05/92] at 125, line 9.)

Defendants will call [Jodie C.] at trial to testify to those very same observations. Thus, for Plaintiffs to claim unfair surprise or prejudice to a witness they knew about before the filing of this suit is baseless and should be overruled by this Court.

11. Defendants would be willing to submit [Jodie C.] to deposition before trial.

Wherefore, Defendants respectfully request the Court to overrule Plaintiffs' objection to [Jodie C.] being called as a witness at trial.

Dated this [5th] day of [February], [1993].

§ 15.8 Motions in Limine

Technically, motions in limine (see **Forms 15–6** to **15–12**) must include not only a request that the court make a determination as to the admissibility or nonadmissibility of certain evidence but also a determination as to the permissibility of asking for it at trial.[3] Unless the second finding is necessary to avoid prejudice from the mere asking of a question, there is no principled reason for deciding the evidentiary question in advance, as opposed to deciding it at trial, when the question is asked. Nevertheless, the increasing emphasis on efficient litigation management and the growing importance of the pre-trial process may make it appropriate to have motions in limine as a part of the pre-trial order drafting step even when the asking of questions or the offering of nontestimonial evidence would not be particularly prejudicial. The authority for motions in limine is generally thought to reside in the inherent power of a trial judge to supervise the trial,[4] in Federal Rule of Civil Procedure 16(c)(3), allowing advance rulings on admissibility, or in Federal Rule of Evidence 103(d), which requires that proceedings be conducted so as to prevent inadmissible evidence from being suggested to the jury by any means.[5]

---

[3] The term *motion in limine* conventionally refers to a motion to exclude evidence. However, for ease of exposition, **Chapter 15** uses the term expansively to refer also to pre-trial motions seeking determinations that evidence is admissible.

[4] *See* Sperburg v. Good Year Tire & Rubber Co., 519 F.2d 708 (6th Cir. 1975) (evaluating pre-trial order in context of overall management of trial).

[5] Oswald v. Laroche Chems., Inc., 894 F. Supp. 998 (E.D. La. 1995) (granting motion in limine in ADA case to exclude evidence of preeffective-date conduct).

§ 15.9   —Motion in Limine to Exclude Videotape

FORM 15–6
SAMPLE MOTION IN LIMINE TO EXCLUDE VIDEOTAPE

MOTION TO EXCLUDE VIDEOTAPE

Plaintiffs filed a motion on [October 24, 1985], to admit a job qualification videotape into evidence. The videotape is intended to show how Plaintiff [name] can perform the essential duties of various office jobs despite significant physical disabilities. Defendant objects to Plaintiffs' motion on the grounds that the videotape is hearsay and will provide only cumulative evidence.

Defendant has several specific objections to the contents of the tape regarding its representational character and potential for undue prejudice. Several aspects of the film indicate that the activities depicted are not typical of those found in Defendant's workplace and are unduly prejudicial toward the Defendant. The filming of the Plaintiff unduly emphasizes telephone conversations with customers and fellow employees, even though these constitute a relatively small part of all of the clerical jobs in Defendant's workplace. Conversation in the unedited version of the film suggests that the photocopying may be done in a way that is totally unlike the requirements of the physical layout of defendant's offices. The edited version of the film minimizes the difficulties Plaintiff would encounter in delivering mail and does not fairly convey the totality of Plaintiff's actual experience. The manner in which Plaintiff is depicted using a personal computer is simply not believable.

The question of permitting the showing of a motion picture film or videotape at trial is one for the sound discretion of the Court. [*Szeliga v. General Motors Corp.,* 728 F.2d 566, 567 (1st Cir. 1984)]. The propriety of allowing videotapes of this type into evidence is questionable for several reasons. Almost always, an edited tape necessarily raises issues as to every sequence portrayed of whether the event shown is fairly representative of fact after the editing process, and whether it is unduly prejudicial because of the manner of presentation. Further, the fact that a plaintiff is aware of being videotaped for such a purpose is likely to cause self-serving behavior, consciously or otherwise. *See* [*Haley v. Byers Transportation Co.,* 414 S.W.2d 777, 780 (Mo. 1967)]. Next, use of a videotape for such purposes is troublesome because it dominates evidence more conventionally adduced simply because of the nature of its presentation. "[T]he very obvious impact of these films would have been to create a sympathy for the plaintiff out of proportion to the real relevancy of the evidence." [*Id.*] Finally, such a videotape may serve to distract the jury from other cogent issues which properly must be considered to produce a fair verdict conscientiously derived from an impartial consideration of the evidence with strict attention to applicable principles of law.

Fed. R. Evid. 1001(2) defines "photographs" as inclusive of videotapes and motion pictures, and therefore properly authenticated tapes do not appear to be inadmissible on grounds of hearsay. *See also* [*Grimes v. Employers Mutual Liability*

Insurance Co., 73 F.R.D. 607, 610–11 (D. Alaska 1977)]. However, policy issues akin to hearsay are also raised even if the tapes are not hearsay. Even in instances where the videotaping is attended by opposing counsel, the conduct filmed is not subject to cross-examination at the time it is made and, therefore, lacks some of the safeguards of the adversary system.

For all of the above reasons, videotapes should be admitted as demonstrative evidence only when the tapes convey the observations of a witness to the jury more fully or accurately than, for some specific, articulable reason, the witness can convey them through the medium of conventional, in-court examination. These requirements are not met here. [*Szeliga v. General Motors Corp.*, 728 F.2d 566, at 567]. [Plaintiff] can testify on her own behalf. [Plaintiff] can demonstrate to the jury in open court activities similar to those depicted in the videotape. Further, relatives and physicians of the Plaintiff may offer similar testimony. Vocational rehabilitation specialists can testify as to the capabilities of the Plaintiff and the correspondence between those capabilities and the job functions actually required in Defendant's workplace. Thus, the videotape will be merely cumulative of testimonial evidence which is available to the Plaintiff. *See* [*Helm v. Wismar*, 820 S.W.2d 495, 496 (Mo. 1991) (affirming exclusion of "day in the life" videotape because plaintiff was in court for jury's observation; emphasizing trial judge's discretion)]; [*Bolstridge v. Central Main Power Co.*, 621 F. Supp. 1202, 1203 (D. Me. 1985) (order denying use at trial of "day in the life" videotape because no showing that traditional testimony by plaintiff could not adduce same facts and risk of prejudice because of claims that portrayal was not accurate portrayal of regular activities)]; [*Johnson v. William C. Ellis & Sons Iron Works*, 604 F.2d 950 (5th Cir.), *modified on other grounds*, 609 F.2d 820 (5th Cir. 1979)]; [*Finn v. Wood*, 178 F.2d 583 (2d Cir. 1950)]; [*DeCamp v. United States*, 10 F.2d 984 (D.C. Cir. 1926)]. Also, admission of the tape into evidence will create the risk of distracting the jury and unfairly prejudicing the Defendant, principally, though not exclusively, because the benefit of effective cross-examination is lost. *See* [*Haley v. Byers Transportation Co.*, 414 S.W.2d 777 (Mo. 1967)]. Therefore, it should be excluded under Fed. R. Evid. 403. [*Johnson*, 604 F.2d at 958]. *See also* [*Foster v. Crawford Shipping Co.*, 496 F.2d 788 (3d Cir. 1974)]; [*Finn*, 178 F.2d at 584]; [*DeCamp*, 10 F.2d at 985]; [5 J. Weinstein, M. Berger, Weinstein's Evidence 1001–36 (1983) ("where the motion picture is not necessary to prove or disprove a material proposition, it should not be allowed into evidence")].

This policy is consistent with that set in Fed. R. Civ. P. 32(a)(3), which provides for the admission of videotaped depositions only in instances where the witness is unavailable or "such exceptional circumstances exist as to make it desirable, in the interest of justice and with due regard to the importance of presenting the testimony of witnesses orally in open court."[6]

---

[6] The language of this motion is adapted from the opinion in Bolstridge v. Central Me. Power Co., 621 F. Supp. 1202 (D. Me. 1985) (excluding day-in-the-life videotape in personal injury case).

§ 15.10   —Objection to Use of Videotape Deposition

FORM 15–7
SAMPLE OBJECTION TO USE OF VIDEOTAPE DEPOSITION

IN THE UNITED STATES DISTRICT COURT

FOR THE [NORTHERN] DISTRICT OF [ILLINOIS]

[EASTERN] DIVISION

U.S. EQUAL EMPLOYMENT OPPORTUNITY COMMISSION,

Plaintiff

v.   Civil Action No. [92 C 7330]

[A.I.C. SECURITY INVESTIGATIONS, LTD.];

[A.I.C. INTERNATIONAL, LTD.]; and [unnamed defendant C],

                                            Honorable [Marvin E. Aspen]

Defendants.   Magistrate Judge [Ronald A. Guzman]

DEFENDANTS' OBJECTIONS TO PLAINTIFFS' DEPOSITION
DESIGNATION OF [CHARLES H. WESSEL]

The Defendants, [A.I.C. SECURITY INVESTIGATIONS, LTD.]; [A.I.C. INTERNA-
TIONAL, LTD.]; and [defendant C], by and through their attorneys, [WESSELS &
PAUTSCH, P.C.], by [Charles W. Pautsch], [attorney A], and [attorney B], hereby
object to Plaintiffs' deposition designation to [Charles H. Wessel] based upon the
following:

1.   Defendants maintain their objection to showing the videotape deposition
of [Charles Wessel ("Wessel")] at trial. No portion of this videotape should be used
at trial if [Wessel] is available to testify. The use of this videotape at trial will cause
undue delay, waste of time, and will present unnecessary cumulative evidence.
Fed. R. Evid. 403.

2.   In the event the Court does allow the videotape deposition of [Wessel] to
be played at trial, the following portions should be omitted from evidence as inadmissible hearsay:

a)   page 17, lines 2–13;

b)   page 62, line 12–23; and

c)   page 127, lines 8–18.

3.   In the event the Court does allow the videotape deposition of [Wessel] to be played at trial, the following portions should be added to Plaintiffs' deposition designation in the interest of fairness:

a)   page 30, line 13 to page 31, line 17;

b)   page 74, lines 21–22;

c)   page 73, line 8 to page 74, line 20; and

d)   page 114, lines 30-20.

Respectfully submitted,

[A.I.C. SECURITY INVESTIGATIONS, LTD.];

[A.I.C. INTERNATIONAL, LTD.]; and [unnamed defendant C]

Commentary.   Recent case law provides a wide spectrum of opinions in regard to videotape depositions. For example, in *General Motors Corp. v. Mosely,*[7] the court found it was error to admit a videotape deposition from another case and that, with the videotape deposition, there was no incentive to cross-examine the witness on the point for which the videotape deposition was admitted. However, that opinion can be compared with *Verdict v. State.*[8] In *Verdict,* the videotape deposition of the medical expert was validly admitted at a murder trial because the expert was unavailable. The court affirmed conviction. In *Miller v. Solaglas California, Inc.,*[9] the defendants unsuccessfully argued on appeal that the trial court had erred in refusing to grant a new trial based upon the admission of a videotape deposition in lieu of live testimony, the rejection of certain objections to the showing of the videotape, and the trial judge's leaving the bench in the courthouse during the jury's viewing of the videotape deposition. The use of the deposition was authorized by the Colorado rules and, more importantly, the plaintiff had listed his intention to use the videotape deposition in lieu of live testimony in his "trial data certificate" and the defendant had failed to timely object.[10] On the other point, the defendants had stipulated that the trial judge's presence during the playing of the videotape was unnecessary.[11]

---

[7] 447 S.E.2d 302, 308 (Ga. Ct. App. 1994).

[8] 868 S.W.2d 443 (Ark. 1993).

[9] 870 P.2d 559 (Colo. Ct. App. 1993).

[10] *Id.* at 569–70.

[11] *Id.* at 570.

In *Web v. Thomas,*[12] the court found that no prejudice was shown from a refusal to admit the transcript of the videotape deposition in addition to the videotape deposition itself. In *State v. Vaughn,*[13] the court affirmed conviction. The videotape testimony of witness who was on vacation at time of trial was validly admitted because the witness was under oath and was cross-examined during videotaping. However, in *Carter v. Sowders,*[14] the court overturned a conviction. The only evidence was a video deposition that was improperly admitted because of the refusal of defendant's counsel to participate in the videotaping, and because the use of the videotape deposition violated the confrontation clause. The court, in *Miller v. National Railroad Passenger Corp.,*[15] denied the costs of the videotape deposition because it saved no time and was otherwise unnecessary, and because the medical expert witness was available to testify in person. The *Miller* court disagreed with the court's opinion in *Commercial Credit Equipment Corp. v. Stamps.*[16] The court, in *Kirby v. Ahmad,*[17] found that the expert witness fee of $750 per hour for a videotape deposition was unreasonable, and the fee request was reduced to $250 per hour for all depositions.

§ 15.11   —Motion in Limine to Exclude Evidence

FORM 15–8
SAMPLE MOTION IN LIMINE TO EXCLUDE EVIDENCE

IN THE UNITED STATES DISTRICT COURT

FOR THE [NORTHERN] DISTRICT OF [ILLINOIS]

[EASTERN] DIVISION

U.S. EQUAL EMPLOYMENT OPPORTUNITY COMMISSION,

Plaintiff

v.   Civil Action No. [92 C 7330]

[A.I.C. SECURITY INVESTIGATIONS, LTD.];

---

[12] 873 S.W.2d 875, 878 (Ark. 1992).
[13] 768 P.2d 1051, 1056 (Ariz. Ct. App. 1989).
[14] 5 F.3d 975, 979 (6th Cir. 1993).
[15] 157 F.R.D. 145, 146 (D. Mass. 1994).
[16] 920 F.2d 1361, 1368 (7th Cir. 1990).
[17] 635 N.E.2d 98 (Ohio Ct. C.P. 1994).

[A.I.C. INTERNATIONAL, LTD.]; and [unnamed defendant C],

Honorable [Marvin E. Aspen]

Defendants.   Magistrate Judge [Ronald A. Guzman]

DEFENDANTS' EMERGENCY MOTION IN LIMINE
TO EXCLUDE FROM EVIDENCE PLAINTIFFS' EXHIBIT NO. 26-
"DISABILITY EVALUATION UNDER SOCIAL SECURITY"

The Defendants, [A.I.C. SECURITY INVESTIGATIONS, LTD.]; [A.I.C. INTER-NATIONAL, LTD.]; and [defendant C], by and through their attorneys, [WESSELS & PAUTSCH, P.C.], by [Charles W. Pautsch], [attorney A], and [attorney B], hereby move to exclude from evidence Plaintiffs' Exhibit No. 26- "Disability Evaluation Under Social Security" based upon the following:

1.   On [February 22, 1993], the parties in the above-captioned action submitted a Final Pre-Trial Order to the Court.

2.   Attached as Schedule C-1 to the Final Pre-Trial Order is Plaintiffs' List of Exhibits.

3.   Exhibit No. 26 of Plaintiffs' List of Exhibits is "Disability Evaluation Under Social Security—May, 1992."

4.   Defendants were served with Plaintiffs' Exhibit No. 26 on or about [March 1, 1993].

5.   After having a chance to review Plaintiffs' Exhibit No. 26, Defendants have taken the position that said exhibit should be excluded from evidence at trial for the reasons listed below.

6.   Plaintiffs' Exhibit No. 26 is an incomplete document. Specifically, Plaintiffs have intentionally excluded pages 12, 14, 16–74 and 82–118 from the document labeled "Disability Evaluation Under Social Security" (Plaintiffs' Exhibit No. 26).

7.   Plaintiffs' Exhibit No. 26 cannot be relied upon in evidence as a trustworthy document since major omissions have been made to the document by Plaintiff EEOC's Counsel.

8.   Plaintiffs' Exhibit No. 26 is an out-of-court statement which Defendants believe Plaintiffs will introduce for the truth of the matters asserted in the document; and, therefore, said exhibit is inadmissible hearsay.

WHEREFORE, Defendants respectfully request this Court to exclude from evidence Plaintiffs' Exhibit No. 26—"Disability Evaluation Under Social Security."

Dated this [4th] day of [March], [1993].

[A.I.C. SECURITY INVESTIGATIONS, LTD.];

[A.I.C. INTERNATIONAL, LTD.]; and [defendant C]

By: [attorney A]

§ 15.12   —Response to Motion in Limine

FORM 15–9
SAMPLE RESPONSE TO MOTION IN LIMINE

IN THE UNITED STATES DISTRICT COURT

FOR THE [NORTHERN] DISTRICT OF [ILLINOIS]

[EASTERN] DIVISION

U.S. EQUAL EMPLOYMENT OPPORTUNITY COMMISSION,

Plaintiff

v.   Civil Action No. [92 C 7330]

[A.I.C. SECURITY INVESTIGATIONS, LTD.];

[A.I.C. INTERNATIONAL, LTD.]; and [unnamed defendant C],

                                           Honorable [Marvin E. Aspen]

Defendants.   Magistrate Judge [Ronald A. Guzman]

DEFENDANTS' RESPONSE TO PLAINTIFF'S MOTION IN LIMINE
TO EXCLUDE EVIDENCE OF UNEMPLOYMENT COMPENSATION
AND DISABILITY BENEFITS

INTRODUCTION

[A.I.C. Security Investigations, et al. ("A.I.C.")] hereby opposes the Plaintiff's Motion for the Exclusion of Evidence relating to unemployment compensation, social security disability payments, and private disability payments paid to [Mr. Wessel]. Unemployment compensation is a not a collateral benefit and is subject to deduction from any damage awarded. Furthermore, disability payments, including private disability funded by the employer, do not derive from an independent collateral source and should also be deducted from any damage award.

Evidence of unemployment compensation and disability payments will not be presented by the Defendant solely on the issue of damages. Evidence with regard to these payments is relevant to both the damage award and other matters in the trial. Furthermore, certain discussions relating to the potential for disability payments are relevant as to the motivation of both the Employer and the Plaintiff at the cessation of [Wessel]'s employment.

Under the Americans with Disabilities Act, a Plaintiff may be entitled to receive compensatory damages, including damages for "future pecuniary losses, emotional pain, suffering inconvenience, mental anguish, loss of enjoyment of life and other nonpecuniary losses." 42 U.S.C. § 1981a(b)(3). The Plaintiff in this case has argued that he should receive compensatory damages, and has further indicated that he will argue that his emotional distress was compounded by financial problems. Undoubtedly, his receipt of other income is relevant to these claims.

I. UNEMPLOYMENT COMPENSATION SHOULD BE DEDUCTED FROM ANY DAMAGE AWARD

Back pay awards are within the court's discretion. [*Olshock v. Village of Skokie,* 541 F.2d 1254 (7th Cir. 1976)]. Unemployment compensation should be deducted from any back pay damages due from the employer, as the amount of the benefits paid should be credited to the party who financed them. [*Nottelson v. Smith Steelworkers D.A.L.U.,* 643 F.2d 445 (7th Cir. 1981)]. In the [*Nottelson*] case, the [Seventh] Circuit held, in a Title VII case, that the Plaintiff's back pay award should reflect a credit for the employer for any unemployment benefits paid to the Plaintiff. [*Id.* at 456.] For purposes of a back pay order under Title VII, the sum of the back pay shall be reduced by the amount of any welfare or unemployment compensation received. [*Association Against Discrimination in Employment, Inc. v. Weeks,* 454 F. Supp. 758 (D. Conn. 1978)].

In [*Diaz v. Pan American World Airways,* 346 F. Supp. 1301 (S.D. Fla. 1972)], the court held that the back pay awarded in a Title VII case should be reduced by the amount of unemployment insurance received by the Plaintiff during the relevant back pay period. [*Id.* at 1309].

Defendant also intends to introduce into evidence information on unemployment compensation as relevant to other issues in addition to the award of back pay. Therefore, based on case precedent that back pay should be reduced by unemployment benefits, and that the Defendant intends to utilize this evidence as to other issues, such evidence is relevant and should not be excluded from presentation at trial.

II. DISABILITY PAYMENTS DO NOT CONSTITUTE A COLLATERAL SOURCE

Under the collateral source rule, courts are prohibited from considering payments received from third parties in determining the extent of Plaintiff's damages;

however, when those payments are received from the Defendant, the collateral source rule does not apply. [*Barkanic v. General Administration of Civil Aviation,* 923 F.2d 957, 964 n.8 (2d Cir. 1991)]. The Plaintiff's reliance on [*Whatley v. Skaggs Co.,* 707 F.2d 1129 (10th Cir. 1983)], is misplaced.

In [*Whatley*], the court refused to deduct payments which the Plaintiff received for an on-the-job injury from the total back pay award. This case fails to state what the source of these payments were. However, due to the language in the case, and the fact that it was an on-the-job injury which resulted in the disability payments, one can assume that the payments were made from worker's compensation insurance. However, deductions made under worker's compensation are excluded based on the collateral source rule because they are obligatory benefits paid by the employer. [*Stifle v. Marathon Petroleum Co.,* 876 F.2d 552 (7th Cir. 1989)]. This situation is different as there is no claim for worker's compensation and the disability compensation was not obligatory on the part of the employer.

Plaintiff's reliance on [*Spulak v. K-Mart Corp.,* 894 F.2d 1150 (10th Cir. 1990)], is also misplaced. In [*Spulak*] the court simply held that an award of social security disability benefits to the employee did not extinguish his right to receive damages for wrongful discharge. It is important to note that the social security disability benefits were based on emphysema and back problems, both conditions not related to the termination of his employment. Thus, the [*Spulak*] case does not stand for the proposition alleged by the Plaintiff, and is cited in error.

It is also important to point out that in the Plaintiff's cited case of [*Johnson v. Harris County Flood Control District,* 869 F.2d 1565 (5th Cir. 1989)], the court states that it is within the trial court's discretion to decide what deductions are to be made from the back pay award. Thus, due to the fact that any deductions from a back pay award are within the trial court's discretion, it is appropriate to state as a matter of law that these types of deductions are improper and should be excluded as irrelevant evidence.

Plaintiff also argues in error that, "The Plaintiff should not be penalized for having had the foresight to obtain insurance." This argument is misplaced as the Plaintiff did not pay the premium for the disability insurance—the Employer did. As a result, the funds do not derive from a collateral source and should be deducted from any back pay award.

Where benefits are paid to the Plaintiff from the Defendant, the collateral source rule does not apply. [*Barkanic v. General Administration of Civil Aviation,* 923 F.2d 957 (2d Cir. 1991)]. "The collateral source rule prohibits courts from considering benefits received from third parties in determining the extent of Plaintiff's recovery." [*Id.* at 964 n.8]. Therefore, due to the fact that the disability insurance was provided by the Defendant, the collateral source rule does not apply. Thus, the Defendant is entitled to an offset in an amount of disability payments made to the Plaintiff.

CONCLUSION

Evidence relating to unemployment or disability payments should not be excluded from consideration for two reasons. First, such payments are not from a collateral source and thus should be deducted from a collateral source and any back pay award. Second, such evidence is relevant to other issues to be presented at trial, specifically, Plaintiff's claim for compensatory damages and the motivation of the Defendant and the Plaintiff in the events leading up to the cessation of [Wessel]'s employment. Thus, the jury should not be prohibited from being advised of the fact that unemployment and disability payments were made to the Plaintiff. The refusal to exclude such evidence would not be prejudicial to the Plaintiff. Accordingly, Defendants respectfully request that the motion to exclude evidence of unemployment compensation, social security, or private disability payments made to the Plaintiff, be denied.

[WESSELS & PAUTSCH, P.C.]

By: [attorney A]

[attorney B]

Attorneys for Defendant

§ 15.13   —Defendant's Response to Plaintiff's Motion in Limine

FORM 15–10
SAMPLE DEFENDANT'S RESPONSE TO PLAINTIFF'S MOTION IN LIMINE

IN THE UNITED STATES DISTRICT COURT

FOR THE [NORTHERN] DISTRICT OF [ILLINOIS]

[EASTERN] DIVISION

U.S. EQUAL EMPLOYMENT OPPORTUNITY COMMISSION,

Plaintiff,

v.   Civil Action No. [92 C 7330]

[A.I.C. SECURITY INVESTIGATIONS, LTD.];

[A.I.C. INTERNATIONAL, LTD.]; and [unnamed defendant C],

Judge [Marvin E. Aspen]

Defendants.   Magistrate Judge [Guzman]

DEFENDANTS' RESPONSE TO PLAINTIFFS' MOTION IN LIMINE

Defendants, [A.I.C. SECURITY INVESTIGATIONS, LTD.]; [A.I.C. INTERNA-
TIONAL, LTD.]; and [defendant C], by and through their attorneys, [WESSELS &
PAUTSCH, P.C.], by [Charles W. Pautsch], [attorney A], and [attorney B], hereby
submit to this Honorable Court Defendants' Response to Plaintiffs' Motion in
Limine and states in support hereof as follows:

1.   On [February 22, 1993], the parties to this action filed a Pre-Trial Order
within the Court.

2.   Attached as Schedule N to the Pre-Trial Order is Plaintiffs' Motion in Limine,
which seeks to exclude from evidence the reasons for [David P.]'s termination.

3.   [David P.] will be called as a witness in Plaintiffs' case-in-chief. (Plaintiff
EEOC's First Set of Interrogatories No. 14.)

4.   In an early set of interrogatories sent from the EEOC to Defendants
(Plaintiff EEOC's First Set of Interrogatories No. 14), the reasons for [David P.]'s ter-
mination was requested. These interrogatories were served and answered prior to
[David P.]'s and [defendant C]'s depositions.

5.   Defendants objected to Plaintiff EEOC's Interrogatory No. 14 because it
did not at that time appear to be relevant to this action.

6.   The reasons for [David P.]'s termination may be used on cross-examination by Defendants counsel to impeach his credibility.

7.   Plaintiffs can claim no surprise or unfair prejudice regarding the information about [David P.]'s termination.

8.   Specifically, [David P.] has been a cooperative witness for the EEOC and
filled out and executed an affidavit to support the charges of [Charles Wessel].
Thus, the EEOC could ask [David P.] himself the reasons for his termination.

9.   In addition, counsel for Plaintiff EEOC extensively and exhaustively questioned [defendant C], the person who solely decided to terminate [David P.],
regarding the reasons for his termination. (See Transcript of [defendant C]
Deposition at 46–55 attached hereto and incorporated herein).

Wherefore, Defendants respectfully request the Court deny Plaintiff's Motion In
Limine to exclude evidence regarding [David P.]'s termination and rule that such
evidence may be used at trial.

Dated this [5th] day of [February], [1993].

§ 15.14 —Motion in Limine to Exclude Plaintiff's Expert Witness

FORM 15–11
SAMPLE MOTION IN LIMINE TO EXCLUDE PLAINTIFF'S EXPERT WITNESS

DEFENDANTS' EMERGENCY MOTION IN LIMINE
TO EXCLUDE [Dr. B] FROM TESTIFYING AT TRIAL

The Defendants, [A.I.C. SECURITY INVESTIGATIONS, LTD.]; [A.I.C. INTERNA-TIONAL, LTD.]; and [unnamed defendant C], by and through their attorneys, [WESSELS & PAUTSCH, P.C.], by [Charles W. Pautsch], [attorney A], and [attorney B], hereby move to exclude [Dr. B] from testifying at trial based upon the following:

1. On [February 22, 1993], the parties in the above-captioned action submitted a Final Pre-Trial Order to the Court.

2. Attached as Schedule D-1 to the Final Pre-Trial Order is Plaintiffs' List of Witnesses.

3. [B], M.D. is listed as a "will call" witness in Plaintiffs' List of Witnesses.

4. [Dr. B] was Plaintiff [Wessel]'s primary testing physician.

5. Plaintiffs will attempt at trial to qualify [Dr. B] as an expert witness and to elicit opinions from [Dr. B] to further their claims against Defendants.

6. For the reasons stated in Defendants' Memorandum and Reply Memorandum in Support of Their Motion for Summary Judgment, the Court should hold, as a matter of law, that [Dr. B] is a completely incredible witness and should not be allowed to testify at trial as an expert witness or in any other capacity. (See Defendants' Memorandum in Support of Their Motion for Summary Judgment at 16-17 and Defendants' Reply Memorandum on Summary Judgment at 3-8.)

WHEREFORE, Defendants respectfully request this Court to preclude from trial the testimony of [B], M.D.

Dated this [4th] day of [March], [1993].

§ 15.15   —Motion in Limine to Preclude Testimony on Rebuttal

FORM 15–12
SAMPLE MOTION IN LIMINE TO PRECLUDE TESTIMONY ON REBUTTAL

DEFENDANTS' EMERGENCY MOTION IN LIMINE TO EXCLUDE
[Dr. C] M.D. FROM TESTIFYING AT TRIAL IN REBUTTAL OR OTHERWISE

The Defendants, [A.I.C. SECURITY INVESTIGATIONS, LTD.]; [A.I.C. INTERNATIONAL, LTD.]; and [unnamed defendant C], by and through their attorneys, [WESSELS & PAUTSCH, P.C.], by [Charles W. Pautsch], [attorney A], and [attorney B], hereby move to exclude from testifying at trial [Dr. C], M.D., in rebuttal or otherwise, based upon the following:

1.   On [February 22, 1993], the parties to the above-captioned action to the Court submitted a Final Pre-Trial Order.

2.   Attached as Schedule D-1 to the Final Pre-Trial Order is Plaintiffs' List of Witnesses.

3.   Included in Plaintiffs' List of Witnesses is [Dr. C] as a rebuttal witness.

4.   On or about [February 19, 1993] Defendants filed a Motion to Exclude [Dr. C.] as an expert witness at trial.

5.   Thereafter in open court Plaintiff EEOC's counsel conveyed that [Dr. C.] will not be called in Plaintiffs' case-in-chief. The Court then ruled that [Dr. C.] would be excluded from testifying in Plaintiffs' case-in-chief, but the Court reserved ruling on the issue of whether [Dr. C.] could testify for Plaintiff in rebuttal.

6.   For the reasons stated in Defendants' previous Motion to Exclude [Dr. C] as an expert witness in Plaintiffs' case-in-chief, Defendants now object to his testimony at trial in rebuttal or otherwise.

WHEREFORE, Defendants respectfully request this Court to preclude from trial the testimony of [Dr. C] in rebuttal or otherwise.

Dated this [4th] day of [March], [1993].

§ 15.16   Order to Establish Uncontested and Contested Facts[18]

FORM 15–13
SAMPLE ORDER TO ESTABLISH UNCONTESTED AND CONTESTED FACTS

STATEMENT OF UNCONTESTED AND CONTESTED FACTS

It is ORDERED:

1.   Development of Joint Statement of Uncontested and Contested Facts.

(a)   Plaintiffs' Proposed Facts. By [_____,] 19[__], Plaintiffs shall serve on opposing parties a narrative statement listing all facts proposed to be proved by them at trial in support of their claim(s) as to liability and damage (except on the issue(s) of [_____]).

(b)   Defendants' Response and Proposed Facts. By [_____], 19[__], Defendants shall serve on opposing parties a statement:

(1)   indicating the extent to which they contest and do not contest the Plaintiffs' proposed facts;

(2)   listing all additional facts proposed to be proved by them at trial in opposition to, or in special defense of, the Plaintiffs' claim(s) as to liability and damages; and

(3) listing all facts proposed to be proved by them at trial in support of their counterclaims), cross-claims(s), and third-party claim(s).

(c)   Replies.

(1)   By [_____], 19[__], Plaintiffs shall serve on opposing parties a statement indicating the extent to which they contest and do not contest the Defendants' proposed facts (including defendants' modifications to the facts initially proposed by plaintiffs) and listing all additional facts proposed to be proved by them at trial in opposition to, or in special defense of, the defendants' counterclaims; and

(2)   By [_____], 19[__], Defendants to cross-claims and third-party claims shall serve on opposing parties a statement indicating the extent to which they contest and do not contest the proposed facts of the cross-claimant or third-party

---

[18] These statements are sometimes also known as statements of contentions (and proof) or final pre-trial statements (FPS). **Form 15–13** was adapted from a Sample Order to Establish Uncontested and Contested Facts, Manual for Complex Litigation 2d § 41.6 (1985).

claimant and listing all additional facts proposed to be proved by them at trial in opposition to, or in special defense, of such cross-claims or third-party claims.

(d)   Final Response. By [_____], 19[__], defendants making counterclaims, cross claims, or third-party claims shall serve on opposing parties a statement indicating the extent to which they contest and do not contest their adversary's proposed facts (including modifications to the facts initially proposed by them).

(e)   Joint Statement of Uncontested and Contested Facts. By [_____], 19[__], the parties shall file with the court a joint statement listing the facts that are not contested and those that are contested, indicating as to the latter the precise nature of their disagreement. These facts, both uncontested and contested, will to the extent practicable be organized and collected under headings descriptive of the claim or defense to which they may be relevant (and, where appropriate, subdivide into factual categories descriptive of particular parties and time periods).

2.   Directions.

(a)   Narration of Proposed Facts. In stating facts proposed to be proved, counsel shall do so in simple, declarative, self-contained, consecutively-numbered sentences, avoiding all "color words," labels, argumentative language, and legal conclusions. If a fact is to be offered against fewer than all parties, counsel shall indicate the parties against which the fact will (or will not) be offered. (The facts to be set forth include not only ultimate facts, but also all subsidiary and supporting facts except those offered solely for impeachment purposes.)

(b)   Agreement and Disagreement. Counsel shall indicate that they do not contest a proposed fact if at trial they will not controvert or dispute the fact. In indicating disagreement with a proposed fact, counsel shall do so by deletion or interlineation of particular words or phrases so that the nature of their disagreement (and the extent .of any agreement) will be clear.

(c)   Objections. Objections to the admissibility of a proposed fact (either as irrelevant or on other grounds) may not be used to avoid indicating whether or not the party contests the truth of that fact. (Counsel shall, however, indicate any objections, both to the facts they contest and those they do not contest.)

3.   Annotations. Facts, not evidence, are to be listed by the parties. However, a party may identify in parentheses at the end of a proposed fact the witness(es), deponent(s), documents), or other evidence supporting the truth of the fact. No party, however, will be required to admit or deny the accuracy of such references.

4.   Effect.

(a)   Elimination of Proof. The uncontested facts shall be taken at the trial as established under Fed. R. Civ. P. 36 without the need for independent proof. To the extent relevant to a resolution of the contested facts and otherwise admissible, these facts may be read to the jury. independent proof of the uncontested facts will be allowed only if incidental to the presentation of evidence on the contested facts or if such proof will better enable the jury to resolve the contested facts.

(b) Preclusion of Other Facts. Except for good cause shown, the parties shall be precluded at trial from offering proof of any fact not disclosed in their listing of proposed facts (except purely for impeachment purposes).

5.   Sanctions. Unjustified refusal to admit a proposed factor to limit the extent of disagreement with a proposed fact shall be subject to sanctions under Fed. R. Civ. P. 37(c). Excessive listing of proposed facts (or of the evidence to be submitted in support of or denial of such facts) which imposes an onerous burden on opposing parties shall be subject to sanctions under Rule 16(f).

Dated: [_____], 19[__]

United States District Judge

§ 15.17   Motion to Amend Statement of Facts

FORM 15–14
SAMPLE MOTION TO AMEND STATEMENT OF FACTS

DEFENDANTS' EMERGENCY MOTION FOR LEAVE
TO SUPPLEMENT THEIR STATEMENT OF UNCONTESTED
MATERIAL FACTS

Defendants, [A.I.C. SECURITY INVESTIGATIONS, LTD.]; [A.I.C. INTERNATIONAL, LTD.]; and [unnamed defendant C], by and through their attorneys, [WESSELS & PAUTSCH, P.C.], by [Charles W. Pautsch], [attorney A], and [attorney B], and pursuant to [Rule 12] of the Court's Local Rules, hereby move for leave to supplement their statement of uncontested facts as follows:

1.   On or about [August 5, 1992], just one week after his last day of work at [A.I.C.], [Charles Wessel] applied for disability benefits through Social Security. (Attached hereto and incorporated herein as Exhibit B, following Defendants' previously submitted Exhibits 1–12.)

2.   [Wessel]'s application was signed under penalty of perjury and criminal punishment. (*Id.*)

3.   [Wessel]'s application was not received by Defendants until very recently after his deposition, despite Defendants' efforts to subpoena said documents in [December 1992], because the Social Security Administration refused to release them without [Wessel]'s authorization.

4.   As the disability report states, paragraph 20, daily radiation which [Wessel] underwent between [April 7, 1992], and [July 14, 1993] "caused a reduction in work activity and slowed production time."

WHEREFORE, because the foregoing represents a sworn statement, because Defendants did not have access to the documents until recently in this expedited trial, and finally, because the foregoing evidence is extremely probative as to one of the key issues on summary judgment, Defendants seek leave to submit the attached Exhibit No. 13 as an uncontested fact.

Dated this [1st] day of [March], [1993].

§ 15.18   Pre-Trial Order Draft

FORM 15–15
SAMPLE PRE-TRIAL ORDER DRAFT

FINAL PRE-TRIAL ORDER

This case came before the court at a pre-trial conference held on [date], pursuant to Fed. R. Civ. P. 16, at which [name] appeared as counsel for the plaintiff and [name] appeared as counsel for the defendant. Accordingly, the following Order is hereby entered:

I.   Pleadings and Discovery Material

Only the following pleadings, answers to interrogatories, and depositions listed below will be admitted into evidence. Any objections to such admission are hereby waived unless set forth below:

A.   Pleadings

The complaint, except for Count 6.

B.   All answers to interrogatories except the answer to interrogatory number [_____]. The videotaped deposition of the Plaintiff demonstrating her capacity to engage in word processing and answer the phone.

II.   Witnesses

A.   Plaintiff's Witnesses

1.   Plaintiff will call the following witnesses with respect to liability:

2.   Plaintiff will call the following witnesses with respect to damages:

B.   Defendant's Witnesses

1.   Defendant will call the following witnesses with respect to liability:

2.   Defendant will call the following witnesses with respect to damages:

C.   Expert Witnesses

No expert may testify unless identified in this section. No experts may testify unless their qualifications are summarized in an attachment to this order. No objections to qualifications may be made unless they are summarized in this section. No expert witness may testify unless all opposing counsel had been informed in advance of testimony of the substance of the expert's anticipated testimony.

1.   Plaintiff's expert witnesses and reference to summaries of substance of testimony:

2.   Defendant's objections to the qualifications of any of plaintiff's experts:

3.   Defendant's expert witnesses and reference to written summaries of the substance of their testimony:

4.   Plaintiff's objections to defendant's experts:

III.   Exhibits

Only the exhibits listed in this section may be introduced at trial. Any objection to these exhibits is waived unless summarized in this section. It shall not be necessary to produce the custodian of an exhibit unless that requirement is set forth below:

A.   Plaintiff's Exhibits

1.   Description and number of each exhibit:

2.   Defendant's objections, by number and basis for objection:

B.   Defendant's Exhibits:

1.   Number and description of each exhibit defendant intends to introduce:

2.   Plaintiff's objections, by number and basis for objection:

IV.   Facts

A.   Uncontested Facts [list each uncontested fact, along with a determination of whether it shall or shall not be read to jury at beginning of trial]

B.   Plaintiff's Presentation on Contested Facts

1.   Plaintiff will prove these contested facts with respect to liability:

2.   Plaintiff will prove these contested facts with respect to damages:

C.   Defendant's Proof of Contested Facts

1.   Defendant will prove the following contested facts with respect to liability:

2.   Defendant will prove these contested facts with respect to damages:

V.   Legal Propositions

A.   Uncontested Legal Propositions

B.   Plaintiff's Position on Contested Legal Issues

C.   Defendant's Position on Contested Legal Issues

VI.   Other Trial Management Issues

A.   Length of Trial (including allowance for various stages, such as plaintiff's case-in-chief and defendant's case-in-chief, opening and closing arguments, and jury instructions)

B.   Draft Jury Instructions

C.   Sequestration of Witnesses and of Jury

§ 15.19   Final Pre-Trial Order

FORM 15–16
SAMPLE FINAL PRE-TRIAL ORDER

FINAL PRE-TRIAL ORDER

It is ORDERED:

1.   Rulings on outstanding motions. [Resolve all outstanding motions seeking summary judgment, challenging jurisdiction or venue, requesting transfer, seeking to limit the period of proof, regarding jury demands, and similar matters.]

2.   Trial. Trial is [tentatively] scheduled to commence at [___] A.M. 19[__], at the Federal Courthouse, [_____].

(a)   Consolidation. Under Fed. R. Civ. P. 42(a), the following cases are consolidated for purposes of this trial:

(Define by inclusion or exclusion the cases consolidated for trial. To the extent appropriate, order transfer of cases under 28 U.S.C. §§ 1404 or 1406.)

(b)   Severance. Under Fed. R. Civ. P. 42(b), the following issues are schedule for trial at this time:

(Define the issues to be tried, indicating whether jury or nonjury.)

After this trial has been concluded, the court will establish a schedule for trial of the remaining issue(s) as may be necessary.

(c)   Order of proof. (Special provisions as to the order in which the issues, evidence, or arguments will be presented.)

(indicate any anticipated changes, such as federal holidays, days on which trial will not be held or on which the trial hours will be reduced, any religious holidays to be observed, and any planned recesses.)

(d)   Jury. A jury of [___] persons and [___] alternates shall be selected. The parties shall by [_____], 19[__], file any special voir dire question they request the panel be asked; additional questions may be suggested after the initial examination of the panel. Each side shall be permitted [___] peremptory challenges to the principal jurors and [___] peremptory challenges to the alternate jurors. (By stipulation of the parties under Fed. R. Civ. P. 48, a verdict may be accepted if returned by a unanimous jury of at least jurors.)

(e)   Continuances; deadline for partial settlements. Postponement of trial will be granted only for compelling reasons. Illness or unavailability of counsel will not justify a continuance if other members of their firms or attorneys representing parties with similar interests are available to proceed with the trial.

3.   Witness lists. Plaintiffs shall file and serve by [_____], 19[__], and defendants shall file and serve by [_____], 19[__], a list identifying all persons (including expert and rebuttal witnesses) whose testimony they may offer at trial in person or by deposition. Counsel will separately list their "major" witnesses (whose testimony they expect to offer) and their "minor" witnesses (whose testimony will probably not be needed, but who have been listed merely to preserve the right to offer such testimony should it be needed in the light of developments during trial).

(a)   Witnesses to testify in person. For witnesses to be examined in person, the list will contain an estimate of the time expected to be needed for direct examination and include a brief summary of their expected direct testimony/indicate the subjects on which they are expected to testify. For any witness who is to express any opinion under Fed. R. Evid. 702, the list shall include, if not previously provided, the information prescribed under Fed. R. Civ. P. 26(b)(4)(A)(i).

(b)   Depositions. Each party will attach to the list the pages of any deposition to be used at trial, with the portions to be offered by the proponent indicated by the blue marking in the margin.

(c)   Response. Within [___] days after receiving these lists, each party shall, with respect to witnesses not previously listed by it but listed by another party, file and serve a notice;

(1)   indicating for each witness who is to testify in person the estimated time expected to be needed for cross-examination and [a brief summary of the expected cross-examination/any additional subjects on which the witness will likely be examined on cross-examination] (other than for impeachment); and

(2)   attaching for each witness whose testimony will be presented by deposition the portions of the deposition, marked in yellow, that are objected to (specifying the grounds for the objections) and, marked in red, that in fairness should be considered with the portions already designated or that will be offered as cross-examination. Unless indicated to the contrary in the notice, the party shall be deemed to have agreed that the conditions of Fed. R. Civ. P. 32(a) are satisfied with respect to each person identified in another party's witness list as someone whose testimony will be presented by deposition.

(d)   Effect. Except for good cause shown, the parties will be precluded from offering substantive evidence through any person not so listed. The listing of a witness does not commit the listing party to have such person available at trial or to offer the testimony of such person. Any party may offer the testimony of a witness listed by another party.

4.   Exhibit lists. Plaintiffs shall file and serve by [_____], 19[__], and defendants shall file and serve by [_____], 19[__], a list identifying all writings, recordings, documents, bills, graphs, charts, models, summaries, compilations, reports, records, photographs, and other exhibits (collectively called "exhibits") they expect to offer at trial, to use as demonstrative exhibits, or to be used or referred to by any of their witnesses, including expert witnesses.

(a)   Identification. The list shall describe each exhibit and give its identification number, if any. Although some exhibits may be adequately identified through a group description (for example, "invoices from C.D. Inc., to A.B., dated from [_____], 19[__], to [_____], 19[__], bearing identification #[_____] through #[_____]") general references (for example, "documents identified in the deposition of _____)" are insufficient.

(b)   Exhibition. Unless beyond the party's control (for example, exhibits from an independent third party being obtained through subpoena), the party shall at the time of serving the list make all exhibits not previously produced available to other parties for their inspection and copying at [_____] (city in which trial will be held, or some other convenient location).

(c)   Objections. Except to the extent a party in its listing of exhibits or within [___] days after receiving another party's exhibit list gives notice to the contrary, it shall be deemed to have agreed (for purposes of this trial only) that:

(1)   the originals of the listed exhibits are authentic within Fed. R. Evid. 901 or 902;

(2)   duplicates, as defined in Fed. R. Evid. 1001, of the listed exhibits are admissible to the same extent as the originals;

(3)   any listed exhibits purporting to be correspondence were sent by the purported sender and received by the purported recipients) on approximately the dates shown or in accordance with customary delivery schedules;

(4)   any disputes regarding the accuracy of any of the listed exhibits that purport to the summaries under Fed. R. Evid. 1006 affect only the weight, not the admissibility, of such exhibits;

(5)   any listed exhibits purporting to be records described in Fed. R. Evid. 803(6) meet the requirements of that Rule without extrinsic evidence; and

(6)   any listed exhibits purporting to be public records or reports described in Fed. R. Evid. 803(8) meet the requirements of that Rule.

(d)   Effect. Except for good cause shown, the parties may not offer in evidence, use as demonstrative evidence, or examine any of their witnesses concerning any exhibit not so identified (except solely for impeachment purposes). The listing of any exhibit does not commit the listing party to use it. Subject to any objections that have not been waived under subparagraph (c), any party may use any exhibit that has been listed by another party.

(e)   Rulings. Requests for a ruling under Fed. R. Evid. 104 in advance of trial with respect to any objections made under subparagraph (c) or with respect to any other expected objection to admissibility of evidence must be made by motion filed not later than [_____], 19[__].

5.   Limits on evidence. (Except for good cause shown, counsel may not offer proof of facts not disclosed in the joint statement of uncontested and contested facts previously submitted, nor may they offer independent evidence of the agreed facts except to the extent incidental to the presentation of evidence on the disputed facts.) Counsel are expected to be selective in deciding on (and listing) the witnesses and documents to be presented at trial and in deciding as trial progresses which of the listed witnesses and documents will be offered. If warranted after review of the lists of witnesses or documents, the court will consider (after hearing from the parties) whether to impose any limits on the length of trial, number of witnesses, or number of exhibits.

6.   Briefs. By [_____], 19[__], plaintiffs (and any defendants asserting counterclaims, cross-claims, or third-party claims) shall file and serve comprehensive
trial briefs covering all significant legal issues expected to arise at trial with respect
to their claims and the defenses made to such claims. By [_____], 19[__], defendant (and any plaintiffs against whom counterclaims are asserted) shall file and
serve comprehensive trial briefs responding to the legal contentions of their adver-
saries and covering any additional significant legal issues expected to arise at trial
with respect to the claims against them and their defenses. Any reply briefs shall be
filed by [_____], 19__.

(a)   Suggested preliminary and interim instructions. In a separate section of
their briefs, the parties shall include their suggestions as to the contents of preliminary instructions to be given the jury at the beginning of the trial and of any interim
instructions regarding evidence that will likely be received only for a limited purpose. (The time for filing requests for final jury instructions will be set by the court
during trial).

(b)   Proposals for special verdicts or interrogatories. In a separate section of
their briefs, the parties shall outline the special verdicts or interrogatories that,
depending upon the evidence, may be appropriate for submission to the jury. (The
time for filing revisions to these proposed special verdicts or interrogatories will be
set by the court during trial.)

7.   Administrative Details.

(a)   Facilities. Each side shall by [_____], 19[__], designate a representative
to confer with the Clerk of the court and the [GSA Building Manager] and make
any special arrangements with respect to the courtroom, witness and conference
rooms, facilities for storage of documents, installation of copying machines or
computer equipment, and similar matters.

(b)   Schedule of witnesses and documents. Counsel shall, absent unusual circumstances, give notice to opposing parties at least [___] hours before calling a
witness or offering (or otherwise using) any exhibit during direct examination. This
shall be accomplished during trial by daily providing a schedule, updated as trial
progresses, reflecting the order in which witnesses are expected to be presented
during the next [___] trial days and the exhibits that are expected to be offered or
used during the examination of such witnesses.

(1)   if less than a complete exhibit (or less than all of the portions of a deposition previously designated by the parties) is to be introduced, the schedule shall so
indicate.

(2)   revisions to this projected sequence of witnesses and documents (or to the
portions of the deposition to be read) shall be disclosed as soon as known.

(c)   Interim conferences. A short conference will usually be held at the end of each trial day and [___] minutes before the start of each trial day to consider problems that may be expected to arise, including last-minute revisions in the sequence or scope of evidence to be presented and objections that have not previously been rules on or that should be reconsidered.

(d)   Presentation of exhibits. Exhibits shall be premarked by the proponent. Unless impractical, the proponent shall provide extra copies for the court and for each juror at the time of offering or first referring to an exhibit. Use of an exhibit shall, unless specifically disclaimed or limited, be deemed an offer of the exhibit in evidence; and, unless excluded on objection promptly made, the exhibit shall be deemed received in evidence. If notice of the proposed use has been given under subparagraph (b) or (c), the presentation of evidence shall not be interrupted for opposing counsel to examine the exhibit. Each side shall designate a representative to aid the courtroom deputy in maintaining current lists and indexes of the exhibits that have been received.

9.   Additional conferences. The court will be available to confer with the parties as trial approaches to consider any details of trial not resolved in this order or any part of this order that should be changed.

Dated: [   ]

United States District Judge[19]

§ 15.20   Pre-Trial Order (Mock Trial)

FORM 15–17
SAMPLE PRE-TRIAL ORDER

UNITED STATES DISTRICT COURT FOR THE [EASTERN]

DISTRICT OF [PENNSYLVANIA]

[Steve Lyons],

Plaintiff

v.   Civil Action No. [820130]

[Eastern Pharmaceuticals, Incorporated],

Defendant

---

[19] **Form 15–16** was adapted from the Final Pre-Trial Order Form in Manual for Complex Litigation 2d § 41.7 (1985).

PRE-TRIAL ORDER

It is ORDERED:

1.   Trial is scheduled to commence at [9:00] A.M., [June 29, 1993], at the Federal Courthouse for the [Eastern] District of [Pennsylvania], [Independence Mall West], [Philadelphia], [Pennsylvania].

2.   Subject to further order, the court sessions will be held from 9:00 A.M. until 5:00 P.M. each weekday, except for [Monday] [July 5], on which there will be no session, in honor of the celebration of Independence Day.

3.   A jury of twelve (12) persons and three (3) alternates shall be selected. The parties shall by [June 15, 1993], file any special voir dire questions they request to be presented to the panel. Any additional questions may be suggested after the initial examination of the panel. Pursuant to Fed. R. Civ. P. 47(b) and 28 U.S.C. § 1870, each side shall be permitted three (3) peremptory challenges to the jurors.

4.   In general the Plaintiff claims that he suffers from multiple sclerosis ("MS"), which substantially limits the major life activities of reading, speaking, and walking. He further claims that the defendant employer terminated him due to his disability, without making reasonable accommodations that would allow him to continue to perform his essential job functions, in violation of the Americans with Disabilities Act ("ADA").

5.   In general, the Defendant claims that they did not terminate the Plaintiff due to his alleged ailment. The Defendant does not admit that the Plaintiff suffers from MS, and denies that the ADA applies to this action. Further, the defendant alleges that even if the Plaintiff is given the additional accommodations that he requested, he will still be unable to perform his essential job functions.

6.   The following facts are established by admissions in the pleadings or by stipulations of counsel:

(a)   The Plaintiff is a citizen of the United States, and resides in [Norristown], [Pennsylvania].

(b)   Defendant, [Eastern Pharmaceuticals, Incorporated ("Eastern")], is a [Delaware] corporation with its manufacturing plant and principal place of business in [Fort Washington], [Pennsylvania].

(c)   [Eastern] is a "person," is engaged in "industry affecting commerce," is an "employer," and is a "covered entity," all as defined by the ADA. In addition, [Eastern] employed more than 25 employees for each working day in more than 20 weeks during the preceding year.

(d)   The Plaintiff was hired by [Eastern] on [July 7, 1972], as an accounting clerk. After several promotions, the Plaintiff was employed as a staff accountant in [Eastern]'s finance department. The Plaintiff was promoted to this position on [July 11, 1989], and held the job until he was terminated on [August 5, 1992].

(e)   [Lisa Brown], [Eastern]'s accounting manager was the Plaintiff's direct supervisor at all relevant times. She terminated the Plaintiff on [August 5, 1992].

(f)   The Plaintiff's essential job functions as a staff accountant were: producing financial reports through spreadsheet applications, operating an adding machine to perform various mathematical functions, maintaining the general ledger, and communicating with outside vendors and [Eastern]'s purchasing agents regarding fixed asset acquisitions.

(g)   [Eastern] provided the Plaintiff with a device that magnifies the computer screen, and also rerouted the Plaintiff's incoming calls so that another employee answered the phone for the Plaintiff. After these accommodations were provided, the Plaintiff was able to perform the essential functions of his job as a staff accountant.

7.   The following constitutes the witness lists as they presently stand:

(a)   Plaintiff's witnesses:

(i)   [Steve Lyons], the Plaintiff will be the first witness called. He will be called on the morning of [June 29, 1993].

(ii)   [Dr. Willard Allen], the Plaintiff's expert medical witness, will be the second witness called. He will be called in the afternoon of [June 29, 1993].

(b)   Defendant's witnesses:

(i)   [Henry Bell], the controller at Defendant [Eastern], will be the first witness called by the defense. He will likely be called on the morning of [June 30, 1993].

(ii)   [Arthur Smith], the Defendant's expert, will be the second witness called by the Defendant. He will likely be called in the afternoon of [June 30, 1993].

(c)   In the event that there are any other witnesses to be called at trial, their names and addresses will be reported to opposing counsel at least ten days prior to trial. This restriction shall not apply to rebuttal witnesses, for the need for such testimony cannot reasonably be anticipated prior to the time of trial.

8.   As this is a jury trial, requests for jury instructions must be submitted to the Court at the commencement of the case, subject to the right of counsel to supplement such requests during the course of trial as to matters that cannot reasonably be anticipated.

9.   This pre-trial order has been formulated after a final pre-trial conference, at which counsel for the respective parties appeared. Reasonable opportunity has been given to counsel to submit corrections or additions prior to the signing of the Order by the Court. From this point forward, this Order will control the course of the trial and may not be amended, except by consent of the parties and the Court or by Order of the Court to prevent manifest injustice, pursuant to Fed. R. Civ. P. 16(e). The pleadings will be deemed merged herein. If any provision of this Order proves to be ambiguous, reference may be made to the record of this conference to the extent reported by stenographic notes, and reference may also be made to the pleadings.

10.   The probable length of this trial is ten (10) days. The case is scheduled to commence with a jury on [June 29, 1993], at [10:00] A.M.

11.   The court will be available to confer with the parties as trial approaches to consider any details of the trial not adequately resolved in this order.

Dated this [_____] day of [_____], 19[__].

United States District Judge

§ 15.21   Final Pre-Trial Order (EEOC)

FORM 15–18
SAMPLE FINAL PRE-TRIAL ORDER

IN THE UNITED STATES DISTRICT COURT

FOR THE [NORTHERN] DISTRICT OF [ILLINOIS]

[EASTERN] DIVISION

U.S. EQUAL EMPLOYMENT OPPORTUNITY COMMISSION and

[CHARLES H. WESSEL],

Plaintiff,

v.   Civil Action No. [92 C 7330]

[A.I.C. SECURITY INVESTIGATIONS, LTD.];

[A.I.C. INTERNATIONAL, LTD.]; and [unnamed defendant C]   Judge [Aspen]

Defendants.   Magistrate Judge [Guzman]

FINAL PRE-TRIAL ORDER

This matter is scheduled to be heard before the Court at a pre-trial conference pursuant to Fed. R. Civ. P. ("Rule") 16 on [February 19, 1993], at [2:00 P.M.]. The following attorneys will appear at trial on behalf of Plaintiff, Equal Employ-ment Opportunity Commission (the "EEOC"):

[attorney A]

[attorney B]

Equal Employment Opportunity Commission
[536 South Clark Street], [Room 982]
[Chicago], [IL] [60605]
[(312) 353-7582]

The following attorneys will appear at trial on behalf of Intervening Plaintiff [Charles H. Wessel ("Wessel")]:

[attorney C]

[attorney E]

The following attorneys will appear on behalf of Defendants [A.I.C. Security Investigations, Ltd. ("A.I.C.")], [A.I.C. International, Ltd. ("A.I.C. International")], and [defendant C]:

[Charles W. Pautsch]

[attorney A]

[attorney B]

[Wessels & Pautsch]
[Two Plaza East]
[330 E. Kilbourne Avenue]
[Suite 1475]
[Milwaukee], [WI] [53202]
[(414) 291-0600]

This is an action filed under the Americans With Disabilities Act of 1990 (the "ADA"), 42 U.S.C. § 12101 *et seq.,* in which Plaintiffs allege that Defendants discriminated against [Wessel] by terminating his employment because of his disability, terminal cancer, in violation of the ADA. The jurisdiction of this Court is invoked pursuant to 28 U.S.C. §§ 451, 1331, 1337, 1343 and 1345. Jurisdiction and venue are not disputed.

The following stipulations and statements are attached and are made part of this Order:

SCHEDULE A STATEMENT OF UNCONTESTED FACTS

SCHEDULE B AGREED STATEMENT OF CONTESTED ISSUES OF FACT AND LAW

Schedule B-1 Plaintiffs' Proposed Contested Facts

Schedule B-2 Defendants' Proposed Contested Issues of Law

Schedule B-3 Agreed Statement of Contested Issues of Law

SCHEDULE C EXHIBITS

Schedule C-1 Plaintiffs' List of Exhibits

Schedule C-2 Plaintiffs' Exhibits to Which Defendants do not object

Schedule C-3 Plaintiffs' Exhibits to which Defendants Object, with Defendants' Objections Noted

Schedule C-4 Defendants' List of Exhibits

Schedule C-5 Defendants' Exhibits to Which Plaintiffs Do Not Object

Schedule C-6 Defendants' Exhibits to Which Plaintiffs Object, with Plaintiffs' Objections Noted

SCHEDULE D WITNESSES

Schedule D-1 Plaintiffs' List of Names and Addresses of Potential Witnesses to Be Called (specifying those who will be called and those who may be called), with Defendants' Objections to the Calling or to the Qualifications of Witnesses

Schedule D-2 Defendants' List of Names and Addresses of Potential Witnesses to Be Called (specifying those who will be called and those who may be called), with Plaintiffs' Objections to the Calling or Qualifications of Witnesses

SCHEDULE E STIPULATION OF QUALIFICATIONS OF EXPERT WITNESSES

Schedule E-1 Plaintiffs' Proposed Stipulated Qualifications of Experts

Schedule E-2 Statement of Qualifications of Defendants' Expert Witnesses

SCHEDULE F DEPOSITION DESIGNATIONS

Schedule F-1 Statement of Plaintiffs' Deposition Designations and Defendants' Objections

Schedule F-2 Statement of Defendants' Deposition Designations and Defendants' Objections

SCHEDULE G ITEMIZED STATEMENT OF SPECIAL DAMAGES

Schedule G-1 Defendants' Objections to Statement of Special Damages

SCHEDULE H PLAINTIFFS' TRIAL BRIEF

SCHEDULE I DEFENDANTS' TRIAL BRIEF

SCHEDULE J JURY INSTRUCTIONS

Schedule J-1 Plaintiffs' Proposed Jury Instructions and Verdict Forms

Schedule J-2 Defendants' Proposed Jury Instructions and Verdict Forms

SCHEDULE K LIST OF PROPOSED VOIR DIRE QUESTIONS

SCHEDULE L DEFENDANTS' LIST OF PROPOSED VOIR DIRE QUESTIONS

SCHEDULE M HISTORY OF SETTLEMENT NEGOTIATIONS

SCHEDULE N MOTIONS IN LIMINE (TO BE ADDED IF NECESSARY)

Each party has completed discovery. Except for good cause shown, no further discovery shall be permitted. Trial of this case is expected to take between eight and ten business days. The Court has set trial of this case for [March 8, 1993].

The case will be tried by a six-person jury. Plaintiffs prefer that alternates deliberate. Defendants prefer that alternates not deliberate.

It is the preference of the parties that the issues of liability and damages should not be bifurcated for trial.

The parties have agreed that this case may be tried before a Magistrate Judge.

This Order will control the course of the trial and may not be amended except by consent of the parties and the court, or by order of the Court to prevent manifest injustice.

Possibility of settlement of this case was considered by the parties.

SCHEDULE A
STATEMENT OF UNCONTESTED FACTS

1.   Plaintiff Equal Employment Opportunity Commission (the "EEOC") is the agency of the United States charged with the administration and enforcement of Title I of the Americans With Disabilities Act of 1990, 42 U.S.C. § 12101 *et seq.* ("ADA").

2.   Intervening Plaintiff, [Charles H. Wessel ("Wessel")] is a former employee of [A.I.C. Security Investigations, Ltd.].[20]

3.   At all times relevant to the issues in this lawsuit, Defendant [A.I.C. Security Investigations, Ltd. ("A.I.C.")] has been an [Illinois] corporation doing business in the State of [Illinois] and the City of [Chicago]. At all relevant times [A.I.C.] has had more than 200, but less than 500, employees.

4.   At all times relevant to the issues in this lawsuit, Defendant [A.I.C. International, Ltd. ("A.I.C. International")] has been an [Illinois] corporation doing business in the State of [Illinois] and the City of [Chicago]. At all relevant times [A.I.C. International] has been a holding company holding all shares of [A.I.C.].

5.   Since [June 6, 1992], and to the present, Defendant [C] has owned all shares of stock of [A.I.C. International].

6.   [Wessel] was employed by [A.I.C.] from [February 2, 1986], through [July 31, 1992], as Executive Director.

7.   [Wessel] was diagnosed with lung cancer in [June 1987], at which time he had surgery; he was hospitalized from [June 6, 1987], until [June 19, 1987]. He returned to work at [A.I.C.] on [July 6, 1987].

8.   In [July] of [1991], [Wessel] suffered pneumothorax during a routine biopsy and was hospitalized from [July 29, 1991], until [August 12, 1991]. He returned to work on [August 13, 1991].

9.   In [October 1991], [Wessel] had surgery for lung cancer of the right lung; he was hospitalized from [October 3, 1991], until [October 18, 1991]. He returned to work at [A.I.C.] on approximately [November 4, 1991].

10.   [Wessel] was diagnosed with inoperable metastatic brain cancer in [April 1992]. The condition was and is considered by his doctors to be terminal.

---

[20] This stipulation will be read to the jury, unless the court determines that Wessel has not properly intervened in the case.

11.　[A.I.C. Security Investigations, Ltd.], is the largest of the entities held by [A.I.C. International]. [A.I.C.] provides licensed private security guards for residential and commercial property in the [Chicago] area.

12.　[Wessel] was hired by [Victor V.], owner of [A.I.C. International] in [February 1986] as Executive Director of [A.I.C.].

13.　During all relevant times, the Executive Director position at [A.I.C.] was the top management position of [A.I.C].

14.　[Victor V.], owner of [A.I.C. International], died on [June 5, 1992]. [David P.], President of [A.I.C. International], was involuntarily terminated from his employment on [July 6, 1992].

15.　As of [July 31, 1992], [Wessel] was earning [$46,725.00] per year plus [$350.00] per month designated as car allowance and reported to the IRS on a Form 1099.

16. If [Wessel] had continued to be employed by [A.I.C.], he would have earned a salary of [$3893.75] per month, excluding any miscellaneous income designated as car allowance and any bonuses and raises, for each month during which he remained employed by [A.I.C.], after [July 1992].

17.　Following [July 31, 1992], [Wessel] has received unemployment compensation.

18.　Beginning in [January 1993], and retroactive to [October 29, 1992], [Wessel] has received payments at the rate of 60% of his former salary pursuant to a disability policy maintained by [A.I.C.] for its management employees.

19.　In [August 1992], [Wessel] applied for Social Security disability benefits. He has been found eligible for such benefits beginning in [January 1993].

20.　If [Wessel] had continued to be employed by [A.I.C.], the company would have maintained his health insurance by paying premiums of [$598.84] per month for insurance for himself and his wife, for each month that he continued to be employed by [A.I.C.] after [July 1992].

21.　If [Wessel] had continued to be employed by [A.I.C.], the company would have maintained his life insurance, paying [$237.72] per quarter in premiums for each quarter that he continued to be employed by [A.I.C.] after [July 1992].

22.　Since [July 1987], Dr. [B] has been [Charles Wessel]'s primary treating physician. Dr. [B] is an oncologist and a hematologist.

SCHEDULE B
AGREED STATEMENT OF CONTESTED FACTS

1.   Whether [Wessel] was involuntarily terminated from his employment as Executive Director of [A.I.C.].

2.   Whether, in [July 1992], [Wessel] was able to perform the essential functions of his position as Executive Director, with or without reasonable accommodation.

3.   Whether, since [July 29, 1992], [Wessel] has continued to be able to perform the essential functions of his position as Executive Director, with or without reasonable accommodation.

4.   Whether, and in what amount, [Wessel] suffered emotional pain, suffering, inconvenience, mental anguish, loss of enjoyment of life, or other nonpecuniary losses as a result of his discharge from [A.I.C.].

5.   Whether [Wessel] is an individual with a disability within the meaning of the Americans with Disabilities Act.

6.   Whether throughout his employment with [A.I.C.], [Wessel] met all of the skill and experience requirements for the position of Executive Director of [A.I.C.].

7.   What were the essential functions of [Wessel]'s job as Executive Director of [A.I.C.].

8.   Whether, during the following fiscal years (each ending [July 3]), [A.I.C.] (the security guard division) had net earnings of:

1986 [$1,446,659.00]

1987 [$1,681,644.00]

1988 [$2,188,535.00]

1989 [$2,315,051.00]

1990 [$2,367,729.00]

1991 [$2,267,277.00]

1992 [$2,454,627.00]

9.   Whether [Wessel] received a salary increase and a bonus in each year that he was employed by [A.I.C.], except [1991], when no bonuses were given.

Whether [Wessel] did not receive a raise or bonus in [1992] because no appraisals were performed, or raises or bonuses awarded, by [A.I.C.] prior to [July 31, 1992].

10.   Whether [Wessel] was terminated because he suffers from cancer.

11.   Whether [Wessel] was paid through [July 31, 1992]. Whether he received accrued vacation pay.

12.   Whether [Wessel] had diligently sought employment since his discharge by [A.I.C.].

13.   Whether, at the time of his discharge, [Wessel] did not meet the job-related qualification standards consistent with [A.I.C.]'s business necessity because he posed a direct threat to the health and safety of others in the work place.

14.   Whether [Wessel] was terminated from [A.I.C.] for legitimate business reasons.

15.   Whether [Wessel] was discharged on [July 30, 1992], effective [July 31, 1992].

16.   Whether during his employment with [A.I.C.], [Wessel] did or did not ever request an accommodation in order to perform the essential functions of his position as Executive Director.

SCHEDULE B-1
PLAINTIFFS' PROPOSED CONTESTED FACTS

1.   Whether [defendant C], [A.I.C.] and/or [A.I.C. International] acted with malice or reckless indifference to [Wessel]'s federally protected rights in discharging him.

2.   Whether [Wessel] is a widely recognized leader in the security guard industry. Whether he has worked in the industry for approximately thirty years.

3.   Whether [Wessel] is licensed as a private detective and as a private security contractor by the State of [Illinois]. Whether he holds similar licenses from the State of [Florida].

4.   Whether [Wessel] is a member of, and has served on the Boards of, numerous professional associations, including the [Associated Detectives of Illinois], the [Associated Guard and Patrol Agencies, Inc.], and the [Special Agents Association].

5.   Whether [Wessel] was the principal drafter of the [Illinois] licensing act for private investigators. Whether he served as chair of the [Legislative Rewrite

Committee] which drafted the [Illinois Private Detective, Private Security Contractor, and Private Alarm Act of 1983], the statute which licenses private investigators and security guards in [Illinois].

6.   What were the marginal functions of [Wessel]'s position as Executive Director of [A.I.C.].

7.   Whether the decision to terminate [Wessel]'s employment was made by [defendant C].

8.   Whether, prior to making the decision to terminate [Wessel], [defendant C] did not consult with any employees of [A.I.C.], other than [Beverly K.], who was hired on approximately [June 10, 1992].

9.   Whether, at the direction of [defendant C], [Beverly K.], on [July 29, 1992], advised [Wessel] that [defendant C] had determined that he should retire.

10.   Whether, on [July 30, 1992], [Beverly K.] advised [Wessel] by telephone that he was terminated, effective [July 31, 1992].

11.   Whether [Wessel] was never subjected to any employment performance warnings or disciplinary action prior to his discharge.

12.   Whether [defendant C], [A.I.C.] and [A.I.C. International] were aware of the requirements of the ADA in [July], [1992], at the time [defendant C] made the decision to discharge [Wessel].

SCHEDULE B-2
DEFENDANTS' PROPOSED CONTESTED ISSUES OF FACT OR LAW

1.   Whether [Wessel] was advised by any of his treating physicians in [April 1992], and/or at other subsequent times, that he was not to drive an automobile due to the significant risk posed by his brain cancer and treatment for same.

2.   Whether [Wessel] was offered a driver by [A.I.C.] to get him to and from work in [1991] and [1992].

3.   Whether [Wessel] refused [A.I.C.]'s offer to provide him with a driver to get him to and from work in [1991] and [1992].

4.   Whether [Wessel]'s brain tumors and treatments, including medications and radiation, affected his mental capacities prior to [July 29, 1992], and if so, did the symptoms relate to [Wessel]'s performance of any of the essential functions of his job of Executive Director of [A.I.C.].

5.   Whether [Wessel] was given a parking place next to the entrance at [A.I.C.]'s building as an accommodation to his condition.

6.   Whether [Wessel] was given an office next to the elevator at [A.I.C.]'s building as an accommodation to his condition.

7.   Whether [Wessel] was physically assisted with his walking in and around [A.I.C.]'s premises by [A.I.C.]'s personnel as an accommodation to his condition.

8.   Whether [Wessel] was assisted by [A.I.C.] personnel in obtaining insurance coverage for an air purifier which he kept in his office at [A.I.C.] as an accommodation to his condition.

9.   Whether [Wessel], on account of his terminal illness, personally conducted interviews in or around [May] of [1992] for the purpose of hiring his replacement as Executive Director.

10.   Whether [Wessel] personally, during the course of [1992], turned over to other [A.I.C.] personnel many of the duties which had always been essential functions of the position of Executive Director.

11.   Whether [Wessel]'s position of Executive Director for [A.I.C.] required, as essential functions of the job, regular and predictable full-time attendance.

12.   Whether [Wessel] voluntarily proposed retirement terms of his own choosing on [July 29, 1992], to [Beverly K.], an employee of [A.I.C.].

13.   Whether [A.I.C.] agreed to give [Wessel] the retirement terms he had proposed on [July 29, 1992], and communicated this agreement to [Wessel].

14.   The amount of time [Wessel] missed work during the last year he was employed with [A.I.C.].

15.   Whether [Wessel] determined to file his Charge, and, in fact, did file his Charge with the EEOC before he attempted to provide [A.I.C.] with any information from his treating physicians.

16.   Whether [Wessel] has diligently sought to mitigate any damages claimed in the instant litigation.

17.   Whether, [Wessel] during his employment with [A.I.C.] in the year [1992], told any [A.I.C.] personnel that his doctor had told him not to drive, but he ([Wessel]) was not going to listen and, in fact, [Wessel] did not follow his doctor's instruction.

SCHEDULE B-3
AGREED STATEMENT OF CONTESTED ISSUES OF LAW

1.   Whether [Wessel] was, on [July 29, 1992], a qualified individual with a disability covered by the protections of the Americans With Disabilities Act.

a.   Whether [Wessel]'s condition of terminal cancer constitutes a physical impairment which substantially limits him in one or more major life activities.

b.   Whether, on [July 29, 1992], [Wessel] met the skill and education requirements for his position as Executive Director of [A.I.C.].

2.   Whether [Wessel] was, from [July 29, 1992], to the present, a qualified individual with a disability covered by the protections of the Americans with Disabilities Act.

a.   Whether [Wessel]'s condition of terminal cancer constitutes a physical impairment which substantially limits him in one or more major life activities.

b.   Whether, from [July 29, 1992], to the present, [Wessel] met the skill and education requirements for his position as Executive Director of [A.I.C.].

3.   Whether [Wessel] is "otherwise qualified" in that he satisfies the prerequisites for the position of Executive Director of [A.I.C.], possessing the appropriate educational background, employment experience, skills, licenses, etc.

SCHEDULE C EXHIBITS

SCHEDULE C-1
PLAINTIFFS' LIST OF EXHIBITS

Exhibit #1: Affidavit of [Charles H. Wessel] to EEOC dated [August 11, 1992].

Exhibit #2: Notes of [Charles Wessel] dated [July 29 and 31, 1992].

Exhibit #3: [August 20, 1992], letter from [Phil W.] to [Charles H. Wessel] advising [Wessel] of the cost of continuing his health benefits for him and his wife.

Exhibit #4: [September 14, 1992], letter from [Charles H. Wessel] to [Phil W.] enclosing payment for continuation of health insurance.

Exhibit #5: Memorandum from [Larry R.] to all [A.I.C.] Building Staff regarding [Charles Wessel].

Exhibit #6: [November 25, 1992], letter from [Unum] Insurance Company to [Charles H. Wessel] informing him that [Unum] had not yet received the employer section of his application for his disability insurance.

Exhibit #7: Letter from [A.I.C. attorney B] to [EEOC attorney A] dated [January 25, 1993] regarding discovery.

Exhibit #8: Videotaped deposition of [Charles H. Wessel] #1.

Exhibit #9: Videotaped deposition of [Charles H. Wessel] #2.

Exhibit #10: Resume of [Charles H. Wessel].

Exhibit #11: List of potential employers from whom [Charles H. Wessel] sought employment subsequent to his discharge from [A.I.C.].

Exhibit #12: [February 10, 1993], letter from [Dr. Peter A.L.], M.D. to [A.I.C. attorney B].

Exhibit #13: Letter to Whom It May Concern from Dr. [B].

Exhibit #14: [A.I.C. International, Ltd.] and Subsidiaries Consolidated Financial Statements, Year Ended [July 31, 1986].

Exhibit #15: [A.I.C. International, Ltd.] and Subsidiaries Consolidated Financial Statements, Year Ended [July 31, 1987].

Exhibit #16: [A.I.C. International, Ltd.] and Subsidiaries Consolidated Financial Statements as of [July 31, 1989] and [1988], together with Auditor's Report.

Exhibit #17: [A.I.C. International, Ltd.] and Subsidiaries Consolidated Financial Statements as of [July 31, 1991] and [1990], together with Auditor's Report.

Exhibit #18: [A.I.C. International, Ltd.] and Subsidiaries Consolidated Financial Statements as of [July 31, 1992], together with Auditor's Report.

Exhibit #19: Curriculum Vitae of Dr. [B].

Exhibit #20: Curriculum Vitae of Dr. [A].

Exhibit #21: Amended Charge of Discrimination

Exhibit #22: [Wessel] computer printout—New Local 73 Format–[7-7-92].

Exhibit #23: EEOC First Request for Production of Documents, Requests 10 and 11.

Exhibit #24: Defendants' Response to EEOC's First Request for Production of Documents, Requests 10 and 11.

Exhibit #25: Curriculum Vitae of Dr. [C] (for rebuttal only).

Exhibit #26: "Disability Evaluation under Social Security"—[May 1992].

Exhibit #27: Chart showing annual net revenue from [A.I.C. Security Investigations, Ltd.] and [A.I.C. International, Ltd.].

Exhibit #28: Plaintiff's First Set of Interrogatories, Interrogatory #8; Defendants' Answer to Plaintiff's First Set of Interrogatories, Interrogatory #8.

Plaintiffs reserve the right to offer additional exhibits as impeachment or rebuttal.

SCHEDULE C-2
PLAINTIFFS' EXHIBITS TO WHICH DEFENDANTS DO NOT OBJECT

EXHIBIT NO./DESCRIPTION

1:      Affidavit of [Charles H. Wessel] to EEOC, dated [8/11/92].

2:      Notes of [Charles Wessel], dated [7/29] and [7/31/92].

3:      [8/20/92] Letter from [P.W.] to [C. Wessel] advising [Wessel] of the cost of continuing his health benefits for him and his wife.

4:      [9/14/92] Letter from [C. Wessel] to [P. W.] enclosing payment for continuation of health insurance.

6:      [11/25/92] Letter from [Unum] to [C. Wessel].

7:      [1/25/93] Letter from [A.I.C. attorney B] to [attorney A] regarding discovery. [no 8, 9, in original]

10:     Resume of [C. Wessel].

11:     [C. Wessel]—List of Potential Employers.

12:     [2/10/93] Letter from [Dr. L.] to [A.I.C. attorney B].

13:     Letter from Dr. [B] to Whom It May Concern.

14–18: [A.I.C. International, Ltd.] and Subsidiaries Consolidated Financial Statements Years Ended [7/31/86], [7/31/87], [7/31/89] and [1988], [7/31/91] and [1990], [7/31/92].

19:     Curriculum Vitae of Dr. [B].

20:     Curriculum Vitae of Dr. [A].

21:     Amended Charge of Discrimination.

22:     Computer printout of New Local 73 Format [7/7/91].

SCHEDULE C-3
PLAINTIFF'S EXHIBITS TO WHICH DEFENDANTS OBJECT, WITH DEFEN-
DANTS' OBJECTIONS NOTED

EXHIBIT NO./DESCRIPTION AND OBJECTION

5:      Memo from [Larry R.].

Defendants object because this document was prepared in the course of litigation per specific instructions of counsel and, therefore, is attorney-client privilege and attorney work product which was not produced to Plaintiff by any
proper means.

8:      Videotaped Deposition of [C. Wessel].

Defendants object. This deposition videotape should not be used at trial if [C.
Wessel] is available to testify. If [C. Wessel] is available to testify, the use of his
videotaped deposition at trial will cause undue delay, waste time, and will
needlessly present cumulative evidence. Rule 403, Fed. R. Evid.

9:      Videotape of the Roast of [C. Wessel].

Defendants object. See Schedule N, Defendants' Motion in Limine.

23:     EEOC First Document Requests Nos. 10 and 11.

Defendants object based upon the expedited discovery schedule.

24:     Defendants' Responses to EEOC's First Request for Production of
Documents, Requests Nos. 10 and 11.

Defendants object based upon the expedited discovery schedule.

25:     Curriculum Vitae of Dr. [C.].

Defendants object to Plaintiff's calling Dr. [C.] at trial for the reasons stated in
Defendants' Motion to Exclude Expert Witness. To the extent Dr. [C.] is
excluded, his Curriculum Vitae is irrelevant.

26:     Defendants reserve the right to object to Plaintiffs' Exhibit No. 26.

27:     Chart showing annual net revenue from [A.I.C. Security Investigations,
Ltd.] and [A.I.C. International, Ltd.].

Defendants object based upon lack of foundation and authenticity.

28:    Plaintiff's First Set of Interrogatories, Interrogatory #8; Defendants' Answer to Plaintiff's First Set of Interrogatories, Interrogatory #8.

Defendants object based upon the expedited discovery schedule.

SCHEDULE C-4
DEFENDANTS' LIST OF EXHIBITS

EXHIBIT NO./DESCRIPTION

1:    Social Security Administration Form 2417, Determination of Benefit Rights, undated (2 pages).

2:    Social Security Administration Form 831-U3, Disability Determination and Transmittal, dated [8/31/92] (1 page).

3:    Letter from [Charles Wessel] to Social Security Administration allowing release of records, dated [1/20/93] (1 page).

4:    Social Security Administration computer printout of disability payments made to [Charles Wessel], undated (1 page).

5:    Disability Development Worksheet, dated [8/6/92] to [8/27/92] (2 pages).

6:    Neoplasm Report, Bureau of Disability Determination Services, dated [8/19/92] (2 pages).

7:    [Illinois] Disability Determination Services Medical Release Form, dated [8/5/92] (1 page).

8:    Data Form for Cancer Staging, undated (1 page).

9:    [South Suburban Hospital] Tissue Report, dated [6/10/87] (1 page).

10:    [South Suburban Hospital] Data Form for Cancer Staging—Pathology, undated (1 page).

11:    [South Suburban Hospital], Report of Frozen Section, dated [6/10/87] (1 page).

12:    [South Suburban Hospital], Tissue Report, dated [6/12/87] (2 pages).

13:    [South Suburban Hospital], Cytology (Form 11), dated [6/10/87] (1 page).

14:    [South Suburban Hospital], Data Form for Cancer Staging, Pathology, undated (1 page).

15:    [South Suburban Hospital], Data Form for Cancer Staging, Pathology, undated (1 page).

16:    [South Suburban Hospital], Tissue Report, dated [6/11/87] (1 page).

17:    [Loyola University Hospital] Admission/Discharge Record, dated [10/18/91] (1 page).

18:    [Loyola University Hospital] Admission Discharge Summary, dated [11/23/91] (1 page).

19:    [Loyola University Hospital], Report of Operation, dated [10/16/91] (1 page).

20:    [Loyola University Hospital], Clinical Laboratory Summary Report dated [10/19/91] (4 pages).

21:    [Loyola University Hospital], Final Report, dated [10/10/91] (4 pages).

22:    [Loyola University Hospital], Progress Notes, dated [10/3/91] to [10/11/91] (34 pages).

23:    [Illinois] Bureau of Disability Determination Services, Records Request to [South Suburban Hospital], dated [8/11/92] (1 page).

24:    [Illinois] Bureau of Disability Determination Services, Records Request to [Palos Community Hospital], dated [8/11/92] (1 page).

25:    [Illinois] Bureau of Disability Determination Services, Records Request to [Loyola University Hospital], dated [8/11/92] (1 page).

26:    [Illinois] Bureau of Disability Determination Services, Records Request to [Ingalls Memorial Hospital], dated [8/11/92] (1 page).

27:    [Illinois] Bureau of Disability Determination Services, Records Request to [SWC Cancer Center], dated [8/11/92] (1 page).

28:    [Illinois] Bureau of Disability Determination Services, Records Request to [Craig A.], M.D., dated [8/11/92] (1 page).

29:    [Illinois] Bureau of Disability Determination Services, Records Request to [B], M.D., dated [8/11/92] (1 page).

30:    [Palos Community Hospital], Surgical Pathology Report, dated [7/30/91] (1 page).

31:   Social Security Administration Form 3368-13K, Disability Report, dated [8/5/92] (8 pages).

32:   Preliminary Information Sheet—Disability Claim, dated [8/5/92] (1 page).

33:   Application for Disability Insurance Benefits, dated [8/5/92] (4 pages).

34:   Progress Notes of [Susan L., M.D.], dated [6/2/92], [11/5/92], [5/5/92] (2 pages).

35:   Report of Consultation and Operation from [Susan L.], M.D., dated [8/2/91] (2 pages).

36:   [Dependicare Home Health, Inc.], Initial Contact Sheet, dated [1/24/92] (1 page).

37:   [Dependicare] Patient Evaluation, dated [10/25/91] (1 page).

38:   [Dependicare] Initial Sheet, dated [1/18/91] (1 page).

39:   [Dependicare] Service Pickup Form, dated [10/17/91] (1 page).

40:   [Dependicare] Service Order Form, dated [10/19/91] (1 page).

41:   Letter to Dr. [C] from [Dependicare], dated [10/28/91] (1 page).

42:   [Dependicare] Certificate of Medical Necessity, dated [9/7/92] (1 page).

43:   [Dependicare] Certificate of Medical Necessity, undated (1 page).

44:   [Dependicare] Certificate of Medical Necessity, undated (1 page).

45:   [Guardian] Health Insurance Claim Form, dated [10/27/92] (1 page).

46:   [Guardian] Health Insurance Claim Form, dated [9/29/92] (1 page).

47:   [Guardian] Health Insurance Claim Form, dated [8/28/92] (1 page).

48:   [Guardian] Health Insurance Claim Form, dated [7/28/92] (1 page).

49:   [Guardian] Health Insurance Claim Form, dated [6/29/92] (1 page).

50:   [Guardian] Health Insurance Claim Form, dated [5/27/92] (1 page).

51:   [Guardian] Health Insurance Claim Form, dated [7/21/92] (1 page).

52:   [Guardian] Health Insurance Claim Form, dated [4/28/92] (1 page).

53:    [Guardian] Health Insurance Claim Form, dated [6/18/92] (1 page).

54:    [Guardian] Health Insurance Claim Form, dated [3/27/92] (1 page).

55:    [Guardian] Health Insurance Claim Form, dated [2/27/92] (1 page).

56:    [Guardian] Health Insurance Claim Form, dated [1/28/92] (1 page).

57:    [Guardian] Health Insurance Claim Form, dated [12/27/91] (1 page).

58:    [Guardian] Health Insurance Claim Form, dated [11/26/91] (1 page).

59:    [Guardian] Health Insurance Claim Form, dated [11/15/91] (1 page).

60:    [Guardian] Health Insurance Claim Form, dated [10/24/91] (1 page).

61:    [Guardian] Health Insurance Claim Form, dated [10/31/91] (1 page).

62:    [Radiation Therapy Consultants, Ltd. (SWC Cancer Center)], description of treatments and billings, dated [11/11/92] (3 pages).

63:    [SWC Cancer Center] Progress Notes, dated [6/26/87] to [6/29/92] (6 pages).

64:    Letter of Consultation from [S.R.], M.D., dated [6/9/87] (1 page).

65:    Letter to Dr. [B] from Dr. [A], dated [7/17/92] (1 page).

66:    Letter to Dr. [B] from Dr. [A], dated [6/23/92] (1 page).

67:    Letter to Dr. [B] from Dr. [A], dated [5/19/92] (1 page).

68:    Letter to Dr. [B] from Dr. [G.], dated [8/25/87] (1 page).

69:    Letter to Dr. [B] from Dr. [G.], dated [7/8/87] (11 page).

70:    Letter to Dr. [B] from Dr. [A], dated [4/15/92] (11 page).

71:    [Center for Magnetic Imaging] Report of Examination, dated [6/3/92] (1 page).

72:    [Palos Community Hospital] Report of Examination, dated [4/7/92] (11 page).

73:    [Palos Community Hospital] Report of Examination, dated [4/30/92] (1 page).

74:   [Center for Magnetic Imagining] Report of Examination, dated [4/14/92] (1 page).

75:   Pulmonary Function Laboratory, [South Suburban Hospital] Test Result, dated [6/9/87] (1 page).

76:   [SWC Cancer Center] Authorization of Administration of Radiation, dated [4/13/92] (1 page).

77:   [Illinois] Bureau of Disability Determination Services Neoplasm Report, dated [8/19/92] (1 page).

78:   [SWC Cancer Center], Plan of Radiation Therapy, dated [6/18/92] (1 page).

79:   [SWC Cancer Center], Record of Radiation Therapy, dated [6/16/92] to [7/2/92] (2 pages).

80:   [SWC Cancer Center] Plan of Therapy, dated [4/13/92] (1 page).

81:   [SWC Cancer Center] Record of Radiation Treatments, dated [4/14/92] to [5/11/92] (2 pages).

82:   [SWC Cancer Center] Plan of Therapy, dated [6/26/87] (1 page).

83:   [SWC Cancer Center] Record of Radiation Treatments, dated [7/10/87] to [8/19/87] (2 pages).

84:   [SWC Cancer Center] Computer Diagram of Brain, dated [4/28/92] (1 page).

85:   Progress Note from [C.A.], M.D., dated [6/29/92] (1 page).

86:   Report from [C.A.], M.D., dated [7/31/91] (3 pages).

87:   Report from Pulmonary Function Lab of [Palos Community Hospital], dated [9/11/91] (2 pages).

88:   Report of Operation by [C.A.], dated [9/6/91] (2 pages).

89:   Excerpt from [Unum Insurance] Policy (4 pages).

90:   [Unum] form record of payment, undated (1 page).

91:   Letter from [Unum] to [Wessel], dated [12/18/92] (1 page).

92:   [Unum] Benefit Memo, dated [12/18/92] (1 page).

93:   Letter to [Unum] from [Charles M.], dated [11/2/92] (1 page).

94:   Letter to [Unum] from [Wessel], dated [10/26/92] (1 page).

95:   [Unum] Application for Disability Benefits, dated [10/26/92] (1 page).

96:   [Unum] Application for Disability Benefits, dated [9/27/92] (1 page).

97:   [Unum] Notes of Telephone Call to [A.I.C.], dated [12/18/92] (1 page).

98:   [Unum] Benefit Memo, dated [12/15/92] (1 page).

99:   [Center for Magnetic Imaging] Report of Examination, dated [8/12/92] (1 page).

100:   [July 1992] Letter to Dr. [B] from Dr. [A] (1 page).

101:   Report from Dr. [B], dated [10/7/92] (1 page).

102:   [Unum]—Employer's Statement, dated [11/27/92] (4 pages).

103:   [SWC Cancer Center] Letter to Dr. [B] from Dr. [G], dated [8/25/87] (1 page).

104:   [SWC Cancer Center] Letter to Dr. [B] from Dr. [G], dated [7/8/87] (1 page).

105:   [South Suburban Hospital] Consultation Report, dated [6/9/87] (1 page).

106:   [South Suburban Hospital] Radiology Report, dated [6/9/87] (1 page).

107:   [South Suburban Hospital] Admission Summary, dated [6/19/87] (1 page).

108:   [South Suburban Hospital] Consultation Report, dated [6/7/87] (1 page).

109:   [South Suburban Hospital] Pulmonary Function Report, dated [6/9/87] (2 pages).

110:   [Palos Community Hospital] Outpatient Record, dated [9/6/91] (1 page).

111:   [Palos Community Hospital] Consent for Procedure Form, dated [9/6/91] (1 page).

112:   [Palos Community Hospital] Outpatient Registration, dated [8/13/92] (1 page).

113: [Palos Community Hospital] Report of Examination, dated [8/13/92] (1 page).

114: [Palos Community Hospital] Report of Examination, dated [9/24/92] (1 page).

115: [Palos Community Hospital] Report of Examination, dated [9/28/92] (1 page).

116: [Palos Community Hospital] Report of Examination, dated [7/22/91] (1 page).

117: [Palos Community Hospital] Report of Examination, dated [4/30/92] (1 page).

118: [Palos Community Hospital] Report of Examination, dated [4/7/92] (1 page).

119: [Palos Community Hospital] Report of Examination, dated [12/31/90] (1 page).

120: [Palos Community Hospital] Report of Examination, dated [9/27/88] (1 page).

121: [Palos Community Hospital] Record of Admission, dated [7/29/91] (1 page).

122: [Palos Community Hospital] Discharge Summary, dated [8/12/91] (1 page).

123: [Palos Community Hospital] Emergency Department Assessment, dated [7/29/91] (1 page).

124: [Palos Community Hospital] Admission History, dated [7/29/91] (1 page).

125: [Palos Community Hospital] Physical Examination Report, dated [7/29/91] (1 page).

126: [Palos Community Hospital] Consultant's Report, dated [7/29/91] (2 pages).

127: [Palos Community Hospital] Consultant's Report, dated [7/31/91] (3 pages).

128: [Palos Community Hospital] Consultant's Report, dated [8/2/91] (1 page).

129: [Palos Community Hospital] Report of Examination, dated [7/29/91] (1 page).

130: [Palos Community Hospital] Report of Examination, dated [7/30/91] (1 page).

131: [Palos Community Hospital] Report of Examination, dated [7/31/91] (1 page).

132: [Palos Community Hospital] Report of Examination, dated [8/1/91] (1 page).

133: [Palos Community Hospital] Report of Examination, dated [8/2/91] (1 page).

134: [Palos Community Hospital] Report of Examination, dated [7/31/91] (1 page).

135: [Palos Community Hospital] Report of Examination, dated [8/3/91] (1 page).

136: [Palos Community Hospital] Report of Examination, dated [8/4/91] (1 page).

137: [Palos Community Hospital] Report of Examination, dated [8/6/91] (1 page).

138: [Palos Community Hospital] Report of Examination, dated [8/7/91] (1 page).

139: [Palos Community Hospital] Report of Examination, dated [8/8/91] (1 page).

140: [Palos Community Hospital] Report of Examination, dated [8/9/91] (1 page).

141: [Intermed Oncology Associates] List of appointments and billings, dated [8/26/87] to [11/5/91] (27 pages).

142: [Intermed Oncology Associates] List of appointments and billings, dated [12/30/91] to [2/25/92] (5 pages).

143: [South Suburban Hospital] Discharge Summary, dated [12/27/87] (1 page).

144: [South Suburban Hospital] History and Physical, dated [12/31/87] (1 page).

145: [Dr. G.]'s Radiology Report, dated [8/3/88] (1 page).

146: [Dr. G.]'s Radiology Report, dated [3/6/89] (1 page).

147: [South Suburban Hospital] Consultation Report, dated [10/18/87] (2 pages).

148: Letter to Dr. [B] from [Wessel] dated [10/22/91] (1 page).

149: [Illinois] Bureau of Disability Determination Services Letter to Dr. [B], dated [8/11/92] (3 pages).

150: [Illinois] Bureau of Disability Determination Services, Neoplasm Report, dated [8/24/92] (1 page).

151: Letter to Dr. [B] from [Wessel], dated [9/27/92] (1 page).

152: Memorandum to Dr. [B] from [Wessel], dated [9/27/92] (3 pages).

153: Letter from Dr. [B] to Whom It May Concern, dated [9/2/92] (1 page).

154: [Palos Community Hospital] Report of Examination, dated [6/29/92] (1 page).

155: [Palos Community Hospital] Admission History, dated [9/27/88] (1 page).

156: [Palos Community Hospital] Admission History, dated [7/29/91] (1 page).

157: [Wessel] Medical Notes, dated [2/19/89] (1 page).

158: [Loyola University Hospital] Outpatient Registration, dated [8/24/91] (1 page).

159: [Loyola University Hospital] Provisional Discharge Summary, dated [10/18/91] (11 page).

160: [Loyola University Hospital] Examination Report, dated [11/26/91] (1 page).

161: [Loyola University Hospital] Examination Report, dated [9/23/91] (1 page).

162: Letter from Dr. [G] to Dr. [A], dated [8/29/91] (1 page).

163: [Loyola University Hospital] [Wessel] Patient Record, dated [10/3/91] (2 pages).

164: [Loyola University Hospital] Admission—Discharge Record, dated [10/3/91] (1 page).

165: [Loyola University Hospital] Discharge Summary, dated [10/18/91] (1 page).

166: [Loyola University Hospital] Pulmonary Function Report, dated [9/5/91] (1 page).

167: [Loyola University Hospital] Final Report, dated [10/3/91] (1 page).

168: [Loyola University Hospital] Final Report, dated [10/4/91] (1 page).

169: [Loyola University Hospital] Final Report, dated [10/5/91] (1 page).

170: [Loyola University Hospital] Final Report, dated [10/6/91] (1 page).

171: [Loyola University Hospital] Final Report, dated [10/7/91] (1 page).

172: [Loyola University Hospital] Final Report, dated [10/8/91] (2 pages).

173: [Loyola University Hospital] Final Report, dated [10/9/91] (1 page).

174: [Loyola University Hospital] Final Report, dated [10/10/91] (1 page).

175: [Loyola University Hospital] Final Report, dated [10/11/91] (1 page).

176: [Loyola University Hospital] Patient Data Base, dated [10/3/91] (4 pages).

177: [Loyola University Hospital] Discharge Medication Schedule, dated [10/3/91] (1 page).

178: Letter to [Charles Wessel] from [Vince G.], dated [1/29/92] (1 page).

179: Letter to [Vince G.] from [Charles Wessel], dated [1/27/92] (1 page).

180: Letter to [Charles Wessel] from [Phyllis M.], dated [11/23/92] (1 page).

181: Determination of Unemployment Insurance Benefits to [Wessel], dated [1/16/93] (1 page).

182: Letter from [Unum] to [Wessel], dated [1/5/93] (1 page).

183: Letter to [A.I.C. attorney B] from Dr. [M], dated [1/18/93] (2 pages).

184: Letter to [A.I.C. attorney B] from Dr. [M], dated [2/8/93] (1 page).

185: Letter to [A.I.C. attorney B] from Dr. [L], dated [2/10/93] (2 pages).

186: Notes of Dr. [M], undated (1 page).

187: Updated Curriculum Vitae of Dr. [M], undated (4 pages).

188: Curriculum Vitae of Dr. [M], undated (4 pages).

189: Curriculum Vitae of Dr. [L], undated (12 pages).

190: Letter to [defendant C] from [Richard F.], dated [8/4/92] (1 page).

191: [Advocare] Bill to [Guardian] Insurance Company, dated [9/1/92] (1 page).

192: [Advocare] Memorandum to Attorneys for [Wessel], dated [11/16/92] (1 page).

193: [Advocare] Initial Report, dated [12/13/91] (5 pages).

194: [Advocare] Letter to [Alice Wessel], dated [12/11/91] (1 page).

195: [Advocare] Provider Agreement, dated [1/3/92] (1 page).

196: [Advocare] Bill to [Guardian] Insurance Company, dated [10/30/91] to [12/16/91] (1 page).

197: [Advocare] Interim Report, dated [9/1/92] (2 pages).

198: [Shay Health] Care Services Letter to [Wessel], dated [12/12/91] (1 page).

199: [Shay Health] Carrier Inquiry Sheet, dated [12/12/91] (1 page).

200: [Shay Health] Home Health Certification and Plan of Treatment, dated [10/18/91] (1 page).

201: [Shay Health] Progress Notes, dated [11/1/92] to [12/12/92] (6 pages).

202: [Loyola University Hospital] Community Nursing Referral Form, undated (2 pages).

203: [Shay Health] Nurses Notes, dated [10/18/91] to [10/22/91] (4 pages).

204: [Shay Health] Admit Note, dated [10/18/91] (1 page).

205: [Shay Health] Patient Assessment form, dated [10/18/91] (8 pages).

206: Medicine List and Times, dated [4/27/92] (1 page).

207: Medicine List and Times, dated [8/4/92] (1 page).

208: Medical Information List for [Wessel], dated [10/26/92] (4 pages).

209: Telephone notes of [Janice D.], undated, and fax cover sheet, dated [1/22/93] (2 pages).

210: Letter to [Judy A.] from [Wessel], dated [9/7/92] (1 page).

211: Fax Transmittal Sheet from [Wessel] to [A.I.C. attorney D], dated [9/13/90] (1 page).

212: EEOC Initial Determination, dated [9/10/92] (2 pages).

213: EEOC Charge of Discrimination, dated [8/3/92] (1 page).

214: Letter to [Wessel] from [Judy A.], dated [9/3/92] (1 page).

215: [Wessel] EEOC Affidavit, dated [8/11/92] (4 pages).

216: List of General Accommodations Given to [Wessel], undated (2 pages).

217: Statement of [defendant C], dated [9/8/92] (5 pages).

218: Letter to [John R.] from [Lawrence R.], dated [8/20/92] (1 page).

219: Signed EEOC Affidavit of [Ken B.] (1 page).

220: Unsigned EEOC Affidavit of [Ken B.] (1 page).

221: Unsigned EEOC Affidavit of Dr. [B] (1 page).

222: Signed EEOC Affidavit of Dr. [B] (1 page).

223: Memo to [Larry R.] from [Charles B.], dated [9/1/92] (1 page).

224: Medicine List and Times, dated [7/20/92] (1 page).

225: Memo to [Larry R.] from [Ed B.], dated [9/2/92] (1 page).

226: Memo to [Larry R.] from [Jan D.], dated [9/2/92] (2 pages).

227: Letter to [Daniel M.] from [Lawrence R.]

228: Handwritten letter to [David P.] from [Judy A.], dated [9/10/92] (3 pages).

229: Handwritten statements of [Wessel], undated (5 pages).

230: EEOC Interview Notes of [Wessel], dated [8/1//92] (9 pages).

231: EEOC Interview Notes of [Wessel], undated (13 pages).

232: Draft Affidavit of Dr. [B], undated (1 page).

233: Draft EEOC Charge of Discrimination of [Wessel], undated (1 page).

234: Handwritten EEOC Affidavit of [Wessel] with Attachments, undated (6 pages).

235: Draft Affidavit of [Ken B.] and Facsimile Cover Sheets of EEOC and [Premisys Real Estate Services, Inc.], dated [9/10/92] (4 pages).

236: Facsimile Cover Sheet and Letter to Dr. [B] from [Judy A.], dated [9/2/92] (2 pages).

237: [A.I.C. International, Ltd.] Drug and Alcohol Abuse Policy, undated (3 pages).

238: [A.I.C. International, Ltd.] Drug Free Awareness Program, undated (1 page).

239: [A.I.C. International, Ltd.] AIDS Policy, undated (2 pages).

240: [A.I.C. International, Ltd.] Drug and Alcohol Abuse Policy and Procedures for Applicants (2 pages).

241: [A.I.C. International, Ltd.] Drug and Alcohol Abuse Policy and Procedures for Employees, undated (5 pages).

242: Memo to [A.I.C. International, Ltd.] from [law firm] re: Drug Free Workplace Act Obligations.

243: Life Threatening Illness Policy, dated [1/1/90] (1 page).

244: Facsimile Cover Sheet and Attachments from [Wessel] to [A.I.C. attorney D], dated [9/10/90] (7 pages).

245: Letter from Social Security Administration to [Wessel], dated [9/8/92] (3 pages).

246: [Wessel]'s W-2 Wage and Tax Statements for [1992] from [Unum] Insurance Company (1 page).

247: [IDES] Benefit Payment Stub and Explanation, dated [12/12/92] to [1/2/93] (2 pages).

248: [Wessel]'s Personal Automobile Policy Premium Statements, dated [3/12/92], [6/17/92], [9/12/92] (3 pages).

249: EEOC Case Log, Charge No. [210922899], dated [8/3/92] to [9/10/92] (2 pages).

250: Memorandum to [Beverly K.] from [Wessel], dated [7/21/92] (1 page).

251: Memorandum to [David P.] from [Wessel], dated [2/6/91] (1 page).

252: Memorandum to [David P.] from [Wessel] re: Drug Free Workplace Policy, dated [9/18/90] (1 page).

253: Memo to [David P.] from [Wessel] re: vacation, dated [5/8/90] (1 page).

254: Vacation/Day Off Requisition of [Wessel], dated [5/7/90] (1 page).

255: Memo to [David P.] from [Wessel] re: medical checkup, dated [1/27/88] (11 page).

256: Memo to [David P.] from [Wessel], dated [7/18/86] (1 page).

257: Letter to [A.I.C. attorney B] from [A.I.C. attorney D] re: [Wessel]'s Answers to Defendants' First Set of Interrogatories to Plaintiff [Wessel], dated [2/15/93] (14 pages).

258: Plaintiff [Wessel]'s Responses to Defendants' First Set of Interrogatories (24 pages).

259: List of [Wessel]'s Assets (3 pages).

260: [Randall Wessel]'s Notes regarding [8/3/92] (4 pages).

261: Resume Questionnaire of [Wessel], dated [8/16/92] (6 pages).

262: [Wessel] Resume List, dated [8/6/92] to [10/22/92] (3 pages).

263: Resume of [Wessel], undated (2 pages).

264: EEOC's Answers to Defendants' First Set of Interrogatories to Plaintiff EEOC, dated [12/4/92] (18 pages).

265: Letter to [Wessel] from [Phil W.], dated [8/12/92] (1 page).

266: Letter to [Wessel] from [Phil W.], dated [8/20/92] (1 page).

267: [Wessel]'s [1991] Income Tax Return with Attachments (14 pages).

268: [Wessel]'s [1990] Income Tax Return with Attachments (9 pages).

269: [Wessel]'s [1989] Income Tax Return with Attachments (6 pages).

270: [Wessel]'s [1988] Income Tax Return with Attachments (7 pages).

271: [Wessel]'s [1987] Income Tax Return with Attachments (14 pages).

272: Medicine List as of [11/21/92] (1 page).

273: Description Notes of dental work performed on [Wessel] (7 pages).

274: [Wessel] Resume ([1984]) (2 pages).

275: [Wessel] Application for Employment, dated [2/19/86] (5 pages).

276: [Shay Health] Care Services notes re: habits and behavior, undated (1 page).

277: [Wessel] Resume draft ([1992]) (3 pages).

278: Letter to [David P.] from [Jack H.], dated [3/3/92] (1 page).

279: [A.I.C. International, Ltd.] and Subsidiaries Consolidated Financial Statements, Year Ended [7/31/86] (13 pages).

280: [A.I.C. International, Ltd.] and Subsidiaries Consolidated Financial Statements, Year Ended [7/31/87] (14 pages).

281: [A.I.C. International, Ltd.] and Subsidiaries Consolidated Financial Statements, Year Ended [7/31/89] (12 pages).

282: [A.I.C. International, Ltd.] and Subsidiaries Consolidated Financial Statements, Year Ended [7/31/91] (9 pages).

283: [A.I.C. International, Ltd.] and Subsidiaries Consolidated Financial Statements, Year Ended [7/31/92] (11 pages).

284: Statement of [Lawrence R.], dated [9/4/92] (5 pages).

285: Memo to [Phil W.] from [Wessel], dated [7/24/92] (1 page).

286: Memo to [Phil W.] from [Wessel], dated [7/27/92] (1 page).

287: EEOC Telephone Interview Notes of conversation with Dr. [A], dated [8/25/92] (1 page).

288: EEOC Telephone Notes of conversation with Dr. [B], dated [8/25/92] (1 page).

289: [Local 73] Wage/Revenue Spread Sheet, dated [7/7/92] (2 pages).

290: [A.I.C. Security Investigations, Ltd.] List of Duties of Executive Director [1986]–[1992] (2 pages).

291: [A.I.C. Security Investigations, Ltd.] List of Reassignment of Duties [1987]–[1992] (7 pages).

292: Memo to [Larry R.] from [R.E.B.] and [Jan D.], dated [8/28/92] (2 pages).

293: [Illinois] Bureau of Disability Determination Services, Signed Records Request to [SWC Cancer Center], dated [8/11/92] (1 page).

294: [Shay Health] Care Services Nurses Notes, dated [10/18/91] to [10/22/91] (4 pages).

295: List of [Wessel]'s health care providers, dated [10/20/92] (4 pages).

296: EEOC Intake Questionnaire, dated [8/3/92] (1 page).

297: List of Medicine and Doctors, undated (1 page).

298: Handwritten Note to [EEOC attorney A] from [Judy A.], re: [Ken B.], dated [9/9/92] (3 pages).

299: Notes of [Judy A.], dated [8/13/92] (3 pages).

300: [Unum] Disability Insurance Policy (23 pages).

301: [Guardian] Group Health Insurance Policy (83 pages).

302: Memo from [David P.] to All Employees, dated [1/1/89] (3 pages).

303: Moving Violation Driving Citation [Wessel] received in [1992] (referred to in [Wessel]'s second deposition).

Defendants reserve the right to introduce as exhibits additional medical records regarding [Charles Wessel] obtained after the time period encompassed in his health care providers' responses to previous discovery subpoenas served in late [1992]. Defendants also reserve the right to introduce exhibits in rebuttal.

SCHEDULE C-5
DEFENDANTS' EXHIBITS TO WHICH PLAINTIFFS DO NOT OBJECT

Exhibit 152: Memorandum to Dr. [B] from [Wessel]—[4-27-92].

Exhibit 153: Letter from Dr. [B] To Whom It May Concern—[9-2-92].

Exhibit 181: Determination of Unemployment Insurance Benefits to [Wessel], dated [1-16-93].

Exhibit 185: Letter to [A.I.C. attorney B] from Dr. [L], dated [2-10-93].

Exhibit 188: Curriculum Vitae of Dr. [M].

Exhibit 189: Curriculum Vitae of Dr. [L].

Exhibit 206: Medicine List and Times, dated [4-27-92].

Exhibit 207: Medicine List and Times, dated [8-4-92].

Plaintiffs do not object to admission of evidence concerning [Wessel]'s health after [July 31, 1993], for the limited purpose of determining whether he remained able to work and is, therefore, entitled to back pay for the period.

Exhibit 208: Medical Information List for [Wessel], dated [10-26-92].

See qualification to admission of Exhibit 207.

Exhibit 210: Letter to [Judy A.] from [Wessel]—[9-7-92].

Exhibit 212: EEOC Letter of Determination—[9-10-92].

Exhibit 213: EEOC Charge of Discrimination—[8-3-92].

Exhibit 215: [Wessel] EEOC Affidavit—[8-11-92].

Exhibit 224: Medicine List and Times, dated [7-20-92].

Exhibit 229: Handwritten statement of [Wessel].

Exhibit 230: EEOC Interview Notes of [Wessel]—[8-11-92].

Exhibit 231: EEOC Interview Notes of [Wessel].

Exhibit 233: Draft EEOC Charge of Discrimination of [Wessel].

Exhibit 234: Handwritten EEOC Affidavit of [Wessel] with Attachments. (Plaintiffs anticipate no objection; but are unable to identify the attachments.)

Exhibit 246: [Wessel]'s W-2 Statements for [1992].

Exhibit 250: Memorandum to [Beverly K.] from [Chuck Wessel]—[7-21-92].

Exhibit 251: Memorandum to [David P.] from [Chuck Wessel]—[2-6-91].

Exhibit 253: Memo from [Wessel] to [David P.] re: vacation—[5-8-90].

Exhibit 254: Vacation/Day Off Requisition of [Wessel]—[7-18-86].

Exhibit 255: Memo to [David P.] from [Wessel] re: medical checkup—[1-27-88].

Exhibit 256: Memo to [David P.] from [Wessel]—[7-18-86].

Exhibit 260: [Randall Wessel]'s Notes—[8-30-92].

Exhibit 261: Resume Questionnaire of [Wessel]—[8-16-92].

Exhibit 262: [Wessel] Resume List—[8-6-92].

Exhibit 263: Resume of [Wessel].

Exhibit 265: Letter to [Wessel] from [Phil W.]—[8-12-92].

Exhibit 266: Letter to [Wessel] from [Phil W.]—[8-20-92].

Exhibit 272: Medicine List as of [11-21-92].

See qualification to admission of Exhibit 207.

Exhibit 274: [Wessel] Resume ([1984]).

Exhibit 275: [Wessel] Application for Employment—[2-6-86].

Exhibit 277: [Wessel] Resume Draft ([1992]).

Exhibit 279: [A.I.C. International, Ltd.] and Subsidiaries Consolidated Financial Statements, Year Ended [7-31-86].

Exhibit 280: [A.I.C. International, Ltd.] and Subsidiaries Consolidated Financial Statements, Year Ended [7-31-87].

Exhibit 281: [A.I.C. International, Ltd.] and Subsidiaries Consolidated Financial Statements, Year Ended [7-31-89].

Exhibit 282: [A.I.C. International, Ltd.] and Subsidiaries Consolidated Financial Statements, Year Ended [7-31-91].

Exhibit 283: [A.I.C. International, Ltd.] and Subsidiaries Consolidated Financial Statements, Year Ended [7-31-92].

Exhibit 285: Memo to [Phil W.] from [Wessel]—[7-24-92].

Exhibit 286: Memo to [Phil W.] from [Wessel]—[7-27-92].

Exhibit 289: [Local 73] Wage/Revenue spreadsheet—[7-7-92].

Exhibit 295: List of [Wessel]'s healthcare providers—[10-20-92].

See qualification to admission of Exhibit 207.

Exhibit 296: EEOC Intake Questionnaire.

Exhibit 297: List of Medicine and Doctors.

See Qualification to Admission of Exhibit 207.

Exhibit 300: [Unum] Disability Insurance Policy.

Exhibit 301: [Guardian] Group Health Insurance Policy.

Exhibit 302: Memo from [David P.] to All Employees—[1-1-90].

SCHEDULE C-6

DEFENDANTS' EXHIBITS TO WHICH PLAINTIFFS OBJECT, WITH PLAINTIFFS' OBJECTIONS NOTED

Exhibits 1–8: Documents from Social Security Administration File

Plaintiffs object to the Exhibit(s) because the documents submitted to the agency and the proceedings and actions of the agency are pursuant to statutes, rules, and/or regulations different from those applicable to the Plaintiff's claims herein. If the Court allows Defendants to offer the agency documents into evidence, the entire file contents should be admitted with the limiting instruction requested by Plaintiffs.

Exhibits 9–16: Documents from [South Suburban Hospital]

Plaintiffs object because documents are incomplete. If Defendants offer the entire [South Suburban] file, Plaintiffs will withdraw their objection.

Exhibits 17–22: Documents from [Loyola Hospital]

Plaintiffs object because documents are incomplete. If Defendants offer the entire [Loyola Hospital] file, Plaintiffs will withdraw their objection.

Exhibits 23–33: Documents from [Illinois] Bureau of Disability Determination

Plaintiffs object to the Exhibit(s) because the documents submitted to the agency and the proceedings and actions of the agency are pursuant to statutes, rules, and/or regulations different from those applicable to the Plaintiffs' claims herein. If the Court allows Defendants to offer the agency documents into evidence, the entire file contents should be admitted with the limiting instruction requestion by Plaintiffs.

Exhibits 34–35: Documents from [Susan L.], M.D., [Southwest Head and Neck Surgical Association]

Plaintiffs object because documents are incomplete. If Defendants offer the entire file from [Susan L.], M.D., [Southwest Head and Neck Surgical Association], Plaintiffs will withdraw their objection.

Exhibits 36–61: Documents from [Dependicare]

Plaintiffs object because the documents are incomplete. If Defendants offer the entire file from [Dependicare], Plaintiffs will withdraw their objection.

Exhibits 62–84: Documents from Dr. [A], [Southwest Cancer Center]

Plaintiffs object because the documents are incomplete. If Defendants offer the entire file from Dr. [A], [Southwest Cancer Center], Plaintiffs will withdraw their objection.

Exhibits 85–88: Documents from [Craig A.], M.D.

Plaintiffs object because the documents are incomplete. If Defendants offer the entire file from [Dr. A.], Plaintiffs will withdraw their objection.

Exhibits 89–102: Documents from [Unum]

Plaintiffs object because the documents are incomplete. If Defendants offer the entire file from [Unum], Plaintiffs will withdraw their objection.

Exhibits 103–109: Documents from [South Suburban Hospital]

Plaintiffs object because the documents are incomplete. If Defendants offer the entire file from [South Suburban Hospital], Plaintiffs will withdraw their objection.

Exhibits 110–140: Documents from [Palos Hospital]

Plaintiffs object because the documents are incomplete. If Defendants offer the entire file from [Palos Hospital], Plaintiffs will withdraw their objection.

Exhibits 141–151 and 154–157: Documents from Dr. [B], M.D., [Intermed Oncology Associates, P.C.]

Plaintiffs object because the documents are incomplete. If Defendants offer the entire file from Dr. [B], [Intermed Oncology Associates, P.C.], Plaintiffs will withdraw their objection.

Exhibits 158–177: Documents from [Loyola University Hospital]

Plaintiffs object because the documents are incomplete. If Defendants offer the entire file from [Loyola University Hospital], Plaintiffs will withdraw the objection.

Exhibit 178: Letter to [Charles Wessel] from [Vince G.]—[1-29-92]

Plaintiffs object to the extent that the document is intended to support the contention that [Wessel] was unable to perform the essential or the marginal functions of his position. The document was not disclosed in response to EEOC's First Request for Production of documents, Requests 10 and 11, which asked for all documents supporting such contentions. Defendants answered that no such documents existed. Plaintiffs also object to lack of foundation.

Exhibit 179: Letter to [Vince G.] from [Charles Wessel]—[1-27-92]

Plaintiffs object for the reasons set forth in Objection to Exhibit 178. Plaintiffs also object to lack of foundation.

Exhibit 180: Letter to [Charles Wessel] from [Phyllis M.]—[11-23-92]

Plaintiffs object for the reasons set forth in Objection to Exhibit 178. Plaintiffs also object to lack of foundation.

Exhibit 182: Letter from [Unum] to [Wessel], dated [1-5-93]

Objection—See Objection to Exhibits 89–102.

Exhibit 183: Letter to [attorney B] from Dr. [M]—[1-18-93]

Objection—Hearsay.

Exhibit 184: Letter to [attorney B] from Dr. [M]—[2-8-93]

Objection—Hearsay.

Exhibit 186: Notes of Dr. [M], undated

Objection—Hearsay.

Exhibit 187: Undated Curriculum Vitae of Dr. [M].

Objection—Duplicative of Exhibit 190.

Exhibit 190: Letter to [defendant C] from [Richard F.], dated [8-4-92]

Plaintiffs object for the reasons set forth in Objection to Exhibit 178. Plaintiffs also object to lack of foundation.

Exhibits 191–197: Documents from [Advocare] file

Plaintiffs object because the documents are incomplete. If Defendants offer the entire file from [Advocare], Plaintiffs will withdraw their objection.

Exhibits 198–205: Documents from [Shay Health] Care Services

Plaintiffs object because the documents are incomplete. If Defendants offer the entire file from [Shay Health] Care Services, Plaintiffs will withdraw their objection.

Exhibit 209: Telephone Note of [Janice D.], undated, and fax cover sheet, dated [1-22-93]

Objection—Hearsay.

Exhibit 211: Fax transmittal sheet from [Wessel] to [A.I.C. attorney D]—[9-13-90]

Objection—Relevance. See also Objection to Exhibit 178.

Exhibit 214: Letter to [Wessel] from [Judy A.]—[9-3-92]

Objections—Hearsay, Relevance.

Exhibit 216: List of General Accommodations Given to [Wessel]

Objection—Hearsay.

Exhibit 217: Statement of [defendant C]—[9-8-92]

Objection—Hearsay.

Exhibit 218: Letter to [John R.] from [Lawrence R.]

Objection—Hearsay.

Exhibit 219: Signed EEOC Affidavit of [Ken B.]

Objection—Hearsay.

Exhibit 220: Unsigned EEOC Affidavit of [Ken B.]

Objection—Hearsay.

Exhibit 221: Unsigned EEOC Affidavit of Dr. [B]

Objections—Hearsay, Relevance.

Exhibit 222: Signed EEOC Affidavit of Dr. [B]

Objection—Hearsay.

Exhibit 223: Memo from [Larry R.] to [Charles B.]—[9-1-92]

Objection—Hearsay.

Exhibit 225: Memo to [Larry R.] from [Ed B.]—[9-2-92]

Objection—Hearsay.

Exhibit 226: Memo to [Larry R.] from [Jan D.]—[9-2-92]

Objection—Hearsay.

Exhibit 227: Letter to [Daniel M.] from [Lawrence R.]

Objection—Hearsay.

Exhibit 228: Letter to [David P]. from [Judy A.]—[9-10-92]

Objections—Hearsay, Relevance.

Exhibit 232: Draft Affidavit of Dr. [B]

Objections—Hearsay, Relevance.

Exhibit 235: Draft Affidavit of [Ken B.] and facsimile cover sheets—[9-10-92]

Objections—Hearsay, Relevance.

Exhibit 236: Facsimile cover sheet and letter to Dr. [B] from [Judy A.]—[9-2-92]

Objections—Hearsay, Relevance.

Exhibit 237: [A.I.C. International, Ltd.] Drug and Alcohol Abuse Policy

Objection for the reasons set forth in Objection to Exhibit 178; objection to relevance.

Exhibit 238: [A.I.C. International, Ltd.] Drug Free Awareness Program

Objection for the reasons set forth in Objection to Exhibit 178; objection to relevance.

Exhibit 239: [A.I.C. International, Ltd.] AIDS Policy

Objection for the reasons set forth in Objection to Exhibit 178; objection to relevance.

Exhibit 240: [A.I.C. International, Ltd.] Drug and Alcohol Abuse Policy and Procedures for Applicants

Objection for the reasons set forth in Objection to Exhibit 178; objection to relevance.

Exhibit 241: [A.I.C. International, Ltd.] Drug and Alcohol Abuse Policy and Procedures for Employees

Objection for the reasons set forth in Objection to Exhibit 178; objection to relevance.

Exhibit 242: Memo to [A.I.C. International, Ltd.] from [Lindquist & Vennum] re: Drug Free Workplace Act Obligations

Objection for the reasons set forth in Objection to Exhibit 178; objection to relevance.

Exhibit 243: Life-threatening Illness Policy—[1-1-90]

Objection for the reasons set forth in Objection to Exhibit 178; objection to relevance.

Exhibit 244: Facsimile cover sheet and attachments from [Wessel] to [A.I.C. attorney D]—[9-10-90]

Objection for the reasons set forth in Objection to Exhibit 178; objection to relevance.

Exhibit 245: Letter from Social Security Administration to [Wessel]—[9-8-92]

Plaintiffs object to the Exhibit(s) because the documents submitted to the agency and the proceedings and actions of the agency are pursuant to statutes, rules, and/or regulations different from those applicable to the Plaintiffs' claims herein. If the Court allows Defendants to offer the agency documents into evidence, the entire file contents should be admitted with the limiting instruction requested by Plaintiffs.

Exhibit 247: [IDES] Benefit Payment Stub and Explanation

Objection—Relevance.

Exhibit 248: [Wessel]'s personal automobile policy premium statements

Objection—Relevance.

Exhibit 249: EEOC's case log, Charge No. [210922899]

Objections—Hearsay, Relevance.

Exhibit 252: Memorandum to [David P.] from [Wessel] re: Drug-Free Work Place Policy

Objection for the reasons set forth in Objection to Exhibit 178; objection to relevance.

Exhibit 257: Letter to [A.I.C. attorney B] from [A.I.C. attorney D] re: [Wessel]'s Answer to Defendants' First Set of Interrogatories to Plaintiff [Wessel]—[2-15-93]

Objection—Relevance.

Exhibit 258: Plaintiff [Wessel]'s Responses to Defendants' First Set of Interrogatories

Objection—Relevance.

Exhibit 259: List of [Wessel]'s assets

Objection—Relevance.

Exhibit 264: EEOC's Answers to Defendants' First Set of Interrogatories—[12-4-92]

Objection—Relevance.

Exhibit 267: [Wessel]'s [1991] income tax return with attachments

Objection—Relevance.

Exhibit 268: [Wessel]'s [1990] income tax return with attachments

Objection—Relevance.

Exhibit 269: [Wessel]'s [1989] income tax return with attachments

Objection—Relevance.

Exhibit 270: [Wessel]'s [1988] income tax return with attachments

Objection—Relevance.

Exhibit 271: [Wessel]'s [1987] income tax return with attachments

Objection—Relevance.

Exhibit 273: Description notes of dental work performed on [Wessel]

Objection—Relevance.

Exhibit 276: [Shay Health] Care Services notes re: habits and behavior

Plaintiffs object because the documents are incomplete. If Defendants offer the entire file from the [Shay Health] Care Service, Plaintiffs will withdraw their objection.

Exhibit 278: Letter to [David P.] from [Jack H.]—[3-3-92]

Objection—Hearsay, lack of foundation. See also Exhibit 178.

Exhibit 284: Statement of [Lawrence R.]—[9-4-92]

Objection—Hearsay.

Exhibit 287: EEOC Telephone Interview Notes of conversation with Dr. [A]

Objection—Hearsay.

Exhibit 288: EEOC Telephone Notes of conversation with Dr. [B], dated [8-25-92]

Objection—Hearsay.

Exhibit 290: [A.I.C. Security Investigations, Ltd.] List of Duties of Executive Director, [1986]–[1992]

Objection—Hearsay.

Exhibit 291: [A.I.C. Security Investigations, Ltd.] List of Reassignment of Duties, [1987]–[1992]

Objection—Hearsay.

Exhibit 292: Memo to [Larry R.] from [R.E.B.] and [Jan D.]—[8-28-92]

Objection—Hearsay.

Exhibit 293: [Illinois] Bureau of Disability Determination Services, signed records request to [SWC Cancer Center]—[8-11-92]

Plaintiffs object to the Exhibit(s) because the documents submitted to the agency and the proceedings and actions of the agency are pursuant to statutes, rules, and/or regulations different from those applicable to the Plaintiffs' claims herein. If the Court allows Defendants to offer the agency documents into evidence, the entire file contents should be admitted with the limiting instruction requested by Plaintiffs.

Exhibit 294: [Shay Health] Care Services Nurses Notes—[10-18-91]–[10-22-91]

Plaintiffs object because the documents are incomplete. If Defendants offer the entire file from the [Shay Health] Care Service, Plaintiffs will withdraw their objection.

Exhibit 298: Handwritten note to [EEOC attorney A] from [Judy A.] re: [Ken B.] [9-9-92]

Objections—Hearsay, Relevance.

Exhibit 299: Notes of [Judy A]—[8-13-92]

Objections—Hearsay, Relevance.

Exhibit 303: Moving violation driving citation [Wessel] received in [1992]

Plaintiff objects to admission of any documents not identified by number in this.

Order which have not been produced to Plaintiffs.

SCHEDULE D WITNESSES

SCHEDULE D-1

PART I
PLAINTIFFS' LIST OF WITNESSES

Plaintiffs will call as witnesses the following persons:

[names and addresses of witnesses]

Plaintiffs may call as witnesses:

[names and addresses of witnesses]

Plaintiff [Wessel] may call as witnesses:

[names and addresses of witnesses]

Plaintiffs expect to call as a rebuttal witness:

[name and address of witness]

Plaintiffs reserve the right to call any witness named by Defendants and additional witnesses for proposes of impeachment and/or rebuttal.

SCHEDULE D-1

PART TWO
DEFENDANTS' OBJECTIONS TO THE CALLING OR QUALIFICATION OF PLAINTIFFS' WITNESSES

1.   It appears from Plaintiffs' List of Witnesses that Plaintiffs are waiving their right to call at trial Dr. [C]. To the extent Plaintiffs attempt to call Dr. [C] at trial (for rebuttal or otherwise), Defendants object for reasons stated in Defendants' Motion to Exclude Expert Witness.

SCHEDULE D-2

PART I
DEFENDANTS' LIST OF WITNESSES

Witnesses Defendants will call at trial:

[names and addresses of witnesses]

Witnesses Defendants may call at trial:

[names and addresses of witnesses]

Defendants reserve the right to call additional witnesses in rebuttal and/or to verify the authenticity of documents listed in Schedule C-6.

SCHEDULE D-2

PART 2
DEFENDANTS' LIST OF WITNESSES WITH PLAINTIFFS' OBJECTIONS

Witnesses Defendants will call at trial:

[names and addresses of witnesses]

Witnesses Defendants may call at trial:

[names and addresses of witnesses]

Plaintiffs object to the calling of [Scott M.] because he was not identified by Defendants as a person with knowledge of the reasons for [Charles Wessel]'s termination in Defendants' answer to EEOC's First Interrogatories, #3.

Plaintiffs object to calling any witness to authenticate documents where Plaintiffs have not challenged authenticity.

[names and addresses of witnesses]

Defendants reserve the right to call additional witnesses in rebuttal and/or to verify

the authenticity of documents listed in Schedule C-6.

SCHEDULE E STIPULATION OF QUALIFICATIONS OF EXPERT WITNESSES

SCHEDULE E-1
PLAINTIFFS' PROPOSED STIPULATED QUALIFICATIONS OF EXPERTS

[Dr. B] is a doctor of medicine specializing in treatment of cancer patients. He received his M.D. at [name] Medical College in [location] in the year [1963]. He served an internship at [name] Hospital during the years [1965]–[1966]. He performed a residency in the field of internal medicine at [name] Hospital between [1966] and [1968]. He performed a residency in the field of hematology at the [name] Clinic in [city, state] from [1969]–[1971]. In [1971] he was an assistant professor of medicine at the [name] Medical School of the University of [city].

Dr. [B] has been certified as a specialist in internal medicine by the American Board of Internal Medicine since [1972], as a specialist in hematology by the American Board of Hematology since [1972]; and in oncology, that is, the field of cancer treatment, by the American Board of Oncology, since [1975].

Dr. [B] has engaged in the private practice of medicine since [1971]. He has specialized in treatment of cancer patients since [1975]. He is affiliated with [name] Hospital in [city, state]; with [name] Hospital in [city, state]; with [name] Hospital in [city, state]; and with [name] Hospital in [city, state].

Dr. [B] has been [Mr. Wessel]'s primary treating physician since [July 1987]. The substance of Dr. [B]'s testimony is that [Mr. Wessel]'s disability did not significantly interfere with his mental abilities, and that he was able to perform the essential functions of his position as Executive Director.

Dr. [A] is a doctor of medicine specializing in radiation treatment of cancer patients. She obtained her medical degree from the University of [city], in [country], in the year [1972]. She served as a resident at the [name] Hospital from [1974] though [1977] and at the University of [city] Medical Center from [1977] through [1978].

Dr. [A] has been certified as a specialist in the fields of radiology and radiation oncology by the American Board of Radiology and Radiation Oncology since [1978]. Radiation oncology is the branch of oncology that treats cancer patients with radiation treatments, as opposed to medical oncology, which treats cancer patients with chemotherapy.

Between [1978] and [1990] Dr. [A] practiced at the [name] Medical Center and acted as a consultant at several hospitals in that area. Since [1990] Dr. [A] has participated in a group practice at [firm name], providing radiation treatments for patients at [name] Hospital and [name] Hospital.

Dr. [A] has provided radiation treatments to [Mr. Wessel] since [April 1992]. The substance of Dr. [A]'s testimony is that [Mr. Wessel]'s disability and treatment did not significantly interfere with his mental abilities, and that he was able to perform the essential functions of his position as Executive Director.

SCHEDULE E-2
STATEMENT OF QUALIFICATIONS OF DEFENDANTS' EXPERT WITNESSES

Defendants will call as an expert witness [Larry S. M.], M.D., a doctor who specializes in the treatment of cancer patients. [Dr. M.] is a board-certified oncologist, hematologist and doctor of internal medicine. [Dr. M.] received his undergraduate and medical school training from the University of [state] and in [1966] graduated from medical school with high honors. From [1966] to [1968] [Dr. M.] worked as an intern and resident at the University of [state] Hospital in [city]. [Dr. M.] then went on to conduct research at [name] Institute in [city, state] from [1968] to [1970]. From [1970] to [1971] [Dr. M.] worked at [name] Hospital in the hematology department. Thereafter from [1971] to [1972], [Dr. M.] worked for the department of Hematology and Oncology at the University of [state] Hospital.

[Dr. M.]'s professional experience includes, but is not limited to, the following:

1)   Attending physician at [name] and [name] Hospitals;

2)   Private Practice in Hematology and Oncology;

3)   Member Board of Directors of American Cancer Society, [name] and [name] units;

4)   Chairman of the tumor boards at [name] and [name] Hospitals;

5)   President of the American Cancer Society, [name] unit;

6)   Deputy Chief Policy Surgeon, [city] Police Department;

7)   Attending Physician at [name] Hospital.

[Dr. M.] is also a member of the American College of Physicians, American Medical Association, American Society of Hematology and American Society of Clinical Oncology.

Among [Dr. M.]'s many publications are the following:

[list published articles]

[Dr. M.] will testify at trial. The substance of [Dr. M.]'s testimony is that due to brain tumors, respiratory insufficiencies, radiation treatments, and medication, [Charles H. Wessel] was unable to perform the essential functions of his job position in [July] of [1992].

Defendants will also call as an expert witness [Peter H. L.], M.D., a doctor who specializes in the treatment of people with mental diseases and impairments. [Dr. L.] is a board-certified Psychiatrist and Neurologist. [Dr. L.] received his undergraduate and medical school training from [name] University in [state]. From [1975] to [1976] [Dr. L.] worked as a resident in medicine at [name] Hospital, from [1977]–[1980] was a resident in Neurology at [name] Medical Center and from [1979]–[1980] was the chief resident at that facility. From [1980]–[1983] [Dr. L.] worked as a clinical associate at [name] Institute in [city, state]. From [1984] to present [Dr. L.] has been an Associate Professor of Neurology and Psychiatry at [name] School of Medicine in [city, state]. From [1988] to the present, [Dr. L.] has worked at the clinical Neuroscience Program at [name] Hospital.

[Dr. L.] is an elected member of the Academy of Neurology and American Neurological Association, Chairman of the Scientific Program Committee of the [state] Neurological Association, Chairman of the Medical Advisory Board of the [state] Parkinson Foundation, a member of the Medical Advisory Board of the United Parkinson Foundation and a member of the Scientific Advisory Board of the [state] Chapter of the Alzheimer's Disease Association.

Among many professional activities throughout his career, [Dr. L.] was the Director of a Postgraduate Neurology Course for the Foundation of [name] in [city, state] from [1981]–[1982] and was on the faculty of [name] Medical School in [city, state] in [1983].

[Dr. L.] has had over 100 of his works published, including several publications in the *New England Journal of Medicine.*

[Dr. L.] will testify at trial. The substance of [Dr. L.]'s testimony is that due to brain tumors, medication, and high doses of radiation, [Charles H. Wessel] suffered cognitive impairments to his higher mental functions in [July] of [1992]. [Dr. L.] will further testify that such cognitive impairments can affect reasoning, judgment, personality, and memory.

SCHEDULE F DEPOSITION DESIGNATIONS

SCHEDULE F-1

PART ONE
STATEMENT OF PLAINTIFFS' DEPOSITION DESIGNATIONS AND DEFENDANTS' OBJECTIONS

p. 5, line 8—p. 16, line 19

p. 17, line 2—p. 30, line 12

p. 31, line 18—p. 74, line 20

p. 75, line 16—p. 78, line 6

p. 78, line 18—p. 98, line 17

p. 99, line 2—p. 107, line 5

p. 107, line 15—p. 114, line 17

p. 114, line 20—p. 130, line 16

p. 130, line 21—p. 151, line 23

p. 152, line 15—p. 188, line 22

p. 189, line 7—p. 193, line 7

Deposition of [defendant C]—p. 124, lines 14–18

Deposition of [Kenneth D.]—p. 15, lines 7–15

Deposition of [Larry R.]—p. 35, lines 5–22, p. 171, lines 7–14

SCHEDULE F-1 STATEMENT OF PLAINTIFF'S DEPOSITION DESIGNATIONS
AND DEFENDANTS' OBJECTIONS

PART TWO
DEFENDANTS' OBJECTIONS TO PLAINTIFFS' DEPOSITION DESIGNATIONS

1.   Videotape deposition of [Charles Wessel]. Defendants object. No portion of this videotape should be used at trial if [Charles Wessel] is available to
testify. If [Wessel] is available to testify, the use of this videotape will cause
undue delay, waste time, and will needlessly present cumulative evidence. Rule
403, Fed. R. Evid.

2.   Deposition of [defendant C]. Defendants object. No portion of this transcript should be read into evidence at trial if defendants is available to testify. If
[defendant C] is available to testify, the reading of this transcript will cause
undue delay, waste time, and will needlessly present cumulative evidence. Rule
403, Fed. R. Evid.

3.   Deposition of [Ken D.]. Defendants object for the same reasons stated
in paragraph two (2) above.

4.   Deposition of [Larry R.]. Defendants object for the same reasons stated
in paragraph two (2) above.

SCHEDULE G ITEMIZED STATEMENT OF SPECIAL DAMAGES

1.   Lost wages from [August 1, 1992], through [August 1, 1993]—
[$36,013.00]. [$4244.00] per month for eight months; plus 5% raise effective
[November 1, 1992]; plus [$1000.00] bonus

2.   Health insurance premiums through [March 1993]-[4790.72]

3.   Life insurance premiums for two quarters-[$475.44]

4.   Job search expenses-[$100.00]

5.   Prejudgment interest

6.   Emotional distress

7.   Punitive damages

SCHEDULE G-1
DEFENDANTS' OBJECTIONS TO STATEMENT OF SPECIAL DAMAGES

Defendants do not stipulate to the Statement of Special Damages drafted by Plaintiff's attorneys and object to same.

Specifically, Defendants object to Paragraph 1 in Schedule G because it does not apportion [Wessel]'s car allowance and assumes, without foundation, that [Wessel] would have received a raise and bonus in [1992].

Defendants also object to paragraphs 4–7 of Schedule G. Prejudgment interest, emotional distress, and punitive damages are not special damages. Also, Plaintiffs have listed a round figure of [$100.00] for job search expenses without providing any foundation for the calculation this figure.

Defendants list the following as special damages:

1.   Lost wages of [$3,893.75] per month from [August 1, 1992] to a date to be determined at trial, when [Wessel] was no longer able to perform the essential functions of the job position with or without reasonable accommodation.

2.   A car allowance of [$350.00] per month from [August 1, 1992] to a date to be determined at trial, when [Wessel] was no longer able to perform the essential functions of the job position with or without reasonable accommodation.

3.   Health insurance premiums of [$598.84] per month from [August 1, 1992] to date to be determined at trial, when [Wessel] was no longer able to perform the essential functions of the job position with or without reasonable accommodation.

4.   Life insurance premiums of [$237.72] per quarter from [August 1, 1992] to a date to be determined at trial, when [Wessel] was no longer able to perform the essential functions of the job position with or without reasonable accommodation.

5.   Job search expenses of an amount to be proven by Plaintiffs at trial.

SCHEDULE H PLAINTIFFS' TRIAL BRIEFS

(Plaintiffs' trial brief appears in **Chapter 17.**)

SCHEDULE I DEFENDANTS' TRIAL BRIEFS

(Defendants' trial brief appears in **Chapter 16.**)

SCHEDULE J JURY INSTRUCTIONS

(Agreed jury instructions appear in **Chapter 16.**)

SCHEDULE J-1

PLAINTIFFS' PROPOSED JURY INSTRUCTIONS AND VERDICT FORMS

(Plaintiffs' proposed jury instructions appear in **Chapter 16.**)

SCHEDULE J-2

DEFENDANTS' PROPOSED JURY INSTRUCTIONS AND VERDICT FORMS

(Defendants' proposed jury instructions appear in **Chapter 16.**)

SCHEDULE K LIST OF PROPOSED VOIR DIRE QUESTIONS

(Plaintiffs' proposed voir dire questions appear in **Chapter 16.**)

SCHEDULE L DEFENDANTS' LIST OF PROPOSED VOIR DIRE QUESTIONS

(Defendants' list of proposed voir dire questions appears in **Chapter 16.**)

SCHEDULE M HISTORY OF SETTLEMENT NEGOTIATIONS

On [November 16, 1992], counsel for the EEOC wrote a letter to counsel for Defendants setting forth full relief for the violations alleged in the Complaint. On [November 20, 1993], counsel for Defendants wrote a letter to counsel for the EEOC rejecting full relief.

Defendants made a counteroffer to Plaintiff [Wessel] on [January 18, 1993]. That offer was rejected.

Counsel for the parties have discussed the possibility of settlement on [February 17], [February 19], and [February 20, 1993], and agree that further discussions will be pursued.

SCHEDULE N MOTIONS IN LIMINE

IN THE UNITED STATES DISTRICT COURT

FOR THE [NORTHERN] DISTRICT OF [ILLINOIS]

[EASTERN] DIVISION

U.S. EQUAL EMPLOYMENT OPPORTUNITY COMMISSION and

[CHARLES H. WESSEL],

Plaintiffs

v.   Civil Action No. [92 C 7330]

[A.I.C. SECURITY INVESTIGATIONS, LTD.];

[A.I.C. INTERNATIONAL, LTD.]; and [unnamed defendant C],

Defendants.

Judge [Aspen]

Magistrate Judge [Guzman]

PLAINTIFFS' MOTION IN LIMINE

Plaintiffs hereby move for the exclusion of evidence, relating to the reason(s) for [David P.]'s termination as President of [A.I.C. International]. The use of evidence of the reasons for [David P.']s termination is precluded based upon the Court's previous denial of the EEOC's Motion to Compel. Defendants argued in opposition to the Motion to Compel that such evidence was nondiscoverable and not reasonably calculated to lead to the discovery of admissible evidence. Therefore, Defendants cannot now be heard to say that such evidence can be used at trial. A denial of the Motion in Limine would essentially permit Defendants to withhold evidence from the Plaintiffs, arguing that it is not admissible, and thereafter introduce the very same evidence at trial. Surely such an anomalous result cannot be permitted.

The Court's acceptance of the Defendants' argument in denying the Motion to Compel also precludes the use of evidence of the reasons for [David P.]'s termination, because the Court expressly stated that the EEOC had "failed to establish that Interrogatory 14 seeks information that is reasonably calculated to lead to discovery of admissible evidence." Defendants should not be permitted to use evidence at trial which was previously determined not to be admissible.

Finally, the Court's order on the Motion to Compel was partially premised on its understanding that [David P.]'s personnel file would be provided to the EEOC pursuant to Document Request Number 2 to which the Defendants did not raise an objection. In his deposition of [December 8, 1992], [Philip A. W.] testified as follows:

Q: What about personnel files of other management employees; do you have custody of those?

A: Yes.

Q: If you wanted to give them to me, how long would it take you to do that?

A: If I wanted to give them to you?

Q: Right.

A: First I have to see who's there. With the people that have come and gone lately—

Q: What if I wanted, for example, [David P.]'s personnel file?

A: [David P.]'s could be in the other building. That may take a while to find.

Deposition of [Philip A. W.], page 34, lines 12–24. To date, Defendants have not provided the Plaintiffs with a copy of [David P.]'s personnel file, stating that it cannot be located. The Defendants' failure to provide [David P.]'s personnel file, despite the Court's understanding that it had done so, is yet another basis for excluding the admission of any evidence as to the reasons for [David P.]'s termination by the Defendants at trial.

WHEREFORE, Plaintiffs respectfully request that evidence relating to the reasons for [David P.]'s termination be excluded from the evidence presented by Defendants at trial.

[Elaine M. C.]
Trial Attorney
Equal Employment Opportunity Commission
[536 South Clark], [Room 982]
[Chicago], [Illinois] [60605]

DEFENDANTS' MOTION IN LIMINE

MOTION NO. 1: Defendants hereby move to exclude the purported May Roast Videotape of [Charles Wessel] proffered as Exhibit No. 9 by Plaintiff EEOC based upon the following:

1.   The video is of a "roast" held for the benefit of [Charles Wessel] by the security guard association to which he belonged; it has absolutely no relevance to any of the issues involved in this case, including the issue of whether [Wessel] could perform the essential functions of his position of Executive Director. (See Rules 401 and 402, Fed. R. Evid.)

2.   The contents of the video are inadmissible hearsay, especially in view of the fact that many of the individuals speaking at the event—[Wessel] himself, [David P]., [Richard F.]—are named witnesses of the parties, and the other participants in the event are available as witnesses to testify in Court.

3.   The videotaped roast is akin to a eulogy, wherein the various speakers pay tribute to a colleague they know to be terminally ill, and thus, their statements are, as [Wessel] himself indicated at the event, far too generous.

4.   The tenuous value of the videotape at trial is substantially outweighed by the danger of unfair prejudice, confusion of the issues and misleading the jury. (See Rule 403, Fed. R. Evid.)

5.   The video cannot be adequately authenticated and the copy which Defendants obtained during discovery appears to have been only a portion of what actually may have been recorded at this event. (See Rules 901 (a) and 401 (b), Fed. R. Evid.)

WHEREFORE, Defendants respectfully request that this video be excluded from evidence at trial.

By:

[attorney A]

CHAPTER 16

TRIAL MATERIALS

§ 16.1   Introduction and Overview

This chapter contains Americans with Disabilities Act (ADA)[1] trial materials, from motions to exclude (see **Forms 16–1** to **16–2**) to jury verdict forms (see **Form 16–21**). Because there have been relatively few complete ADA jury trials, this chapter relies to a significant extent on materials developed in simulated ADA trials. See **Forms 16–7** to **16–8**, and **Forms 16–15** to **16–22**.

Transcripts of simplified evidentiary proceedings are useful as starting points for developing checklists for witnesses and witness examination. See **Form 16–4**. For that reason, transcribed material is included (see **Forms 16–5** to **16–6** and Forms **16–9** to **16–14**) as well as other types of forms.

§ 16.2   Defendants' Motion to Exclude Expert Witness

FORM 16–1
SAMPLE DEFENDANTS' MOTION TO EXCLUDE EXPERT WITNESS

IN THE UNITED STATES DISTRICT COURT

FOR THE [NORTHERN] DISTRICT OF [ILLINOIS]

[EASTERN] DIVISION

U.S. EQUAL OPPORTUNITY COMMISSION

Plaintiff,   Civil Action No.: No. [92-C-7330]

v.

[A.I.C. SECURITY INVESTIGATIONS, LTD.];

[A.I.C. INTERNATIONAL, LTD.]; AND [unnamed defendant C],

Defendants.   Judge [Marvin E. Aspen]

---

[1] Pub. L. No. 101-336, 104 Stat. 327 (1990) (codified at 42 U.S.C. §§ 12101–12213 (1994); 47 U.S.C. §§ 225, 711 (1994) [hereinafter ADA].

DEFENDANTS' MOTION TO EXCLUDE EXPERT WITNESS

Defendants, [A.I.C. SECURITY INVESTIGATIONS, LTD.]; [A.I.C. INTERNA-TIONAL, LTD.]; and [defendant C], by and through their attorneys, [WESSELS & PAUTSCH, P.C.], [Charles W. Pautsch], [attorney A], and [attorney B], hereby move this Honorable Court to exclude from trial the testimony of [E. Richard B.], M. D., and states in support hereof as follows:

1.   On [November 5, 1992], the Equal Opportunity Commission ("EEOC") filed this instant action alleging that Defendants violated the Americans With Disabilities Act.

2.   Shortly thereafter the Honorable [Marvin E. Aspen] placed this case on an expedited docket.

3.   Subsequently, in [December] of [1992], the Plaintiff EEOC named two expert witnesses, [A], M.D. and [B], M.D.

4.   On [December 2] and [14], [1992] respectively, Defendants disclosed to Plaintiffs their witnesses, Doctors [Larry S. M.] and [Peter A.L.].

5.   On [December 11, 1992], Defendants deposed Dr. [A] and on [December 19, 1992], Defendants deposed Dr. [B].

6.   On [January 22, 1993], discovery closed in this case. On or about [January 21], Plaintiffs canceled their previously scheduled deposition of [Dr. L.] in [Detroit] on [January 22, 1993]. Plaintiffs made no attempts to depose [Dr. M.] during the discovery period.

7.   On [January 29, 1993], all parties came before this Court on various motions, at which this time this Court entertained status issues regarding the progression of this case. During this hearing EEOC Attorney [B] indicated there were no expert witnesses. Defendants' counsel conveyed to the Court that Defendants intended to call their two previously identified medical experts as witnesses at trial; however, because neither witness had been deposed by Plaintiffs during the discovery period, the Court established additional time for Plaintiffs to depose Defendants' named experts.

8.   Accordingly, the parties have scheduled the deposition of [Dr. Larry M.] for [February 11, 1993]; Defendants have tentatively agreed to have [Dr. Peter L.] come to [Detroit] to examine [Charles Wessel], as ordered by the Court, on [February 12, 1993], at which time he could also be deposed by Plaintiffs in [Chicago].

9.   On [February 9, 1993], Plaintiff EEOC sent, via facsimile, Supplemental Responses to Defendants' First Set of Interrogatories to Plaintiff. EEOC now intends to call [E. Richard B.], M.D. as an additional expert witness at trial. (Attached hereto as Exhibit No. 1.)

10.   Plaintiffs have sought no Leave of Court to name any additional expert witnesses at this point in time, long after the discovery cutoff.

11.   Plaintiffs have no right to notice new expert witnesses at this extremely late date, discovery having already closed on [January 22, 1993], and only limited discovery having now been permitted by the Court solely with respect to expert witnesses identified by the Defendants long ago, back in [1992].

Wherefore, defendants respectfully request an Order prohibiting [E. Richard B.], M.D. from testifying at trial.

Dated this [10th] day of [February], [1993].

Respectfully submitted,

[A.I.C. SECURITY INVESTIGATIONS, LTD.];

[A.I.C. INTERNATIONAL, LTD.];

AND [defendant C],

By: [attorney A]

§ 16.3   Defendants' Emergency Motion to Exclude Testimony of Attorney

FORM 16–2
SAMPLE DEFENDANTS' MOTION TO EXCLUDE TESTIMONY OF ATTORNEY

DEFENDANTS' EMERGENCY MOTION IN LIMINE
TO EXCLUDE TESTIMONY OF ATTY. [MICHAEL C.]

The Defendants, [A.I.C. SECURITY INVESTIGATIONS, LTD.]; [A.I.C. INTERNA-TIONAL, LTD.]; AND [unnamed defendant C], by and through their attorneys, [WES-SELS & PAUTSCH, P.C.], by [Charles W. Pautsch], [attorney A], and [attorney B], hereby move to exclude testimony of Atty. [Michael C.] based upon the following:

1.   On [February 22, 1993], the parties in the above-captioned case submitted a Final Pre-Trial Order to the Court.

2.   Within the Final Pre-Trial Order is Plaintiffs' List of Witnesses (Schedule D-11).

3.   In Plaintiffs' List of Witnesses, it is indicated that Plaintiffs will call [Michael C.] as a witness at trial.

4.   [Michael C.] is an attorney practicing law in the [Chicago] area and, upon information and belief, is licensed to practice law in the State of [Illinois].

5.   That, for a period of time prior to [August 1992], [Michael C.] represented and counseled Defendants [A.I.C. International, Ltd.] and [A.I.C. Security Investigations, Ltd.] in numerous matters, including employment law matters.

6.   As a previous attorney for [A.I.C. International, Ltd]. and [A.I.C. Security Investigations, Ltd.], [Michael C.] cannot at trial divulge any information he obtained while acting in the capacity of attorney for Defendants.

7.   In addition, Defendants in this action cannot be forced into a position of having to divulge confidential information in order to effectively cross-examine [Michael C].

8.   If Defendants are forced to choose between effective cross-examination or divulgence of confidential and highly sensitive material, Defendants will be foreclosed from due process of law.

9.   If [Michael C.] testifies at trial against Defendants using information he obtained through his representation of Defendants, he will violate ABA Model Code of Professional Responsibility Canon 4, Disciplinary Rule 4-101—Preservation of Confidences and Secrets of Client. (See [Ill. Rev. Stat. ch. 110A, Rule 4-101].) Moreover, if the testimony of [Michael C.] forces Defendants to use confidential information to effectively cross-examine [Michael C.], then [Michael C.] will still be in violation of [Canon 4] and [Disciplinary Rule 4-101] cited above and will have breached his common law fiduciary duty to Defendants. *See* [*Financial General Bankshares, Inc. v. Metzger,* 680 F.2d 768, 771 (D.C. Cir. 1982)].

10.   Defendants do not intend to waive their attorney-client privilege at trial with regards to information in the possession of [Michael C.]; and, therefore, will be foreclosed from effective cross-examination of [Michael C.] and due process of law.

WHEREFORE, Defendants respectfully request that [Michael C.] be excluded from testifying at trial.

Dated this [4th]day of [March], [1993].

[A.I.C. SECURITY INVESTIGATIONS, LTD.];

[A.I.C. INTERNATIONAL, LTD.];

and [defendant C]

By: [attorney A]

§ 16.4 Demonstrative Evidence

One of the most effective types of evidence in an ADA case can be a videotape demonstration of the plaintiff performing essential job functions. Several sections of this chapter provide forms useful in advocating or opposing that type of evidence. This section summarizes foundational issues.

Real and demonstrative evidence is admissible only after being authenticated. The concept of *authentication* refers to establishing a link between the evidence and the person, place, or thing to which it purportedly relates.[2] Federal Rule of Evidence 901 says that "The requirement for authentication . . . is satisfied by evidence sufficient to support a finding that the matter in question is what its proponent claims."[3] Even though common sense suggests that writings themselves are evidence of their authors, the law of evidence traditionally has required extrinsic evidence to establish the authenticity of a writing.[4] Usually the controversy is over authorship.[5] The examples given in Rule 901 focus largely on authorship.[6]

Authentication is not limited conceptually to writings. McCormick gives the example of an article of clothing found at a crime scene, which cannot be evidence against the defendant unless his ownership or other connection with the clothing is established.

Establishing the defendant connection is an authentication problem.[7] When a party in ADA litigation offers demonstrative evidence of the plaintiff's ability or inability to perform job functions, establishing a connection between the demonstration and the actual job functions is an authentication problem also.

---

[2] L. Packel & A. Poulin, Pennsylvania Evidence (1987) [hereinafter Packel & Poulin] § 901, at 672 (authentication concept); McCormick on Evidence §§ 212-214, 218-228 (3d ed. 1984).

[3] Fed. R. Evid. 901(a), 901(b) (giving examples of authentication of records).

[4] Packel & Poulin § 901.5, at 683 (writing itself insufficient proof of authenticity; when writing supplied by agent, proponent must establish (1) agent actually signed, (2) agent was the agent of the principal, and (3) agent acted within authority). *But see* Fed. R. Evid. 902 (self-authentication of certain documents such as certified copies of public records, newspapers). The authentication requirement originated with illiterate juries. The courts feared that such juries might give either too much weight to written evidence because they were in awe of it, or too little weight because they could not understand it. Hence the authentication rule provided oral testimony on which the jury could rely.

[5] *See, e.g.,* Packel & Poulin § 901.9, at 691 (applying authentication rules for writings to telephone conversations and focusing on identity of speaker). McCormick on Evidence § 218, at 686–87 (3d ed. 1984) (using term authentication in limited sense of proof of authorship).

[6] *See, e.g.,* Fed. R. Evid. 901(b)(2) (handwriting), 901(b)(5) (voice identification), 901(b)(6) (identity of called party in telephone conversation).

[7] McCormick on Evidence § 218, at 686 (3d ed. 1984).

Judge Friendly engaged in a useful review of the authentication concept in *United States v. Sliker*.[8] Most fundamentally, he observed that authentication is a logical requirement that a piece of evidence be what it claims to be.[9] "Evidence admitted as something can have no probative value unless that is what it really is."[10] He noted that the type and quantum of authentication evidence should depend on the purpose for which evidence is offered because authorship may not be the important issue. In Sliker, he found that records of criminal transactions were sufficiently connected to a sham bank regardless of who wrote them. The content and the physical location of the records were the probative authentication evidence.[11] He noted in particular, as appropriate methods of authenticating evidence, distinctive characteristics, combined with other circumstances,[12] contents, and where the evidence was found.[13] He approved the appropriateness of comparing the sound of a voice on an audio tape with the sound of a witness's voice in the trial.[14]

In the actual trial, the proponent of videotape demonstration evidence must have one or more sponsoring witnesses. One sponsor may be the plaintiff.[15] The testimony from these witnesses must establish that the videotape accurately shows: the identity of the plaintiff; the capabilities of the plaintiff; and the requirements of the job.

The ultimate question for the videotape medium is trustworthiness. If the techniques used to create the videotape are apparently reliable, the information should be admitted unless the opponent of admissibility can raise some reasonable factual question undercutting trustworthiness,[16] especially if the opponent of evidentiary use was notified, was present, and thus had an opportunity to object to aspects of the demonstration in time for them to be modified.

The larger battle usually will relate to the accuracy of the portrayal of plaintiff capabilities and job functions, especially the latter.

---

[8] 751 F.2d 477, 488–89 (2d Cir. 1984) (evaluating authentication of records of fraudulent transactions and audio tapes of defendant conversations in reviewing conviction for wire fraud in scheme to defraud banks).

[9] *Id.* at 499.

[10] *Id.* (approving trial judge's listening to audio tape and comparing voices before allowing jury to hear it, although jury ultimately decided fact question of authenticity).

[11] *Id.* at 489 (citing cases where physical proximity authenticated physical evidence).

[12] *Id.* at 500 (citing Fed. R. Evid. 901 (b)(3),(4) advisory committee's notes).

[13] *Id.* (citing case involving letter combined with testimony).

[14] United States v. Sliker, 751 F.2d 477, 500 (2d Cir. 1984).

[15] *See generally* L. Packel & D.B. Spina, Trial Advocacy: A Systematic Approach 97–98 (1984) (sponsoring witnesses for real and demonstrative evidence).

[16] *See* United States v. Hutson, 821 F.2d 1015, 1020 (5th Cir. 1987) (remanding embezzlement conviction, although computer records were admissible under business records exception, despite trustworthiness challenge based on fact that defendant embezzled by altering computer files; access to files offered in evidence was restricted by special code).

§ 16.5   Memorandum Supporting Motion to Admit Videotape Demonstration

The contents of the motion appearing in **Form 16–3** could be used in support of admissibility at the time of objection at trial, as well as in a motion in limine.

FORM 16–3
SAMPLE MOTION IN LIMINE TO ADMIT
VIDEOTAPE DEMONSTRATION

MOTION IN LIMINE TO ADMIT VIDEOTAPE
DEMONSTRATION OF PLAINTIFF'S CAPABILITIES TO
PERFORM JOB FUNCTIONS

Plaintiff moves the court for an order that a videotape showing the Plaintiff performing the essential functions of the job in controversy in this case is admissible into evidence and ordering the Defendant not to object to it.

Rules 403, 611, and 901 of the Federal Rules of Evidence permit demonstrative evidence to be shown to a factfinder under certain conditions. Those conditions are satisfied in this case because the videotape shows the Plaintiff performing the ordinary functions of the job for which Plaintiff applied, under realistic conditions. The following cases support the admissibility of such demonstrative evidence. Under the following cases, the Defendant has not and cannot show any aspect of the videotape that is unduly prejudicial or that is significantly misleading in terms of the functions of the job as the Defendant itself has defined them.

See [*Sterkel v. Fruehauf Corp.*, 975 F.2d 528, 523 (8th Cir. 1992) (affirming denial of mistrial; model of slider pens on truck trailer shown to jury was not exactly correct in its dimension but no showing that jury was misled)]; [*Roland v. Langlois*, 945 F.2d 956, 963 (7th Cir. 1991) (affirming trial court admission of life-sized model of amusement park ride component; no requirement that demonstrative evidence be completely accurate as long as jury is alerted to perceived inaccuracies in personal injury case)]; [*Petty v. Ideco*, 761 F.2d 1146, 1151 (5th Cir. 1985) (affirming admission of videotape showing the functioning of oil well equipment because of failure to object and procedure used at trial permitting stopping of videotape whenever opposing party had any objection)]; [*In re Beverly Hill Fire Litigation*, 695 F.2d 207, 222 (6th Cir. 1982) (affirming admission of model of exterior portions of a wall involved in fire in personal injury action)].

Videotape demonstrations of an ADA plaintiff's capabilities are similar in terms of evidentiary issues to videotapes or movies showing "a day in the life" of an injured plaintiff. Such videotapes regularly are admitted as long as certain conditions are satisfied. *See* [*Bannister v. Town of Nobel*, 812 F.2d 1265, 1268 (10th Cir. 1987) (approving admission of "day in the life" videotape because (1) tape fairly represented facts regarding impact of injuries on plaintiff's day-to-day activities and did not depict victim in unlikely circumstances or performing improbable tasks, (2) no showing of self-serving behavior because of awareness of videotaping and no showing of exaggeration of difficulty in performing tasks, (3) no showing of undue prejudice by dominating evidentiary record in jury's mind, and (4) no showing that inability to cross-examine tape prejudiced deponent; videotape depicted daily routine, including getting around school, getting into car, pumping gasoline for car, and performing different routine tasks at home)]; [*id.*, 812 F.2d 1265, 1270 (affirming admission of videotape showing car like the one involved in accident approaching an inclined ramp, becoming airborne, and landing; videotape not offered as re-creation of accident but as demonstration of certain principles; instruction given that "the film is not being introduced for the purpose of attempting to recreate the accident involved in this case")]; [*id.*, 812 F.2d 1265, 1270 (no error to permit "day in the life" videotape admitted into evidence to be shown during closing argument)]; [*United States v. Sanders*, 696 F. Supp. 334, 335 (N.D. Ill. 1988) (admitting promotional videotapes to help jury understand commodities trading, drawing analogies between them, and "day in the life" videotapes; admissible under catchall exception to hearsay rule)].

Videotape or live demonstrations of the ADA Plaintiff's capability to perform essential functions also are similar to in-court demonstration of [injuries. Such evidence routinely is admitted. *See* [*Monk v. Doctors' Hospital*, 403 F.2d 580, 584 (D.C. Cir. 1968) (permissible for plaintiff to demonstrate injury as long as foundation is laid to prevent undue prejudice and make demonstration realistic)]; [*Lester v. Sayles*, 850 S.W.2d 858, 870 (Mo. 1993) (affirming trial court's allowance of mother's demonstration of physical therapy she performs on daughter; no showing of exaggeration of symptoms or pain)]; [*Fravel v. Burlington Northern Railroad*, 671 S.W.2d 339 (Mo. Ct. App. 1984) (affirming allowance of demonstration by plaintiff of injuries to leg by having physician manipulate leg in front of jury; defense counsel did not make record of alleged grimaces and exclamations of pain)]; [*LeMaster v. Chicago Rock Island & Pacific Railroad Co.*, 343 N.E.2d 65 (Ill. App. Ct. 1976) (affirming trial judge discretion to permit plaintiff to disrobe to bathing suit and demonstrate taking off and putting on arm and leg prostheses and to re-dress, along with a series of photographs showing essentially the same thing)]; [*Bellart v. Martell*, 137 N.W.2d 729 (Wis. 1965) (no error to permit personal injury plaintiff to display arm and leg stump to jury and to demonstrate operation and putting on prostheses)].

Commentary.   In cases involving "day in the life" videotapes, the opponent's usual claim is that the activities portrayed on the videotape are more difficult than activities undertaken in real life. In an ADA case, the person opposing a videotape demonstration would claim that the activities portrayed on the videotape are easier than the activities involved on the job, and real life. In either kind of case, however, the criteria for admissibility are the same: that the videotape accurately portrays the questions in the case, (that is, that the activities portrayed are reasonably similar to the real world activities) and that the jury is instructed and otherwise cautioned in order to minimize the risks of prejudice.

§ 16.6   Checklist for Voir Dire

____ 1.   Basic Juror Attitudes Toward the Disabled

    ____ a.   Have you ever worked with a person who had a physical or mental disability?

    ____ b.   Have you ever had a supervisor with a physical or mental disability?

    [If the potential juror answers yes, explore the experience with questions such as]

        ____ (1)   How closely did you work with the disabled person?

        ____ (2)   What was the nature of the disability?

        ____ (3)   How did the disability affect the person's ability to do his or her job?

        ____ (4)   How did the disability affect relations with coworkers?

        ____ (5)   How did the disability affect relations with the employer?

        ____ (6)   Do you think the employer treated the disabled person fairly? Why or why not?

    ____ c.   Does anyone in your family have a physical or mental disability?

    ____ d.   Have you ever contributed to an organization that has as its goal the protection or support of persons with physical or mental disabilities?

    ____ e.   If you have contributed to such an organization, does it have as its goal the placing of disabled persons in the mainstream of American life, or does it favor separating them and providing support because they do not work?

    ____ f.   What is your reaction when you see wheelchair ramps on buildings and curbs of streets, and when you see special devices on buses for the handicapped?

    ____ g.   Have you ever been waited on by a disabled person?

____ 2.   Attitudes Toward Discrimination and Accommodation

    ____ a.   What kind of disability discrimination do you think present law prohibits?

    ____ b.   What kind of disability discrimination should be prohibited?

    ____ c.   Should a distinction be drawn between discrimination based on physical disabilities and mental disabilities?

_____ d. Under what circumstances do you think it is justifiable to treat persons with physical or mental disabilities differently from nondisabled persons?

_____ e. Should employers consider changing job duties and the organization of work in order to make it possible for a disabled person to perform job functions?

_____ f. What kinds of changes should be considered?

_____ g. What kinds should not be considered?

_____ 3. Attitudes Toward Discrimination and Accommodation in Public Accommodations and Commercial Facilities

_____ a. Do you think that persons with physical or mental disabilities should be allowed to use facilities like movie theaters and retail stores along with everyone else?

_____ b. Should special arrangements be made to make it easier for persons with physical or mental disabilities to use such public places?

_____ c. Do you think any distinction should be drawn between persons who have mobility disabilities, such as being confined to wheelchairs or going on crutches, from those who have visual limitations like blindness or hearing limitations like deafness? What distinctions?

_____ d. Are there any circumstances under which people with physical or mental disabilities should be excluded from public facilities, including stores and places of entertainment like movie theaters?

_____ e. Suppose the disabled people wishing to use such facilities are severely deformed or make unusual noises?

_____ f. Under what circumstances should "socially acceptable behavior" be applied to exclude disabled persons from public places?

_____ g. If you were running a small dress shop, what would be your policy toward use of your shop by persons with physical or mental disabilities?

_____ h. How much trouble would you go to to make sure that disabled persons had access to your place of business?

_____ i. Would it make any difference if you were operating a video game parlor, a movie theater, or a place in which athletic activities such as tennis or ice skating were performed?[17]

---

[17] Many of the ideas for this checklist are adapted from R.B. Conlin, _Effective Voir Dire in Sex Discrimination Cases,_ Trial (July 1993) at p. 23.

§ 16.7   Proposed Voir Dire Questions

FORM 16–4
SAMPLE PROPOSED VOIR DIRE QUESTIONS

PLAINTIFFS' PROPOSED VOIR DIRE QUESTIONS

1.   Are any of you acquainted with any of the parties in this case or any member of their families? The parties in this case are: [names of parties]

2.   To the best of your knowledge, is any member of your family or household or any close friend acquainted with any of the parties?

3.   Have any of you or, again, any member of your family or household or any close friend ever met any of the attorneys in this case or, to your knowledge, any attorney associated in practice with one of those attorneys? The attorneys in this case are: [names of attorneys]

4.   Have any of you or any members of your household or family or any close friends ever had any business dealings with any of the parties involved in this case?

5.   Have any of you or any member of your household or family or any close friend ever met or even heard of any person identified as a possible witness in this case? The following individuals are possible witnesses in this case: [list of witnesses]

6.   Did any of you hear anything about this case before you came into the courtroom this morning?

7.   As you look around this room, do any of you recognize any friends or acquaintances among the other prospective jurors?

8.   What is your occupation and employer? How long have you worked there? What is your position? How long have you held that position?

9.   Have you or a close friend or relative or member of your household ever been a supervisor, manager, or executive? If so, provide the details.

10.   If you have ever been an owner, supervisor, manager, or executive of a business, did you ever terminate or recommend the termination of an employee? If so, provide the details.

11.   If you have been an owner, supervisor, manager, or executive, did any employee under you or in your company ever raise a claim or file a lawsuit for employment discrimination or other employment-related claims? If so, provide the details.

12.   Have you or a close friend or relative or member of your household had any training or employment experience in personnel or human resources?

13.   Please identify the members of your immediate family and anyone else who lives with you.

14.   What is the occupation, employer, and position of each member of your family?

15.   Have any of you or a member of your family or household or any close friend ever been terminated or laid off from any job for a reason that was considered discriminatory or unfair? If so, provide details.

16.   Have you or any member of your family or household or any close friend, or any business you owned or operated, ever been involved in a lawsuit of any kind? Are you now involved in a lawsuit?

17.   Have you or a member of your family or household or a close friend ever made a claim of employment discrimination or other claim relating to employment?

18.   Do you, or does any member of your immediate family suffer from any disability? If so, does that disability interfere with the ability to work?

19.   Have you or any member of your family or any close friend had cancer? Would that fact interfere with your ability to try this case fairly?

20.   From what you have heard thus far about the case—the type of lawsuit, the parties, the witnesses who may testify—do any of you believe you or your family could possibly be affected in any way by the outcome of this case?

21.   Is there anything about the nature of this case that would prevent you from being fair and impartial?

22.   Is there anything else about yourself that would affect your ability to render a fair and impartial verdict based on the evidence and law?

23.   Do you believe you can give both sides a fair trial?

DEFENDANTS' LIST OF PROPOSED VOIR DIRE QUESTIONS

1.   Are any of you acquainted with any of the individual parties in this case or any member of their families? The individual parties in this case are:

[Charles H. Wessel]

[defendant C]

2.   Are any of you acquainted with any of the corporate parties in this case? The corporate parties in this case are:

[A.I.C. International, Ltd.]

[A.I.C. Security Investigations, Ltd.]

3.   To the best of your knowledge, is any member of your family or household or any close friend acquainted with any of the parties?

4.   Have any of you ever filed a charge of discrimination with the Equal Employment Opportunity Commission?

5.   To the best of your knowledge, has any member of your family or household or any close friend filed a charge of discrimination with the Equal Employment Opportunity Commission?

6.   Have you or any member of your family or household or any close friend ever been employed by the Equal Employment Opportunity Commission?

7.   Has any of you or, again, any member of your family or household or any close friend ever met any of the attorneys in this case, or, to your knowledge any attorney associated in practice with one of those attorneys? The attorneys and law firms in this case are:

[list of attorneys and law firms]

8.   Has any of you or any members of your household or family or any close friend ever had any business dealings with any of the parties involved in this case?

9.   Has any of you or any member of your household or family or any close friend ever met or even heard of any person identified as a possible witness in this case? The following individuals are possible witnesses in this case:

[list of witnesses]

10.   Did any of you hear anything about this case before you came into the courtroom this morning? If so, what did you hear?

11.   As you look around this room, do any of you recognize any friends or acquaintances among the other prospective jurors?

12.   What is your occupation and employer? How long have you worked there? What is your position? How long have you held that position?

13.   Please describe the members of your immediate family and anyone else who lives with you.

14.   What is the occupation, employer, and position of each member of your family?

15.   Have any of you or any member of your family or household or any close friend ever been terminated or laid off from any job for a reason that was considered discriminatory or unfair? If so, give details.

16.   Have you or any member of your family or household or any close friend, or any business you owned or operated, ever been involved in a lawsuit of any kind? Are you now involved in a lawsuit?

17.   Have you or any member of your family or household or any close friend ever made a claim of employment discrimination or other claim relating to employment?

18.   Do you, or does any member of your immediate family suffer from any disability? If so, does that disability interfere with the ability to work?

19.   Have you or any member of your family or close friend had cancer, or has anyone close to you died from cancer in the past fifteen years? Would that fact interfere with your ability to render a fair and impartial verdict in this case?

20.   What do you think about women in business and their holding high positions in business?

21.   [Charles Wessel] has been diagnosed as terminally ill with inoperable cancer. Will this make you unable to render a fair and impartial verdict regarding whether [Mr. Wessel] was qualified to remain in his position as Executive Director?

22.   If [Charles Wessel] is hospitalized or dies before or during the course of this trial, would it affect your ability to render a fair and impartial verdict in this case?

23.   Do you have any perceived notions or opinions about cancer, brain cancer, or terminal illness which would prohibit you from rendering a fair and impartial verdict in this case?

24.   From what you have heard thus far about the case—the type of lawsuit, the parties, the witnesses who may testify—do any of you believe you or your family could possibly be affected in any way by the outcome of this case?

25.   Is there anything about the nature of this case that would prevent you from being fair and impartial?

26.   Is there anything else about yourself that would affect your ability to render a fair and impartial verdict based on the evidence and law?

27.   Do you believe you can give both sides a fair trial?

28.   Would the fact that this trial involves individuals from the [name] family, as parties and potential witnesses who have been and are active in City of [Chicago] politics, affect your impartiality at all?

29.   Have you read, seen, or heard any news regarding this case?

§ 16.8   Plaintiffs' Trial Brief

FORM 16–5
SAMPLE PLAINTIFFS' TRIAL BRIEF

IN THE UNITED STATES DISTRICT COURT

FOR THE [NORTHERN] DISTRICT OF [ILLINOIS]

[EASTERN] DIVISION

U.S. EQUAL EMPLOYMENT OPPORTUNITY COMMISSION and [CHARLES H. WESSEL],

Plaintiffs,

v.   Civil Action No. [92 C 7330]

[A.I.C. SECURITY INVESTIGATIONS, LTD.];

[A.I.C. INTERNATIONAL, LTD.]; and [unnamed defendant C],   Judge [Aspen]

Defendants.   Magistrate [Judge Guzman]

PLAINTIFFS' TRIAL BRIEF

Plaintiff, Equal Employment Opportunity Commission (the ["Commission" or "EEOC"), and Intervening Plaintiff, [Charles Wessel], hereby submit this Trial Brief in the above-captioned cause.

I.   Nature of the Case

This action is brought pursuant to Title I of the Americans with Disabilities Act of 1990, 42 U.S.C. § 12101 *et seq.*, and Title I of the Civil Rights Act of 1991, 42

U.S.C. § 1981a. The EEOC and the Intervening Plaintiff, [Charles Wessel] allege that the Defendants, [A.I.C. Security Investigations, Ltd. ("A.I.C.")], [A.I.C. International, Ltd. ("A.I.C. International")], and [defendant C] discriminated against [Wessel] on the basis of his disability, terminal cancer, by discharging him from his position as Executive Director at [A.I.C.].

II.   Factual Summary

[A.I.C.] is a wholly owned subsidiary of [A.I.C. International]. [Defendant C] became the sole shareholder of [A.I.C International] on [June 6, 1992]. Prior to [June 6, 1992], the sole owner of [A.I.C. International] was [Victor V.]. [A.I.C. International] and its subsidiaries have been and are now currently engaged in the business of providing commercial security services, hardware, and investigative services to customers in the [Chicago] area. There are two companies held by [A.I.C. International]: [A.I.C. Security Investigations, Ltd.], the security guard division, and [A.I.C. Security Systems, Inc.], the security systems (hardware) division. In his position of Executive Director, [Charles Wessel] was the Chief Executive of [A.I.C.], responsible for the security guard company.

[Charles Wessel] was hired by [Victor V]. in [February 1986] and reported to [Victor V.] until his death on [June 6, 1992], and to [David P.], President of [A.I.C. International], until [David P.]'s termination on [July 6, 1992]. [Wessel] is a widely recognized leader in the security guard industry, having worked in the industry for approximately thirty years. He is licensed as a private detective and a private security contractor by the State of [Illinois] and the State of [Florida]. [Wessel] is also a member of, and has served on the Boards of, numerous professional associations within the security industry, including the Associated Detectives of [Illinois], the Associated Guard and Patrol Agencies, Inc., and the Special Agents Association. In addition, [Wessel] served as the principal drafter of the [Illinois] Licensing Act for private investigators and security guards.

In [June 1987], [Wessel] was diagnosed with lung cancer. Following surgery and recuperation, Wessel returned to work at [A.I.C.]. In [July 1991], [Wessel] suffered pneumothorax during a biopsy and went into respiratory arrest. Thereafter, [Wessel] was again diagnosed with lung cancer, this time affecting his right lung. Surgery was performed, and following a period of treatment and recuperation, [Wessel] again returned to work as Executive Director at [A.I.C.]. In [April 1992], [Wessel] was diagnosed with metastatic brain cancer. [Wessel]'s doctors consider his condition to be terminal. [Wessel] received radiation treatments. Some of the treatments were scheduled late in the afternoon. [Wessel] continued to work at [A.I.C.] throughout the course of the treatments and did not miss an entire day of work in [July 1992], although on the days when the radiation treatments were scheduled in the afternoon, he had to leave work at approximately [2:30 P.M.].

On [June 6, 1992], [Victor V.] died. After his death, [Victor V.]'s widow, [defendant C], became sole shareholder of [A.I.C. International] and [A.I.C.]. On or about [June 10, 1992], [defendant C] hired [Beverly K.] to work for [A.I.C.] On [July 29,

1992],[Beverly K.] had a meeting with [Wessel]. During that meeting, [Beverly K.] apprised [Wessel] that [defendant C] had decided that it was time for [Wessel] to retire. At that time, [Wessel] expressed his unwillingness to retire. On [July 30, 1992], [Beverly K.] advised [Wessel] by telephone that his employment at [A.I.C.] was terminated effective [July 31, 1992]. [Wessel] was paid through [July 31, 1992]. Prior to his termination from [A.I.C.], [Wessel] was never subject to any warnings relating to his performance or any disciplinary action. There is also no evidence to suggest that either [Victor V.] or [David P.], [Wessel]'s supervisors during most of the time he was employed at [A.I.C.], ever expressed any dissatisfaction with [Wessel]'s performance. Similarly, there is no evidence that any customer of [A.I.C.] ever expressed any dissatisfaction with [Wessel]'s performance of his duties throughout his tenure at [A.I.C.]. [Wessel] received a merit salary increase and a bonus in each year he was employed by [A.I.C.], except [1991], when no bonuses were given to any employees, and [1992], because he was not given a review prior to his termination.

III. Legal Analysis

A. Plaintiffs' Prima Facie Case

The initial burden on the Plaintiffs in this case is to prove by a preponderance of the evidence that [Wessel] was a qualified individual with a disability within the meaning of the Americans with Disabilities Act ("ADA") at the time of his termination. Disability under the ADA is defined as a "physical or mental impairment that substantially limits one or more of the major life activities of such individual." 42 U.S.C. § 12102(2)(A). A physical or mental impairment is defined as "a physiological disorder or condition, cosmetic disfigurement, or anatomical loss affecting one or more of several body systems . . . or any mental or psychological disorder . . ." 29 C.F.R. § 1630.2(h). Major life activities are defined as "functions such as caring for oneself, performing manual tasks, walking, seeing, hearing, speaking, breathing, learning, and working." 29 C.F.R. § 1630.2(i). The term "substantially limits" means "unable to perform a major life activity that the average person in the general population can perform or significantly restricted as to the condition, manner, or duration under which an individual can perform a particular major life activity as compared to the condition, manner, or duration under which the average person in the general population can perform that same major life activity." 29 C.F.R. § 1630.2(j). In addition, the Plaintiffs must establish that at the time of his discharge, [Wessel] was otherwise qualified for the position of Executive Director at [A.I.C.]. That is, that except for his disability, [Wessel] possesses the necessary qualifications for the position, such as the requisite educational background, experience, skills, and other job-related factors.

In this instance, undisputed evidence demonstrates that [Wessel] was a qualified individual with a disability within the meaning of the ADA as a matter of law. It is undisputed that [Wessel] has been diagnosed with terminal metastatic brain cancer. It is similarly indisputable that, as a result of his cancer, [Wessel] was limited in his ability to perform strenuous physical activity as compared with the average person in the general population. Therefore, at the time of his discharge, [Wessel] was "disabled" within the meaning of the ADA, in that he had a physiological disorder, cancer, affecting his neurological and respiratory systems, which restricted the condition, manner, or duration under which he could perform the major life activities of performing manual tasks, walking, speaking, and breathing as compared with the condition, manner, or duration under which the average person in the general population could perform the same major life activities.

The plaintiffs will also be able to establish that [Wessel] was otherwise qualified for the position of Executive Director at [A.I.C.], in that he possessed the necessary education, experience, and skills to perform his job functions. In fact, the evidence will establish that [Wessel] was a recognized leader in the security industry with approximately thirty years' experience, who is licensed as a private detective and a private security contractor in the state of [Illinois] and the State of [Florida]. Similarly, the evidence will demonstrate a long history of involvement with professional associations within the industry. Finally, the evidence will establish that [Wessel] was the principal drafter of the licensing act for private investigators and security guards in the state of [Illinois], further demonstrating that, except for his disability, [Wessel] possessed the necessary skills to perform the job of Executive Director at [A.I.C.].

The Plaintiffs will, thereafter, have to establish by a preponderance of the evidence that [Wessel] could perform the essential functions of the position of Executive Director of [A.I.C.].[18] The evidence as to what tasks comprise the essential functions of the position of Executive Director at [A.I.C.] and whether [Wessel] could perform those functions is in dispute. The Plaintiffs intend to prove that the essential functions of [Wessel]'s job were comprised of activities associated with the overall administration and operation of the guard division. Specifically, the essential functions included supervision of day-to-day security guard operations, maintenance of profitability, decision-making and problem-solving, delegation of duties and responsibilities to mid-level management, supervision of mid-level management, discipline, policymaking, and customer contact. Deposition of [Larry J. R.] (p. 35, lines 5–22 and p. 171, lines 7–14). The Plaintiffs further intend to prove that at the time of his discharge, [Wessel] was performing all of the essential functions of his job without the need for any accommodation.[19]

---

[18] Under the ADA, the definition of whether a disabled individual can perform the essential functions of the job at issue refers to a consideration of whether the individual can perform such functions with or without reasonable accommodation. However, as will be more fully discussed in the 'Undue Hardship" section of this brief, there is no need for a consideration of accommodations here. At the time of his discharge, Wessel was able to perform the essential functions of the job without accommodation. In addition, there is no evidence that Wessel ever requested any accommodation from the defendants. Consequently, there is no issue of accommodation in this case, except as it may relate to a time after Wessel's discharge, for the consideration of damages.

[19] It is also anticipated that the defendants will attempt to rely on the finding of the Social Security Administration that Wessel was entitled to Social Security Disability Benefits

Finally, Plaintiffs will have to demonstrate that [Wessel]'s disability was a motivating factor in the decision to terminate his employment. Plaintiffs are not required to prove that [Wessel]'s disability was the sole motivation or primary motivation for Defendants' decision to terminate [Wessel]. The Plaintiffs need only prove that [Wessel]'s disability played a part in the decision. The Plaintiffs do not anticipate that the nexus between [Wessel]'s disability and the termination decision will be contested. Although the Plaintiffs and Defendants disagree as to whether or not [Wessel]'s performance deteriorated in this case as a result of his cancer, the Defendants have never asserted that there was some other cause of any alleged performance deterioration other than [Wessel]'s cancer. Therefore, it does not appear that Defendants are actually challenging the causal connection between [Wessel]'s cancer and his termination, despite their assertions that [Wessel] could not perform the essential functions of his job, that his disability could not be reasonably accommodated without undue hardship, and that his continued presence constituted a direct threat to the safety of others.[20]

B.   Undue Hardship

It is anticipated that in making their argument that [Wessel] could not perform the essential functions of his job, the Defendants will attempt to rely on the undue hardship defense, arguing that reasonable accommodation of [Wessel]'s disability would have created an undue hardship. However, the undue hardship defense is not at issue in this case. The Plaintiffs will prove that [Wessel] could perform the essential functions of his job without accommodation, as that term is defined for purposes of the ADA. Therefore, there need be no lengthy consideration of accommodation and undue hardship as none was requested in this instance and, in fact, no accommodation was given or required.

---

after July 29, 1992, to support their argument that Wessel could not perform the essential functions of his job as Executive Director at A.I.C. Although the statements made by Wessel and his treating physicians in support of his application of disability benefits are admissible and can be considered along with other relevant evidence, the finding is not entitled to preclusive effect. Instead, as the Seventh Circuit noted in Overton v. Reilly, 977 F.2d 1190 (7th Cir. 1992), the finding of disability by the Social Security Administration "may be relevant evidence of the severity of [plaintiff]'s handicap, but it can hardly be construed as a judgment that [plaintiff] could not do his job. . . ." *Id.* at 1196. That conclusion is strengthened in this case, as it was in *Overton,* because Wessel was awarded disability benefits based on the finding that he met the criteria for a listed disability and was not working without the Social Security Administration's making an inquiry into the ability to find work within the national economy. *Id.* (citing Garfield v. Schweiker, 732 F.2d 605, 607 (7th Cir. 1984)).

[20] The parties disagree as to whether the plaintiffs must prove that Wessel's disability was a motivating factor or the sole factor in the termination decision. However, that issue need not be resolved for purposes of this case, because each of the defendants' stated reasons for the termination—inability to perform the essential functions of the job, undue hardship, and direct threat—unquestionably relate to Wessel's disability. That is, none of the defendants' assertions in this case challenge the causal nexus between Wessel's disability and his termination.

44444433333333

C. Direct Threat

It is also anticipated that Defendants will argue that [Wessel] did not meet job-related qualification standards consistent with [A.I.C.]'s business necessity because he posed a direct threat to the health and safety of others in the workplace. In so arguing, Plaintiffs anticipate that Defendants will assert that [Wessel] posed a direct threat to the safety of others because his medical condition prevented him from safely operating a motor vehicle. That assertion is contested by Plaintiffs, because [Wessel] was not under any driving restriction by his treating physicians. However, even if it were assumed that [Wessel]'s driving created a significant risk of imminent, substantial harm, Defendants cannot prevail on a direct threat defense. Direct threat is defined as "a significant risk of substantial harm to the health and safety of the individual or other that cannot be eliminated or reduced by reasonable accommodation. The determination that an individual poses a 'direct threat' shall be based on an individual assessment of the individual's present ability to safely perform the essential functions of the job." 29 C.F.R. § 1630.2(r).

Initially, and most significantly, Defendants' direct threat defense is without merit because Defendants cannot establish that driving was an essential function of the position of Executive Director at [A.I.C.]. Therefore, any inability to drive could not serve as the basis for asserting the defense. In order to rely on a safety requirement to screen out disabled individuals, the employer must demonstrate that the requirement, as applied to the individual, satisfies the direct threat standard under the ADA in order to show that the requirement is job-related and consistent with business necessity. 29 C.F.R. § 1630.15 and EEOC Interpretive Guidance thereto. In this instance, the Defendants cannot demonstrate that driving was an essential function of [Wessel]'s job; therefore, they cannot use any existing driving restrictions as a basis for asserting the direct threat defense in that they cannot satisfy the element of job-relatedness.

Even if Defendants were able to demonstrate that there was some driving that [Wessel] performed within the scope of his employment, Defendants cannot prevail on a direct threat defense because they never told [Wessel] not to drive. Certainly, such an order would be required before the Defendants could terminate [Wessel]'s employment. The conclusion that Defendants were required to apprise [Wessel] of their concern and to order him to stop driving (and, potentially, consider transportation accommodations for him) prior to being permitted to rely on a direct threat defense is bolstered by the ADA's requirement that an employer engage in good faith consideration of any accommodation that would have eliminated or reduced the threat before permitting reliance on the direct threat defense. 29 C.F.R. § 1630.2(r).

D. Punitive Damages

Section 1981 a of the Civil Rights Act of 1991 provides that a Plaintiff under the Americans with Disabilities Act may recover punitive damages against a Defendant if the Plaintiff demonstrates that the Defendant "engaged in a discriminatory practice or discriminatory practices with malice or with reckless indifference to the federally protected rights of an aggrieved individual." 42 U.S.C. § 1981a(b)(1). This standard is the same as that applied by courts under § 1981. *See, e.g.,* [*Rowlett v. AnheuserBusch, Inc.,* 832 F.2d 194 (1st Cir. 1987) ("reckless or callous indifference to the federally protected rights of others')]; [*Beauford v. Sisters of Mercy-Province of Detroit, Inc.,* 816 F.2d 1104 (6th Cir. 1987)]. In[*Rowlett*], the court also noted that Congress intended damage awards in civil rights actions to "be governed by the same principles as damage awards under the common law." The Supreme Court, as noted in [*Pacific Mutual Life Insurance Co. v. Haslip,* ____ U.S. ____, 111 S. Ct. 1032, 113 L. Ed. 2d 1 (1991)], has more than once approved the common law method for assessing punitive damage awards:

> It is a well-established principle of the common law. . . a jury may inflict what are called exemplary, punitive or vindictive damages upon a defendant, having in view the enormity of his offense rather than the measure of compensation to the plaintiff. . . . [I]f repeated judicial decisions for more than a century are to be received as the best exposition of what the law is, the question will not admit of argument.

[*Id.* at ____ U.S. ____, ____, 113 L. Ed. 2d 1, 14].

The legislative history for § 1981a states that:

> Compensatory and punitive damages will not give back to a plaintiff, in many cases, the career that they [sic] lost or the ability to rise further in that career. Congress doesn't have the ability to do that. It's a lasting permanent damage. I think what the increased remedies under the bill will do, however, is primarily act as a deterrent. . . . It is the deterrent value that is so important. Allowing full compensatory and punitive damages . . . would provide a stronger incentive for employers to implement effective remedies for intervention and prevention, which I think is the real goal. Data suggests that employers do indeed implement measures to interrupt and prevent employment discrimination when they perceive that there is increased liability.

[H.R. Rep. No. 400(I), 102d Cong., 1st Sess., *reprinted in* 1991 U.S.C.C.A.N. 607 (quoting testimony of [Nancy E.] and [Dr. Freada K.], respectively)].

Although the statements were made with respect to gender and race discrimination, they are equally true for disability discrimination. When Congress enacted the Americans with Disabilities Act, it stated that the purpose of the Act was to "provide a clear and comprehensive national mandate for the elimination of discrimination against individuals with disabilities" and to "provide clear, strong, consistent, enforceable standards addressing discrimination against individuals with disabilities." 42 U.S.C. § 12101 *et seq.* Thus, punitive damages are clearly available in this case.

The Supreme Court has previously discussed the "reckless disregard" standard under the Age Discrimination in Employment Act. In [*Trans World Airlines v.*

Thurston, 469 U.S. 111 (1985)], it was stated that "a violation is 'willful' if 'the employer knew or showed reckless disregard for the matter of whether its conduct was prohibited by the ADEA.' . . . We hold that this is an acceptable way to articulate a definition of 'willful.'" A similar standard is appropriate under the Americans with Disabilities Act. The Defendants showed reckless disregard for the matter or whether its conduct was prohibited by the Americans with Disabilities Act; therefore, [Wessel]'s entitlement to punitive damages should be submitted to the jury.

IV.   Conclusion

The Plaintiffs' proof will, therefore, establish that:

(1)   [Charles Wessel] had, at the time of his termination, a disability, as that term is defined in the ADA;

(2)   He was "otherwise qualified" for the position he held. This element requires proof by the Plaintiffs, by a preponderance of the evidence, that, except for [Wessel]'s disability, [Wessel] possesses the necessary qualifications for the position, such as educational background, experience, skills, and other job-related factors;

(3)   [Wessel] was capable of performing all of the essential functions of the position, either with or without a reasonable accommodation by the employer;

(4)   [Wessel]'s disability did not prevent him from performing the essential functions of the position, such that any functions he could not perform because of his disability were merely marginal functions not essential to performance of the job of Executive Director; and

(5)   [Wessel]'s disability was a motivating factor in the decision to discharge him.

§ 16.9   Defendants' Trial Brief

FORM 16–6
SAMPLE DEFENDANTS' TRIAL BRIEF

IN THE UNITED STATES DISTRICT COURT

FOR THE [NORTHERN] DISTRICT OF [ILLINOIS]

[EASTERN] DIVISION

U.S. EQUAL EMPLOYMENT OPPORTUNITY COMMISSION and [CHARLES H. WESSEL],

Plaintiffs,

v.   Civil Action No. [92 C 7330]

[A.I.C. SECURITY INVESTIGATIONS, LTD.];

[A.I.C. INTERNATIONAL, LTD.]; and [unnamed defendant C],

Defendants.   Honorable [Marvin E. Aspen]

DEFENDANTS' TRIAL BRIEF

I.   NATURE OF THE CASE

This action is brought pursuant to Title I of the Americans With Disabilities Act
(ADA). 42 U.S.C. § 12111 *et seq.* This law, as it pertains to Defendants [A.I.C.
SECURITY INVESTIGATIONS, LTD.]; [A.I.C. INTERNATIONAL, LTD].; and
[unnamed defendant C] (hereinafter jointly "[A.I.C.]" unless otherwise specified),
took effect on [July 26, 1992]. *Id.* Plaintiffs allege that Defendants unlawfully discriminated against [Charles Wessel] by discharging him on account of his disability, cancer. Defendants assert that this action is without merit because [Wessel] is
not a qualified individual with a disability and therefore he is afforded no cause of
action under ADA. Furthermore, Defendants assert that their challenged actions
were for legitimate, nondiscriminatory business reasons.

II.   FACTUAL SUMMARY

[Charles Wessel] worked as the Executive Director of [A.I.C. Security Investigations, Ltd.], the security guard division of [A.I.C. International, Ltd.], from [February
1986] to [July 1992]. [Mr. Wessel] suffered from emphysema during the entire
course of his employment with [A.I.C.] and, for five of the six-plus years he spent
at [A.I.C.], he battled cancer in various locations in his body.

In [1987], he first experienced cancer in his left lung, and he had approximately
one-third of that lung removed through surgery. For a period of time following his
surgery upon his return to work, [Wessel] was driven to and from his home and
work by an employee of [A.I.C.]. In [1991], [Wessel] experienced a recurrence of
cancer, this time in his right lung, and he had approximately one-third of that lung
removed in late [1991]. Upon his eventual return to work, [Wessel] was again
offered a driver from [A.I.C.] to get him to and from work; however, he declined.

In early [April 1992], [Wessel] was diagnosed with two inoperable brain tumors
which multiplied to four tumors in various parts of his brain by the end of [June
1992]. [Wessel] indicated to [A.I.C.] management that he had been instructed not
to drive, yet he continued to drive to, from, and during work. [Wessel] took part in
arrangements for his own replacement, interviewing candidates for his position

from outside [A.I.C.] and, on [July 22, 1992], promoted [Jan D.] from within [A.I.C.] to a position as his heir apparent.

During his last year with [A.I.C.], [Wessel] was absent from work roughly 25% of the time due to hospitalizations, convalescence, and treatments which included periods of daily radiation treatments between [April] and [July 1992]. On [July 29, 1992], [Wessel] indicated to [Beverly K.], a managerial employee of [A.I.C.] that he reported to, that he would retire immediately if the company provided him with certain severance terms which he proposed. When his terms were subsequently accepted, [Wessel] rejected the agreement, and named additional terms which would require [A.I.C.]'s disability insurance provider to pay a higher amount than [Wessel] would otherwise be entitled to under the plan.

[Wessel] was thereafter excluded from his position of Executive Director on or about [July 30, 1992]. He did not provide any medical information to [A.I.C.] when asked, nor would he or his treating physicians supply adequate information regarding his condition, including driving restrictions.

III.   LEGAL ANALYSIS

At this time, there exists little or no case law specifically regarding the ADA that may provide the Court with any guidance in the instant action. However, the ADA expressly contemplates that the voluminous precedent arising out of § 504 of the Rehabilitation Act of 1973 (29 U.S.C. § 794 *et seq.*) may serve as guidance for determinations involving the ADA. *See* 42 U.S.C. § 12117(b).

In these regards, case law under the Rehabilitation Act has loosely followed the shifting of burdens of proof enunciated in [*McDonnell Douglas Corp. v. Green*, 411 U.S. 792 (1973)], [*Texas Department of Community Affairs v. Burdine*, 450 U.S. 248 (1981)], and their progeny, although these cases are almost never referred to in Rehabilitation Act case law.[21] A prima facie case under the ADA, however, will necessarily differ from that of an action under Title VII of the Civil Rights Act due to the substantial differences in the two statutes.

The ADA proscribes in pertinent part discrimination "against a qualified individual with a disability because of the disability of such individual. . . ." 42 U.S.C. § 12112(a). A "qualified individual with a disability" is defined as "an individual

---

[21] The Equal Employment Opportunity Commission [hereinafter EEOC] Rules implementing Title I, ADA §§ 101–107, 42 U.S.C. §§ 12111–12117 (1994) [hereinafter Title I], of the ADA suggest that the *McDonnell Douglas, Burdine* analysis "may" apply to ADA cases. 29 C.F.R. § 1630.15(a). *But see* Pushkin v. Regents of Univ. of Colo., 658 F.2d 1372, 1384–85 (10th Cir. 1981) (Rehabilitation Act of 1973 (29 U.S.C. §§ 701–709, 720–724, 730–732, 740, 741, 750, 760–764, 770–776, 780–787, 790–794 (1994) [hereinafter Rehabilitation Act of 1973]) contemplates neither a disparate treatment nor a disparate impact analysis because the law, similarly to the ADA, "sets forth its own criteria for scrutinizing claims . . . "). *See also* Title VII of the Civil Rights Act of 1964, 42 U.S.C. §§ 2000e-2000e-16 (1994) [hereinafter Title VII].

with a disability who, with or without reasonable accommodation, can perform the essential functions of the employment position that such individual holds or desires." 42 U.S.C. § 12111(8).

Thus, similar to the analysis used in Rehabilitation Act cases,[22] the Plaintiff has the burden of showing:

(1)   [Charles Wessel] is an "individual with a disability";

(2)   He was "qualified" (i.e., he could perform the essential functions of his position of Executive Director for Defendants [A.I.C.]'s guard division, with or without reasonable accommodation);

(3)   He was excluded from his position solely because of his disability; and

(4)   Defendants are subject to the ADA.

See [Overton v. Reilly, 977 F.2d 1190, 1193 (7th Cir. 1992) (Rehabilitation Act Plaintiff "may not maintain an action . . . unless he is 'qualified'")]; [Carr v. Barr, 59 Empl. Prac. Dec. (CCH) para. 41,651 (ex. 1) (D.D.C. 1992) (handicapped plaintiff must initially show that he is "otherwise qualified" and excluded from position solely because of that handicap, and, if this is shown, "the burden shifts to defendants to demonstrate job-related criteria and that 'reasonable accommodation' is not feasible. if defendants meet their showing, the burden would shift once again to the plaintiff, requiring him to rebut the employer's evidence by showing that the accommodation of the handicapped imposes no undue hardship upon the defendant.")].

The first and second elements of the Plaintiffs' foregoing prima facie burden of proof are explicitly stated in the ADA. 42 U.S.C. § 12111(8).[23] The parties have a divergence of opinion as to the third element listed above, since the EEOC will argue that Plaintiffs need only demonstrate that [Mr. Wessel]'s disability was a motivating factor rather than the sole factor for his exclusion from his position.

Virtually all of the cases concerning the Rehabilitation Act have held that the Plaintiff must prove that his or her handicap was the sole basis for an exclusion from a position. See [School Board of Nassau County v. Arline, 480 U.S. 273, 275 (1987)]; [Ristoff v. United States, 839 F.2d 1242, 1244 (7th Cir. 1988)]; [Carter v. Casa Central, 849 F.2d 1048, 1053 (7th Cir. 1988)]; [Pesterfield v. TVA, 941 F.2d

---

[22] The phrase "qualified individual with a disability" from the ADA is comparable to an individual who is "otherwise qualified" under the Rehabilitation Act of 1973. See 29 C.F.R. § 1630.2(m) (1996). Both laws treat "qualified" in the identical terms of one who "with or without reasonable accommodation can perform the essential functions" of a particular position. Compare 42 U.S.C. § 12111(8) (1994), with 29 C.F.R. § 1613.702(f) (1996).

[23] There remains, however, some issues under the law concerning the identification and reasonableness of accommodations, the burdens of proof, and the determination of essential functions.

437, 441 (6th Cir. 1991)]; [*Doe v. New York University*, 666 F.2d 761, 774 (2d Cir. 1981) (adopted in *Norcross v. Sneed*, 755 F2d 113, 117–18 (8th Cir. 1985))]; [*Pushkin v. Regents of University of Colorado*, 658 F.2d 1372 (10th Cir. 1981)]; [*Treadwell v. Alexander*, 707 F.2d 473, 475 (11th Cir. 1983)].

The United States Court of Appeals for the [Eighth] Circuit articulated the underlying logic behind the necessity that handicap discrimination be shown to be the Defendants' sole motive when it stated:

> Thus both the language of the statute and its interpretation by the Supreme Court indicate that [the Rehabilitation Act] was designed to prohibit discrimination within the ambit of an employment relationship in which the employee is potentially able to do the job in question.

[*Beauford v. Father Flanagan's Boys' Home*, 831 F.2d 768, 771 (8th Cir. 1987)]. This, then, represents the key distinction between a handicap or disability and those classes (race, color, religion, sex, etc.) which are protected under Title VII— the Rehabilitation Act and ADA protect only persons who are "qualified," whereas Title VII proscribes all levels of class-based differentiation.

Accordingly, individuals who are handicapped, or, for purposes of ADA, disabled, are afforded only an equal footing to compete for jobs with others, and a plaintiff is entitled to no preferential treatment where other nondiscriminatory motives factor into the challenged action. This conclusion is supported by the congressional findings stated in § 2(q) of ADA, 42 U.S.C. § 12101(9), that "the continuing existence of unfair and unnecessary discrimination and prejudice denies people with disabilities the opportunity to compete on an equal basis and to pursue those opportunities for which our free society is justifiably famous . . . ."

In addition to the overwhelming case law under the Rehabilitation Act, another compelling reason for requiring Plaintiffs to prove that unlawful discrimination was the sole reason rather than a reason for Defendants' action, is that the ADA was excluded from recent federal legislation on this very issue.

The Civil Rights Act of 1991 (Public L. 102-166, 105 Stat. 1071) made sweeping amendments to civil rights laws, including the recently enacted ADA which, at the time, in many respects had not yet become effective. Specifically, § 107 of the 1991 Act added subsection (m) to § 703 of Title VII. Thus, 42 U.S.C. § 2000e-2 now reads at the newly added subsection (m):

> . . . an unlawful employment practice is established when the complaining party demonstrates the race, color, religion, sex, or national origin was a motivating factor for any employment practice, even though other factors also motivated the practice.

Conspicuously absent from the amendments of the Civil Rights Act of 1991 is any similar language applicable to the ADA. Clearly, Congress did not intend to interrupt the well-reasoned and thoroughly developed body of law that existed under the Rehabilitation Act which, again, Congress intended would apply in ADA actions.

The instant action may bring to the fore the issue of what burdens each of the parties should bear as to accommodation. Defendants submit that if [Charles Wessel] is determined to be totally disabled under the law, then accommodation does not become an issue. *See* [*Byrne v. Board of Education, School District of West Allis*, 741 F. Supp. 167, 169 (E.D. Wis. 1990)].

As recently as [October] of [1992], however, the [Seventh] Circuit Court of Appeals declined to allocate the burden of proof regarding reasonable accommodations under the Rehabilitation Act. [*Overton v. Reilly*, 977 F.2d 1190, 1194 (7th Cir. 1992)]. Distinguishing between §§ 501 and 504 of the Act (§ 504 being, of course, more similar to the ADA), the court held that "section 504 . . . may require the plaintiff to show that a proposed accommodation is reasonable, although the case law on this issue is, to say the least, complex" (citations omitted). [*Id.*]

Thus, the [Seventh] Circuit Court of Appeals at least has implied some duty on the part of the plaintiff to come forward with some evidence on the issue of accommodation.

The [Eleventh] Circuit Court, in [*Treadwell v. Alexander*, 707 F.2d 473, 478 (11th Cir. 1983)], was more elaborate:

> Although the plaintiff initially has the burden of coming forward with evidence to make at least a facial showing that his handicap can be accommodated, the . . . employer has the ultimate burden of persuasion in showing an inability to accommodate.

The foregoing analysis conforms to the language of the ADA, since the Plaintiff must initially show that he is "qualified," which, by its very definition, incorporates the idea of performance "with or without reasonable accommodation." 42 U.S.C. § 12111(8). It reasonably follows that the employer bears the shifting burden of demonstrating the unreasonableness of or any "undue hardship" involved with any proposed accommodations. 42 U.S.C. § 12111(10).

The express language of the ADA further supports the foregoing placements of burdens. In construing the term "discriminate," 42 U.S.C. § 12112(b)(5)(A) states that unlawful conduct under the Act could include, inter alia:

> not making reasonable accommodations to the known physical or mental limitations of an otherwise qualified individual with a disability who is an applicant or employee, unless such covered entity can demonstrate that the accommodation would impose undue hardship . . . .

The foregoing language of the ADA imposes a duty to accommodate only "known" limitations, which can only be lawfully avoided by "demonstrating" undue hardship, i.e. that the accommodation is not reasonable. The burdens of the parties are self-evident from this language.[24]

To determine the overall issue of whether Plaintiff was "qualified," this Court should adhere to the Supreme Court's holding in [*Arline*, 480 U.S. 273], that in most cases, an "individualized inquiry" must be made under the particular circumstances of this case, giving appropriate weight to the Defendants' legitimate business concerns.[*Id.* at 287].

B.   DEFENDANTS' BURDEN OF PROOF

If the Plaintiff can establish a prima facie case that he was disabled, qualified, and excluded from his former position based upon his disability, then the burden shifts to the Defendants to articulate a legitimate, nondiscriminatory reason for their challenged actions, or to rebut the prima facie showing that Plaintiff is disabled or qualified.

The ADA defines a qualified individual in terms of ability to perform the "essential functions" of the position; however, the Act provides that "consideration shall be given to the employer's judgment as to what functions of a job are essential. . . ." 42 U.S.C. § 12111(8). Thus, Defendants' burden of proof in rebuttal of Plaintiffs' prima facie case would include evidence of essential functions ignored by the Plaintiff, and that the Plaintiff could not perform. The employer's judgment must, by law, be considered in these regards.

Finally, a specific defense which applies to the instant action is provided for in the ADA, at 42 U.S.C. § 12113, if an employer "den[ies] a job or benefit to an individual with a disability" because he poses "a direct threat to the health or safety of other individuals in the workplace." The EEOC guidelines for Rules, at 29 C.F.R. § 1630.2(r), interpret this provision as follows:

> An employer may require, as a qualification standard, that an individual not pose a direct threat to the health or safety of himself/herself or others.
>
> * * *
>
> The risk can only be considered when it poses a significant risk, i.e., high probability, of substantial harm . . . .
>
> Where accommodation is not at issue, an employer may lawfully discharge an employee who poses such a "direct threat."

[*Id.*]

---

[24] Moreover, punitive and compensatory damages made available by the recent Civil Rights Act of 1991 (42 U.S.C. §§ 1981a, 2000e–2000e-17 (1994) [hereinafter Civil Rights Act of 1991]) may not be awarded unless the person with the disability "has informed the covered entity that accommodation is needed . . . ."

C.   DAMAGES RECOVERABLE UNDER ADA

Section 12117 of the ADA provides, in subsection (A), that:

> The powers, remedies, and procedures set forth in Section 705, 706, 707, 709 and 710 of the Civil Rights of 1964 (42 U.S.C. §§ 2000e-4, 2000e-5, 2000e-6, 2000e-8 and 2000e-9) shall be the powers, remedies, and procedures this title provides to the commission . . . or to any person alleging discrimination on the basis of disability in violation of any provision of this chapter, or . . . concerning employment.

Section 706(g)(1) of the Civil Rights Act, as amended in 1991, provides in pertinent part:

> If the court finds that the respondent has intentionally engaged in . . . an unlawful employment practice charged in the complaint, the court may enjoin the respondent from engaging in such unlawful employment practice, and order such affirmative action as may be appropriate, which may include, but is not limited to, reinstatement or hiring of employees, with or without back pay . . . or any other equitable relief as the court deems appropriate.
>
> *   *   *
>
> Interim earnings or amounts earnable with reasonable diligence by the person or persons discriminated against shall operate to reduce the back pay otherwise allowable.

42 U.S.C. § 2000e-5(g)(1).

Section 706(g)(2)(A) restricts the right of reinstatement and back pay with the following qualifications:

> No order of the court shall require the . . . reinstatement . . . of an individual as an employee, or the payment to him of any back pay, if such individual was suspended or discharged for any reason other than discrimination.

Subsection (B) of Section 706(g)(2) goes on to provide essentially that where the defendant demonstrates that it would have taken the same action in the absence of any impermissible motivating factor establishing by the plaintiff, the court:

> (i) may grant declaratory relief injunctive relief (except as provided in clause (ii)), and attorneys' fees and costs demonstrated to be directly attributable only to the pursuit of a claim under Section 703(m); and
>
> (ii) shall not award damages or issue an order requiring any admission, reinstatement . . . or payment described in subparagraph (A).

Finally, subsection (k) goes on to provide:

> In any action or proceeding under this subchapter, the court, in its discretion, may allow the prevailing party, other than the commission . . . a reasonable attorney's fee (including expert fees) as part of the costs, and the commission . . . shall be liable for costs the same as a private person.

42 U.S.C. § 2000e-5(k).

The Civil Rights Act of 1991 provides (at 42 U.S.C. § 1981a(a)(2)) that if a respondent is shown to have engaged in unlawful intentional discrimination (not an employment practice that is unlawful because of its disparate impact, rather, intentional disparate treatment) violative of § 102 of the ADA (42 U.S.C. § 12112), or committed a violation of § 102(B)(5) of the Act, against an individual, then the complaining party may potentially recover:

> compensatory and punitive damages as allowed in Subsection (B), in addition to any relief authorized by Section 706(G) of the Civil Rights Act of 1964, from the respondent.

Subsection (B) goes on to provide that:

> (1) Punitive Damages—to recover punitive damages, the complaining party must demonstrate "that the respondent engaged in a discriminatory practice or discriminatory practices with malice or with reckless indifference to the federally protected rights of an aggrieved individual"
>
> (2) Compensatory Damages—Compensatory damages may not include back pay, interest, or any other type of relief authorized under § 706(G) of the Civil Rights Act of 1964;
>
> (3) Limitations—[Compensatory and punitive damages are limited, in this action, under 42 U.S.C. § 1981 a(b)(3)(C) to $200,000.00 based upon the uncontested fact that only Defendant AIC Security Investigations, Ltd. employs any employees, and more than 200 but fewer than 501 in number].[25]

It is important to note, however, that no compensatory or punitive damages may be awarded in this action where Defendants demonstrate "good faith efforts," in consultation with the person with the disability who has informed the covered entity that accommodation is needed, "to identify and make a reasonable accommodation that would provide such individual with an equally effective opportunity and would not cause an undue hardship on the operation of the business." 42 U.S.C. § 1981a(a)(3). This exclusion of compensatory and punitive damages is denominated in the statute as the "reasonable accommodation and good faith effort" defense, applicable in actions "where a discriminatory practice involves the provision of a reasonable accommodation." Id. Reasonable accommodation is involved in any action where the individual with a disability invokes some reasonable accommodation in order to meet his or her burden of demonstrating that they are qualified.

Finally, Defendants submit that no claim for punitive damages is at issue because no claims for such damages have been properly joined in this action. In support of this contention, Defendants submit:

---

[25] 42 U.S.C. § 1981a(4)(c)(2) (1994) provides that "the court shall not inform the jury of the limitations described in subsection (b)(3)," but shall simply cap any verdict of the jury subsequent to its decision.

(1)   The Complaint of the EEOC is the only pleading properly joined in this action, and it seeks no remedy of punitive damages.

(2)   Although [Charles Wessel] has filed a motion to intervene as a party Plaintiff, he never filed nor served his Complaint following the Court's Order granting his motion to intervene.[26]

§ 16.10   Plaintiff's Opening Statement (Mock Trial)

FORM 16–7
SAMPLE PLAINTIFF'S OPENING STATEMENT

This case presents the story of [Steve Lyons]. [Steve Lyons] worked for Defendant [Eastern Pharmaceuticals] for over [20] years until his employment was terminated last [August.] [Steve Lyons] was a staff accountant at the time of his termination.

In the summer of [1991], [Steve Lyons] began to experience blurry vision and slurred speech. In [June] of that year, he was diagnosed as having Multiple Sclerosis ("MS"). Although diagnosed with MS, [Steve] was able to continue his work at [Eastern]. All that he needed was magnification device for his computer and someone to answer his incoming calls.

In late [July] of last year, [Steve Lyons] suffered another, more severe MS attack. After this attack, his vision and speech were worse than they had been before and he began to have some problems walking and coordinating muscle movement. [Steve] reasonably requested that the defendant provide him with the following accommodations:

(a)   a reader who would communicate written messages and computer information to him,

(b)   a speaker who would communicate oral messages from him, and

(c)   [Eastern] would have to make the office area 'handicapped friendly."

[Eastern] refused to make such reasonable accommodations and on [August 5, 1992], [Lisa Brown], [Eastern]'s Accounting Manager, fired [Steve Lyons].

The Americans with Disabilities Act ("ADA") was promulgated to protect people like [Steve Lyons] from this type of discrimination. People with disabilities have long been excluded from normal life activities. In passing the ADA, Congress estimated

---

[26] Charles Wessel's motion to intervene specifically sought leave of court for permission to file a complaint by attaching a "proposed" copy to the motion. The motion was granted in open court on December 20, 1992, yet no complaint was filed or served by Charles Wessel.

that disabled people are unemployed at a rate of approximately 66 percent. Congress found that often there was not a justifiable reason for this, as many disabled people are qualified not only to work, but also to participate in activities from which they are regularly excluded. Such is the case here. [Steve Lyons] is capable of performing essential job functions provided that [Eastern] provide him with the reasonable accommodations that he requested. They refused to do so, and terminated his employment. [Eastern] has blatantly violated the ADA.

You will hear two witnesses testify today. The first witness will be [Steve Lyons], the plaintiff. He will testify about his role as staff accountant at [Eastern Pharmaceuticals], and what transpired after his diagnosis with MS when he requested the second set of accommodations which were denied prior to his termination.

The second testimony that you will hear will come from [Dr. Willard Allen], a neurologist with expertise in the field of Multiple Sclerosis. He will testify about the plaintiff's capabilities, general symptoms, and progression of the disease.

After you have heard all of the evidence it will be clear that the defendant has violated the Americans with Disabilities Act by terminating the plaintiff's employment when they refused to make reasonable accommodations that would not have caused undue hardship.

§ 16.11   Defendant's Opening Statement
(Mock Trial)

FORM 16–8
SAMPLE DEFENDANT'S OPENING STATEMENT

Good morning ladies and gentlemen of the jury. My name is [John Black] and I represent the defendant in today's case, [Eastern Pharmaceuticals]. [Eastern Pharmaceuticals] is a drug manufacturing company which produces many drugs which allow us to live longer and better lives. [Eastern] was brought into court today by the plaintiff [Steve Lyons].

Obviously, [Mr. Lyons] suffers from physical ailments which limit his eyesight, his speech, and his motor skills. To protect disabled individuals from discrimination, the government has enacted the Americans with Disabilities Act (ADA), as opposing counsel has advised you.

It is true that [Mr. Lyons] is disabled. it is true that he was terminated from his position at [Eastern]. However, to sustain a cause of action under the ADA, the individual must also prove that he was discriminated against. [Mr. Lyons] will be unable to meet this burden. In fact, I will prove to you today through the testimony of the controller of [Eastern], [Mr. Henry Bell], that [Mr. Lyons] was terminated because of his subpar performance. His disability played no role whatsoever in his termination.

[Mr. Lyons], on the other hand, will claim that he was discriminated against because the accommodations which he sought were not provided by [Eastern]. However, [Arthur Smith], a partner at [Eastern]'s auditing firm—[Ernst & Young]—will show that it would have been an undue hardship to [Eastern] to provide these accommodations. The ADA permits an employer not to provide accommodations if doing so would cause the entity to suffer an undue hardship. In [Mr. Lyons]' case, the cost difference between providing the accommodations and keeping [Mr. Lyons] on board and hiring someone else to do his job was astronomical. Also, the nature of the pharmaceutical industry is highly dependent upon reinvesting any available funds back into the company for research and development purposes. Any cut whatsoever in these funds will have an immediate impact on both the company's short-term and long-run possibilities for developing drugs, and survival for that matter. Therefore, providing [Mr. Lyons] with the accommodations he sought would cause [Eastern] to suffer an undue hardship.

Furthermore, it will be demonstrated that even if the accommodations were provided for [Mr. Lyons], he still would not be able to perform the essential functions of his job. Therefore, even with the protection of the ADA, [Lyons] has no substantial cause of action.

In conclusion, it is true that [Mr. Lyons] suffers from a disability and that he was terminated from his job at [Eastern]; however, he was not discriminated against. If [Mr. Lyons] were not disabled, he still would have been let go. [Lyons] cannot be allowed to recover under the ADA.

§ 16.12   Testimony by Plaintiff in HIV Case

The testimony in **Form 16–9** was presented in the trial of the case of *Doe v. Kohn Nast & Graf, P.C.*[27]

FORM 16–9
SAMPLE PLAINTIFF'S TESTIMONY IN HIV CASE

BEFORE: HONORABLE [ROBERT S. GAWTHROP III], J.

JURY TRIAL—DAY 2

[JOHN DOE]—DIRECT]

Page 188

BY [MR. EPSTEIN]:

---

[27] No. 93-4510 (E.D. Pa.). This testimony was presented on the second and third days of trial in Philadelphia, Pennsylvania.

Q. Did he ever raise any other subject of any type as the reason for the nonre-newal of your contract at the end of the year?

A. No.

Q. You started to say you loved your job, you wanted to stay there. What did you resolve to do to effect that end?

A. I wanted to work for other attorneys in the firm, just do as good a job as I could on those tasks, so that I would continue to work there at that firm.

Q. Did you believe that at that time, that the statements of [Steven A.] were a final resolution of your employment at the [Kohn] firm?

A. There was no indication that that was the case, no.

Q. Why?

A. I had not received written notice and I was still under a contract. He had told me to find a job as soon as possible, but I thought I could change peo-ple's mind by working really hard.

Q. During the month of [January], did [Steven A.] do anything that made you feel uncomfortable?

A. It was starting in [December] through [January].

[JOHN DOE]—DIRECT

Page 189

He stayed his distance. Our offices were two offices apart, and he would not come by, say hello. He would not talk to me. He avoided me. One point, he wouldn't use the phone. There were no phone calls in [January]. At one point, he wanted to give me an assignment. He said, I want to assign you something, but he had his secretary type the assignment up, and had the secretary come in, lay it in my office.

I did the assignment. Gave it back to him. And then he gave his secretary a note and the secretary came and laid the note in my office. No direct contact at all.

Q. Where was your office in this suite at the [Kohn] firm in connection with [Steven A.]'s office in the [Kohn] firm?

A. [Mr. A.]s office—[Steve] would probably be at the end of that jury box. My office would be at this end of this jury box.

Q. About how much distance is there between that?

A. Twenty feet maybe.

Q. Had [Steven A.] ever, before [January] of [1993], ever given you assign-
    ments where he would actually just give it to you in writing, and hand it
    through his secretary?

                              *   *   *

[JOHN DOE]—DIRECT

Page 193

    prepared and gave to [Dianne N.] at the end of [January] of [1993]?

A. Yes, it is.

Q. Were the statements made in this memorandum truthful statements at the
    time that you made them?

A. Yes.

Q. Had you, on or about [January twenty-ninth, 1993], had any contact with
    any lawyer regarding bringing an action against the firm?

A. At this time, no.

Q. On or about [January twenty-ninth, 1993], had you taken any steps to com-
    plain about the firm's behavior toward you, to the organization that we have
    acronymed as the EEOC or the Equal Employment Opportunity Commission?

A. At this time, no.

Q. Had you complained to any state agency, and, specifically, the [Pennsylvania]
    Human Relations Commission, about any behavior or treatment of you at the
    [Kohn] firm?

A. No.

Q. Would you please read into the record this document, as it appears at para-
    graph four, starting with the word, beginning—by the way, so the record
    reflects, who's the memorandum to?

                              *   *   *

[JOHN DOE]—DIRECT

Page 222

hour and the jurors are reminded of my prior admonition. (Court was thereupon recessed at [3:35 P.M.] After the recess, the following proceedings were held commencing at [3:50 P.M.])

THE COURT: [Mr. Epstein], I'd ask that you avoid speaking directly to the jury.

[MR. EPSTEIN]: I wasn't aware that I did it and if I did it, I apologize to the Court, Your Honor.

THE COURT: Except for stipulations or summations.

(To the Clerk) Bring in the jury, please.

(The jury entered the courtroom.)

BY [MR. EPSTEIN]:

Q. During this same general time period in early [February 1993], did something occur that made you realize that [Steven A.] knew of your infection with the AIDS virus?

A. Yes.

Q. Can you please tell the jury what happened in the beginning of [February 1993] that led you to this conclusion?

[JOHN DOE]—DIRECT

Page 223

A. I had been asked to obtain a copy of a memorandum of understanding between Canada and France. It's a legal document. And I went to the file which was outside [Mr. A.]'s office and it wasn't there and I thought maybe [Mr. A.] had a copy of this document in his office where we routinely kept documents which weren't in the file.

I went into his office and I went to the back of his desk where he had the credenza table. I was looking through the documents of various pleadings that we were working on them were laying there and I came across a copy of my letter from [Dr. John B.] from [Johns Hopkins] and a copy of my policy.

Q. Did you give [Steven A.] any right to have either one of those documents?

A. No, I did not.

Q. Did you provide him with either copies or the original documents for him to copy at any time?

A. No, I did not.

Q. Had you authorized anyone to do that on your behalf?

A. No, I did not.

Q. Do you have any idea how [Steven A.] rightfully came into possession of those documents

[JOHN DOE]—DIRECT

Page 224

when you found them in his office?

A. I have no idea how [Mr. A.] obtained them.

Q. When you saw the two documents, the one regarding your disability policy and the one regarding the letter from [Dr. B.] in his office, what was your reaction?

A. I was angry and my heart dropped. I felt like: Oh my God. This is what it's all about. I know now that—Well, my fear was was reality. Even though I tried not to let anyone know that I was HIV positive, the explanation for the behavior now was clear.

Q. What did you do after you discovered these documents in his office?

A. I called the AIDS Law Project in [Pennsylvania]; I contacted the Equal Employment Opportunity Commission, the [Pennsylvania] Relations Commission and I sought legal counsel.

Q. The documents that you saw copies of, were the originals still in the office?

A. I believe the originals were still at my desk, yes.

Q. In your desk where you had originally told us they were before?

A. Yes.

[JOHN DOE]—DIRECT

Page 225

Q. Did you consider confronting [Steven A.] with this revelation that you had just made that he had documents from your desk drawer?

A. No. It was clear. No.

Q. After you talked to the AIDS Law Project, what did you do as a result of that conversation or in addition to that conversation?

A. I sought legal counsel in [Washington, D.C.].

Q. I'd like you again to turn to, and if it's not readily available to you, the document that has previously been marked as P-39. Is that in fact one of the documents which you found in [Mr. A.]'s office?

A. No, this not the document.

Q. P-40. Excuse me. I'll have to get a copy of that. Was it the letter from [Dr. B.] that you were talking about?

A. Yes.

Q. Was this the document that you found in [Mr. A.]'s office?

A. I saw a copy of that document laying on the table, yes.

Q. And this the document that's been marked as P-40?

[JOHN DOE]—DIRECT

Page 226

A. Yes.

Q. And in addition to that, did you also see a copy of the document relating to your disability insurance that the jury viewed earlier?

A. Yes. Mr. [A.] and I had been talking about the disability and a copy of that policy in his possession when it shouldn't have been.

Q. Getting back to what I asked you before, did you also take action beyond calling the AIDS Law Project?

A. I retained a lawyer to seek legal advice.

Q. Who was that lawyer?

A. It was [Deborah K.] of the firm of [Bernabei] and [Katz] in [Washington, D.C.].

Q. Will you please tell us how you came to choose a [Washington, D.C.] firm instead of a firm that was located in the [Philadelphia] area?

A. There were two reasons. I wanted this problem resolved by good attorneys and I wanted it outside of the [Philadelphia] community. I didn't want my career ruined.

Q. Why did you think having—going to a [Philadelphia] lawyer wouldn't resolve the problem?

A. [Pat P.] had told me in [January] and a couple times throughout this period that if I sued

                              *   *   *

[JOHN DOE]—DIRECT

Page 234

Honor, may I have it admitted into evidence?

    THE COURT: Without objection it is admitted?

A. It reads: "PERSONAL CONFIDENTIAL" bold and underlined.

"[Nicole M.], Esquire, [Barnabei] and [Katz], [1773 T. Street, N.W.] [Washington, D.C]. [20009].

"Dear [Ms. M.]: I am interested in retaining [Ms. Lynne B.] to representing me in an employment discrimination case. "I prepared the attached memorandum setting forth the facts of the situation and potential claims. I am a commercial litigator and not attorney adept in this field so my memorandum does not profess to include all the potential claims that may be asserted.

"I have included the relevant documents to provide you further insight. After you have an opportunity to review the materials, please contact me so that we can discuss whether your firm is interested in pursuing this matter on my behalf and to arrange for a meeting.

"Thank you for your consideration

"Very truly yours."

Q. And did you send that letter out with the

[JOHN DOE—DIRECT]

                              *   *   *

Page 255

character with you as [S.]?

A.   No, I wouldn't have said that.

Q.   Now did you send copies of the chronological history that you prepared for your lawyers just a the history not the materials but did you send a copy of the chronological materials that you sent your lawyers to anyone else?

A.   Yes, I sent a copy of the narrative telling what was going on at the firm and how they were treating me to four news sources and believe it was [ABC], [CBS], [PBS], the [Front Line] and [NBC].

Q.   [S.], why did you do that?

A.   I did it because I wanted to the expose the law firm, what they were doing.

Q.   Why?

A.   Because it was wrong.

Q.   Were you mad?

A.   I was angry, yes.

Q.   Were you angry that they were violating the law?

    [MR. SWEENEY]: Objection, Your Honor.

    THE COURT: I'll sustain that

    BY [MR. EPSTEIN]:

Q.   Did you send to any news source any documentation regarding the allegations that you

[JOHN DOE—DIRECT]

Page 256

    were making of discrimination based on your disability?

A.   Can you repeat that, please?

Q.   Did you send any documentation along with those letters to the news sources where you alleged that you were the victim of unlawful discrimination?

A.   No. I sent a cover letter, the narrative and an article about [Lynne B.] and [Deborah K.].

Q.   In the opening statements of counsel, they alleged that you offered, and in fact I think I stated this in my opening as well, that you offered to receive money for giving them your story. Is that true?

A.   No. That's incorrect. I did I think what Mr. [Mr. Sweeney] said. I asked them if they would help finance my litigation to oppose discrimination at this firm. I knew when I was at the law firm the kind of practice that they had. They would have a psychiatrist pick a jury like they did the other day; that they would have fancy computers like this.

    MR. SWEENEY: Objection.

    THE COURT: State your grounds.

    [MR. O'BRIEN]: May we see you at side bar,

* * *

JURY TRIAL–DAY 3

[JOHN DOE]—DIRECT

and this envelope until I requested the [Kohn] firm, through the course of this litigation, to produce to me all documents, all mail, that I had received which they had not provided me. And they gave me a copy of this document.

Q.   Did you ever receive a copy of this letter?

A.   I never received this envelope or the ability to respond to a job at [Cohen Shapiro], because I never received this.

Q.   Did you ever give them permission to return to sender mail that was directed to you?

A.   No. I explicitly had given them my mail address. I knew that they had my address. The knew where I was located. I expected any mail that was personal and confidential to be forwarded to me at my home.

Q.   In fact, on occasion, they did mail letters to you, did they not, so they knew where you were?

A.   Yes, they did.

Q.   After you were expelled from the [Kohn] firm, did you take any action to file your claim with any State or Federal agencies?

A.   Yes, I contacted the EEOC and the [Pennsylvania] Human Relations Commission.

Q.   On what basis did you file with these agencies,

[JOHN DOE]—DIRECT

Page ___

what was the basis of your claim, stated basis of your claim, as to why you were filing?

A.   I subsequently filed other claims, other commissions, but at the time I filed these claims, I filed a claim with the EEOC and the [PHRC]. That's what we call those commissions for short, for discrimination, on the basis of my disability, being infected with the human immunodeficiency virus.

Q.   Why did you go to these agencies? Did you go to the Federal agencies, the agency, the EEOC, the [Pennsylvania] Human Relations Commission, as opposed to just coming right into this Court? You're a lawyer?

A.   In order to allow these matters sometimes to be investigated and conciliated peacefully among the parties, those commissions have been charged by the legislators of the Federal Government, or the state government, to try to resolve the matters. And they require me to get a letter from them giving me permission to bring the action in a Court of law.

Q.   Is it a prerequisite to coming into this courtroom that you first file with both of those agencies?

MR. SWEENEY: Objection, Your Honor, leading.

[JOHN DOE]—DIRECT

THE COURT: I will sustain it.

BY MR. EPSTEIN:

Q.   What are the prerequisites to coming into this courtroom and filing a claim under either the [Pennsylvania] Human Relations Act or Title 7, or the ADA, Americans with Disabilities Act?

A.   In order for me to stop the discrimination and get my claims redressed, I have to get what is called, a right to sue letter from the [PHRA], [PHRC] and the EEOC, which will permit me to file a complaint in Court, in either the [Common Pleas] Court or the United States District Court, which brought me here.

Q. Again, I ask you, does that mean that it is a prerequisite to come into this courtroom?

A. Yes, it is what we called exhaustion of our administrative remedies.

Q. Were you aware of that when you filed with those agencies?

A. Yes, I was.

Q. Did you, in fact, receive a notice of right to sue from the EEOC?

A. Yes, I did.

Q. I'm going to show you a document that has previously been marked as one of the defendant's

[JOHN DOE]—DIRECT

pendency of litigation cannot be used against someone? Somebody can confess to a murder in the middle of trial, you can hold that against them.

[MS. O'CONNELL]: It reserves all defense claims.

THE COURT: That, if anything, is helpful to your cause, is it not there?

[MS. O'CONNELL]: Yes, sir.

THE COURT: If that is an objection, I think it is overruled.

[MS. O'CONNELL]: Thank you, sir.

(Side-bar.)

BY [MR. EPSTEIN]:

Q. Would you please read to the jury, and for the record, the statements made by [Mr. K.] that are dated here [September twenty-fourth, 1993]?

A. It reads, "Pursuant to paragraph twelve of the employment agreement, dated [September seventeenth, 1991], between you and the undersigned firm, this will confirm in writing the notice, previously given to you orally by [Mr. A.], that the agreement has not been renewed for the period subsequent to [December thirty-one, 1993].

This notice is given as a precaution only and is without prejudice to our understanding and

JOHN DOE—DIRECT

Page ___

> position that no such written notice is necessary under paragraph twelve in light of your prior acts and the fact that your employment relationship withthe firm ended in [March 1993]. Further, we expressly reserve the right to assert any and all defenses and claims against you under the agreement and otherwise."

BY [MR. EPSTEIN]:

Q.   Does this letter confirm your understanding that, in fact, [Mr. K.] had ended your employment relationship in [March 1993]?

A.   I understood this to be saying—

> [MR. SWEENEY]: Objection.

> THE COURT: Sustain that as leading.

BY [MR. EPSTEIN]:

Q.   What did you understand [Mr. K.] to be saying about that subject?

A.   I understood him to be telling me that when he threw me out—

> [MR. SWEENEY]: Objection, Your Honor.

> THE COURT: State your grounds.

> [MR. SWEENEY]: It is a conclusion.

> THE COURT: Sure it is. I think a proper one. Overruled. Proper, that is to say, under the Rules of Evidence. I comment not upon its veracity.

[JOHN DOE] –DIRECT

Page 82

> THE WITNESS: I understood him to be saying that, although I threw you out of my firm on [March] of [1993], I'm giving you this notice confirming the fact that you are not a member of this firm and your contract is not being renewed for the following year there.

> [MR. SWEENEY]: Move to strike, Your Honor.

THE COURT: Motion denied.

BY [MR. EPSTEIN]:

Q. You filed a lawsuit in this matter, did you not?

A. Yes, I did.

Q. Were you, at that time, represented by the law firm that you had hired in Washington, [Bernabei & Katz]?

A. No. Come [August] of [1993], I was no longer represented by them.

Q. Why?

A. By that time, I had exhausted my financial resources. And my parents were taking a second mortgage on their home, no longer had any money to help me, so I could not pay for my lawyers.

Q. What did you do in order to file this lawsuit, who filed it on your behalf?

A. I filed the lawsuit by myself, what we call pro

[JOHN DOE]—DIRECT

se.

Q. Did you continue in that status until [March] of [1994]?

A . Yes.

Q. And, thereafter, did you continue to be pro se even after the intervention of the EEOC?

A. Yes. In [March] of [1994], the EEOC certified this case, and the Court granted them permission to intervene. But I still did not have private counsel so I continued assisting the EEOC in prosecuting this case.

Q. In the context of this lawsuit, can you tell the jury what your claims are in brief, just what the complaint states you claim under, which acts with regard to your claim of disability discrimination?

[MR. SWEENEY]: Objection, Your Honor.

THE COURT: State your grounds.

[MR. SWEENEY]: The obligation of the Court to instruct the jury on the law not the witness.

[MR. EPSTEIN]: I'm not going to ask him what the law is, merely what the five areas of claim are before he gets off the witness stand.

THE COURT: I'm going to permit him to do that. That objection is overruled.

[JOHN DOE]—DIRECT

THE WITNESS: I filed a complaint in this United States Court alleging Federal violations of my Federal rights, and also several state common law claims.

Under the Federal laws, I'm alleging that these defendants, [Harold K.], [Steven A.], and [Kohn, Nast & Graf], violated my Federal rights under the Americans with Disabilities Act. Specifically, they discharged me on the basis that I was infected with HIV, a disability, that they retaliated against me when they found out that I was going to sue the law firm. That they coerced me, interfered and intimidated with my rights to oppose a discrimination.

[MR. SWEENEY]: Objection, Your Honor.

THE COURT: State your grounds, sir.

[MR. SWEENEY]: I think we are getting into the area that we discussed at side-bar.

BY [MR. EPSTEIN]:

Q. Can you keep it broader?

A. Okay. That I brought a claim, third claim under the ADA for intimidation, interference and coercion. That I brought a fourth claim under the Americans with Disabilities Act for improper medical inquiry.

[JOHN DOE]—DIRECT

Q. Were those same claims, and those same types of claims brought under the [Pennsylvania] Human Relations Act?

A. Yes. There are parallel claims under the [Pennsylvania] Human Relations Act.

Q. Now, in addition to those claims, did you bring any claims regarding your contract of employment?

A. Well, I had also a Federal claim under the Equal—under the insurance laws of the Federal Government for discrimination, for deprivation of my right to have disability insurance.

    And then I also—

Q. That is under what act, sir?

A. We call it the ERISA Act, the employment Retirement Insurance Act.

Q. And?

A. Employer.

Q. Security Act?

A. Security Act, thank you.

Q. Now, in addition to that, were there claims brought, pursuant to the terms of that contract, for the years nineteen,—the balance of the year of [1993], and the entire year of [1994]?

A. Yes, sir.

Q. How about the other common law claims, what are

[JOHN DOE]—DIRECT

    they, what other two claims do you have?

A. The present claims that I understand are pending before this Court—I don't want to misstate this.

Q. I don't want you to go into deeply. What two category of claim?

A. I believe I have a defamation claim and I have invasion of privacy claim.

Q. With regard to the defamation, as you were leaving the offices, you saw the reaction of the individuals who were watching you leave, did you not?

A. Yes.

Q. What was your—what was your belief, based upon their reaction to your leaving under those circumstances?

[MR. SWEENEY]: Objection, Your Honor.

THE COURT: State your grounds.

[MR. SWEENEY]: No foundation.

THE COURT: What foundation do you want? Do you want him to articulate, verbalize what their reactions were, sir?

[MR. SWEENEY]: No, sir, the basis for him having an understanding of what was inside someone else's mind.

§ 16.13 Transcript of Plaintiff Testimony

The following testimony from *Stone v. Entergy Services, Inc.*,[28] albeit taken at a deposition rather than at trial, is a good example of the direct examination of an ADA plaintiff. This case involved a plaintiff who suffered from such post-polio residuals as "muscle weakness, partial paralysis, one leg [being] longer than the other and one foot [being] longer than the other."[29] This testimony occurred when the plaintiff was asked about his present limitations.

A: I have limited endurance. If I'm climbing stairs, I have to stop after about two flights and rest. I'm unable to run, which means there are a number of sports that I can't participate in. I have limited motion in my body. When I go to bend over, I try to make sure that I either bend from the knees or support myself by holding on to a window sill, piece of furniture, something like that. If I'm walking in a group, if the group does not pace itself to me, I am left far behind. Certain activities I know I'm limited, so I try not to put myself in a position where balance would be a particular problem. Walking down stairs, my right foot won't really support me. I can't lift my right heel off the ground, so in handling stairs, I have to be careful to put my whole foot on the stair when I'm going up; otherwise I've got a problem.

Q: We talked about your limited endurance, you get winded after about two flights of stairs. You have trouble handling stairs in general because of your right foot?

A: That's correct.

Q: You have limited body motion which results in your needing to bend from the knees or have a support?

A: Yes.

---

[28] Civ. A. No. 94-2669, 1995 WL 368473 at *4 (E.D. La. June 20, 1995) ("Although plaintiff cannot walk briskly, and has some trouble climbing stairs," plaintiff's "ability to walk is not substantially limited nor significantly restricted . . . .").

[29] *Id.* at *3.

Q: And you need to pace yourself slower than the average person when you're walking?

A: Significantly.

Q: And you do have some trouble with balance?

A: Occasionally.

Q: Not all the time?

A: Not all the time.

Q: Other than these problems, is there any other way you differ from the average person because of your polio residuals?

A: I already told you I can't do a situp. That's about it.[30]

Commentary. Despite the presence of such limitations, the *Stone* court concluded that plaintiff did "not have a physical impairment that substantially limits a major life activity."[31]

§ 16.14   Transcript of Testimony (Mock Trial)

Q. Plaintiff calls [Steve Lyons]. Please state your name, address, and occupation for the court.

A. My name is [Steve Lyons] and I was a staff accountant at [Eastern] until I was fired on [August 5, 1992]. My address is [2222 22d Street], [Lower Merion], [Pennsylvania] [22222].

Q. Are you currently employed?

A. No, I am not.

Q. What is your educational background?

A. I have a economics degree from [Georgetown University], and I received my CPA before I started with [Eastern] on [July 7, 1972].

Q. When were you first diagnosed with Multiple Sclerosis?

A. Around [June 20th] I had problems with blurry vision and slurred speech and at that time I went and talked with my normal physician, who referred me to [Dr. Allen], a neurologist. [Dr. Allen], on [June 26th], was the first to diagnose that I had Multiple Sclerosis.

Q. Excuse me. [June 26th] of which year was this?

A. [1991].

Q. Has MS affected any of your major life activities? By major life activities I mean functions which you perform every day?

A. Yes, MS has substantially limited my ability to read, speak, and walk.

Q. Thank you. When were you first hired by [Eastern]?

A. I was hired as an accounting clerk on [July 7, 1972], and since that time I had received several promotions and on [July 11, 1989], I was promoted to staff accountant and since then I have been working [20] years for the company as a loyal employee.

---

[30] *Id.* (emphasis added) (citation omitted).

[31] Stone v. Entergy Servs., Inc., Civ. A. No. 94-2669, 1995 WL 368473 at *4 (E.D. La. June 20, 1995).

Q. What were your essential job functions as staff accountants?

A. My essential job functions as a staff accountant included producing financial reports using spreadsheet applications and computers, operating an adding machine to perform various mathematical functions and maintaining the general ledger and communicating the results with outside vendors and [Eastern]'s purchasing agents regarding the fixed asset acquisitions.

Q. What initial accommodations were made to deal with your blurry vision and slurred speech?

A. Initially, when I noticed the blurry vision and slurred speech, I approached [Ms. Lisa Brown], the Accounting Manager, and at that time my vision was not as bad as it is today and they were able to accommodate me by giving me a magnifying glass so that I could read the computer screen and other papers.

Q. What accommodation, if any, did they make to deal with your slurred speech?

A. For my slurred speech, all my incoming calls was rerouted to another employee to answer my calls.

Q. Who did you say [Lisa Brown] was?

A. She was [Eastern]'s Accounting Manager and my supervisor.

Q. Was she your supervisor during your whole time at [Eastern] or just during the time you were staff accountant?

A. During the period that I was staff accountant.

Q. When did you inform her that you suffer from MS?

A. I initially informed her after I received my diagnosis on [June 26, 1991]. After I had informed her of my MS, she made the necessary accommodations for me soon afterwards.

Q. Prior to your diagnosis with MS, had you ever received any unfavorable job evaluations?

A. No, I had not. I had always received satisfactory or above-average job performance.

Q. What was your most recent job evaluation?

A. My most recent job evaluation, which was in [1991], was that my work was satisfactory.[32]

Q. Was this prior to or after your diagnosis?

A. Prior to my most recent attack of MS.

Q. OK, but subsequent to the initial diagnosis?

A. That's correct.

Q. In [July of 1992], you suffered another MS attack?

A. Yes, I did. With this attack, my eyesight and speech deteriorated further and I had difficulty with walking and coordination of muscle movements at that time. At that time I approached [Ms. Brown] to request further accommodations, which included having a reader communicate written messages and computer information to me, having a speaker communicate oral messages from me, and having the office area of [Eastern]'s facility made "handicapped friendly." At that time, [Ms. Brown] informed me that the accommodations

---

[32] The witness's answer regarding the contents of the job evaluation is hearsay.

were unreasonable and would create undue financial hardship for [Eastern]. Soon thereafter she fired me from my job.

Q. Do you believe that you can perform the essential job functions of staff accountant if you were provided with the reasonable accommodations that you requested?

A. Yes, I believe I can. As an accountant, I believe that most of my functions relate to the mental abilities and the MS has not affected any of my mental faculties, just my vision and speech.

Q. Did [Ms. Brown] give you any indication aside from the undue financial burden as to the reason for the company terminating your employment?

A. She mentioned that I can no longer perform my essential job functions and she also suggested that there were other healthy individuals who could perform the job without the changes I have requested.

Q. As far as you know, are there any other people working for [Eastern] who suffer from Multiple Sclerosis?

A. No one else that I know of. No.

Q. Nothing further.

Cross-Examination of Plaintiff

Q. I just have a couple questions for you, [Mr. Lyons]. Do you have an employment contract with [Eastern Pharmaceuticals]?

A. No, I don't.

Q. So is it fair to say that you are an employee at will?

A. Yes, but I was given . . . .

Q. Thank you. It is "yes" or "no." OK. You said that your last evaluation was in [1991]. When exactly in [1991]?

A. Yes, that is correct. It was toward the end of the year, so it was around [December 31st]. That is when [Eastern] provides all its employees with employee evaluations.

Q. So it was a full eight months between the time of your last evaluation and the time you were terminated?

A. That is correct.

Q. Since your termination from [Eastern] have you gotten another job?

A. No, I have not.

Q. Have you looked for another job?

A. Yes, I have. [33]

Q. What is happening when you look for jobs?

A. Most people I assume look at my disability and have assumed that I cannot perform the functions without the accommodations necessary and have determined that it would be an undue hardship for them. [34]

Q. They told you this, that it would be an undue hardship?

A. No, they haven't.

---

[33] Counsel would have been better advised not to ask the question that produced this answer.

[34] These answers are more helpful to defense counsel.

Q. You just have that impression?

A. That's correct. When I first go and meet with the potential employers and they first learn that I can't speak, that my speech is slurred, they react differently than if I could speak normally.

Q. Do you bring lawsuits against them for not hiring you?

A. No, I haven't.

Q. Isn't it true that at the time of your firing you were engaging in the illegal use of drugs?

A. No, that is not true.

Q. No further questions.

Re-Direct

Q. Did you receive any indication after your review in [December] of [1991] and prior to your termination in [August] of [1992] that either [Eastern] or [Ms. Brown] felt that your performance was subpar or that they were unhappy with anything that you were doing?

A. No. I had not gotten that impression or a verbal communication saying that to me.

Q. When did you get the impression that they were dissatisfied with your work?

A. The first indication that they felt my performance was subpar was with the actual termination.

Q. Thank you. Nothing further.

By the Court

Q. In what way did you communicate your request for accommodation just before you were terminated?

A. In what way? I verbally requested to [Ms. Brown] that the following accommodations that I mentioned earlier be made available to me: a reader, a speaker, and making it "handicapped friendly."

Q. So you didn't request this in writing?

A. No, I didn't.

Plaintiff Calls [Dr. Willard Allen]

Q. Please state your name, address, and occupation for the court.

A. My name is [Dr. Willard Allen], [3333 3d Boulevard], [Upper Merion], [PA] [33333]. I am Chief of Neurology at [Jefferson Hospital], where I have been the Chief of Neurology for five years.

Q. How long have you been a neurologist?

A. I have been a neurologist for 15 years. I graduated with a [B.S.] degree in [Biology] from the University of [Pennsylvania] and I received my medical degree from [Harvard University] Medical School. Afterwards, I was a resident at the [Massachusetts General Hospital], where I also did a fellowship in neurology.

Q. Are you licensed to practice medicine in this state?

A. Yes, I am licensed to practice medicine in [Pennsylvania], [New York], [Maryland], [New Jersey], and [Massachusetts].

Q. Have you had much contact with MS patients?

A. Yes, I have. As I stated previously, my area of specialization is neurology, and I have done extensive research on MS, and have also published many materials regarding MS, including articles on the effects of MS on patients and society's negative reaction to the disease.

Q. Have you been involved in any clinical studies of MS patients?

A. Yes. And in my published materials I used results of clinical studies that I have done on MS patients.

Q. What are the effects and common symptoms of MS?

A. MS is a chronic degenerative disease of the central nervous system in which gradual destruction of the myelin occurs throughout the brain or the spinal cord or both. Basically, myelin is a sheath that surrounds a nerve fiber that facilitates the transmission of nerve impulses. MS basically interferes with the transmission and causes muscular weakness, loss of coordination, and speech and visual disturbances. Now that doesn't mean a patient who suffers from MS has all of these symptoms, for there can be variations and some people might suffer from one or the other and the symptoms can be more severe to less severe.

And generally, MS attacks occur, remit, and then recur. The studies show it seems to happen randomly and there is no pattern that develops on how these attacks occur. Basically, the flare-ups are greatest during the first three to four years of the disease, but afterwards another attack might not happen for the next 10 to 20 years. And during typical episodes the symptoms worsen over a period of a few days to a few weeks and then remit. During the remission period, the recovery is usually rapid over a period of weeks, although at times it may extend over several months and, again, the extent of the recovery varies from person to person and the remission may be complete or it might be partial.

Q. Do you know the plaintiff in this case?

A. Yes, I do. He has been a patient of mine since [June 1991], when I diagnosed him with MS.[35]

Q. Did you know the plaintiff prior to this diagnosis?

A. No, I did not.

Q. What were the results of your initial examination of the plaintiff?

A. The initial examination showed that the plaintiff suffered a mild MS attack in which he had slurred speech and blurry vision and afterwards it remitted. He was able basically to recover all of his functionality except for a slight vision problem.

Q. Doctor, is there a known cause for MS?

---

[35] It is more common to present a medical expert who is not the treating physician, both to protect doctor-patient privilege and to avoid any inference of bias in favor of the plaintiff by the physician. There is no reason, however, why the treating physician cannot be the only expert, if the physician qualifies as an expert.

A.   At this time there is no cause for it. We are currently in the research area trying to determine the actual cause of it.

Q.   OK. Is there a known cure for MS?

A.   No. There is no actual cure for MS. There have been certain drugs that we can give to try to make the attacks less frequent, but at this time there is no effective cure for it.

Q.   On average, how long does a typical MS patient live with the disease?

A.   The patient lives approximately 30 years after the onset of the disease, it being the rare case where a patient may die within a few years.

Q.   I believe you said before that it is possible that MS will remit and then recur randomly over the course of many years?

A.   That is correct.

Q.   So can one say with any scientific accuracy that the plaintiff's condition will only deteriorate with no hope of remission ?[36]

A.   No. I think it is the exact opposite. Scientific experience has shown that after an attack, the majority of the patients would become better before having another attack which would worsen their condition.

Q.   In your expert opinion Doctor, do you believe that if the plaintiff is provided with the accommodations that he requested, he can perform the essential job functions of staff accountant?

A.   Yes, he could. Again, MS basically is a disease that causes muscular weakness loss of coordination, and speech and visual disturbances. It has nothing to do with impairment of mental capacity.

Q.   Doctor, the plaintiff testified that his essential job functions as staff accountant were as follows: producing financial reports through spreadsheet applications, operating an adding machine to perform various mathematical functions, maintaining the general ledger, and communicating with outside vendors and [Eastern]'s purchasing agents regarding fixed asset acquisitions. Assuming that those are his essential job functions, do you believe that the plaintiff, if provided with the accommodations that he requested, can perform those functions as staff accountant?

A.   Yes. In my medical opinion, I believe that he can perform the essential job functions because, again, the disease only causes the muscular weaknesses, loss of coordination, and speech and visual disturbances. It does not affect his mental abilities which I deem as the essential function of the staff accountant position.

Q.   Thank you. Nothing further.

By the Court

Q.   Before you start, Counsel, do you stipulate to his qualifications as an expert?

A.   Yes.

---

[36] The question is leading, but did no harm because of the answer.

By Defense Counsel

Q. Is [Mr. Lyons] still a patient of yours, [Dr. Allen]?
A. Yes, he is.
Q. So, in other words, you have a financial stake in having him continue to be a patient of yours which is directly correlated with his employment and benefits?
A. No. That is not really true because even if he was not employed by [Eastern], he is still a patient. If he can't pay by [Eastern]'s medical coverage, then the government will pay by disability insurance.
Q. You said that the plaintiff could perform the essential job functions because they all just required no physical abilities, right?
A. Yes.
Q. But the functions, computer work and operating the adding machine require some degree of manual dexterity, don't they?
A. I suppose so.
Q. Doctor, what are the criteria for coverage by Social Security disability?
A. I have no idea.
Q. Nothing further.

By the Court

Q. Any redirect?
A. No.

Commentary.   At this point, Defense moved for a judgment as a matter of law as no reasonable jury could find for the plaintiff on its claim of discrimination in violation of the ADA. The motion was denied.

DEFENDANT'S CASE-IN-CHIEF

By Defense Counsel

Defense Calls [Henry Bell]

Q. Please state your name and address for the record.
A. My name is [Henry Bell], [4444 44th Street], [Lower Radnor], [Pennsylvania] [44444].
Q. What is your position?
A. I am controller of [Eastern Pharmaceuticals].
Q. Please tell us about your background and qualifications.
A. I am 37 years old and I graduated from [Villanova] with a Bachelor's Degree in Accountancy in [May 1977]. I obtained my CPA certificate in [1979]. Right out of school I worked eight years with [Deloitte Haskins & Sells], an independent public accounting firm. Following those eight years, I obtained a

position with [Eastern] in their accounting department. I served as controller for the last four years.

Q. You said you graduated from [Villanova] in [1977] and you obtained your CPA certificate in [1979]. How come there is a two-year delay?

A. There is a two-year practice requirement. You have to pass the exam and then practice as an independent public accountant for two years before you can obtain your certificate.

Q. So that is as soon as you could be qualified, two years later?

A. Yes.

Q. To the best of your knowledge, how many people work at [Eastern]?

A. [Eastern] employs approximately 300 people.

Q. Please tell us about some of the products which [Eastern] produces.

A. Major products manufactured by [Eastern] include drugs which minimize the risk of infection during organ transplant operations, such as [Governor C.]'s recent operation. We are also on the cutting edge of AIDS research and we have a product on the market that helps prevent the risk of skin cancer.

Q. How many people use these drugs?

A. These are drugs which help many people every day.

Q. Do you supervise anyone?

A. Yes.

Q. What supervising roles do you perform as controller?

A. I have overall responsibility for the accounting department, including the staff accountants.

Q. Could you please describe the essential functions of the staff accountant at [Eastern]?

A. The essential job functions of the staff accountant include producing financial reports through spreadsheet applications, operating an adding machine to perform various mathematical functions, maintaining a computerized general ledger system, communicating with outside vendors and [Eastern] purchasing agents concerning fixed asset acquisitions.

Q. Could [Mr. Lyons] perform these essential functions when he was terminated?

A. No.

Q. Why not?

A. We have had various problems with [Mr. Lyons], including the fact that he is unable to keep up with the hectic pace of [Eastern]'s demanding financial reporting schedule. We issue financial reports at the end of every month and for regulatory agencies at the end of every fiscal quarter and at the end of the financial year. The accounting department operates in a real nonflexible deadline-oriented atmosphere with minimal room for error. [Mr. Lyons] is not able to produce these required reports in a timely manner.

Q. In addition to the essential job functions you discussed earlier, are there any continuing education requirements which the staff accountant at [Eastern] is required to maintain?

A. To maintain his certification as a CPA in [Pennsylvania] he needs a minimum amount of continuing education each year and basically this, involves keeping abreast of current financial reporting literature and also any tax requirements as they relate to his job calculating depreciation of fixed assets and things of that nature. So yes, there are various continuing education requirements.

Q. Did you have occasion to talk to [Mr. Lyons] about his compliance with the continuing education requirements?

A. Yes, I did.

Q. And what, if anything, did he say about his compliance with the continuing education requirements ?[37]

A. [Mr. Lyons] told me that he had not been keeping up with his continuing education requirements.

Q. If the accommodations which [Mr. Lyons] requested were met by [Eastern], would this enable him to perform his essential job function?[38]

A. If he was provided with the accommodations, no, he couldn't perform the essential job functions.

Q. What effect would an intermediary between [Lyons] and his computer and his adding machine have on his performance?

A. Although in most instances two heads are better than one, I think accounting is unique in that aspect because any time you insert more people into a process the risk of error is greater as far as transposing a number or miscommunicating, and we are in a position where we can't afford to have any type of clerical errors in our financial data.

Q. Is it your practice to give employees who have performance difficulties warnings before you fire them for those performance difficulties?

A. Warnings, not in the sense of necessarily written evaluations because our written evaluation process is done annually, but verbally as projects are turned in and we find errors.

Q. Was that done in [Mr. Lyons]' case?

A. Yes.

Q. Why was [Lyons] terminated from his position as staff accountant at [Eastern]?

A. [Mr. Lyons] was terminated because he could not adequately perform his essential job functions. His work was illegible, we had caught some errors in his work, it was not completed in a timely manner and we were getting some complaints from outside vendors.

Q. Did [Mr. Lyons]' termination have anything to do with the fact that he was disabled?

A. No.

Q. Since [Mr. Lyons]' termination has he ever sought a recommendation letter from you to help him with his job search?

A. No. He has never asked for a recommendation.

Q. Is it common for ex-employees to ask you for a recommendation letter?

A. Yes.

---

[37] This is hearsay, but it is admissible under an exception to the Hearsay Rule because it is an admission by a party opponent.

[38] This calls for a speculative answer by the witness. However, because this witness is the supervisor and is responsible for establishing or not establishing or, at least, policing compliance with the various job requirements, it is probably within the knowledge of this witness to answer the question, and, therefore, should be allowed.

Q. Wouldn't it make it much more difficult for someone to get a job without a letter of recommendation from its former employer?[39]

A. I would think so.

Cross-Examination by Plaintiff Counsel

Q. Have you ever allowed any of your accountants of [Mr. Lyons]' level to use support personnel to assist them in using their computers or adding machines?

A. Yes.

Q. Doesn't that raise the same risk of error?

A. No, because you have [Mr. Lyons] in a review function then and nothing is . . . [Mr. Lyons] is at a level where he would be the last review of financial data for the area that he covers. So anybody who did work for him, he would review for accuracy.

Q. So your testimony is that the people that you have allowed to use support personnel in conjunction with their computer and adding machine functions have been in jobs different from [Mr. Lyons]?

A. Yes.

Q. And there is something special about [Mr. Lyons]' position in which the introduction of such a support person would increase the risk of error-more than use of a support person at other levels?[40]

A. Yes, this is true.

Q. Do you have any reason to question Dr. Allen's diagnosis of the plaintiff's condition?

A. No.

Q. Do you suspect then that possibly the illegible writing problem may be tied into the MS symptoms rather than just his incompetency or whatever it is that you said caused this?

A. I have no medical background or basis to make that determination.

Q. Regarding the accommodations that he requested, you commented that he is in a special position so that having two heads will not be better than one. Isn't it possible that [Lyons] could check for accuracy the work of his accommodator so that it really would be his work, he would just be directing him or her in the various functions of operating the computer or the adding machine so that it would be the same result as if he did it himself; he just wouldn't be doing the actual typing?

A. I would say that yes, he could check the accuracy, but the problem comes in with meeting the deadlines and I don't think he could perform the job on a timely basis.

Q. How direct is your supervision on [Mr. Lyons]?

A. I am not the direct supervisor of [Mr. Lyons]—there is an intermediary between [Mr. Lyons] and myself.

---

[39] This question may be subject to objection as calling for speculation.

[40] It would have been better not to ask this question, because it gives the witness an opportunity to explain an otherwise obscure and possibly illogical position.

Q. Aside from what [Ms. Brown] has told you, do you first-hand know anything about [Mr. Lyons] and his employment problems over the past year or year and a half?

A. Yes, I do, because as I indicated, nobody reviews [Mr. Lyons]' work. It would come directly to me as controller.

Q. Isn't it true that his last review a year ago was nothing but favorable, or was at least satisfactory—there was no indication that he had subpar performance?

A. This is true.

Q. Switching the scope a little bit: Does [Eastern] have wheelchair access ramps, wheelchair bathrooms, or anything?

A. No.

Q. Do you realize that that may not be in compliance with the laws as they stand today?

A. I am not legal counsel.

Q. Are you aware of any continuing education accommodations that are made for people with disabilities? Obviously, if someone has trouble getting around, I would suspect that there may be some accommodations that can be made in terms of the continuing education?

A. I am not aware.

Q. But you have no reason to doubt that it is possible that there could be such an accommodation?

A. It is possible.

Q. So you testified that your company employs approximately 300 people?

A. Yes.

Q. So it is probable that there is someone or some two people at the company who have enough free time on their hands so that it wouldn't be that the company would have to hire someone to do the accommodations requested by [Mr. Lyons], there could just be some shifting around of job functions and possibly someone could move in to do that on a part-time basis and continue to do his or her other job when the accommodations are not needed.

A. I don't believe that is true. I think we are a pretty streamlined operation and everybody works eight full hours a day. So I would say no.

Q. Including the people who answer the telephones? They never have any free time as far as you know?

A. No.

Q. You mentioned that [Mr. Lyons] was the staff accountant. He was in the position of last review work of the accounting information?

A. Yes.

Q. Does that not mean that you would have to have trust and faith in his abilities such that he is the last reviewer?

A. Yes.

Q. You testified, sir, that it would take too long if you made the accommodations that [Mr. Lyons] requested, is that what you said?

A. Yes.

Q. Did you try it out? Did you try out his accommodations to see how long it would take?

A. No, we did not.

Q. You didn't conduct any experiments to see.

A. No.

Q. Do you do all your own typing?

A. No, I do not.

Q. Do you do all your own data entry on the computer?

A. I do not have in my position . . . I don't have much data entry from a pure clerical standpoint.

Q. When you get reports and documents from your subordinates—you do get such things?

A. Yes.

Q. Do you check the addition and the other arithmetic on all of those you saw personally?

A. No.

Q. So it is possible that by delegating these functions to these support personnel, that some errors could be introduced? Isn't that true? Isn't it possible?

A. It is possible, yes.

Q. But you have concluded that it is tolerable. That possibility of error is tolerable.

A. Well, it is being performed from me and it's coming back to me. Yes.

Q. Did you or anyone at [Eastern] consider possibly moving [Mr. Lyons] to another position maybe that has lesser responsibility, possibly going back to as he was as a clerk? Something so that the fact that he moves more slowly than he used to wouldn't be a problem if he had fewer things to do?

A. He never asked that.

Q. You never thought about doing that either?

A. No.

Q. OK. Nothing further. Any re-direct?

By Defense Counsel

Q. Yes. Have you noticed a change in [Mr. Lyons]' performance between the time of his most recent evaluation eight months prior to his termination and the date of his termination?

A. Yes, a marked decrease.

Q. Are there generally spare days each month and each quarter between the date a report is completed and the due date of that report?

A. No.

Q. So what effect would an additional step in the report-generating process have?[41]

A. We would probably have a more difficult time meeting our inflexible due dates and probably miss a couple of them.

Q. Nothing further.

---

[41] This question might be considered speculative.

Defense Calls [Arthur Smith] as an Expert Witness

Q. Please state your name for the record.

A. My name is [Arthur Smith].

Q. Please tell us about your background and qualifications, [Mr. Smith].

A. I am 45 years old. I have a Bachelor's Degree in Accountancy from [Lehigh University]. I obtained that in [May] of [1970]. I also have an MBA with concentrations in Finance and Accounting from [Wharton School of Business] at [Penn]. I obtained that in [May 1980]. I have been a CPA since [1972]. I have worked at [Ernst & Young International Accounting Tax & Consulting Firm] for 23 years, the last 12 as a partner. I specialize in manufacturing with a concentration in the pharmaceutical industry.

Q. What is your relationship with [Eastern]?

A. [Ernst & Young] has audited [Eastern] for the past 15 years and I have been the partner in charge of the audits for the past six years.

Q. Were you here when [Mr. Lyons] testified?

A. Yes.

Q. In your opinion as an expert, what would it cost in dollars for [Eastern] to meet these accommodations that [Lyons] has requested ?[42]

A. About [$64,000] per year.

Q. How does that break down?

A. Well, the cost of employing [Lyons] was [$54,000] per year. He makes [$45,000] in salary and there is an extra [$9,000] in benefits that [Eastern] pays for him. The approximate cost of a reader or an intermediary to do his work would be [$25,000] per year. The cost of making the building handicapped friendly is [$250,000]. Depreciated over ten years, this turns into an expense of [$25,000] a year. It is also important to remember the cash flow impact of that [$250,000].

On the other hand, the cost of replacing [Lyons] is [$40,000] per year, [$33,000] in salary and [$7,000] in benefits, so when you add and subtract all those factors, [Eastern]'s annual incremental cost of accommodating [Lyons] would be [$64,000] per year.

Q. Is there any other possible expenses connected with this?

A. Yes. One other possible expense is an increase in [Eastern]'s audit fees because of the increased audit risk resulting from having an intermediary help [Lyons] with his work.

Q. You testified earlier that you and your firm have audited [Eastern]'s financial statements for the past number of years. Over the past five years, what has [Eastern]'s net income averaged?

A. Approximately [$500,000] per year.

---

[42] The Federal Rules of Evidence 703 and 705 permit an expert to testify as to the expert's conclusion without laying the factual foundation that leads to the conclusion, so this question and the anticipated answer is permissible. But if the expert should be asked on cross-examination to disclose the facts on which he bases his conclusion, Federal Rule of Evidence 705 requires that the expert disclose those facts.

Q. What would be the effect on net income of providing the accommodations for [Lyons]?

A. As I said earlier, net income would decline by [$64,000], which is more than a 10 percent decrease.

Q. What difference does it make if net income goes down?

A. Funds available for research and development purposes vary directly with net income. Therefore, when net income decreases, so do the funds for research and development purposes. Research and development is crucial to a pharmaceutical company's success and survival.

[Eastern] never even pays dividends because it reinvests all of its net income into research and development to maintain its market share. Again, they really have no alternative from this strategy if they wish to maintain their position and actually survive as a pharmaceutical company.

Q. So what effect would a decrease in net income of [$64,000] a year have?

A. That would have a direct dollar-for-dollar impact on [Eastern]'s budgeted research and development and would be a threat on the continuing existence of the company. A [$64,000] decrease in net income reduces funds available for research and development purposes by the sum of [$64,000].

Q. In your opinion, would you consider this to be an undue hardship to [Eastern]?

A. Certainly. It would threaten their continuing existence.

Q. Has [Lyons] ever asked you for a reference letter or to work at your firm?

A. No.

Q. What is the practice of employees at firms which you audit regarding recommendation letters?

Q. It is often typical that employees of entities that we audit ask for recommendation letters from our firm concerning their performance and even inquire about jobs working for us.

A. [Mr. Lyons] did not do this?

Q. No, he did not.

Cross-Examination

Q. You testified previously that the reasonable accommodations requested by [Mr. Lyons] were in your mind unreasonable. What accommodations do you recollect [Mr. Lyons] requesting?

A. [Mr. Lyons] requested that [Eastern] make the building handicap accessible. That [Eastern] make the building handicap accessible and also that [Eastern] provide him with an intermediary who could do reading for him and also communicate to other parties for him.

Q. You also testified that a replacement could be brought in for [Mr. Lyons] for [$40,000]?

A. Yes.

Q. Isn't it possible that once people achieve a certain status of seniority, they can always be replaced with cheaper and younger help, so it is just a fact that you can bring in someone for a smaller salary? Isn't it possible that that person also lacks the expertise that [Mr. Lyons] acquired over the years working at [Eastern]?

A.   It is possible that [Lyons] has familiarity with the organization that is of some benefit but it would not take any significant amount of time for a replacement familiar with the industry to overcome that capability of [Mr. Lyons].

Q.   You testified that it is possible that [Eastern] would suffer an increase in audit fees because of the presence of [Mr. Lyons] in the accounting department. It seems unlikely that many large companies in this country do not have handicapped people working in their accounting departments. I can't imagine from a policy standpoint that your firm can get away with charging people more money because they are accommodating people with disabilities by offering them employment.

A.   Our audits are risk-based audits so when there is ever an increased audit risk, no matter how that risk gets there, it is going to take us more time to do our job effectively and we can certainly justify increasing audit fees.

Q.   Suppose that there is a handicapped person working in the manufacturing plant at [Eastern] as opposed to the accounting department, so the risk is in the manufacturing of the drugs and possible lawsuits and products liability and things of that sort. How do you handle that in your audit? Do you look purely at the numbers and who is putting the numbers together for you? Are you looking at a whole picture of the company?

A.   We do look at a whole picture of the company. That wouldn't necessarily require more audit effort but it would just result in us increasing a reserve for lawsuits.

Q.   You also testified that you believe that the reasonable accommodation would cause an undue hardship based on the comparison to the net income of the company?

A.   Yes.

Q.   If you use profit at the bottom line for everything, it is conceivable that you can have a company with a billion dollars in revenue that is turning no profits. Would you say that for them to spend an extra $50,000 would also be an undue hardship?

A.   I would have to be more familiar with that, it is possible.[43]

*   *   *

A.   I think in this industry it is all driven with cash flow.

Q.   Is [Eastern] a private company or do they issue stock?

A.   It is a closely held company, so they have financial reporting requirements but are not traded publicly.

Q.   The investment is all internal?

A.   Yes.

Q.   So it may be less important to them than to a company for instance that is doing an IPO or is publicly traded, where word of the decrease in profit could drive the shares down.

---

[43] It is important to understand that gross income also plays a part in deciding whether something is a reasonable accommodation; therefore, the questions about gross income are pertinent for issues other than tthe issue of profitability.

A. I don't think our risk here is decrease in profits as much as a decrease in cash flow and investment.

Q. Last question: I realize auditing is done independently and is very quantitative and mathematical, but is there some human factor that comes into play here? There are millions and millions of people in the country who are disabled and from an accounting standpoint you could exclude them completely from employment because they will have an adverse effect on the balance sheets, but from the policy standpoint, it is not really possible and many laws have been enacted to actually prevent this. So do you believe that some human factor should also go into the analysis that you are doing, or is this is strictly quantitative?

A. Well . . . .

Q. If a qualified person in a wheelchair came to your company seeking a position would you hire them?

A. Yes.

Q. And if that is the case, would you not also have to make the place handicap friendly to accommodate his wheelchair access?

A. Yes.

Q. Then does that not sort of invalidate your charge when you were calculating approximately [$50,000], you were looking at that cost into [Mr. Lyons] individually? Is that not sort of not correct then, you can't really charge that to [Mr. Lyons], you have to sort of make it a general company expense that you would have to do as a cost of doing business. Is that not correct?

A. Well, yes, it is a-cost of doing business that directly affects the cash flow of the company.

Q. But in a sense you cannot charge that to [Mr. Lyons] directly. It is a general company cost.

A. If [Eastern] were to have to make its building handicap friendly, it would cost [$250,000] no matter if it was [Mr. Lyons] or someone else.

Q. Besides that, has it been a practice of [Eastern] to bring in no salary replacements for its senior employees?

A. I am not familiar with that.

§ 16.15   Expert Testimony:
Psychological Evaluation

In this hypothetical,[44] the plaintiff Mr. SDT (schizophrenic decompensating[45] telemarketer) has been denied a job "out of hand" as a telemarketer due to the fact that he is schizophrenic and has a history of not taking his medication. Under the circumstances, liability appears relatively easy to establish

---

[44] This hypothetical and the testimony in §§ **16.16** and **16.17** were drafted by Charles Fisher on June 6, 1993. Mr. Fisher was an assistant to Henry H. Perritt, Jr.

[45] *Decompensation* is the term commonly used to describe a schizophrenic's progressive returns to premedication morbidity as a result of a failure either to take prescribed medication or to take the medication in the manner prescribed.

although certain employment contracting and insurance issues might arise. **Sections 16.16** and **16.17** contain sample expert testimony for the plaintiff and the defendant, respectively.

§ 16.16   —Expert Testimony for the Plaintiff

Q. Please state your name, address, and occupation for the court.

A. My name is [Dr. Robert Smith], [5555 55th Street], [Upper Treddyffrin], [Pennsylvania] [55555], and I am a practicing psychiatrist.

Q. How long have you been a psychiatrist?

A. Ten years.

Q. What is your educational background?

A. I received Bachelor of Arts degrees in both psychology and prelaw from the [University of Washington] in [Seattle]. I received my M.D. from [Hahnemann School of Medicine] in [Philadelphia].

Q. Where did you do your residency?

A. I did my residency at [Hahnemann University] Hospital in [Philadelphia], specializing in the areas of psychology and psychiatric medicine.

Q. Are you licensed to practice medicine in this state?

A. Yes.

Q. Are you licensed to practice in states other than [Pennsylvania]?

A. Yes, I am licensed to practice in [Delaware], [Maryland], [New Jersey], [New York], and the [District of Columbia].

Q. What is your area of specialization?

A. I deal primarily with patients suffering from schizophrenia.

Q. Approximately how many schizophrenic patients have you treated in your career, Doctor?

A. I have diagnosed and treated over 100 schizophrenic patients over the last 10 years.

Q. Have you been involved with any clinical studies of patients suffering from schizophrenia?

A. I have been involved in no less than seven such studies.

Q. Have you published any material based on schizophrenia or schizophrenic patients?

A. Yes, I have authored several articles and two books on the subject.

Q. Are you familiar with the literature concerning schizophrenia?

A. Yes. The literature on this subject is extensive, but I stay abreast of the latest findings in order to give proper treatment to my patients.

Q. Do you know [Mr. SDT], the plaintiff, in this case?

A. Yes, I have examined [Mr. SDT].

Q. What is your clinical impression of the plaintiff?

A. The plaintiff suffers from a relatively moderate case of schizophrenia.

Q. When you say moderate, what do you mean?

A. I mean that [Mr. SDT] is high functioning from a cognitive standpoint and that with proper medication[46] he is capable of overcoming the debilitating effects of his condition.

Q. What does that mean in terms of [Mr. SDT], compared with someone who is not schizophrenic?

A. When [Mr. SDT] is properly medicated, his abilities are much the same as someone who does not suffer from the disorder.

Q. Could the plaintiff work the phones as a telemarketer as long as he was properly medicated?

A. Yes, I believe that [Mr. SDT] is fully capable of performing the tasks of a telemarketer when he is medicated.

Q. Are there side effects of his medication that would cause trouble with performing the duties of a telemarketer?

A. Patients often complain of excessive tiredness when they are taking medication for schizophrenia. This tiredness generally disappears after about three weeks. Patients can also experience a stiffness in the tongue but this can be successfully treated in most cases with cogentin.

Q. What would happen if [Mr. SDT] stopped taking his medication?

A. His cognitive functioning would deteriorate and he would begin to experience symptoms of the disorder. This process is known as decompensation.

Q. What is [Mr. SDT]'s history with respect to taking his medication?

A. He has a history of not taking his medication.

Q. Wouldn't this cause problems if he were employed by the defendant?

A. If the plaintiff were not taking his medication, he would not be able to perform his job responsibilities satisfactorily.

Q. Based on the plaintiff's history, wasn't it prudent for the defendant to deny him employment?[47]

A. The plaintiff is capable of performing the required duties of the position for which he applied. He is also completely capable of understanding that taking his medication as prescribed would be a requirement of his being hired and his continued employment.

Q. What would be the effect if [Mr. SDT] were made aware by the defendant that failure to take his medication in the prescribed manner would result in his being fired?[48]

A. He would understand the meaning and gravity of such a statement.

Q. Would the defendant be able to tell if [Mr. SDT] stopped taking his medication?

---

[46] Because this is mock testimony, there is no reason to overcomplicate the text with a discussion of what medication the plaintiff might be taking. Haldol, prolixin, loxitane, and thorozene are all possible choices, though there are others. It should be noted that haldol and prolixin can be administered by intramuscular injection once a month rather than by daily oral ingestion and that this would greatly facilitate efforts to guarantee that the patient is taking his medication.

[47] This is a leading question, but there is no prejudice because it suggests an answer favoring the opponent.

[48] *See* § **4.45** regarding last chance agreements.

A. Yes, the symptoms of decompensation are very apparent.

Q. Would the defendant need to have the plaintiff's supervisor specially trained to recognize the symptoms of decompensation?

A. No. In the early stages of decompensation there would be noticeable changes in the plaintiff's mood, personality, and behavior.

Q. What type of changes would be typical?

A. The most likely red flag changes would be that the plaintiff would become suspicious and/or withdrawn. In the later stages of decompensation, the plaintiff might begin to talk to himself (respond to internal stimuli) and would verbalize feelings of paranoia.

Q. Could these symptoms of early decompensation be due to things other than failing to take his medication?

A. Of course, [Mr. SDT] might simply not feel like talking one day and therefore appear withdrawn. But due to his special circumstances, it seems that the prudent thing to do would be to play it safe and test his blood or urine to see if he is taking his medication.

Q. Is it possible that the plaintiff could decompensate without any of these symptoms to put the defendant on notice of a problem?

A. Decompensation without notice is possible but highly unlikely with high function schizophrenics like [Mr. SDT].

Q. Is [Mr. SDT] capable of safely and competently performing the duties of a telemarketer in the defendant's employ?

A. Yes.

§ 16.17 —Expert Testimony for the Defense

Q. Doctor, have you had an opportunity to examine [Mr. SDT]?

A. Yes.

Q. What is your clinical opinion as to the plaintiff's condition?

A. The plaintiff suffers from schizophrenia.[49]

Q. Do you believe that the plaintiff is capable of working the phones as a telemarketer?

A. No. While it is true that the plaintiff is high-functioning when properly medicated, his history indicates that when he begins to feel okay following a period of relatively normal functioning, he discontinues taking his medication and it is this medication that allows him to function with the degree of clarity and concentration that would be required for the telemarketing position.

Q. You heard [Dr. Smith] say that there would be indications that the plaintiff was not taking his medication and that his supervisor would be able to know if the plaintiff was decompensating. Do you agree?

A. While I agree that there are noticeable symptoms of decompensation in most cases, I do not believe that the plaintiff's supervisor would be able to spot the often subtle symptomatology of the early stages of decompensation.

---

[49] The testimony concerning Mr. SDT's degree of debilitation has been omitted because this hypothetical is based on a high-functioning schizophrenic.

Additionally, the plaintiff's cognitive functioning, and thereby his ability to do the job, might well be affected long before any noticeable symptomatology appeared.

Q. Could the plaintiff's ability to interact effectively with potential customers be eroded before anyone knew he was not taking his medication?

A. Yes.[50]

§ 16.18 Plaintiff's Closing Argument (Mock Trial)

FORM 16–10
SAMPLE PLAINTIFF'S CLOSING ARGUMENT

Ladies and gentlemen of the jury. [Steve Lyons] is afflicted with MS. This disease substantially limits the major life activities of reading, speaking, and walking. Thus, according to the ADA, [Steve Lyons] is disabled. It has been shown that although [Steve Lyons] is disabled he would have been able to continue in his position as staff accountant at [Eastern] had they not refused to make the reasonable accommodations that he requested.

Defendant [Eastern] has failed to prove that it would constitute an undue hardship if they were required to make the reasonable accommodations requested by [Steve Lyons]. All that [Steve Lyons] requested was a reader to communicate written and computer information to him, a speaker to communicate oral messages from him, and the addition of a ramp and other things to make the building handicap friendly.

Given the size of the company, it is likely that [Eastern] could find someone already employed to serve as [Steve Lyons]' reader and speaker. As for [Eastern]'s contention that it will cost them [$250,000] to make their building handicap friendly, they cannot place this expense squarely on the shoulders of [Steve Lyons]. [Steve Lyons] may not be the first and certainly will not be the last disabled person to work at [Eastern]. The addition of wheelchair ramps and other renovations is inevitable regardless of the outcome of this case. As the jury, you need to send a strong message to employers like [Eastern] that discrimination against qualified individuals with disabilities will no longer be tolerated.

[Steve Lyons] suffers from a mysterious disease. As [Dr. Allen] testified, little is known about what causes MS and there is no cure. What is known is that the average MS patient lives 30 years with the disease. MS affects the motor skills of the person but has no effect on the cognitive abilities and functions. [Steve Lyons] is as mentally sharp today as he was prior to his diagnosis. He simply has trouble with his eyesight, speech, and muscle coordination.

---

[50] The testimony concerning the expert's qualifications and experience in the field of psychiatry has been omitted to avoid needless redundancy.

[Steve Lyons] was wrongfully terminated by [Eastern]. He was fired because he has MS. The defendant claims that [Steve Lyons] was fired for subpar job performance, yet [Steve Lyons] never had anything but satisfactory year-end employment reviews. To find for the defendant in this case is to give credence to the many stereotypes that are cast upon people with disabilities. Because it is apparent that [Steve Lyons] is not at all disabled mentally, it is just as apparent that he was wrongfully terminated. This is a blatant violation of the ADA. It is up to you the jury to correct this manifest injustice.

§ 16.19   Defense's Closing Argument (Mock Trial)

FORM 16–11
SAMPLE DEFENSE'S CLOSING ARGUMENT

Ladies and gentlemen of the jury, it is now time for you to make your decision in this case. As in all cases, this decision will not be an easy one. My only words of advice to you are to make this decision with your minds and not your hearts. It might make each of you feel good or even feel less guilty about the way you treated a disabled individual in the past if you were to hold in favor of [Mr. Lyons]. But the decision based on these factors will not be a just and equitable one. Rather, each of you must detach your emotions from this case and perform an analysis considering both the facts of the case which you have heard and the relevant law.

The relevant law in this case is the Americans with Disabilities Act. This law prohibits employers from discriminating against disabled workers. Applying the facts to this law, it is true that [Mr. Lyons] is disabled. It is true that [Eastern] was [Mr. Lyons]'s employer. It is also true that [Eastern] terminated [Mr. Lyons]'s employment, but it is not true that [Eastern] discriminated against [Mr. Lyons].

[Mr. Lyons] was let go because his work was subpar. His work was illegible, his work was inaccurate, and his work was late. Outside vendors lodged complaints against [Mr. Lyons] and the quality of his work.

[Mr. Lyons] on the other hand would have you believe that he was let go because [Eastern] didn't want to provide the accommodations which he sought. If this were true, [Mr. Lyons] would have a good case for himself but there are two substantial holes in this theory.

First, as you heard [Arthur Smith] a partner at an international accounting firm testify, providing the accommodations which [Mr. Lyons] requested would have caused [Eastern] to suffer an undue hardship. The ADA does not require that an employer provide accommodations if they will thereby suffer an undue hardship. The pharmaceutical industry is ultra dependent upon research and development. Even a minimal decrease in the funds available for R&D purposes has a monumental effect on the firm's health and ability to survive in the market. Forcing [Eastern] to provide [Mr. Lyons] with the accommodations he sought would most probably put [Eastern] out of business, taking with them the drugs which they manufacture to enable us to live longer and better lives.

Second, as you heard [Mr. Lyons]' supervisor [Henry Bell] testify, [Mr. Lyons] would not be able to perform the essential functions of his job even if [Eastern] provided him with every accommodation he requested. The work of an accountant must be precise and exact. There is no room for error. Close enough is not good enough.

As I have demonstrated for you analytically, applying the facts of the case to the relevant law, [Mr. Lyons] cannot sustain his cause of action under the ADA because [Eastern] did not discriminate against him.

Therefore you must find for the defendant, [Eastern Pharmaceuticals], and deny [Mr. Lyons]' request for damages. Thank you.

§ 16.20   Agreed Jury Instructions (EEOC)

FORM 16–12
SAMPLE AGREED JURY INSTRUCTIONS

AGREED JURY INSTRUCTIONS

PRELIMINARY INSTRUCTION

AGREED INSTRUCTION 1

MEMBERS OF THE JURY:

You have now been sworn as the jury to try this case. As the jury you will decide the disputed questions of fact.

In this case there are two Plaintiffs, the Equal Employment Opportunity Commission and [Charles Wessel]. The Equal Employment Opportunity Commission (or EEOC) as many of you may know, is a government agency. [Charles Wessel] is a former Executive Director for [A.I.C. Security Investigations, Ltd.], who claims that his employer discriminated against him on the basis of his disability, cancer. In this case the EEOC's claims are the same as those of [Mr. Wessel], and [Mr. Wessel] and the EEOC will be jointly presenting the Plaintiffs' case. The EEOC is participating in this lawsuit as a Plaintiff, not as an impartial government agency or an expert in disability discrimination. You should not infer that discrimination on the basis of disability has occurred because the EEOC chose to participate, nor should you attach any special significance to this case because of the EEOC's participation. The EEOC is required to meet the same burden of proof in this case as must be met by a private Plaintiff.

The Defendants in this lawsuit are [A.I.C. Security Investigations, Ltd.], [A.I.C. International, Ltd.], and [defendant C]. [A.I.C. Security Investigations, Ltd.] is a wholly owned subsidiary of [A.I.C. International, Ltd.]. [Defendant C] is the sole shareholder of [A.I.C. International Ltd.] [A.I.C. Security Investigations, Ltd.] provides commercial security services, hardware, and investigative services to customers in the [Chicago] area.

As the judge, I will decide all questions of law and procedure. From time to time during the trial and at the end of the trial, I will instruct you on the rules of the law that you must follow in making your decision.

Soon, the lawyers for each of the parties will make what is called an opening statement. Opening statements are intended to assist you in understanding the evidence. What the lawyers say is not evidence.

After the opening statements, the Plaintiffs will call witnesses and present evidence. Then, the Defendants will have an opportunity to call witnesses and present evidence. After the parties' main case is completed, the Plaintiffs may be permitted to present rebuttal evidence. After all the evidence is completed, the lawyers will again address you to make final arguments. Then I will instruct you on the applicable law. You will then retire to deliberate on a verdict.

Keep an open mind during the trial. Do not decide any fact until you have heard all of the evidence, the closing arguments, and my instructions.

Pay close attention to the testimony and evidence. Even though the court reporter is making stenographic notes of everything that is said, a typewritten copy of the testimony will not be available for your use during deliberations. On the other hand, any exhibits received in evidence will be available to you during you deliberations.

If you would like to take notes during the trial, you may do so. If you do not take notes, be careful not to get so involved in not taking notes that you become distracted and miss part of the testimony. Your notes are to be used only as aids to your memory, and if your memory should later be different from your notes, you should rely on your memory and not on your notes. if you do not take notes, rely on your own independent memory of the testimony. Do not be unduly influenced by the notes of other jurors. A juror's notes are not entitled to any greater weight than the recollection of each juror concerning the testimony.

Until this trial is over, do not discuss this case with anyone and do not permit anyone to discuss the case in your presence. Do not discuss the case even with the other jurors until all of the jurors are in the jury room actually deliberating at the end of the case. If anyone should attempt to discuss this case or to approach you concerning the case, you should inform the Court immediately. Hold yourself completely apart from the people involved in the case-the parties, the witnesses, the attorneys, and the persons associated with them. It is important not only that you be fair and impartial but that you also appear to be fair and impartial.

Do not make any independent investigation of any fact or matter in this case. You are to be guided solely by what you see and hear in this trial. Do not learn anything about the case from any other source. In particular, do not read any newspaper account of this trial or listen to any radio or television newscast concerning it. Do not listen to any local radio or television newscast until this trial is over, or read any local newspaper unless someone else first removes any possible reference to this trial.

During the trial, it may be necessary for me to confer with the lawyers out of your hearing or to conduct a part of the trial out of your presence. I will handle these matters as briefly and as conveniently for you as I can, but you should remember that they are a necessary part of any trial.

It is now time for the opening statements.

Adapted from Pattern Jury Instructions (Civil Cases), U.S. Fifth Circuit District Judges Association (1991), Instruction 1.1.

Given:
Denied:
Given as Modified:

AGREED INSTRUCTION 2
STIPULATION OF FACT

The parties have agreed, or stipulated, the following facts. This means that both sides agree that these are facts. You must therefore treat these facts as having been proved.

Adapted from Pattern Jury Instructions (Civil Cases), U.S. Fifth Circuit District Judges Association (1991), Instruction 2.3.

Given:
Denied:
Given as Modified:

AGREED INSTRUCTION 3
GENERAL INSTRUCTION

MEMBERS OF THE JURY:

You have heard the evidence in this case. I will now instruct you on the law that you must apply. It is your duty to follow the law as I give it to you. On the other hand, you the jury are the judges of the facts. Do not consider any statement that I have made in the course of trial or make in these instructions as an indication that I have any opinion about the facts of this case.

You have heard the closing arguments of the attorneys. Statements and arguments of the attorneys are not evidence and are not instructions on the law. They are intended only to assist the jury in understanding the evidence and parties' contentions.

Answer each question from the facts as you find them. Your answers and your verdict must be unanimous.

You must answer all questions from a preponderance of the evidence. By this I mean the greater weight and degree of credible evidence before you. In other words, a preponderance of the evidence just means the amount of evidence that persuades you that a claim is more likely so than not so. In determining whether any fact has been proved by a preponderance of the evidence in the case, you may, unless otherwise instructed, consider the testimony of all witnesses, regardless of who may have called them, and of all exhibits received in evidence, regardless of who may have produced them.

In determining the weight to give to the testimony of a witness, you should ask yourself whether there was evidence tending to prove that the witness testified falsely concerning some important fact, or whether there was evidence that at some other time the witness said or did something, or failed to say or do something, that was different from the testimony the witness gave before you during the trial.

You should keep in mind, of course, that a simple mistake by a witness does not necessarily mean that the witness was not telling the truth as he or she remembers it, because people may forget some things or remember other things inaccurately. So, if a witness has made a misstatement, you need to consider whether that misstatement was an intentional falsehood or simply an innocent lapse of memory; and the significance of that may depend on whether it has to do with an important fact or with only an unimportant detail.

While you should consider only the evidence in this case, you are permitted to draw such reasonable inference from the testimony and exhibits as you feel are justified in the light of common experience. In other words, you may make deductions and reach conclusions that reason and common sense lead you to draw from the facts that have been established by the testimony and evidence in the case.

The testimony of a single witness may be sufficient to prove any fact, even if a greater number of witnesses may have testified to the contrary, if, after considering all the other evidence, you believe that single witness.

There are two types of evidence that you may consider in properly finding the truth as to the facts in the case. One is direct evidence—such as testimony of an eyewitness. The other is indirect or circumstantial evidence—the proof of a chain of circumstances that indicates the existence or nonexistence of certain other facts. As a general rule, the law makes no distinction between direct and circumstantial evidence, but simply requires that you find the facts from a preponderance of all the evidence, both direct and circumstantial.

Any notes that you have taken during this trial are only aids to memory. If your memory should differ from your notes, then you should rely on your memory and not on the notes. The notes are not evidence. A juror who has not taken notes should rely on his or her independent recollection of the evidence and should not be unduly influenced by the notes of other jurors. Notes are not entitled to any greater weight than the recollection or impression of each juror about the testimony.

When you retire to the jury room to deliberate on your verdict, you may take these instructions with you as well as the stipulations of fact and the exhibits which the Court has admitted into evidence. Select your Foreperson and conduct your deliberations; follow all of the instructions that the Court has given you about your conduct during the trial. if you recess during your deliberations, follow all of the instructions that the Court has given you about/on your conduct during the trial. After you have reached your unanimous verdict, your Foreperson is to fill in on the form your answers to the questions. Do not reveal your answers until such time as you are discharged, unless otherwise directed by me. You must never disclose to anyone, not even to me, your numerical division on any question.

If you want to communicate with me at any time, please give a written message or question to the bailiff, who will bring it to me. I will then respond as promptly as possible either in writing or by having you brought into the courtroom so that I can address you orally. I will always first disclose to the attorneys your question and my response before I answer your question.

After you have reached a verdict, you are not required to talk with anyone about the case unless the Court orders otherwise.

Adapted from Pattern Jury Instructions (Civil Cases), U.S. Fifth Circuit District Judges Association (1991), Instruction 3.1.

Given:
Denied:
Given as Modified:

AGREED INSTRUCTION 4
BURDEN OF PROOF

In this case Plaintiffs must prove every essential part of their claim by a preponderance of the evidence.

A preponderance of the evidence simply means evidence that persuades you that the Plaintiffs' claim is more likely true than not true.

In deciding whether any fact has been proven by a preponderance of the evidence, you may, unless otherwise instructed, consider the testimony of all witnesses, regardless of who may have called them, and all exhibits received in evidence, regardless of who may have produced them.

If the proof fails to establish any essential part of the Plaintiffs' claim by a preponderance of the evidence, you should find for the Defendant as to that claim.

Adapted from Pattern Jury Instructions (Civil Cases), U.S. Fifth Circuit District Judges Association (1991), instruction 2.20.

Given:
Denied:
Given as Modified:

AGREED INSTRUCTION 5
DISABILITY—DEFINITION

Disability, as defined by the Americans with Disabilities Act, means

(1)   a physical or mental impairment that substantially limits one or more major life activities;

(2)   a record of such impairment; or

(3)   being regarded as having such impairment.

29 C.F.R. § 1630.2(g)

Given:
Denied:
Given as Modified:

AGREED INSTRUCTION 6
MENTAL OR PHYSICAL IMPAIRMENT—DEFINITION

The term mental or physical impairment is defined as:

(1)   any physiological disorder or condition, cosmetic disfigurements, anatomical loss affecting one or more of the following body systems: neurological; neuromuscular; special sense organs; cardiovascular; reproductive; digestive; genito-urinary; hemic and lymphatic; skin; and endocrine; or

(2)   any mental or psychological disorder, such as mental retardation, organic brain syndrome, emotional or mental illness, and specific learning disabilities.

29 C.F.R. § 1630.2(h)

Given:
Denied:
Given as Modified:

AGREED INSTRUCTION 7
MAJOR LIFE ACTIVITY—DEFINITION

The term "major life activity" refers to basic life activities that an average person can perform with little or no difficulty, such as caring for one's self, performing manual tasks, walking, seeing, hearing, speaking, breathing, learning, working, sitting, standing, lifting and reaching.

29 C.F.R. § 1630.2(i)

Given:
Denied:
Given as Modified:

AGREED INSTRUCTION 8
SUBSTANTIALITY LIMITS—DEFINITION

A physical or mental impairment "substantially limits" one or more of a person's major life activities when it:

(1)   renders the individual unable to perform a major life activity that the average person in the population could perform, or

(2)   significantly restricts, as to condition, manner, or duration, the individual's ability to perform a particular major life activity as compared to the condition manner, or duration under which the average person in the general population could perform the same major life activity.

The question of whether the individual's impairment substantially limits a major life activity depends on the impairment's

(1)   nature and severity;

(2)   duration or expected duration;

(3)   expected or actual permanent or long term impact.

29 C.F.R. § 1630.2(i).

Given:
Denied:
Given as Modified:

§ 16.21   Plaintiffs' Proposed Jury Instructions (EEOC)

FORM 16–13
SAMPLE PLAINTIFFS' PROPOSED JURY INSTRUCTIONS

PLAINTIFFS' PROPOSED JURY INSTRUCTIONS

PLAINTIFFS' PRELIMINARY INSTRUCTION 1
LIMITING INSTRUCTION

The testimony (or exhibit) being offered relates to [Mr. Wessel]'s medical condition at a time after the date on which he left his employment with Defendants. As I will instruct you at the end of the trial, this will be relevant to the amount of back pay to which [Mr. Wessel] is entitled, if your verdict is for the Plaintiffs. You may not consider the testimony with respect to the question of whether [Wessel] was able to perform his job on [July 29, 1992].

Given:
Denied:
Given as Modified:

PLAINTIFFS' INSTRUCTION 2
EXPERT WITNESS

When knowledge of technical subject matter may be helpful to the jury, a person who has special training or experience in that technical field—an expert witness—is permitted to state his opinion on those technical matters. However, you are not required to accept that opinion. As with any other witness, it is up to you to decide whether to rely upon it.

In deciding whether to accept or rely upon the opinion of an expert witness, you may consider any bias of the witness, including any bias you may infer from evidence that the expert witness has been or will be paid for reviewing the case and testifying, or from evidence that he testifies regularly as an expert witness and his income such testimony represents a significant portion of his income.

Adapted from Pattern Jury Instructions (Civil Cases), U.S. Fifth Circuit District Judges Association (1991), Instruction 3.1.

Given:
Denied:
Given as Modified:

PLAINTIFFS' INSTRUCTION 3
AMERICANS WITH DISABILITIES ACT

This is an action brought under the Americans With Disabilities Act. The purpose of the Act is to provide a clear and comprehensive national mandate for the elimination of discrimination against individuals with disabilities. The Act makes it unlawful for an employer to discriminate against a qualified individual with a disability by terminating him from his employment because of his disability.

Adapted from Americans With Disabilities Act, 42 U.S.C. § 12101(b)(1); 42 U.S.C. § 12112(a).

Given:
Denied:
Given as Modified:

PLAINTIFFS' INSTRUCTION 4
PARTIES' CONTENTIONS

In this case, Plaintiffs contend that [Charles Wessel] was unlawfully terminated from his position as Executive Director at [A.I.C. Security Investigations] because of his disability, cancer.

The Defendants deny that they unjustifiably discharged [Wessel] from his employment on account of his disability. The Defendants instead contended that their request that [Wessel] remove himself from the position of Executive Director was justified because he could no longer perform the essential functions of Executive Director of [A.I.C. Security Investigations, Ltd.], with or without reasonable accommodation. Defendants also contend that Plaintiff posed a direct threat to the health or safety of himself or others in the workplace.

Adapted from Pattern Jury Instructions (Civil Cases), U.S. Fifth Circuit District Judges Association (1983), Federal Claims Instruction No. 10 (1983).

Given:
Denied:
Given as Modified:

PLAINTIFFS INSTRUCTION 5
PLAINTIFFS' PRIMA FACIE CASE

The Plaintiff in an Americans With Disabilities Act case has the burden of proving by a preponderance of the evidence the following elements:

(1)   That he had at the time of his termination, a disability, as that term is defined in the ADA.

(2)   That he was "otherwise qualified" for the position he held. This element requires proof by the Plaintiffs, by a preponderance of the evidence, that, except for [Wessel]'s disability, [Wessel] possesses the necessary qualifications for the

position, such as educational background, experience, skills, and other job-related factors.

(3)   That [Wessel] was capable of performing all of the essential functions of the position, with or without reasonable accommodation;

(4) That [Wessel]'s disability did not prevent him from performing the essential functions of the position, such that any functions he could not perform because of his disability were merely marginal functions not essential to performance of the job of Executive Director; and

(5)   That [Wessel]'s disability was a motivating factor in the decision to discharge him.

Plaintiffs are not required to prove that [Wessel]'s disability was the sole motivation or the primary motivation for Defendants' decision. The Plaintiffs need only prove that [Wessel]'s disability played a part in the decision. In addition, Plaintiffs are not required to produce direct evidence of unlawful motive. Intentional discrimination, if it exists, is seldom admitted, but is a fact which you may infer from the existence of other facts.

Adapted from [*Chiari v. City of League City,* 920 F.2d 311, 315–18 (5th Cir. 1991)]; [*Prewitt v. United States Postal Service,* 662 F.2d 292, 309–10 (5th Cir. 1981)]; Devitt & Blackmar, Federal Jury Practice and Instructions, Ch. 104.01 *et seq.*

Given:
Denied:
Given as Modified:

PLAINTIFFS' INSTRUCTION 6
OTHERWISE QUALIFIED—DEFINITION

An individual is otherwise qualified within the meaning of the Americans With Disabilities Act if he satisfies the prerequisites for the position, such as possessing the appropriate educational background, employment experience, skills, licenses, etc.

29 C.F.R. § 1630.2(m); EEOC Interpretive Guidance to Regulations at 29 C.F.R. § 1630(2)(m).

Given:
Denied:
Given as Modified:

PLAINTIFFS' INSTRUCTION 7
QUALIFIED INDIVIDUAL

The determination of whether [Wessel] was qualified, in that he was able to perform the essential functions of his position, with or without reasonable accommodation, must be made with respect to the time of the employment decision. The determination should be based on whether he was capable of performing the essential functions of his position as Executive Director at the time of the decision to terminate him, and should not be based on speculation that he might have become unable to perform the essential functions of the position in the future or might have caused increased health insurance premiums of workers' compensation costs.

Adapted from EEOC interpretive Guidance to Regulations at 29 C.F.R. § 1630(2)(m).

Given:
Denied:
Given as Modified:

PLAINTIFFS' INSTRUCTION 8
LIMITING INSTRUCTION

You will recall that during the course of this trial I have admitted certain evidence in the form of testimony and exhibits which related to [Mr. Wessel]'s medical condition at a time after he left his employment with Defendants. You may consider such evidence only for the limited purpose of determining the appropriate back pay to which [Mr. Wessel] is entitled, if your verdict is for the Plaintiffs. You may not consider such evidence for the purpose of determining whether [Wessel] was a qualified individual at the time of his discharge.

Adapted from Pattern Jury Instructions (Civil Cases), U.S. Fifth Circuit District Judges Association (1991), Federal Claims Instruction No. 2.15 (1991).

Given:
Denied:
Given as Modified:

PLAINTIFFS' INSTRUCTION 9
ESSENTIAL FUNCTIONS—DEFINITION

The term "essential functions" means the fundamental job duties of the employment position the individual with a disability holds. The term "essential functions" does not include the marginal functions of the position. Whether a particular function is essential is a factual determination that must be made on a case-by-case basis. in determining whether or not a particular function is essential, all relevant evidence should be considered.

Adapted from EEOC Regulation 29 C.F.R. § 1630.2(n); EEOC Interpretive Guidance to 29 C.F.R. § 1630.2(n).

Given:
Denied:
Given as Modified:

PLAINTIFFS' INSTRUCTION 10
SOCIAL SECURITY DISABILITY AND UNEMPLOYMENT COMPENSATION

   The definition of disability under the Americans With Disabilities Act is not the
same as the definition of disability in other laws, such as state workers' compensation laws or other federal or state laws that provide benefits for people with disabilities and disabled veterans. Therefore, in making your determination of whether
[Charles Wessel] was disabled and/or unable to perform the essential functions of
his job as Executive Director of [A.I.C. Security Investigations, Ltd.], because of his
disability, you may consider the determination of the Social Security
Administration that [Charles Wessel] was entitled to disability benefits as evidence
to be considered in conjunction with all other relevant evidence in resolving the
question; however, you cannot consider the determination of the Social Security
Administration as a definitive finding that [Wessel] could or could not perform the
essential functions of his job.

   Similarly, the fact that the [Illinois] Department of Employment Security has
found that [Wessel] is eligible for unemployment compensation, based on a finding that he is able to work and is diligently seeking employment, may be considered by you in conjunction with all other relevant evidence in determining
whether he was or was not able to perform, and whether he continues to be able
to perform, the essential functions of his job as Executive Director. However, you
cannot consider the determination of the [Illinois] Department of Employment
Security as a definitive finding that [Wessel] was able, or not, to work, and was
actively seeking employment following his termination from [A.I.C. Security
Investigations, Ltd.].

   Adapted from EEOC Interpretive Guidance, 29 C.F.R. § 1630.2(k); EEOC
Technical Assistance Manual,§ 2.2; [Overton v. Reilly, 977 F.2d 1190, 1196 (7th
Cir. 1992)]; [Mitchell v. Humana Hospital-Shoals, 942 F.2d 1581, 1583 n.2 (11th
Cir. 1991)].

Given:
Denied:
Given as Modified:

PLAINTIFFS' INSTRUCTION 11
THREAT TO SAFETY DEFENSE

   If you find that the Plaintiffs have established each of the elements of their claim,
then you will consider the Defendants' defense, which the Defendants must establish by a preponderance of the evidence. It is Defendants' defense that [Charles

Wessel] poses a direct threat to the health or safety of himself or others in the workplace.

You may find that [Charles Wessel] poses a direct threat only if the Defendants have proved, more likely than not, that [Charles Wessel] poses a significant risk of substantial harm to the health and safety of himself or others in the workplace that cannot be eliminated or reduced by reasonable accommodation. The threat must relate to the work environment, [Wessel]'s activities outside of the work environment are irrelevant.

A significant risk is more than an elevated risk of injury on the job. A significant risk is a specific risk having a high probability of imminent, substantial harm. In determining whether [Wessel] posses a significant risk, you must consider the following factors:

1.   The duration of the risk;

2.   The nature and severity of the potential harm;

3.   The likelihood that potential harm will occur; and

4.   The imminence of the potential harm.

If an individual poses a direct threat as a result of his disability, the employer must determine whether a reasonable accommodation would either eliminate the risk or reduce it to an acceptable level.

Adapted from Americans with Disabilities Act, 42 U.S.C. §§ 12113(b), 12111(3); EEOC Interpretive Guidance, 29 C.F.R. § 1630.2(r); [*School Board of Nassau County v. Arline,* 480 U.S. 273 (1987)]; [*Mantolete v. Bolger,* 767 F.2d 1416 (9th Cir. 1985)]; [*Strathie v. Department of Transportation,* 716 F.2d 227 (3d Cir. 1983)]; [*New York State Ass'n for Retarded Citizens v. Carey,* 612 F.2d 644 (2d Cir. 1979)]; 56 Fed. Reg. 35, 745 (1991).

Given:
Denied:
Given as modified:

Commentary.   In *EEOC v. A.I.C. Security Investigations, Ltd.*[51] the Seventh Circuit held that it was error for the district court to give the following direct threat instruction, a slightly different one from either instruction originally tendered by the parties:

[I]t is the defendant's defense that Charles Wessel posed a threat to the health and safety of himself or others in the workplace. You may find that Charles

---

[51] 55 F.3d 1276 (7th Cir. 1995).

Wessel posed a direct threat only if the defendants have proven by a preponderance of the evidence that, more likely than not, Charles Wessel in the performance of an essential function of his job posed a significant threat of substantial harm to himself or others in the workplace that could not be eliminated or reduced by a reasonable accommodation.[52]

The court of appeals held that the limitation of the defense to "in the performance of an essential function of his job" was error because it invited the jury to consider whether Wessel had to drive to accomplish his job, a question which should have been confined as a subset of the question of accommodation. Nevertheless, the court of appeals thought that the relatively minor error did not prejudice the jury's consideration of the case and rejected this basis for overturning the jury verdict in the plaintiff's favor.[53]

PLAINTIFFS' INSTRUCTION 12
CONSIDER DAMAGES ONLY IF NECESSARY

If the Plaintiffs have proven their claim against the Defendants by a preponderance of the evidence, you must determine the damages to which [Charles Wessel] is entitled. You should not interpret the fact that I have given instructions about [Wessel]'s damages as any indication in any way that I believe that the Plaintiffs should, or should not, win this case. it is your task first to decide whether the Defendants are liable. I am instructing you on damages only so that you will have guidance in the event you decide that the Defendants are liable and that [Wessel] is entitled to recover money from the Defendants.

Adapted from Pattern Jury Instructions (Civil Cases), U.S. Fifth Circuit District Judges Association (1991), Instruction 3.1.

Given:
Denied:
Given as Modified:

PLAINTIFFS' INSTRUCTION 13
DEFENDANTS' LIABILITY

If you find that the Plaintiffs have proved that the Defendants discriminated against [Wessel] on the basis of his disability, the three Defendants together will be liable for any back pay, future out-of-pocket expenses, or compensatory damages which are proven.

---

[52] *Id.* at 1283–84.
[53] *Id.* at 1284–85.

PLAINTIFFS' INSTRUCTION 14
DAMAGES

If you find that the Defendants are liable to [Charles Wessel], then you must also determine an amount that is fair compensation for all of the injuries that he suffered because of the discrimination. The purpose of damages is to make the plaintiff whole—that is, to compensate the plaintiff for the damage that the plaintiff has suffered. Under the Americans with Disabilities Act, damages include: (1) lost salary and benefits, (2) future out-of-pocket expenses, and (3) compensatory damages for intangible losses. Intangible losses may include, but are not limited to, emotional pain, suffering, inconvenience, mental anguish, humiliation, shame, loss of self-esteem, fear, embarrassment, depression, and injury to reputation or professional standing which plaintiff has suffered or may suffer in future.

You may award damages only for injuries that the Plaintiffs prove were caused by the Defendants' allegedly discriminatory conduct. The damages that you award must be fair compensation for all of [Wessel]'s damages, no more and no less. Damages are not allowed as a punishment and cannot be imposed or increased to penalize the Defendants. You should not award damages for speculative injuries, but only for those injuries which [Charles Wessel] has actually suffered or is reasonably likely to suffer in the future.

You must use sound discretion in fixing an award of damages, drawing reasonable inferences where you find them appropriate from the facts and circumstances in evidence.

You should consider the following elements of damages, to the extent you find them proved by a preponderance of the evidence:

Adapted from Pattern Jury Instructions (Civil Cases), U.S. Fifth Circuit District Judges Association (1991), Instruction 15.2, and 42 U.S.C. § 1981a.

Given:
Denied:
Given as Modified:

PLAINTIFFS' INSTRUCTION 15
BACK PAY AND BENEFITS

One element of the damages that you must consider is back pay and benefits. That is, as part of a damage recovery, you must award [Charles Wessel] an amount equal to the pay and benefits that he would have received from the Defendants had he not been discharged, from the time that he was discharged until the date of trial, unless you find that [Charles Wessel] became unable to perform the essential functions of the position of Executive Director with or without reasonable accommodation at some point following his discharge and prior to the date of trial. If you so find, then you should calculate back pay and benefits from the date of discharge up to the date that he became unable to perform the essential functions of the position of Executive Director. The parties have stipulated that [Wessel] would have earned [$3,893.75] per month for each month he continued to work for [A.I.C.]. The parties have stipulated that [Wessel] was receiving [$350.00] per month designated as a car allowance from [A.I.C.], but disputes whether he would have continued to receive it for each month that he continued to be employed by EEOC. The parties have also stipulated that Defendants would have paid [$598.84] per month in health insurance premiums and [$247.72] per quarter in life insurance premiums as long as [Wessel] had remained employed. You may include in the calculation all forms of compensation [Wessel] would have earned, including salary, car allowances, bonuses, raises, vacation pay, and health insurance benefits.

Plaintiffs are not required to prove with unrealistic precision the amount of lost earnings, if any, due to [Wessel]. Any ambiguities in determining what he would have earned should be resolved against the Defendants.

If Defendants prove that [Charles Wessel] unjustifiably failed to take a new job of like kind, status, and pay which was available to him, or failed to make reasonable efforts to find a new job, you should subtract from his damages any amount he could have earned in a new job after his discharge.

Adapted from Devitt and Blackmar, Federal Jury Practice and Instruction, § 106.07.

Given:
Denied:
Given as modified:

PLAINTIFFS' INSTRUCTION 16
REASONABLE ACCOMMODATION

In this case Plaintiffs do not claim that Defendants should have provided a reasonable accommodation to [Wessel] prior to his discharge. [Wessel] never requested a reasonable accommodation, and claims that he was able to perform the essential functions of his position without accommodation. However, if you determine that Plaintiffs have proven that [Wessel] was unlawfully terminated because of his disability, then you may consider the question of reasonable accommodation in determining the back pay to which [Wessel] is entitled. Back pay should include lost earnings for the period during which [Wessel] could have continued to perform the essential functions of his position, with or without reasonable accommodation.

The term reasonable accommodation means modification or adjustment to the work environment, or to the manner or circumstances under which a job is customarily held or performed.

Required reasonable accommodations may include: making existing facilities used by employees readily accessible to and usable by individuals with disabilities; job restructuring; part-time or modified work schedules; reassignment to a vacant position; modification of examinations, training materials, or policies; the provision of qualified readers or interpreters; and other similar accommodations for individuals with disabilities. The list is not exhaustive, but is intended to provide general guidance about the reasonable accommodation concept.

42 U.S.C. § 12111(9) (1991); 29 C.F.R. § 1630.2(o).

Given:
Denied:
Given as Modified:

PLAINTIFFS' INSTRUCTION 17
FUTURE OUT-OF-POCKET EXPENSES

If you find for Plaintiffs, you should also consider future out-of-pocket expenses. These include the reasonable expected costs for expenses such as insurance premiums and other consequential damages which will result from Defendants' discriminatory conduct.

Given:
Denied:
Given as Modified:

PLAINTIFFS' INSTRUCTION 18
COMPENSATORY DAMAGE FOR INTANGIBLE INJURY

No evidence of the monetary value of intangible things, such as mental or physical pain and suffering, has been, or need be, introduced. You are not trying to determine value, but an amount that will fairly compensate [Wessel] for the damages he has suffered. There is no exact standard for fixing the compensation to be awarded for these elements of damage. Any award that you make should be fair in light of the evidence.

If you find that [Wessel] is entitled to compensatory damages for intangible losses, you should be guided by dispassionate common sense. Computing damages may be difficult, but you must not let that difficulty lead you to engage in arbitrary guesswork. On the other hand, the law does not require that the Plaintiffs prove the amount of [Wessel]'s losses with mathematical precision, but only with as much definiteness and accuracy as the circumstances permit.

Adapted from Pattern Jury Instructions (Civil Cases), U.S. Fifth Circuit District Judges Association (1991), Instruction 15.4.

Given:
Denied:
Given as Modified:

PLAINTIFFS' INSTRUCTION 19
PUNITIVE DAMAGES

If you find that the Defendants are liable for [Wessel]'s injuries, you must award the compensatory damages Plaintiffs have proven. You also may award punitive damages, if the Plaintiffs have proved that a Defendant acted with malice or willfulness or with reckless indifference to the rights of [Wessel]. One acts willfully with respect to the rights of others if the Defendant knew or should have known that [Wessel]'s rights would be violated by the discriminatory acts proven.

Punitive damages, unlike back pay and benefits, out-of-pocket expenses and other compensatory damages, should be considered for each Defendant separately. If you determine that a Defendant acted with malice or with reckless indifference to [Wessel]'s right as to justify an award of punitive damages, you may exercise your discretion to award those damages. In making any award of punitive damages, you should consider that the purpose of punitive damages is to punish the Defendant for malicious or reckless conduct, and to deter the Defendant and others from engaging in similar conduct in the future. The law does not require you to award punitive damages, however. If you decide to award punitive damages, you must use sound reason in setting the amount of the damages. The amount of an award of punitive damages must not reflect bias, prejudice, or sympathy toward any party. However, the amount can be as large as you believe necessary to fulfill the purposes of punitive damages. You may consider the financial resources of the Defendant in fixing the amount of punitive damages, and may impose punitive damages against one or more of the Defendants, and not others, or against more than one Defendants in different amounts.

Adapted from Pattern Jury Instructions (Civil Cases), U.S. Fifth Circuit District Judges Association (1991), Instruction 15.13, 42 U.S.C. § 1981a(b)(1)(1991).

Given:
Denied:
Given as Modified:

PLAINTIFFS' INSTRUCTION 20
VERDICT FORMS

Upon retiring to the jury room, you will select one of your number to act as Foreperson. The Foreperson will preside over your deliberations, and will be your spokesperson here in Court.

Verdict forms have been prepared for your convenience.

If you find in favor of [Wessel] and against the Defendants, you should calculate damages, using the jury verdict form which reads as follows:

We the jury find that the Defendants violated the Americans with Disabilities Act by discharging [Charles Wessel] on the basis of his disability.

Having found in favor of [Wessel] and against Defendants, we further assess damages in the following amount:

___ Back pay and benefits

___ Future out-of-pocket expenses

___ Compensatory damages for intangible losses.

If you find that the Defendants violated the ADA, and you further find that the Defendants or any of them engaged in a discriminatory practice with malice or with reckless indifference to the federally protected rights of [Wessel], you may award punitive damages, using the jury verdict form which reads as follows:

We the jury find that [the Defendant] violated the Americans with Disabilities Act by discharging [Charles Wessel] on the basis of his disability.

Having found in favor of [Wessel] and having further found that [the Defendant] engaged in a discriminatory practice with malice or with reckless indifference to the federally protected rights of [Wessel], we assess punitive damages in the amount of [____].

If you find in favor of the Defendants and against [Wessel], you should use the jury verdict form which reads as follows:

We the jury find that the Defendant did not violate the Americans with Disabilities Act by discharging [Charles Wessel], and therefore find for the Defendants and against the Plaintiffs.

You will take the verdict forms to the jury room and, when you have reached unanimous agreement as to your verdict, you will have your Foreperson fill in, date and sign the form which sets forth the verdict upon which you unanimously agree; and then return with your verdict to the courtroom.

Adapted from Devitt, Blackmar and Wolff, Federal Jury Practice and Instruction, § 74.04.

Given:
Denied:
Given as modified:

PLAINTIFFS' VERDICT FORM (ALL DEFENDANTS)

We the jury find that the Defendants violated the Americans with Disabilities Act by discharging [Charles Wessel] on the basis on his disability.

Having found in favor of [Wessel] and against Defendants, we further assess damages in the following amounts:

___ Back pay and benefits

___ Future out-of-pocket expenses

___ Compensatory damages for intangible losses.

[Foreperson]

PLAINTIFFS' VERDICT FORM ([A.I.C. SECURITY INVESTIGATIONS, LTD.])

We the jury find that the Defendant [A.I.C. Security Investigations, Ltd.] violated the Americans with Disabilities Act by discharging [Charles Wessel] on the basis on his disability.

Having found in favor of [Wessel] and having further found that [A.I.C. Security Investigations, Ltd.] engaged in a discriminatory practice with malice or with reckless indifference to the federally protected rights of [Wessel], we assess punitive damages in the amount of [___].

[Foreperson]

PLAINTIFFS' VERDICT FORM ([A.I.C. INTERNATIONAL, LTD.])

We the jury find that the Defendant [A.I.C. International, Ltd.] violated the Americans with Disabilities Act by discharging [Charles Wessel] on the basis on his disability.

Having found in favor of [Wessel] and having further found that [A.I.C. International, Ltd.] engaged in a discriminatory practice with malice or with reckless indifference to the federally protected rights of [Wessel], we assess punitive damages in the amount of [___].

[Foreperson]

PLAINTIFFS' VERDICT FORM (DEFENDANT C)

We the jury find that Defendant [C] violated the Americans with Disabilities Act by discharging [Charles Wessel] on the basis on his disability.

Having found in favor of [Wessel] and having further found that [defendant C] engaged in a discriminatory practice with malice or with reckless indifference to the federally protected rights of [Wessel], we assess punitive damages in the amount of [___].

[Foreperson]

PLAINTIFFS' VERDICT FORM

We the jury find that the Defendants did not violate the Americans with Disabilities Act by discharging [Charles Wessel], and therefore find for the Defendants and against the Plaintiffs.

[Foreperson]

§ 16.22   Defendants' Proposed Jury Instructions (EEOC)

FORM 16–14
SAMPLE DEFENDANTS' PROPOSED JURY INSTRUCTIONS

DEFENDANTS' PROPOSED JURY INSTRUCTIONS

PRELIMINARY INSTRUCTION—PART ONE

DEFENDANTS' INSTRUCTION 1
EXPERT WITNESSES

A witness who has special knowledge, skill, experience, or training of education in a certain field may give his or her opinion as an expert to any matter in which he or she is skilled. in determining the weight to be given to the experts' opinions, you should consider the qualifications and reliability of the expert and the reasons given for his or her opinion. Consider how extensive each expert's educational background is in the field. You are not bound by an expert's opinion merely because he or she is an expert; you may accept or reject it, as in the case of other witnesses. Give it the weight you deem it entitled.

Given:
Denied:
Given as Modified:

DEFENDANTS' INSTRUCTION 2
AMERICANS WITH DISABILITIES ACT

This is an action brought under the Americans with Disabilities Act. The Act makes it unlawful for an employer to discriminate against a qualified individual with a disability. The Act provides no protection to an individual with a disability who is not qualified.

A qualified individual with a disability is a person who, with or without reasonable accommodation, can perform the essential functions of the employment position.

DEFENDANTS' INSTRUCTION 3
CONTENTIONS OF THE PARTIES

In this case, Plaintiffs claim that, because of [Charles H. Wessel]'s disability, he was unjustifiably discharged from his position as Executive Director at [A.I.C. Security Investigations, Ltd.].

The Defendants deny that they unjustifiably discharged [Wessel] from employment on account of his disability. The Defendants instead contend that [Wessel] was justifiably excluded from the position of Executive Director because he could no longer perform the essential functions of the position of Executive Director at [A.I.C. Security Investigations, Ltd.] with or without reasonable accommodation. Defendants also contend that [Wessel] was excluded from his position as Executive Director due to legitimate business reasons. In addition, Defendants contend that they, in good faith, offered [Charles H. Wessel] further reasonable accommodations, provided to [Charles H. Wessel] reasonable accommodations, and that any further accommodation beyond those offered would have imposed an undue hardship upon the business [A.I.C. Security Investigations, Ltd.]. Defendants also contend that Plaintiff posed a direct threat to the health or safety of himself or others in the workplace.

Adapted from Pattern Jury Instructions (Civil Cases), U.S. Fifth Circuit District Judges Association (1983), Federal Claims Instruction No. 10 (1983).

Given:
Denied:
Given as Modified:

DEFENDANTS' INSTRUCTION 4
PLAINTIFFS' PRIMA FACIE CASE

The Plaintiff in an Americans with Disabilities Act (the "ADA") case has the burden of proving by a preponderance of the evidence all of the following elements:

1)   That [Wessel] has a "disability," as that term is defined in the ADA;

2)   That he is "otherwise qualified" for the position he held. This element requires proof by the Plaintiffs, by a preponderance of the evidence, that, except for [Wessel]'s disability, [Wessel] possessed the necessary qualifications for the

position, such as educational background, experience, skills, and other job-related factors;

3)   That [Wessel] was capable of performing all of the essential functions of the position of Executive Director either with or without reasonable accommodation by the employer;

4)   That [Wessel]'s disability did not prevent him from performing the essential functions of the position, such that any functions he could not perform because of his disability were marginal functions not essential to performance of the job of Executive Director; and

5)   That [Wessel]'s disability was the sole motivating factor in the decisions ending [Wessel]'s employment with [A.I.C. Security Investigations].

Adapted from [*School Board of Nassau County v. Arline*, 480 U.S. 273, 275 (1987)]; [*Ristoff v. United States*, 839 F.2d 1242 (7th Cir. 1988)].

Given:
Denied:
Given as Modified:

DEFENDANTS' INSTRUCTION 5
DEFENDANTS' REBUTTAL OF PLAINTIFF'S PRIMA FACIE CASE—INTENTIONAL DISABILITY DISCRIMINATION

If you find that Plaintiff has shown the foregoing elements, then you should consider Defendants' explanation for its conduct toward Plaintiff.

Defendants have contended that their actions toward [Wessel] were taken for reasons unrelated to [Wessel]'s disability. Therefore, Defendants need only articulate to you a legitimate, nondiscriminatory reason for their conduct towards [Charles Wessel]. With respect to such reasons, Plaintiff, in order to prevail, must then convince you by a preponderance of the evidence either that an unlawfully discriminatory reason was the sole motivating factor for the decision, or that Defendants' stated reasons were mere pretext. Pretext is shown if you find that the stated reasons are false or are unworthy of belief.

If Plaintiff has so satisfied you, you should find for Plaintiff. If not, you should find for Defendants.

Adapted from Federal Claims Instruction No. 10, Pattern Jury Instructions-Civil Cases (U.S. Fifth Circuit District Judges Ass'n 1983); [*School Board of Nassau County v. Arline*, 480 U.S. 273, 275 (1987)]; [*Ristoff v. United States*, 839 F.2d 1242 (7th Cir. 1988)]. *See* [*McDonnell Douglas Corp. v. Green*, 411 U.S. 792, 802–06 (1973)]; [*Texas Department of Community Affairs v. Burdine*, 450 U.S. 248, 256–69 (1981)].

Given:
Denied:
Given as Modified:

DEFENDANTS' INSTRUCTION 6
DEFENDANTS' REBUTTAL OF PLAINTIFF'S PRIMA FACIE CASE—REASONABLE
ACCOMMODATION AND DEFENSE OF UNDUE HARDSHIP

Defendants will be excused from liability if Defendants prove by a preponderance of the evidence the following: that [Wessel]'s disability prevented him from performing essential functions of the job; and that there is no accommodation Defendants could have made without undue hardship that would enable [Wessel] to perform all essential functions of the job.

If you find that [Wessel]'s disability was the sole motivating factor in that decision, Defendants will be excused from liability if they prove by a preponderance of the evidence the following: that [Wessel]'s disability prevented him from performing any of the essential functions of the job; and that there is no further reasonable accommodation Defendants could have made without undue hardship that would enable [Wessel] to perform all essential functions of the job.

Here, this affirmative defense of Defendants' inability to make further reasonable accommodations without undue hardship that would enable [Wessel] to perform the essential functions of the job is claimed by Defendants as the basis for their employment decisions regarding [Wessel].

To determine whether Defendants have met their burden of proof on this affirmative defense as to each of these employment decisions, you must consider the following issues: the essential functions of the Executive Director job, reasonable accommodation, and undue hardship. I will explain the significance of each of these issues in turn.

42 U.S.C. §§ 12111, 12113; 29 C.F.R. §§ 1630.2(m)–(p), 1630.9, 1630.15(b)–(d) and guidelines; [*School Board of Nassau County v. Arline*, 480 U.S. 273, 275 (1987)]; [*Chiari v. City of League City*, 920 F.2d 311, 315–19 (5th Cir. 1991)]; [*Prewitt v. United States Postal Service*, 662 F.2d 292, 307–10 (5th Cir. 1981)]; [*Strathie v. Department of Transportation*, 716 F.2d 227, 230–31 (3d Cir. 1983)].

Given:
Denied:
Given as Modified:

DEFENDANTS' INSTRUCTION 7
ADA: ESSENTIAL FUNCTIONS OF THE JOB

Job functions may be considered essential for any of several reasons, such as the following:

1) The employer's judgment as to what functions of a job are essential;

2) The reason the position exists is to perform that function;

3) A limited number of employees are available among whom the performance of the function may be distributed; or

4) The function is highly specialized so that the incumbent is hired for his or her expertise or ability to perform that particular function.

Evidence of whether a particular function is essential also includes the amount of time the employee must spend performing the function; the consequences of not requiring the incumbent to perform the function; and the work experiences of incumbents in similar jobs. To the extent such evidence is before you, you may consider all of these factors in determining whether any particular function is essential to the job in question. Defendants have the burden of proving by a preponderance of the evidence that any particular function is essential to the job in question.

42 U.S.C. § 12111(8). 29 C.F.R. § 1630.2(n)(2)(3).

Given:
Denied:
Given as Modified:

DEFENDANTS' INSTRUCTION 8
ADA: PERFORMANCE STANDARDS

It is important to note that the inquiry into essential functions is not intended to second-guess an employer's business judgment with regard to performance standards, whether qualitative or quantitative, or to require employers to lower such standards.

29 C.F.R. § 1630. (interpretive Guidance on Title I of the Americans with Disabilities Act, *id.* § 1630.2(n)).

Given:
Denied:
Given as Modified:

DEFENDANTS' INSTRUCTION 9
ADA: REASONABLE ACCOMMODATION

An accommodation is a modification or adjustment to the work environment, or to the manner or circumstances under which the position held or desired is customarily performed, that enables a qualified individual with a disability to perform the essential functions of the job. Plaintiffs bear the initial burden of coming forward with evidence that a proposed accommodation is reasonable and that such an accommodation could permit the essential functions of the job to be performed where, without such accommodation, they could not be performed.

An employer would not be required to make an accommodation if the accommodation is unreasonable. A proposed accommodation is unreasonable if it would alter the essential nature of the position or reallocate essential functions of the job to another individual. Defendants bear the burden of proving by a preponderance of the evidence if the accommodation is reasonable. Defendants would not have to implement the accommodation if it would impose an undue hardship on the business of [A.I.C. Security Investigations].

[*Overton v. Reilly,* 977 F.2d 1190, 1194 (7th Cir. 1992)]; [*Treadwell v. Alexander,* 707 F.2d 473, 478 (11th Cir. 1983)]; 42 U.S.C. § 12111(9); 29 C.F.R. § 1630.2(o) and guidelines thereto.

Given:
Denied:
Given as Modified:

DEFENDANTS' INSTRUCTION 10
ADA: UNDUE HARDSHIP

A proposed accommodation would impose an undue hardship on [A.I.C. Security Investigations], and Defendants would not be liable for failing to implement such an accommodation, if the accommodation would impose significant difficulty and expense on the business of [A.I.C. Security Investigations]. In determining whether any proposed accommodation would create an undue hardship, you may consider the following factors to the extent there is evidence of them before you:

1)   The nature and net cost of the accommodation needed, taking into consideration the availability of tax credits and deductions or outside funding;

2)   The overall financial resources of employer's facility or facilities involved in the provision of the accommodation, the number of persons employed at such facility, and the effect on the employer's expense and resources;

3)   The overall financial resources of the employer as a whole, the overall size of the business with respect to its total number of employees, and the number, type, and location of its facilities;

4)   The type of operation or operations of employer, including the composition, structure, and functions of the work force, and the geographic separateness and administrative or fiscal relationship of the facility or facilities in question to the employer; and

5)   The impact of the accommodation on the operation of the facility involved, including the impact on the ability of the other employees to perform their duties and the impact on the facility's ability to conduct business.

Defendants also bear the burden of proving by a preponderance of the evidence that a proposed accommodation would create undue hardship on the business of [A.I.C. Security Investigations].

42 U.S.C. § 12111(10)(b); 29 C.F.R. § 1630.2(p) and guidelines thereto.

Given:
Denied:
Given as Modified:

DEFENDANTS' INSTRUCTION 11
ADA: FAILURE TO PERFORM ESSENTIAL FUNCTION OF JOB

If Plaintiffs do not prove to your satisfaction by a preponderance of the evidence that [Wessel] could perform all of the essential functions of the job of Executive Director for [A.I.C.], even with any reasonable accommodation that would not cause an undue hardship on the business of [A.I.C.] presented in the evidence during this trial, you must find in favor of Defendants.

[*Chiari v. City of League City*, 920 F.2d 311, 318 (5th Cir. 1991)]; [*Prewitt v. United States Postal Service*, 662 F.2d 292, 308 (5th Cir. 1981)].

Given:
Denied:
Given as Modified:

DEFENDANTS' INSTRUCTION 12
ADA: LIMITATION ON DAMAGES—GOOD FAITH AND INDEPENDENT JUSTIFICATION

If your finding is that Defendants discriminated against [Wessel] by failing to provide any reasonable accommodation that [A.I.C. Security Investigations] could have provided without undue hardship to itself, then you will be asked to answer two further questions. First, you will be asked to determine whether the Defendants have proved by a preponderance of the evidence that they made a good faith effort to identify and make a reasonable accommodation.

Second, you will be asked to determine whether Defendants have proved by a preponderance of the evidence that [Wessel] would not have remained employed, even in the absence of discrimination, because of [Wessel]'s disability. That is, you must also determine whether Defendants have shown by a preponderance of the evidence that disability discrimination was not the sole factor in the decision.

Your answer to these questions will have a bearing on the relief available to [Wessel], which need not concern you at this time, and about which you should not speculate.

42 U.S.C. § 1981a(a)(3).

Given:
Denied:
Given as Modified:

DEFENDANTS' INSTRUCTION 13
THREAT TO SAFETY DEFENSE

If you find that the Plaintiffs have established each of the elements of their claim, then you will consider this defense, which the Defendants must establish by a preponderance of the evidence. It is the Defendants' defense that [Charles Wessel] poses a threat to the health or safety of himself or others in the workplace.

You may find that [Charles Wessel] poses a direct threat only if the Defendants have proved, more likely than not, that [Charles Wessel] poses a significant risk to the health and safety of himself or others in the workplace that cannot be eliminated or reduced by reasonable accommodation.

If an individual poses a direct threat as a result of his disability, the employer must determine whether a reasonable accommodation would either eliminate the risk or reduce it to an acceptable level.

Adapted from Americans with Disabilities Act, 42 U.S.C. §§ 12113(b), 12111(3); [*School Board of Nassau County v. Arline*, 480 U.S. 273, 275 (1987)]; [*Mantolete v. Bolger*, 767 F.2d 1416 (9th Cir. 1985)]; [*Strathie v. Department of Transportation*, 716 F.2d 227 (3d Cir. 1983)].

Given:
Denied:
Given as Modified:

DEFENDANTS' SPECIAL INTERROGATORIES
FIRST SET OF SPECIAL INTERROGATORIES

1)   Do you find that Plaintiffs have proved by a preponderance of the evidence that [Charles H. Wessel] was able to perform the essential functions of the position of Executive Director with or without reasonable accommodation?

Yes [___] No [___]

If your answer to question 1 is "Yes," answer question 2.

If your answer to question 1 is "No," skip questions 2, 3, and 4.

2)   Do you find that Plaintiffs have proved by a preponderance of the evidence that Defendants discharged [Charles H. Wessel] from his position of Executive Director solely because of [Wessel]'s disability?

Yes [___] No [___]

If your answer to question 2 is "No," skip questions 3 and 4.

If your answer to question 2 is "Yes," answer question 3.

3)   Do you find that Defendants have proved by a preponderance of the evidence that there is no reasonable accommodation it could have made without undue hardship to [A.I.C. Security Investigations] that would have enabled [Wessel] to perform all of the essential functions of the job of Executive Director?

Yes [___] No [___]

If your answer to question 3 is "Yes," skip question 4.

If your answer to question 3 is "No," answer question 4.

4)   Do you find that Defendants have proved by a preponderance of the evidence that they would have discharged [Charles Wessel] from his position as Executive Director due to legitimate business reasons in the absence of any discrimination on the basis [Wessel]'s disability?

Yes [___] No [___]

INSTRUCTIONS TO BE FOLLOWED AFTER ANSWERING FIRST SET OF SPECIAL INTERROGATORIES

If you answered "Yes" to Interrogatories 1 and 2 above and "No" to Interrogatories 3 or 4 above, then complete Verdict Form 2 which follows. If you answered "No" to Interrogatories 1 and 2 above or "Yes" to Interrogatories 3 or 4 above, then complete Verdict Form 1 which follows. If you complete Verdict Form 2, you must answer the Second Set of Interrogatories.

VERDICT FORM 1

We the jury find that the Defendants did not violate the Americans with Disabilities Act, and therefore find for the Defendants and against the Plaintiffs.

[Foreperson]

NOTE: If you answered this verdict form, then do not answer Second Set of Special Interrogatories and return this form to the judge immediately.

VERDICT FORM 2

We the jury find that the following Defendants violated the Americans with Disabilities Act (place an "X" by each Defendant you find liable):

[A.I.C. Security Investigations, Ltd.] [___]
[A.I.C. International, Ltd.] [___]
[Defendant C] [___]

[Foreperson]

NOTE: If you completed this verdict form, then answer Second Set of Special Interrogatories.

SECOND SET OF SPECIAL INTERROGATORIES

1)   Do you find that Defendants have proved by a preponderance of the evidence that they made a good faith effort to make a reasonable accommodation to enable Plaintiff to perform the job of Executive Director?

Yes [___] No [___]

[Foreperson]

NOTE: Now please go on to the Jury Instructions pertaining to damages.

DAMAGES

DEFENDANTS' INSTRUCTION 14
INSTRUCTION NOT TO BE TAKEN AS INDICATION OF LIABILITY: PLAINTIFF MUST PROVE DAMAGES

I will now instruct you on the issue of damages. My charge to you on the law of damages must not be taken as any indication that you must decide for the Plaintiffs. It is for you to decide on the evidence presented and the rules of law I give you whether [Charles H. Wessel] is entitled to recover anything from the Defendants. If you decide that [Charles H. Wessel] is not entitled to recover, your verdict will be for the Defendants and you need not go further. Only if you decide that [Charles H. Wessel]'s rights under the Americans With Disabilities Act ("ADA") have been violated by the intentional acts of the Defendants, will you then consider the measure of damages. In other words, if you find that the Plaintiffs have failed to prove any one of the elements of proof which are essential to their claim by a preponderance of the evidence, then your verdict must be against the Plaintiffs and in favor of Defendants of this claim. In this case, the Plaintiff EEOC is seeking compensatory damages for [Charles H. Wessel]. Plaintiff [Wessel] is seeking compensatory and punitive damages. It is the Plaintiffs' burden to prove that [Charles H. Wessel] actually suffered damages and that such damages were directly caused by Defendants. It is Plaintiffs' burden to prove the amount of such damages by a preponderance of the credible evidence.

[*Memphis Community School District v. Stachura,* 106 S. Ct. 2537 (1986)]; [*Carey v. Piphus,* 435 U.S. 247, 264–65 (1978)].

Given:
Denied:
Given as Modified:

DEFENDANTS' INSTRUCTION 15
COMPENSATORY DAMAGES

If you find that the Defendants are liable to [Charles H. Wessel], then you must also determine an amount that is fair compensation for his damages. The purpose of compensatory damages is to make [Wessel] whole—that is, to compensate him for the damage that he has suffered. Compensatory damages are not limited to expenses that [Wessel] may have incurred. If Defendants are found liable, Plaintiff is entitled to compensatory damages for physical injury, pain and suffering, mental anguish, shock, and discomfort that he has suffered as a direct result of Defendants' conduct.

You can award compensatory damages only for injuries that the Plaintiffs prove were the proximate result of the Defendants' allegedly wrongful conduct. The damages that you award must be full compensation for all of [Charles H. Wessel]'s damages, no more and no less. Compensatory damages are not allowed as a punishment and cannot be imposed or increased to penalize the Defendant. You should not award compensatory damages for speculative injuries, but only for those injuries which [Charles H. Wessel] has actually suffered or is reasonably likely to suffer in the future.

If you decide to award compensatory damages, you should be guided by dispassionate common sense. Computing damages may be difficult, but you must not let that difficulty lead you to engage in arbitrary guesswork. On the other hand, the law does not require that the Plaintiffs prove the amount of [Wessel]'s losses with mathematical precision, but only with as much definiteness and accuracy as the circumstances permit.

You must use sound discretion in fixing an award of damages, drawing reasonable inferences where you find them appropriate from the facts and circumstances in evidence.

Adapted from Pattern Jury Instructions (Civil Cases), U.S. Fifth Circuit District Judges Association (1991), Instruction 15.2; 42 U.S.C. § 1981a.

Given:
Denied:
Given as Modified:

DEFENDANTS' INSTRUCTION 16
BACK PAY AWARD

One element of the damages that you must consider is back pay. That is, as part of a damage recovery, you must award [Charles H. Wessel] an amount equal to the pay and benefits that he would have received from the Defendants had he not been discharged until the date of trial, unless you find that [Charles H. Wessel] became unable to perform the essential functions of the position of Executive Director with or without reasonable accommodation at some point following his discharge and prior to the date of trial. If you so find, then you should calculate back pay and benefits from the date of discharge up to the date that he became unable to perform the essential functions of the position of Executive Director. The parties have stipulated that [Wessel] would have earned [$3,893.75] per month for each month he continued to work for [A.I.C.]. The parties have also stipulated that Defendants would have paid [$598.84] per month in health insurance premiums and [$247.72] per quarter in life insurance premiums as long as he had remained employed.

There are certain deductions and offsets which must be made relative to any back pay award.

First, you must deduct from any back pay award any amount which could have been earned by [Wessel] through the exercise of reasonable diligence from the time of his layoff.

Second, all unemployment, Social Security, Supplemental Unemployment, and other benefits received by [Wessel] must be deducted from any back pay award.

Third, you may not include back pay for any period during which [Wessel] merely drew unemployment compensation and did not actively seek employment.

Adapted from Devitt & Blackmar, Federal Jury Practice and Instructions §§ 87.14 and 87.19 (Supp. 1980); [*Schulz v. Hickok Manufacturing Co.,* 358 F. Supp. 1208 (N.D. Ga. 1973)]; [*Dunlop v. Hawaiian Telephone Co.,* 415 F. Supp. 330 (D. Haw. 1976)]; 29 C.F.R. § 60.110(19); [*Bowe v. Colgate-Palmolive Co.,* 416 F.2d 711 (7th Cir. 1969)]; [*Bradford v. Sloan Paper Co.,* 383 F. Supp. 1157 (N.D. Ala. 1974)]; [*Peters v. Missouri Pacific Railroad,* 483 F.2d 490 (5th Cir.), *cert. denied,* 414 U.S. 1002 (1973)]; [*Buick v. Board of Education,* 10 Empl. Prac. Dec. ¶ 10,363 (E.D.N.Y. 1975)]; [*Doe v. Osteopathic Hospital of Wichita, Inc.,* 330 F. Supp. 1357 (D. Kan. 1971)]; [*Ainsworth v. United States,* 399 F.2d 176 (Ct. Cl. 1968)].

Given:

Denied:
Given as Modified:

DEFENDANTS' INSTRUCTION 17
EFFECT OF FAILURE TO MITIGATE DAMAGES

You are instructed that any person who claims damages as a result of alleged discrimination has a duty under the law to mitigate those damages—that is, to take advantage of any reasonable opportunity he may have had under the circumstances to reduce or minimize the loss or damage. An employee who believes he has been wrongfully dismissed has a duty to make every reasonable effort to seek and accept other employment. It was [Wessel]'s duty to earn what he could from the time he was no longer working for [A.I.C. Security Investigations].

So, if you should find from a preponderance of the evidence that [Wessel] failed to seek out and take advantage of an employment that was reasonably available to him under all the circumstances, as shown by the evidence, then you should reduce the amount of his damages by the amount he could have reasonably realized if he had taken advantage of such an opportunity. You must not compensate [Wessel] for any portion of his damages which resulted from his failure to use ordinary care to minimize his damages and to seek other employment.

Adapted from Devitt & Blackmar, Federal Jury Practice and Instructions §§ 1, 86.06 (Supp. 1980); 42 U.S.C. § 2000e-5(g); 8 Am. Jur. Pleading and Practice Forms (Damages), Form 335 (Rev. 1969); [*Higgins v. Lawrence PC*, 107 Mich. App. 178, 181, 309 N.W.2d 194 (1981)]; [*Taylor v. Safeway Stores, Inc.*, 524 F.2d 263 (10th Cir. 1975)].

Given:
Denied:
Given as Modified:

DEFENDANTS' INSTRUCTION 18
DUTY TO MITIGATE—DEFINITION

If you find that [Wessel] failed to mitigate his damages, you must reduce the sum you award to [Wessel] by the amount he could have earned. By mitigating damages I mean that [Wessel] exercised reasonable care and diligence to obtain suitable alternative employment.

If you find that [Wessel] did not make any efforts to obtain suitable alternative employment and you find that other jobs for which [Wessel] was qualified were available, [Wessel] would have failed to mitigate his damages. Any amounts that he could have earned should be deducted from his back pay award. Similarly, if you find [Wessel] refused employment, any interim jobs, then you must reduce the back pay awarded by the amount he could have earned had he not refused or voluntarily terminated employment.

[*Coleman v. City of Omaha,* 714 F.2d 804 (8th Cir. 1983)]; [*Jackson v. Shell Oil Co.,* 702 F.2d 197 (9th Cir. 1983)]; [*EEOC v. Sandia Corp.,* 639 F.2d 600 (10th Cir. 1980)]; [*Wehr v. Burroughs Corp.,* 619 F.2d 276 (3d Cir. 1980)]; [*United States v. Lee Way Motor Freight, Inc.,* 625 F.2d 918 (10th Cir. 1979)].

Given:
Denied:
Given as Modified:

DEFENDANTS' INSTRUCTION 19
CALCULATION OF FUTURE DAMAGES

If you should find that [Wessel] is reasonably certain to suffer damages in the future from his injuries, then you should award him the amount you believe would fairly compensate him for such future damages, unless you find that [Wessel] became unable to perform the essential functions of the position of Executive Director at some point following his discharge and prior to the date of trial.

If you so find, you should stop calculating damages as of that point in time. In the alternative, if you find that [Wessel] will be unable to perform the essential functions of the position of Executive Director at some point in time after trial, then you should stop calculating damages as of that date. An award of future damages requires that payment be made now for a loss that the Plaintiff will not actually suffer until some future date. If you should find that the Plaintiff is entitled to future damages, including future earnings, then you must determine the present worth in dollars of such future damages.

If you award damages for loss of future earning, you must consider two particular factors:

1)   You should reduce any award by the amount of the expenses that the Plaintiff would have incurred in making those earnings.

2)   If you make an award for future loss of earnings, you must reduce it to present value by considering the interest that the Plaintiff could earn on the amount of the award if he made a relatively risk-free investment. The reason you must make this reduction is because an award of an amount representing future loss of earnings is more valuable to the Plaintiff if he receives it today than if he received it in the future, when he would otherwise have earned it. It is more valuable because the Plaintiff can earn interest on it for the period of time between the date of the award and the date he would have earned the money. Thus, you should adjust the amount of interest that the Plaintiff can earn on that amount in the future.

If you make any award for future medical expenses, you should adjust or discount the award to present value in the same manner as with loss of future earnings.

However, you may not make any adjustment to present value for any damages you may award for future pain and suffering or future mental anguish.

Pattern Jury Instructions (Civil Cases), U.S. Fifth Circuit District Judges Association (1991), Instruction 13.3.

Given:
Denied:
Given as Modified:

DEFENDANTS' INSTRUCTION 20
PUNITIVE DAMAGES

If Defendant were found liable to [Charles H. Wessel], you must award [Wessel] the compensatory damages that Plaintiffs have proven. You also may award punitive damages, if [Wessel] has proved that Defendants acted with malice or reckless indifference to the civil rights of [Wessel]. "Malice" means conduct which is intended by the Defendants to cause in jury to [Wessel] or carried on by the Defendants with a conscious disregard of the rights or safety of [Wessel] when they are aware of the probable dangerous consequences of his or her conduct and willfully and deliberately fail to avoid those consequences.

If you determine that the Defendants acted with reckless indifference to [Wessel]'s civil rights as to justify an award of punitive damages, you may exercise your discretion to award those damages. In making any award of punitive damages, you should consider that the purpose of punitive damages is to punish a Defendant for malicious conduct, and to deter the Defendants and others from engaging in similar conduct in the future. The law does not require you to award punitive damages; however, if you decide to award punitive damages, you must use sound reason in setting the amount of damages. The amount of an award of punitive damages must not reflect bias, prejudice, or sympathy toward any party. However, the amount can be as large as you believe necessary to fulfill the purposes of punitive damages. You may consider the financial resources of the Defendants in fixing the amount of punitive damages.

Pattern Jury Instructions (Civil Cases), U.S. 5th Circuit District Judges Association (1991), Instruction 15.13; 42 U.S.C. § 1981a.

Given:
Denied:
Given as Modified:

VERDICT FORMS

Upon retiring to the jury room, you will select one of your members to act as foreperson. The foreperson will preside over your deliberation, and will be your spokesperson here in Court.

Verdict forms have been prepared for your convenience.

If you find in favor of [Wessel] and against the Defendants you should calculate damages, using the jury verdict form which reads as follows:

VERDICT FORM 1

We the jury find that the Defendants violated the Americans With Disabilities Act by discharging [Charles Wessel] on the basis of his disability.

Having found in favor of [Wessel] and against the Defendant, we award [Wessel] back pay in the following amount: [___].

We would enter the above award of back pay against the following Defendants in the following amounts:

NOTE: You are to apportion the above award of back pay among the Defendants.

    [A.I.C. International, Ltd.] [___]
    [A.I.C. Security Investigations, Ltd.] [___]
    [defendant C] [___]

[Foreperson]

If you find that the Defendants violated the ADA, and you further find that Defendants did not prove that they demonstrated good faith efforts to reasonably accommodate [Charles Wessel]'s disability, then you should use jury Verdict Form 2 instead of jury Verdict Form 1. Jury Verdict Form 2 reads as follows:

VERDICT FORM 2

We the jury find that the Defendants violated the Americans With Disabilities Act by discharging [Charles Wessel] on the basis of his disability.

Having found in favor of [Wessel] and having further found that Defendants did not prove that they demonstrated good faith efforts to reasonably accommodate [Charles Wessel]'s disability, we assess damages as follows:

Back pay [___]

We would enter the above back pay award against the following Defendants:

NOTE: You are to apportion the above award of back pay among the Defendants.

    [A.I.C. International, Ltd.] [___]

[A.I.C. Security Investigations, Ltd.] [___]
[defendant C] [___]
Compensatory damages [___]

[Foreperson]

If you find that the Defendants violated the ADA, and you further find that:

(a)   Defendants did not prove that they demonstrated good faith efforts to reasonably accommodate [Charles Wessel]'s disability; and

(b)   Defendants engaged in a discriminatory practice with malice or with reckless indifference to the federally protected rights of [Wessel], you should use Jury Verdict Form 3 instead of either Jury Verdict Forms 1 or 2.

Jury Verdict Form 3 reads as follows:

VERDICT FORM 3

We the jury find that the Defendants violated the Americans With Disabilities Act by discharging [Charles Wessel] on the basis of his disability.

Having further found that Defendants did not prove that they demonstrated good faith efforts to reasonably accommodate [Charles Wessel]'s disability and that the Defendant engaged in a discriminatory practice with malice or with reckless indifference to the federally protected rights of [Wessel], we assess damages as follows:

Back pay -

We would enter the above back pay award against the following Defendants:

NOTE: You are to apportion the above award of back pay among the Defendants.

[A.I.C. International, Ltd.] [___]
[A.I.C. Security Investigations, Ltd.] [___]
[defendant C] [___]
Compensatory damages [___]
Punitive damages [___]

[Foreperson]

You will take the verdict forms to the jury room and, when you have reached unanimous agreement as to your verdict, you will have your foreperson fill in the date, sign the form which sets forth the verdict upon which you unanimously agree, and then return with your verdict to the courtroom.

Adapted from Devitt and Blackmar, Federal Jury Practice and Instruction § 74.04.

Given:
Denied:
Given as Modified:

§ 16.23   Plaintiff's Jury Instructions (Mock Trial)

FORM 16–15
SAMPLE PLAINTIFF'S JURY INSTRUCTIONS:
ECONOMIC BURDEN

PROPOSED JURY INSTRUCTIONS ON ECONOMIC BURDEN
(PLAINTIFF'S REQUEST)

The Plaintiff claims that the Defendant discriminated against him by terminating his employment due to his disability. Specifically, the Plaintiff claims that after the onset of multiple sclerosis ("MS"), he requested certain accommodations from the Defendant employer. Minor accommodations were made initially after the Plaintiff's diagnosis, but once the Plaintiff's vision and speech worsened, the Plaintiff's second request for accommodations was denied. Shortly thereafter, his employment with the Defendant was terminated.

The defendant denies that the Plaintiff was terminated due to his disability, but rather asserts that the subpar job performance of the Plaintiff was the reason for the termination. The Defendant also claims that it would be an undue hardship on the company to provide the accommodations requested by the Plaintiff.

In order to prevail in this case, the Plaintiff must prove by a preponderance of the evidence each of the following:

(1)   that the Plaintiff is an individual with a "disability," for his ailment substantially limits major life activities,

(2)   that the Plaintiff is a "qualified individual with a disability," and therefore can perform his essential job functions with or without the Defendant's providing "reasonable accommodations," and

(3)   that the Defendant is an "employer," "covered entity," "person," and engaged in an "industry affecting commerce" as defined by the ADA.

The Defendant has admitted that it is an "employer," etc., as defined by the ADA. The Defendant has not admitted, however, that the Plaintiff has a "disability," nor has it admitted that the Plaintiff is a "qualified individual with a disability." The

Plaintiff has presented two witnesses that have testified as to these matters. If you find that the Plaintiff has established these two elements, you must find for the Plaintiff, unless you believe the undue hardship defense asserted by the Defendant.

The Defendant asserts that to provide the accommodations requested by the Plaintiff would cause the company an undue hardship, both financially and competitively. The Defendant's expert witness has testified to this. The ADA allows the undue hardship defense only when the cost of the accommodation to the employer is disproportionate to the overall financial resources, size, and type of operation of the defendant employer. The ADA was written so that the undue hardship defense would be applicable only in limited circumstances. The burden of proof for establishing economic hardship is on the Defendant. Absent conclusive evidence by the Defendant that an undue hardship exists, you cannot allow this defense, and must find in favor of the Plaintiff. Even if you believe that the accommodations requested by the Plaintiff would cause a burden on the defendant, and if you believe that the burden would not be severe, then you must find in favor of the Plaintiff, so long as the Plaintiff has met his burden of proof.

FORM 16–16
SAMPLE JURY INSTRUCTIONS: QUALIFIED INDIVIDUAL WITH A DISABILITY

PROPOSED JURY INSTRUCTIONS ON "QUALIFIED INDIVIDUAL WITH A DISABILITY" (PLAINTIFF'S REQUEST)

The Plaintiff claims that the Defendant discriminated against him by terminating his employment due to his disability. Specifically, the Plaintiff claims that after the onset of multiple sclerosis ("MS"), he requested certain accommodations from the Defendant employer. Minor accommodations were made initially after the Plaintiff's diagnosis, but once the Plaintiff's vision and speech worsened, the Plaintiff's second request for accommodations was denied. Shortly thereafter, his employment with the Defendant was terminated.

The Defendant denies that the Plaintiff was terminated due to his disability, but rather asserts that the subpar job performance of the Plaintiff was the reason for the termination.

Under the ADA, a "qualified individual with a disability" is one who suffers from a disability, but is able, either with or without reasonable accommodations, to perform the essential job functions of the employment position.

In this case, the Plaintiff was a staff accountant at the time of his termination. Both parties agree that the essential job functions of the Plaintiff were as follows: (i) producing financial reports through spreadsheet applications, (ii) operating an adding machine to perform various mathematical functions, (iii) maintaining the general ledger, and (iv) communicating with outside vendors and [Eastern]'s purchasing agents regarding fixed asset acquisition.

It is up to you to decide whether, based on the testimony, the Plaintiff is capable of performing the essential job functions, either with or without the accommodations requested. If you answer in the affirmative, then you will find the Plaintiff to be a "qualified individual with a disability."[54]

§ 16.24   Defendant's Jury Instructions: Establishing Plaintiff as a Qualified Individual with a Disability (Mock Trial)

FORM 16–17
SAMPLE DEFENDANT'S JURY INSTRUCTIONS: ESTABLISHING PLAINTIFF AS QUALIFIED INDIVIDUAL WITH A DISABILITY

In this case, the Plaintiff must prove that he is a qualified individual with a disability within the meaning of the Americans With Disabilities Act.

To find that the Plaintiff is a qualified individual with a disability, the Plaintiff must prove by a preponderance of the evidence that:

1.   the Plaintiff has a disability, and

2.   the Plaintiff can, with or without the accommodations he requested, perform the essential functions of the staff accountant position that he formerly held.

If you find that the Plaintiff is not a qualified individual with a disability, then your verdict should be for the Defendant.

§ 16.25   Approved Jury Instructions in Title II Case

The instruction in **Form 16–18** was approved as appropriate in an ADA Title II case involving the rejection of a nursing home applicant because of the behavioral manifestations of the applicant's Alzheimer's disease:

FORM 16–18
SAMPLE APPROVED JURY INSTRUCTIONS FOR TITLE II CASE

Now, the law also requires, however, that a nursing home facility such as [Fair Acres] make reasonable accommodations to the known physical and mental limitations of an otherwise-qualified handicapped person. But they [*sic*] are not

---

[54] The jury instructions in both **Forms 16–15** and **16–16** were drafted on July 14, 1993, by Brian Sopinsky and Marc Lisker, former assistants to Henry H. Perritt, Jr.

required to make fundamental or substantial modifications to their program. In other words, they are not required to become something other than what they purport to be; that is, a skilled long-term nursing home with certain admission criteria which they believe they are entitled to use and determine who should be admitted and who should not be admitted. The accommodation that the law requires them to make must be reasonable; it can't be unreasonable. This is just an analogy, it may not be applicable in this case, but they cannot make a nursing home—turn it into a burn center or a psychiatric institution or something like that, because that would require substantial or fundamental modification of the program which they have in existence. But on the other hand, if their program would accommodate [Mrs. Wagner] with only inconsequential or nonsubstantial changes, then under the law they are required to do that. So that if you find that a fundamental or substantial modification is necessary in order to accommodate the plaintiff, the Rehabilitation Act does not apply. On the other hand, if they can accommodate her with reasonable changes in their program, then of course the Act does apply.[55]

§ 16.26   Jury Instructions: Expert's Basis for Opinion (Mock Trial)

FORM 16–19
SAMPLE JURY INSTRUCTIONS: EXPERT'S BASIS FOR OPINION

You have heard the Defendant's expert testify as to whether providing the accommodations sought by the Plaintiff would cause an undue hardship on the Defendant. His opinion is based on his personal knowledge of the Defendant's financial condition. In general, the opinion of an expert has value only when you accept the facts upon which it is based. This is true whether the facts are assumed hypothetically by the expert, come from his personal knowledge of the defendant, from some other proper source, or from a combination of these.[56]

§ 16.27   —Establishing Undue Hardship (Mock Trial)

FORM 16–20
SAMPLE JURY INSTRUCTIONS: ESTABLISHING UNDUE HARDSHIP

In its defense, the Defendant claims that even if you should find that the Plaintiff has proven all the necessary elements of his claim, the Defendant has not violated

---

[55] Wagner v. Fair Acres Geriatric Ctr., 49 F.3d 1002, 1019 n.19 (3d Cir. 1995) (remanding for consideration of decision to allow new trial).

[56] *See* Gordon v. State Farm Life Ins. Co., 203 A.2d 320 (Pa. 1964) (quoting Jackson v. United States Pipe Line Co., 191 A. 165 (Pa. 1937)); Pennsylvania Bar Inst., Pennsylvania Suggested Standard Jury Instructions (Civil), para. 5.31 (1984).

the ADA by refusing to provide reasonable accommodations because providing such accommodations would cause the Defendant undue hardship.

To determine whether the reasonable accommodations requested by the Plaintiff would cause undue hardship, you must determine that the accommodations require significant difficulty or expense in light of:

1.   the overall financial resources of the Defendant;

2.   the number of persons employed by the Defendant;

3.   the effect on expenses and resources, or the impact otherwise of such accommodation upon the Defendant's operations;

4.   the nature and cost of the accommodation needed by the Defendant; and

5.   the type of operation of the covered entity, including the composition, structure, and functions of the Defendant's workforce.

If you find that providing the reasonable accommodations suggested by the Plaintiff would cause the Defendant undue hardship, then your verdict should be for the Defendant.

§ 16.28   Plaintiff's Proposed Findings (Mock Trial)

FORM 16–21
SAMPLE PLAINTIFF'S PROPOSED FINDINGS

UNITED STATES DISTRICT COURT FOR THE [EASTERN]

DISTRICT OF [PENNSYLVANIA]

[Steve Lyons],

Plaintiff

v.   Civil Action No. [820130]

[Eastern Pharmaceuticals, Incorporated],

Defendant.

PROPOSED FINDINGS OF FACT

The Plaintiff requests that the court make the following findings of fact in this action:

1.   The Plaintiff is afflicted with multiple sclerosis ("MS").

2.   MS substantially limits the Plaintiff in the major life activities of reading, speaking, and walking, and therefore the Plaintiff has a "disability" as defined by the ADA.

3.   The Plaintiff, with the reasonable accommodations of (i) having a reader communicate written and computer information to him, (ii) having a speaker communicate oral messages from him, and (iii) having the office area of [Eastern] made "handicapped friendly," can perform the essential functions of his job as staff accountant in [Eastern]'s finance department.

4.   Because the Plaintiff can perform his essential job function with the reasonable accommodations, he is a "qualified individual with a disability" as defined by the ADA.

5.   The Plaintiff was diagnosed with MS on [June 26, 1991].

6.   At the time of the diagnosis of MS, the Plaintiff suffered from blurry vision and slurred speech.

7.   Immediately after the Plaintiff's diagnosis of MS on [June 26, 1991], he informed his supervisor, [Lisa Brown], [Eastern]'s Accounting Manager, of his condition.

8.   On [July 28, 1992], the Plaintiff suffered another MS attack. After this attack, the Plaintiff's eyesight and speech deteriorated further and he began having difficulty walking and coordinating muscle movement.

9.   After the second MS attack, the plaintiff requested the following reasonable accommodations: (i) a reader to communicate written messages and computer information to him, (ii) a speaker to communicate oral messages from him, and (iii) having the office area of [Eastern]'s facility made "handicapped friendly."

10.   [Ms. Brown] refused to make the reasonable accommodations requested by the plaintiff for his disability, and she terminated him on [August 5, 1992].

11.   The decisions made and the actions taken by [Ms. Brown] in refusing the request for accommodations and terminating the Plaintiff were within the course and scope of her employment.

Dated: [Philadelphia], [Pennsylvania]

[July 14, 1993]

Signed: [_____]

[Louis Watt]
Attorney for the Plaintiff
[1234 Main Street]
[Villanova], [Pennsylvania] [19085]
[(215) 555-1212]

§ 16.29   Defendant's Proposed Findings
(Mock Trial)

FORM 16–22
SAMPLE DEFENDANT'S PROPOSED FINDINGS

UNITED STATES DISTRICT COURT FOR THE [EASTERN]

DISTRICT OF [PENNSYLVANIA]

[Steven Lyons],

Plaintiff

v.   Civil Action, File Number [820130]

[Eastern Pharmaceuticals, Incorporated],

Defendant.

PROPOSED FINDINGS OF FACT AND CONCLUSIONS OF LAW

The following findings of fact and conclusions of law have been organized such that each cardinal number represented by an arabic symbol (e.g., "1.") states a proposed conclusion of law and each indented letter of the Roman alphabet (e.g., "a.") states a proposed finding of fact. Each proposed finding of fact supports the conclusion of law preceding it. The final conclusion of law is supported by each of the preceding conclusions of law.

1.   [Eastern] did not provide reasonable accommodations for [Lyons].

a.   [Lyons] requested that [Eastern]: (1) provide him with a reader to communicate written messages and computer information to him, (2) provide him with a speaker to communicate oral messages from him, and (3) make the office area of [Eastern]'s facility "handicapped friendly."

b.   [Lyons]' request that [Eastern]: (1) provide him with a reader to communicate written messages and computer information to him, (2) provide him with a speaker to communicate oral messages from him, and (3) make the office area of

Eastern's facility "handicapped friendly" was a request for reasonable accommodations.[57]

c.   [Eastern] did not: (1) provide [Lyons] with a reader to communicate written messages and computer information to him, (2) provide Lyons with a speaker to communicate oral messages from him, nor (3) make the office area of [Eastern]'s facility "handicapped friendly."

2.   [Eastern] knew that [Lyons] had a physical limitation.

a.   Multiple sclerosis ("MS") is a physical limitation.

b.   [Lyons] suffers from MS.

c.   [Lyons] has a physical limitation.

d.   [Lisa Brown] was [Lyons]' supervisor at [Eastern].

e.   [Lyons] informed [Lisa Brown] that he had MS.

f.   [Lyons] informed [Eastern] that he had MS.

3.   [Lyons] is an individual with a disability.

a.   MS is a physical impairment.

b.   [Lyons] has MS.

c.   [Lyons] has a physical impairment.

d.   MS substantially limits [Lyons]' ability to read, speak, and walk.

e.   Reading, speaking, and walking are major life activities of [Lyons].

f.   MS substantially limits some of [Lyons]' major life activities.

4.   [Lyons] is not a qualified individual with a disability.

a.   The essential job functions of the staff accountant at [Eastern] are: (1) producing financial reports through spreadsheet applications, (2) operating an adding machine to perform various mathematical functions, (3) maintaining the general ledger, and (4) communicating with outside vendors and [Eastern]'s purchasing agents regarding fixed asset acquisitions.

---

[57] This fact would have been proven by submission into evidence of the EEOC's determination letter.

b.   [Lyons] was staff accountant at [Eastern].

c.   [Lyons]' essential job functions were: (1) producing financial reports through spreadsheet applications, (2) operating an adding machine to perform various mathematical functions, (3) maintaining the general ledger, and (4) communicating with outside vendors and [Eastern]'s purchasing agents regarding fixed asset acquisitions.

d.   [Lyons] requested reasonable accommodations to perform his essential job functions.

e.   With the reasonable accommodations, [Lyons] would not have been able to perform his essential job functions.

5.   Providing [Lyons] with the reasonable accommodations he requested would have been an undue burden to [Eastern].

a.   Providing the reasonable accommodations would have cost [Eastern] [$64,000] per year.

b.   Spending [$64,000] per year would cause a dollar-for-dollar decrease in net income.

c.   A [$64,000] per year decrease in net income would negatively impact monies available for research and development purposes.

d.   Providing the reasonable accommodations would have negatively impacted monies available for research and development purposes.

e.   Pharmaceutical companies must, at a minimum, maintain at a constant level monies available for research and development purposes in order to survive.

f.   Providing the reasonable accommodations would negatively affect [Eastern]'s ability to survive.

6.   [Eastern] did not discriminate against [Lyons] because of his known physical limitation and disability by not providing him with the reasonable accommodations he sought, because he is not a qualified individual with a disability and/or providing [Lyons] with the reasonable accommodations he requested would have caused an undue burden to [Eastern].

[John Black], Attorney for Defendant
[1111 Cherry Street]
[Philadelphia], [Pennsylvania] [19105]

§ 16.30   Actual Jury Verdict Form (EEOC)

FORM 16–23
SAMPLE ACTUAL JURY VERDICT FORM

We the jury find the following Defendants violated the Americans With Disabilities Act.

[Place an "X" by each Defendant you find liable]

[A.I.C. Security Investigations, Ltd.] [X]
[defendant C] [X]

Having found in favor of [Wessel] and against Defendants, we further assess damages in the following amounts.

Back pay and Benefits [$22,000]
Compensatory Damages [$50,000]

[signatures of seven jury members]

We the jury find, as to punitive damages, for the Plaintiff and against the Defendants in the following amounts as to each Defendant individually.

[A.I.C. SECURITY INVESTIGATIONS, LTD.] [$250,000]
[defendant C] [$250,000]

[signatures of seven jury members]

CHAPTER 17

REMEDIES

§ 17.1   Introduction and Overview

This chapter contains material relating to remedies in Americans with Disabilities Act (ADA)[1] cases. It considers not only post-trial relief in the form of judgments (see **Form 17–14**) and decrees, but also judicial relief available without trial—consent judgments (see **Forms 17–4** and **17–5**) and decrees (see

---

[1] Pub. L. No. 101–336, 104 Stat. 327 (1990) (codified at 42 U.S.C. §§ 12101–12213 (1994); 47 U.S.C. §§ 225, 711 (1994)) [hereinafter ADA].

Forms 17–6 and **17–7**), interlocutory relief, particularly preliminary injunctions (see **Forms 17–1** through **17–3**), the implementation of judicial orders through the contempt process (see **Forms 17–8** through **17–10**), and judgment-related motions (see **Forms 17–11** through **17–13**) and documents, including an ADA judgment notice for employees (see **Form 17–17**).

§ 17.2   Preliminary Injunction Order to Show Cause

FORM 17–1
SAMPLE PRELIMINARY INJUNCTION ORDER TO SHOW CAUSE

UNITED STATES DISTRICT COURT

[judicial district] OF [state]

[name]

Plaintiff,

v.   CIV. NO. [case number]

[state] BOARD OF LAW EXAMINERS,

Defendant.

ORDER TO SHOW CAUSE

Upon the affidavit of [plaintiff], sworn to [date], the affidavit of [Hobart L.], M.D., sworn to [date], and the Summons and Complaint herein,

LET THE DEFENDANT SHOW CAUSE before the Honorable [name], United States Courthouse, [address] on [date] at [time] in the forenoon of that day, or as soon thereafter as counsel may be heard, as to why an Order should not be entered herein pursuant to the Americans with Disabilities Act (ADA), 42 U.S.C. § 12101 *et seq.,* granting a preliminary injunction directing the [state] Board of Law Examiners to allow Plaintiff to take the [state] Bar Examination, which is scheduled to commence on [date], with certain accommodations. Under the requested preliminary injunction, the Plaintiff would be allowed:

a.   To take the examination in a separate room, isolated from other Bar candidates;

b.   To hand mark answers as opposed to filling in the computer-scored answer sheet with respect to multiple choice questions;

c.   To be provided with a large print exam and to be allowed to use a straight edge ruler; and

d.   To be allotted time to take the examination over a four-day period, with approximately five hours of testing each day, plus 15-minute breaks on the hour, if needed, and a lunch break.

SUFFICIENT CAUSE APPEARING THEREFOR, let service of a conformed copy of this Order to Show Cause and the papers upon which it is granted upon the [state] Board of Law Examiners be deemed good and sufficient service thereof if made by personal delivery thereof to the Office of the [state] Board of Law Examiners not later than [date], and by sending a copy thereof by certified mail, return receipt requested to the [state] Board of Law Examiners at [address], not later than [date].

§ 17.3   Preliminary Injunctions in Title I Cases

Preliminary injunctions in ADA Title I[2] cases present some special problems. These problems are the same ones encountered in Title VII[3] litigation.[4] The first question is whether such relief is available to a private party before the party has exhausted Equal Employment Opportunity Commission (EEOC) procedures. The answer is yes.[5] The second question refers to the procedures to be followed. Federal Rule of Civil Procedure 65 provides the answer. The third question is how irreparable injury can be established.[6] Irreparable injury can be established when a preliminary injunction is sought against altering or removing records,[7] hiring or promoting third parties when that might foreclose meaningful relief for plaintiffs,[8] retaliating against the plaintiff for asserting ADA rights,[9] and preventing psychic injury that could not be compensated by a later injunction or a money judgment.[10]

---

[2] ADA §§ 101–108, 42 U.S.C. §§ 12111–12117 (1994) [hereinafter Title I].

[3] 42 U.S.C. §§ 2000e–2000e-16 (1994) [hereinafter Title VII].

[4] ADA § 107(a), 42 U.S.C. § 12117(a) (1994) (incorporating by reference remedial provisions of Title VII). *See generally* Henry H. Perritt, Jr., Labor Injunctions (John Wiley & Sons 1986) [hereinafter Perritt] § 14.3.

[5] Hicks v. Dothan City Bd. of Educ., 814 F. Supp. 1044, 1049 (M.D. Ala. 1993) (EEOC procedures not being exhausted, plaintiff must show irreparable harm if preliminary injunction is not granted).

[6] White v. Carlucci, 862 F.2d 1209 (5th Cir. 1989) (establishing irreparable injury as matter of fact in Title VII cases).

[7] EEOC v. Recruit USA, Inc., 939 F.2d 746 (9th Cir. 1991).

[8] Black Fire Fighters Ass'n v. City of Dallas, 905 F.2d 63, 66 (5th Cir. 1990) (affirming denial of preliminary injunction but accepting general proposition stated in text).

[9] Baker v. Buckeye Cellulose Corp., 856 F.2d 167 (11th Cir. 1988) (reversing denial of preliminary injunction and requiring evidentiary hearing on retaliation allegations).

[10] Gutierrez v. Municipal Court, 838 F.2d 1031, 1045 (9th Cir. 1988) (approving preliminary injunction against enforcement of English-only rule).

§ 17.4   Memorandum Opposing
Preliminary Injunction

FORM 17–2
SAMPLE MEMORANDUM OPPOSING
PRELIMINARY INJUNCTION

UNITED STATES DISTRICT COURT

[judicial district] OF [state]

[name],

Plaintiff,

v.   [case number]

[state] BOARD OF LAW EXAMINERS,

Defendant.

DEFENDANT'S MEMORANDUM OF LAW

PRELIMINARY STATEMENT

The plaintiff herein, [name] (hereafter "Plaintiff"), has commenced this action pursuant to the Americans with Disabilities Act (42 U.S.C. § 12101 *et seq.;* hereafter "the ADA"). The essential allegations are that Plaintiff is a law school graduate with a severe visual impairment and that the defendant has not made the [state] Bar Examination, scheduled for [date], accessible to Plaintiff, as required by the ADA. The defendant [state] Board of Law Examiners (hereafter "the Board") has been ordered to show cause why a preliminary injunction should not issue which would require the Board to make a number of special accommodations to the Plaintiff with reference to this examination.

FACTS

The Plaintiff suffers from a long-standing, severe, and uncorrectable visual impairment (see Affidavit of [plaintiff], ¶¶ 3-5; Affidavit of [Hobart A. L.], M.D., ¶¶ 3-5). This impairment lengthens the amount of time the Plaintiff requires to read testing materials, and requires her to rest her eyes more frequently in order to reduce eye fatigue ([plaintiff] Affidavit, Exhibit H).

In anticipation of Plaintiff's graduating from the [name] Law School in [month, year], the Plaintiff applied in [month] of that year to take the [month, year] [state] Bar Examination ([plaintiff] Affidavit, ¶¶ 13, 14). The Plaintiff, supported by documentation from her ophthalmologist, requested that the Board grant her a number of accommodations, including time and one-half to take the exam ([plaintiff] Affidavit, ¶ 16, Exhibit D). All of these accommodations were granted by the Board, with the exception of the color of the paper available to her during the exam[11] ([plaintiff] Affidavit, Exhibit E).

Following the exam, but prior to the publication of the test results, the Plaintiff wrote a letter to [James T. F.], Executive Secretary to the Board. In Plaintiff's letter, the Plaintiff complained at considerable length about the conduct of the exam proctor and another candidate taking the test (see Affidavit of [James T. F.], Exhibit A). However, at no time did the Plaintiff claim that, despite the accommodations made, she had been denied adequate time to complete the exam. Quite the contrary, the Plaintiff explicitly stated:

"In fact, I am extremely grateful. I honestly feel that the special conditions, especially the large-print exam and the additional time were necessary for me to be able to take and complete the exam." ([James T. F.] Affidavit, Exhibit A, p.3).

Pointedly, the Plaintiff requested that, should she have to retake the exam, the same accommodations be extended to her:

"Secondly, if I did not pass the exam and am not waived in, I should have the same testing accommodations (sic) as I had for the [month] exam, with the extra time and the large-print exam." ([James T. F.] Affidavit, Exhibit A, p.3).

Similarly, the Plaintiff made no complaints of a lack of adequate time in her contacts with other members of the Board's staff (see Affidavit of [Mary G.]).

Further evidence of a lack of time pressure during the [month] examination is provided by an analysis of the Plaintiff's exam booklets (see [James T. F.] Affidavit, ¶ 10). The Plaintiff apparently completed each of the essay questions, writing a considerable amount in response to each of the questions and even adding an unnecessary "end of question" at the end of each response ([James T. F.] Affidavit, ¶ 10). Additionally, the Plaintiff completed all of the short-answer questions in the exam, and there is no evidence that Plaintiff lacked sufficient time to do so ([James T. F.] Affidavit, ¶ 10).

It was only after the Plaintiff was notified that she had failed the [month] bar examination that Plaintiff asserted for the first time that she did not have adequate time to complete the examination. In applying to retake the exam in [month, year], in addition to the other accommodations requested, the Plaintiff added a request that she be permitted to take the exam over a four-day period, with only five hours of testing per day ([Dr. L.] Affidavit, ¶ 13).[12]

---

[11] The color of the paper is apparently no longer at issue and the plaintiff does not address this request in her motion for a preliminary injunction.

[12] In point of fact, the plaintiff's actual request for accommodation for the examination only asks for "extra time (for rest and for work)." *See* James T. F. Affidavit, Exhibit B.

The Board reviewed the Plaintiff's application for accommodations and considered all relevant factors, including the requirements of the ADA, the Board's prior experience in accommodating blind and visually handicapped candidates, the availability of aural compensatory aids such as audiotapes and readers/writers, the importance of the time element of the examination in the determination of minimal competence and the comparability of examination results, considerations of examination security, the fact that the Plaintiff had apparently completed the [month] examination within the time allotted, and the fact that the medical documentation submitted by the Plaintiff did not indicate any change in her medical condition. On [date], the Board advised the Plaintiff that all of her requests, with the exception of the four-day extension, had been granted ([James T. F.] Affidavit, Exhibit D). Specifically, the Board made the following accommodations:

1.   A separate testing room with enhanced lighting. The Plaintiff would be free to bring any additional lighting she wished.

2.   A large-print copy of the exam.

3.   The Plaintiff would be permitted to use a ruler to assist in reading.

4.   The Plaintiff would be permitted to write the answers to the multiple-choice and Multi-State Bar Examination questions in the question books, to be transcribed onto computer sheets by Board staff.

Although the Board declined to grant the Plaintiff a four-day examination, it took the unprecedented step of offering Plaintiff the option of specifying the hours that she wished to take the exam during the two days during which it was being conducted ([James T. F.] Affidavit, Exhibit D, ¶ [5]). In addition, although not requested by the Plaintiff, the Board offered to make available an audiotaped copy of the examination and an amanuensis to serve as a reader/writer.

The Plaintiff thereafter petitioned the Board for reconsideration of her request for a four-day examination ([James T. F.] Affidavit, Exhibit D, ¶ [2]). The Board reconsidered the Plaintiff's situation and concluded that the extensive accommodations made by it were reasonable and sufficient to compensate for the Plaintiff's vision deficit. Accordingly, Plaintiff's petition was denied ([James T. F.] Affidavit, Exhibit F). This action was subsequently commenced by the Plaintiff.

DISCUSSION

The Plaintiff bears a "heavy burden" of demonstrating a "clear entitlement" to an injunction ([*New York v. Nuclear Regulatory Commission,* 550 F.2d 745, 755 (2d Cir. 1977)]). The Board respectfully submits that the Plaintiff has failed to carry her burden of demonstrating her entitlement to a preliminary injunction which, as the

---

The plaintiff's ophthalmologist, Dr. Hobart L., made the specific request for a four-day examination.

Court of Appeals for this Circuit has observed, is a broad and potentially drastic remedy (see [*General Fireproofing Co. v. Wyman,* 444 F.2d 391, 393 (2d Cir. 1971)]).

It is well-settled in this Circuit that a party seeking injunctive relief must establish (a) that the injunction is necessary to prevent irreparable harm and (b) either that (i) it is likely to succeed on the merits on the underlying claim or (ii) there are sufficiently serious questions going to the merits of the claim as to make them a fair ground for litigation, together with a balance of hardships tipping decidedly in favor toward the movant ([*Abdul Wali v. Coughlin,* 754 F.2d 1015,1025 (2d Cir. 1985)]). An application of this standard to the facts before the Court amply demonstrates the Plaintiff's lack of entitlement to a preliminary injunction.

A.   An Injunction Is Not Necessary to Prevent "Irreparable Harm."

Clearly, the Court's intervention is not necessary in order to provide the Plaintiff with the first three accommodations she seeks in the Order to Show Cause (see Order to Show Cause, dated [date], subparagraphs a, b, and c). As it did prior to the Plaintiff's taking the [month, year] examination, the Board has unequivocally and irrevocably offered the Plaintiff the opportunity to take the upcoming examination in a separate room, to hand mark her answers as opposed to marking a computer-scored answer sheet, to be provided a large print exam and to utilize a straight edge ruler (see [Plaintiff] Affidavit, Exhibits E and I; [James T. F.] Affidavit, Exhibit D; Affidavit of [Charles T. B., Jr., Esq.]).[13] Thus, there is no necessity to invoke the drastic injunctive power of the court with reference to these three accommodations.

With reference to the Plaintiff's remaining request to take the examination for five hours per day for four days, an examination of the proofs submitted to the Court indicates serious doubt as the likelihood of "irreparable injury" as well as the necessity for the unusual accommodations Plaintiff seeks.

The Plaintiff's argument that she will suffer "irreparable injury" is premised upon two contentions: first, that without the four-day schedule Plaintiff will be unable to pass the exam, and, second, that such a failure constitutes an irreparable injury. Both of these assumptions lack merit.

A review of the Plaintiff's [month] exam reveals that she was apparently under no time pressure to complete the examination and did, in fact, complete all portions (see [James T. F.] Affidavit, ¶ 10). More compelling proof, however, comes from the Plaintiff. First, Plaintiff made no request for a four-day exam prior to the [month, year] examination and made no objection to the Board's offer that she be allowed time and one-half to take the exam. Although Plaintiff now proffers the

---

[13] Indeed, the Board had already voluntarily offered the plaintiff more accommodations than she requested in the order to show cause (that is, a tape-recorded copy of the examination and an amanuensis to serve as a reader/writer).

excuse that she believed that this was the maximum amount of time allowed by the Board, this is unpersuasive. If Plaintiff believed that she required four days and that the ADA mandated such an accommodation, Plaintiff could have commenced an action under the ADA, or a special proceeding under [statute] to compel such an accommodation. Indeed, that is precisely what Plaintiff has done now, and offers no excuse as to why she did not do so previously if she felt aggrieved. More critically, perhaps, is the fact that the Plaintiff never complained about the time given to complete the examination until after she was advised that she had failed. In Plaintiff's [date], letter to the Board (approximately 9 weeks after the [month, year] exam but prior to the publication of the results), the Plaintiff complained at considerable length about the conduct of the exam proctor and another candidate taking the test. However, at no time did the Plaintiff claim that, despite the accommodations made for her, she had been denied adequate time to complete the exam. Quite the contrary, Plaintiff thanked the Board for the accommodations it extended, specifically noting the additional time Plaintiff had been given. Critically, the Plaintiff stated in her letter that, if she failed, she wanted the same accommodations on the next exam. Not only is the Board prepared to give the Plaintiff those accommodations that she found so satisfactory, it is willing to accommodate Plaintiff even further with a schedule to be designed by her, a tape-recorded copy of the exam, and/or an amanuensis to read any or all of the exam to Plaintiff and record her responses. Given the Plaintiff's previous unsolicited expression of satisfaction with the [month] accommodations, her present assertion that additional accommodations are necessary to prevent irreparable injury rings particularly hollow.

A similar problem exists with reference to the assertions now made by the Plaintiff's ophthalmologist. Although [Dr. L.] now states that the Plaintiff requires four days, prior to the [month, year] examination [Dr. L.] stated that ". . . she needs more time to take an exam—possibly half again as much time." ([plaintiff] Affidavit, Exhibit D). At no time prior to Plaintiff's taking the first bar exam did [Dr. L.] state or even imply that she required four days to take the exam.

We submit that the Plaintiff will not suffer any injury should the court refrain from issuing an injunction which would in effect grant Plaintiff most, if not all, the relief she seeks in the underlying action. As noted above, the Board has offered the Plaintiff virtually all the accommodations sought by her, plus several others Plaintiff has not even requested. Because the Plaintiff expends much time and effort in reading, Plaintiff may avail herself of an amanuensis to read some or all of the questions to her, and record any or all of her answers. The Board has taken the unprecedented step of offering the Plaintiff the opportunity to set her own schedule for the exam, which Plaintiff may take at any time during the two-day period within which it is given. Thus, we submit that the court's intervention is not required to prevent any alleged injury to the plaintiff.

However, even assuming, arguendo, that the Plaintiff might be detrimentally affected by the Board's determination, Plaintiff's assertion that she is entitled to an injunction remains without merit. In order for an injunction to issue, the alleged injury must be actual and imminent, as opposed to remote or speculative ([*New York v. Nuclear Regulatory Commission,* 550 F.2d 745, 755 (2d Cir. 1977)], quoted at [*Jackson Dairy, Inc. v. HY Hood & Sons, Inc.,* 596 F.2d 70, 72 (2d Cir. 1979)]). Whether the Plaintiff will fail the exam unless given a four-day schedule, as opposed to the alternative schedule and additional accommodations offered by the Board, is indeed speculative, especially in view of the fact that the Plaintiff was apparently able to complete the [month] exam without any difficulties with the time factor. Secondly, the harm which may be visited upon the Plaintiff is not the type which justifies the issuance of an injunction. Thus, the Plaintiff's possible inability to be admitted to practice law involves issues relating to employment and Plaintiff's ability to secure an income. As the Court of Appeals for this Circuit has observed, loss of income and the concomitant loss of reputation "is not the sort of irreparable harm which is an essential predicate to the issuance of injunctive relief." ([*Curtin v. Henderson,* 514 F. Supp. 16, 19 (E.D.N.Y. 1980), (citing [*New York v. Nuclear Regulatory Commission,* 550 F.2d 745, 755 (2d Cir. 1977))]].

Based upon the following, we respectfully submit that the Plaintiff has failed to demonstrate that an injunction is necessary to prevent irreparable injury to her.

B.   The Plaintiff Is Unlikely to Succeed on the Merits

The Plaintiff's case rests upon her assertion that the Defendant has violated Titles II and III of the ADA. An examination of the relevant law as applied to the facts of this case lends no support to this claim.

The Plaintiff's Title III claim is premised upon 42 U.S.C. § 12189, which provides that:

> Any person that offers examinations or courses related to applications, licensing, certification, or credentialing for secondary or postsecondary education, professional, or trade purposes shall offer such examinations or courses in a place and manner accessible to persons with disabilities or offer alternative accessible arrangements for such individuals.

An examination of the implementing regulations make it clear that this title is inapplicable to the case at bar. As set forth in 28 C.F.R. § 36.101:

> Purpose. The purpose of this part is to implement title III of the Americans with Disabilities Act of 1990, 42 U.S.C. § 12181, which prohibits discrimination on the basis of disability by public accommodations and requires places of public accommodation and commercial facilities to be designed, constructed, and altered in compliance with the accessibility standards established by this part.

Although Plaintiff selectively quotes from 28 C.F.R. § 36.309 in support of her contention that Title III applies to the Board, a review of the full contents of that section reveals its obvious inapplicability to governmental agencies:

(a) General. Any private entity that offers examinations or courses related to applications, licensing, certification, or credentialing for secondary or postsecondary education, professional, or trade purposes shall offer such examinations or courses in a place and manner accessible to person with disabilities or offer alternative accessible arrangements for such individuals.

The subsections which apply this general standard all specify their applicability to private entities only (see 28 C.F.R. §§ 36.309 (b)(1), (3), and (c)(1), (3)).

Critically, the United States Department of Justice, Civil Rights Division, Office on the Americans with Disabilities Act, which is the agency given the mandate of ensuring compliance with the ADA, has specifically recognized the inapplicability of Title III to governmental entities (see The Americans with Disabilities Act, Title III Technical Assistance Manual, annexed hereto).

The reed to which the Plaintiff clings in this regard is an obviously ambiguous reference to bar examinations in Appendix B to 28 C.F.R. § 36.309, which states: "Examinations covered by this section would include a bar exam or the Scholastic Aptitude Test prepared by the Educational Testing Service."

Any attempt to shoehorn this language into the facts of this case runs afoul of the clear language of the section itself, which, as the Department of Justice has asserted, specifies its applicability only to private entities. More critically, it also runs afoul of subsection (a) of Appendix B, § 36.309, which also specifies that the section applies only to private entities. The only reasonable interpretation of the subsection relied upon by the Plaintiff is that the drafters believed that the bar exam was prepared by the [Educational Testing Service], as is the [Scholastic Aptitude] test. No other interpretation comports with the clear language of the regulation, which renders Title III inapplicable to governmental entities.

The Plaintiff fares no better under Title II, which does apply to governmental entities (see 42 U.S.C. §§ 12131(l)(B)). Pursuant to that section and § 12132, the Board must make "reasonable modification" to its policies and provide auxiliary aids and services to disabled individuals such as the Plaintiff. We respectfully submit a review of the Board's actions demonstrates that it has been more than reasonable in its efforts to accommodate the Plaintiff. In response to Plaintiff's requests, the Board has allowed Plaintiff to take the exam in a separate testing room, enjoying an absence from distractions not provided to other candidates. Not only will the room have enhanced lighting, the Plaintiff will be able to bring whatever additional illumination she desires. Plaintiff will be provided a large-print copy of the exam and allowed to bring a ruler to assist her in following the print. Plaintiff will be permitted to make her answers to multiple choice and Multi-State Bar Examination questions in a separate book, to be transcribed by Board staff following the exam. In short, the only accommodation not granted by the Board is the Plaintiff's request for a four-day exam, based upon legitimate concerns for the validity of the testing process and the security of the examination. However, as a compromise, and despite the questionable necessity for such accommodations in light of Plaintiff's previous bar exam experience, the Board has offered the plaintiff a tape-recorded copy of the examination, an amanuensis to read any or all of the exam to her and record her answers, and the unprecedented opportunity to make her own schedule for the two days of the examination so as to allow Plaintiff to take as much time as she wished with the exam, interspersed with whatever rest times Plaintiff desired. The Plaintiff has apparently rejected all of these proposed accommodations. Given the legitimate concerns of the Board and their statutory mandate to ensure the admission of qualified applicants to the bar, we submit their proposed accommodations are more than reasonable and amply satisfy the mandates of Title II.

C.   The "Balancing of the Hardships."

Even if one were to assume that there exist sufficiently serious questions going to the merits of the claim as to make them a fair ground for litigation, in order to be entitled to an injunction, the Plaintiff must still prove that the equities of the situation tip "decidedly" in favor ([*Abdul Wali v. Coughlin*, 754 F.2d 1015 (2d Cir. 1985)]).

Unquestionably, the Plaintiff paints a sympathetic picture of her situation. Plaintiff has obviously struggled throughout her life to overcome her disability and achieve the lofty goals she has set for herself. The plaintiff asserts that the only remaining obstacle to passing the bar exam is this one accommodation and that "neither the Law Examiners nor the bar examination will be harmed by allowing the requested accommodation" (Plaintiff's Memorandum of Law, p. 13). As tempted as one might be to be swayed by this argument, it must be rejected.

The Board of Law examiners bears the burden of assuring that all attorneys admitted to practice in [state] are competent to serve the public who seeks their services. To this end, the Board has established the bar examination to assure minimal competence. While the Board has the legal obligation to "level the playing field" for all examination candidates with disabilities, it has a concomitant obligation to ensure that no candidate, whether disabled or not, has an advantage over any other. The Board, upon a detailed consideration of the Plaintiff's condition and the alternatives available to her, has determined that the accommodations offered to the plaintiff will provide her with a fair opportunity to demonstrate her knowledge and abilities within the time constraints that the practice of law mandates. We respectfully submit that should this Court substitute its judgment for that of the Board, it will not have leveled the playing field but, rather, tipped it in favor of the plaintiff. To do so would possibly result in the admission of an unqualified candidate.[14] Given the potential harm that such an admission could cause both to the public and the Plaintiff herself, we submit that the equities of this situation hardly tip "decidedly" in favor of the Plaintiff.

---

[14] This is especially true because, as noted above, the plaintiff failed her previous bar exam when the evidence suggests that she had sufficient time to complete the exam.

CONCLUSION

The Plaintiff has failed to carry her heavy burden of demonstrating her entitlement to a preliminary injunction and, consequently, Plaintiff's application should be denied.

§ 17.5 Affidavit Opposing Preliminary Injunction

FORM 17–3
SAMPLE AFFIDAVIT OPPOSING PRELIMINARY INJUNCTION

UNITED STATES DISTRICT COURT

[judicial district] OF [state]

[name]

Plaintiff,

v.

[state] BOARD OF LAW EXAMINERS,

Defendant.

AFFIDAVIT OF [CHARLES T. B.]

IN OPPOSITION TO MOTION FOR PRELIMINARY INJUNCTION

STATE OF [state]

COUNTY OF [name]

[Charles T. B.], being duly sworn deposes and says:

1.   I am a member of the [state] Board of Law Examiners ("Board"), and I submit this affidavit in response to the application made on Plaintiff's behalf for an order directing that, in addition to the extensive accommodations the Board has granted to Plaintiff in taking the bar examination on [dates], Plaintiff be given four full days to complete the examination instead of the two days normally prescribed for candidates. The Board has agreed to provide Plaintiff with (1) a separate testing room with enhanced lighting; (2) a large-print copy of the examination, and, if requested, a taped copy of the examination and the services of an amanuensis to serve as a reader/writer; (3) a ruler; (4) freedom to write the answers to short answer questions on the question book themselves; and (5) as much time as the candidate wishes to spend during the two days when the exam is to be regularly

administered. The only requested accommodation denied by the Board was the administration of the exam over four days instead of the regular two days.

2.   In brief summary, the position of the Board in defense of this action, and the essential thrust of this affidavit, is that the Board, having been entrusted pursuant to the [state] Judiciary Law with the responsibility for composing and administering the bar examination, has a duty to make judgments about the accommodations to be extended to applicants who seek special accommodations to account for physical or mental disabilities and not simply to defer to medical conclusions about the extent of such accommodations. The practice of law, as the Court is well aware, is largely time driven: court deadlines must be met, work must be done and decisions must be made promptly to protect clients' interests, and legal fees must usually be based on time spent. The bar examination thus reflects the need to absorb, analyze, and resolve issues within a limited time. In determining whether accommodations requested in respect of a disability are reasonable, the Board must consider the need to preserve the essential purpose and integrity of the bar examination process as a fair measurement of minimum competence to practice law. In carrying out that duty, the Board believes that neither the Americans with Disabilities Act nor the Board's other legal responsibilities call for it to abdicate to the medical profession the making of judgments about how much accommodation each disabled individual should be accorded. While the Board is not competent to make medical judgments, neither is the medical profession competent to judge how much variation from regular examination procedures can be granted without compromising the objective of administering examinations on fair and equal terms to all candidates. Thus, while a medical doctor may be fully qualified to diagnose the nature and extent of a disability, the Board cannot leave it to the diagnosing doctor to determine how much time and other accommodations may be appropriate. In this case, in full recognition of the medial diagnosis, the Board has concluded that granting additional time, beyond the two days prescribed for all candidates who have no disabilities, would not be a reasonable accommodation of Plaintiff's disability.

3.   Although not required by law, the membership of the Board has always been comprised of practicing lawyers. The Board, appointed by the Court of Appeals, has established a set of rules for administering the examination and procedures for composing the so-called [state] portion of the exam (which consists of all of the essay questions and 50 short answer questions, excluding the Multi-state portion which consists of 200 short answer questions composed under the auspices of the National Conference of Bar Examiners). The Board must make judgments about the kinds of conditions under which the examinations are given, the scheduling of the examination and the amount of time allowed. in composing the examination, the Board must be conscious of the number of issues projected and the amount of time required of candidates to read and understand the questions, and, in the case of essay questions, to write complete answers dealing with all of the issues.

4.   The members of the Board must exercise their judgment of what is required to demonstrate minimum competence to practice law. As practicing attorneys, their background and experience provide a basis for the judgments they must make. The background and experience of the present Board are as follows:

[list names and qualifications of Board attorneys]

5.   The letters and affidavits from physicians submitted on [plaintiff's] behalf unquestionably demonstrate a substantial visual disability which has rendered Plaintiff unable to read at a normal pace for extended periods of time and requires Plaintiff to rest at intervals. The Board does not dispute Plaintiff's demonstration of disability. It does, however, question the conclusion of Plaintiff's doctors that she requires four days to take the bar examination. The doctors' analyses of Plaintiff's condition nowhere support that specific conclusion. They might as easily have said that Plaintiff requires six or eight days. Nor do the physicians address the relief from eyestrain that can be afforded by the provision of an audiotape of the examination text or a reader/writer. The Board has offered to extend such accommodations, which have been utilized successfully in the past by blind and other severely visually impaired bar examination candidates, to Plaintiff. And, of course, the doctors, understandably, nowhere purport to make a judgment about whether or not the allowance of four days for the taking of the examination would maintain the fairness and integrity of the examination process.

6.   Notably a number of applicants who are completely blind have over the years successfully completed the examination, and many have done so without having been given additional time. Some have used a braille or a taped version of the examination or used an amanuensis. Blind or other visually impaired persons have been granted special accommodations for many years, long pre-dating the adoption of the Americans with Disabilities Act. The Board has determined that [plaintiff] may use a taped version of the examination and an amanuensis who will be permitted to read the examination questions to her and, if Plaintiff wishes, transcribe her answers, both to the short answer and essay questions, so that Plaintiff need not consume undue amounts of time reading the questions.

7.   During the two days on which the examination is regularly administered, [plaintiff] will be allowed as much time as she wishes. Plaintiff's doctor suggests that this only aggravates Plaintiff's problems because extended hours only add to her fatigue. However, there is no apparent reason why Plaintiff cannot allocate her time between work on the examination and rest. The whole purpose of allowing as much time as a candidate may wish on a single day is not to impose an intolerable burden of continuous work over ten or fifteen hours or more, but rather to enable the candidate to use the time effectively with appropriate rest periods.

8.   The security and integrity of the examination process are of vital concern to the Board, and that is the primary reason why the Board cannot readily accede to requests for time exceeding the two days when the exam is regularly administered. it is no reflection upon [plaintiff]'s character to note that administration of the exam over four days affords opportunities for compromising the examination which cannot be effectively controlled. Obviously, the Board cannot make individual judgments about whether each candidate can be trusted to observe the constraints against giving help to or obtaining help from others in completing the examination.

9.   From the time the Board of Law Examiners came into existence, it has granted four days for completion of the examination in only five instances. In all of those cases, extreme and extraordinary health conditions were demonstrated which, in the view of the Board, warranted the unusual accommodation. In one case, the applicant was, functionally, a quadriplegic and could write only with the use of a stick held in his mouth. In another case, the applicant was allowed to take the examination in a room close to his hospital where medication could be administered, if necessary. In two other cases, accommodations were provided pursuant to stipulations in the context of expedited litigation, without prejudice in future litigation. In one or more of those instances, it might have been argued that too much time was given or alternatively that enough time was accorded, but the Board exercised its best judgment in light of all of the medical information before it and the need to maintain fairness in the examination process.

10.   The difficulty which now faces the Board, particularly under the Americans with Disabilities Act, is the tendency for more and more applicants to seek what they know to be the maximum amount of additional time the Board has ever allowed to obtain a medical recommendation which coincides exactly with that maximum time. Unless the Board is to wholly abdicate its responsibility to make judgments about the extent of accommodation to be granted, it cannot simply accept at face value a medical judgment, however well intended, which states that four days are needed, and thereupon to grant that accommodation in every case. The Board does not believe that the Americans with Disabilities Act or other applicable law compels the Board to subordinate its judgment concerning time requirements to whatever medical authority may be submitted.

[Charles T. B.]

§ 17.6   Consent Judgment

FORM 17–4
SAMPLE CONSENT JUDGMENT

IN THE [type] COURT OF [location]

[John Jones],

Plaintiff,

v.   No. [case number]

[XYZ, Inc.],

Defendant.

JUDGMENT BY CONSENT

Upon consideration of the attached agreement [not included herein], hereby incorporated by reference, between Plaintiff, [John Jones], and Defendant, [XYZ, Inc.], to settle this case, it is ordered that judgment is entered for Plaintiff against Defendant in the amount of [$10, 000].

Judge [name]

Dated [date]

§ 17.7   Consent Judgment Memorandum

FORM 17–5
SAMPLE CONSENT JUDGMENT MEMORANDUM

I. Facts

On [July 5, 1992] [John Jones], then an employee of [XYZ, Inc. ("XYZ")], requested reasonable accommodations from [XYZ]'s management to accommodate [Jones]'s recent loss of vision. [XYZ] refused to grant [Jones]'s request and fired him. In response to the firing, [Jones] sued [XYZ] in federal court under the Americans With Disabilities Act ("ADA"). Shortly thereafter, [Jones] and [XYZ] agreed to a consent judgment. Under the terms of the consent judgment, [XYZ] agreed to pay [Jones] [$10,000] in consideration for Jones's promise to forfeit all legal claims related to [XYZ]'s refusal to provide reasonable accommodations.

II. Discussion

A consent judgment is a method for settling disputes after a lawsuit has been filed.[15] A consent judgment incorporates features of a contract and a judgment. The first half of this memorandum describes the common attributes of consent judgments. The second half of this memorandum discusses construing and enforcing a consent judgment and related issues attributable to the instrument's dual character as a contract and a judgment.

---

[15] This memorandum discusses only consent judgments. Due to the procedural merger of law and equity in the federal and most state courts, the term "judgment" now includes the term "decree." Fed. R. Civ. P. 54(a). However, consent judgments and consent decrees must be distinguished. A *consent judgment* incorporates features of a contract and a judgment, but a *consent decree* incorporates features of a contract and an injunction. The distinction between a judgment and an injunction is in the method of enforcement. Once a court issues a judgment, the parties to the original lawsuit control the execution process. Perritt at 16. Conversely, when a court issues an injunction, the court retains authority to enforce the injunction, primarily through the court's inherent contempt powers.

A.   Consent Judgments in General

A *consent judgment* is a contract to end a lawsuit in which the relief to be provided
by the judgment and the wording to effectuate that relief are agreed to by the parties.[16] Consent judgments are a desirable means of settling a dispute when parties
can agree upon the terms of the settlement, but want their agreement to have the
force of a judgment. A consent judgment serves this unique purpose because of its
dual character. Not only is a consent judgment a contract settling the underlying
dispute and providing for the entry of judgment in a pending or contemplated
action,[17] but it is also a judgment.[18] As a contract, a consent judgment embodies the
intent of the parties. Accordingly, consent judgments vary greatly depending upon
the needs of the parties in a particular situation. However, no matter how complex
the underlying agreement, the court has no duty to inquire into the wisdom of the
parties entering the bargain.[19]

B. Construction and Enforcement of Consent Judgments

The scope of a consent judgment's effect depends upon how a court construes the
judgment and to what extent the judgment is binding. Ordinarily, consent judgments are enforceable in the same manner as other judgments. However, since the
underlying agreement is the product of the parties and not the court, construing the
judgment may become a crucial prelude to enforcing it. Since the court's construction of the agreement ultimately determines the effect of the consent judgment,
parties should carefully consider contract principles when drafting the agreement
underlying the consent judgment.

In addition to its contractual qualities, a consent judgment represents a final decision on the merits. Therefore it has res judicata effect.[20] A more debated issue is the
extent to which consent judgments may be subject to collateral attack. Strict application of the doctrine of collateral estoppel suggests that no issues should be barred
from subsequent collateral attack because no issues in a consent judgment have
been litigated.[21] Two fact scenarios seem to bring this proposition into question. The

---

[16] Interspace, Inc. v. Morris, 650 F. Supp. 107, 109 (S.D.N.Y. 1986).

[17] James Fleming, Jr., *Consent Judgments as Collateral Estoppel,* 108 U. Pa. L. Rev. 173,
175 (1959).

[18] Consent judgments are distinguishable from confession of judgments. A *confession of
judgment* involves the unilateral concession by the defendant that the plaintiff's cause is
right. In contrast, a consent judgment is in the nature of a bilateral contract as to how the
underlying dispute should be resolved. National Hygienics, Inc. v. Southern Farm
Bureau Ins. Co., 707 F.2d 183 (5th Cir. 1983).

[19] Risk v. Director of Ins., 3 N.W.2d 922 (Neb. 1942).

[20] Assuming, of course, that the other essential requirements of res judicata exist. Epic
Metals Corp. v. H.H. Robertson Co., 870 F.2d 1574, 1576 (Fed. Cir. 1989) (for res judicata purposes, consent judgments have the same force and effect as judgments entered
after a trial on the merits).

[21] United States v. International Bldg. Co., 345 U.S. 502, 505 (1953). *See* 18 C. Wright, A.
Miller, & E. Cooper, Federal Practice & Procedure § 4443 (1981).

first contemplates the parties to the underlying agreement requesting that the court determine the propriety of the agreement prior to entering judgment. Regardless of whether the court ultimately concludes on the correctness of the agreement, no issues have been litigated so collateral estoppel does not apply. The second scenario exists when the parties have stipulated the existence or nonexistence of certain facts and the judgment expressly or impliedly recites these facts. Although once again none of these facts was litigated, authority exists supporting the proposition that the doctrine of collateral estoppel requires that these issues be given binding effect.[22] Regardless of the doctrine of collateral estoppel, contract law ordinarily ensures that these issues are binding if a court finds that it was the parties' intention to be bound.

In summary, a consent judgment provides an alternative to litigation when the parties to the dispute can successfully negotiate their own settlement, but want their contract to have the status of a judgment issued by the court.

§ 17.8   Consent Decree

FORM 17–6
SAMPLE CONSENT DECREE

IN THE [type] COURT OF [location]

[John Jones],

Plaintiff,

v.   No. [Case number]

[XYZ, Inc.],

Defendant.

DECREE

Defendant, [XYZ, Inc.], is hereby ordered to comply with the terms of the attached agreement [not included herein] by immediately hiring [Robert Jones], son of Plaintiff, [John Jones], as a management trainee in Defendant's corporate management training program. In addition, Defendant must continue to employ [Robert Jones] until at least [July 5, 1998], provided that [Robert Jones]' job performance in the Defendant's management training program does not fall below the level of "fully as expected," as defined in the Defendant's employee handbook currently in force.

---

[22] *See* Restatement (Second) of Judgments § 27 cmt. e (1982).

Judge [name]

Dated [date]

§ 17.9   Consent Decree Memorandum

FORM 17–7
SAMPLE CONSENT DECREE MEMORANDUM

I. Facts

On [July 5, 1992], [John Jones], then an employee of [XYZ, Inc. ("XYZ")], requested reasonable accommodations from [XYZ]'s management to accommodate Jones's recent loss of vision. [XYZ] refused to grant [Jones]'s request and fired him. In response to the firing, [Jones] sued [XYZ] in federal court under the Americans With Disabilities Act ("ADA"). Shortly thereafter [Jones] and [XYZ] agreed to settle their lawsuit via a consent decree. Under the terms of the agreement, [XYZ] agreed to hire [Jones]'s twenty-three-year-old son, [Robert], as a management trainee in [XYZ]'s corporate management training program. Further, [XYZ] promised [Jones] that [XYZ] would continue to employ [Robert] at least until [July 5, 1998], provided that [Robert]'s job performance did not fall below the level of "fully as expected."[23] As consideration for [XYZ]'s promise, [Jones] promised to waive all legal claims related to [XYZ]'s refusal to provide him with reasonable accommodations for his blindness.

II. Discussion

A consent decree is a method for settling disputes, after a lawsuit has been filed, that has attributes of a contract and an injunction.[24] This memorandum discusses the general nature of a consent decree, construction and enforcement of consent decrees, and the validity of consent decrees under the ADA.

A *consent decree* is an agreement of the parties in settlement of litigation which the court approves and embodies in an order.[25] Although the terms of the agreement are the product of the parties' negotiations, the trial court must approve the agreement. In deciding whether to approve or deny the issuance of a consent decree, the court has the duty to decide whether the decree is fair, adequate, and reasonable.[26] However, as long as the agreement is otherwise reasonable, a court

---

[23] "Fully as expected" is the phrase used in XYZ's employee handbook to describe an average performer.

[24] *See* Local No. 93, Int'l Ass'n of Firefighters v. City of Cleveland, 478 U.S. 501, 519 (1986).

[25] Lloyd C. Anderson, *Implementation of Consent Decrees in Structural Reform Litigation,* 1986 U. Ill. L. Rev. 727.

[26] United States v. Colorado, 937 F.2d 505, 509 (10th Cir. 1991).

need not require that the agreement serve the best interests of the public.[27] Thus, a court's review of a consent decree is more than a rubber stamping. After court approval, the agreement takes on the status of a consent decree. Inherent in this status is the trial court's retention of authority to modify or enforce its decree even without a provision in the decree stating that the court shall retain jurisdiction over the matter to insure compliance.[28] Accordingly, a consent decree might be best characterized as a judgment subject to continued judicial proceeding.[29]

Despite this characterization, a consent decree is principally an agreement between the parties that will be construed as a contract and interpreted to give effect to what the parties agreed to, as reflected in the decree itself or in the documents incorporated in the decree by reference.[30] Accordingly, the parties to the lawsuit should always heed contract principles when drafting the agreement.

As a judicial act, though, a consent decree is considered a final judgment on the merits.[31] A consent decree is also given res judicata effect.[32] Concerning collateral estoppel, a consent decree is similar to a consent judgment in that no issues have been litigated. Accordingly, a consent decree should be barred from collateral attack only when the parties intend for their agreement to have this effect.

One final issue peculiar to consent decrees in settlement of ADA claims arises because the ADA incorporates by reference the enforcement provisions of the Civil Rights Act of 1964.[33] The question arises as to whether consent decrees are valid in the context of litigation under the Civil Rights Act, given the Act's prohibition against court orders requiring an employer to give relief to an employee who suffers adverse job action if such action was taken for any reason other than discrimination.[34] The Supreme Court has held that consent decrees are not included among these prohibited court orders.[35] Accordingly, consent orders are also a permissible mode of settlement for lawsuits brought under the ADA.

---

[27] United States v. Oregon, 913 F.2d 576, 581 (9th Cir. 1990).

[28] Picon v. Morris, 933 F.2d 660, 662 (8th Cir. 1991).

[29] United States v. Oregon, 913 F.2d 576, 580 (9th Cir. 1990).

[30] SEC v. Levine, 881 F.2d 1165, 1178–79 (2d Cir. 1989).

[31] Vanguards of Cleveland v. City of Cleveland, 753 F.2d 479, 484 (6th Cir. 1985), *aff'd*, 478 U.S. 501 (1986).

[32] United States v. Fisher, 864 F.2d 434, 439 (7th Cir. 1988).

[33] ADA § 107(a) 42 U.S.C. § 12117(a) (1994). *See also* Civil Rights Act of 1964, 42 U.S.C. Ch. 21 (1994) [hereinafter Civil Rights Act of 1964].

[34] 42 U.S.C. § 2000e-5(g) (1994).

[35] Local No. 93, Int'l Ass'n of Firefighters v. City of Cleveland, 478 U.S. 501, 523 (1986).

§ 17.10   Contempt Motion

FORM 17–8
SAMPLE CONTEMPT MOTION

UNITED STATES DISTRICT COURT

FOR THE [EASTERN] DISTRICT OF [PENNSYLVANIA]

[John Jones]

Plaintiff,

v.   Civil Action No. [case number]

[XYZ, Inc.]

Defendant

MOTION FOR ORDER TO SHOW CAUSE WHY EMPLOYER IN ADA ACTION SHOULD NOT BE PUNISHED FOR CONTEMPT

Mr. [John Jones], by his undersigned counsel, respectfully moves this Court for an Order requiring the Defendant to show cause why this Court should not hold the Defendant in contempt for failing to comply with this Court's Order of [January 2, 1993]. As grounds for this motion, [Mr. Jones] shows the Court:

1.   On [January 2, 1993], this Court entered an Order requiring that, within fifteen days of the Order, the Defendant reinstate [Mr. Jones] as a telemarketing assistant and make reasonable accommodations for [Mr. Jones]' disability by changing his job requirements.

2.   As of [January 30, 1993], the Defendant has failed to reinstate [Mr. Jones] and otherwise comply with this Court's Order of [January 2, 1993].

Accordingly, [Mr. Jones] respectfully requests that this Court issue an Order directing the Defendants to show cause why this Court should not hold them in contempt for failing to comply with this Court's Order of [January 2, 1993].

Respectfully Submitted,

[attorney for plaintiff]

§ 17.11   Memorandum of Law Supporting
Contempt Motion

FORM 17–9
SAMPLE MEMORANDUM OF LAW SUPPORTING CONTEMPT

I.   FACTS

From [January 1987] through [July 5, 1992], [XYZ, Inc. ("XYZ")], employed [John Jones] as a telemarketing assistant. On [July 4, 1992], [Jones] injured himself during a backyard barbecue, rendering himself completely and permanently blind. On [July 5, 1992], when [Jones] informed [XYZ] of his misfortune, [XYZ] terminated him. At the time of his termination, [Jones] had a good work record that showed above average performance in his position. In response to [XYZ]'s actions, [Jones] filed suit under the Americans with Disabilities Act ("ADA") in federal court, alleging that [XYZ] terminated him because of his disability, therefore discriminating against him.[36] [Jones] sought a permanent injunction requiring [XYZ] to reinstate him in the telemarketing position he formerly held.

On [January 2, 1993], the Court granted [Jones]' request and issued an order requiring that [XYZ] reinstate [Jones] in his former position within fifteen days and provide reasonable accommodations for [Jones]' disability by changing his job requirements. As of [January 30, 1993], [XYZ] had not complied with the Court's order. Accordingly, [Jones] petitioned the Court for an order to show cause why the Court should not hold [XYZ] in contempt.

II.   DISCUSSION

This memorandum discusses contempt proceedings as they relate to the ADA. The first part of the memorandum describes the general nature of contempt by distinguishing between civil and criminal contempt, the two types of contempt. The second part of the memorandum discusses judicial procedure peculiar to civil and criminal contempt. Although civil contempt proceedings are more relevant than criminal contempt proceedings in ADA cases in which the employer refuses to comply with a court order, both are discussed in detail. Finally, this memorandum concludes with a discussion of impossibility, a complete defense to civil contempt.

A.   The Nature of Contempt

Courts may use their contempt powers to ensure that an employer honors an injunction issued as a result of an ADA lawsuit.[37] Although the ADA does not

---

[36] *See* ADA § 102(b)(1), 42 U.S.C. § 12112(b)(1) (1994).

[37] Bessette v. W.B. Conkey Co., 194 U.S. 324, 327 (1904).

specifically discuss the use of contempt to enforce injunctions,[38] contempt is a remedy available for violation of a ADA-related injunction.[39]

An employer may be charged with civil or criminal contempt when it refuses or fails to obey an ADA injunction. The purpose and character of the potential punishment distinguishes civil from criminal contempt.[40] Whether a particular contumacious act is classified as civil or criminal contempt is important because the procedural protections are much greater for one accused of criminal contempt.[41] Civil contempt punishes to enforce the rights of a litigant,[42] and the nature of the punishment is to force future compliance with the injunction.[43] In addition, a private litigant prosecutes civil contempt proceedings, and the proceedings usually result either in the imposition of money penalties payable to the private complainant, or in the incarceration of the defendant for an indefinite period pending compliance with the court order.[44] Penalties for civil contempt are considered conditional because the contemnor can avoid remission of a monetary penalty or secure release from custody by complying with the terms of the court order.[45]

In contrast with civil contempt, criminal contempt punishes to vindicate public authority.[46] In addition, criminal contempt punishes the offender for past contempt, is punitive, and cannot be ended by any act of the contemnor.[47] Punishment for criminal contempt may include incarceration and a fine payable to the United States, which serves as the prosecutor in criminal contempt proceedings in federal court.

Moreover, contempt is subdivided into direct and indirect contempt. This distinction is important because direct contempt may be punished summarily by the judge

---

[38] The ADA enforcement provisions at ADA § 107, 42 U.S.C. § 12117 (1994); ADA § 203, 42 U.S.C. § 12133 (1994); ADA § 308, 42 U.S.C. § 12188 (1994) make no mention of contempt.

[39] Perritt at 445 (contempt is remedy available for violation of any court order). Because the ADA authorizes injunctive relief, a court presented with an ADA case could issue an order which, if violated, would be punishable by contempt.

[40] Gompers v. Bucks Stove & Range Co., 221 U.S. 418, 441 (1911).

[41] *Id.* at 446. Criminal contempt would be involved only if a prosecutor exercised the discretion to prosecute for contempt. It is far more likely that a victim of an ADA violation would seek civil contempt.

[42] Penfield Co. v. SEC, 330 U.S. 585, 590 (1947).

[43] Perritt at 446.

[44] Gompers v. Bucks Stove & Range Co., 221 U.S. 418, 418 (1911).

[45] *Id.* In UMWA v. Bagwell, ___ U.S. ___, 114 S. Ct. 2552 (1994), the Supreme Court made this analytical framework less certain. It reversed the Virginia Supreme Court and held that, under the facts of that case, contempt penalties announced in advance and assessed only after further noncompliance occurred were criminal rather than civil. *Id.* at 2562. The Court suggested that coercive penalties are likely to be found to be criminal in nature unless they have a compensatory purpose.

[46] Carbon Fuel Co. v. UMWA, 517 F.2d 1348, 1349 (4th Cir. 1975).

[47] *Id.*

in whose presence the contumacious acts occurred. Indirect contempt may be punished only through a factfinding process that determines whether or not out-of court conduct was contumacious.[48] Direct contempt covers acts committed under the eye and within the hearing of the court.[49] In a summary proceeding to punish such direct contempt, a court need not hear evidence on contempt committed within its sight or hearing before punishing the contemnor.[50] Given this distinction between direct and indirect contempt, an employer's refusal to obey an ADA-related court order would almost always be treated as indirect contempt when the refusal occurred away from the court house. The only ADA context in which direct contempt could plausibly arise is if a witness refused an order to testify at a trial or hearing.

Despite the different classifications of contempt and the possibility that contempt related to an ADA injunction could be classified as either direct or indirect contempt, the most likely classification in ADA cases is civil contempt. The purpose and character of the punishment test confirms this conclusion because the private plaintiff in this proceeding seeks future compliance with the injunction. Most contempt proceedings related to an employer's refusal to obey a court order resulting from an ADA lawsuit should be characterized as civil contempt.[51]

B.   Proceedings to Punish Contempt

1.   Criminal Contempt Proceedings

Federal Rule of Criminal Procedure 42 governs criminal contempt proceedings. Subsection (a) of Rule 42 states that criminal contempt may be punished summarily if the judge certifies that the judge saw or heard the conduct constituting the contempt, and that it was committed in the actual presence of the court.[52] Subsection (a) addresses only direct criminal contempt.

Subsection (b) addresses all other criminal contempt and requires three procedural stages:

1.   Proper notice of the criminal nature of the contempt citation

2.   Trial by jury when "an act of Congress so provides"

3.   Trial before an impartial (nondisqualified) judge.[53]

---

[48] *In re* Heathcock, 696 F.2d 1362, 1365 (11th Cir. 1983).

[49] United States v. Marshall, 451 F.2d 372, 374 (9th Cir. 1971).

[50] United States v. Vague, 697 F.2d 805, 808 (7th Cir. 1983).

[51] In addition to civil contempt proceedings, the court may institute criminal proceedings against the defendant to the civil contempt proceeding based on the same conduct. United States v. UMWA, 330 U.S. 258, 303 (1947).

[52] Fed. R. Crim. P. 42(a).

[53] *Id.* 42(b); Perritt at 614.

Commencing criminal contempt proceedings under Rule 42(b) requires only notice.[54] Although criminal contempt proceedings have been commenced by indictment or information, this is not required.[55] For the notice to be adequate, it must state the time and place of hearing and allow reasonable time for preparation of a defense.[56] Further, the notice must state the essential facts constituting the criminal contempt charged and describe it as such.[57] A jury trial is required in a criminal contempt proceeding only when the contempt is considered a serious offense.[58] Criminal contempt is a serious offense when it is punishable by more than six months in prison.[59] Thus, an employer is entitled to a jury trial in all ADA criminal contempt cases in which conviction would result in a sentence greater than six months.

The final procedural requirement of an impartial judge arises when the contempt involved disrespect to, or criticism of, a judge.[60] In these instances, the alleged contemnor is entitled to a full hearing before a different judge.[61]

Distinct from the procedural requirements of a criminal contempt proceeding are the mechanics for initiating those proceedings. Criminal contempt proceedings may be initiated in three ways:

1.   the court may bring charges on its own motion,

2.   a private party may petition the court to prosecute another for criminal contempt,[62] or

3.   the local United States Attorney may initiate the criminal contempt proceeding.

A court usually brings charges on its own motion only in summary proceedings pursuant to Rule 42(a). The court may bring contempt charges at the time of the contumacious act or at some later time.[63] Local prosecuting authorities usually initiate contempt proceedings for indirect criminal contempt. A private party may ask the U.S. Attorney to prosecute another for criminal contempt. Similarly, the local

---

[54] Fed. R. Crim. P. 42(b).

[55] United States v. Mensik, 440 F.2d 1232, 1234 (4th Cir. 1971).

[56] Fed. R. Crim. P. 42(b).

[57] *Id.*

[58] Codispoti v. Pennsylvania, 418 U.S. 506, 511 (1974).

[59] *Id.*

[60] *See* United States v. Prugh, 479 F.2d 611, 613 (8th Cir. 1973).

[61] United States v. Meyer, 462 F.2d 827, 842 (D.C. Cir. 1972).

[62] *See* Charles B. Blackmar, West's Federal Forms § 7766 (1971) (example of a Petition for Prosecution of Criminal Contempt).

[63] United States v. Schiffer, 351 F.2d 91, 94–95 (6th Cir. 1965).

prosecuting authority may initiate criminal contempt proceedings in accordance with local criminal procedure.

2.   Civil Contempt Proceedings

Notice and the opportunity to be heard are the essential characteristics of civil contempt proceedings.[64] The requirements for notice vary based upon the rules of procedure used by the court in which the litigant initiates the contempt proceedings. The rules of procedure used in the contempt proceedings should be the same ones used in the lawsuit that originally gave rise to the court order in dispute. This is because courts consider a proceeding for contempt to enforce a remedy in a civil action a proceeding in that original civil action.[65] Because the contempt proceeding involves new issues, the alleged contemnor is entitled to notice of the facts alleged in the contempt proceeding. Nevertheless, a new civil action is not involved. Rather, the first step in initiating civil contempt proceedings is to file a motion or "order to show cause," depending on local practice, with the clerk of the court with jurisdiction over the main action. The adequacy of the contents of this initial document will, of course, be determined by the rules of civil procedure used by the court in which the complaint is filed. Since lawsuits under the ADA involve federal subject matter jurisdiction,[66] this memorandum addresses only the form and content of the motion for an order to show cause under the Federal Rules of Civil Procedure.[67]

Under the Federal Rules of Civil Procedure, a motion to the court for an order to show cause why an employer in an ADA action should not be punished for contempt must:

1.   be made in writing,

2.   state with particularity the grounds therefor, and

3.   set forth the relief or order sought.[68]

---

[64] Perritt at 448. This discussion assumes that the employer was the defendant in the initial ADA lawsuit and is also charged with contempt. Accordingly, no new process is required when the employer is already subject to the jurisdiction of the court, because the contempt proceeding is considered a continuation of the original proceeding. C.A. Wright & A.R. Miller, Federal Practice and Procedure § 2960 (1973) [hereinafter Wright & Miller] at 589.

[65] Gompers v. Bucks Stove & Range Co., 221 U.S. 418, 444–45 (1947). This makes sense because a litigant commences proceedings for civil contempt to enforce rights which that litigant has gained as a result of a prior legal action.

[66] The plaintiff may always obtain federal question jurisdiction in a lawsuit filed under the ADA. 28 U.S.C. § 1331 (1994). In contrast, if the plaintiff brings the initial action in state court, whether the lawsuit eventually ends up in federal court depends upon the defendant's success in removing the lawsuit. *Id.* § 1441.

[67] See the applicable state rules of procedure for ADA injunctions issued by state courts.

[68] Fed. R. Civ. P. 7(b)(1).

No difficulties exist with the requirements of a writing or the relief or order sought. The purpose of the particularity requirement is to provide the defendant with notice of the grounds upon which the motion is based and the relief sought. Further, the movant must provide the defendant with adequate information for the defendant to process the motion correctly.[69]

Once the plaintiff has filed its motion, and the motion's contents comply with the appropriate court's standards, formal civil contempt procedure commences. As stated earlier, the essential attributes of these proceedings are notice and the opportunity to be heard.

The proper or permissible form of notice varies with the local practice[70] and should comport with the appropriate federal or state rule of civil procedure governing pleadings or motions, as appropriate.

The appropriate form of the requisite hearing in a civil contempt proceeding is flexible. The opportunity to be heard contemplates that the person have an opportunity to present argument and evidence on possible defenses.[71] Form varies with the issues.[72] Regardless of the desirability and expediency of summary proceedings, they must always comport with the requirements of due process.[73]

C.   Impossibility

Impossibility is a defense to civil contempt for violation of an injunction.[74] Impossibility occupies a unique position in an ADA-related civil contempt proceeding because it not only serves as a potential defense to contempt charges, but also may be used in the original ADA lawsuit when an employer attempts to establish undue hardship. For example, in attempting to establish undue hardship an employer might attempt to show that financial constraints prevent it from providing reasonable accommodations. If a court rejects this argument and fails to find undue hardship, the question arises as to whether the employer may relitigate this issue when he asserts the defense of impossibility in the contempt proceedings. In *Maggio v. Zeitz*,[75] the Supreme Court ruled that it is not permissible to relitigate the legal or factual basis of the order alleged to have been disobeyed.[76] However, the Court stated that if the two disputes may be characterized as asking the same question (i.e., the

---

[69] Registration Control Sys., Inc. v. Compusystems, Inc., 922 F.2d 805 (Fed. Cir. 1990).

[70] Wright & Miller at 588.

[71] *See* Washington Metro. Area Transit Auth. v. Transit Union, 531 F.2d 617, 621–22 (D.C. Cir. 1976) (reversing contempt for failure to consider defenses adequately).

[72] Wright & Miller at 590.

[73] Shillitani v. United States, 384 U.S. 364, 371 (1966).

[74] United States v. Rylander, 460 U.S. 752, 757, *reh'g denied,* 462 U.S. 1112 (1983) (contempt for failure to produce records pursuant to an IRS subpoena).

[75] 333 U.S. 56, 69 (1948).

[76] *Id.* at 74.

employer's financial capability to provide reasonable accommodations) at two different points in time, then the latter issue must be tried just as any other issue.

Another, related, issue concerns burdens of proof in establishing undue hardship and impossibility. The structure of ADA § 102(b)(5) and the ADA's legislative history make it clear that the employer has the burden of establishing undue hardship.[77] Similarly, in establishing the defense of impossibility, the initial burden of production lies with the alleged contemnor. However, the burden of persuasion shifts back to the party seeking the contempt order when the contemnor has satisfied its burden of production of evidence establishing his present inability to comply. As applied to an ADA lawsuit, this means that the employer has a greater evidentiary burden in establishing undue hardship in the original lawsuit than in establishing impossibility in the contempt proceedings. Although strategically an employer might be tempted to relitigate the burdensomeness of making accommodation in the civil contempt proceeding, the law-of-the-case doctrine is likely to prevent relitigation of this issue if it was decided in the context of an undue burden defense in establishing liability or in proceedings on a preliminary injunction.[78]

§ 17.12   Motion to Reduce Coercive Civil Contempt Fines to a Judgment

FORM 17–10
SAMPLE MOTION TO REDUCE FINES TO A JUDGMENT

In the [type] Court of [location]

[John Jones],

Plaintiff,

v.   No. [case number]

[XYZ, Inc.],

Defendant.

Plaintiff, [John Jones], by his undersigned counsel, respectfully moves the court for further relief in the above-referenced cause. As grounds for this motion, Plaintiff shows the court the following:

---

[77] See § **4.47.**

[78] Maggio v. Zeitz, 333 U.S. 56, 68 (1948) (original proceeding is separate from contempt proceeding; when original proceeding terminates in final order, it becomes res judicata and not subject to collateral attack in contempt proceedings). Res judicata would not, of course, preclude relitigation in a subsequent criminal contempt proceeding because the burden of proof is more demanding in the criminal context.

1.   On [February 1, 1993], this court found the defendant, [XYZ, Inc. ("XYZ")], in contempt for failing to comply with this court's [January 2, 1993], order requiring that the Defendant reinstate the Plaintiff in his former position as a telemarketing assistant with [XYZ].

2.   In its [February 1, 1993], order, this court ordered [XYZ] fined prospectively [one-thousand dollars] per day for each day after [February 1, 1993], that [XYZ] failed to reinstate [John Jones] as a telemarketing assistant at [XYZ]. In the same order this court also stated that the purpose of this fine was to coerce [XYZ] to comply with this court's [January 2, 1993], order.

3.   Plaintiff now advises the court that as of the date of this motion, the defendant has not yet reinstated [Jones] to his position as a telemarketing assistant.

Plaintiffs respectfully pray:

a.   that the court issue an order directing the defendant to show cause why it should not be fined [ten thousand] dollars pursuant to the prospective fine schedule included in this court's [February 1, 1993], order,

b.   that this court hold an assessment hearing to assess fines in the amount of [ten thousand] dollars against the defendant, and

c.   that, upon conclusion of the assessment hearing, this court enter a judgment in favor of the plaintiff for [ten thousand] dollars.

Respectfully Submitted,

[attorney for the plaintiff]

[address]

§ 17.13   Assessment and Collection of Civil Contempt Fines

A court assesses coercive civil contempt fines when an employer fails to comply with a contempt order whose terms expressly provide for such fines. This section discusses not only the procedure for assessing and collecting coercive contempt fines but also the arguments used to avoid paying coercive contempt fines.

Understanding how an employee gets to the point of collecting coercive civil contempt fines requires some knowledge of the events preceding the assessment of those fines. This series of events consists of three distinct stages. In the first stage, the court issues an injunction as a result of an ADA lawsuit. In the second stage, the employer violates the injunction and the court issues a contempt order that specifies prospective monetary penalties or "fines" if the employer violates the contempt order. In the third stage, the employer violates the contempt order, the related fines accrue pursuant to the fine provision in the order, and the employee tries to collect the fines.

The first stage in assessing coercive civil contempt fines is for a court to issue an injunction. A court must issue either an injunction to compel or to prohibit certain conduct by the employer.

The second stage of the assessment process begins when the employer fails to comply with the terms of the injunction. To force compliance with the injunction, courts use their civil contempt powers. In a civil proceeding, a private plaintiff must invoke these powers. Accordingly, the employee commences civil contempt proceedings by filing a "show cause" motion with the court. Provided that the court finds the contents of this motion adequate, the court then issues a "show cause" order. This order commands the defendant to appear at a hearing to defend himself against the contempt charges. If the employer is unsuccessful in defending himself against these charges, the court issues a contempt order. Although the circumstances of each case determine the contents of the contempt order, at a minimum, the order should reiterate the terms of the original injunction and order future compliance with the injunction. If the defendant's previous noncompliance has injured the employee, the court may order compensatory fines.[79] In any event, the court uses the threat of fines to coerce compliance, and thus includes a provision in the order mandating that the employer be fined for each day or occurrence of future noncompliance.[80]

The final stage of the assessment process begins when the employer violates the contempt order. When the employee has evidence of the employer's prohibited conduct, the employee may move the court to assess fines pursuant to the prospective fine schedule set forth in the contempt order. This motion should describe both the violation and the relief sought by the employee. The court then orders the employer to appear before the court and defend itself against these new contempt allegations. If the court finds the employer in contempt, the court enters a judgment in favor of the employee for the amount of the accrued fines and issues a new order with provisions similar to, or more

---

[79] Compensatory actions are essentially backward-looking, seeking to compensate the employee through the payment of money for damages caused by the employer's past acts of disobedience of the court's order. Latrine Steel Co. v. United Steelworkers, 545 F.2d 1336, 1344 (3d Cir. 1976) (coercive contempt order could not survive invalidation of underlying injunction and, thus, was subject to being vacated).

[80] Coercive sanctions, in contrast to compensatory sanctions, look to the future and are designed to aid the plaintiff by bringing a defiant party into compliance with the court order or by assuring that a potentially contumacious party adheres to an injunction by setting forth in advance the penalties the court will impose if the party deviates from the path of obedience. *Id.* The court order may also include a provision mandating that the employer be incarcerated either until the employer complies or for future noncompliance.

stringent than, the first contempt order. Having a judgment in hand, the employee then executes the judgment to collect the fines.[81]

In order to avoid paying the fines, counsel for the employer may make either or both of two arguments. First, the employer might characterize coercive fines as a criminal sanction by asserting that courts assess coercive fines because of past contumacy and that the court failed to provide the employer with the usual criminal procedure safeguards. Because a court cannot impose criminal sanctions without providing the employer with all of the procedural safeguards owed to a criminal defendant, this argument leads to the conclusion that the fines must be revoked because the employer was denied due process. The employee's counsel can refute this argument by asserting that the fine was prospective at the time the employer received notice of it[82] and that the purpose of the fine was to coerce compliance with the injunction, thereby making it civil in nature.

Secondly, the employer might argue that even if the fines are civil they become moot after the employer complies with the injunction because compliance was the ultimate goal of initially assessing the fines. Accepting this argument means that any employer subject to coercive contempt fines could avoid payment of the fines by postponing actual collection until after the employer complied with the injunction. Such a rule provides no incentive for compliance with the court order and courts reject it as undermining public respect for the judiciary.[83]

---

[81] *But see id.* at 1346 (describing coercive contempt fines as payable into court or public treasury and not to complainant). In UMWA v. Bagwell, ____ U.S. ____, 114 S. Ct. 2552 (1994), the Supreme Court made this analytical framework less certain. It reversed the Virginia Supreme Court and held that, under the facts of that case, contempt penalties announced in advance and assessed only after further noncompliance occurred were criminal rather than civil. *Id.* at 2562. The Court suggested that coercive penalties are likely to be found to be criminal in nature unless they have a compensatory purpose.

[82] If the employer had complied with the injunction upon receiving notice of it, the court would not have fined the employer.

[83] Bagwell v. UMWA, 423 S.E.2d 349, 357 (Va. 1992), *rev'd,* ____ U.S. ____, 114 S. Ct. 2552 (1994).

§ 17.14   Plaintiffs' Motion for Entry of Judgment (EEOC)

FORM 17–11
SAMPLE PLAINTIFF'S MOTION FOR ENTRY OF JUDGMENT

IN THE UNITED STATES DISTRICT COURT

FOR THE [NORTHERN] DISTRICT OF [ILLINOIS]

[EASTERN] DIVISION

U.S. EQUAL EMPLOYMENT OPPORTUNITY COMMISSION and [CHARLES H. WESSEL],

Plaintiffs,

v.   Civil Action No.: [92 C 7330]

[A.I.C. SECURITY INVESTIGATIONS LTD.];

[A.I.C. INTERNATIONAL, LTD.]; and [unnamed defendant C],

Defendants.

Magistrate Judge [Guzman]

PLAINTIFFS' MOTION FOR ENTRY OF JUDGMENT

Plaintiffs, Equal Employment Opportunity Commission and [Charles H. Wessel], respectfully move the Court, pursuant to Rule 58 of the Federal Rules of Civil Procedure, for entry of judgment on the verdicts rendered on [March 19, 1993], and for equitable relief. A draft judgment, incorporating the claims for relief of each Plaintiff, is attached.

[certificate of service]

[draft judgment]

§ 17.15   Motion in Opposition to Judgment for Damages

FORM 17–12
SAMPLE MOTION IN OPPOSITION TO JUDGMENT FOR DAMAGES

IN THE UNITED STATES DISTRICT COURT

FOR THE [NORTHERN] DISTRICT OF [ILLINOIS]

[EASTERN] DIVISION

U.S. EQUAL EMPLOYMENT OPPORTUNITY COMMISSION,

Plaintiff,

v.   Civil Action No. [92 C 7330]

[A.I.C. SECURITY INVESTIGATIONS, LTD.];

[A.I.C. INTERNATIONAL, LTD.]; and [unnamed defendant C],

Honorable [Marvin E. Aspen]

Defendants.   Magistrate Judge [Ronald A. Guzman]

DEFENDANTS' MOTION IN OPPOSITION TO
PLAINTIFFS' PROPOSED JUDGMENT ON DAMAGES

The Defendants, [A.I.C. SECURITY INVESTIGATIONS, LTD. (hereinafter "A.I.C.")] and [defendant C], by and through their attorneys, [WESSELS & PAUTSCH, P.C.], by [Charles W. Pautsch], [attorney A], and [attorney B], upon order of the Court hereby move in opposition to the draft judgment submitted by Plaintiffs and move that the jury verdict on damages be effected in the final judgment[84] as follows:

1.   The jury verdict of [$50,000.00] in compensatory damages is speculative and excessive and goes against the weight of the evidence at trial.

2.   The jury verdict of [$250,000.00] in punitive damages against [A.I.C.], and [$250,000.00] in punitive damages against [defendant C], is excessive and goes against the weight of the evidence at trial.

---

[84] The defendants are submitting this motion on the limited issue of damages pursuant to the court's express request that such issues be addressed prior to its entry of judgment in this action. The defendants reserve the right to bring any postjudgment motions on these or any other issues deemed appropriate.

3.   Pursuant to 42 U.S.C. § 1981a(b)(3), the Court is charged to reduce the sum of compensatory and punitive damages Plaintiffs may recover not to exceed the statutory maximum of [$200,000.00] based upon the parties' stipulation in the pre-trial order that [A.I.C.] employs more than 200 but less than 500 employees.

WHEREFORE, Defendants [A.I.C. SECURITY INVESTIGATIONS, LTD.] and [defendant C] request, without waiver of their rights to file any postjudgment motions as provided for in the Federal Rules of Civil Procedure, that the Court first apply the statutory cap of $200,000.00 to the total compensatory and punitive damages awarded by the jury, and secondly, that the Court exercise its discretion in further reducing the jury's award of compensatory and punitive damages on the basis of the record at trial and the guidance afforded by other case law cited in the accompanying memorandum.

Dated this [26th] day of [March, 1993].

[A.I.C. SECURITY INVESTIGATIONS, LTD.] and [defendant C]

By:

[attorney A]

§ 17.16   Objections to Entry of Judgment

FORM 17–13
SAMPLE OBJECTIONS TO ENTRY OF JUDGMENT

IN THE UNITED STATES DISTRICT COURT

FOR THE [NORTHERN] DISTRICT OF [ILLINOIS]

[EASTERN] DIVISION

U.S. EQUAL EMPLOYMENT OPPORTUNITY COMMISSION,

Plaintiff,

v.   Civil Action No.: [92 C 7330]

[A.I.C. SECURITY INVESTIGATIONS, LTD.];

[A.I.C. INTERNATIONAL, LTD.];

and [unnamed defendant C],   Honorable [Marvin E. Aspen]

Defendants.   Magistrate Judge [Guzman]

DEFENDANTS' OBJECTIONS TO PLAINTIFFS' MOTION
FOR ENTRY OF JUDGMENT

Defendants, [A.I.C. SECURITY INVESTIGATIONS, LTD.] and [defendant C], by and through their attorneys, [WESSELS & PAUTSCH, P.C.], by [Charles W. Pautsch], [attorney A], and [attorney B], hereby object to the Plaintiffs' Motion for Entry of Judgment in the above-captioned action based upon the following:

1.   Defendants object to paragraph two (2) of Plaintiffs' draft judgment because the jury award of [$50,000.00] in compensatory damages is excessive and goes against the weight of the evidence at trial.[85]

2.   Defendants further object to paragraph two (2) of Plaintiffs' draft judgment because it impermissibly fails to aggregate "the sum of the amount of compensatory damages awarded . . . and the amount of punitive damages awarded" for purposes of the statutory caps on such damages. See 42 U.S.C. § 1981a(b)(3).

3.   Defendants object to paragraphs three (3) and four (4) of Plaintiffs' draft judgment because they fail to aggregate "the sum of the amount of compensatory damages awarded . . . and the amount of punitive damages awarded" for purposes of the statutory caps on such damages. 42 U.S.C. § 1981a(b)(3).

4.   Defendants further object to paragraph four (4) of Plaintiffs' draft judgment because it wholly ignores 42 U.S.C. § 1981a(b)(3) in that total compensatory and punitive damages recoverable by [Wessel] "shall not exceed" $200,000.00 because the parties have stipulated in the Pre-Trial Order that this is a case of a Respondent who has more than 200 but fewer than 500 employees; as detailed in the accompanying memorandum, Plaintiffs' apparent position that the Civil Rights Act of 1991 places no cap on the compensatory or punitive damages [Wessel] may recover from [defendant C] is contrary to the law.

5.   Defendants further object to paragraphs three (3) and four (4) of Plaintiffs' draft judgment because the jury award of [$250,000.00] in punitive damages against [A.I.C.] and [defendant C], each, is excessive and goes against the weight of the evidence at trial.

6.   Defendants object to paragraphs five (5) through ten (10) of the Plaintiffs' draft judgment because the requested injunctive relief would be punitive in its effect and would not serve any principles of equity since no one other than [Wessel] has complained against Defendants, Defendants remain subject to the law under the ADA regardless of any equitable relief, and the peculiar circumstances of this case do not justify the broad injunctive remedies sought by Plaintiffs.

---

[85] This position is argued more fully in the defendants' accompanying memorandum of law on damages, which the defendants are submitting pursuant to the court's request. The defendants' submission of said memorandum does not constitute a waiver of their right to submit any postjudgment motions they may deem appropriate.

7.   Defendants further object to paragraphs (5) through ten (10) of the Plaintiffs' draft judgment because it seeks punitive measures such as postings at the property of its clients which is intrusive to such parties and would effectively cause the loss of many such clients, and further any notices, posted or hand-delivered to employees, would serve no equitable purpose in light of the massive media attention and publicity given to this action since its inception.

8.   Defendants further object to paragraphs five (5) through (10) of the Plaintiffs' draft judgment because the three-year period Plaintiffs seek for any injunctive relief is excessive and punitive, especially under these circumstances, where the jury in effect determined that [Wessel] was not qualified and was not entitled to backpay beyond [November] and thus could have been permissibly discharged after [November], but not [July], of [1992].

9.   Defendants object to paragraph six (6) of Plaintiffs' draft judgment because, in addition to the foregoing objections, Plaintiffs seek injunctive relief which is nonsensical in that it would apply to "any person" filing a charge, opposing an unlawful practice under the ADA, etc.; Defendants are already prohibited by law from retaliating against their employees or applicants, 42 U.S.C. § 2000e-3, and the proposed judgment of the Plaintiffs is impracticable and unnecessary.

Respectfully submitted on this [26th] day of [March], [1993].

§ 17.17   Judgment

FORM 17–14
SAMPLE JUDGMENT

IN THE UNITED STATES DISTRICT COURT

FOR THE [NORTHERN] DISTRICT OF [ILLINOIS]

[EASTERN] DIVISION

U.S. EQUAL EMPLOYMENT OPPORTUNITY COMMISSION,

Plaintiff,

v.   Civil Action No. [92 C 7330]

[A.I.C. SECURITY INVESTIGATIONS, LTD.];

[A.I.C. INTERNATIONAL, LTD.];

and [unnamed defendant C],

Defendants.   Magistrate Judge [Guzman]

JUDGMENT

The Court hereby enters judgment upon the verdicts of the jury, rendered [March 18, 1993], in favor of Plaintiff Equal Employment Opportunity Commission ("EEOC") and Intervening Plaintiff [Charles H. Wessel ("Wessel")] and against Defendants [A.I.C. Security Investigations, Ltd. ("A.I.C.")] and [defendant C]. Pursuant to the Court's ruling of [March 17, 1993], Defendant [A.I.C. International, Ltd.] is dismissed as a Defendant.

The Court orders that judgment be entered in favor of EEOC and [Wessel] and against the Defendants as follows:

1.   [A.I.C.] shall pay [Wessel] the sum of [$22,000.00] as back pay based on the jury award, plus interest at the rate of [six percent (6%)], compounded annually, to the date of judgment, in accordance with 42 U.S.C. § 2000e-5, incorporated by reference into the Americans With Disabilities Act ("ADA"), 42 U.S.C. § 12117.

2.   [A.I.C.] and [defendant C], jointly and severally, shall pay [Wessel] the sum of [$50,000.00] as compensatory damages, based upon the jury award, in accordance with 42 U.S.C. § 1981a(b).

The Court further orders that judgment be entered in favor of [Wessel] and against the Defendants as follows:

3.   [A.I.C.] and [defendant C], jointly and severally, shall pay [Wessel] the sum of [$150,000.00] as punitive damages, reduced from the jury award of [$500,000.00] in accordance with 42 U.S.C. § 1981a(b).

The Court further orders, pursuant to 42 U.S.C. § 2000e-5, incorporated by reference into the ADA, 42 U.S.C. § 12117, equitable relief in favor of the Equal Employment Opportunity Commission and against Defendants [A.I.C.] and [defendant C] as follows:

4.   [A.I.C.], its officers, agents, employees, successors, and all those in active concert or participation with them, or any of them; and [defendant C], are enjoined from engaging in any employment practice which discriminates against any qualified individual on the basis of disability, including, but not limited to, discharging any qualified employee because of his or her disability.

5.   [A.I.C.], its officers, agents, employees, successors, and all those in active concert or participation with them, or any of them; and [defendant C], shall not engage in retaliation or reprisal of any kind against any person because of such

person's opposition to any practice made unlawful under the ADA; because of such person's filing a charge, testifying, or participating in any manner in any investigation, proceeding, or hearing under the ADA; because such person was identified as a potential witness for the EEOC in this action; or in the investigation giving rise to this action; or because such person asserts any right under this Judgment.

6.   Within seven (7) days of the entry of this Judgment, [A.I.C.] and [defendant C] shall provide a copy of the Notice attached as Exhibit A to every employee of [A.I.C.]. In addition, [A.I.C.] and [defendant C] shall post a copy of the Notice on the premises of [A.I.C.] in a conspicuous location. Further, all new employees of [A.I.C.] are to be given a copy of this notice in [A.I.C.]'s Employee Handbook or Training Manual.

7.   [A.I.C.] and [defendant C] shall maintain, and keep available for inspection and copying by the EEOC, records providing the following information with respect to any employee who is disabled within the meaning of the ADA: name, address, telephone number, social security number, date of hire, date of disciplinary action, if applicable, date of discharge, if applicable, and reason for any adverse employment action.

8.   Every six (6) months for the duration of this Judgment, [A.I.C.] and [defendant C] shall provide to the EEOC a report including the information set forth in the records described in Paragraph 7.

9.   For the purposes of paragraphs four through eight above, this judgment shall remain in effect for a period of three years from the date of entry.[86]

§ 17.18   Preliminary Injunction

Form 17–15 represents the text of a typical injunction granted under the ADA. This order was issued as part of the proceedings in *Thomas v. Davidson Academy.*[87]

---

[86] EEOC v. A.I.C. Sec. Investigations, Ltd., 823 F. Supp. 571, 581 (N.D Ill. 1993) (judgment), *aff'd in part, rev'd in part*, 55 F.3d 1276 (7th Cir. 1995) (affirming compensatory damages award of $50,000 and punitive damages award of $150,000 against corporation, but reversing award against individual).

[87] 846 F. Supp. 611, 620 (M.D. Tenn. 1994) (preliminary injunction based on failure to exercise leniency with respect to student's outburst caused by fear of bleeding associated with blood disorder).

FORM 17–15
SAMPLE PRELIMINARY INJUNCTION

ORDER

On [February 1, 1994], the Court held a consolidated trial and hearing pursuant to Fed. R. Civ. P. 65(a)(2) on plaintiff's application for a preliminary injunction in the above-styled matter.

Consistent with the contemporaneously filed Memorandum, the Court hereby GRANTS [Miss Thomas]' application for preliminary injunction. Accordingly, a preliminary injunction is ENTERED PROHIBITING defendant [Davidson Academy] from enforcing the decision to expel [Miss Thomas] or otherwise to interfere with her continued enrollment at [Davidson Academy]; and PROHIBITING [Davidson Academy] and its officials and employees from retaliating, coercing, intimidating, threatening, or interfering with [Miss Thomas] in the exercise and enjoyment of her rights as granted under the Americans with Disabilities Act of 1990 and the Rehabilitation Act of 1973. The Court waives any requirement for security under Fed. R. Civ. P. 65(c). Furthermore, the Court retains jurisdiction of this case through the remainder of the [1993-94] academic calendar.

§ 17.19   Temporary Restraining Order in Title II Case

Form 17–16 represents a temporary restraining order from an actual ADA Title II[88] case. The source of this restraining order is *Heather K. v. City of Mallard.*[89]

FORM 17–16
SAMPLE TEMPORARY RESTRAINING ORDER IN TITLE II CASE

TEMPORARY RESTRAINING ORDER

WHEREAS, pursuant to Fed. R. Civ. P. 65(b), the court finds that the exceptions to the ban on open burning found in [Ordinance 105.05] of the [City of Mallard] pose a threat of irreparable harm to the life and health of plaintiff [Heather K.] in violation of Title II of the Americans with Disabilities Act, 42 U.S.C. §§ 12131 *et seq.,* the following sections of [City of Mallard] [Ordinance 105.05] are, for the [10] days following issuance of this order, hereby temporarily restrained and enjoined upon the terms stated.

---

[88] ADA §§ 201–246, 42 U.S.C. §§ 12131–12165 (1994) [hereinafter Title II].

[89] 887 F. Supp. 1249 (N.D. Iowa 1995).

1. [Ordinance 105.05], [subparagraph 1.], which permits "recreational fires" defined as open fires for cooking, heating, recreation and ceremonies, provided they comply with the limits for emissions of visible air contaminants established by the State Department of Natural Resources . . . is temporarily restrained and enjoined, with the exception that recreational fires pursuant to this subparagraph shall be permitted on [Sunday], [May 28, 1995], and [Monday], [May 29, 1995], in observance of the National Holiday of Memorial Day. Nothing in this court's order shall be construed as restraining or enjoining the ordinary use of outdoor cooking appliances such as charcoal or gas grills, barbecues, or hibachis, and like outdoor cooking fire receptacles at any time during the effective period of this temporary restraining order.

2. [Ordinance 105.05], [subparagraph 2.], which permits "backyard burning," defined as backyard burning of residential waste at dwellings of four-family units or less . . . is temporarily restrained and enjoined in its entirety for the duration of this temporary restraining order.

3. [Ordinance 105.05], [subparagraph 3.], which permits "training fires," defined as fires set for the purpose of bona fide training of public or industrial employees in <u>fire</u> fighting methods, provided that the Executive Director receives notice in writing at least one week before such action commences . . . is temporarily restrained and enjoined only to the extent that the [City of Mallard] shall provide notice by personal service to plaintiffs herein of the occurrence of any such training fires not less than 24 hours before any such fires are scheduled to commence.

4. [Ordinance 105.05], [subparagraph 4.], which permits any "variance" in the following terms: Any person wishing to conduct open burning of materials not permitted herein may make application for a variance to the Executive Director . . . is temporarily restrained and enjoined only to the extent that the [City of Mallard] shall provide notice by personal service to plaintiffs herein of the occurrence of any such variance fires not less than 24 hours before any such fires are scheduled to commence.

This temporary restraining order shall be binding upon the parties to this action, their officers, agents, servants, employees, and attorneys, and upon those persons in active concert or participation with them who receive actual notice of the order.

The [City of Mallard], [Iowa], shall provide notice of this temporary restraining order by posting notice copies of this temporary restraining order in such public places as are reasonably calculated to give reasonable notice to the citizens of [Mallard] of the existence and terms of the temporary restraining order not later than 24 hours following the date and time on which this order is signed and filed with the Clerk of Court for the [Northern] District of [Iowa].

IT IS SO ORDERED.

§ 17.20   Notice to Employees

FORM 17–17
SAMPLE NOTICE TO EMPLOYEES

IN THE UNITED STATES DISTRICT COURT

FOR THE [NORTHERN] DISTRICT OF [ILLINOIS]

[EASTERN] DIVISION

U.S. EQUAL EMPLOYMENT OPPORTUNITY COMMISSION,

Plaintiff,

v.   Civil Action No. [92 C 7330]

[A.I.C. SECURITY INVESTIGATIONS, LTD.];

[A.I.C. INTERNATIONAL, LTD.];

and [unnamed defendant C],

Defendants.   Magistrate Judge [Guzman]

NOTICE TO ALL EMPLOYEES OF [A.I.C.]

This Notice is being posted by order of the Court in a lawsuit brought against [A.I.C. Security Investigations, Ltd ("A.I.C.")] and [defendant C] by the Equal Employment Opportunity Commission ("EEOC") and [Charles H. Wessel]. In the suit a federal jury has determined that [A.I.C.] and [defendant C] violated the Americans With Disabilities Act ("ADA") by discharging [Charles H. Wessel] from his position as Executive Director of [A.I.C.] because of his disability. [A.I.C.] and defendants have been ordered by the Court to pay to [Charles H. Wessel] back pay, compensatory damages including damages for mental distress, and punitive damages.

Under the Court's Judgment, [A.I.C.] and [defendant C] have been ordered not to discriminate against any qualified employee or applicant for employment because of his or her disability. The Court has also ordered [A.I.C.] and [defendant C] not to retaliate against any person who participated in the EEOC's investigation or trial of the case, or who exercises his or her rights under this Notice.

Should you have any complaints of discrimination on the basis of disability, you can contact the EEOC at [536 South Clark Street], [Room 982], [Chicago], [Illinois] [60605]. EEOC charges no fee for their services, and has employees that speak languages other than English. EEOC's offices are accessible to the disabled.

THIS IS AN OFFICIAL NOTICE AND MUST NOT BE DEFACED BY ANYONE

This Notice must remain posted for three (3) years from the date shown above and must not be altered, defaced or covered by any other material. Any questions concerning this Notice or compliance with its provisions should be directed to the EEOC, at the address shown above.[90]

---

[90] EEOC v. A.I.C. Sec. Investigations, Ltd., 823 F. Supp. 571, 582 (N.D. Ill. 1993), *aff'd in part, rev'd in part,* 55 F.3d 1276 (7th Cir. 1995) (affirming compensatory damages award of $50,000 and punitive damages award of $150,000 against corporation, but reversing award against individual).

CHAPTER 18

PREVENTIVE MATERIALS

§ 18.1 Introduction and Overview

The purpose of the Americans with Disabilities Act (ADA)[1] is not to increase the number of lawsuits brought by disabled persons, but to change behavior by public and private institutions to increase the opportunities available to the disabled. Accordingly, as important as the legal theories and the institutional procedures analyzed in other parts of this book are the practical steps that can be taken by employers, governmental entities, and places of public accommodation to improve opportunities for the disabled. This chapter outlines some of those practical steps. Following these steps not only will

---

[1] Pub. L. No. 101–336, 104 Stat. 327 (1990) (codified at 42 U.S.C. §§ 12101–12213 (1994); 47 U.S.C. §§ 225, 711 (1994)) [hereinafter ADA].

increase opportunities for the disabled but also will reduce the likelihood of being sued and losing.

Section 18.2 suggests some matters of general philosophy that apply to all kinds of entities covered by the ADA. The chapter then provides materials that employers, government entities, and places of public accommodation can use to avoid the need for the rest of the materials in this book. There is a significant amount of strategic and tactical analysis in terms of how personnel procedures and employee handbooks should be written, in addition to actual language that can be adapted to particular employer circumstances. See **Forms 18–6, 18–7, 18–18** and **18–19,** and **Forms 18–21** through **18–23.** In addition to substantive rules, employer commitments, and policy statements (see **Form 18–2**), this chapter also provides language by which employers can avoid legal liability based on breach of contract, model procedures for handling claims of disability discrimination, and requests for accommodation of disabilities.

§ 18.2   Matters of General Philosophy

Compliance with the spirit of the ADA requires adherence to the following principles:

1. To accept the proposition that the majority of physically and mentally disabled persons can participate meaningfully in employment and other kinds of activities and programs from which they historically were excluded

2. To identify specific barriers to meaningful participation by physically and mentally disabled persons

3. To evaluate necessity of these barriers to the essential nature of the activity

4. To be willing to remove nonessential barriers when that can be done at reasonable costs

5. To engage in a dialogue with disabled persons and their representatives to understand the kinds of barrier removal and other accommodation that might improve opportunities for the disabled without imposing great costs on institutions.

§ 18.3   Overview of Employer Attitudes and Action

The first step is to understand the basics of the ADA, as explained in earlier chapters. The core employment requirements of the ADA are:

1. Not disqualifying disabled applicants or employees because of their inability to perform marginal or nonessential job functions
2. Requiring employers to demonstrate the job-relatedness and business necessity of the requirements or selection criteria that tend to screen out disabled applicants
3. Requiring employers to make reasonable accommodations to assist disabled applicants or employees in meeting legitimate criteria.[2]

Employers who seek to develop an implementation plan can use the following basic approach:[3]

1. Employers should identify barriers to equal employment opportunities for disabled applicants and employees
2. Employers should identify possible accommodations
3. Employers should assess the reasonableness of each accommodation
4. Employers should implement the accommodation that is most reasonable for both the employer and the employee.[4]

This four-step process should be applied with respect to each stage of the employment relationship, beginning with the recruitment process.

§ 18.4 Employment Contacts

Employers should review the major types of communication they initiate with the outside world in connection with employment. The types of communication are described in §§ **18.5** through **18.13.**

§ 18.5 Policy Statement on Disability Discrimination in Employment

The statement in **Form 18–1** is suited for publication as an internal personnel policy direction to personnel specialists and supervisors. It also could be included in employee handbooks.

---

[2] H.R. Rep. No. 485, 101st Cong., 2d Sess., pt. 2 (1990) [hereinafter House Labor Report] at 71.

[3] *Id.* at 66; S. Rep. No. 116, 101st Cong., 1st Sess. (1989) [hereinafter Senate Report] at 35.

[4] House Labor Report at 66; Senate Report at 35. **Section 18.7** elaborates on the suggestion by Congress and the Equal Employment Opportunity Commission [hereinafter EEOC] that the process of reasonable accommodation should be an interactive one involving both the employer and the disabled employee.

FORM 18–1
SAMPLE DISABILITY DISCRIMINATION POLICY STATEMENT

The employer takes its obligations under the Americans with Disabilities Act and applicable state disability and handicap discrimination statutes seriously. Accordingly, it does not refuse to hire, dismiss from employment, or discriminate in compensation or other terms of employment because of an otherwise qualified employee's or applicant's mental or physical disability.

Employees must, however, be able to perform the essential functions of their jobs. It is not illegal discrimination to require that all employees, including those with disabilities, be able to perform the essential functions of their jobs or jobs for which they apply.

It is the employer's responsibility and prerogative to define job functions.

[Include this paragraph only if the reasonable accommodation statement in § 18.7 and the reasonable accommodation procedure in § 18.20 are also included.] If an employee (you) believe that job functions have been defined in a way that is inconsistent with the essential character of the job or if an employee (you) believe that you have been the victim of discrimination in violation of this policy statement, the employee (you) may request reasonable accommodation as explained in [§ ____] of this policy.

§ 18.6   Disability Discrimination and Harassment Policy Statement

FORM 18–2
SAMPLE DISABILITY DISCRIMINATION AND HARASSMENT POLICY STATEMENT

DISABILITY DISCRIMINATION AND HARASSMENT
POLICY STATEMENT

[Company name] has adopted a policy which forbids disability discrimination, including harassment in either a business or personal context. The policy applies to all workplace relationships, not solely to persons in a management or supervisory capacity. Thus, it also applies to people in the same job grade or department. The behavior could relate to physical actions or verbal or visual communications. It could be open or subtle. But if it is offensive to another, it is forbidden. Violations of the policy subject an employee to the full range of the [company]'s disciplinary policies.

It is the policy of [company] to maintain an employment atmosphere free of any pressures on employees relating to mental or physical disability. Consistent with applicable federal and state laws, [company] endorses the objective that employees, be free of situations where disability forms the basis for business decisions.

Disability discrimination or harassment will not be tolerated at [company], and employees who engage in such conduct are subject to the full range of [company]'s disciplinary policies.

§ 18.7   Reasonable Accommodation Policy Statement

The language in **Form 18–3** is suitable for inclusion either in a statement of personnel policies for internal use by personnel specialists and supervisors or in an employee handbook.

FORM 18–3
SAMPLE REASONABLE ACCOMMODATION POLICY STATEMENT

The employer takes seriously its obligations under the Americans with Disabilities Act and applicable state disability and handicap discrimination laws to provide reasonable accommodation to the mental and physical disabilities of employees and applicants for employment. Accordingly, when an employee or applicant requests reasonable accommodation, the employer gives serious consideration to the possibility of special arrangements such as modified work schedules, allowing the employee to use employee-provided special equipment, and modification in job responsibilities. Each request for reasonable accommodation must be considered on its own merits, in light of the particular job, of other related jobs, of the capabilities of the particular employee, and of the specific accommodation requested.

When the employer makes accommodation to the needs of a particular employee, the employer does not make any commitment that these special arrangements are permanent or that they automatically will be extended to any other employee. Rather, the employer must retain its flexibility to reorganize work and to redefine job requirements in light of the overall needs of its business.

[Include the following language only if the reasonable accommodation procedure provided in § **18.20** is included.] These case-by-case evaluations are made under the procedure described in [§ ___] of this policy statement (handbook), which is commenced by an individual employee's request for accommodation.

§ 18.8 Employment Advertisements

Advertisements for positions should state that the employer does not discriminate based on disability. See **Form 18–4.** A more specific statement like the following should also be considered:

The employer will not refuse to hire a disabled applicant who is capable of performing the essential requirements of the job with reasonable accommodation.

§ 18.9 Job Advertisement Language

FORM 18–4
SAMPLE JOB ADVERTISEMENT LANGUAGE

The [name] company does not discriminate based on physical or mental disability, and makes reasonable accommodation to permit disabled persons to perform essential job functions.

§ 18.10 Job Applications

Employment application forms should repeat the same nondiscrimination notice selected by the employer for advertisements. In addition, the application should invite applicants to identify any disability for which the applicant seeks accommodation.

Requesting information about disabilities on applications is tricky. The request must be framed so as to avoid violating the ADA's limitations on requiring information (see **Chapter 4**). Nevertheless, inviting voluntary disclosure puts both the employer and the applicant in a better practical position to assess the feasibility of accommodating disabilities. It also may put the employer in a better position to defend the claim of disability discrimination by an employee who failed to disclose the disability.

Language like the following should be considered:

You are not required to disclose information about physical or mental limitations that you believe will not interfere with your capability to do the job. On the other hand, if you want the employer to consider special arrangements to accommodate a physical or mental impairment, you may identify that impairment in the space provided and suggest the kind of accommodation that you believe would be appropriate.

Permitting the employee to suggest the kind of accommodation the employee believes to be appropriate is responsive to the language in the ADA's legislative history on the best way to begin a dialogue about reasonable accommodation.[5]

Title I,[6] the employment title, of the ADA forces employers to design job application procedures differently than most employers have designed them in the past. The ADA requires the elimination of all potential sources of discrimination against disabled individuals during job application procedures.[7] (See **Form 18–5.**) This requirement certainly extends to questions asked in job applications.

Employers have traditionally asked applicants about their physical and mental well-being in job applications. Under the ADA, however, employers can no longer ask applicants about their health or medical history.[8] These restrictions are designed to make employers base their selection decisions solely on the qualifications of the applicants. The intent of the ADA requirements is, therefore, to try to ensure that employers will hire the most qualified applicant, the applicant who is able to perform the essential job functions, with or without reasonable accommodations, for all vacant positions.

To adhere to the ADA requirements and thereby minimize the risk of discrimination claims by disabled individuals, employers must be attentive to what must be excluded from job applications rather than to what is included in them. Employers must eliminate all inquiries in job applications which could possibly be interpreted as seeking information about disabilities suffered by the applicants. Furthermore, an application may not ask if the applicant will need reasonable accommodations to perform the essential job functions because a disabled applicant could perceive this information as discriminatory.[9]

Only after an employer offers a position to an applicant should the applicant's need for reasonable accommodations be brought up. At this point, the

---

[5] House Labor Report at 65–66 (suggesting problem-solving approach involving affected employee).

[6] ADA §§ 101–108, 42 U.S.C. § 12111–12117 (1994) [hereinafter Title I].

[7] ADA §§ 102(a)–(b), 42 U.S.C. §§ 12112(a)–(b) (1994).

[8] ADA § 102(c)(1)(A), 42 U.S.C. § 12112 (c)(1)(A) (1994). The entity can, however, inquire about an applicant's ability to perform job-related functions. ADA § 102(c)(1)(B), 42 U.S.C. § 12112(c)(1)(B) (1994). Nonetheless, an applicant can be excluded from consideration for a position only if the applicant will not be able to perform the essential job functions after reasonable accommodations have been made for the applicant's disability.

[9] An example of an acceptable job application inquiry is: "Can you lift a fifty-pound box with or without reasonable accommodations for any disability from which you may suffer (answer "yes" or "no" only)?" It is important to note that this question does not require an individual to disclose whether he or she is disabled. A disabled individual who can perform the essential job function only after reasonable accommodations have been made for that individual's disability will answer this question with the same response ("yes") as a nondisabled individual who requires no accommodations. Therefore, the employer has no way of telling whether the applicant is disabled.

employer will have already selected the most qualified applicant for the job, and reasonable accommodations must be made for that applicant to perform the essential job functions as long as providing the accommodations does not cause an undue hardship to the entity.

A goal of the ADA is to prevent a job applicant's disability from being a source of discrimination against the applicant by a potential employer. The ADA does not require that employers give preference to disabled job applicants. However, it does require that employers give them the same opportunities for employment as are given to nondisabled applicants. The best way of ensuring that employers treat all applicants equally is to eliminate all possible sources of discrimination against disabled individuals. Because job applications are one of the first and most important communications between a job applicant and an employer, it is imperative that the employer adhere to the antidiscrimination requirements of the ADA when drafting job applications. The possible repercussions of a discrimination claim against an employer far outweigh any benefits from the additional knowledge an employer may gain through even borderline discriminatory questions in a job application.

§ 18.11   Interviews and Disability Checklist

Interviews are inherently harder to manage than applications and advertisement because there is a greater risk of conflicting post hoc testimony regarding what went on in the interview. Employers should consider supplying explicit guidelines to all persons conducting employment interviews, with strict instructions not to deviate from those guidelines on the subject of disabilities.

The following checklist is a starting point:

_____   Do not ask about mental or physical impairments unless the employee brings up the subject explicitly or unless the employee has disclosed a disability on the employment application.

_____   State emphatically the employer's commitment to provide a discrimination-free workplace for disabled applicants and employees, including the making of reasonable accommodation to disabilities, as soon as the subject of disability comes up.

_____   Limit preemployment inquiries to asking whether an applicant can perform particular job functions. EEOC and Department of Justice Questions and Answers (Q&A) say that employers should not make preemployment inquiries on application forms or in interviews regarding whether individuals are disabled. "If the applicant has a disability known to the employer, the employer may ask how he or she can perform job functions that the employer considers difficult or impossible to perform because of the disability, and whether an accommodation would be needed."[10]

_____ Emphasize that the only purpose for discussing a mental or physical impairment is to ascertain the employee's view on how the disability does not interfere with the performance of essential job functions and the nature of accommodation by the employer that should be considered.[11]

The specific requirements of the job should be discussed and, to the extent the applicant is willing to do so, compared with the applicant's capabilities. If the applicant is rejected for the position, a statement should be given to the applicant explaining how the disability influenced the decision not to hire. This statement should be reviewed with counsel.

The advantage of this approach is that it builds a specific documentation base showing rational consideration of the employer's obligation not to discriminate based on disability. There are major disadvantages, however. For example, the guidelines governing verbal conduct also serve to establish the employer's awareness and consideration of the disability. A determined applicant almost certainly can fashion an argument on how a discriminatory inference can be drawn from the conversation at the interview or from any statement of reasons for rejection.

Employers, therefore, should consider an alternate approach under which the regular interviewers are instructed not to discuss mental or physical impairments under any circumstance. This strategy would instruct the regular interviewers to refer an applicant wishing to discuss the impact of a disability to specialized equal employment counselors. The advantage of this approach is that training on the appropriate treatment of disabled applicants can be focused on a smaller number of personnel. There are, however, two obvious disadvantages: (1) only a large employer can afford this specialized personnel; and (2) requiring disabled applicants to undergo a more demanding interview protocol arguably is discriminatory because it represents an additional barrier to employment.

---

[10] U.S. Department of Justice, Questions and Answers (Rev. Sept. 1992) [hereinafter Q+A] at 5.

[11] If this guideline is subsequently challenged, the employer can point to the language in the ADA's legislative history encouraging such a dialogue. *See* House Labor Report at 65–66.

§ 18.12   Use of Interview Checklist

A good checklist for interviews is contained in the § **18.11.** Interviewers should not only be trained and rehearsed in the use of these do's and don'ts but should also have copies readily available for reference during the interviewing process.

§ 18.13   Job Description

Form 18–5 is a good example of a carefully worded job description. It is worded so as to permit auxiliary aids and equipment to accommodate disabilities, and states performance expectations (for example, words per minute and making visitors comfortable).

FORM 18–5
SAMPLE JOB DESCRIPTION

Secretary

Supports senior lawyer in all functions.

Transcribes dictation.

Uses word processing hardware and software to process 75 words per minute.

Makes appointments using the telephone.

Keeps schedule and provides attorney with copies daily.

Welcomes visitors and makes them feel comfortable.

Keeps track of deadlines and due dates error-free, advising attorney in advance when actions must be taken.

Records attorney time.

§ 18.14   Previous Employment References

Policies and procedures should be developed for checking references and other background investigation inquiries on disabled (and nondisabled) applicants. Those making inquiries on behalf of the employer should be instructed not to discuss mental or physical impairments, except strictly according to the following guidelines. As suggested in § **18.11,** inquiries relating to a disability may be directed to specialized equal employment personnel.

1.   The inquiry about the applicant's disability should begin with an emphatic restatement of the employer's commitment to provide equal opportunity for disabled applicants, and should explain that the only reason for asking about the disability is to facilitate making reasonable accommodation

2.   The inquiry should determine as specifically as possible the requirements of the previous job, and any overlap between those requirements and the applicant's impairments

3.   The inquiry should determine as specifically as possible what changes in job duties or assignments were made in order to accommodate the applicant's disability

4.   The inquiry should ascertain as specifically as possible the applicant's previous performance and conduct without regard to the disability, and aspects of performance or conduct on which the disability may have had some influence.

§ 18.15   Employment Testing

The categories of employment testing covered in §§ **18.16** through **18.18** should be undertaken only in conjunction with a clear statement as to the legitimate business need for the testing procedure. This statement need not be disclosed to employees, but it should be available, and it should be in force prior to the filing of any discrimination claim.

§ 18.16   —Medical Tests

Medical testing should not be undertaken unless it can be justified on one of the following grounds:

1.   It is a preemployment examination that focuses on the ability to perform essential job functions not on the disabilities of employees or applicants

2.   It is an employment entrance examination uniformly required of all employees, and produces information that is maintained in confidence to inform supervisors, first aid and safety personnel, and government enforcement personnel about the implications of disabilities

3.   It is another type of medical examination or inquiry and is part of a voluntary employee wellness program, or is aimed solely at determining

the ability to perform job-related functions, and can be shown to be job-related and consistent with business necessity.[12]

§ 18.17   —Blood Tests

When blood testing or medical testing is justified for drug abuse prevention reasons, the employer should be able to justify the particular procedures used, based on the case law relating to drug testing under federal constitutional constraints and collective bargaining agreements.

Human Immunodeficiency Virus (HIV) testing for AIDS is particularly difficult to justify. The risk of the invasion of privacy due to inappropriate or inadvertent disclosure is enormous and, because the condition is neither very contagious nor curable, the affirmative reasons for testing are difficult to discover.

§ 18.18   —Skill Testing

Skill testing should be undertaken only if the employer has detailed justification for each aspect of the test, and can relate each aspect to an essential function of the job for which an employee/applicant is being tested. Skill tests should be adaptable in order to respond appropriately both to any job requirement identified by the applicant as nonessential and subject to modification as a part of the employer's duty reasonably to accommodate, and to any functions, the performance of which is called into question by the applicant's limitations.

§ 18.19   Employee Handbooks and Policy Statements

Whenever an employer decides to maintain written employment policies and to give written information to employees in the form of handbooks, the employer and its counsel must navigate among conflicting forces. The purpose of having the written documents is to communicate. Good communication requires clarity and precision, two qualities that are difficult to achieve at the same time. Moreover, especially when the intended audience is the work force in general, the objective of communicating will be limited by the desire not to stir up problems. For example, a handbook might explain disability discrimination most clearly and precisely by outlining, in some detail, the steps to file a charge with the EEOC or a state agency and then to file suit

---

[12] *See* ADA § 102(c), 42 U.S.C. § 12112(c) (1994).

after a right to sue letter is received. It also might explain the different theories of disability discrimination that might be asserted.

Very few employers would want to do this, however. Such detailed explanation of litigation might have the effect of encouraging employees to litigate over borderline cases rather than working them out through internal employer procedures. Indeed, any reference to the rights granted by the ADA might tend to increase litigation beyond what it would be if the employees were wholly ignorant of their rights. Nevertheless, few employers would take the position that disability and other forms of discrimination should never be mentioned in materials prepared for employee consumption.

Striking a balance between these extremes cannot be accomplished mechanically or with a single solution fitting all employers and all situations. Rather, in the end, the language of an employee handbook must feel right to the employer and its counsel. The material presented in this chapter generally strikes a compromise between broad generalities such as "We treat everyone fairly," and extensive detail similar to a statute, administrative regulation, or formal contract. When major alternatives clearly exist with respect to specificity, the chapter points them out.

There is another matter regarding style. Precision can be the enemy of simplicity and clarity. A good, airtight contract does not necessarily make a good employee handbook, although there is a growing recognition in the legal profession that clarity is clarity regardless of whether legal or ordinary writing is involved and that plain language is a desirable goal in all kinds of writing. The drafter of handbook language must be conscious of writing for a general audience, frequently with limited education and reading comprehension.

The inherent tensions are less with respect to personnel policy statements and manuals intended for internal use by personnel specialists and supervisors. This audience's economic interests and legal claims do not diverge from those of the employer as an entity, so the risk of putting ideas into people's heads is not a significant concern. Also, these audiences usually have somewhat more formal education than the general work force and can comprehend more complex language and legal explanations.

Still, there is not much point in having separate personnel policy documents that reiterate statutes, administrative regulations, and contracts. The purpose of such separate documents is to simplify, explain, interpret, and define institutional positions. See **Forms 18–8** through **18–15.** When the details of a legal document are important, it is usually better to quote just the applicable excerpt than to paraphrase the actual document.

If an employer has both an internal personnel policy statement designed for use by personnel specialists and supervisors, and an employee handbook distributed to the work force in general, the relationship between the two must be considered. In most cases, it is desirable to include the actual, verbatim language of the employee handbook in the personnel policy statement,

followed or preceded by additional explanation intended for the policy statement only. Such an approach ensures that the employer is saying the same
thing to the general work force and to supervisors and personnel specialists.
It is also more efficient for supervisors and personnel specialists, who need
not be inconvenienced by referring to two different documents whenever an
issue comes up. Even if the style of the policy statement is more technical
and more sophisticated, the pertinent language from the employee handbook
can be excerpted and quoted in the policy statement.

§ 18.20   Reasonable Accommodation Procedure

The language in **Form 18–6** regarding reasonable accommodation is suitable
for inclusion in either a statement of personnel policies for internal use by
personnel specialists and supervisors or an employee handbook.

FORM 18–6
SAMPLE REASONABLE ACCOMMODATION LANGUAGE

If you believe that you have been the victim of discrimination in hiring, compensation, or with respect to other terms of employment, or if you believe that
you are about to be laid off or terminated because of a mental or physical disability despite the fact that you are otherwise qualified, you may request review
by the [personnel department/human resources department/person to whom
your supervisor reports/office of the president].

Also, if you believe that specific accommodation of your mental or physical
disability would permit you to perform the essential functions of the job, you
may request accommodation through the same procedures.

If you use these procedures, it is your responsibility to identify the specific
decision or decisions that you think discriminate against you and/or to suggest
the specific changes in work organization or job requirements that would permit you to perform the essential functions of the job despite your disability.

§ 18.21   Post-Complaint/Request
Procedure Language

The language in **Form 18–7** is appropriate for a personnel policy statement
designed for internal use by personnel specialists and supervisors. It is not,
however, as suitable for an employee handbook.

FORM 18-7
SAMPLE POST-COMPLAINT/REQUEST PROCEDURE LANGUAGE

Whenever a complaint of disability discrimination or a request for accommodation is received, it must be forwarded immediately to [the entity or person responsible for coordinating ADA compliance]. The employee should be contacted promptly and a meeting arranged to discuss the complaint or request.

If intentional discrimination is alleged, it may be desirable to schedule an initial meeting without the participation of any supervisor involved in the alleged discrimination. Otherwise, and in all cases when accommodation is requested, the immediate supervisor should participate in the initial meeting. The initial meeting has the following purposes:

(1) To clarify the employee's complaint or request

(2) To identify any difficulties in remedying the alleged discrimination or in making the requested accommodation

(3) To discuss other feasible alternatives presenting fewer difficulties for the employer

(4) To establish an action plan for follow-up, with specific responsibilities assigned to the participants.

Ordinarily, it is desirable to list any matters agreed to and any follow-up steps at the end of the meeting and have the employee initial the summary. It is not necessary, and probably better, that the list not be typed and formalized.

The participants should not commit themselves in this meeting to the existence of discrimination or to specific changes in work organization or job requirements until further review can be done after the meeting.

§ 18.22   Disability Discrimination or Harassment Complaint Procedure

FORM 18-8
SAMPLE DISABILITY DISCRIMINATION OR HARASSMENT COMPLAINT PROCEDURE

PROCEDURE FOR THE FILING AND DISPOSITION OF COMPLAINTS OF DISABILITY DISCRIMINATION OR HARASSMENT

I.   Introduction

[Name] University has issued a policy statement condemning disability discrimination as violative of its own standards and those of applicable federal and state law. This procedure provides the structure for the filing and resolution of complaints of disability discrimination relating to the employment life of its employees and educational experience of its students. All allegations of disability discrimination which occur subsequent to the date on which the underlying policy is adopted by the board of trustees shall be subject to this procedure, except where neither complainant or respondent have any role as an evaluator one of the other. In cases covered by this exception, the procedure set forth in the University's student handbook or applicable "Code of Conduct" shall apply.

II.   Established Resources and Considerations

Confidentiality is essential in any effort to investigate and resolve allegations of disability discrimination. The interests of both the complainant and the respondent must be protected as information is gathered and evaluated. Therefore, only persons who have a "need to know" within the investigation and resolution of complaints and appropriate senior administrative officials are entitled to information in the application of this procedure. University employees or students who disclose to persons not in the "need to know" chain information which is obtained within the informal or formal steps of this procedure will be subject to disciplinary action.

The president shall make a standing appointment of one or more members of the faculty, administration, or staff to serve as the complaint officer. This person is responsible to determine at the first formal step if alleged disability discrimination may have occurred. As provided in this procedure, the complaint officer also is responsible to convene the review board and to provide such administrative assistance as the board may request. However, it is the expectation that the officer would not attend the proceedings of the board.

A review board may be established as provided in this procedure. The board's function is to review referrals from the complaint officer and also any appeals of the decisions of the complaint officer as provided for in this procedure. The review board is comprised of three members: one is appointed by the complainant, one by the respondent, and the third person to serve as chairperson is appointed by the complaint officer. The board is empowered to convene appropriate hearings and to keep its own records in a format determined for each respective case. The board's procedures may include by example, but are not limited to, such approaches as open or closed hearings, individual interviews, and the examination of written documentation.

However, the board is not bound by rules of judicial or administrative hearing procedures or by formal rules of evidence.

III.   Informal Procedure

The university encourages its members to attempt informal resolution of complaints of disability discrimination. The university has many offices and individuals who may be able to provide counseling on a confidential basis for a person who believes that he or she is the victim of disability discrimination. The departments of [names of departments] are staffed with caring and experienced human resource and development specialists who may be able to help resolve concerns on an ad hoc and confidential basis.

IV.   Formal Procedure

When a person is unable to resolve a problem of disability discrimination informally, the following procedure may be invoked for the formal examination of the allegation:

1.   A formal, written complaint, utilizing the university's standard form, shall be submitted to the university complaint officer. The purpose of the complaint form is to assist the complainant in formulating a concise statement of his/her concern and to assist the complaint officer to see the basic facts of the allegation, along with the complainant's requested remedy. The complaint must be filed no later than [six months] from the date on which the subject conduct allegedly occurred.

2.   The complaint officer shall review the charges made in the complaint with the complainant, shall provide guidance and counseling as to the complainant's options and available procedures, and shall make such investigation of the charges as the officer may deem appropriate. In order to achieve a complete review of the case, the officer shall notify the respondent of the complaint and confer as necessary with the respondent. With the approval of both the complainant and the respondent, the complaint officer may attempt private mediation in an effort to resolve the alleged problem without the need for additional proceedings.

3.   Within [20] business days of receiving the complaint, the complaint officer shall issue a written report on the case to the complainant and respondent.

a)   If the complaint officer finds that the case cannot reasonably be construed to constitute disability discrimination or that there is insufficient information to conclude that disability discrimination may have occurred, the complaint officer shall file a report closing the case and stating the reasons why the complaint should be dismissed. The complaint officer shall also advise the complainant in the written report that the decision may be appealed to the review board. The complainant must notify the complaint officer of his/her desire to appeal the decision within [five] business days of the officer's decision.

b)   If the complaint officer decides that the case can reasonably by construed to have constituted disability discrimination, the complaint officer shall convene a review board.

4.   The complainant and the respondent will each designate his/her board member, and the complaint officer will designate the chairperson of the board, all within [15] business days of the issuance of the complaint officer's report. Within [10] business days of the appointment of the board, the board shall begin its proceedings.

In appearances before the board, the complainant and the respondent may each be accompanied by an adviser of their own choosing who is a member of the university community (current faculty member, administrator, staff member, or student).

The board will render its conclusions in a written report no later than [20] business days from the date of the board's initiation of the proceedings. The board's report shall be limited to findings of fact and the conclusions of whether or not disability discrimination occurred. The report shall be delivered to the complaint officer and to the vice president responsible for the area in which the respondent employee is assigned, or to the judicial affairs officer if the respondent is a student and the complainant is not.

The vice president and/or the judicial affairs officer shall communicate the board's conclusions to the complainant and the respondent. It is the sole responsibility of the vice president or judicial affairs officer to determine and take any disciplinary action based on the report provided by the board.

5.   When the vice president or judicial affairs officer takes disciplinary action against the respondent, the respondent may utilize the existing applicable university grievance procedure to dispute the discipline.

§ 18.23   Disability Discrimination Complaint Form

FORM 18–9
SAMPLE DISABILITY DISCRIMINATION COMPLAINT FORM

[name] UNIVERSITY

COMPLAINT OF DISABILITY DISCRIMINATION

INFORMATION ON COMPLAINANT:

Name: [_____]

Campus Department/Campus/Home: [_____]

Home Address: [_____]

Telephone: [_____]

INFORMATION ON RESPONDENT:

Name: [_____]

Campus: [_____]

Department Address: [_____]

Explain the actions, events, or other factors and the dates and times of such occurrences which lead you to make this complaint: [_____]

State the action requested to resolve this problem: [_____]

Date: [_____]

Received by: [_____]

Date: [_____]

Signed: [_____]

§ 18.24 Internal Report of Accommodation Request

FORM 18–10
SAMPLE INTERNAL REPORT OF ACCOMMODATION REQUEST

[name] CORPORATION

AMERICANS WITH DISABILITIES ACT

ACCOMMODATION CONSIDERATION

Name [_____] Employee No. [_____]

Dept. [_____] Craft [_____] Location [_____]

Description of Disability: [_____]

Description of Essential Job Functions: [_____]

Nature of Impact of Disability on Essential Function Performance: [_____]

Has the employee requested an accommodation? If so, explain and comment:
[_____]

Please Return to: [_____]

    [address]

(If there is not adequate space, use reverse side or attach other documentation.)

§ 18.25   Post-Complaint/Request Procedure

After the initial meeting, the personnel specialist, the supervisor, and other management and human resources or position control and compensation personnel should consider the differences between the job requirements or work organization as it existed up to that point and the work organization or job requirements suggested by the employee or applicant. The following questions must be addressed:

1. Should accommodation be made only for this individual, or is it appropriate to redefine the work organization or job requirements permanently in order to reduce the likelihood of future problems?

2. What are the costs of making the requested accommodation, both in quantitative dollar terms and in other less quantifiable terms?

3. Are there other ways to accommodate the particular disability at lower cost?

4. What is the possibility of significant ripple effects if the request accommodation for alternative accommodation is made? (Will it destabilize the compensation structure? Will it make position descriptions in general and job titles incoherent?)

5. What are the estimates of the likely costs of not providing accommodations when there are major costs associated with the requested accommodation?[13] More precise estimates may require assistance of counsel.

When there are major conflicts between the accommodation that appears necessary to prevent major ADA claim costs and other needs of the entity with respect to compensation and position control policy, the conflicts should be explained in writing, the major alternatives should be identified, and a recommendation should be made to the lowest level authority in the employing entity that has authority over both of the conflicting functions. For example, if the conflict is between the compensation policy and the management of employee discrimination claim risks, the matter should be referred up the chain of command until an officer is reached who has authority over both the compensation policy and employee claims risk management functions.

---

[13] When precise cost estimates are needed, the assistance of counsel may be required.

§ 18.26   Handbook on Requests for Accommodation

FORM 18–11
SAMPLE HANDBOOK ON REQUESTS FOR ACCOMMODATION

A GUIDE FOR [corporation name] EMPLOYEES:

UNDERSTANDING TITLE I OF THE AMERICANS WITH DISABILITIES ACT

EFFECTIVE: JULY 26, 1992

RESOURCE DEVELOPMENT

JULY, 1992

[name] CORPORATION

EQUAL EMPLOYMENT OPPORTUNITY

It has always been the policy of [name] Corporation to afford equal employment opportunity to all qualified individuals regardless of race, sex, age, national origin, religion, sexual orientation, and disability. It is also the policy of the Corporation to make reasonable accommodation for otherwise qualified individuals with disabilities.

It is critical to [corporation] success that it values employees who desire to be productive partners in helping the Corporation attain its goals. Accordingly, and in keeping with our obligation under the Americans with Disabilities Act, we will support our employees and those candidates for employment who are affected by physical or mental impairments which may limit their opportunities to be productive. As appropriate, we will work to eliminate artificial or real barriers to productive employment and to afford qualified individuals with opportunities to pursue available employment to the full extent of their abilities and talents.

ALL EMPLOYEES are expected to cooperate and to support actively the efforts to ensure that this policy will be effective. Employees with questions about the policy or its interpretation and implications should not hesitate to contact their supervisors/managers, the field personnel staff of the Labor Relations Department, and members of the Human Resources and Health Services sections of the Resource Development Department.

[name]

CHAIRMAN, PRESIDENT & C.E.O.

INTRODUCTION TO THE AMERICANS WITH DISABILITIES ACT

On July 26, 1990, President Bush signed into law the Americans with Disabilities Act ("ADA"). The implications of this law are immense and it can be considered the most important civil rights statute enacted since the Civil Rights Act of 1964. There are five sections included in the Act:

Title I—Employment

Title II—Public Services and Transportation

Title III—Public Accommodations/Commercial Facilities

Title IV—Telecommunications

Title V—Miscellaneous

While each of these sections may affect [corporation] and its employees, Titles I and III have the most significant impact. Title III covers buildings and facilities that are accessible to the public and Title I establishes provisions for equitable dealing with employees or candidates for employment. Title I will be the principal focus of these guidelines.

Title I makes it unlawful to discriminate in all aspects of employment against a qualified individual with a disability, as long as that individual can perform the ESSENTIAL FUNCTIONS of the job. This includes an obligation for employers to provide REASONABLE ACCOMMODATION for individuals with disabilities unless doing so would cause an UNDUE HARDSHIP on the operation of the business.

All employees need to understand the Americans with Disabilities Act and how it affects them at work. The following section defines a number of the critical terms included in Title I.

DEFINITIONS

Qualified Individual with a Disability: A qualified individual with a disability is a person who can perform those functions/tasks which are essential to the job, with or without reasonable accommodation, and who can satisfy job requirements such as education, experience, skills, licenses, and any other job-related qualification standards.

Disability: A disability is a physical or mental impairment that substantially limits one or more major life activities.

- Examples of physical or mental impairments include:

Orthopedic Impairments

Visual Impairments

Speech Impairments

HIV Infection

Cancer

Heart Disease

Hearing Impairments

Cerebral Palsy

Muscular Dystrophy

Multiple Sclerosis

Specific Learning Disabilities

Diabetes

Mental Retardation

Emotional Illness

Alcoholism

Epilepsy

- Major life activities include hearing, seeing, walking, speaking, breathing, performing manual tasks, caring for oneself, learning, and working.

Essential Functions: Essential functions are those job functions which the individual who holds the position must be able to perform unaided or with a reasonable accommodation.

- Factors in considering whether a job function is essential:

___Employer's established job description.

___Actual work experience of other incumbents of the same position.

___Amount of time spent performing the function.

___Consequences of not requiring employee to perform the function.

Reasonable Accommodation: A reasonable accommodation is any modification or adjustment to the work environment or to the manner in which a job is customarily performed which enables a qualified individual with a disability to perform the essential functions of the job.

- Reasonable accommodation need not be made if it would impose an undue hardship on the employer:

___Undue hardship means more than a minimal expense or inconvenience.

___Difficulty or expense must be significant not to be reasonable.

- An accommodation need not be the best or most expensive one available, so long as it is effective.

- An employer is not required to provide an accommodation which is primarily for personal use.

MORE INFORMATION ABOUT THE DISABLED AND ADA

According to U.S. government statistics, there are 43 million Americans with disabilities and, of these, approximately 30 percent are of working age. Almost 70 percent of that group are unemployed, but, as a group, they may be the best-educated group of unemployed people. When the disabled have been employed, they have generally established better attendance, productivity and accident records, and have less turnover, than those employees who are not disabled.

Here are some questions and answers that may help you understand how the ADA will affect [corporation] and its employees:

Q: Will [corporation] be required to hire a certain number of people with disabilities?
A: No. There are no quotas, minimum hiring standards, or special reporting requirements. However, [corporation] is required to make hiring decisions based on an individual's abilities, not his/her disabilities.
Q: Does ADA affect only the hiring process?
A: No. It impacts on all aspects of employment including testing, evaluation, discipline, training, promotion, medical examinations, termination, leaves of absence, benefits, compensation, and layoff/furlough.
Q: If an employee is returning from layoff/furlough with restrictions/disabilities, does [corporation] have to employ them?
A: Yes, if the employee can perform the essential functions of the job, with or without accommodation. The ADA applies to employees returning to active service just as it applies to candidates for employment.
Q: Won't ADA increase litigation and [corporation]'s liability?
A: Because of the way the law is written (not all regulations and remedies are clearly defined), some litigation is inevitable. The most effective protection is complete and voluntary compliance with ADA.

Q: What kind of steps have to be taken to comply with ADA?
A: There are too many steps to outline all of them in this booklet, but some of the more critical steps are:

___Establish job descriptions which differentiate between essential and marginal functions for each job or group of jobs.

___Provide procedures for determining whether an accommodation is appropriate and reasonable.

___Train employees to focus on a person's abilities and not on his/her disabilities.

___Change certain medical examination processes.

___Establish a resource which supervisors and employees can contact for clarification and advice on ADA requirements.

Q: How will job descriptions be developed and what are the specific uses for which they are used?
A: Job descriptions will be developed for each unique job or group of jobs using a panel of job function "experts." The Association of [name] has a computer database and application program developed to assist [member businesses] in this effort.

Once a job description is finalized, it will be available to aid in the determination of whether an employee can perform the essential functions of the position with or without reasonable accommodations. The job description also can be used in assisting in the determination of whether a reasonable accommodation can be made in the duties of the job and will be helpful to our Health Services personnel in the areas of rehabilitation and job-oriented physical examinations.

DO'S AND DON'TS WHEN INTERVIEWING

The ADA imposes certain new responsibilities, and prohibits certain areas of discussion, in regard to preemployment interviews and examinations. Every employee whose duties involve any participation in a selection process must be familiar with these requirements and prohibitions. It should be noted that these provisions apply to all selection processes, whether they involve new hirings or existing employees.

An employer may not make any preemployment inquiries regarding disability, but may ask questions about the ability to perform specific job functions and may, with certain limitations, ask individuals with a disability to describe or demonstrate how they would perform those functions.

Some examples of questions that may be asked are:

___DO inquire about an individual's ability to perform specific (both essential and marginal) job functions, tasks, or duties, as long as these questions are not phrased in terms of a disability.

___DO ask, "Are you able to perform these tasks with or without an accommodation?" (if the individual indicates that the tasks can be performed with an accommodation, then you may ask, "How would you perform the tasks, and with what accommodation(s)?"

___DO describe or demonstrate a particular job function and inquire whether the individual can perform that function with or without a reasonable accommodation.

___DO say, "Our business hours are 9:00 A.M. to 5:00 P.M. Will you be able to work those hours?"

___DO say, "These are the tasks of the job. How would you complete each task?"

___DO ask, "Is there any reason you cannot perform the requirements of the job?"

___DO ask, "Can you lift 50 pounds (or 100 pounds) without difficulty?" (But only if those lifting requirements are an essential function of the job.)

The following questions and similar questions are not to be used:

___DON'T make an inquiry about a disability, or about the nature or severity of a disability. (Such an inquiry must not be done directly, in writing, or in background or reference checks.)

___DON'T ask about the condition causing the disability.

___DON'T ask, "Do you have any physical defects which preclude you from performing certain kinds of work?"

___DON'T ask, "Do you have any disabilities or impairments which may affect your performance in the position for which you are applying?"

___DON'T ask, "Are you taking any prescribed drugs?"

___DON'T ask, "Have you ever been treated for drug addiction or alcoholism?"

___DON'T make any medical inquiry or give a preemployment medical examination prior to making a conditional offer of employment.

___DON'T ask whether an individual has a disability.

___DON'T ask how a particular individual became disabled or the prognosis of the individual's disability.

___DON'T ask, "Have you ever been hospitalized? If so, for what condition?"

___DON'T ask, "Have you ever been treated by a psychiatrist or psychologist? if so, for what condition?"

___DON'T ask, "Is there any health-related reason you may not be able to perform the job for which you are applying?"

___DON'T ask, "Do you expect to go to the doctor frequently?"

___DON'T ask, "Have you ever submitted a claim for Workers' Compensation?"

___DON'T ask, "How many days were you absent from work because of illness last year?"

___DON'T ask, "Do you have a disability that would prevent you from doing the job?"

___DON'T ask, "Do you have a bad back that would prevent you from doing heavy lifting?"

If an individual has a known disability that might interfere or prevent performance of job functions, they may, however, be asked to describe or demonstrate how these functions will be performed, with or without an accommodation.

If a known disability would not interfere with performance of job functions, an individual may be required to describe or demonstrate how they will perform a job only if this is required of all applicants for the position.

THE REASONABLE ACCOMMODATION PROCESS

REASONABLE ACCOMMODATIONS

An employer must provide a reasonable accommodation to the known physical or mental limitations of a qualified applicant or employee with a disability, unless it can show that the accommodation would cause an undue hardship on the operation of its business.

The reasonable accommodation process will require the close cooperation between the hiring department, human resources, and health services.

WORKING THROUGH THE REASONABLE ACCOMMODATION PROCESS

Once it is acknowledged/understood that an accommodation must be considered, the following steps should be taken:

___Analyze the particular job and determine its essential functions.

___Confer with the individual with a disability and ascertain:

- The job-related limitations; and

- How a reasonable accommodation would lessen those limitations.

___Identify possible accommodations and assess the cost and effectiveness of each.

___Determine which reasonable accommodations would not create an undue hardship.

___Ask the individual with a disability about his or her preference for a reasonable accommodation.

___Select the accommodation which is most appropriate for both the employer and the disabled applicant or employee. It is the employer's right to select among alternative accommodations, but the preference of the qualified individual with a disability should be weighed carefully.

EXAMPLES OF REASONABLE ACCOMMODATIONS

___Making facilities readily accessible to, and usable by, an individual with a disability.

___Restructuring a job by reallocating or redistributing marginal job functions.

___Altering when or how an essential job function is performed.

___Establishing part-time or modified work schedules.

___Obtaining or modifying equipment or devices.

___Modifying examinations, training materials, or policies.

___Providing qualified readers or interpreters.

___Reassigning the individual to a vacant position.

___Permitting use of accrued paid leave or unpaid leave for necessary treatment.

___Providing reserved parking for a person with a mobility impairment.

___Allowing an employee to utilize equipment or devices that an employer is not required to provide.

EXAMPLES OF FACILITY ACCOMMODATIONS

___Installation of ramps.

___Removal of raised thresholds.

___Rearranging office furniture and equipment.

___Making accessible, and providing accessible "path of travel" to, equipment and facilities used by an employee, such as to copying machines, meeting rooms, washrooms, lunchrooms, and lounges.

EXAMPLES OF EQUIPMENT ACCOMMODATIONS

___TDDs (Telecommunication Devices for the Deaf) make it possible for people with hearing and/or speech impairments to communicate over the telephone.

___Telephone amplifiers are useful for people with hearing impairments.

___Special software for standard computers and other equipment can enlarge print or convert print documents to spoken words for people with vision and/or reading disabilities.

___Desks or work stations can be modified to accommodate specific physical impairments.

[Corporation]'S INTERNAL DISCRIMINATION COMPLAINT PROCEDURE

[Corporation], since its inception, has fostered the underlying principles of Equal Employment Opportunity and does not condone any acts of discrimination because of age, race, sex, religion, national origin, sexual orientation, or physical or mental disability. Neither does it condone any forms of sexual harassment. In looking towards the future, [corporation] is committed to valuing people for their abilities and contributions.

However, it is recognized that from time to time, there are occurrences which may cause some of us to believe that we are being treated unfairly because of age, sex, race, disability, etc. Each employee has the right and the obligation to bring these occurrences to the attention of the company. [Corporation]'s Administrative Instruction [AI-26], "International Resolution of Discrimination Complaints" provides a method for any employee to have a complaint investigated and, if justified, have the basis for the complaint corrected.

Based on where employees are located, individuals who believe they have a well-founded complaint may file such a complaint with the Personnel Manager at [city, state] or [city, state] or the Manager—Equal Employment, [city, state]. [Corporation] will conduct a confidential investigation of the complaint and advise of a finding on the complaint within [45] days. If individuals wish to appeal the findings, they may appeal to the Assistant Vice President—Human Resources.

This procedure is not intended to diminish nor replace other courses of action available to the individual. Rather, it is an attempt to allow [corporation] to ensure that its commitment to valuing employees and complying with the Law is diligently pursued throughout the Corporation.

For further information and guidance, please contact the office of the Assistant Vice President-Human Resources.

The information from the Accommodation Consideration Form[14] is reviewed by an ADA Accommodation Panel made up of representatives from the Law, Safety, Medical, Claims, Human Resources (part of Resource Development) departments, and a departmental expert/coordinator from each department where an accommodation is requested.

§ 18.27   Employer Guidelines: Requests for Reasonable Accommodations

FORM 18–12
SAMPLE EMPLOYER GUIDELINES: REQUESTS FOR REASONABLE ACCOMMODATIONS

TABLE OF CONTENTS

SECTIONS

§ 1. Scope

§ 2. How Requests for Reasonable Accommodations Are Made

---

[14] See § **18.21.**

§ 3. When Requests for Reasonable Accommodations Must Be Made

§ 4. Receipt of Form [RRA.1] by Personnel Department

§ 5. Composition of Review Team

§ 6. Guidelines for Review Team Determinations

§ 7. Communication of Review Team Determination to Disabled Individual

§ 8. Actions Taken after Approval of Reasonable Accommodations by Review Team

§ 9. Rights of the Disabled Individual after Rejection of Request for Reasonable Accommodations

FORMS

REQUEST FOR REASONABLE ACCOMMODATIONS: [FORM 6]

§ 1. Scope

These sections govern the procedure applicable to a request by a disabled individual for reasonable accommodations due to his or her disability. These sections cover both current employees and individuals who have been extended offers of employment (Hirees). These sections are based on the provisions of the employment title of the Americans with Disabilities Act of 1990 (ADA).

§ 2. How Requests for Reasonable Accommodations Are Made

A request for reasonable accommodations by a disabled individual must be made by submitting a Request for Reasonable Accommodations Form [(Form RRA.1)] to the employer's or prospective employer's personnel department. A Hiree may submit a [Form RRA.1] to his or her interviewer. The interviewer is considered an authorized representative of the prospective employer's personnel department.

§ 3. When Requests for Reasonable Accommodations Must Be Made

A request for reasonable accommodations by a disabled individual to his or her employer or prospective employer must be made as soon as reasonably possible. The personnel department must provide every applicant for employment with a [Form RRA.1] along with an application for employment. The personnel department must inform the applicant that the [Form RRA.1] is to be submitted to the entity only if the applicant receives an offer of employment.

A memorandum on the personnel department bulletin board shall notify all employees of the availability of [Form RRA.1] in the personnel department. The disabled employee may pick up this form from the personnel department, or can request that the personnel department mail him or her the form. If an employee's direct supervisor has reason to know that an employee has become disabled and has not yet returned to work, the supervisor may forward a copy of the form to the employee by mail. The disabled individual must return the [Form RRA.1] to the personnel department within a reasonable time after the disability has been incurred.

§ 4. Receipt of [Form RRA.1] by Personnel Department

Upon receipt of [Form RRA.1], the personnel department shall perform four functions. First, the personnel department shall mail an acknowledgement of the receipt of the [Form RRA.1] to the disabled individual. Second, the personnel department shall forward a copy of the [Form RRA.1] to the review team. Third, the personnel department shall enter the relevant data from the [Form RRA.1] with the relevant data from all other such forms in the log designated for this purpose. The log shall be updated periodically to reflect the status and/or disposition of all requests for reasonable accommodations. Fourth, the personnel department shall permanently maintain the original [Form RRA.1] in the disabled individual's personnel file.

§ 5. Composition of Review Team

The review team is comprised of [five (5)] members. There are [three (3)] permanent members and [two (2)] temporary members. The permanent members are: the human resources manager, the corporate controller, and the building engineer. The two temporary members are selected from volunteers from within the entity. The temporary members are selected randomly from the pool of volunteers. Each temporary member serves a term of [three] years on the review team. After a term on the review team, the temporary member must wait [three] years before volunteering to be a temporary member of the review team again.

§ 6. Guidelines for Review Team Determinations

The review team shall approve a request by a disabled individual for reasonable accommodations if three requirements are met. First, the reasonable accommodations must be required due to the individual's disability. Second, the reasonable accommodations must enable the individual to perform his or her essential job functions. And third, the reasonable accommodations must not impose an undue hardship upon the operations of the entity. The review team may request from the disabled individual, or acquire by other means, any evidence which the review team deems necessary to make its determination. The review team may also call any witness it deems necessary. Evidence obtained by the review team regarding both the disabled individual's ability to perform the essential job functions after reasonable accommodations have been made and the potential undue hardship which the entity will suffer must be recorded. The criteria in the written job description, so long as they are job-related and consistent with business necessity, shall be the sole basis for determining the essential job functions. The review team determination must be based exclusively on the evidence considered.

§ 7. Communication of Review Team Determination to Disabled Individual

The review team shall notify the disabled individual by mail that a decision has been reached regarding his or her request for reasonable accommodations. The notification must inform the disabled individual that he or she must schedule a meeting with the review team to learn the status of his or her request. If the disabled individual does not request a meeting with the review team within [thirty] days of the mailing of the notification, the review team shall send a notification by certified mail to the disabled individual, stating that he or she has [thirty] more days in which to schedule a meeting or else his or her request will be considered abandoned.

At the meeting, the review team shall communicate its determination to the disabled individual both orally and through a written memorandum. The communications must include the findings of fact and the reasons for the decision. If the review team rejects the request for reasonable accommodations, the communications must inform the disabled individual of his or her rights as provided in § 9. The review team shall also forward a copy of the determination to the personnel department for inclusion in the disabled individual's personnel file.

§ 8. Actions Taken after Approval of Reasonable Accommodations by Review Team

The review team is authorized to request the approved reasonable accommodations for the disabled individual through the entity's prescribed means for such requests.

§ 9. Rights of the Disabled Individual after Rejection of Request for Reasonable Accommodations

The disabled individual has the right to review all evidence considered by the review team. The disabled individual may seek a hearing with the review team to refute the evidence considered by the review team or to submit additional material evidence. The disabled individual must notify the review team within [thirty] days of the determination meeting if he or she desires a hearing. The review team, upon a showing of excusable neglect or good cause, may extend the time for notification by the disabled individual upon a request by him or her received not later than [sixty] days after the determination meeting. If the disabled individual requests a hearing, the review team must hold the hearing as soon as reasonably possible. The review team shall base its final decision on the same guidelines as provided in § 6. Within two weeks of the hearing, there view team shall issue a final determination through the same process as provided in § 7 based on any new evidence. If the disabled individual's request for reasonable accommodations is rejected for a second time, his or her sole recourse shall be through the courts.

FORM 18–13
SAMPLE REQUEST FOR REASONABLE
ACCOMMODATIONS FORM

REQUEST FOR REASONABLE ACCOMMODATIONS FORM ([FORM RRA.1])

(1)   Date: [_____]

(2)   Name of employee or applicant for employment: [_____]

(3)   Department: [_____]

(4)   Current position: [_____]

(5)   Position applied for: [_____]

(6)   Nature of disability: [_____]

(7)   Accommodations sought-check all that apply:

   ( )   Alterations to existing facilities.

   ( )   Job restructuring.

   ( )   Part-time or modified work schedule.

   ( )   Reassignment to a vacant position.

   ( )   Acquisition or modification of equipment or devices.

   ( )   Adjustment or modification of examinations, training materials, or policies.

   ( )   Provision of qualified readers or interpreters.

   ( )   Other

(8)   For each item checked in (7), please provide a detailed description of the exact accommodations sought: [_____]

(9)   Are you currently engaging in the illegal use of drugs? ( ) yes ( ) no

Signature: [_____]

§ 18.28 Requests for Reasonable Accommodation

Inherent in a request for reasonable accommodations by a disabled individual are two competing interests: (1) the interests of the disabled individual to work to the individual's full potential, and (2) the interests of the entity to minimize expenses and maximize profits. Title I, the employment title favors the interests of the individual over those of the entity.[15] The ADA requires the entity to make reasonable accommodations[16] for the individual's disability as long as the individual will thereby be able to perform his or her essential job functions without causing an undue hardship[17] to the entity.[18]

The procedural guidelines in **Forms 18–12** to **18–14** are designed to facilitate the goals of the ADA. As with any other set of guidelines, cost-benefit judgments play an important part in their development. Even though there are no due process issues involved with such internal procedures, a procedural fairness evaluation[19] is useful in appraising the guidelines. Judge Friendly's list of procedural elements[20] serves as a useful tool in analyzing the procedural provisions in the request for reasonable accommodations guidelines. Under the analytical framework set forth in *Manhews v. Eldridge,*[21] each procedural element is evaluated in the following terms:

1. The marginal utility in the factfinding accuracy that the element affords
2. The seriousness of the deprivation to the disabled individual if a factual error is made
3. The burden to the entity that results from providing the procedural element.

The seriousness of the deprivation to the disabled individual is a constant in requests for reasonable accommodations. The effect of factfinding accuracy and the burden to the entity vary depending on the procedural element and how that element is implemented. The following procedural elements should be considered:

1. An unbiased tribunal
2. A notice of the proposed action and the grounds asserted

---

[15] *See* ADA § 102(a), 42 U.S.C. § 12112(a) (1994).

[16] ADA § 101(9), 42 U.S.C. § 12111(9) (1994).

[17] ADA § 101(10), 42 U.S.C. § 12111(10), ADA § 102, 42 U.S.C. § 12112 (1994).

[18] *Id.*

[19] For a similar analysis, *see* Henry H. Perritt, Jr., Employee Dismissal Law and Practice § 8.13 (John Wiley & Sons, 4th ed. 1997) (procedural fairness evaluation of employer dismissal procedures) [hereinafter Employee Dismissal Law and Practice].

[20] See Friendly, *Some Kind of Hearing,* 123 U. Pa. L. Rev. 1267 (1973).

[21] 424 U.S. 319 (1976).

3. A reason why the proposed action should not be taken

4. A right to present evidence, including the right to call witnesses

5. A right to know opposing evidence and to cross-examine adverse witnesses

6. A decsions based exclusively on the evidence considered

7. A right to counsel

8. A record of the evidence considered by the tribunal

9. A right to the tribunal's written findings of fact and reasons for its decision

10. An appellate review.

An unbiased tribunal.   An unbiased tribunal is an essential element of accurate factfinding. The review team is designed to constitute an unbiased tribunal. The three management-level review team members should not be biased toward either the individual or the immediate supervision because they are employed midway between the entity's hierarchical extremes. The review team is in direct contact with neither the average employee nor the top management. Even if the disabled individual does not perceive the permanent team members as completely unbiased, that disabled individual cannot plausibly question the motives of the two randomly selected members of the review team. Also, the additional diversity which the temporary review team members provide serves to dispel further any possible perceived biases.

The entity will suffer a burden by having at least three of its key personnel take time from their normal duties to perform review team functions. However, the burden and expense the entity would suffer by employing an outside tribunal to evaluate requests for reasonable accommodations would be far greater. Therefore, the review team accomplishes the essential requirement of an unbiased tribunal through a minimum of burden to the entity.

A notice of the proposed action and the grounds asserted.   The disabled individual sets the reasonable accommodations evaluation process in motion by submitting a request for reasonable accommodations form. The form itself provides a notice of what information is material to the subsequent decisions of the request.

A reason why the proposed action should not be taken.   The disabled individual is the party initiating the evaluation process and thus provides the reasons on the form.

A right to present evidence, including the right to call witnesses.   The guidelines do not permit the disabled individual to present any evidence or call any witnesses prior to the review team's determination. Rather, the review team determines which evidence it will consider. It is empowered to call any witnesses and request any evidence, from the disabled individual or others, which it deems necessary.

The fact that the review team, not the disabled individual, determines what evidence and which witnesses are to be considered does not impair factfinding accuracy. The review team is an unbiased investigatory tribunal and has no reason either not to request relevant evidence or not to call relevant witnesses the disabled individual would have presented or called. Therefore, the same information is considered in the review team's determination, just as if the disabled individual had submitted it.

The burden to the entity of allowing the disabled individual to present evidence and call witnesses would be substantial. The determination process would be converted from an efficient factfinding mechanism into a quasi-trial. This quasi-trial could continue for days, keeping some of the entity's key employee's from their daily, "profitable" tasks and duties.

A right to know opposing evidence and to cross-examine adverse witnesses. As explained previously, neither the disabled individual nor the entity present any evidence. Rather, the review team acquires the evidence it deems necessary to make its determination. Therefore, there is no true opposing evidence, only relevant evidence. Allowing the disabled individual to know the relevant evidence to be considered by the review team prior to its determination would provide no improvements to factfinding accuracy.

Based on the same reasoning, the cross-examination of adverse witnesses is also not required.

A decision based exclusively on the evidence considered. A decision based exclusively on the evidence considered is a fundamental requirement of procedural fairness because it enhances accurate fact finding. Any burden, if there is one, of providing this procedure pales in comparison to its utility.

A right to counsel. The guidelines do not authorize a disabled individual to have the assistance of counsel because the determination process is generally neither technical nor complex. Therefore, the right to counsel does not promote factfinding accuracy. If the disabled individual were allowed representation by counsel, the determination process could be converted from a mechanism for making decisions into a quasi-trial, dramatically increasing the burden to the entity.

A record of the evidence considered by the tribunal. The preparation of a record of the considered evidence is essential to the appellate review procedure provided for by the guidelines. Absent this record, the disabled individual would not be able to refute the evidence considered by the review team in making its determination. Furthermore, the burden to the entity of maintaining this record is so minimal that even if appellate review were not permitted, the record should be maintained to assist future review team determinations.

A right to the tribunal's written findings of fact and reasons for its decision. This requirement also facilitates appellate review by the disabled individual. The benefits to factfinding accuracy and the burden to the entity of providing this procedure are similar to those relating to the decision based on the record.

An appellate review. The guidelines provide for automatic appellate review if the disabled individual desires it. Appellate review gives the disabled individual the opportunity to refute any evidence considered by the review team and/or to submit any additional relevant evidence the review team did not consider. Therefore, it greatly enhances factfinding accuracy. This procedure makes up for any possible shortcomings of procedural fairness at the initial stages of the determination process by providing for them at the end of the process. Even though automatic appellate review imposes a substantial burden upon the entity, the possible repercussions of an erroneous determination warrant its implementation.[22]

§ 18.29   Requests for Reemployment

FORM 18–14
SAMPLE EMPLOYER GUIDELINES: REQUESTS FOR REEMPLOYMENT

TABLE OF CONTENTS

SECTIONS

---

[22] The material in this section was developed with the help of Brian Sopinsky, assistant to Henry H. Perritt, Jr.

FORMS

REQUEST FOR REEMPLOYMENT FORM

§ 101.   Scope

These sections govern requests for reemployment by an individual who suffered an injury covered by workers' compensation statutes. These sections cover requests both by individuals who have fully recovered from their injuries and by those who continue to suffer disabilities.

§ 102.   How Requests for Reemployment Are Made

An individual who was injured must submit a Request for Reemployment Form ([Form WCRR.1]) to the entity's personnel department to be considered for reemployment.

§ 103. When Requests for Reemployment Must Be Made

The personnel department shall forward [Form WCRR.1] to the injured employee as soon as reasonably possible after the entity becomes aware of the employee's work-related injury. The personnel department shall also forward a Request for Reasonable Accommodations Form ([Form RRA.1]) to the injured individual at the same time as the [Form WCRR.1]. The entity may transmit the forms to the employee by mail.

The individual seeking reemployment may submit [Form WCRR.1] as soon as he or she is capable of performing the essential duties of the position requested.

§ 104.   How Requests for Reemployment Are Treated by the Entity

The entity shall treat a request for reemployment by a fully recovered individual in the same manner as any other request for employment. A request for reemployment by a fully recovered individual is not to be afforded any better or worse treatment than other requests for employment. If a position is available, the entity must award it to the most qualified applicant.

The entity shall grant all requests for reemployment by disabled individuals. The entity shall also provide all reasonable accommodations requested by the individual due to his or her disability, provided that such accommodations do not cause an undue hardship to the entity (see Employer Guidelines: Requests for Reasonable Accommodations § 6).[23]

§ 105.   When Requested Position Is Unavailable but Alternate Position is Available

---

[23] See § **18.17.**

The entity shall utilize its pool of reemployment requests to fill all employment openings. The entity shall use an employment request to fill the job requested as well as all vacant positions at or below the level of the requested position. Alternate positions are awarded based on the same criteria as requested positions (see § 102). The provision of an alternate position may be considered a reasonable accommodation for a disabled individual.

§ 106.   Status of Rejected Requests for Reemployment

All individuals who request reemployment but are not awarded positions shall have their requests for reemployment retained by the entity for [six (6)] months. The entity shall use the requests for reemployment to fill future vacant positions as provided in §§ 102 and 103. The entity shall notify the individual requesting reemployment of this procedure.

The entity shall also provide all individuals requesting reemployment with a list of available positions at other entities. The list shall be based on the physical capabilities and skills of the applicant.

FORM 18–15
SAMPLE REQUEST FOR REEMPLOYMENT FORM

REQUEST FOR REEMPLOYMENT FORM

[FORM WCRR.1]

(1) Date [_____]

(2) Name [_____]

(3) Department (prior to injury) [_____]

(4) Position (prior to injury) [_____]

(5) Position requested [_____]

(6) If you will require reasonable accommodation to perform the position requested, please complete the enclosed Request for Reasonable Accommodations Form ([Form RRA.1]). [_____]

Signature [_____]

§ 18.30   Negligent Hiring

Employers should be alert to the possibility that stretching to accommodate an employee's disability may open up possible liability for negligent hiring. For example, if an employer hires someone with limited dexterity to perform a job that requires considerable dexterity in order to avoid risks of injury to other employees, an accident involving that employee almost certainly will result in a claim that the employer breached a duty to other employees when it hired the disabled employee. Similarly, if an employee with a mental impairment engages in conduct that injures other employees, customers, or suppliers, the same kind of allegation can be made.

The best way to address this conflict is to identify specifically what risks may exist to other personnel, and to evaluate how to protect against this risk.

The ADA, as discussed in **Chapter 4,** permits excluding disabled employees and applicants in order to prevent injury to others.[24]

§ 18.31   Privacy of Personnel Files

Any source of information about physical or mental impairments, including employment applications, results of interviews or investigations, or test procedures should be carefully controlled by the employer to minimize the potential for inappropriate disclosure. Any records pertaining to treatment for alcohol or drug abuse must be kept strictly confidential to prevent discrimination as a byproduct of seeking help for personal problems.[25]

The EEOC permits employers to supply medical information to workers' compensation offices under sections of the ADA relating to the confidentiality of information obtained from a medical examination or inquiry.[26] The EEOC also prohibits questions about an applicant's history of workers' compensation claims in the EEOC's Interpretive Guidance for 29 C.F.R. § 1630.13(a) of the regulations concerning preemployment medical examinations and inquiries.[27]

---

[24] *See generally* Lutz v. Cybularz, 607 A.2d 1089 (Pa. Super. Ct. 1992) (affirming summary judgment for newspaper distributor on negligent hiring claim based in part on the physical disabilities of truck driver who was determined to be independent contractor.) *Cf.* Crabtree v. Montana State Library, 665 P.2d 231 (Mont. 1983) (refusing to validate state statute affording public employment preference to veterans and disabled civilians notwithstanding potential risk of negligent hiring lawsuits).

[25] *Cf. In re* Collester, 599 A.2d 1275 (N.J. 1992).

[26] *Id. See* ADA § 102(c)(3)(B), 42 U.S.C. § 12112(c)(3)(B) (1994) (information of medical condition or history treated as confidential medical record).

[27] 56 Fed. Reg. 35,750 (July 26, 1991) (codified at 29 C.F.R. pt. 1630 app. § 1630(a) (1996)). *See* ADA § 102(c)(2)(A), 42 U.S.C. § 12112(c)(2)(A) (1994) (prohibition against medical examination or inquiry relating to disability status).

Such an inquiry is prohibited even though arguably job-related and consistent with business necessity.[28]

§ 18.32   Rules of Conduct

The employer should have counsel review its rules of conduct to identify any rules that may have an unjustifiable adverse impact on disabled applicants or employees.

§ 18.33   Performance Standards

Employers should review the existing performance standards for each major job classification to determine those standards that may have an unjustifiable adverse impact on disabled applicants or employees.

§ 18.34   Counseling and Periodic Evaluation

Employers should supplement their regular counseling and periodic evaluation practices to ensure that no evaluator or counselor makes remarks that might be construed as discriminatory based on disabilities. Conversely, the employers should inquire of any employee already known to be disabled as to whether the employee believes that the disability is being accommodated reasonably.

§ 18.35   Progressive Discipline

Employers should consider implementing or expanding existing progressive discipline procedures. Under these progressive procedures, the employees whose disciplinary problems are associated with physical or mental impairments covered by the ADA are given appropriate opportunities to conform their conduct to what the employer reasonably may require, and the employer is given reasonable opportunity to consider steps toward the reasonable accommodation the employee may wish to suggest. The progressive discipline may include "last chance agreements" (see **§ 4.45**).

---

[28] 56 Fed. Reg. 35,732 (July 26, 1991) (preamble to final EEOC regulations explaining changes to 29 C.F.R. § 1630.13 (1996)). *See* ADA § 102(c)(2)(B), 42 U.S.C. § 12112(c)(2)(B) (1994) (preemployment inquiry permitted regarding ability to perform job-related function).

§ 18.36 Changes in Organization of Work

After a request for accommodation is made, employers should consult with the disabled individual to decide on the appropriate accommodations.[29] In addition, the Senate Report suggests taking the following four informal steps:

1. Identify the barriers to equal opportunity, distinguishing between essential and nonessential job tasks, and both the abilities and the limitations of the disabled individual

2. Identify possible accommodations, by consulting the disabled individual, the state and federal agencies, and other opportunities

3. Assess the reasonableness of each possible accommodation in terms of effectiveness and equal opportunity

4. Implement the accommodation that is most appropriate for the employee and the employer and does not impose an undue hardship on the employer's operation; or permit the employee to provide his or her own accommodation if it does not impose an undue hardship.[30]

The expressed choice of the applicant should be given primary consideration "unless another effective accommodation exists that would provide a meaningful equal opportunity or that the accommodation requested would pose an undue hardship."[31]

§ 18.37 Interactive Problem Solving

The EEOC guidelines suggest an interactive approach, involving the disabled employee applicant in exploring the possibilities for accommodating the disability.[32] This interactive approach considers the following factors:

1. Analysis of the particular job, determining both the purpose and essential functions

2. Consultation with the disabled individual not only to ascertain the precise job-related limitations imposed by the disability but also to determine how the limitations could be overcome with reasonable accommodation

---

[29] Senate Report at 34.

[30] *Id.* at 35.

[31] *Id.*

[32] 29 C.F.R. pt. 1630 app. § 1630.9 (1996) (process of determining the appropriate reasonable accommodation).

3. Identification of potential accommodations in consultation with the disabled employee and assessment of the effectiveness each would have in enabling performance of the essential functions of the position

4. Consideration of the preference of the disabled employee and selection of the accommodation that is most appropriate for both the employee and the employer.[33]

The EEOC guidelines proceed to give a concrete illustration of the interactive determination of reasonable accommodation. The illustration involves a consultation between a sack handler, who handles 50-pound sacks but has a back problem, and an employer. The consultation results in a conclusion that the essential job requirement is not the mere lifting and carrying of the sacks, but the requirement that the job holder move the sacks from the loading dock to the storage room. The illustration describes the employer and employee considering the various kinds of vehicles that could carry the sacks, the particular function the employee cannot perform, the exclusion of a cart as one possibility because no suitable carts are available. This discussion is followed by the ultimate agreement that a dolly is an appropriate reasonable accommodation.[34]

§ 18.38   Affirmative Action

The approach suggested by this chapter encourages employers to take affirmative action in complying with ADA requirements. Employers may also wish to consider outreach efforts to communities or facilities for the disabled. This may be particularly appropriate and serve employer self-interest well when labor shortages are encountered.

§ 18.39   Advisory Committee

Large employers who employ a significant numbers of disabled employees, or who anticipate employing significant numbers of disabled applicants, should consider establishing a disability accommodation advisory committee. If carefully selected, such committees can provide useful practical information to employers both on the limitations likely to be associated with different types of disabilities and on cost-effective ways of accommodating these limitations.[35] In addition, an advisory committee can play a useful role in reviewing particular

---

[33] *Id.*

[34] 29 C.F.R. pt. 1630 app. § 1630.9 (1996) (reasonable accommodation process illustrated).

[35] *See generally* House Labor Report at 66 (suggesting consultation with disabled employee or applicant and establishing governmental advisory groups).

cases, either encouraging the employer to change its decision or encouraging employees to accept the outcome of employer decisions.

§ 18.40   Economic Impact

The Preliminary Regulatory Impact Analysis (PRIA) contained in the preamble to the EEOC's proposed regulations justifies the requirements of Title I through the use of economic analysis. The PRIA indicates that failure to implement the ADA's provisions mandating nondiscrimination against disabled persons in employment could result in lost benefits to the economy of approximately $400 million.[36] The proposed regulations (and, by implication, the substantially similar final regulations) were not expected to impact significantly the economic viability of smaller entities.[37] Economists studying discrimination in the workplace have variously concluded that discriminatory employment practices result in suboptimal human capital investments which reduce overall societal productivity and increase economic costs to employers and taxpayers.[38] Economic analysis suggests that continued discrimination against individuals with disabilities in employment lowers the competitiveness of the potential work-force pool by reducing the number of available workers, drains the public purse through entitlements and support payments, and allocates inefficiently the costs of reasonable accommodations for disabled persons.[39]

---

[36] 56 Fed. Reg. 8579 (1991). The $400 million figure is composed of estimated reasonable accommodation expenses of $16 million, productivity gains of more than $164 million, and decreased support payments and increased tax revenues totaling about $222 million. *Id.* The PRIA was not revised when the final regulations were issued. Rather, comments were solicited in preparation for a January 1, 1992 revision. 56 Fed. Reg. at 35,734 (1991) (preamble to final EEOC regulations).

[37] 56 Fed. Reg. 8579 (1991). Not only are smaller entities less likely to be required to make reasonable accommodations, but also a combination of factors, including the two-year exemption period, the availability of tax credits, and the lack of reporting requirements, ensures that disadvantageous economic effects to such entities should be minimal. *Id.*

[38] *Id.* at 8581. Economic rationales for the efficacy of nondiscrimination policies include the theory of discrimination coefficients, the theory of short-run profit maximizing (based on marginal productivity), the theory of imperfect market information, and a characterization of the problem as one of internalizing the costs of externalities. *See id.* at 8580–81.

[39] *Id.* at 8580. Becker's analysis indicates that discriminatory employment practices result in suboptimal hiring practices because individuals who are potentially more qualified are excluded from consideration for positions, thus suggesting that the resulting work force is less efficient than it would be with the more qualified, but excluded, individuals. *Id.* Clearly, attaining higher levels of employment of individuals with disabilities would result in lower welfare and unemployment payments to such individuals because they would be more capable of financially supporting themselves. *Id.* Finally, because employers are more likely to be able to afford the cost of making reasonable accommodations in the workplace, such accommodations are more likely to be made, and because

§ 18.41   Disclaimers

Under the common law of contracts in virtually every state, unilaterally adopted employer policy statements may be contractually enforceable.[40] The same theories that lead to enforcement also permit employers to negate contractual status for such statements by including prominent disclaimers (see **Forms 18–16** and **18–17**) in any statement or employee handbook or manual.[41] In many cases, an employee's breach of contract claim is premised not on a written communication, but on oral statements from lower-level employees. Disclaimers can eliminate the apparent authority of lower-level employees to make such promises.

To be effective, a statement similar to the following samples from *Employee Dismissal Law and Practice* should be included in employment applications or other written documents communicated to employees when they first enter service.

FORM 18–16
SAMPLE DISCLAIMER #1

I understand that no store manager or representative of the company, other than the president or vice president of the Company, has any authority to enter into any agreement for employment for any specified period of time, or to make any agreement contrary to the foregoing (reservation of employment at will).[42]

FORM 18–17
SAMPLE DISCLAIMER #2

I agree my employment and compensation can be terminated, with or without cause, and with or without notice, at any time I understand that no representative of your company has any authority to enter into any other agreement with me . . . .[43]

---

an employer may be able to reuse the benefit of the reasonable accommodation expense for another employee as well, the net cost of the accommodation is reduced commensurately. *Id.*

[40] *See* Employee Dismissal Law and Practice, Ch. 4 (contract theories for wrongful dismissal).

[41] *See* Swanson v. Liquid Air Corp., 826 P.2d 664, 673 (Wash. 1992) (analytical framework for disclaimer assessment; allowing jury to decide if disclaimer on page six of 200-page handbook was effectively communicated to employee).

[42] *Id.*

[43] *Id.*

Commentary. As an example, in *Shelby v. Zayre Corp.,*[44] an employee claimed that the assistant manager who hired her had promised that she would have permanent employment, knowing that the representation of permanent employment was false. The employee had quit her previous job in reliance on that representation. The Supreme Court of Alabama affirmed judgment for the employer, finding that any reliance on the supervisor's statement was unreasonable because the plaintiff admitted reading and understanding the quoted provision of the employment application. The language limiting authority was outcome-determinative.

§ 18.42   Limiting Relief to Internal Remedies

Employers also may wish to limit employees to internal procedures, regardless of whether these procedures are contractual entitlements. The general principles of contract construction are consistent with literal enforcement of the following sample language from *Employee Dismissal Law and Practice.*

FORM 18–18
SAMPLE LANGUAGE LIMITING RELIEF

In consideration of my employment, I understand and accept that "cause" for my termination will be determined to exist or not to exist within the sole discretion of my employer. I waive any rights I may have to obtain court determination or review of an employer's finding that there is cause for my dismissal.[45]

If an employer elects either to require pretermination exhaustion of certain procedures or to afford an internal complaint procedure, the employer may wish to limit an employee's right to relitigate the dismissal in the courts. This can be accomplished by the inclusion of language similar to the language in **Form 18–19.**

FORM 18–19
SAMPLE LANGUAGE LIMITING EMPLOYEE'S RIGHT
TO RELITIGATE

In consideration of my employer's affording me certain rights to obtain higher-level review of supervisory actions adverse to me, including a possible decision to terminate my employment, and decisions on reasonable accommodation of disabilities, I waive any rights I may have to obtain court review of the appropriateness of such adverse action, and will utilize the internal company

---

[44] 474 So. 2d 1069, 1071 (Ala. 1985).

[45] Employee Dismissal Law and Practice at § 8.9 at 167.

procedures as the exclusive means of protesting adverse supervisory action, including discharge and refusal of accommodation. The internal procedures provide an adequate opportunity for the true facts to be determined and for me to present my side of any controversy. I will accept the determination resulting from such internal procedures as final and binding, and waive any right I may have to protest such a determination or to obtain review of it in any proceeding outside the company.[46]

Thus, as a result of this language, the employees are required to exhaust internal remedies as a matter of basic contract doctrine.

If the internal procedures terminate in arbitration (see **Form 18–20**), an employee's agreement to be bound by the arbitration should be enforceable in any jurisdiction that has adopted the Uniform Arbitration Act[47] under a trend in the federal cases. In *Gilmer v. Interstate/Johnson Lane Corp.,*[48] the United States Supreme Court approved the enforcement of an individual employee contract provision sending controversies over the legitimacy of termination to arbitration even though the controversy required the application of statutory law. Under the Employee Polygraph Protection Act,[49] the Ninth Circuit reached a similar result.[50] The Seventh Circuit held, however, that conditioning the use of internal procedures on refraining from filing an Age Discrimination in Employment Act charge with the EEOC constitutes retaliation for asserting rights under the ADEA.[51] This raises questions on any contractual election-of-remedies provision when federal nondiscrimination rights are involved.

Even if a purported waiver is found to be legally ineffective in subsequent litigation, any arbitration award in the employer's favor should be entitled to some evidentiary weight in a wrongful dismissal lawsuit.[52] Accordingly,

---

[46] *Id.*

[47] Unif. Arb. Act § 1–25.

[48] 500 U.S. 20 (1991).

[49] 29 U.S.C. §§ 2001–2009 (1994).

[50] *See* Saari v. Smith Barney, Harris Upham & Co., 968 F.2d 877, 881–82 (9th Cir. 1992) (vacating district court refusal to order arbitration of federal Polygraph Protection Act claim under broker-dealer agreement arbitration clause). *But see* Hillding v. McDonnell Douglas Helicopter Co., 59 Fair Empl. Prac. Cas. (BNA) 869 (D. Ariz. 1992) (denying res judicata effect to binding decision of employee grievance committee under Alexander v. Gardner-Denver Co., 415 U.S. 36 (1974); distinguishing *Gilmer,* but granting summary judgment on Title VII (42 U.S.C. §§ 2000e–2000e-16 (1994) [hereinafter Title VII]) and contract claims on other grounds).

[51] 29 U.S.C. §§ 621–634 (1994) [hereinafter ADEA]; EEOC v. Board of Governors, 957 F.2d 424, 431 (7th Cir. 1992) (reversing summary judgment; grievance processing was suspended when employee filed ADEA claim).

[52] *See* Barrentine v. Arkansas-Best Freight Sys., Inc., 450 U.S. 728, 743 n.22 (1981) (quoting Alexander v. Gardner-Denver, 415 U.S. 36, 59 n.21 (1974), to same effect); Darden v. Illinois Bell Tel. Co., 797 F.2d 497, 504 (7th Cir. 1986) (approving "great weight" given to arbitration award by district judge in deciding to dismiss Title VII claim;

waiver language also should be included prominently on forms used to commence an internal review of an adverse employment action and on any settlement document. Failure to follow the recommendations of internal review entities can produce liability.[53]

The procedural model developed under the Employee Retirement Income Security Act (ERISA)[54] for handling claims for employee benefits is useful for a broader range of employment disputes. The model requires that employees be given notice of adverse determinations with sufficient specificity to allow the employee to make pertinent arguments or to present pertinent data as to why the determination should be changed. ERISA, however, does not require any particular mode or formality for the notice or associated procedures.[55]

§ 18.43   Arbitration Agreement

FORM 18-20
SAMPLE ARBITRATION AGREEMENT

1.   Under this agreement, the employee and employer agree to use the dispute resolution procedure specified in this agreement as the exclusive means of resolving disputes over employee rights and employer obligations under the Americans with Disabilities Act (ADA). The employee understands that, absent this agreement, the employee would be entitled to assert ADA rights by filing charges with the Equal Employment Opportunity Commission (EEOC) or state or local human rights agencies and ultimately to file a lawsuit in state or federal court or both. Understanding these rights, the employee elects to waive them and prefers the machinery described in this agreement.

2.   This agreement and the arbitration procedure described in it apply to any and all claims connected with mental or physical disability and the impact of such

---

arbitrator fully considered race discrimination under collective agreement prohibiting discrimination); Gonzalez v. Southern Pac. Transp. Co., 773 F.2d 637, 645 (5th Cir. 1985) (on rehearing) (Railway Labor Act (45 U.S.C. §§ 151–185 (1994) arbitrator's award deciding outcome-determinative facts entitled to preclusive effect in suit for retaliation under federal railroad liability act).

[53] *See* Mace v. Charleston Area Medical Ctr. Found., 422 S.E.2d 624, 632 (W. Va. 1992) (failure to follow recommendation of internal grievance committee was single piece of evidence most supportive of $230,000 jury verdict finding retaliation for asserting veterans' reemployment rights).

[54] 29 U.S.C. § 1133 (1994). *See also* Employment Retirement Income Security Act, 29 U.S.C. §§ 1001–1461 (1994) [hereinafter ERISA].

[55] Halpin v. W.W. Grainger, Inc., 962 F.2d 685, 693–94 (7th Cir. 1992) (ERISA required reversal of denial of long-term disability benefits because plan's procedure was arbitrary and capricious and violated regulatory requirements for notice of appeal rights, including specific reasons for initial denial).

disabilities on the employee's qualification to perform job duties, and any and all accommodation that might be requested by the employee or undertaken by the employer. It specifically covers refusals of promotion, pay increase, transfer, change in job duties, or termination of employment because of limitations on performance of in job duties, or termination of employment because of limitations on perform job functions due to mental or physical disabilities.

3.   Procedure. If the employee or employer wishes to present a dispute or assert a claim under this agreement, the claim or dispute must be presented under the following steps. Any dispute over compliance with these procedures shall be resolved by the arbitrators appointed under paragraph 5.

Step 1. The employee informs either his immediate supervisor or the designated ADA officer in the human resources department of the employee's claim or dispute. This may be done orally, in which case the supervisor or ADA officer will make a brief written record. If the employer wishes to present a dispute, the first step necessitates informing the employee in writing.

Step 2. If the complaint or dispute is resolved by informal discussion between employer representative and employee, the resolution shall be recorded in writing and signed by the employee and either the supervisor or the designated ADA officer.

Step 3. If the dispute or claim is not resolved informally in steps 1 and 2, it may be presented by either party to the employer's ADA compliance committee.

Step 4. If the ADA compliance committee resolves the claim or dispute on terms acceptable to both employee and employer, the resolution shall be recorded in writing and signed by the employee and the chairman of the employer ADA compliance committee.

Step 5. If the claim or dispute is not resolved in the preceding steps, either employee or employer may present the claim in writing for final and binding arbitration selected in accordance with this agreement.

4.   Claim Form. The following form shall be used for presenting claims and disputes:

Name of employee: [_____]

Type of disability: [_____]

Accommodation requested: [_____]

Means by which accommodation was requested: [_____]

Accommodation offered by employer: [_____]

Remedy desired by person presenting claim or dispute: [_____]

5.   Methodology for Selecting Arbitrator. The employee or employer may suggest a particular individual to serve as arbitrator. If the other party agrees on that person and the person agrees to serve, that person shall be the arbitrator. If there is no agreement on a specific individual, either employee or employer may request the appointment on a specific individual, either employee or employer may request the appointment of an arbitrator by the American Arbitration Association in New York, and the parties agree to use and be bound by the decisions of an arbitrator appointed by that association. If these methods for selecting an arbitrator fail, the parties agree that a state or federal court may appoint an arbitrator under the provisions of the Federal Arbitration Act or any version of the Uniform Arbitration Act in the state of employment.

6.   Both employee and employer may be represented by counsel or other representatives.

7.   Costs. An employee requesting arbitration shall pay [$100.00], unless the arbitrator finds that payment of such amount would represent undue hardship for the employee. The employer shall pay any remaining costs. If the arbitrator finds that frivolous claims or bad faith conduct have been presented in the arbitration proceeding, the arbitrator may allocate the cost differently from the allocation provided in this section.

8.   Scope of Arbitrator Authority. The arbitrator may resolve any questions of jurisdiction and any procedural issues. The arbitrator shall make a final and binding decision on the claim or dispute as it was presented.

9.   The arbitrator may determine remedies to be applied, but if reorganization of work or change in job duties is part of the remedy selected by the arbitrator, the arbitrator shall give the employer an election to pay a monetary sum instead of making the changes.

10.   The arbitrator may not impose monetary compensation in excess of [five] years' compensation.

11.   Procedures. Burdens of proof shall be those applied under the ADA. The employee has the burden of establishing a disability and qualifications to perform essential functions of the desired position; the employer has the burden of establishing undue hardship in making requested accommodation.

12.   Both employee and employer may be present throughout the hearing. Both employer and employee shall be allowed a brief opening statement.

13.   Both employee and employer may present witnesses indicated on witness lists submitted at the commencement of the hearing, except that the arbitrator may exclude repetitive or cumulative testimony. The employer shall make available any employee witnesses at no loss in pay as directed by the arbitrator.

14.   Both employer and employee may examine and cross-examine witnesses.

15.   Both employer and employee may present documentary and demonstrative evidence as appropriate to the issues.

16.   The rules of evidence shall not be applied strictly, but the arbitrator may give little or no weight to hearsay.

17.   Both employee and employer may make brief closing statements.

18.   The arbitrator shall issue a written decision, making specific findings of fact and conclusions, within [ninety] days after the conclusion of the hearing.

19.   Judgment may be entered on the arbitration award in any court.

Commentary.   The American Arbitration Association (AAA) makes it easy to write arbitration agreements that are enforceable without specifying great detail about the arbitration process.[56] The AAA recommends the following language in **Form 18–21** be included in employment contracts, personnel manuals or policy statements, employment applications or "other agreements."[57]

FORM 18–21
SAMPLE LANGUAGE REQUIRING ARBITRATION

Any controversy or claim arising out of or relating to this contract, or the breach thereof, shall be settled by arbitration in accordance with the employment dispute resolution rules of the American Arbitration Association and judgment on the award rendered by the arbitrators may be entered in any court having jurisdiction thereof.[58]

The AAA recommends the language in **Form 18–22** for the arbitration of existing disputes.

FORM 18–22
SAMPLE LANGUAGE: ARBITRATION OF EXISTING DISPUTES

We, the undersigned parties, hereby agree to submit to arbitration under the Employment Dispute Resolution Rules of the American Arbitration Association the following controversy: [cite briefly].

---

[56] *See* AAA, Resolving Employment Disputes: A Manual on Drafting Procedures (1993) (available from AAA Headquarters, 140 West 51st St., New York, NY 10020-1203; (212) 484-4000; (fax) (212) 307-4387); AAA, 1993 Employment Dispute Resolution Rules (Jan. 1, 1993) (including mediation and arbitration rules).

[57] AAA, 1993 Employment Dispute Resolution Rules 3–4 (Jan. 1, 1993).

[58] *Id.* at 4.

We further agree that the above controversy be submitted to [1]/[3] arbitrators selected from the panels of arbitrators of the American Arbitration Association. We further agree that we will faithfully observe this agreement and the rules, and that we will abide by and perform any award rendered by the arbitrators and that a judgment of the court having jurisdiction may be entered on the award.[59]

The AAA suggests the options in **Forms 18–23** through **18–25** as alternative language if the parties desire discovery in arbitration.

FORM 18–23
SAMPLE DISCOVERY PROVISIONS: OPTION #1

The parties shall cooperate in the voluntary exchange of such documents and information as will serve to expedite the adjudication. Discovery shall be conducted in the most expeditious and cost-effective manner possible and shall be limited to that which is relevant and for which each party has a substantial, demonstrable need. Upon request, the employee shall be entitled to a true copy of his or her personnel records kept in the ordinary course of business and at least one deposition of an employer representative designated by the employee.[60]

FORM 18–24
SAMPLE DISCOVERY PROVISIONS: OPTION #2

Each party shall have the right to take the deposition of one individual and any expert witness designated by another party. Each party also shall have the right to propound requests for production of documents to any party. Additional discovery may be had only when the arbitrator so orders, upon a showing of substantial need.[61]

FORM 18–25
SAMPLE DISCOVERY PROVISIONS: OPTION #3

In preparation for the arbitration hearing, each party may utilize all methods of discovery authorized by the procedural rules and statutes of this state, and may enforce the right to such discovery in the manner provided by said rules and statutes and/or by the arbitration law of this state.[62]

---

[59] *Id.* The pamphlet does not explain why the existing-agreement language goes further in specifying who the arbitrators are and expressly commits to observe the agreement, the rules, and the award, because other suggested language for future claims does not have these provisions.

[60] AAA, Resolving Employment Disputes: A Manual on Drafting Procedures 11–12 (1993).

[61] *Id.* at 12.

[62] *Id.*

§ 18.44   Releases

Disclaimers are preventive in character; they attempt to preclude the possibility of a legal right to employment security arising in the first place. An *employee release* is a contract in which a discharged employee abandons claims against a former employer after they have arisen in exchange for benefits such as severance pay or continuation of salary and benefits for a period of time. See **Forms 18–26** and **18–27**. Employee releases generally are effective in barring implied-in-fact contract claims against employers, but may not be as effective in barring statutory claims.[63]

The scope of employee releases is limited to the intentions of the parties as set forth on the face of the agreement. The mere acceptance of termination payments does not necessarily show that the employee intends to give up rights to litigate the validity of the termination. Similarly, the acceptance of one kind of accommodation to a disability does not necessarily waive the right to assert ADA claims with respect to the refusal of other kinds of accommodation.

§ 18.45   —Release Agreement

FORM 18–26
SAMPLE RELEASE AGREEMENT

THIS AGREEMENT, made this [date], by and between [employer name] (hereinafter "Employer"), and [employee name] (hereinafter "Employee") is intended by the parties to be a settlement and release whereby [employer] and [employee] extinguish their respective rights and claims against one another as hereinafter enumerated.

FOR VALUABLE CONSIDERATION, receipt of which is hereby acknowledged, Employee agrees as follows:

1.   Employee agrees upon the execution of this Agreement to surrender to legal counsel for Employer all [employer] information in whatever form it is possessed by

---

[63] Stroman v. West Coast Grocery Co., 884 F.2d 458, 462 (9th Cir. 1989) (reversing district court and finding that release waived Title VII claims despite lack of explicit reference to Title VII and absence of attorneys; based on employee understanding); Riley v. American Family Mut. Ins. Co., 881 F.2d 368, 373 (7th Cir. 1989) (affirming district court conclusion that release negotiated in connection with settlement of state law claim barred Title VII claim because knowing and voluntary; extensive review of cases and different standards); Myers v. Health Specialists, S.C., 587 N.E.2d 494, 499 (Ill. App. Ct. 1992) (reversing summary judgment; relase, properly construed as "general release," did not bar claim for failure to buy malpractice insurance; generally analyzing principles for construing releases).

Employee, including but not limited to, computer printouts, index cards, mailing labels, floppy disk(s) or other methods of computer storage, photostatic, typewritten, and handwritten copies of the same.

2.   Employee releases and discharges Employer, its successors and assigns, directors, officers, shareholders, and employees, from all rights, claims, and causes of action which Employee now has, or may hereafter have, which arose, arise, or may arise out of any action, contract, conduct, or course of conduct whatsoever at any time prior to the date of the signing of this Agreement, specifically, but not limited to, any and all claims and causes of action arising out of or pertaining to Employee's employment by Employer and its termination.

3.   Employee specifically releases and discharges Employer, its successors and assigns, directors, officers, shareholders and employees, from all rights, claims, and causes of action which Employee now has, or may hereafter have, which arose, arise, or may arise out of any action, contract, conduct, or course of conduct whatsoever at any time prior to the date of the signing of this Agreement, pertaining to any physical or mental disability Employee may have had during employment or any steps taken by the employer to accommodate such disabilities or refusal to accommodate such disabilities. Employee subscribes to this paragraph after having consulted legal counsel about applicable rights under the Americans with Disabilities Act and state and local law protecting disabled employees.

4.   In consideration of the foregoing promises of Employee and notwithstanding any other provision of the Agreement, Employer agrees that Employee may retain the [number] clients listed on the two handwritten pages attached hereto, collectively designated Exhibit B, and incorporated herein by reference.

5.   The parties, in executing this Agreement, do not rely on any inducements, promises, or representations made by any other party, or a party's agents or attorneys, other than those expressed herein. The parties have read this Agreement, consisting of [__] pages and have had the consequences explained by their respective attorneys. In executing this Agreement the parties intended to be legally bound.

By: [_____]

Commentary.   The introductory paragraph of this release makes it clear that the agreement is a waiver and that it is intended to extinguish rights. This sort of preamble buttresses agreement validity against a subsequent challenge that a signatory did not know that he or she was waiving rights by signing the agreement.

Paragraph two is extremely broad and might be subject to the defense that it does not call to the signatory's attention particular kinds of employment law claims. For example, an age discrimination claim probably would not be waived by this paragraph.[64] In comparison, paragraph three specifically refers to the ADA, and if its recitation that counsel was consulted is true, it is much more likely to be given effect regarding an ADA claim.

Paragraph four strengthens the agreement against any attack that it is not supported by consideration or is not fair. Paragraph five is useful to reduce the likelihood of "fraud in the inducement" claims.

§ 18.46   —Refusal to Accommodate Release

FORM 18–27
SAMPLE RELEASE FOR REFUSAL TO ACCOMMODATE

RELEASE FROM LIABILITY FOR EMPLOYER'S REFUSAL TO PROVIDE REASONABLE ACCOMMODATIONS

In consideration of [amount] paid by [Employer] on [date], the receipt of which is hereby acknowledged, I, [Employee], my heirs, legal representatives, successors, and assigns, release [Employer] from all lawsuits arising out of [Employer's] refusal to provide reasonable accommodations, as defined by the Americans with Disabilities Act ("ADA"), for my blindness. This release includes all lawsuits I ever had, presently have, or may have in the future pertaining to [Employer's] refusal to provide reasonable accommodations. In addition, this release includes, but is not limited to, lawsuits potentially arising under the ADA, all state or federal statutes governing discrimination against handicapped individuals, and all wrongful termination claims, whether based on tort or contract theories of recovery.

I understand the terms of this release and have executed it voluntarily. in witness whereof, I execute this release on [date], at [city, state].

[Signature of Releasor]

§ 18.47   —Hypothetical Release and Commentary

Hypothetical.   On July 5, 1992, John Jones, then an employee of XYZ, Inc. ("XYZ"), requested reasonable accommodations from XYZ's management to accommodate Jones's recent lost of vision. XYZ refused to grant Jones's request and fired him. In response to the firing, Jones threatened to sue XYZ under the Americans with Disabilities Act ("ADA"). In turn, XYZ offered Jones $10,000 in exchange for a signed statement by Jones releasing XYZ

---

[64] *See* Employee Dismissal Law and Practice, §§ 2.6, 8.10.

from all liability related to their refusal to provide reasonable accommodations for him. Jones accepted XYZ's offer and signed a release drafted by XYZ's counsel.[65]

Commentary.   As § **18.44** explains, a release[66] is a contract an employer uses to protect itself from pending or potential lawsuits arising from the employer's past conduct. This section discusses the essential elements of an ADA claim release and suggests additional provisions that practitioners might want to include in their releases.

To be valid, a release must be supported by consideration and release only those claims the law permits parties to release. In addition, the releasor must voluntarily and knowingly enter into the release.

Because a release is a contract, the release must meet all requirements of a contract, including the requirement of consideration. Further, the parties must determine what consideration is adequate given the legal remedies forfeited by the employee. In addition, it is prudent for the parties to state that the release is supported by consideration and specify the consideration for the release.[67]

Besides the contractual requirements, waivers of certain claims may be limited by law.[68] For example, an employee cannot waive claims under the

---

[65] See § **18.25.**

[66] This memorandum makes no distinction between a release and a covenant not to sue. Although both documents are contracts, a *release* is a covenant that surrenders a right of action, while a *covenant not to sue* is an agreement not to enforce a right of action. W. Prosser & P. Keeton, Prosser and Keeton on Torts § 49, at 332–36 (5th ed. 1984) [hereinafter Prosser & Keeton]. In jurisdictions that distinguish between the two documents, the distinction is important as a matter of procedure and when joint tortfeasors are involved. As a matter of procedure, a release is an affirmative defense, Fed. R. Civ. P. 8(c), but a breach of a covenant not to sue would not affect the lawsuit brought in violation of the covenant. Instead, the amount recovered in a lawsuit brought in violation of a covenant not to sue would be used to compute damages in a subsequent lawsuit based on the employee's breach of that covenant not to sue. Prosser & Keeton at 334. When joint tortfeasors are the defendants in a lawsuit, the distinction between a release and a covenant not to sue has import in determining which of the tortfeasors the document legally releases. Jurisdictions have varied views concerning the distinction between and related legal effect of releases and covenants not to sue. *See id.* at 332–36.

[67] One practitioner suggests that the recital of consideration should also include statements that the consideration is "good and valuable" and that the consideration is "hereby received and acknowledged." Such a statement would support the argument that the consideration is adequate and help enforce a release signed by and delivered to an employee who might try to renege on the release by returning the settlement check. J.H. Carey, *A Checklist for Drafting Employee Releases,* Prac. Law. 21, 27 (Apr. 1989). It is dubious that such formal boilerplate makes much difference, except psychologically in discouraging suit.

[68] In addition, the release must not be contrary to public policy or unconscionable. *See* Bartel Dental Books Co. v. Schultz, 786 F.2d 486, 488 (2d. Cir.), *cert. denied,* 478 U.S. 1006 (1986).

Fair Labor Standards Act[69] except in settlements supervised by the Wage and Hour Administration of the Department of Labor.[70] In the case of claim releases under the ADA, such a statutory limitation is not at issue because the ADA itself does not expressly prohibit the use of releases. Moreover, the Civil Rights Act of 1964,[71] whose enforcement powers, remedies, and procedures are the enforcement powers, remedies, and procedures available to plaintiffs under the ADA,[72] permits the use of releases.[73]

Related to the requirement that the law must permit the release is the idea that the substantive terms of the release should not conflict with any other agreement to which the employer is bound. An example of such agreements includes any labor contract, such as a collective bargaining agreement.[74]

Finally, in addition to the requirements and limitations concerning the substantive terms of the contract, the employee must knowingly and voluntarily agree to the terms of the release.[75]

The more carefully a release is drafted, the more likely it is that the document will have the effect intended by the parties.[76] Depending upon the needs and complexity of a particular release, counsel should consider including in their releases provisions addressing some or all of the following concerns:

1. A recital of facts that led to the release
2. The specific legal identity of parties released
3. The purpose of the document
4. The specific claims released by the employee
5. A confidentiality clause[77]
6. A clause in which the employer specifies that entering into the agreement is not an admission of fault

---

[69] 29 U.S.C. §§ 201–219 (1994).

[70] J.H. Carey, *A Checklist for Drafting Employee Releases,* Prac. Law. 21–24 (Apr. 1989) (citing D.A. Schulte, Inc. v. Gangi, 328 U.S. 108, 114–15 (1946)).

[71] 42 U.S.C. Ch. 21 (1994) [hereinafter Civil Rights Act of 1964].

[72] ADA § 107(a), 42 U.S.C. § 12117(a) (1994).

[73] Wright v. Southwestern Bell Tel. Co., 925 F.2d 1288, 1292 (10th Cir. 1991) (Title VII claims may be waived by agreement, but the waiver must be knowing and voluntary).

[74] *See* W.R. Grace & Co. v. Local Union 759, Int'l Union of United Rubber Workers of Am., 461 U.S. 757 (1983) (employer entered into a conciliation agreement with the EEOC that conflicted with the seniority provisions of the employer's existing collective bargaining agreement with the union).

[75] Wright v. Southwestern Bell Tel. Co., 925 F.2d 1288, 1292 (10th Cir. 1991).

[76] Bartel Dental Books Co. v. Schultz, 786 F.2d 486, 488 (2d Cir. 1986) (stating that contract principles apply to interpretation of releases).

[77] Such a clause is useful if the employer does not want other employees to know how much the employer paid the employee to execute the release.

7. An amicable resolution of disputed claims statement, supporting an argument that the release is an offer of settlement inadmissible in any other legal proceedings

8. A statement that if any terms of the agreement are inoperative, for any reason, those provisions are severable and the remaining provisions retain full effect

9. An integration clause stating that the release constitutes the entire agreement between the parties

10. The presence of choice of law and forum clauses

11. Any other additional commitments.[78]

§ 18.48 Title III Materials

Title III[79] involves relationships that are less formal than employer-employee relationships. Accordingly, there is less opportunity for internal governance documentation to reduce the exposure to ADA liability. There are, however, certain kinds of documents that promote Title III compliance, as presented in §§ **18.49** and **18.53.**

§ 18.49 Strategies for Private Places of Public Accommodation: Existing Facilities

Private places of public accommodation can fulfill the duties under Title III of the ADA by developing a basic compliance strategy that includes actions with respect both to existing facilities and services, and to new facilities.

With respect to existing facilities and services, the enterprise should do at least the following:

1. Erect signs indicating the enterprise's commitment to afford access to the disabled and instructing how someone should request assistance or accommodation

2. Train all employees about how to handle requests for assistance or accommodation

3. Establish a procedure for handling complaints that accommodation has not been forthcoming, and make sure that all employees know this procedure

---

[78] *See* J.H. Carey, *A Checklist for Drafting Employee Releases,* Prac. Law. 21, 26–30 (Apr. 1989), for a more detailed discussion of these clauses and additional suggestions.

[79] ADA §§ 301–310, 42 U.S.C. §§ 12181–12189 (1994) [hereinafter Title III].

4. Work with trade associations and organizations for the disabled to establish local or regional help desks and conciliation programs to work out problems between the disabled and individual merchants

5. Evaluate existing facilities against Department of Justice (DOJ) and Architectural and Transportation Barriers Compliance Board (ATBCB) guidelines (considered in **Chapter 6**) and make necessary modifications, especially in parking lots, stairways, and restrooms.

§ 18.50   —New Facilities

Whenever a private place of public accommodation plans a new facility or an addition to an existing facility, one of the first subjects in interviewing architects should be compliance with the ADA. The architects should be knowledgeable about the requirements of the ATBCB guidelines and creative in identifying alternative ways to meet those requirements. It almost certainly will be cheaper to build a new facility to provide for disabled access than to modify the facility after it has been built.

When particular accommodations are ruled out in the design stages, the cost implications of the rejected alternatives should be documented carefully with an eye toward sustaining an unreasonableness or undue hardship defense as discussed in §§ **6.14** through **6.16.**

§ 18.51   Public Accommodation and Commercial Facility Notice

The notice in **Form 18–28** does not add to the obligations imposed by the ADA itself. It can build goodwill and channel complaints or requests for accommodation to the management rather than to a lawyer. The only significant disadvantage would occur if a notice like this were posted and if the person handling inquiries were unavailable or unresponsive. Any such notice should be coupled with appropriate instructions to employees, like those presented in **Form 18–29.**

FORM 18–28
SAMPLE PUBLIC ACCOMMODATION AND COMMERCIAL FACILITY NOTICE

We take our obligations under the Americans with Disabilities Act seriously. We do not discriminate based on physical or mental disability, and we strive to make our facility accessible to the disabled. If you are disabled and have a specific request or suggestion, please contact [name].

§ 18.52   Directions to Employees Regarding
Disabled Customers

Employees of entities covered by Title III should be instructed about their obligations under the ADA lest, out of ignorance, they act in a way that causes liability for the entity.

FORM 18–29
SAMPLE DIRECTIONS TO EMPLOYEES REGARDING
DISABLED CUSTOMERS

The Americans with Disabilities Act and similar state statutes and local ordinances obligate us to make our facilities accessible to persons with physical and mental disabilities. We take these obligations seriously, and have caused notices to be posted on the premises informing the public that we do. An important part of your job responsibility is to be sensitive and responsive to persons with disabilities. Sometimes, accessibility to the disabled can be improved by physical changes in design and layout of the premises. To some extent we have made those design and layout changes.

In other instances, the most effective way to ensure accessibility is to provide special personal assistance.

You may be requested to provide such assistance either by a disabled customer or by your supervisor. In either event, you must take such a request seriously. You must be considerate and you must not act so as to cause undue commotion or embarrassment to the disabled customer.

In many instances, suggestion by the disabled person is the best guide as to how to be helpful. You should not override a request with your own judgment about what is "best" for the disabled customer.

In many instances, the simplest and best response to a request is to do what the customer asks. An easy example is helping someone in a wheelchair over a curb or through a doorway.

Occasionally, however, you may receive a request from a customer that seems to you like it would create a risk to other customers to yourself, to employees, or would interfere with your performance of your other job responsibilities in a major way. You should not take it upon yourself to refuse the request. Instead, you should make every effort to obtain instructions of advice from your supervisor or from the designated ADA compliance officer.

§ 18.53   Private Dispute Resolution

Section 513 of the ADA[80] provides for the use of alternative means of dispute resolution, including settlement negotiations, conciliation, facilitation, mediation, factfinding, minitrials, and arbitration. In the House Judiciary Report,[81] the House and Senate Conference Committee adopted language in the House Judiciary Report[82] noting that "the use of these alternative dispute resolution procedures is completely voluntary. Under no condition would an arbitration clause in a collective bargaining agreement or employment contract prevent an individual from pursuing their rights under the ADA."[83]

The range of internal dispute resolution procedures that may be useful to employers in avoiding the high costs of court litigation is considered in a current book, *Employee Dismissal Law and Practice.*[84] Such procedures are particularly appropriate for potential claims of disability discrimination because they offer an opportunity for the employer and employee to work things out through the employer's reasonable accommodation or the employee's better understanding of essential job functions. Employers should consider new internal dispute resolution procedures, including mediation, advisory committees (see §§ **18.42** and **18.43**), and arbitration, as they prepare to conform to the ADA.

Alternative dispute resolution is not limited to employment disputes; it also may be used for disputes arising over governmental service and access to places of public accommodation. In the governmental setting, alternative dispute resolution merges with the reform of administrative procedures. In this setting, however, agencies should consider the value of mediation and arbitration, compared with traditional agency hearings.[85]

In the Title III context, most requests for accommodation are addressed informally. It might be helpful, however, for trade associations and chambers of commerce to consider developing alternative dispute resolution programs in conjunction with organizations for the disabled. Such programs must provide a well-publicized point of intervention to which a complaint may be referred

---

[80] 42 U.S.C. § 12213 (1994).

[81] H.R. Rep. No. 485, 101st Cong., 2d Sess., pt. 3 (1990) [hereinafter House Judiciary Report].

[82] H.R. Conf. Rep. No. 596, 101st Cong., 2d Sess., *reprinted in* 136 Cong. Rec. H4582 (daily ed. July 12, 1990) [hereinafter House Conference Report] at para. 81.

[83] *Id.*

[84] Employee Dismissal Law and Practice, Ch. 9.

[85] *See* Administrative Conference of the United States, Recommendation 95–7, 60 Fed. Reg. 43,108 (1995) (recommending agency use of mediation for ADA disputes).

when a disabled person believes that a merchant is not accommodating a disability appropriately. Then, representatives from trade associations and organizations for the disabled can become involved to conciliate a resolution.

Such a program could be combined with a "help line" or "help desk" for disabled seeking accommodation in places of public accommodation.